The Oxford Dictionary of
Idioms

The Oxford Dictionary of

Idioms

SECOND EDITION

Edited by
JUDITH SIEFRING

OXFORD
UNIVERSITY PRESS

OXFORD
UNIVERSITY PRESS

Great Clarendon Street, Oxford OX2 6DP

Oxford University Press is a department of the University of Oxford.
It furthers the University's objective of excellence in research, scholarship,
and education by publishing worldwide in

Oxford New York

Auckland Cape Town Dar es Salaam Hong Kong Karachi
Kuala Lumpur Madrid Melbourne Mexico City Nairobi
New Delhi Shanghai Taipei Toronto

With offices in

Argentina Austria Brazil Chile Czech Republic France Greece
Guatemala Hungary Italy Japan Poland Portugal Singapore
South Korea Switzerland Thailand Turkey Ukraine Vietnam

Published in the United States
by Oxford University Press Inc., New York

© Oxford University Press 1999, 2004, 2005

First published 1999
Second published 2004
Second edition issued as an Oxford University Press paperback 2005

British Library Cataloguing in Publication Data

Data available

Library of Congress Cataloging-in-Publication Data

Data available

Designed by Jane Stevenson
Typeset in Swift and Frutiger by SPI Publisher Services, Pondicherry, India
Printed in Great Britain by Clays Ltd, St Ives plc.

ISBN 978-0-19-861055-7

4

Contents

Preface

The aim of the *Oxford Dictionary of Idioms* is to provide clear definitions of phrases and sayings for those who do not know what they mean, but also to offer the curious reader interesting facts about the origins of phrases and examples of their use. This second edition of the *Oxford Dictionary of Idioms* is based on the first edition, edited by Jennifer Speake. It maintains the first edition's focus on contemporary and historical phrases, sayings, and proverbs, and uses a combination of definition and (where required) explanatory note and illustrative quotation to provide a rounded picture of idiomatic usage. The coverage of the previous edition has been extended by the inclusion of more than 350 new idioms, and a great many contemporary illustrative quotations have also been added. These quotations have been taken from a vareity of sources: from novels to travel guides, broadsheet newspapers to teenage magazines. They help to give the reader a better understanding of how an idiom is used: a typical context, a certain tone, or a particular resonance. The formation of new phrases and sayings is one of the most colourful aspects of language development, and by adding idioms such as **chew the scenery, be in like Flynn**, and **give someone the hairy eyeball**, and quotations from the likes of Anthony Bourdain, Arundhati Roy, Melvin Burgess, and Tom Clancy, the new edition hopes to reflect this colour.

A new index section at the end of the book groups together idioms which share a common theme or subject, so giving readers a vivid snapshot of those areas and aspects of life that have generated a particularly rich variety of figurative expressions.

My thanks must go to Richard Jones for his work on sourcing quotations, to Georgia Hole for proofreading, and above all to Sara Hawker for her help and insight throughout the project.

JUDITH SIEFRING

A

A 1 excellent; first-rate.

> ℹ The full form of this expression is *A1 at Lloyd's*. In Lloyd's Register of Shipping, the phrase was used of ships in first-class condition as to the hull (A) and stores (1). The US equivalent is *A No. 1*; both have been in figurative use since the mid 19th century.

from A to B from your starting point to your destination; from one place to another.

> **1987 K. Rushforth** *Tree Planting & Management* The purpose of street tree planting is to...make the roads and thoroughfares pleasant in their own right, not just as places used to travel from A to B.

from A to Z over the entire range; in every particular.

> **1998** *Salmon, Trout & Sea-Trout* In order to have seen Scotland's game fishing in its entirety, from A to Z, visiting 30 stretches of river and 350 lochs a year, you would have to be travelling for a hundred years.

aback

take someone aback shock, surprise, or disconcert someone.

> ℹ The phrase is frequently used in the passive form (*be taken aback*): this was adopted in the mid 19th century from earlier (mid 18th-century) nautical terminology, to describe the situation of a ship with its sails pressed back against the mast by a headwind, preventing forward movement.

> **1991 Kathleen Jones** *Learning Not To Be First* They were taken aback by the shabbiness of the hotel and lack of cleanliness in the city generally.

ABC

as easy (or simple) as ABC extremely easy or straightforward.

> ℹ From the 15th to the 17th century, a child's first spelling and reading book was commonly called an *ABC*, and this led to the development of its metaphorical use, 'the basic elements or rudiments of something'.

abdabs

give someone the screaming abdabs induce an attack of extreme anxiety or irritation in someone.

> ℹ *Abdabs* (or *habdabs*) is mid 20th-century slang whose origin is unknown. The word is sometimes also used to mean an attack of delirium tremens.

abet

aid and abet: *see* AID.

about

know what you are about be aware of the implications of your actions or of a situation, and of how best to deal with them. informal

> **1993** *Ski Survey* He ran a 3-star guest house before this, so knows what he is about.

above

above yourself conceited; arrogant.

> **1999 Frank McCourt** *'Tis* Many a man made his way in America by the sweat of his brow and his strong back and it's a good thing to learn your station in life and not be getting above yourself.

not be above — be capable of stooping to an unworthy act.

> **1991 Maureen Duffy** *Illuminations* The copyist was not above turning author or forger and several MSS from this period must be viewed as highly suspect.

Abraham

in Abraham's bosom in heaven, the place of rest for the souls of the blessed. dated

> ℹ The phrase is taken from Luke 16:22: 'And it came to pass, that the beggar died, and was carried by the angels into Abraham's bosom'. In the Bible, *Abraham* was the Hebrew patriarch from whom all Jews traced their descent.

acceptable

the acceptable face of the tolerable or attractive manifestation or aspect of.

1996 *New York Review of Books* He presents himself as the acceptable face of gambling...the man who, almost single-handedly, has turned a huckster's paradise into a gangster-free zone.

accident

an accident waiting to happen ❶ a potentially disastrous situation, usually caused by negligent or faulty procedures. **❷** a person certain to cause trouble.

> **❶ 1997** *Times* Accidents are often said to be 'waiting to happen'. It does not take much imagination to see that the chaotic start to the Whitbread round-the-world race...could easily have ended in tragedy.

accidents will happen however careful you try to be, it is inevitable that some unfortunate or unforeseen events will occur.

> **ℹ** This phrase is a shortened form of the early 19th-century proverb 'accidents will happen in the best regulated families'.

a chapter of accidents: *see* CHAPTER.

accord

of your own accord voluntarily or without outside intervention.

account

give a good (*or* bad) account of yourself make a favourable (*or* unfavourable) impression through your performance or actions.

settle (*or* square) accounts with someone ❶ pay money owed to someone. **❷** have revenge on someone.

accounting

there's no accounting for tastes it's impossible to explain why different people like different things, especially those things which the speaker considers unappealing. proverb

> **ℹ** Since the late 18th century, this has been the usual English form of the Latin expression *de gustibus non est disputandum* 'there is no disputing about tastes'.

ace

have an ace up your sleeve have an effective resource or piece of information kept hidden until it is necessary to use it; have a secret advantage.

> **ℹ** The ace is the highest playing card in its suit in many card games, so a cheating player might well hide one to use against an unwary opponent. A North American variant is *an ace in the hole*. The next two idioms are also based on this meaning of *ace*.

hold all the aces have all the advantages.

play your ace use your best resource.

within an ace of very close to.

> **ℹ** *Ace* here has the figurative meaning of 'a tiny amount' and is used with reference to the single spot on the playing card. The phrase was first recorded in the early 18th century.

Achilles

an Achilles heel a person's only vulnerable spot; a serious or fatal weakness.

> **ℹ** In Greek mythology, the nymph Thetis dipped her infant son Achilles in the water of the River Styx to make him immortal, but the heel by which she held him was not touched by the water; he was ultimately killed in battle by an arrow wound in this one vulnerable spot.

1998 *Times* The inclination to outlaw that of which it disapproves...is, if not the cloven hoof beneath the hem of Tony Blair's Government, certainly its Achilles heel.

acid

the acid test a situation or event which finally proves whether something is good or bad, true or false, etc.

> **ℹ** The original use of the phrase was to describe a method of testing for gold with nitric acid (gold being resistant to the effects of nitric acid).

1990 *Which?* These deals are designed to encourage impulse buying, so the acid test is whether you would have bought anyway.

come the acid be unpleasant or offensive; speak in a caustic or sarcastic manner.

put the acid on someone try to extract a loan or favour from someone. Australian & New Zealand informal

acquaintance

have a nodding acquaintance with someone or something: *see* NODDING.

scrape acquaintance with: *see* SCRAPE.

acre

God's acre: *see* GOD.

across

across the board applying to all.

> ❶ In the USA, this expression refers to a horse-racing bet in which equal amounts are staked on the same horse to win, place, or show in a race.

> **1999** *Wall Street Journal* The decline for the euro across the board was mainly attributed to the further erosion of global investors' confidence toward the euro-zone economy.

be across something fully understand the details or complexity of an issue or situation. Australian

act

act your age behave in a manner appropriate to your age and not to someone much younger.

act the goat: *see* GOAT.

act of God an instance of uncontrollable natural forces in operation.

> ❶ This phrase is often used in insurance contracts to refer to incidents such as lightning strikes or floods.

a class act: *see* CLASS.

clean up your act: *see* CLEAN.

do a disappearing act: *see* DISAPPEARING.

get your act together organize yourself in the manner required in order to achieve something. informal

> **2002** *New York Times* There are still many who think all that the dirty, homeless man on the corner talking to himself needs is just to get his act together.

a hard (or tough) act to follow an achievement or performance which sets a standard difficult for others to measure up to.

> **1996** *Independent* Her determination and championing of tourism will be a tough act to follow.

in on the act involved in a particular activity in order to gain profit or advantage. informal

> **1997** *What Cellphone* Conference calls are becoming big business for the fixed-line operators, and now there are signs that the mobile networks are getting in on the act.

read someone the riot act: *see* READ.

action

action stations an order or warning to prepare for action.

> ❶ Originally, this was an order to naval personnel to go to their allocated positions ready to engage the enemy.

man of action a man whose life is characterized by physical activity or deeds rather than by words or intellectual matters.

a piece of the action: *see* PIECE.

where the action is where important or interesting things are happening. informal

> **1971** *Gourmet* You can dine outside, weather permitting, or in the bar where the action is.

actual

your actual — the real, genuine, or important thing specified. informal

> **1968 Kenneth Williams** *Diary* There's no doubt about it, on a good day, I look quite lovely in your actual gamin fashion.

Adam

not know someone from Adam not know or be completely unable to recognize the person in question. informal

the old Adam unregenerate human nature.

> ❶ In Christian symbolism, *the old Adam* represents fallen man as contrasted with *the second Adam*, Jesus Christ.

> **1993** *Outdoor Canada* It is the Old Adam in us. We are descendants of a long line of dirt farmers, sheepherders … and so forth.

add

add fuel to the fire: *see* FUEL.

add insult to injury: *see* INSULT.

adder

deaf as an adder: *see* DEAF.

admirable

an admirable Crichton a person who excels in all kinds of studies and pursuits, or who is noted for supreme competence.

> ❶ This expression originally referred to James Crichton of Clunie (1560–85?), a Scottish nobleman renowned for his intellectual and physical prowess. In J. M. Barrie's play *The Admirable Crichton* (1902), the eponymous hero is a butler who takes charge when his master's family is shipwrecked on a desert island.

a

adrift

cast (or cut) someone adrift ❶ leave someone in a boat or other craft which has nothing to secure or guide it. ❷ abandon or isolate someone.

> ❷ **1998** *Oldie* The various dissenting movements... should be cut adrift and left to their own devices.

advance

any advance on —? any higher bid than —?

> ❶ This phrase is said by an auctioneer to elicit a higher bid, and so is used figuratively as a query about general progress in a particular matter.

advocate

play devil's advocate: *see* DEVIL.

afraid

afraid of your own shadow: *see* SHADOW.

Africa

for Africa in abundance; in large numbers. South African informal

> **1980 C. Hope** *A Separate Development* An entire museum of vintage stuff including... Bentleys for Africa.

after

be after doing something be on the point of doing something or have just done it. Irish

> **1988 Roddy Doyle** *The Commitments* I'm after rememberin'. I forgot to bring mine back. It's under me bed.

age

act your age: *see* ACT.

the awkward age: *see* AWKWARD.

come of age ❶ (of a person) reach adult status. ❷ (of a movement or activity) become fully established.

feel your age: *see* FEEL.

a golden age: *see* GOLDEN.

under age: *see* UNDER.

agenda

a hidden agenda: *see* HIDDEN.

agony

pile on the agony: *see* PILE.

prolong the agony: *see* PROLONG.

agree

agree to differ cease to argue about something because neither party will compromise or be persuaded.

agreement

a gentleman's agreement: *see* GENTLEMAN.

ahead

ahead of the game ahead of your competitors or peers in the same sphere of activity.

> **1996** *Daily Telegraph* The smart money headed for Chinatown, where you can pick up all those Eastern looks the designers are promoting for next spring ahead of the game.

ahead of your (or its) time innovative and radical by the standards of the time.

streets ahead: *see* STREET.

aid

aid and abet help and encourage someone to do something wrong, especially to commit a crime.

> ❶ *Abet* comes from an Old French term meaning 'to encourage a hound to bite'.

> **1986 Frank Peretti** *This Present Darkness* She strained to think of... any friend who would still aid and abet a fugitive from the law, without questions.

in aid of in support of; for the purpose of raising money for. chiefly British

> **1999** *Teesdale Mercury* A wine and savoury evening in aid of cancer research will be held... on Friday.

what's all this in aid of? what is the purpose of this? British informal

air

airs and graces an affected manner of behaving, designed to attract or impress. British

give yourself airs act pretentiously or snobbishly.

> **1948 Christopher Bush** *The Case of the Second Chance* It was said she gave herself airs, and it was also hinted that she was no better—as they say—than she might be.

> ❶ *Air* in the sense of 'an affected manner' has been current since the mid 17th century; from the early 18th century the plural form has been more usual in this derogatory sense.

hot air: *see* HOT.

up in the air (of a plan or issue) still to be settled; unresolved.

1995 *Scientific American* Prospects for federal research and development are up in the air as Republicans looking for budget cuts take control on Capitol Hill.

on (*or* off) the air being (*or* not being) broadcast on radio or television.

take the air go out of doors.

walk on air feel elated.

> **1977 Bernard MacLaverty** *Secrets* 'I'm sure you're walking on air,' my mother said to Paul at his wedding.

aisle

have people rolling in the aisles ❶ make an audience laugh uncontrollably. **❷** be very amusing. informal

> **❶ 1940 P. G. Wodehouse** *Quick Service* I made the speech of a lifetime. I had them tearing up the seats and rolling in the aisles.

aitch

drop your aitches: *see* DROP.

Aladdin

an Aladdin's cave a place full of valuable objects.

an Aladdin's lamp a talisman that enables its owner to fulfil every desire.

> **❶** In the *Arabian Nights* tale of Aladdin, the hero finds a magic lamp in a cave. He discovers that rubbing it summons a powerful genie who is able to carry out all his wishes.

alarm

alarms and excursions confused activity and uproar. humorous

> **❶** *Alarm* was formerly spelled *alarum*, representing a pronunciation with a rolling of the 'r'; the phrase was originally a call summoning soldiers to arms. The whole phrase is used in stage directions in Shakespeare to indicate a battle scene.

alight

set the world alight: *see* SET.

alive

alive and kicking prevalent and very active. informal

> **1991 Mark Tully** *No Full Stops in India* You deliberately choose unknown actors, although India is a country where the star system is very much alive and kicking.

alive and well still existing or active (often used to deny rumours or beliefs that something has disappeared or declined).

1990 *Times* Thatcherism may be dying on its feet in Britain, but it is alive and well in foreign parts.

all

all and sundry everyone.

> **1991** *Sunday Times* In the manner of an Oscar-winner, she thanks all and sundry for their help.

all comers anyone who chooses to take part in an activity, typically a competition.

> **1992 Al Gore** *Earth in the Balance* He has traveled to conferences and symposia in every part of the world, argued his case, and patiently taken on all comers.

all-in ❶ with everything included. **❷** exhausted. British informal

all my eye and Betty Martin: *see* EYE.

all of as much as (often used ironically of an amount considered very small by the speaker or writer).

> **1995 Bill Bryson** *Notes from a Small Island* In 1992, a development company . . . tore down five listed buildings, in a conservation area, was taken to court and fined all of £675.

be all one to make no difference to someone.

all out using all your strength or resources.

all over the place in a state of confusion or disorganization. informal

> **❶** Other variants of this phrase include *all over the map* and *all over the lot* which are North American, and *all over the shop* which is mainly British.

> **1997** *Spectator* The government . . . proposed equalising standards and making them comparable . . . there could be no clearer admission that standards are all over the place.

all the rage: *see* RAGE.

all round ❶ in all respects. **❷** for or by each person.

all-singing, all-dancing with every possible attribute; able to perform any necessary function. British informal

> **❶** This phrase is used particularly in the area of computer technology, but it was originally used to describe show-business acts. Ultimately, it may come from a series of 1929 posters which advertised the addition of sound to motion pictures. The first Hollywood musical, MGM's *Broadway Melody*, was promoted with the slogan *All Talking All Singing All Dancing*.

1991 *Computing* Each of the major independents launched an all-singing all-dancing graphics-oriented version last year.

all systems go: *see* SYSTEM.

be all that be very attractive or good. US informal

> **2002** *Guardian* I can't believe how she throws herself at guys, she thinks she's all that.

not all there not in full possession of your mental faculties. informal

be all things to all men: *see* THING.

— and all used to emphasize something additional that is being referred to. informal

> **1992 Kenichi Ohmae** *The Borderless World* You can whip up nationalist passions and stage-manage protectionist rallies, bonfires and all.

be all go: *see* GO.

be all up with: *see* UP.

for all — in spite of —.

> **1989** *Independent* For all their cruel, corrupt and reckless vices, the Maharajahs were worshipped as gods by tens of thousands of their subjects.

all of a sudden: *see* SUDDEN.

on all fours: *see* FOUR.

all-clear

give (or get) the all-clear indicate (or get a sign) that a dangerous situation is now safe.

> ❶ In wartime a signal or siren is often sounded to indicate that a bombing raid is over.

alley

a blind alley: *see* BLIND.

up your alley: *see* **up your street** *at* STREET.

ally

pass in your ally: *see* PASS.

along

along about round about a specified time or date. North American informal or dialect

> **1989** *Motor Trend* Along about this time, it had started raining, so they red-flagged the race for a change to rain tires.

alpha

alpha and omega ❶ the beginning and the end. ❷ the essence or most important features.

> ❶ *Alpha* and *omega* are respectively the first and last letters of the Greek alphabet. Christians use the phrase as a title for Jesus Christ, taking it from Revelation 1:8: 'I am Alpha and Omega, the beginning and the ending, saith the Lord'.

> ❷ **1994** *BBC Holidays* At Cambridge ... you'll find the alpha and omega of American academic life: historic Harvard and space-age MIT (Massachusetts Institute of Technology).

altar

sacrifice someone or something on the altar of make someone or something suffer in the interests of someone or something else.

> **1994** *Post* (Denver) The cherished goal of a color-blind society ... has been sacrificed on the altar of political expediency.

altogether

in the altogether without any clothes on; naked. informal

> **1991** *Today* The mothers ... have agreed to pose in the altogether.

American

as American as apple pie typically American in character.

> **1995** *New York Times Magazine* To reward people for something beyond merit is American as apple pie.

the American dream the ideal by which equality of opportunity is available to any American, allowing the highest aspirations and goals to be achieved.

amok

run amok behave uncontrollably and disruptively.

> ❶ *Amok*, formerly also spelt *amuck*, comes from the Malay word *amuk*, meaning 'in a homicidal frenzy', in which sense it was first introduced into English in the early 16th century.

> **1990** *New York Review of Books* Hersh's article is sensationalism run amok. It does no credit to him or to *The New York Times Magazine*.

analysis

in the final analysis when everything has been considered (used to suggest that the following statement expresses the basic truth about a complex situation).

ancient

ancient as the hills: see HILL.

the ancient of Days a biblical title for God, taken from Daniel 7:9.

angel

the angel in the house a woman who is completely devoted to her husband and family.

> ❶ This was the title of a collection of poems on married love by Coventry Patmore (1823–96), and it is now mainly used ironically.

on the side of the angels on the side of what is right.

> ❶ In a speech in Oxford in November 1864 the British statesman Benjamin Disraeli alluded to the controversy over the origins of humankind then raging in the wake of the publication of Charles Darwin's *On the Origin of Species* (1859): 'Is man an ape or an angel? Now I am on the side of the angels' (*The Times* 26 Nov. 1864).

angry

angry young man a young man who feels and expresses anger at the conventional values of the society around him.

> ❶ Originally, this term referred to a member of a group of socially conscious writers in Britain in the 1950s, in particular the playwright John Osborne. The phrase, the title of a book (1951) by Leslie Paul, was used of Osborne in the publicity material for his play *Look Back in Anger* (1956), in which the characteristic views of the angry young men were articulated by the anti-hero Jimmy Porter.

answer

the answer's a lemon: see LEMON.

a dusty answer: see DUSTY.

ante

up (or raise) the ante increase what is at stake or under discussion, especially in a conflict or dispute.

> ❶ *Ante* comes from Latin, in which it means 'before'. As an English noun it was originally (in the early 19th century) a term in poker and similar gambling games, meaning 'a stake put up by a player before drawing cards'.

> **1998** *New Scientist* This report ups the ante on the pace at which these cases need to be identified and treated.

ant

have ants in your pants be fidgety or restless. informal

any

not be having any of it be absolutely unwilling to cooperate. informal

anyone

anyone's game an evenly balanced contest.

be anyone's (of a person) be open to sexual advances from anyone. informal

anything

anything goes: see GOES.

apart

be poles apart: see POLE.

come apart at the seams: see SEAM.

ape

go ape go wild; become violently excited. informal

> ❶ Originally mid 20th-century North American slang, this expression possibly refers to the 1933 movie *King Kong*, which stars a giant ape-like monster.

apology

an apology for a very poor example of.

> **1998** Imogen de la Bere *The Last Deception of Palliser Wentwood* It's an apology for a bridge, built of left-over stones.

with apologies to used before the name of an author or artist to indicate that something is a parody or adaptation of their work.

> **2001** *This Old House* With apologies to Robert Frost, boundary expert Walter Robillard says, 'Good fences on the proper line make good neighbours'.

appeal

appeal from Philip drunk to Philip sober ask someone to reconsider, with the suggestion that an earlier opinion or decision represented only a passing mood.

> ❶ This phrase comes from an anecdote told by the Roman historian and moralist Valerius Maximus concerning an unjust judgement given by King Philip of Macedon: the woman condemned by Philip declared that she would appeal to him once again, but this time when he was sober.

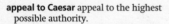

appeal to Caesar appeal to the highest possible authority.

> ❶ The allusion is to the claim made by the apostle Paul to have his case heard in Rome, which was his right as a Roman citizen: 'I appeal unto Caesar' (Acts 25:11).

appearance

keep up appearances maintain an impression of wealth or well-being.

to (or by) all appearances as far as can be seen.

> **1991 Eric Lax** *Woody Allen* To all appearances, theirs was a unique case of sibling amity.

apple

apple of discord a subject of dissension.

> ❶ This expression refers to the Greek myth in which a golden apple inscribed 'for the fairest' was contended for by the goddesses Hera, Athene, and Aphrodite.

the apple of your eye a person or thing of whom you are extremely fond and proud.

> ❶ In Old English, the phrase referred to the pupil of the eye, considered to be a globular solid body; it came to be used as a symbol of something cherished and watched over.

apples and oranges (of two people or things) irreconcilably or fundamentally different. North American

a rotten (or bad) apple a bad person in a group, typically one whose behaviour is likely to have a corrupting influence on the rest. informal

she's apples used to indicate that everything is in good order and there is nothing to worry about. Australian informal

> ❶ *Apples and spice* or *apples and rice* is Australian rhyming slang for *nice*.

apple cart

upset the apple cart wreck an advantageous project or disturb the status quo.

> ❶ The use of a cart piled high with apples as a metaphor for a satisfactory but possibly precarious state of affairs is recorded in various expressions from the late 18th century onwards.

> **1996** *Business Age* The real test will be instability in China … Another Tiananmen Square could really upset the apple cart.

apple pie

as American as apple pie: *see* AMERICAN.

apropos

apropos of nothing having no relevance to any previous discussion or situation.

approval

seal (or stamp) of approval an indication or statement that something is accepted or regarded favourably.

> ❶ This expression stems from the practice of putting a stamp (or formerly a seal) on official documents.

apron

tied to someone's apron strings too much under the influence and control of someone (especially used to suggest that a man is too much influenced by his mother).

area

a grey area: *see* GREY.

a no-go area: *see* NO-GO.

argue

argue the toss dispute a decision or choice already made. informal, chiefly British

> ❶ The *toss* in this phrase is the tossing of a coin to decide an issue in a simple and unambiguous way according to the side of the coin visible when it lands.

ark

out of the ark extremely old-fashioned.

> ❶ The ark referred to is the biblical Noah's ark (Genesis 6–7), in which Noah endeavoured to save his family and two of every kind of animal from the Flood.

arm

a call to arms a call to make ready for confrontation.

cost an arm and a leg be extremely expensive. informal

give an arm and a leg for pay a high price for.

keep someone or something at arm's length avoid intimacy or close contact with someone or something.

the long arm of coincidence the far-reaching power of coincidence.

the long (or strong) arm of the law the police seen as a far-reaching or intimidating power.

as long as your arm very long. informal

put the arm on attempt to force or coerce someone to do something. North American informal

up in arms about protesting angrily about something.

> **1994** *Asian Times* A lack of checks and balances ... or legal redress for workers have trade unions up in arms.

with open arms with great affection or enthusiasm.

would give your right arm for be willing to pay a high price for; greatly desire to have or do. informal

armchair

an armchair critic a person who knows about a subject only by reading or hearing about it and criticizes without active experience or first-hand knowledge.

> ❶ The phrase *armchair critic* is first recorded in 1896, but the concept was around at least a decade earlier: in 1886 Joseph Chamberlain sneered at opponents as 'arm-chair politicians'. Another common variant is *armchair traveller*, meaning 'someone who travels in their imagination only'.

armed

armed at all points prepared in every particular.

armed to the teeth ❶ carrying a lot of weapons. ❷ heavily equipped.

armpit

up to your armpits deeply involved in a particular unpleasant situation or enterprise. chiefly US

army

you and whose army? used to express disbelief in someone's ability to carry out a threat. informal

around

have been around have a lot of varied experience of the world, especially a lot of sexual experience. informal

arrow

an arrow in the quiver one of a number of resources or strategies that can be drawn on or followed.

arrow of time (or time's arrow) the direction of travel from past to future in time considered as a physical dimension.

a straight arrow an honest or genuine person. North American

arse vulgar slang

go arse over tit fall over in a sudden or dramatic way.

kiss my arse: see KISS.

kiss someone's arse: see KISS.

lick someone's arse: see LICK.

not know your arse from your elbow be totally ignorant or incompetent.

a pain in the arse: see PAIN.

art

art for art's sake the idea that a work of art has no purpose beyond itself.

> ❶ This phrase is the slogan of artists who hold that the chief or only aim of a work of art is the self-expression of the individual artist who creates it.

be art and part of be an accessory or participant in; be deeply involved in.

> ❶ *Be art and part of* was originally a Scottish legal expression: *art* referred to the bringing about of an action and *part* to participation in it.

have something down to a fine art: see FINE ART.

state of the art: see STATE.

article

an article of faith a firmly held belief.

> ❶ *Article* is here used in the sense of 'a statement or item in a summary of religious belief'.

> **1994 Paul Ormerod** *The Death of Economics* It is an article of faith in orthodox economics that free trade between nations is wholly desirable.

the finished article: see FINISHED.

the genuine article: see GENUINE.

as

as and when used to refer to an uncertain future event.

> **1996** *She* The single most important strategy you can adopt to boost your energy levels is to learn to deal with an issue as and when it rears its head.

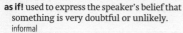

as if! used to express the speaker's belief that something is very doubtful or unlikely. informal

as it were in a way (used to be less precise).

> **1991** *Atlantic* Jazz audiences permit older musicians to go on suiting up, as it were, until they drop.

ascendant

in the ascendant rising in power or influence.

> ❶ This expression has been in figurative use since the late 16th century. Literally, in technical astrological use, an *ascendant* is the sign of the zodiac that is just rising above the eastern horizon at a particular moment.

ash

dust and ashes: see DUST.

rake over the ashes: see RAKE.

rise from the ashes: see RISE.

turn to ashes in your mouth become bitterly disappointing or worthless.

> ❶ This phrase alludes to the Dead Sea fruit, a legendary fruit which looked appetizing but turned to smoke and ashes when someone tried to eat it. The fruit are described in the *Travels* attributed to the 14th-century writer John de Mandeville.

> **1995** *Guardian* Those who marvelled at the phenomenal climbing feats of Pedro Delgado in the 1988 Tour found words such as 'heroic' and 'Herculean' turn to ashes in their mouths during the probenecid (a masking agent) scandal.

ask

ask for the moon: see MOON.

ask me another! used to say emphatically that you do not know the answer to a question. informal

ask no odds: see ODDS.

a big ask a difficult demand to fulfil. informal

don't ask me! used to indicate that you do not know the answer to a question and that you are surprised or irritated to be questioned. informal

I ask you! an exclamation of shock or disapproval intended to elicit agreement from your listener. informal

asking

be asking for trouble (*or* **be asking for it**)

behave in a way that is likely to result in difficulty for yourself. informal

for the asking used to indicate that someone can easily have something if they want it.

> **1991 Mark Tully** *No Full Stops in India* Second helpings come automatically, and third helpings are there for the asking.

asleep

asleep at the wheel not attentive or alert; inactive. informal

> ❶ The image here is of falling asleep while driving a car. A North American variant is *asleep at the switch*, which refers to the points lever or switch on a railway.

> **2003** *Guardian* Rowling has not been asleep at the wheel in the three years since the last Potter novel, and I am pleased to report that she has not confused sheer length with inspiration.

ass North American vulgar slang

bust your ass try very hard to do something.

chew someone's ass reprimand someone severely.

cover your ass take steps to protect yourself.

drag (*or* **haul**) **ass** hurry or move fast.

get your ass in gear hurry.

kick (some) ass (*or* **kick someone's ass**): see KICK.

kiss ass: see KISS.

kiss someone's ass: see KISS.

no skin off your ass: see SKIN.

not give a rat's ass not care at all about something.

a pain in the ass: see PAIN.

a piece of ass: see PIECE.

put someone's ass in a sling get someone in trouble.

whip (*or* **bust**) **someone's ass** use physical force to beat someone in a fight.

at

at it engaged in some activity, typically a reprehensible one.

> **1993 G. F. Newman** *Law & Order* Oh, don't take me for a complete idiot, Jack. I know you're at it.

at that in addition; furthermore (used for emphasis at the end of a statement).

> **1994** *Sunday Times* The sensitivity to social change may play its part, but in reality fashion is a business, and a hard-nosed one at that.

where it's at the most fashionable place, possession, or activity. informal

> **1990 Ellen Feldman** *Looking for Love* New York is where it's at, stylewise.

atmosphere

an atmosphere that you could cut with a knife a general feeling of great tension or malevolence.

attendance

dance attendance on: *see* DANCE.

auld

for auld lang syne for old times' sake.

> ❶ The phrase literally means 'for old long since', and is the title and refrain of a song by Robert Burns (1788).

auspice

under the auspices of with the help, support, or protection of.

> ❶ *Auspice* (since the late 18th century almost always used in the plural), comes from the Latin word *auspicium*, which means the act of divination carried out by an *auspex* in ancient Rome. The *auspex* observed the flight of birds in order to foretell future events. If the omens were favourable he was seen as the protector of the particular enterprise foretold.

authority

have something on good authority have ascertained something from a reliable source.

away

away with something used as an exhortation to overcome or be rid of something.

get away with you! used to express scepticism. Scottish

far and away: *see* FAR.

out and away: *see* OUT.

awkward

the awkward age adolescence.

the awkward squad a squad composed of recruits and soldiers who need further training.

> ❶ Shortly before his death Robert Burns is reported to have said, 'Don't let the awkward squad fire over me'. Nowadays, the expression is often used to refer to a group of people who are regarded as tiresome or difficult to deal with.

axe

have an axe to grind have a private, sometimes malign, motive for doing or being involved in something.

> ❶ The expression originated in a story told by Benjamin Franklin and was used first in the USA, especially with reference to politics, but it is now in general use.

> **1997** *Times* I am a non-smoker, and have no personal axe to grind.

aye

the ayes have it the affirmative votes are in the majority.

> ❶ *Aye* is an archaic or dialect word meaning 'yes', now used in standard speech only when voting. Compare with **the noes have it** (*at* NO).

> **2000** *Guardian* The arguments will continue. But we think the 'ayes' have it.

Bb

B

plan B an alternative strategy.

> **1999** *8 Days* And if that doesn't work, well, there's always Plan B.

babe

babes in the wood inexperienced people in a situation calling for experience.

> ⓘ The *babes in the wood* are characters in an old ballad *The Children in the Wood*, which dates from the 16th century. The two children are abandoned in the wood by their wicked uncle who wishes to steal their inheritance. The children die of starvation and robins cover their bodies with leaves; the uncle and his accomplice are subsequently brought to justice.

baby

be someone's baby (of a project) be instigated and developed by one particular person; be someone's creation or special concern. informal

be left holding the baby: *see* HOLDING.

throw the baby out with the bathwater discard something valuable along with other things that are inessential or undesirable.

> ⓘ This phrase is based on a German saying recorded from the early 16th century but not introduced into English until the mid 19th century, by Thomas Carlyle. He identified it as German and gave it in the form, 'You must empty out the bathing-tub, but not the baby along with it.'

> **1998** *New Scientist* It is easy to throw out the baby with the bathwater when it comes to UFO books—there are some seriously bad titles out there.

back

at the back of your mind not consciously or specifically thought of or remembered but still part of your general awareness.

back in the day in the past; some time ago.

a back number ❶ an issue of a periodical before the current one. ❷ a person whose ideas or methods are out of date and who is no longer relevant or useful.

back o'Bourke the outback. Australian informal

> ⓘ *Bourke* is the name of a town in northwest New South Wales.

the back of beyond a very remote or inaccessible place.

> **1998 Sanjida O'Connell** *Angel Bird* This is London, Niall, not some poky wee place in the back of beyond.

back to the drawing board used to indicate that an idea or scheme has been unsuccessful and a new one must be devised.

> ⓘ An architectural or engineering project is at its earliest phase when it exists only as a plan on a *drawing board*.

> **1991** *Discover* Even as Humphries fine-tunes his system, however, he realizes that NASA could send him back to the drawing board.

back to square one back to the starting point, with no progress made.

> ⓘ *Square one* may be a reference to a board game such as Snakes and Ladders, or may come from the notional division of a football pitch into eight numbered sections for the purpose of early radio commentaries.

back the wrong horse make a wrong or inappropriate choice.

be on (*or* **get off**) **someone's back** nag (*or* stop nagging) someone. informal

by the back door using indirect or dishonest means to achieve an objective.

get someone's back up make someone annoyed or angry.

> ⓘ This phrase developed as an allusion to the way a cat arches its back when it is angry or threatened.

get your own back: *see* GET.

know something like the back of your hand be entirely familiar with something.

not in my back yard: *see* NOT.

on your back in bed recovering from an injury or illness.

put your back into approach a task with vigour.

see the back of be rid of an unwanted person or thing. British informal

someone's back is turned someone's attention is elsewhere.

> **1989 Orson Scott Card** *Prentice Alvin* That prentice of yours look strong enough to dig it hisself, if he doesn't lazy off and sleep when your back is turned.

take a back seat take or be given a less important position or role. Compare with **in the driver's seat** (*at* DRIVER).

with your back to (*or* **up against**) **the wall** in a desperate situation.

backbone

put backbone into someone encourage someone to behave resolutely.

> ❶ As a metaphor for 'firmness of character', *backbone* dates from the mid 19th century.

> **1998** *Spectator* There is a widespread belief that if only Mrs Thatcher had still been in No. 10, she would have put backbone into Bush and got rid of Saddam.

back-seat

a back-seat driver ❶ a passenger in a vehicle who constantly gives the driver unwanted advice on how to drive. ❷ someone who lectures and criticizes the person actually in control of something.

backwards

bend over backwards to do something make every effort, especially to be fair or helpful. informal

know something backwards be entirely familiar with something.

> **1991 William Trevor** *Reading Turgenev* People who lived in the town knew it backwards.

bacon

save someone's bacon: *see* **save someone's skin** *at* SAVE.

bring home the bacon ❶ supply material provision or support. ❷ achieve success. informal

> ❶ This phrase probably derives from the much earlier *save your bacon*, recorded from the mid 17th century. In early use *bacon* also referred to fresh pork, the meat most readily available to rural people.

❷ **1997** *Spectator* Mr Montgomery was able to sack Mr Hargreaves, who had evidently not brought home the bacon.

bad

bad blood: *see* BLOOD.

a bad quarter of an hour a short but very unpleasant period of time; an unnerving experience.

> ❶ *A bad quarter of an hour* is a translation of the French phrase *un mauvais quart d'heure*, which has also been current in English since the mid 19th century.

a bad workman blames his tools: *see* WORKMAN.

be bad news: *see* NEWS.

my bad used to acknowledge responsibility for a mistake. North American informal

turn up like a bad penny: *see* PENNY.

bag

bag and baggage with all your belongings.

a bag of bones an emaciated person or animal. Compare with **be skin and bone** (*at* SKIN).

a bag (*or* **bundle**) **of nerves** a person who is extremely timid or tense. informal

a bag (*or* **whole bag**) **of tricks** a set of ingenious plans, techniques, or resources. informal

be left holding the bag: *see* **be left holding the baby** *at* HOLDING.

in the bag ❶ (of something desirable) as good as secured. ❷ drunk. US informal

pack your bag: *see* PACK.

bait

fish or cut bait: *see* FISH.

rise to the bait: *see* RISE.

baker

a baker's dozen thirteen.

> ❶ This expression arose from the former bakers' practice of adding an extra loaf to a dozen sold to a retailer, this representing the latter's profit.

balance

turn the balance: *see* **turn the scales** *at* SCALE.

weigh something in the balance carefully

ponder or assess the merits and demerits of something.

> ❶ The image is of a pair of old-fashioned scales with two pans in which the positive and negative aspects of something can be set against each other. The expanded phrase *weighed in the balance and found wanting* meaning 'having failed to meet the test of a particular situation' is also found, and is an allusion to the biblical book of Daniel, where such a process formed part of the judgement made on King Belshazzar.

bald

as bald as a coot completely bald.

> ❶ The coot (*Fulica atra*) has a broad white shield extending up from the base of its bill. The history of the word *bald* is somewhat obscure, but analogies with other northern European languages suggest a connection with the idea of 'having a white patch or streak'.

ball

a ball and chain a severe hindrance.

> ❶ Originally, *a ball and chain* referred to a heavy metal ball attached by a chain to the leg of a prisoner or convict to prevent their escape.

the ball is in someone's court it is that particular person's turn to act next.

> ❶ This expression is a metaphor from tennis or a similar ball game where different players use particular areas of a marked court.

a ball of fire a person who is full of energy and enthusiasm.

> ❶ In the early 19th century this phrase was also used to mean 'a glass of brandy'.

behind the eight ball: *see* EIGHT.

have a ball enjoy yourself greatly; have fun. informal

have the ball at your feet have your best opportunity of succeeding.

have a lot on the ball have a lot of ability. US

keep the ball rolling maintain the momentum of an activity.

keep your eye on (or take your eye off) the ball keep (or fail to keep) your attention focused on the matter in hand.

on the ball alert to new ideas, methods, and trends. informal

1998 Romesh Gunesekera *Sandglass* It's big business now, you know. You have to be on the ball: go, go, go all the time.

play ball work willingly with others; cooperate. informal

> ❶ The literal sense is of *play ball* is 'play a team ball game such as baseball or cricket'.

start the ball rolling set an activity in motion; make a start.

the whole ball of wax everything. North American informal

a whole new ball game a completely new set of circumstances. informal

> ❶ The phrase originated in North America, where a *ball game* is a baseball match.

1989 *Looks* Making the film was a whole new ball game ... for Kylie.

ballistic

go ballistic fly into a rage. informal

1998 *New Scientist* The French nuclear industry, local authorities around La Hague and some government agencies went ballistic. Viel was fiercely condemned for his findings.

balloon

go down like a lead balloon: *see* LEAD.

when (or before) the balloon goes up when (or before) the action or trouble starts. informal

> ❶ The balloon alluded to is probably one released to mark the start of an event.

1959 *Punch* The international rules of war are apt to be waived when the balloon goes up.

ballpark

in the ballpark in a particular area or range. informal

> ❶ The phrase originated in the USA, where a *ballpark* is a baseball ground.

bamboo

the bamboo curtain an impenetrable political, economic, and cultural barrier between China and non-Communist countries.

> ❶ Formed on the pattern of **the iron curtain** (*see at* IRON), this phrase dates back to the 1940s.

banana

banana republic a small tropical state,

especially one in central America, whose economy is regarded as wholly dependent on its fruit-exporting trade. derogatory

go bananas ❶ become extremely angry or excited. ❷ go mad. informal

> ❶ **1992 Jim Lehrer** *A Bus of My Own* I predicted John Erlichman would probably go bananas when he testified the next day.

second banana the second most important person in an organization or activity. informal, chiefly North American

top banana the most important person in an organization or activity. informal, chiefly North American

> ❶ The two expressions above originated in US theatrical slang. The *top banana* was originally the comedian who topped the bill in a show, while the *second banana* was the supporting comedian.

banana skin

slip on a banana skin: *see* SLIP.

band

when the band begins to play when matters become serious.

bandwagon

jump on the bandwagon join others in doing something or supporting a cause that is fashionable or likely to be successful.

> ❶ *Bandwagon* was originally the US term for a large wagon able to carry a band of musicians in a procession.

bang

bang for your (or the) buck value for money; performance for cost. US informal

> **1995** *Desktop Publishing Journal* These additions to RunShare ... will surely give you the most productive network, the most 'bang for your buck'.

bang goes — used to express the sudden or complete destruction of something, especially a plan or ambition.

> **1895 George Bernard Shaw** *Letter* Somebody will give a surreptitious performance of it: and then bang goes my copyright.

bang on exactly right. British informal

bang people's heads together reprimand people severely, especially in the attempt to make them stop arguing.

get a bang out of derive excitement or pleasure from. North American informal

> **1931 Damon Runyon** *Guys and Dolls* He seems to be getting a great bang out of the doings.

go with a bang happen with obvious success.

bank

break the bank ❶ (in gambling) win more money than is held by the bank. ❷ cost more than you can afford. informal

banner

under the banner of ❶ claiming to support a particular cause or set of ideas. ❷ as part of a particular group or organization.

baptism

a baptism of fire a difficult introduction to a new job or activity.

> ❶ A *baptism of fire* was originally a soldier's initiation into battle.

> **1998** *Times* Opposition spokesmen do not normally face a baptism of fire, but the Bank of England's unexpected decision ... provided the Shadow Chancellor with an opportunity to make an early mark.

bar

bar none with no exceptions.

> **1866 M. E. Braddon** *Lady's Mile* Your 'Aspasia' is the greatest picture that ever was painted— 'bar none'.

bare

the bare bones the basic facts about something, without any detail.

bargepole

would not touch someone or something with a bargepole used to express an emphatic refusal to have anything to do with someone or something. informal

> ❶ A *bargepole* is used to propel a barge and to fend off obstacles. The equivalent US expression substitutes a *ten-foot pole*.

bark

bark at the moon: *see* MOON.

bark up the wrong tree pursue a mistaken or misguided line of thought or course of action. informal

> ❶ The metaphor is of a dog that has mistaken the tree in which its quarry has taken refuge and is barking at the foot of the wrong one.

1969 Arnold Bennett *Forty Years On* For sovereign states to conclude agreements on the basis of a mutual fondness for dogs seems to me to be barking up the wrong tree.

someone's bark is worse than their bite someone is not as ferocious as they appear or sound.

> ❶ A similar association between barking and biting occurs in the proverb *a barking dog never bites*, which can be traced back through 13th-century French (*chascuns chiens qui abaie ne mort pas*, dogs that bark don't bite) to Latin (*canem timidum vehementius latrare quam mordere*, a timid dog barks more furiously than it bites).

barn

round Robin Hood's barn: *see* ROBIN HOOD.

barred

no holds barred: *see* HOLD.

barrel

a barrel of laughs a source of fun or amusement. informal

> **1996** *Mail on Sunday* Seeing so many old people gathered all in one place was hardly a barrel of laughs.

get someone over a barrel get someone in a helpless position; have someone at your mercy. informal

> ❶ This phrase perhaps refers to the condition of a person who has been rescued from drowning and is placed over a barrel to clear their lungs of water.

scrape the barrel: *see* SCRAPE.

with both barrels with unrestrained force or emotion. informal

> ❶ The barrels in question are the two barrels of a firearm.

barrelhead

on the barrelhead: *see* **on the nail** *at* NAIL.

barricade

man (or go to) the barricades strongly protest against a government or other institution or its policy.

base

get to first base achieve the first step towards your objective. informal, chiefly North American

> **1962 P. G. Wodehouse** *Service with a Smile* She gives you the feeling that you'll never get to first base with her.

off base mistaken. North American informal

> **1947** *Time* Your Latin American department was off base in its comparison of the Portillo Hotel in Chile with our famous Sun Valley.

touch base briefly make or renew contact with someone or something. informal

> **1984 Armistead Maupin** *Babycakes* In search of a routine, he touched base with his launderette, his post office, his nearest market.

> ❶ *Base* in these three phrases refers to each of the four points in the angles of the 'diamond' in baseball, which a player has to reach in order to score a run.

basic

back to basics abandoning complication and sophistication to concentrate on the most essential aspects of something.

> ❶ *Back to basics* is often used to suggest the moral superiority of the plain and simple, as in a speech made in 1993 by the British Conservative leader John Major, who spearheaded the government's campaign for the regeneration of basic family and educational values in the 1990s.

bat

blind as a bat: *see* BLIND.

have bats in the (or your) belfry be eccentric or crazy. informal

> ❶ This expression refers to the way in which bats in an enclosed space fly about wildly if they are disturbed.

> **c1901 G. W. Peck** *Peck's Red-Headed Boy* They all thought a crazy man with bats in his belfry had got loose.

like a bat out of hell very fast and wildly. informal

> **1995 Patrick McCabe** *The Dead School* Like a bat out of hell that Joe Buck gets on out of the apartment and doesn't stop running till he reaches Times Square.

not bat an eyelid (or eye) show no emotional or other reaction. informal

> ❶ *Bat* in this sense is perhaps a dialect and US variant of the verb *bate* meaning 'lower or let down'. The variant *not blink an eye* is also found.

> **1997 James Ryan** *Dismantling Mr Doyle* She did not bat an eyelid when Eve spelled out the unorthodox details of the accommodation they required.

off your own bat at your own instigation; spontaneously. British

> ❶ The *bat* referred to in this phrase is a cricket bat.

> **1995 Colin Bateman** *Cycle of Violence* She doesn't have me doing anything, Marty. It's all off my own bat.

right off the bat at the very beginning; straight away. North American

bated

with bated breath in great suspense; very anxiously or excitedly.

> ❶ *Baited*, which is sometimes seen, is a misspelling, since *bated* in this sense is a shortened form of *abated*, the idea being that your breathing is lessened under the influence of extreme suspense.

bath

an early bath the sending off of a sports player during a game. British informal

> ❶ The allusion is to the bath or shower taken by players at the end of a match.

take a bath suffer a heavy financial loss. informal

> **1997** *Bookseller* When the yen drops in value, as it is doing right now, we take a bath. There is no way to change the prices fast enough.

baton

pass (or hand) on the baton hand over a particular duty or responsibility.

> ❶ In athletics, the *baton* is the short stick or rod passed from one runner to the next in a relay race. The related phrases *pick up* or *take up the baton* mean 'accept a duty or responsibility'. Compare with **hand on the torch** (at TORCH).

under the baton of (of an orchestra or choir) conducted by.

> ❶ The *baton* here is the rod used by the conductor.

batten

batten down the hatches prepare for a difficulty or crisis.

> ❶ *Batten down the hatches* was originally a nautical term meaning 'make a ship's hatches secure with gratings and tarpaulins' in expectation of stormy weather.

> **1998** *Oldie* They endured the hard pounding of the Seventies, when Labour battened down the hatches, and soldiered through the follies of the early Eighties.

battery

recharge your batteries: see RECHARGE.

battle

battle of the giants a contest between two pre-eminent parties.

> ❶ This expression may be a reference to the battle between the giants and gods in Greek mythology.

battle royal a fiercely contested fight or dispute.

> **1997 Fred Chappell** *Farewell, I'm Bound to Leave You* The boys told no one about the fight … it was a battle royal and went on from two o'clock in the afternoon until sundown.

battle stations used as a command or signal to military personnel to take up their positions in preparation for battle. chiefly US

half the battle an important step towards achieving something.

a losing battle: see LOSING.

a pitched battle: see PITCHED.

a running battle: see RUNNING.

bay

bay for blood demand punishment or retribution.

bring someone or something to bay trap or corner a person or animal being hunted or chased.

> ❶ This phrase was originally a medieval hunting term, referring to the position of the quarry when it is cornered by the baying hounds. An animal cornered in this way is said to *stand at bay*.

hold (or keep) someone or something at bay prevent someone or something from approaching or having an effect.

be

-to-be of the future.

> **1993** *Mother & Baby* Many mums-to-be report that small frequent snacks are easier to keep down than three large meals a day.

be there for someone be available to support or comfort someone who is experiencing difficulties or adversities.

the be-all and end-all a feature of an activity or a way of life that is of greater importance than any other. informal

bead

draw (or get) a bead on take aim at with a gun. chiefly North American

> **1994** *Ontario Out of Doors* Few moose will pose majestically right at the water's edge while you draw a bead on them.

beam

a beam in your eye a fault that is greater in yourself than in the person you are finding fault with.

> ℹ This phrase comes from Matthew 7:3: 'Why beholdest thou the mote that is in thy brother's eye, but considerest not the beam that is in thy own eye?' For **a mote in someone's eye**, see MOTE.

broad in the beam: *see* BROAD.

off (or way off) beam on the wrong track; mistaken. informal

> ℹ Originally, this phrase referred to the radio beam or signal used to guide aircraft.

> **1997 Anthony Barnett** *This Time* I sample the press coverage to illustrate how large sections of the Fourth Estate were way off beam in their conviction that voters want the country steered back towards 'Great Englishness'.

on your beam ends near the end of your resources; desperate.

> ℹ The *beam* referred to here is one of the main horizontal transverse timbers of a wooden ship; compare with **broad in the beam** (at BROAD). The phrase originated as the nautical term *on her beam ends*, and was used of a ship that had heeled over on its side and was almost capsizing.

bean

full of beans lively; in high spirits. informal

> ℹ This phrase was originally used by people who work with horses, and referred to the good condition of a horse fed on beans.

give someone beans scold or deal severely with a person. informal

a hill (or row) of beans something of little importance or value. informal

> **1999** *SL (Cape Town)* I think that what your friends and family think shouldn't amount to a hill of beans.

know how many beans make five be intelligent; have your wits about you. British informal

not have a bean be penniless. informal

> ℹ *Bean* was an early 19th-century slang term for a golden guinea or sovereign. In the sense of 'a coin', it now survives only in this phrase.

spill the beans: *see* SPILL.

bear

bear the brunt of: *see* BRUNT.

grin and bear it: *see* GRIN.

have your cross to bear: *see* CROSS.

like a bear with a sore head (of a person) very irritable. British informal

loaded for bear fully prepared for any eventuality, typically a confrontation or challenge. North American informal

> ℹ The image here may be of a hunting gun loaded and ready to shoot a bear.

beard

beard the lion in his den (or lair) confront or challenge someone on their own ground.

> ℹ This phrase developed partly from the idea of being daring enough to take a lion by the beard and partly from the use of *beard* as a verb to mean 'face', i.e. to face a lion in his den.

beat

beat a hasty retreat withdraw, typically in order to avoid something unpleasant.

> ℹ In former times, a drumbeat could be used to keep soldiers in step while they were retreating.

beat about the bush discuss a matter without coming to the point; be ineffectual and waste time.

> ℹ This phrase is a metaphor which originated in the shooting or netting of birds; compare with **beat the bushes** below.

> **1992 Barry Unsworth** *Sacred Hunger* I don't want to beat about the bush. Mr Adams is threatening to leave us.

beat someone at their own game use someone's own methods to outdo them in their chosen activity.

beat your breast: *see* BREAST.

beat the bushes search thoroughly. North American informal

> ⓘ This expression originates from the way in which hunters walk through undergrowth wielding long sticks which are used to force birds or animals out into the open where they can be shot or netted.

beat the clock perform a task quickly or within a fixed time limit.

beat the daylights out of: *see* DAYLIGHT.

beat the drum for: *see* DRUM.

beat your (*or* the) meat (of a man) masturbate. vulgar slang

beat the pants off prove to be vastly superior to. informal

> **1990 Paul Auster** *The Music of Chance* 'Not bad, kid,' Nashe said. 'You beat the pants off me.'

beat a path to someone's door (of a large number of people) hasten to make contact with someone regarded as interesting or inspiring.

> ⓘ This phrase developed from the idea of a large number of people trampling down vegetation to make a path: compare with **off the beaten track** (*at* BEATEN).

beat the system succeed in finding a means of getting round rules, regulations, or other means of control.

beat someone to it succeed in doing something or getting somewhere before someone else, to their annoyance.

if you can't beat them, join them if you are unable to outdo rivals in some endeavour, you might as well cooperate with them and gain whatever advantage possible by doing so. humorous.

miss a beat: *see* MISS.

to beat the band in such a way as to surpass all competition. North American informal

> **1995 Patrick McCabe** *The Dead School* He was polishing away to beat the band.

beaten

beaten (*or* pipped) at the post defeated at the last moment.

> ⓘ The *post* alluded to here is the marker at the end of a race.

off the beaten track (*or* path) ❶ in or into an isolated place. ❷ unusual.

> ❷ **1992 Iain Banks** *The Crow Road* 'Your Uncle Hamish...' She looked troubled. 'He's a bit off the beaten track, that boy.'

beautiful

the beautiful people ❶ fashionable, glamorous, and privileged people. ❷ (in the 1960s) hippies.

> ❶ **1995** *Singapore: Rough Guide* The coolest address in town, and a magnet for the beautiful people.

the body beautiful an ideal of physical beauty.

> **1992** *Mother Jones* About 75,000 women a year elect to have cosmetic surgery, spurred on by ubiquitous images of the body beautiful.

beaver

work like a beaver work steadily and industriously. informal

> ⓘ The beaver is referred to here because of the industriousness with which it constructs the dams necessary for its aquatic dwellings. The image is similarly conjured up by the phrase *beaver away* meaning 'work hard'.

beck

at someone's beck and call always having to be ready to obey someone's orders immediately.

> ⓘ *Beck* in the sense of 'a significant gesture of command' comes from the verb *beck*, a shortened form of *beckon*. It is now found mainly in this phrase.

bed

bed and breakfast ❶ overnight accommodation and breakfast next morning as offered by hotels etc. ❷ designating financial transactions in which shares are sold and then bought back the next morning.

a bed of nails a problematic or uncomfortable situation.

> ⓘ A *bed of nails* was originally a board with nails pointing out of it, lain on by Eastern fakirs and ascetics.

a bed of roses a situation or activity that is comfortable or easy.

get out of bed on the wrong side be bad-tempered all day long.

in bed with ❶ having sexual intercourse with. ❷ in undesirably close association with. informal

> ❷ **2000** *Snowboard UK* Jackson lies like an oasis of culture and good coffee in a state that is otherwise firmly in bed with gun culture.

you have made your bed and must lie in it
you must accept the consequences of your
own actions.

bedpost

**between you and me and the bedpost (*or*
the gatepost *or* the wall)** in strict
confidence. informal

> ❶ The *bedpost*, *gatepost*, or *wall* is seen as
> marking the boundary beyond which the
> confidence must not go.

bedside

bedside manner a doctor's approach or
attitude to a patient.

> **1993 Bill Moyers** *Healing & the Mind* Are you
> just talking about the old-fashioned bedside
> manner of a doctor who comes around and
> visits you when you need him?

bee

the bee's knees something or someone
outstandingly good. informal

> ❶ The *bee's knees* was first used to refer to
> something small and insignificant, but it
> quickly developed its current, completely
> opposite meaning.

have a bee in your bonnet have an obsessive
preoccupation with something. informal

> ❶ This expression, along with *have bees in
> the head* or *bees in the brain*, was first used to
> refer to someone who was regarded as crazy
> or eccentric.

beeline

make a beeline for go rapidly and directly
towards.

> ❶ The phrase refers to the straight line
> supposedly taken instinctively by a bee
> returning to its hive.

> **1997** *Bookseller* And when he heard that people
> might like him to sign copies of his new
> novel…he cut the small talk and made a
> beeline for the stall.

been

been there, done that: *see* THERE.

beer

beer and skittles amusement. British

> ❶ This phrase comes from the proverb *life
> isn't all beer and skittles*. The game of skittles
> is used as a prime example of a form of light-
> hearted entertainment.

beg

beg the question ❶ raise a point that has not
been dealt with; invite an obvious
question. ❷ assume the truth of an
argument or of a proposition to be proved,
without arguing it.

> ❶ The original meaning of the phrase *beg
> the question* belongs to the field of logic and
> is a translation of Latin *petitio principii*,
> literally meaning 'laying claim to a principle',
> i.e. assume the truth of something that
> ought to be proved first. For many
> traditionalists this remains the only correct
> meaning, but far commoner in English today
> is the first sense here, 'invite an obvious
> question'.

beggar

beggar belief (*or* description) be too
extraordinary to be believed (*or* described).

beggar on horseback a formerly poor person
made arrogant or corrupt through
achieving wealth and luxury.

> ❶ Compare with the mid 17th-century
> proverb *set a beggar on horseback and he'll
> ride to the devil*, meaning that a person not
> used to power will use it unwisely.

beggars can't be choosers people with no
other options must be content with what is
offered. proverb

begging

go begging ❶ (of an article) be available.
❷ (of an opportunity) not be taken.

beginner

beginner's luck good luck supposedly
experienced by a beginner at a particular
game or activity.

beginning

the beginning of the end the event or
development to which the conclusion or
failure of something can be traced.

> **1992 H. Norman Schwartzkopf** *It Doesn't Take a
> Hero* I heard about D-Day on the radio. The
> announcer quoted Ohio governor John
> Bricker's now-famous line that this was 'the
> beginning of the end of the forces of evil'.

bejesus informal

beat the bejesus out of someone hit
someone very hard or for a long time.

scare the bejesus out of someone frighten
someone very much.

2001 *GQ* This place is going to scare the bejesus out of the fuddy-duddy Sloaney-Pony set.

> ❶ *Bejesus* is an alteration of the exclamation *by Jesus!* It is often found in its Anglo-Irish form *bejasus* or *bejabers*.

bell

bell, book, and candle a formula for laying a curse on someone.

> ❶ This expression alludes to the closing words of the rite of excommunication, 'Do to the book, quench the candle, ring the bell', meaning that the service book is closed, the candle put out, and the passing bell rung, as a sign of spiritual death.

bell the cat take the danger of a shared enterprise upon yourself.

> ❶ *Bell the cat* alludes to the fable in which mice or rats have the idea of hanging a bell around the cat's neck so as to have warning of its approach, the only difficulty being to find one of their number willing to undertake the task.

bells and whistles attractive additional features or trimmings. informal

> ❶ The *bells and whistles* originally referred to were those found on old fairground organs. Nowadays, the phrase is often used in computing jargon to mean 'attractive but superfluous facilities'.

saved by the bell: *see* SAVED.

as clear (*or* sound) as a bell perfectly clear (*or* sound).

> **1993** *Independent* We spent a few thousand on redecoration, but basically the place was sound as a bell.

give someone a bell telephone someone. British informal

ring a bell revive a distant recollection; sound familiar. informal

with bells on enthusiastically. North American informal

> **1989 Mary Gordon** *The Other Side* So, everybody's waiting for you with bells on.

belle

belle of the ball the most admired and successful woman on a particular occasion.

> ❶ The *belle of the ball* was originally the girl or woman regarded as the most beautiful and popular at a dance.

belly

go belly up go bankrupt. informal

> ❶ The implied comparison is with a dead fish or other animal floating upside down in the water.

> **1998** *Times: Weekend* The single currency could well go belly-up within two or three years.

bellyful

have a bellyful of become impatient after prolonged experience of someone or something. informal

below

below stairs in the basement of a house, in particular as the part occupied by servants. British dated

belt

below the belt unfair or unfairly; not in keeping with the rules.

> ❶ In boxing a blow *below the belt* is a low, and therefore unlawful, blow.

belt and braces (of a policy or action) providing double security by using two means to achieve the same end. British

> ❶ This meaning developed from the idea of a literal *belt* and *braces* holding up a pair of loose-fitting trousers.

> **2002** *Digital Photography Made Easy* Oddly, the manual is also on CD, which seems a bit belt and braces (though useful if you lose the original).

tighten your belt cut your expenditure; live more frugally.

under your belt ❶ (of food or drink) consumed. ❷ safely or satisfactorily achieved, experienced, or acquired.

bend

bend someone's ear talk to someone, especially with great eagerness or in order to ask a favour. informal

bend your elbow drink alcohol. North American

bend over backwards: *see* BACKWARDS.

round the bend (*or* twist) crazy; mad. informal

> **1998** *Spectator* She combines a fondness for holidays in Switzerland with an amiable husband . . . who saves her from going completely round the bend.

b

bended

on bended knee kneeling, especially when pleading or showing great respect.

> ❶ *Bended* was the original past participle of *bend*, but in Middle English it was superseded in general use by *bent*. It is now archaic and survives only in this phrase.

benefit

give someone the benefit of — explain or recount to someone at length (often used ironically when someone pompously or impertinently assumes that their knowledge or experience is superior to that of the person to whom they are talking).

> **1999** *Stage* Our courses are delivered by 2 current TV personalities who will give you the benefit of their 6 years experience.

the benefit of the doubt a concession that someone or something must be regarded as correct or justified, if the contrary has not been proved.

Benjamin

a Benjamin's portion (*or* **mess**) the largest share or portion.

> ❶ In the Bible, Benjamin was the youngest son of the Jewish patriarch Jacob. When Jacob's sons encountered their long-lost brother Joseph in Egypt, where he had become a high official, they failed to recognize him, but Joseph generously entertained them: 'And he took and sent messes [servings of food] unto them from before him: but Benjamin's mess was five times so much as any of their's' (Genesis 43:34).

bent

bent out of shape angry or agitated. North American informal

> **1994 David Spencer** *Alien Nation 6: Passing Fancy* Max Corigliano was there … and bent out of shape about having been made to wait so long.

berth

give someone or something a wide berth stay away from someone or something.

> ❶ *Berth* is a nautical term which originally referred to the distance that ships should keep away from each other or from the shore, rocks, etc., in order to avoid a collision. Therefore, the literal meaning of the expression is 'steer a ship well clear of something while passing it'.

besetting

besetting sin a fault to which a person or institution is especially prone; a characteristic weakness.

> ❶ The verb *beset* literally means 'surround with hostile intent', so the image is of a sin besieging or pressing in upon a person.

> **1974 Donal Scannell** *Mother Knew Best* Mother said vanity was a besetting sin which Amy resented, to say the least of it.

beside

beside yourself overcome with worry, grief, or anger; distraught.

best

best bib and tucker: *see* BIB.

the best thing since sliced bread: *see* BREAD.

put your best foot forward: *see* FOOT.

with the best will in the world: *see* WILL.

the best of both worlds: *see* WORLD.

the best of British used to wish someone well in an enterprise, especially when you are almost sure it will be unsuccessful. informal

> ❶ This phrase is an abbreviation of *the best of British luck to you*.

give someone or something best admit the superiority of; give way to. British
> **1990** *Birds Magazine* He finally decided to give us best and took himself off.

make the best of it ❶ derive what limited advantage you can from something unsatisfactory or unwelcome. ❷ use resources as well as possible.

> ❶ The first sense is often found in the form *make the best of a bad job*, meaning 'do something as well as you can under difficult circumstances'.

your best bet the most favourable option available in particular circumstances.

six of the best a caning as a punishment, traditionally with six strokes of the cane.

> ❶ *Six of the best* was formerly a common punishment in boys' schools, but it is now chiefly historical in its literal sense and tends to be used figuratively or humorously.

bet

all bets are off the outcome of a particular situation is unpredictable. informal

don't bet on it used to express doubt about an assertion or situation. informal

you can bet your boots (or **bottom dollar** or **life**) you may be absolutely certain. informal

bet the farm risk everything that you own on a bet, investment, or enterprise. North American informal

a safe bet a certainty.

> ❶ *A safe bet* originally referred to a horse that was confidently expected to win a race.

> **2002** *Observer* It is a safe bet that as the Western world gets fatter, the people on its television screens will continue to get thinner.

better

against your better judgement: *see* JUDGEMENT.

the — the better used to emphasize the importance or desirability of the quality or thing specified.

> **1986** Patrick Leigh Fermor *Between the Woods & the Water* He had a passion for limericks, the racier the better.

better the devil you know it's wiser to deal with an undesirable but familiar person or situation than to risk a change that might lead to a situation with worse difficulties or a person whose faults you have yet to discover.

> ❶ This phrase is a shortened form of the proverb *better the devil you know than the devil you don't know.*

better late than never it's preferable for something to happen or be done belatedly than not at all.

better safe than sorry it's wiser to be cautious and careful than to be hasty or rash and so do something that you may later regret.

> ❶ Apparently the expression is quite recent in this form (mid 20th century); *better be sure than sorry* is recorded from the mid 19th century.

> **1998** *New Scientist* The meeting is to be commended for taking a 'better safe than sorry' attitude, and drawing up a baseline list of measures to be put in place when disease breaks out.

the better to — so as to — better.

> **1986 Peter Mathiessen** *Men's Lives* Francis ran both motors with their housings off, the better to tinker with them.

get the better of win an advantage over someone; defeat or outwit someone.

go one better ❶ narrowly surpass a previous effort or achievement. ❷ narrowly outdo another person.

no better than you should (or **ought to**) **be** regarded as sexually promiscuous or of doubtful moral character.

> ❶ This phrase dates back to the early 17th century. Used typically of a woman, it is now rather dated.

> **1998** *Spectator* 'She's no better than she ought to be'. (British mothers of my generation... often used that enigmatic phrase. They would use it about female neighbours of whom they disapproved, or women in low-cut dresses on television.)

your better half your husband or wife. humorous

seen better days: *see* DAY.

so much the better: *see* MUCH.

betting

the betting is that it is likely that. informal

between

between the devil and the deep blue sea: *see* DEVIL.

between a rock and a hard place: *see* ROCK.

betwixt

betwixt and between neither one thing nor the other. informal

> ❶ *Betwixt* is now poetic or archaic and is seldom found outside this phrase.

beyond

the back of beyond: *see* BACK.

it's beyond me it's too astonishing, puzzling, etc. for me to understand or explain. informal

bib

your best bib and tucker your best clothes. informal

> ❶ *Bib and tucker* originally referred to certain items of women's clothing. A *bib* is a garment worn over the upper front part of the body (e.g. the bib of an apron), and a *tucker* was a decorative piece of lace formerly worn on a woman's bodice.

stick (or **poke**) **your bib in** interfere. Australian & New Zealand informal

bicky

big bickies a large sum of money Australian informal

> ❶ *Bickies* is an abbreviation of *biscuits*.

1981 *Canberra Times* Appearance money is another claim which we think will succeed...Just showing up is worth big bickies.

bide

bide your time wait quietly for a good opportunity.

> ❶ *Bide* in the sense of *await* is now only found in this expression. It has been superseded by *abide* in most of its other senses.

1991 Gillian Slovo *The Betrayal* And so he bided his time, waiting, plotting, planning, looking for the signs that would be good for him.

big

Big brother: *see* BROTHER.

the big C: *see* C.

a big cheese an important and influential person. informal

> ❶ Other versions of this phrase substitute *fish*, *gun*, *noise*, *shot*, or *wheel* for *cheese*. These are mainly self-explanatory, with the exception of *cheese* itself, which is of doubtful origin but may be from Persian and Urdu *chīz* meaning 'thing'. As a phrase, *big cheese* seems to have originated in early 20th-century US slang, as did *big noise*. *Big wheel* in this metaphorical sense (as opposed to the fairground ride known as a Ferris wheel) and *big shot* are similarly US in origin (mid 20th century). *Big fish* may have connotations either of something it is desirable for you to catch or of the metaphorical expression a *big fish in a small pond*.

big deal ❶ an important or impressive event. ❷ used as an ironic exclamation to indicate that you do not think something is as important or impressive as another person has suggested. informal

the big five a name given by hunters to the five largest and most dangerous African mammals: rhinoceros, elephant, buffalo, lion, and leopard.

the big lie a gross distortion or misrepresentation of the facts, especially when used as a propaganda device by a politician or official body.

the big smoke ❶ London. British informal ❷ any large town. chiefly Australian

the big Three, Four, etc. the dominant group of three, four, etc. informal

1998 *Sunday Telegraph* The notion that someone outside the so-called 'Big Four'—the ministerial group which meets before Cabinet —might be given such status is uplifting.

big white chief: *see* CHIEF.

give someone the big e reject someone, typically in an insensitive or dismissive way. British informal

> ❶ The *e* in the phrase is from *elbow*: *give someone the big elbow* has the same meaning.

make it big become very successful or famous. informal

talk big talk confidently or boastfully. informal

think big be ambitious. informal

too big for your boots conceited. informal

bike

get off your bike become annoyed. Australian & New Zealand informal

> **1939 Xavier Herbert** *Capricornia* 'I tell you I saw no-one.' 'Don't get off your bike, son.—I know you're tellin' lies.'

on your bike! ❶ go away! ❷ take action! British informal

> ❶ Sense 2 became a catchphrase in 1980s Britain, when it was used as an exhortation to the unemployed to show initiative in their attempt to find work. It was taken from a speech by the Conservative politician Norman Tebbit in which he said of his unemployed father: 'He did not riot, he got on his bike and looked for work.'

bill

bill and coo exchange caresses or affectionate words; behave or talk in a very loving or sentimental way. informal, dated

> ❶ The image is of two doves, a long-established symbol of mutual love.

a clean bill of health a declaration or confirmation that someone is healthy or something is in good condition.

> ❶ In the mid 18th century, a *bill of health* was an official certificate given to the master of a ship on leaving port; if *clean*, it certified that there was no infection either in the port or on board the vessel.

fit (or fill) the bill be suitable for a particular purpose.

> ❶ *Bill* in this context is a printed list of items on a theatrical programme or advertisement.

foot the bill be responsible for paying for something.

sell someone a bill of goods deceive or swindle someone, usually by persuading them to accept something untrue or undesirable.

> ❶ A *bill of goods* is a consignment of merchandise.

> **1968** *Globe & Mail* (Toronto) There was no production bonus...We were sold a bill of goods.

top (*or* **head**) **the bill** be the main performer or act in a show, play, etc.

billy-o

like billy-o very much, hard, or strongly. British informal

> **1995 John Banville** *Athena* This skin tone is the effect of cigarettes, I suspect, for she is a great smoker...going at the fags like billy-o.

bird

the bird has flown the person you are looking for has escaped or gone away.

a bird in hand something that you have securely or are sure of.

> ❶ This phrase refers to the proverb *a bird in hand is worth two in the bush*, current in English since the mid 15th century.

a bird of passage someone who is always moving on.

> ❶ Literally, a *bird of passage* is a migrant bird.

a bird's-eye view a general view from above.

the birds and the bees basic facts about sex and reproduction as told to a child. informal

birds of a feather people with similar tastes, interests, etc.

> ❶ This phrase comes from the proverb *birds of a feather flock together*, which has been current in this form since the late 16th century. Its origins may ultimately lie in the Apocrypha: 'the birds will resort unto their like' (Ecclesiasticus 27:9).

do bird serve a prison sentence. British informal

> ❶ In this phrase *bird* comes from rhyming slang *birdlime* 'time'.

early bird: *see* EARLY.

flip someone the bird stick your middle finger up at someone as a sign of contempt or anger. US informal

> **1994** *Washington Post Magazine* We could simultaneously honour America, break the law and flip the bird to all the do-gooders.

give someone (*or* **get**) **the bird** boo or jeer at someone (*or* be booed or jeered at). British informal

> ❶ This phrase first appeared in early 19th-century theatrical slang as *the big bird*, meaning 'a goose'. This was because the hissing of geese could be compared to the audience's hissing at an act or actor of which it disapproved.

have a bird be very shocked or agitated. North American informal

> **1992** *Globe & Mail* (Toronto) The Washington press corps would have a bird if the president-to-be appointed his wife to a real job.

kill two birds with one stone: *see* KILL.

a little bird told me used as a teasing way of saying that you do not intend to divulge how you came to know something.

strictly for the birds not worth consideration; unimportant. informal

> ❶ This expression was originally US army slang. It may be an allusion to the way in which birds eat the droppings of horses and cattle.

birthday

in your birthday suit naked. humorous

biscuit

have had the biscuit be no longer good for anything; be done for. Canadian informal

> **1994** *Equinox* I thought I'd had the biscuit. I was more than 12 kilometres from camp, I didn't have a coat...and it was about 40 below.

take the biscuit: *see* TAKE.

bit

a bit much somewhat excessive or unreasonable.

a bit of all right a pleasing person or thing, especially a woman regarded sexually. British informal

bit of fluff (*or* **skirt** *or* **stuff**) a woman regarded in sexual terms. British informal

> **1937 W. Somerset Maugham** *Theatre* It was strangely flattering for a woman to be treated as a little bit of fluff that you just tumbled on to a bed.

bit of rough: *see* ROUGH.

bit on the side ① a person with whom you are unfaithful to your partner. **②** a relationship involving being unfaithful to your partner. **③** money earned outside your normal job. informal

bits and pieces (*or* **bobs**) an assortment of small or unspecified items.

do your bit make a useful contribution to an effort or cause. informal

> **ⓘ** The exhortation to *do your bit* was much used during World War 1, but the expression was current in the late 19th century.

get the bit between your teeth begin to tackle a problem or task in a determined or independent way.

> **ⓘ** The metal bit in a horse's mouth should lie on the fleshy part of its gums; if a headstrong horse grasps the bit between its teeth it can evade the control of the reins and its rider.

to bits very much. informal

> **1998** *Times* A succession of elderly ladies explained how, as young women, they had fancied him to bits.

bite

bite someone's head off respond curtly or angrily.

a bite at the cherry: *see* CHERRY.

bite the big one die. North American informal

> **1996 Tom Clancy** *Executive Orders* The Premier of Turkmenistan bit the big one, supposedly an automobile accident.

bite the bullet face up to doing something difficult or unpleasant; stoically avoid showing fear or distress.

> **ⓘ** This phrase dates from the days before anaesthetics, when wounded soldiers were given a bullet or similar solid object to clench between their teeth when undergoing surgery.

> **1998 Joyce Holms** *Bad Vibes* Once he accepted it as inevitable he usually bit the bullet and did what was required of him with a good grace.

bite the dust ① be killed. **②** fail. informal

bite the hand that feeds you deliberately hurt or offend a benefactor; act ungratefully.

> **1994 Warren Farrell** *The Myth of Male Power* When this is combined with the fact that women watch more TV in every time slot, shows can't afford to bite the hand that feeds them.

bite off more than you can chew take on a commitment you cannot fulfil.

bite your tongue make a desperate effort to avoid saying something.

put the bite on blackmail; extort money from. North American & Australian informal

> **1955 Ray Lawler** *Summer of the Seventeenth Doll* Your money's runnin' out you know you can't put the bite on me any more.

take a bite out of reduce by a significant amount. informal

biter

the biter bit (*or* **bitten**) a person who has done harm has been harmed in a similar way.

> **ⓘ** *Biter* was a late 17th-century term for a fraudster or trickster. In this sense it now survives only in this phrase.

> **2000** *Locus* The most common plot device in Lee's stories is the classic 'biter bitten' resolution.

bitten

be bitten by the bug: *see* BUG.

I could have bitten my tongue off used to convey that you profoundly and immediately regret having said something.

once bitten, twice shy: *see* ONCE.

bitter

a bitter pill: *see* PILL.

to the bitter end persevering to the end, whatever the outcome.

black

beat someone black and blue hit someone so severely that they are covered in bruises.

be in someone's black books be in disfavour with someone.

> **ⓘ** Although a *black book* was generally an official book in which misdemeanours and their perpetrators were noted down, this phrase perhaps originated in the black-bound book in which evidence of monastic scandals and abuses was recorded by Henry VIII's commissioners in the 1530s, before the suppression of the monasteries.

beyond the black stump: *see* STUMP.

black box an automatic apparatus, the internal operations of which are mysterious to non-experts.

> **ⓘ** *Black* does not refer to the colour of the device but to the arcane nature of its functions. Originally Royal Air Force slang for

a navigational instrument in an aircraft, the phrase is now used in aviation specifically to refer to the flight recorder.

a black mark against someone something that someone has done that is disliked or disapproved of by other people.

> ❶ The literal meaning of the phrase is a black cross or spot marked against the name of a person who has done something wrong.

the black sheep a person considered to have brought discredit upon a family or other group; a bad character.

a black spot a place that is notorious for something, especially a high crime or accident rate.

> **1992** *Radio Times* Jonathon Porritt meets the 'green warriors' who are spearheading campaigns to clean up some of the world's worst pollution black spots.

in the black not owing any money; solvent.

in black and white ❶ in writing or in print, and regarded as more reliable than by word of mouth. ❷ in terms of clearly defined opposing principles or issues.

not as black as you are painted not as bad as you are said to be. informal

> ❶ The proverb *the devil is not as black as he is painted*, first recorded in English in the mid 16th century, was used as a warning not to base your fears of something on exaggerated reports.

blank

a blank cheque unlimited scope, especially to spend money.

> ❶ A *blank cheque* is literally one in which the amount of money to be paid has not been filled in by the payer.

draw a blank elicit no response; be unsuccessful.

> ❶ A *blank* was originally a lottery ticket that did not win a prize.

firing blanks (of a man) infertile. informal

blanket

born on the wrong side of the blanket illegitimate. dated

a wet blanket: *see* WET.

blarney

have kissed the blarney stone be eloquent and persuasive.

> ❶ A stone at Blarney Castle near Cork in Ireland is said to give the gift of persuasive speech to anyone who kisses it; from this comes the verb *blarney*, meaning 'talk in a flattering way'.

blast

a blast from the past something powerfully nostalgic, especially an old pop song. informal

> **1997** *Time Out N.Y.* Tonight's act is a tribute to Curtis Mayfield, featuring three blasts from the past: The Impressions . . . The Stylistics and The Dramatics.

blaze

blaze a trail be the first to do something and so set an example for others to follow.

> ❶ *Blaze* in this sense comes ultimately from an Old Norse noun meaning 'a white mark on a horse's face'. In its literal sense, *blazing a trail* refers to the practice of making white marks on trees by chipping off bits of their bark, thereby indicating your route to those who are following you.

like blazes very fast or forcefully. informal

> ❶ *Blazes* in this context refers to the flames of hell; *go to blazes!* is a dated equivalent of *go to hell!*

blazing

with guns blazing: *see* GUN.

bleed

bleed someone dry (*or* white) drain someone of all their money or resources.

> ❶ Since the late 17th century *bleeding* has been a metaphor for extorting money from someone. *White* refers to the physiological effect of losing blood.

> **1982 William Haggard** *The Mischief-Makers* Her husband had been a wealthy man, the lady's solicitors sharp and ruthless, and her husband had been bled white to get rid of her.

bleeds

my heart bleeds for you I sympathize very deeply with you.

> ❶ This image was used by Chaucer and Shakespeare to express sincere anguish. Nowadays, the phrase most often indicates the speaker's belief that the person referred to does not deserve the sympathy they are seeking.

bless

not have a penny to bless yourself with: *see* PENNY.

blessing

a blessing in disguise an apparent misfortune that eventually has good results.

count your blessings: *see* COUNT.

a mixed blessing: *see* MIXED.

blind

a blind alley a course of action that does not deliver any positive results.

> **1997** *New Scientist* The next person looking for the same information has to go through the process all over again—even if 1000 people have already been up the same blind alleys.

as blind as a bat having very bad eyesight. informal

> ❶ This expression probably arose from the bat's nocturnal habits and its disorientated flutterings if disturbed by day. The poor eyesight of bats (and less frequently, moles) has been proverbial since the late 16th century.

a blind bit of — the smallest bit of—; no — at all. informal

> **1995 Patrick McCabe** *The Dead School* Not that it made a blind bit of difference what they thought, considering the way their lives were about to go.

a blind date a social meeting, usually with the object of starting a romance, between two people who have not met each other before.

the blind leading the blind a situation in which the ignorant or inexperienced are instructed or guided by someone equally ignorant or inexperienced.

> ❶ This phrase alludes to the proverb *when the blind lead the blind, both shall fall into the ditch*, quoting Matthew 15:14.

a blind spot ❶ an area into which you cannot see. ❷ an aspect of something that someone knows or cares little about.

> ❶ These general senses appear to have developed from a mid 19th-century cricketing term for the spot of ground in front of a batsman where a ball pitched by the bowler leaves the batsman undecided whether to play forward to it or back.

blind someone with science use special or technical knowledge and vocabulary to confuse someone.

go it blind act recklessly.

rob someone blind: *see* ROB.

turn a blind eye pretend not to notice.

> ❶ This phrase is said to be a reference to Admiral Horatio Nelson (1758–1805), who lifted a telescope to his blind eye at the Battle of Copenhagen (1801), thereby ensuring that he failed to see his superior's signal to discontinue the action. A less usual version, referring directly to this story, is *turn a Nelson eye*.

blinder

play a blinder: *see* PLAY.

blinding

effing and blinding: *see* EFFING.

blink

in the blink of an eye very quickly. informal

> **1995** *Daily Mail* It also has an unnerving way of flipping over from comedy to tragedy, or from tragedy to comedy, in the blink of an eye.

on the blink (of a machine) not working properly; out of order. informal

block

a chip off the old block: *see* CHIP.

a new kid on the block a newcomer to a particular place or sphere of activity. informal

> ❶ This phrase was originally American: the *block* referred to is a block of buildings between streets.

> **1998** *Times* Andrew Flintoff has displaced Ben Hollioake as the new kid on the block.

have been around the block a few times (of a person) have a lot of experience. North American informal

on the block for sale at auction. chiefly North American

> ❶ The *block* in this phrase was the platform on which, in former times, a slave stood to be auctioned.

put the blocks on prevent from proceeding.

> ❶ A *block* of wood or other material placed in front of a wheel prevents forward movement.

put your head (*or* **neck**) **on the block** put your position or reputation at risk by proceeding with a particular course of action. informal

> ❶ This phrase alludes to the *block* of wood on which a condemned person was formerly beheaded.

blood

blood and guts violence and bloodshed, especially in fiction. informal

blood and iron military force rather than diplomacy.

> ❶ *Blood and iron* is a translation of German *Blut und Eisen*, a phrase particularly associated with a speech made by the German statesman Bismarck (1815–98) in the Prussian House of Deputies in 1886.

blood and thunder unrestrained and violent action or behaviour, especially in sport or fiction. informal

> ❶ *Blood and thunder* is often used to describe sensational literature, and in the late 19th century gave rise to *penny bloods* as a term for cheap sensational novels.

blood is thicker than water family loyalties are stronger than other relationships.

blood on the carpet used to refer in an exaggerated way to a serious disagreement or its aftermath.

> **1984** *Times* The last thing I want now is blood on the boardroom carpet.

blood, sweat, and tears extremely hard work; unstinting effort.

> ❶ In May 1940 Winston Churchill made a speech in the House of Commons in which he declared : 'I have nothing to offer but blood, toil, tears, and sweat.'

blood will tell family characteristics cannot be concealed. proverb

first blood the first point or advantage gained in a contest.

> ❶ *First blood* is literally 'the first shedding of blood', especially in a boxing match or formerly in duelling with swords.

have blood on your hands be responsible for the death of someone.

in cold blood: *see* COLD.

in your blood ingrained in or fundamental to your character.

like getting blood out of a stone extremely difficult and frustrating.

> ❶ A North American variant of this expression is *like getting blood out of a turnip*.

make your blood boil infuriate you.

make your blood curdle fill you with horror.

make your blood run cold horrify you.

> ❶ The previous three phrases all come from the medieval physiological scheme of the four humours in the human body (melancholy, phlegm, blood, and choler). Under this scheme blood was the hot, moist element, so the effect of horror or fear in making the blood run cold or curdling (solidifying) it was to make it unable to fulfil its proper function of supplying the body with vital heat or energy. The blood boiling was a supposedly dangerous overreaction to strong emotion.

new (*or* young) blood new (*or* younger) members of a group, especially those admitted as an invigorating force.

someone's blood is up someone is in a fighting mood.

sweat blood: *see* SWEAT.

taste blood achieve an early success that stimulates further efforts.

there is bad blood between — there is long-standing hostility between the parties mentioned.

> **2001 Hugh Collins** *No Smoke* There are occasional square-gos sometimes, but there's no bad blood between rival gangs.

bloody

bloody (*or* bloodied) but unbowed proud of what you have achieved despite having suffered great difficulties or losses.

bloom

the bloom is off the rose something is no longer new, fresh, or exciting. North American

blot

blot your copybook tarnish your good reputation. British

> ❶ A *copybook* was an exercise book with examples of handwriting for children to copy as they practised their own writing.

a blot on the escutcheon something that tarnishes your reputation.

> ❶ An *escutcheon* was a family's heraldic shield, and so also a record and symbol of its honour.

a blot on the landscape something ugly that spoils the appearance of a place; an eyesore.

> **1962** *Listener* Charabancs and monstrous hordes of hikers are blots upon the landscape.

blouse

big girl's blouse a weak, cowardly, or oversensitive man. British informal

blow

blow someone away ❶ kill, destroy, or defeat someone. ❷ have a very strong effect on someone. informal

> ❷ **1998** *Times* It blows me away the way she [a 13-year-old] is already moving through her life.

blow away the cobwebs: see COBWEB.

blow your cool lose your composure; become angry or agitated. informal

blow the doors off be considerably better or more successful than. North American informal

blow a fuse (or gasket) lose your temper. informal

> ❶ The metaphor is of the failure of an electrical circuit or engine as a result of overheating.

blow the gaff: see GAFF.

blow great guns: see GUN.

blow hot and cold alternate inconsistently between two moods, attitudes, or courses of action; be sometimes enthusiastic, sometimes unenthusiastic about something.

> ❶ This phrase refers to a fable involving a traveller who was offered hospitality by a satyr and offended his host by blowing on his cold fingers to warm them and on his hot soup to cool it.

blow the lid off: see LID.

blow someone's mind affect someone very strongly. informal

> ❶ *Blow someone's mind* was originally a mid 20th-century expression for the effect of hallucinatory drugs such as LSD.

blow off steam: see STEAM.

blow your own horn: see HORN.

blow your own trumpet: see TRUMPET.

blow a raspberry: see RASPBERRY.

blow someone's socks off: see SOCK.

blow something sky-high destroy something completely in an explosion. informal

blow your top lose your temper.

> ❶ Two, chiefly North American, variants are *blow your lid* and *blow your stack*.

blow up in your face (of an action, plan, or situation) go drastically wrong with damaging effects to yourself.

blow the whistle on: see WHISTLE.

blow with the wind act according to prevailing circumstances rather than a consistent plan.

soften (or cushion) the blow make it easier to cope with a difficult change or upsetting news.

which way the wind blows how a situation is likely to develop.

blow-by-blow

a blow-by-blow account a detailed narrative of events as they happened.

blown

be blown away be extremely impressed. informal

be blown off course have your plans disrupted by some circumstance.

> ❶ This phrase is a nautical metaphor: contrary winds turn a sailing ship away from its intended course.

be blown out of the water (of a person, idea, or project) be shown to lack credibility or viability.

> **1997** *Daily Mail* Things finally seem to be looking up for Kelly—which is more than can be said for Biff, whose romantic plans are blown out of the water by Linda.

blue

between the devil and the deep blue sea see DEVIL.

a bolt from the blue: see BOLT.

do something until you are blue in the face persist in trying your hardest at an activity but without success. informal

once in a blue moon very rarely; practically never. informal

> ❶ The colour *blue* was an arbitrary choice in this phrase. To say that the moon is blue is recorded in the 16th century as a way of indicating that something could not be true.

out of the blue without warning; very unexpectedly. informal

> **ⓘ** This phrase refers to a blue (i.e. clear) sky, from which nothing unusual is expected.

scream blue murder: *see* MURDER.

talk a blue streak speak continuously and at great length. North American informal

> **ⓘ** A *blue streak* refers to something like a flash of lightning in its speed and vividness.

true blue genuine.

> **ⓘ** The sense of someone being *true blue* may derive from the idea of someone being genuinely aristocratic, or having 'blue blood'. In recent times, the term *true blue* has become particularly associated with loyal supporters of the British Conservative party.

the wide (*or* wild) blue yonder the sky or sea; the far or unknown distance.

> **ⓘ** The phrase comes from 'Army Air Corps' (1939), a song by Robert Crawford: 'Off we go into the wild blue yonder, Climbing high into the sun'.

blue-eyed

a blue-eyed boy the favourite of someone in authority.

> **ⓘ** The significance of *blue eyes* may be their association with the innocence and charm of a very young child. The term is first recorded in a novel by P. G. Wodehouse in 1924.

> **1998** *Spectator* Of the three, the arrest of Osborne, one of the blue-eyed boys of British racing, was the most striking.

blue-sky

blue-sky research research that is not directed towards any immediate or definite commercial goal.

> **1997** *New Scientist* Bell Labs and IBM are well known for blue-sky research. They have people who are paid just to sit around and think—not about products.

bluff

call someone's bluff challenge someone to carry out a stated intention, in the expectation of being able to expose it as a false pretence.

> **ⓘ** In the game of poker (which was formerly also known by the name of *bluff*), *calling someone's bluff* meant making an opponent show their hand in order to reveal that its value was weaker than their heavy betting suggested.

blush

spare (*or* save) someone's blushes refrain from causing someone embarrassment.

board

above board honest; not secret.

> **ⓘ** *Above board* was originally a gambling term, indicating fair play by players who kept their hands above the *board* (i.e. the table).

across the board: *see* ACROSS.

go by the board (of something planned or previously upheld) be abandoned, rejected, or ignored.

> **ⓘ** In former times, *go by the board* was a nautical term meaning 'fall overboard' and was used of a mast falling past the *board* (i.e. the side of the ship).

on board as a member of a team or group. informal

> **ⓘ** *On board* literally means on or in a ship, aircraft, or other vehicle, or (of a jockey) riding a horse.

take something on board fully consider or assimilate a new idea or situation. informal

tread (*or* walk) the boards appear on stage as an actor. informal

boat

be in the same boat be in the same unfortunate or difficult circumstances as others. informal

burn your boats: *see* BURN.

off the boat recently arrived from a foreign country, and by implication naive or an outsider. informal, often offensive

push the boat out be lavish in your spending or celebrations. British informal

> **ⓘ** *Push the boat out* apparently originated as mid 20th-century naval slang meaning 'pay for a round of drinks'.

rock the boat say or do something to disturb an existing situation and upset other people. informal

> **1999** *Times* The six candidates are so determined not to rock the boat that they are in danger of saying nothing of interest.

bob

bob and weave make rapid bodily movements up and down and from side to side.

Bob's your uncle everything is fine; problem solved. British informal

> ℹ️ *Bob* is a familiar form of the name *Robert*. The origin of the phrase is often said to be in the controversial appointment in 1887 of the young Arthur Balfour to the important post of Chief Secretary for Ireland by his uncle Lord Salisbury, whose first name was Robert. The problem with this explanation is that the phrase is not recorded until the 1930s.

> **1996 Colin Bateman** *Of Wee Sweetie Mice and Men* I couldn't believe how easy it was to get. Just walked into a shop, signed a piece of paper, and Bob's your uncle.

bodkin

ride bodkin travel squeezed between two other people. dated

body

body and soul involving every aspect of a person; completely.

keep body and soul together manage to stay alive, especially in difficult circumstances.

know where the bodies are buried have the security deriving from personal knowledge of an organization's confidential affairs and secrets. informal

over my dead body: see DEAD.

boil

go off the boil pass the stage at which interest, excitement, activity, etc. is at its greatest.

it all boils down to it amounts to or is in essence.

> ℹ️ *Boiling down* a liquid means reducing its volume and concentrating it by evaporation.

> **1998** *Times* And why are deals getting more complex? Unsurprisingly it all boils down to profit.

make your blood boil: see BLOOD.

boiling

keep the pot boiling maintain the momentum or interest value of something.

bold

as bold as brass confident to the point of impudence.

> ℹ️ *Brass* is used in this phrase as a metaphorical representation of a lack of shame, as it was in the old expression *a brass face*, meaning 'an impudent person'.

bolt

a bolt from the blue a sudden and unexpected event or piece of news.

> ℹ️ The phrase refers to the unlikelihood of a thunderbolt coming out of a clear blue sky.

have shot your bolt have done all that is in your power. informal

> ℹ️ In this idiom, the *bolt* referred to is a thick, heavy arrow for a crossbow.

> **1998** *Spectator* The Britpop boom has ended, the Spice Girls have shot their bolt.

make a bolt for try to escape by moving suddenly towards something.

> ℹ️ A *bolt* here is a sudden spring or start into rapid motion, typically that made by a horse breaking into an uncontrollable gallop.

bomb

go down a bomb be very well received. British informal

> ℹ️ This phrase is especially used of entertainment and in this context is the opposite of **go down like a lead balloon** (see LEAD).

go like a bomb ❶ be very successful. ❷ (of a vehicle or person) move very fast. British informal

Bondi

give someone Bondi attack someone savagely. Australian informal

> ℹ️ A *bondi* (also spelled *boondie*, *bundi*, or *bundy*) is a heavy Aboriginal club.

bone

a bag of bones: see BAG.

the bare bones: see BARE.

a bone of contention a subject or issue over which there is continuing disagreement.

> ℹ️ The idea is of a bone thrown into the midst of a number of dogs and causing a fight between them.

a bone in your leg (*or* **head**) a (feigned) reason for idleness. informal

close to (*or* **near**) **the bone** ❶ (of a remark) penetrating and accurate to the point of causing hurt or discomfort. ❷ (of a joke or story) likely to cause offence because near the limit of decency.

cut (*or* **pare**) **something to the bone** reduce something to the bare minimum.

have a bone to pick with someone have reason to disagree or be annoyed with someone. informal

> ❶ A *bone to pick* (or *gnaw*) has been a metaphor for a problem or difficulty to be thought over since the mid 16th century.

in your bones felt, understood, or believed very deeply or instinctively.

make no bones about something have no hesitation in stating or dealing with something, however unpleasant, awkward, or distasteful it is.

> ❶ This expression, which dates back to the 16th century, may originally have referred to eating a bowl of soup in which no bones were found and which was therefore easily eaten.

not a — bone in your body not the slightest trace of the specified quality.

> **1999 Scott Turow** *Personal Injuries* I mean, I like Betty. Not a mean bone in her body.

point the bone at betray someone; cause someone's downfall. Australian

> ❶ The phrase comes from an Australian Aboriginal ritual, in which a bone is pointed at a victim so as to curse them and cause their sickness or death.

to the bone ❶ (of a wound) so deep as to expose the victim's bone. ❷ affecting a person in a very penetrating way.

to your bones (*or* **to the bone**) in a very fundamental way (used to emphasize that a person possesses a specified quality as an essential or innate aspect of their personality).

> **2003 Eve** Gloria is known today to be a conservative to her bones—a true monarchist.

work your fingers to the bone work very hard.

boo

wouldn't say boo to a goose (of a person) very shy or reticent.

> **1948 P. G. Wodehouse** *Uncle Dynamite* She looks on you as a . . . poor, spineless sheep who can't say boo to a goose.

booay

up the booay completely wrong or astray. Australian & New Zealand

> ❶ Literally, the *booay* are remote rural districts. The origin of the term is uncertain, though *Puhoi*, the name of a district in North Auckland, New Zealand, has been suggested as the source.

book

be in someone's black books: *see* BLACK.

bring someone to book bring someone to justice; punish someone.

by the book strictly according to the rules.

close the books make no further entries at the end of an accounting period; cease trading.

a closed book: *see* CLOSED.

cook the books: *see* COOK.

in someone's bad (*or* **good**) **books** in disfavour (*or* favour) with someone.

make (*or* **open**) **a book** take bets and pay out winnings on the outcome of a race or other contest or event.

on the books contained in a list of members, employees, or clients.

read someone like a book: *see* READ.

suit someone's book be convenient or acceptable to someone. British

take a leaf out of someone's book: *see* LEAF.

throw the book at charge or punish someone as severely as possible or permitted. informal

boot

boots and all completely. Australian & New Zealand informal

> **1947 D. M. Davin** *The Rest of Our Lives* The next thing he'll do is counter-attack, boots and all.

the boot is on the other foot the situation has reversed.

> ❶ A North American variant is *the shoe is on the other foot*.

die with your boots on: *see* DIE.

get the boot be dismissed from your job or position. informal

> ⓘ *Get the boot* comes from the idea of being literally kicked out, as does *give someone the boot*. A facetious expansion of this idiom is *get the Order of the Boot*.

hang up your boots: *see* HANG.

put the boot in treat someone brutally, especially when they are vulnerable. British informal

> ⓘ The literal sense is 'kick someone hard when they are already on the ground'.

seven-league boots the ability to travel very fast on foot.

> ⓘ This phrase comes from the fairy story of Hop o' my Thumb, in which magic boots enable the wearer to travel seven leagues at each stride.

to boot as well; in addition. informal

> ⓘ *Boot* here has nothing to do with footwear but comes from an Old English word meaning 'good, profit, or advantage'. It survives for the most part only in this phrase and in *bootless* meaning 'unavailing or profitless'.

> **1998** *New Scientist* It's an ideal first-year programming book, covering both Java and programming concepts clearly, with humour to boot.

tough as old boots: *see* TOUGH.

you can bet your boots: *see* BET.

your heart sinks into your boots used to express a feeling of sudden sadness or dismay.

> ⓘ This idiom has given rise to the adjective *heartsink*, used in the medical profession to describe a patient who causes their medical practitioner to experience such a feeling, usually as a result of making frequent visits to the surgery to complain of persistent but unidentifiable ailments.

bootstrap
pull (or drag) yourself up by your own bootstraps improve your position by your own efforts.

> ⓘ A *bootstrap* is sometimes sewn into the back of boots to help with pulling them on. This idiom has given rise to the computing term *bootstrapping*, meaning the process of loading a program into a computer by means of a few initial instructions which enable the introduction of the rest of the program from an input device. We now refer to the process of starting a computer as *booting* or *booting up*.

booty
shake your booty dance energetically. informal

borak
poke borak at make fun of someone. Australian & New Zealand, dated

> ⓘ *Borak* was used in 19th-century Australian to mean 'nonsense or rubbish'. It was originally a pidgin term and was based on an Aboriginal word meaning 'no, not'.

> **1960 Eric North** *Nobody Stops Me* I . . . subscribed to his ravings about women, while everybody else about the place poked borak at him.

born
be born with a silver spoon in your mouth: *see* SILVER.

born and bred by birth and upbringing.
> **1991 Sharon Kay Penman** *The Reckoning* I was being tended by a most unlikely nurse, an Irish sprite who spoke French as if she was Paris born and bred.

born in the purple: *see* PURPLE.

not know you are born be unaware how easy your life is. informal

there's one (or a sucker) born every minute there are many stupid or gullible people about (used as a comment on a particular situation in which someone has been or is about to be deceived). informal

to the manner born: *see* MANNER.

I wasn't born yesterday used to indicate that you are not foolish or gullible.

borrow
borrow trouble take needless action that may have bad effects. North American

borrowed
living on borrowed time continuing to survive against expectations (used with the implication that this will not be for much longer).

borrowed plumes a pretentious display not rightly your own.

> ⓘ This phrase refers to the fable of the jay which dressed itself in the peacock's feathers.

boss
show someone who's boss make it clear that it is yourself who is in charge.

both

cut both ways: *see* CUT.

have it both ways benefit from two incompatible ways of thinking or behaving.

> **1998** *New Scientist* It is only now dawning on the legislators that they cannot have it both ways—that cleanliness and ecological friendliness are incompatible.

bothered

hot and bothered in a state of anxiety or physical discomfort, especially as a result of being pressured.

bottle

have (*or* show) a lot of bottle have (*or* show) boldness or initiative. British informal

> ⓘ The mid 19th-century slang phrase *no bottle*, meaning 'no good or useless', is the probable origin of *bottle*'s current sense of 'courage or nerve'. Nowadays we also find the expressions *lose your bottle* meaning 'lose your nerve' and *bottle out* meaning 'fail to do something as a result of losing your nerve'.

hit (*or* be on) the bottle start to drink alcohol heavily, especially in an attempt to escape from one's problems. informal

bottom

be bumping along the bottom (of an economy or industry) be at the lowest point in its performance without improving or deteriorating further.

bottom drawer: *see* DRAWER.

the bottom falls (*or* drops) out of something something fails or collapses totally.

the bottom line: *see* LINE.

from the bottom of your heart: *see* HEART.

scrape the bottom of the barrel: *see* SCRAPE.

touch bottom: *see* TOUCH.

you can bet your bottom dollar: *see* **you can bet your boots** *at* BET.

bought

have bought it be killed. informal

bounce

bounce an idea off someone share an idea with another person in order to get feedback on it and refine it. informal

bounce off the walls be full of nervous excitement or agitation. North American informal

a dead cat bounce: *see* DEAD.

on the bounce ❶ as something rebounds. ❷ in quick succession. informal

> ❷ **2001** *Greyhound Star* He has now won twelve races on the bounce, including three big competitions.

bound

duty-bound: *see* DUTY.

honour-bound: *see* HONOUR.

bounden

a bounden duty a responsibility regarded by yourself or others as obligatory.

> ⓘ *Bounden* as the past participle of *bind* is now archaic in all contexts and is seldom found except in this phrase.

bow

bow and scrape behave in an obsequious way to someone in authority.

bow down in the house of Rimmon pay lip service to a principle; sacrifice your principles for the sake of conformity.

> ⓘ *Rimmon* was a god worshipped in ancient Damascus; the source of this phrase is Naaman's request in 2 Kings 5:18, 'when I bow down myself in the house of Rimmon, the Lord pardon thy servant in this thing'.

have a second string to your bow: *see* STRING.

make your bow make your first formal appearance in a particular role.

take a bow ❶ (of an actor or entertainer) acknowledge applause after a performance. ❷ used to tell someone that they should feel themselves worthy of applause.

a warning shot across the bows a statement or gesture intended to frighten someone into changing their course of action.

> ⓘ Literally, a shot fired in front of the bows of a ship is one which is not intended to hit it but to make it stop or alter course.

bowl

a bowl of cherries: *see* CHERRY.

box

black box: *see* BLACK.

box clever act so as to outwit someone. British informal

> **1950 Alexander Baron** *There's No Home* If you box clever and keep your mouth shut … you ought to be able to count on a suspended sentence.

be a box of birds be fine or happy. Australian & New Zealand

a box of tricks an ingenious gadget. informal

in the wrong box placed unsuitably or awkwardly; in difficulty or at a disadvantage.

> ❶ This phrase perhaps arose with reference to an apothecary's boxes, from which a mistaken choice might have provided poison instead of medicine.

out of the box unusually good. Australian & New Zealand informal

out of your box intoxicated with alcohol or drugs. British informal

Pandora's box: *see* PANDORA.

think outside the box have ideas that are original, creative, or innovative. informal

box seat

in the box seat in an advantageous position. Australian & New Zealand

boy

boys in blue policemen; the police. informal

boys will be boys childish, irresponsible, or mischievous behaviour is typical of boys or young men. proverb

jobs for the boys: *see* JOB.

the old boy network: *see* NETWORK.

one of the boys accepted by a group of men.

sort out the men from the boys: *see* MAN.

brain

have something on the brain be obsessed with something. informal

pick someone's brains: *see* PICK.

rack your brains: *see* RACK.

brass

brass monkey used in various phrases to refer to extremely cold weather.

> ❶ *Brass monkey* comes from the mid 20th-century vulgar slang expression 'cold enough to freeze the balls off a brass monkey', the origin of which has been debated. One suggestion relates it to brass trays known as *monkeys* on which cannon balls were once stowed aboard warships.

> **1994** *Camping Magazine* David will be doing his best to show you how to keep warm under canvas even if the temperature outside has dipped to brass monkey level.

the brass ring success, especially as a reward for ambition or hard work. North American informal

> ❶ This phrase refers to the reward of a free ride on a merry-go-round given to the person who succeeds in hooking a brass ring suspended over the horses.

brass neck cheek or effrontery. informal

get down to brass tacks start to consider the essential facts or practical details; reach the real matter in hand. informal

> **1932 T. S. Eliot** *Sweeney Agonistes* That's all the facts when you come to brass tacks: Birth, and copulation, and death.

not a brass farthing no money or assets at all. informal

part brass rags with: *see* RAG.

brave

brave new world a new and hopeful period in history resulting from major changes in society.

> ❶ This phrase comes ultimately from Shakespeare's *The Tempest*, but is more often used with allusion to Aldous Huxley's ironical use of the phrase as the title of his 1932 novel *Brave New World*.

put a brave face on something: *see* FACE.

breach

step into the breach take the place of someone who is suddenly unable to do a job or task.

> ❶ In military terms a *breach* is a gap in fortifications made by enemy guns or explosives. In this context, to *stand in the breach* is to bear the brunt of an attack when other defences or expedients have failed.

bread

the best (or greatest) thing since sliced bread a notable new idea, person, or thing (used to express real or ironic appreciation). informal

> ❶ This phrase alludes to the mid 20th-century advertising promotions for packed, pre-sliced loaves.

bread and circuses material benefits and entertainment employed by rulers or political parties to keep the masses happy and docile.

> ❶ *Bread and circuses* is a translation of the Latin phrase *panem et circenses*, which appeared in Juvenal's *Satires*, and which alludes to the Roman emperors' organization of grain handouts and gladiatorial games for the populace.

break bread with share a meal with someone. dated

cast your bread upon the waters do good without expecting gratitude or immediate reward.

> ❶ This expression comes from Ecclesiastes 11:1: 'Cast thy bread upon the waters: for thou shalt find it after many days'.

eat the bread of idleness eat food that you have not worked for. literary

> ❶ This phrase appears in the description of the virtuous woman in Proverbs 31:27: 'She . . . eateth not the bread of idleness'.

have your bread buttered on both sides be in a state of easy prosperity.

know on which side your bread is buttered know where your advantage lies.

man cannot live by bread alone people have spiritual as well as physical needs.

> ❶ This phrase comes from Matthew 4:4 (quoting Deuteronomy 8:3), where the passage continues 'but by every word that proceedeth out of the mouth of God'.

someone's bread and butter someone's livelihood; routine work to provide an income.

> **1998** *Times* It is not that the smaller deal has disappeared—they remain the bread and butter of this industry.

take the bread out of people's mouths deprive people of their livings, especially by competition or unfair working practices.

want your bread buttered on both sides want more than is practicable or than is reasonable to expect. informal

bread-and-butter

a bread-and-butter letter a guest's written thanks for hospitality.

break

break the back of ❶ accomplish the main or hardest part of a task. ❷ overwhelm or defeat.

break the bank: *see* BANK.

break a butterfly on a wheel use unnecessary force in destroying something fragile or insignificant.

> ❶ In former times, *breaking someone upon the wheel* was a form of punishment or torture which involved fastening criminals to a wheel so that their bones would be broken or dislocated.

> **1998** *Times* But why break a butterfly upon a wheel? What harm does the Liberal Democrat leader do? Unfortunately he may be about to do a great deal.

break a leg! good luck! theatrical slang

break cover: *see* COVER.

break the ice: *see* ICE.

break the mould: *see* MOULD.

break new (or fresh) ground do pioneering work.

break rank: *see* RANK.

break ship fail to rejoin your ship after absence on leave.

give me a break! used to express contemptuous disagreement or disbelief about something that has been said.

give someone a break stop putting pressure on someone about something. informal

make a break for make a sudden dash in the direction of, usually in a bid to escape.

make a clean break remove yourself completely and finally from a situation or relationship.

that's (or them's) the breaks that's the way things turn out (used to express resigned acceptance of a situation). North American informal

breakfast

a dog's breakfast: *see* DOG.

have someone for breakfast deal with or defeat someone with contemptuous ease. informal

breast

beat your breast make a great show of sorrow or regret.

make a clean breast of something: *see* CLEAN.

breath

a breath of fresh air ❶ a small amount of or a brief time in the fresh air. ❷ a refreshing change, especially a new person on the scene.

the breath of life a thing that someone needs or depends on.

> ❶ *Breath of life* is a biblical phrase: 'And the Lord God formed man of the dust of the ground, and breathed into his nostrils the breath of life' (Genesis 2:7).

don't hold your breath used to indicate that something is very unlikely to happen.

save your breath not bother to say something because it is pointless.

take someone's breath away inspire someone with awed respect or delight; astonish someone.

> **1988 Janet Frame** *The Carpathians* The speed of the process took everyone's breath away.

waste your breath talk or give advice without effect.

breathe

breathe down someone's neck ❶ constantly check up on someone. ❷ follow closely behind someone.

breathe your last die.

breed

a breed apart a kind of person or thing that is very different from the norm.

a dying breed: *see* DYING.

brick

a brick short of a load (of a person) stupid. informal

> ❶ This is one of a number of humorous variations on the theme of someone not possessing their proper share of brains or intelligence; compare, for example, with **a sandwich short of a picnic** (*at* SANDWICH).

come down like a ton of bricks exert crushing weight, force, or authority against someone. informal

come up against (*or* hit) **a brick wall** encounter an insuperable problem or obstacle while trying to do something.

make bricks without straw try to accomplish something without proper or adequate material, equipment, or information.

> ❶ The allusion here is to Exodus 5:6–19 where 'without straw' meant 'without having straw provided', as the Israelites were required to gather straw for themselves in order to make the bricks required by their Egyptian taskmasters. A misinterpretation has led to the current sense.

bridge

burn your bridges: *see* **burn your boats** *at* BURN.

cross that bridge when you come to it deal with a problem when and if it arises.

> **1998** *Spectator* As to what would happen to the case for non-proliferation when the Cold War was won, the allies would cross that bridge when they came to it, which seemed at the time well beyond any foreseeable future.

brief

hold no brief for not support or argue in favour of.

> ❶ The *brief* referred to is the summary of the facts and legal points in a case given to a barrister to argue in court.

bright

bright and early very early in the morning.

as bright as a button intelligently alert and lively. informal

> ❶ There is a play here on *bright* in its Old English sense of 'shiny' (like a polished metal button) and *bright* in its transferred sense of 'quick-witted', found since the mid 18th century.

the bright lights the glamour and excitement of a big city.

bright spark a clever person (often used ironically to or of a person who has done something you consider stupid). British informal

bright young thing a wealthy, pleasure-loving, and fashionable young person.

> ❶ The term was originally applied in the 1920s to a member of a young fashionable group of people noted for their exuberant and outrageous behaviour.

look on the bright side be optimistic or cheerful in spite of difficulties.

bright-eyed

bright-eyed and bushy-tailed alert and lively; eager. informal

bring

bring home the bacon: *see* BACON.

bring the house down make an audience respond with great enthusiasm, especially as shown by their laughter or applause.

bring something home to someone: *see* HOME.

bring something into play cause something to begin to have an effect.

bring someone to book: *see* BOOK.

British

the British disease a problem or failing supposed to be characteristically British, especially (formerly) a proneness to industrial unrest. informal

broad

broad in the beam fat round the hips. informal

> ❶ A *beam* was one of the horizontal transverse timbers in a wooden ship, and so the word came to refer to a ship's breadth at its widest point. It is from this sense that the current meaning of *broad in the beam* developed.

in broad daylight used generally to express surprise or outrage at someone's daring to carry out a particular act, especially a crime, during the day, when anyone could see it.

it's as broad as it's long there's no significant difference between two possible alternatives. informal

broke

go for broke risk everything in an all-out effort. informal

broken

a broken reed: *see* REED.

broo

on the broo claiming unemployment benefit. Scottish informal

> ❶ *Broo*, also spelt *buroo*, is a colloquial alteration of *bureau*, meaning a labour exchange or social security office.

broom

a new broom a newly appointed person who is likely to make far-reaching changes.

> ❶ This phrase comes from the proverb *a new broom sweeps clean*.

broth

a broth of a boy a lively boy. Irish

too many cooks spoil the broth: *see* COOK.

brother

Big brother the state perceived as a sinister force supervising citizens' lives.

> ❶ *Big brother* comes from the slogan *Big Brother is watching you* in George Orwell's novel *1984*.

brown

as brown as a berry (of a person) very suntanned.

in a brown study in a reverie; absorbed in your thoughts.

> ❶ The earliest meaning of *brown* in English was simply 'dark'. From this, an extended sense of 'gloomy or serious' developed and it is apparently from this sense that we get the phrase *in a brown study*.

> **2001** *New York Review of Books* When he isn't stirring up mischief, or conniving for gold, or composing beautiful poetry, he's apt to be sunk in a brown study.

brownie

brownie point an imaginary award given to someone who does good deeds or tries to please. informal

> ❶ The *Brownies* are the junior wing of the Guides; the organization awards points and badges for proficiency in various activities.

brunt

bear the brunt of be the person to suffer the most (as the result of an attack, misfortune, etc.).

> ❶ The origin of *brunt* is unknown, and may be onomatopoeic. The sense has evolved from the specific ('a sharp or heavy blow') to the more general ('the shock or violence of an attack').

bubble

burst someone's bubble: *see* BURST.

on the bubble (of a sports player or team) occupying the last qualifying position in a team or for a tournament, and liable to be replaced by another. North American informal

> ❶ This expression comes from *sit on the bubble*, with the implication that the bubble may burst.

buck

the buck stops here (or with someone) the responsibility for something cannot or should not be passed to someone else. informal

ⓘ Famously, *the buck stops here* was the wording of a sign on the desk of US President Harry S. Truman. Compare with **pass the buck** below.

buck up your ideas make more effort; become more energetic and hardworking. informal

ⓘ *Buck* here refers to the lively action of a horse jumping with all its feet together and its back arched. *Buck up* in its modern senses of 'cheer up' and 'hurry up' is first found in late 19th-century school slang.

make a fast buck earn money easily and quickly. informal

pass the buck shift the responsibility for something to someone else. informal

ⓘ A *buck* is an object placed as a reminder in front of the person whose turn it is to deal in the game of poker.

1998 *New York Review of Books* The legislation left the main decisions to the individual states which may well pass the buck to the large cities where most of the problem is.

bucket

a drop in a bucket: *see* DROP.

kick the bucket: *see* KICK.

Buckley

Buckley's chance a forlorn hope; no chance at all. Australian & New Zealand informal

ⓘ The phrase is often shortened simply to *Buckley's*. Who or what *Buckley* was remains uncertain: the name is sometimes said to refer to William Buckley, a convict transported to Australia in 1802 who escaped and lived with the Aborigines for many years, despite dire predictions as to his chances of survival.

1948 Vance Palmer *Golconda* Buckley's chance we have of getting our price if we're left to face the companies alone.

buff

in the buff naked. informal

ⓘ The original meaning of *buff* in English was 'buffalo', and it later came to mean 'ox hide' or 'the colour of ox hide'. *In the buff* itself comes from *buff* leather, a type of yellowish-beige ox hide formerly used in military uniform, the colour of which was regarded as comparable to that of human skin.

bug

have (or be bitten by) the bug develop a sudden strong enthusiasm for something.

bugger vulgar slang

bugger all nothing.

bugger me used to express surprise or amazement.

play silly buggers act in a foolish way.

Buggins

Buggins' turn: *see* TURN.

built

built on sand without secure foundations; liable to collapse.

ⓘ This phrase comes from the biblical parable contrasting the wise man who built his house on rock with the fool who built his on sand (Matthew 7:24–7).

bulge

have (or get) the bulge on have or get an advantage over. British informal

bulging

bulging at the seams: *see* SEAM.

bull

like a bull at a gate hastily and without thought.

like a bull in a china shop behaving recklessly and clumsily in a place or situation where you are likely to cause damage or injury.

a red rag to a bull: *see* RED.

take (or grab) the bull by the horns deal bravely and decisively with a difficult, dangerous, or unpleasant situation.

2000 Andrew Calcutt *Brit Cult* The government has failed to take the bull by the horns, thereby granting 'hunt sabs' a new lease of life.

bullet

bite the bullet: *see* BITE.

sweat bullets: *see* SWEAT.

bully

bully for —! well done! good for (you, them, etc.)!

ⓘ This expression takes its origin from the US colloquial sense of *bully* meaning 'first-rate', recorded since the mid 19th century.

bum

bums on seats the audience at a theatre, cinema, or other entertainment, viewed as a source of income. informal

give someone (*or* get) the bum's rush ❶ forcibly eject someone (*or* be forcibly ejected) from a place or gathering. ❷ abruptly dismiss someone (*or* be abruptly dismissed) for a poor idea or performance. chiefly North American

> ❶ **1998** *Spectator* When . . . James Cameron wrote an uproariously funny piece about the hotel's iniquities . . . he was promptly given the bum's rush.

on the bum travelling rough and with no fixed home; vagrant. North American

bump

things that go bump in the night: *see* THING.

bumper

bumper-to-bumper ❶ very close together, as cars in a traffic jam. ❷ (chiefly of an insurance policy) comprehensive; all-inclusive.

bun

have a bun in the oven be pregnant. informal

take the bun: *see* TAKE.

bunch

bunch of fives ❶ a fist. ❷ a punch. British informal

bundle

a bundle of nerves: *see* **a bag of nerves** *at* BAG.

a bundle of fun (*or* laughs) something extremely amusing or pleasant. informal

drop your bundle panic or lose one's self-control. Australian & New Zealand informal

> ⓘ This expression comes from an obsolete sense of *bundle* meaning 'swag' or 'a traveller's or miner's bundle of personal belongings'.

go a bundle on be very keen on or fond of. British informal

> ⓘ In this idiom, *bundle* is being used in the late 19th-century US slang sense of a bundle of money, i.e. a large sum. To *go a bundle on* was originally early 20th-century slang for betting a large sum of money on a horse.

> **1968 Adam Diment** *Bang Bang Birds* I don't go a bundle on being told I'm a pro.

bung

go bung ❶ die. ❷ fail or go bankrupt. Australian & New Zealand informal

> ⓘ In this sense *bung* comes from Yagara, an extinct Aboriginal language.

> ❷ **1951** J. Devanny *Travel in North Queensland* 'The stations would go bung without the Abos', one of the missionaries told me.

burden

the white man's burden the task, believed by white colonizers to be incumbent upon them, of imposing Western civilization on the black inhabitants of European colonies. dated

> ⓘ *The white man's burden* comes from Rudyard Kipling's poem of that title (1899), originally referring specifically to the United States' role in the Philippines.

burl

give it a burl attempt to do something. Australian & New Zealand informal

> **1953 T. A. G. Hungerford** *Riverslake* Well you want to give it a burl—you want to come?

burn

burn your boats (*or* bridges) commit yourself irrevocably.

> ⓘ In a military campaign, burning your boats or bridges would make escape or retreat impossible.

burn the candle at both ends ❶ lavish energy or resources in more than one direction at the same time. ❷ go to bed late and get up early.

burn daylight: *see* DAYLIGHT.

burn your fingers: *see* FINGER.

burn the midnight oil read or work late into the night.

burn rubber: *see* RUBBER.

go for the burn push your body to the extremes when practising a form of physical exercise. informal

> ⓘ The *burn* referred to is the burning sensation caused in muscles by strenuous exertion.

have money to burn: *see* MONEY.

someone's ears are burning: *see* EAR.

slow burn a state of slowly mounting anger or annoyance. informal

burner

on the back (or front) burner having low (or high) priority. informal

> ❶ The metaphor here is from cooking on a stove with several burners of varying heat: food cooking at a lower temperature on a back burner receives or requires less frequent attention than that cooking at a high temperature on a front burner. Compare with the mainly North American expression *cook on the front burner* meaning 'be on the way to rapid success'.

burnt

burnt to a cinder (or crisp) completely burnt through, leaving only the charred remnant.

burr

a burr under (or in) your saddle a persistent source of irritation. North American informal

burst

burst someone's bubble shatter someone's illusions about something or destroy their sense of well-being.

bursting

bursting at the seams: *see* SEAMS.

Burton

go for a Burton meet with disaster; be ruined, destroyed, or killed. British informal

> ❶ This phrase first appeared in mid 20th-century air force slang, meaning 'be killed in a crash'. It has been suggested that it refers to Burton's, the British men's outfitters, or to Burton, a kind of ale, but these are folk etymologies with no definite evidence to support them, and the origin of the phrase remains uncertain.

bury

bury the hatchet end a quarrel or conflict and become friendly.

> ❶ This expression makes reference to an Native American custom of burying a hatchet or tomahawk to mark the conclusion of a peace treaty.

bury your head in the sand ignore unpleasant realities; refuse to face facts.

> ❶ This expression alludes to the belief that ostriches bury their heads in the sand when pursued, thinking that as they cannot see their pursuers the pursuers cannot see them.

bush

beat about the bush: *see* BEAT.

beat the bushes: *see* BEAT.

bush telegraph: *see* TELEGRAPH.

go bush leave your usual surroundings; run wild.

> ❶ *Bush* in the sense of 'wild, wooded, or uncleared country' became current among English speakers during 19th-century British colonial expansion. In South Africa it may have been adopted directly from Dutch *bosch*.

bushel

hide your light under a bushel: *see* HIDE.

business

the business end the part of a tool, weapon, etc. that carries out the object's particular function. informal

> **1936 Richmal Crompton** *Sweet William* The business end of a geometrical compass was jabbed into Douglas's arm.

do the business ❶ do what is required or expected; achieve the desired result. British informal ❷ have sexual intercourse. vulgar slang

like nobody's business in no ordinary way; to an extremely intense degree. informal

> **1991 Elspeth Barker** *O Caledonia* They spread like nobody's business. They're a really pernicious weed.

busman

a busman's holiday a holiday or form of recreation that involves doing the same thing that you do at work.

> ❶ From the late 19th century, a popular form of working-class recreation was to take an excursion by bus.

busted

a busted flush someone or something that has not fulfilled expectations; a failure. US informal

> ❶ In the game of poker, *a busted flush* is a sequence of cards of one suit that you fail to complete.

busy

as busy as a bee very busy or industrious.

butcher

the butcher, the baker, the candlestick-maker people of all kinds.

> **ⓘ** This phrase comes from the traditional nursery rhyme *Rub-dub-dub, Three men in a tub*.

have a butcher's have a look. British informal

> **ⓘ** *Butcher's* comes here from *butcher's hook*, rhyming slang for 'look'.

butter

look as if butter wouldn't melt in your mouth appear deceptively gentle or innocent. informal

butterfingers

have (or be a) butterfingers be unable to catch deftly or hold securely.

> **ⓘ** This phrase comes from the idea that hands covered with butter will be slippery, making holding on to anything difficult. There was also a dialect sense of 'unable to handle anything hot', as if your fingers were made of melting butter. *Butterfingers!* is often jeeringly shouted at someone who has failed to catch a ball in a game.

butterfly

the butterfly effect the phenomenon whereby a minute localized change in a complex system can have large effects elsewhere.

> **ⓘ** The expression comes from chaos theory. In 1979, Edward N. Lorenz gave a paper to the American Association for the Advancement of Science entitled 'Does the flap of a butterfly's wings in Brazil set off a tornado in Texas?'

have butterflies in your stomach have a queasy feeling because you are nervous. informal

button

button your lip remain silent. informal

on the button ❶ punctually. ❷ exactly right. informal, chiefly US

press the button initiate an action or train of events. informal

> **ⓘ** During the cold war period, this expression was often used with reference to the possible action of the US or Soviet presidents in starting a nuclear war.

push (or press) someone's buttons be successful in arousing or provoking a reaction in someone. informal

buy

buy the farm die. North American informal

> **ⓘ** This expression originated as US military slang, probably with the meaning that the pilot (or owner) of a crashed plane owes money to the farmer whose property or land is damaged in the crash.

buy time adopt tactics which delay an event temporarily so as to have longer to improve your own position.

by

by and large on the whole; everything considered.

> **ⓘ** Originally this phrase was used in a nautical context, describing the handling of a ship both to the wind and off it.

by the by (or bye) incidentally; parenthetically.

bygones

let bygones be bygones forgive and forget past offences or causes of conflict.

Cc

C

the big C cancer. informal

caboodle

the whole caboodle (*or* **the whole kit and caboodle**) the whole lot. informal

> ❶ *Caboodle* may come from the Dutch word *boedel* meaning 'possessions'.

cackle

cut the cackle stop talking aimlessly and come to the point. informal

cadenza

have a cadenza be extremely agitated. South African informal

> ❶ *Cadenza* is an Italian term for a virtuoso solo passage near the end of a piece of music. This informal sense probably comes from Danny Kaye's humorous 1940s recording 'The Little Fiddle'.

> **1991** D. Capel *Personality* The Conservative party is having a cadenza about 'subliminal messages' on the SABC's news logo.

Caesar

appeal to Caesar: *see* APPEAL.

Caesar's wife a person who is required to be above suspicion.

> ❶ This expression comes ultimately from Plutarch's account of Julius Caesar's decision to divorce his wife Pompeia. The libertine Publius Clodius, who was in love with Pompeia, smuggled himself into the house in which the women of Caesar's household were celebrating a festival, thereby causing a scandal. Caesar refused to bring charges against Clodius, but divorced Pompeia; when questioned he replied 'I thought my wife ought not even to be under suspicion'.

cahoots

in cahoots working or conspiring together, often dishonestly; in collusion. informal

> ❶ *In cahoots* is recorded in the early 19th century, in the south and west of the USA, in the sense of 'partnership'. The origin of *cahoot* is uncertain; it may come either from

the French word *cahute* meaning 'a hut' or from *cohort*.

> **1998** *Spectator* Labour knows that. So do the Tories and that's why the two of them are in cahoots.

Cain

mark of Cain: *see* MARK.

raise Cain create trouble or a commotion. informal

> ❶ The sense of *raise* in this expression is that of summoning a spirit, especially an evil one; similar sayings include *raise the Devil* and *raise hell*. A mid 19th-century expression originating in the USA, the particular form *raise Cain* is possibly a euphemism to avoid using the words *Devil* or *hell*. Cain, according to the biblical book of Genesis, was the first murderer.

cake

cakes and ale merrymaking.

> **1601** William Shakespeare *Twelfth Night* Dost thou think because thou art virtuous there shall be no more cakes and ale?

you can't have your cake and eat it you can't enjoy both of two desirable but mutually exclusive alternatives. proverb

the icing on the cake: *see* ICING.

a piece of cake something easily achieved. informal

sell (*or* **go**) **like hot cakes** be sold quickly and in large quantities.

a slice of the cake: *see* SLICE.

take the cake: *see* TAKE.

> ❶ In most of these idioms *cake* is used as a metaphor for something pleasant or desirable.

calf

a golden calf: *see* GOLDEN.

kill the fatted calf: *see* FATTED.

call

call someone's bluff: *see* BLUFF.

call it a day: *see* DAY.

call someone names: *see* NAME.

call of nature: *see* NATURE.

call the shots (*or* **tune**) take the initiative in deciding how something should be done; be in control. informal

> **ⓘ** *Call the shots* was originally an American phrase, first recorded in the 1960s. *Call the tune* comes from the saying *he who pays the piper calls the tune*, which dates from the late 19th century.

> **1996** *Sunday Telegraph* Britain is no longer run from Downing Street. It's Brussels that calls the shots.

don't call us, we'll call you used as a dismissive way of saying that someone has not been successful in an audition or job application. informal

good call (*or* **bad call**) used to express approval (*or* criticism) of a person's decision or suggestion. informal

> **ⓘ** Originally *good call* or *bad call* referred to decisions made by referees or umpires in a sports match.

call a spade a spade: *see* SPADE.

too close to call: *see* CLOSE.

can

carry the can: *see* CARRY.

in the can completed and available for use.

> **ⓘ** In recording or film-making, something that is *in the can* has been captured on tape or film.

open up a can of worms discover or bring to light a complicated matter likely to prove awkward or embarrassing. informal

> **1998** *New Scientist* UN officials readily accept that they have opened a can of worms, and their guidelines will only have an effect, they say, if governments act on them.

candle

burn the candle at both ends: *see* BURN.

cannot hold a candle to be nowhere near as good as. informal

> **ⓘ** In the 16th century, an assistant would literally *hold a candle to* his superior by standing beside him with a candle to provide enough light for him to work by. The modern version suggests that the subordinate is so far inferior that he is unfit to perform even this humble task.

not worth the candle not justifiable because of the trouble or cost involved.

> **ⓘ** The idea behind this idiom is that expenditure on a candle to provide light for an activity would not be recouped by the profits from that activity. The expression comes from the French phrase *le jeu ne vaut pas la chandelle*, 'the game is not worth the candle'.

> **1998** *New Scientist* But what if, instead of one … five, fifteen or fifty people … have to endure such an existence? At what point does the game cease to be worth the candle?

cannon

a loose cannon: *see* LOOSE.

canoe

paddle your own canoe: *see* PADDLE.

canter

at a canter without much effort; easily. British

> **ⓘ** *At a canter* is a horse-racing metaphor: a horse has to make so little effort that it can win at the easy pace of a canter rather than having to gallop.

canvas

by a canvas by a small margin.

> **ⓘ** The tapered front end of a racing boat was formerly covered with canvas to prevent water being taken on board. In this context, to win *by a canvas* meant to win by the length between the tip of the bow and the first oarsman.

cap

cap in hand humbly asking for a favour.

> **ⓘ** To have your cap in your hand, and therefore to have your head uncovered, is a mark of respect and also of subordination. The idea of a cap as a begging bowl into which coins can be dropped may also be present. A North American version of this expression is *hat in hand*.

if the cap fits, wear it used as a way of suggesting that someone should accept a generalized remark or criticism as applying to themselves.

> **ⓘ** Early examples of this saying show that the *cap* in question was originally a fool's cap. The variant *if the shoe fits, wear it* is also found, mainly in North America.

set your cap at try to attract as a suitor. dated

capital

with a capital — used to give emphasis to the word or concept in question.

1991 **Nesta Wyn Ellis** *John Major* He is not a personality with a capital P, not flamboyant, not it seems an angry man.

card

get your cards be dismissed from your employment. British informal

> ❶ *Cards* are the national insurance card and other documents relating to an employee that are retained by the employer during the period that the employee works for them. *Give someone their cards* means 'make someone redundant'.

have a card up your sleeve have a plan or asset that is kept secret until it is needed. British

hold all the cards be in the strongest or most advantageous position.

keep your cards close to your chest (*or* **vest**) be extremely secretive and cautious about something. informal

> ❶ The previous two idioms both refer to a hand of cards in a card game. If you hold all the cards you have a winning hand, while card players who hold their cards close to their bodies ensure that no opponent can look at them.

mark someone's card: *see* MARK.

on the cards possible or likely.

> ❶ This phrase, a North American variant of which is *in the cards*, probably refers to the practice of using playing cards or tarot cards to foretell the future.

play the — card exploit the specified issue or idea mentioned, especially for political advantage.

> ❶ This expression comes from the view expressed in 1886 by Lord Randolph Churchill that, concerning Irish Home Rule, 'the Orange card would be the one to play'.

1998 *Edinburgh Student* The SNP, who dominate the Scottish independence campaign, argue that they do not play the race card.

play your cards right make the best use of your assets and opportunities.

put (*or* **lay**) **your cards on the table** be completely open and honest in declaring your resources, intentions, or attitude.

care

not care two straws care little or not at all.

carpet

a magic carpet a means of sudden and effortless travel.

> ❶ In fairy tales, a *magic carpet* is able to transport a person sitting on it to any place they desire.

on the carpet ❶ (of a topic or problem) under discussion. ❷ (of a person) being severely reprimanded by someone in authority. informal

> ❶ *Carpet* in both these senses originally meant 'table covering', and referred to 'the carpet of the council table', a table around which a problem was debated (as in sense 1) or before which a person would be summoned for reprimand (as in sense 2). The informal use of *carpet* as a verb meaning 'reprove' dates from mid 19th century.

sweep something under the carpet hide or ignore a problem or difficulty in the hope that it will be forgotten.

1996 **Iain Pears** *Death & Restoration* Many others would merely have swept all our problems under the carpet, and left them until they became too difficult to solve.

carrot

carrot and stick the promise of reward combined with the threat of force or punishment.

> ❶ The image in this expression is of offering a carrot to a donkey to encourage it to move and using a stick to beat it if it refuses to budge.

1998 *New Scientist* And if your powers of persuasion prove insufficient, here's a carrot and stick policy.

carry

carry the can take responsibility for a mistake or misdeed. British informal

> ❶ The origin of this expression and the nature of the *can* involved are both uncertain, though the idiom appears to have started life as early 20th-century naval or military slang.

1998 *Times* Was this the same Mr Cook who danced on the Tories' graves for not carrying the can for errors of their officials?

carry the day: *see* DAY.

cart

in the cart in trouble or difficulty. British informal

> ⓘ A cart was formerly used to take convicted criminals to the public gallows and to expose prostitutes and other offenders to public humiliation in the streets.

put the cart before the horse reverse the proper order or procedure of something.

> ⓘ A medieval version of this expression was *set the oxen before the yoke*. The version with *horse* and *cart* dates from the early 16th century.

> **1998** *Spectator* It's putting the cart before the horse. All history shows that if you want to create a political union, you do that first and the single currency follows.

carved

be carved in stone: *see* STONE.

case

be on (*or* get off) someone's case start (*or* stop) criticizing or hounding someone. informal

cash

cash in your chips die. informal

> ⓘ The counters used in various gambling games are called *chips*. They are converted into cash at the conclusion of the game.

cash in hand payment for goods and services by money in the form of notes and coins.

> ⓘ *Cash in hand* is mainly used to distinguish between cash payment and payment by cheque, especially with reference to being paid in this way in order to avoid having to declare the amount earned to the tax authorities.

cast

be cast in a — mould be of the type specified.

> **1991** **Jean Bow** *Jane's Journey* He was certainly not cast in a common mould. She had never met anyone like him before.

cast someone adrift: *see* ADRIFT.

cast your bread upon the waters: *see* BREAD.

cast the first stone: *see* STONE.

cast something in someone's teeth reject defiantly or refer reproachfully to a person's previous action or statement.

castle

build castles in the air (*or* in Spain) have a visionary and unattainable scheme; daydream.

> ⓘ The concept was known to St Augustine (354–430), who uses the phrase *subtracto fundamento in aere aedificare* meaning 'build on air without foundation'. *Castles in the air* has been the version predominant in English since the late 16th century, but *castles in Spain*, from Old French *châteaux en Espagne*, was used in the late medieval period and occasionally in more recent times. The form of the saying in Old French, known from the 13th century, may refer to the fact that much of Spain in the Middle Ages was under Moorish control, so any scheme to build castles there was clearly unlikely to succeed.

cat

all cats are grey in the dark the qualities that distinguish people from one another are obscured in some circumstances, and if they can't be perceived they don't matter. proverb

> ⓘ The US version of this proverb is *at night all cats are gray*.

bell the cat: *see* BELL.

the cat has got someone's tongue someone is remaining silent.

a cat may look at a king even a person of low status or importance has rights. proverb

> **1998** *Times* A cat may look at a king. The cat may be wrong in its conclusions, but others, following its gaze, can draw their own.

a dead cat bounce: *see* DEAD.

enough to make a cat laugh extremely ridiculous or ironic. informal

> ⓘ This expression dates from the mid 19th century and is associated with the story of Puss in Boots.

fight like cat and dog (of two people) be continually arguing with one another.

> **1995** **Edward Toman** *Dancing in Limbo* Her desertion of him hadn't come as a total surprise ... for the pair of them had been fighting like cat and dog for the best part of a year.

let the cat out of the bag reveal a secret, especially carelessly or by mistake.

> ⓘ A similar metaphorical use of *bag* may be found in the French phrase *vider le sac*, literally 'empty the bag', meaning 'tell the whole story'.

> **1996** **Bernard Connolly** *The Rotten Heart of Europe* Tim Renton ... at odds with his leader on Europe, let the cat out of the bag when he told a television audience, 'we need a strong

Europe to maintain our independence from the United States and the Pacific Rim'.

like a cat on a hot tin roof (*or* **on hot bricks**) very agitated, restless, or anxious.

like the cat that's got (*or* **who's stolen**) **the cream** self-satisfied; having achieved your objective. informal, chiefly British

like a scalded cat: *see* SCALDED.

like something the cat brought in (of a person) very dirty, bedraggled, or exhausted. informal

> **1996 Frank McCourt** *Angela's Ashes* One of them says we look like something the cat brought in and Malachy has to be held back from fighting them.

no room to swing a cat: *see* ROOM.

not a cat in hell's chance no chance at all. informal

> ❶ This expression is often shortened to *not a cat's chance*.

> **2001 James Hamilton-Paterson** *Loving Monsters* There isn't, of course, a cat in hell's chance that I shall ever see 1999 as you, I and Dr Faruli know perfectly well.

play cat and mouse with manoeuvre in a way designed alternately to provoke and thwart an opponent.

> ❶ The image here is of the way that a cat toys with a mouse, pretending to release it and then pouncing on it again.

put the cat among the pigeons say or do something that is likely to cause trouble or controversy. British

> ❶ This expression was first recorded in J. Stevens's *New Spanish and English Dictionary* (1706), where it is explained as referring to a man coming into the company of a group of women. The idiom **flutter the dovecotes** (*see* FLUTTER) is based on the same idea of a group of pigeons as a tranquil or harmless community.

> **1998** *New Scientist* The ... study has firmly put the cat among the pigeons by claiming that most of the therapeutic effects of expensive antidepressant pills ... can be mimicked by dummy pills.

see which way the cat jumps see what direction events are taking before committing yourself.

> **1990 Dennis Kavanagh** *Thatcherism* She borrowed Kipling's words: 'I don't spend a lifetime watching which way the cat jumps. I know really which way I want the cat to go.'

that cat won't jump that suggestion is implausible or impracticable. informal

> **1965 Simon Troy** *No More a-Roving* If you're telling me she fell in, just like that—oh no! That cat won't jump.

turn cat in pan change sides; be a traitor.

> ❶ The origin of this phrase is unknown. It was used in the 16th century in the form *turn the cat in the pan* with the sense of 'reverse the proper order or nature of things', but this was replaced by the modern sense in the early 17th century.

when the cat's away, the mice will play people will naturally take advantage of the absence of someone in authority to do as they like. proverb

catbird

in the catbird seat in a superior or more advantageous position. North American informal

> ❶ This expression is said to have originally referred to a baseball player in the fortunate position of having no strikes and therefore three balls still to play (a reference made in James Thurber's short story *The Catbird Seat*).

catch-22

a catch-22 situation a dilemma or difficulty from which there is no escape because of mutually conflicting or dependent conditions.

> ❶ The classic statement of this situation is in Joseph Heller's novel *Catch-22* (1961), from which the expression is taken: 'Orr would be crazy to fly more missions and sane if he didn't, but if he was sane he had to fly them. If he flew them he was crazy and didn't have to; but if he didn't want to he was sane and had to.'

> **1997** *New Scientist* It's a catch-22 situation: you cannot get the job without having the relevant experience and you cannot get the experience without having first done the job.

catch

catch at straws: *see* STRAW.

catch a cold: *see* COLD.

catch your death: *see* DEATH.

catch the sun ❶ be in a sunny position. ❷ become tanned or sunburnt. British

catch a Tartar encounter or get hold of a person who can neither be controlled nor got rid of; meet with a person who is unexpectedly more than your match.

> ❶ The Tartars (or Tatars), a combined force of central Asian people including Mongols and Turks, established a vast empire during the Middle Ages under the leadership of the warlord Genghis Khan, and were a byword for ferocity.

catch-up

play catch-up try to equal a competitor in a sporting event.

cat's whiskers

the cat's whiskers an excellent person or thing. informal

> ❶ Other similar phrases include *the cat's pyjamas* and the chiefly North American *the cat's miaou*.

cause

make common cause with unite with in order to achieve a shared aim.

> **1997 A. Sivanandan** *When Memory Dies* I was sorry that the crows, proud kings of the dung-heap, should make common cause with house-sparrows under the eaves of roofs.

a rebel without a cause: *see* REBEL.

caution

throw caution to the wind (*or* winds) act in a completely reckless manner.

cave

keep cave act as lookout. school slang

> ❶ *Cave* is a Latin word meaning 'beware!' Pronounced as one or two syllables, *cave* was the traditional warning uttered by a schoolchild to let others know that a teacher was approaching.

caviar

caviar to the general a good thing that is not appreciated by the ignorant.

> ❶ This phrase comes from Shakespeare's *Hamlet*, where Hamlet commends a play with the words: 'the play, I remember, pleased not the million; 'twas caviar to the general'.

Cerberus

a sop to Cerberus: *see* SOP.

ceremony

stand on ceremony insist on the observance of formalities; behave formally.

without ceremony without preamble or politeness.

cess

bad cess to a curse on. chiefly Irish

> ❶ The origin of *cess* in this expression is probably linked to the historical requirement for Irish households to provide the soldiers of their English overlords with provisions at the low prices 'assessed' by the government.

chafe

chafe at the bit: *see* **champ at the bit** *at* CHAMP.

chaff

be caught with chaff be easily deceived.

> ❶ *Chaff* is the husks of corn separated from the grain by threshing. *Be caught with chaff* has been used since the late 15th century as metaphor for being easily fooled or trapped.

separate the wheat from the chaff: *see* WHEAT.

chain

pull (*or* yank) someone's chain tease someone, especially by leading them to believe something that isn't true. US informal

chalice

a poisoned chalice: *see* POISONED.

chalk

as different as chalk and cheese fundamentally different or incompatible. British

> ❶ The opposition of *chalk* and *cheese* hinges on their being totally different in all qualities other than their rather similar appearance.

by a long chalk by far. British

> ❶ This expression is based on the old custom of marking up points scored in a game with chalk on a blackboard, as is its opposite *not by a long chalk* meaning 'by no means; not at all'.

chalk and talk teaching by traditional methods focusing on the blackboard and presentation by the teacher as opposed to more informal or interactive methods. British

walk the chalk: *see* WALK.

champ

champ (*or* chafe) at the bit be restlessly impatient, especially to start doing something.

> ❶ *Champ at the bit* is used literally of a spirited horse that tugs at the bit in its mouth in its eagerness to move.

chance

chance your arm (*or* **luck**) undertake something although it may be dangerous or unsuccessful; take a risk. British informal

chance would be a fine thing used to express a belief that something desirable that has just been mentioned is unlikely to happen. informal

in the last chance saloon: *see* LAST.

not a cat in hell's chance: *see* CAT.

not a chance in hell: *see* HELL.

not a Chinaman's chance: *see* CHINAMAN.

on the off chance just in case.

> **1992** Neal Stephenson *Snow Crash* They upload staggering quantities of useless information to the database, on the off chance that some of it will eventually be useful.

a sporting chance: *see* SPORTING.

change

change horses in midstream: *see* HORSE.

a change is as good as a rest a change of work or occupation can be as restorative or refreshing as a period of relaxation. proverb

a change of heart a move to a different opinion or attitude.

change your tune express a very different opinion or behave in a very different way, usually in response to a change in circumstances.

get no change out of fail to get information or a desired reaction from. British informal

ring the changes vary the ways of expressing, arranging, or doing something.

> ❶ In bell-ringing, the *changes* are the different sequences in which a peal of bells may be rung.

chapter

chapter and verse an exact reference or authority.

> ❶ *Chapter and verse* was originally used to refer to the numbering of passages in the Bible. It is now also used more generally to refer to any (usually written) authority for something.

a chapter of accidents a series of unfortunate events.

> ❶ This expression was apparently coined by Lord Chesterfield in a letter to Solomon Dayrolles in 1753: 'The chapter of knowledge is a very short, but the chapter of accidents is a very long one'.

charge

return to the charge make a further attempt at something, especially in arguing a point. dated

> ❶ *Charge* here is used in the sense of a headlong rush forward, usually associated with attacking soldiers in a battle.

charity

charity begins at home a person's first responsibility is for the needs of their own family and friends. proverb

cold as charity: *see* COLD.

charm

work like a charm be completely successful or effective.

> ❶ *Charm* here means a magic spell or lucky talisman.

chase

chase the dragon take heroin (sometimes mixed with another smokable drug) by heating it in tinfoil and inhaling the fumes through a tube or roll of paper.

> ❶ *Chase the dragon* is reputedly a translation from Chinese. The expression apparently refers to the undulating movements of the fumes up and down the tinfoil, resembling those of the tail of a dragon, a creature found in many Chinese myths.

go and chase yourself! go away! informal

chattering

the chattering classes articulate and educated people considered as a social group given to the expression of liberal opinions about society and culture. derogatory

cheap

cheap and cheerful simple and inexpensive. British

cheap and nasty of low cost and bad quality. British

cheap at the price well worth having, regardless of the cost.

> ⓘ A frequently heard variant of this expression, *cheap at half the price*, while used to mean exactly the same, is, logically speaking, nonsense, since *cheap at twice the price* is the actual meaning intended.

check

check someone or something skeef give someone or something a dirty look; look askance at someone or something. South African

check you goodbye. South African informal

cheek

cheek by jowl close together; side by side.

> ⓘ *Jowl* here is used in the sense 'cheek'; the phrase was originally *cheek by cheek*.

turn the other cheek refrain from retaliating when you have been attacked or insulted.

> ⓘ This expression comes from Matthew 5:39: 'But I say unto you, That ye resist not evil: but whosoever shall smite thee on thy right cheek, turn to him the other also'.

cheer

of good cheer cheerful or optimistic. archaic

> ⓘ The exhortation to *be of good cheer* occurs in several passages of the New Testament in the Authorized Version of the Bible (for example in Matthew 9:2, John 16:33, and Acts 27:22). In Middle English, *cheer* had the meaning 'face'. This sense of *cheer* is now obsolete, but the related senses of 'countenance' and 'demeanour as reflected in the countenance' survive in a number of phrases, including *in good cheer* and the archaic *what cheer?* (how are you?).

three cheers for — three successive hurrahs expressing appreciation or congratulation of someone or something.

> ⓘ Qualified approval or mild enthusiasm is sometimes expressed by *two cheers for —*, as in the title of E. M. Forster's book *Two Cheers for Democracy* (1951).

> **1998** *Zest* So three cheers for The Body Shop's Community Trade programme, which is helping organic bergamot farms thrive once more.

cheese

a big cheese: *see* BIG.

hard cheese used to express sympathy over a petty matter. British informal

say cheese said by a photographer to encourage the subject to smile.

chequered flag

take the chequered flag finish first in a race.

> ⓘ In motor racing a *chequered flag* is used to signify that the winner has passed the finishing post.

cherry

a bite at the cherry an attempt or chance to do something.

> ⓘ This phrase is often used in the negative, to express the idea that you will not get a second chance (*a second bite at the cherry*). If you take two attempts to do something, especially some quite small task, this is taking *two bites at the (same) cherry* or *another bite at the cherry*.

a bowl of cherries a very pleasant or enjoyable situation or experience.

the cherry on the cake a desirable feature perceived as the finishing touch to something that is already inviting or worth having.

pop someone's cherry have sexual intercourse with a girl or woman who is a virgin. informal

Cheshire

grin like a Cheshire cat have a broad fixed smile on your face.

> ⓘ The Cheshire cat with its broad grin is best known for its appearance (and disappearance) in Lewis Carroll's *Alice's Adventures in Wonderland* (1865), but the expression, which is of uncertain origin, is recorded from the first half of the 19th century.

chest

hope chest: *see* HOPE.

get something off your chest say something that you have wanted to say for a long time, resulting in a feeling of relief. informal

chestnut

an old chestnut a joke, story, or subject that has become tedious and boring as a result of its age and constant repetition.

❶ The most likely source for this sense of *chestnut* is in the following exchange between two characters, Zavior and Pablo, in William Dimond's play *Broken Sword* (1816): ZAVIOR . . . When suddenly from the thick boughs of a cork tree— PABLO. (Jumping up) A chesnut, Captain, a chesnut . . . Captain, this is the twenty-seventh time I have heard you relate this story, and you invariably said, a chesnut, until now.

pull someone's chestnuts out of the fire succeed in a hazardous undertaking for someone else's benefit.

❶ This expression refers to the fable of a monkey using a cat's paw (or in some versions a dog's paw) to rake out roasting chestnuts from a fire. *Cat's paw* is sometimes used as a term for someone who is used by another person as a tool or stooge.

chew

chew the cud: see CUD.

chew the fat (or rag) chat in a leisurely way, usually at length. informal

1986 Tom Clancy *Red Storm Rising* Four-star admirals didn't chew the fat with newly frocked commanders unless they had nothing better to do.

chew the scenery (of an actor) overact. informal

chick

neither chick nor child no children at all. North American or dialect

chicken

a chicken-and-egg problem an unresolved question as to which of two things caused the other.

❶ This expression comes from the traditional riddle: 'which came first, the chicken or the egg?'

chickens come home to roost your past mistakes or wrongdoings will eventually be the cause of present troubles.

❶ This phrase comes from the proverb *curses, like chickens, come home to roost.*

1997 Arundhati Roy *The God of Small Things* He knew, had known, that one day History's twisted chickens would come home to roost.

count your chickens: see COUNT.

running (or rushing) about like a headless chicken acting in a panic-stricken manner and not thinking clearly about what should be done.

❶ A decapitated chicken may continue to flap about for a few moments before finally expiring.

chief

big white chief a person in authority. humorous

❶ This expression supposedly represents Native American speech, and also occurs as *great white chief.*

1971 Roger Busby *Deadlock* You'd think he was the bloody big white chief instead of an OB technician.

chief cook and bottle-washer a person who performs a variety of important but routine tasks. informal

too many chiefs and not enough Indians used to describe a situation where there are too many people giving orders and not enough people to carry them out.

child

child's play a task which is very easily accomplished.

chin

keep your chin up remain cheerful in difficult circumstances. informal

take it on the chin endure or accept misfortune courageously.

❶ The image here is of a boxing blow taken squarely on the chin.

1998 *Times* The occasional 'bad 'un' [i.e. decision] is inevitable, and when it comes . . . the players must take it on the chin.

Chinaman

not a Chinaman's chance not even a very slight chance.

1952 Frank Yerby *A Woman Called Fancy* You haven't a Chinaman's chance of raising that money in Boston.

chink

a chink in someone's armour a weak point in someone's character, arguments, or ideas which makes them vulnerable to attack or criticism.

chip

a chip off the old block someone who resembles their parent, especially in character. informal

> ❶ A *chip* in this expression means something which forms a portion of, or is derived from, a larger or more important thing, and which retains the characteristic qualities of that superior thing. In 1781 Edmund Burke commented on Pitt the Younger's maiden speech in Parliament by saying he was: 'Not merely a chip of the old "block", but the old block itself'.

a chip on your shoulder a strong and usually long-standing inclination to feel resentful or aggrieved, often about a particular thing; a sense of inferiority characterized by a quickness to take offence. informal

> ❶ In 1830 the *Long Island Telegraph* described the practice which gave rise to this expression: 'When two churlish boys were *determined* to fight, a *chip* would be placed on the shoulder of one, and the other demanded to knock it off at his peril'.

have had your chips be dead, dying, or out of contention. British informal

when the chips are down when you find yourself in a very serious and difficult situation. informal

> ❶ *Chips* in this phrase, and in **have had your chips** above, are gambling chips.

choice

Hobson's choice no choice at all.

> ❶ Thomas Hobson, to whom this expression refers, was a carrier at Cambridge in the early 17th century, who would not allow his clients their own choice of horse from his stables as he insisted on hiring them out in strict rotation. They were offered the 'choice' of the horse nearest the door or none at all. *Hobson's choice* is also mid 20th-century British rhyming slang for *voice*.

chop

bust someone's chops nag or criticize someone. North American informal

bust your chops exert yourself. North American informal

chop and change change your opinions or behaviour repeatedly and abruptly, often for no good reason. British informal

> ❶ Both *chop* and *change* originally had the sense of 'barter', 'exchange', or 'buy and sell', but as this sense of *chop* became dated the meaning of the whole expression shifted to its present one.

chop logic argue in a tiresomely pedantic way; quibble.

> ❶ *Chop* is here used in the 16th-century sense meaning 'bandy words'. This sense is now obsolete, and the sense of *chop* used in this phrase was later wrongly understood as 'cut something into small pieces'.

not much chop no good; not up to much. Australian & New Zealand informal

> ❶ The sense of *chop* in this expression originated in the Hindi word *chāp* meaning 'official stamp'. Europeans in the Far East extended the use of the word to cover documents such as passports to which an official stamp or impression was attached and in China it came to mean 'branded goods'. From this, in the late 19th century, *chop* was used to refer to something that had 'class' or had been validated as genuine or good.

1947 Dan Davin *The Gorse Blooms Pale* I know it's not been much chop so far but we're only getting started.

chord

strike (*or* touch) a chord say or do something which affects or stirs the emotions of others.

strike (*or* touch) the right cord skilfully appeal to or arouse a particular emotion in others.

chuck

chuck it down rain heavily. informal

chump

off your chump crazy. British informal

> ❶ The literal sense of *chump* meaning 'a broad, thick block of wood' led in the mid 19th century to its humorous use to mean 'head', with the implication of 'blockhead'.

cigar

close but no cigar (of an attempt) almost but not quite successful. North American informal

> ❶ This phrase possibly originated as a consoling comment to or about a man who put up a good, but not winning, performance in a competition or contest of strength in which the prize was a cigar.

1995 Nick Hornby *High Fidelity* But, you know … you did not represent my last and best chance of a relationship. So, you know, nice try. Close, but no cigar.

cinder

burnt to a cinder: see BURNT.

circle

circle the wagons (of a group) unite in defence of a common interest. North American informal

> ⓘ In South Africa the Afrikaans word *laager*, meaning 'a defensive circle of ox wagons', is used in similar metaphorical contexts.

come (or turn) full circle return to a past position or situation, often in a way considered to be inevitable.

go round in circles do something for a long time without achieving anything but purposeless repetition. informal

run round in circles be fussily busy with little result. informal

the wheel has turned (or come) full circle the situation has returned to what it was in the past, as if completing a cycle.

> ⓘ This phrase comes from Shakespeare's *King Lear*: 'The wheel is come full circle'. The wheel referred to is that which the goddess Fortune was said to turn as a symbol of random luck or change.

circus

a three-ring circus ❶ a circus with three rings for simultaneous performances. ❷ a public spectacle, especially one with little substance.

> ❷ **1998** *Spectator* Along the way, these meetings have lost all that might have made them worthwhile … and have turned into a travelling three-ring circus.

citizen

citizen of the world a person who is at home in any country.

civilization

the end of civilization as we know it: see END.

claim

claim to fame a reason for being regarded as unusual or noteworthy (often used when the reason cited is comical, bizarre, or trivial).

clam

happy as a clam: see **happy as a sandboy** at HAPPY.

clanger

drop a clanger: see DROP.

clap

clap eyes on: see EYE.

clap hold of grab someone or something roughly or abruptly. informal

clap someone in jail (or irons) put someone in prison (or in chains).

> ⓘ The meaning of *clap* in these idioms is somewhat removed from the original one of 'make a sudden explosive sound'. Over time the word developed the additional sense of 'make a sudden action', without necessarily implying any sound.

clapper

like the clappers very fast or very hard. British informal

> ⓘ *Clappers* may refer to the striking part of a bell, or it may refer to a device in a mill for striking or shaking the hopper in order to make the grain move down to the millstones. The phrase *like the clappers* developed as mid 20th-century RAF slang, and is sometimes found in the form *like the clappers of hell*.

> **1992 Jeff Torrington** *Swing Hammer Swing!* Why should a hearse be going like the clappers through the streets of Glasgow at this time of night?

claret

tap a person's claret make a person's nose bleed by a blow with the fist. informal

class

a class act a person or thing displaying impressive and stylish excellence. informal

claw

get your claws into enter into a possessive relationship with someone (used especially of a woman who dominates or manipulates a man). informal

clay

have feet of clay: see FOOT.

clean

clean as a whistle ❶ extremely clean or clear. ❷ free of incriminating evidence. informal

a clean bill of health: see BILL.

a clean sheet (or slate) an absence of existing restraints or commitments.

2003 *Guardian* Given a clean slate and an impressive budget, I would love to programme a festival...that exposed audiences to completely new forms of music-making at their best and most diverse.

clean someone's clock ❶ give someone a beating. **❷** defeat or surpass someone decisively. North American informal

> ❶ *Clock* is used here in the slang sense of 'face'.

clean house eliminate corruption or inefficiency. North American

clean up your act behave in a more acceptable manner. informal

come clean be completely honest and frank. informal

have clean hands (*or* **keep your hands clean**) be uninvolved and blameless with regard to an immoral act.

keep a clean sheet (in a football match) prevent the opposing side from scoring.

keep your nose clean: *see* NOSE.

make a clean breast of something (*or* **of it**) confess your mistakes or wrongdoings.

> ❶ In former times, many people believed that the breast or chest was where a person's conscience was located. The breast is still used metaphorically to represent the seat of the emotions.

make a clean sweep ❶ remove all unwanted people or things ready to start afresh. **❷** win all of a group of similar or related sporting competitions, events, or matches.

Mr Clean an honourable or incorruptible politician.

cleaner

take someone to the cleaners ❶ take all of someone's money or possessions in a dishonest or unfair way. **❷** inflict a crushing defeat on someone.

clear

clear the air defuse or clarify an angry, tense, or confused situation by frank discussion.

> ❶ This expression comes from the idea that a thunderstorm makes the air less humid.

clear as a bell: *see* BELL.

as clear as day very easy to see or understand.

clear as mud not at all easy to understand. informal

clear the decks prepare for a particular event or goal by dealing beforehand with anything that might hinder progress.

> ❶ In the literal sense, *clear the decks* meant to remove obstacles or unwanted items from the decks of a ship before a battle at sea.

in clear not in code.

> **1966 Robert Sheckley** *Mindswap* Thus, he crosscircuited his fear of embarrassment, and spoke to his oldest friend in clear.

in the clear ❶ no longer in danger or suspected of something. **❷** with nothing to hinder someone in achieving something.

out of a clear (blue) sky as a complete surprise.

> **1992** *New Yorker* The latest revelations... about the marriage of the Prince and Princess of Wales may have induced disbelief, but they did not come out of a clear blue sky.

cleft

be (*or* **be caught**) **in a cleft stick** be in a difficult situation, when any action you take will have adverse consequences. chiefly British

> ❶ *Cleft* is one of the forms of the past participle of *cleave*, in its basic meaning of 'divide with a cutting blow' or 'split'. The other form still current in standard English is *cloven*, and the two words tend to be used in different contexts: we find a *cleft stick* and a *cleft palate* but a *cloven hoof*.

clever

too clever by half annoyingly proud of your intelligence or skill. informal

click

click into place become suddenly clear and understandable.

> ❶ *Click into place* is used literally of an object, especially part of a mechanism, to mean 'fall smoothly into its allotted position'.

click your fingers at: *see* snap your fingers at *at* FINGER.

climb

have a mountain to climb: *see* MOUNTAIN.

climbing

be climbing the walls feel frustrated, helpless, and trapped. informal

clip

at a clip at a time; all at once. US informal

> **2000 Anthony Bourdain** *Kitchen Confidential* I peeled 75 pounds of shrimp at a clip.

clip someone's wings prevent someone from acting freely.

> ❶ *Clip someone's wings* comes from the phrase *clip a bird's wings*, which means 'trim the feathers of a bird so that it cannot fly'.

clock

round (*or* around) the clock all day and all night; ceaselessly.

> **1992 Susan Sontag** *The Volcano Lover* The mountain was ... guarded round the clock by a ring of armed soldiers mounted on nervous horses.

turn back the clock return to the past or to a previous way of doing things.

watch the clock wait eagerly for the end of working hours.

> ❶ It is from this expression that the word *clock-watcher* has developed, referring to someone who is determined not to work more than their allotted hours.

clog

clogs to clogs in three generations the return of a family to poverty after one generation of prosperity.

close

close to the bone: *see* BONE.

close the door on: *see* DOOR.

close to home: *see* HOME.

close your mind to: *see* MIND.

close ranks: *see* RANK.

close shave (*or* call) a narrow escape from danger or disaster. informal

close to (*or* close on) (of an amount) almost; very nearly.

run someone close almost match the same standards or level of achievement as someone else.

too close for comfort dangerously or uncomfortably near.

too close to call (of a contest, race, etc.) so evenly balanced that it is impossible to predict the outcome with confidence. informal

closed

behind closed doors (of an action) done in a secretive or furtive way; hidden from public view.

a closed book a thing of which you have no knowledge or understanding.

> **1944 Frank Clune** *The Red Heart* The desert is an open book to the man of the Vast Open Spaces, but to the schoolmaster it was a closed book.

closet

out of the closet out into the open. informal

> ❶ *Closet*, the normal North American term for 'cupboard' or 'wardrobe', is used in the Bible to typify privacy and seclusion (for example in Luke 12:3: 'that which ye have spoken in the ear in closets shall be proclaimed upon the housetops'). *Come out of the closet* means 'cease hiding a secret about yourself' or 'make public your intentions'. It is now most commonly, though not always, used in connection with someone making their homosexuality public.

> **1998** *Spectator* The Prime Minister's entourage could not conceal its glee at the results of their boss coming out of the closet.

cloud

on cloud nine extremely happy.

> ❶ *On cloud nine* refers to a ten-part classification of clouds in which *nine* was second highest. A dated variant of the expression is *on cloud seven*.

a silver lining: *see* SILVER.

under a cloud under suspicion or discredited.

> **1992 Alasdair Gray** *Poor Things* The career of this once famous soldier began as well as ended under a cloud.

with your head in the clouds (of a person) out of touch with reality; daydreaming.

cloven hoof

a cloven hoof a symbol or indication of evil.

> ❶ Traditional pictures of the Devil show him with the head and torso of a man but the legs and cloven hoofs of a goat. Therefore, a *cloven hoof* is a giveaway sign of the Devil.

> **1959 François Mauriac** *A Woman of Pharisees* She had been a trial to him from the beginning, and now the cloven hoof was beginning to show.

clover

in clover in ease and luxury.

> ℹ This sense of the phrase is a reference to clover's being particularly attractive to livestock, as in the expression *happy as a pig in clover*.

club

in the club (*or* **the pudding club**) pregnant. British informal

> **1993** Carl MacDougall *The Lights Below* Must be serious if you're drinking with the old man. Did you stick her in the club?

join (*or* **welcome to**) **the club** used as a humorous exclamation to express solidarity with someone else who is experiencing problems or difficulties that the speaker has already experienced.

clutch

clutch at straws: *see* STRAW.

coach

drive a coach and horses through make something entirely useless or ineffective. British.

> ℹ An early example of this idiom is found in this statement by the Irish lawyer Stephen Rice (1637–1715): 'I will drive a coach and six horses through the Act of Settlement'. Early versions of the phrase also refer to a space big enough to *turn a coach and six* (or *four*) (i.e. horses) in, but the context, following Rice's declaration, is very often that of rendering a law or regulation ineffective.

> **1997** *Spectator* A coach and horses was driven through one of the guiding principles of American statecraft.

coal

coals to Newcastle something brought or sent to a place where it is already plentiful.

> ℹ Coal from Newcastle-upon-Tyne in northern England was famously abundant in previous centuries, and *carry coals to Newcastle* has been an expression for an unnecessary activity since the mid 17th century.

haul someone over the coals reprimand someone severely.

> ℹ This expression originated in a form of torture that involved dragging the victim over the coals of a slow fire.

heap coals of fire on someone's head go out of your way to cause someone to feel remorse. British

> ℹ This phrase is of biblical origin: 'if thine enemy hunger, feed him; if he thirst, give him drink: for in so doing thou shalt heap coals of fire on his head' (Romans 12:20).

coalface

at the coalface engaged in work at an active rather than a theoretical level in a particular field. British

> **1998** *Town and Country Planning* Workers at the coalface of sustainable development need these success stories.

coast

the coast is clear there is no danger of being observed or caught.

> ℹ *The coast is clear* originally meant that there were no enemies guarding a sea coast who would prevent an attempt to land or embark.

coat-tail

on someone's coat-tails undeservedly benefiting from another's success.

> **1964** *Economist* Mr Robert Kennedy cannot be sure of riding the coat-tails of Mr Johnson in New York.

cob

have (*or* **get**) **a cob on** be annoyed or in a bad mood. British informal

cobweb

blow (*or* **clear**) **away the cobwebs** banish a state of lethargy; enliven or refresh yourself.

cock

a cock-and-bull story a ridiculous and implausible story.

> ℹ The expression 'talk of a cock and a bull' is recorded from the early 17th century, and apparently refers to an original story or fable which is now lost.

at full cock: *see* FULL.

at half cock: *see* HALF.

cock a snook at: *see* SNOOK.

cock of the walk someone who dominates others within a group.

> ℹ The places in which cocks bred for fighting were kept were known as *walks*: one cock would be kept in each walk and would tolerate no other birds in its space.

cock your ear listen attentively to or for something.

> ❶ The image here is of a dog raising its ears to an erect position.

cocked hat

knock something into a cocked hat ❶ put a definitive end to something. ❷ be very much better than someone or something.

> ❶ A *cocked hat* is a hat with the brim permanently turned up, especially a style of three-cornered hat worn from the late 18th century to the early 19th century.

cockle

warm the cockles of someone's heart give someone a comforting feeling of pleasure or contentment.

> ❶ This phrase perhaps arose as a result of the resemblance in shape between a heart and a cockleshell.

cocoa

I should cocoa (or coco) I should say so. British rhyming slang

> **1996 Melvin Burgess** *Junk* He said, 'Someone'll really buy it and it'll be theirs then.' 'I should coco,' I said.

code

bring something up to code renovate an old building or update its features in line with the latest building regulations. North American

coign

coign of vantage a favourable position for observation or action. literary

> ❶ The literal sense of a *coign of vantage* is 'a projecting corner of a wall or building'; the phrase appears in Shakespeare's *Macbeth* in Duncan's description of the nesting places of the swifts at Macbeth's castle. The word *quoin* meaning 'an external angle of a building' still exists in English, but the archaic spelling *coign* survives mainly in this phrase.

coil

shuffle off this mortal coil die. literary

> ❶ *Shuffle off this mortal coil* is a quotation from Shakespeare's *Hamlet*. *This mortal coil* is sometimes used independently to mean 'the fact or state of being alive', with the suggestion that this is a troublesome state, since *coil* retains here its archaic sense of 'turmoil'.

> **1986 Dudley Moore** *Off-Beat* He was just one of a number of distinguished composers who have shuffled off their mortal coil in a variety of unusual ways.

coin

the other side of the coin the opposite or contrasting aspect of a matter. Compare with **the reverse of the medal** (*at* MEDAL).

pay someone back in their own coin retaliate by similar behaviour.

to coin a phrase ❶ said ironically when introducing a banal remark or cliché. ❷ said when introducing a new expression or a variation on a familiar one.

coincidence

the long arm of coincidence: *see* ARM.

cold

catch a cold (*or* **catch cold)** ❶ become infected with a cold. ❷ encounter trouble or difficulties, especially financial ones. informal

> ❷ **2001** *Financial Times* Most observers expect house prices to rise . . . depending on whether the UK economy continues to grow smoothly or whether it catches a cold from the US.

as cold as charity very cold.

cold comfort poor or inadequate consolation.

> ❶ This expression, together with the previous idiom, reflects a traditional view that charity is often given in a perfunctory or uncaring way. The words *cold* (as the opposite of 'encouraging') and *comfort* have been associated since the early 14th century, but perhaps the phrase is most memorably linked for modern readers with the title of Stella Gibbons's 1933 parody of sentimental novels of rural life, *Cold Comfort Farm*.

cold feet loss of nerve or confidence.

in the cold light of day when you have had time to consider a situation objectively.

the cold shoulder a show of intentional unfriendliness; rejection.

> ❶ The verb *cold-shoulder*, meaning 'reject or be deliberately unfriendly', comes from this phrase.

go cold turkey suddenly and completely stop taking drugs.

> ❶ The image is of one of the possible unpleasant side effects of this, involving bouts of shivering and sweating that cause

goose flesh or goose pimples, a bumpy condition of the skin which resembles the flesh of a dead plucked turkey.

have someone cold have someone at your mercy. US informal

> **1988 Rodney Hall** *Kisses of the Enemy* He waited in his office for news of violence, knowing that then he would have the troublemakers cold.

in cold blood without feeling or mercy; ruthlessly.

> ❶ According to medieval physiology blood was naturally hot, and so this phrase refers to an unnatural state in which someone can carry out a (hot-blooded) deed of passion or violence without the normal heating of the blood. Compare with **make your blood curdle** and **make your blood run cold** (at BLOOD).

leave someone cold fail to interest or excite someone.

left out in the cold ignored; neglected.

out cold completely unconscious.

pour (or throw) cold water on be discouraging or negative about a plan or suggestion.

> **1998 New Scientist** When I put it to...the health minister, that perhaps all clinical trial results should be published, she threw cold water on the idea.

collar

feel someone's collar arrest or legally apprehend someone.

> ❶ The image here is of using a person's collar as a means of getting a secure grip on them.

collision

on a collision course adopting an approach that is certain to lead to conflict with another person or group.

> ❶ This phrase is also used literally to mean 'going in a direction that will lead to a violent crash with another moving object or person'.

colour

lend (or give) colour to make something seem true or probable.

> **1991 J. Rusbridger** *The Intelligence Game* Nothing should be done that would lend colour to any suggestion that it [the Security Service] is concerned with the interests of any particular section of the community.

see the colour of someone's money receive some evidence of forthcoming payment from a person.

colours

nail (or pin) your colours to the mast declare openly and firmly what you believe or favour.

sail under false colours disguise your true nature or intentions.

show your (true) colours reveal your real character or intentions, especially when these are disreputable or dishonourable.

with flying colours: *see* FLYING.

> ❶ The distinguishing ensign or flag of a ship or regiment was known as its *colours*, and the word is used in this sense in these four idioms. A ship on illegal business or in time of war may fly a bogus flag in order to deceive and would therefore be *sailing under false colours*.

column

dodge the column: *see* DODGE.

fifth column: *see* FIFTH.

come

as — as they come used to describe someone or something that is a supreme example of the quality specified.

> **1991 Daily Telegraph** The petrol-engined V-8 was as silky as they come.

come the — play the part of; behave like. informal

> **1992 Jeff Torrington** *Swing Hammer Swing!* Don't come the innocent with me.

come the acid: *see* ACID.

come apart at the seams: *see* SEAM.

come clean: *see* CLEAN.

come in from the cold gain acceptance. informal

> **1998 New Scientist** Considering that the intracavity technique got off to such a slow start, it may, at last, have come in from the cold.

come it over seek to impose on or to impress deceptively. informal

come it strong go to excessive lengths; use exaggeration. informal

come of age: *see* AGE.

come off it! said when vigorously expressing disbelief. informal

come to grief: *see* GRIEF.

come the old soldier over someone seek to impose something on someone, especially on grounds of greater experience or age. informal

come to that (*or* **if it comes to that**) said to introduce an additional significant point. informal

> **1998 Martin Booth** *The Industry of Souls* I am sure you would not wish your son to hear of his father's waywardness. Or your wife, come to that.

come to think of it said when an idea or point occurs to you while you are speaking.

come up smelling of roses: *see* SMELLING.

comfort

too — for comfort causing physical or mental unease by an excess of the specified quality.

> **1994 Janice Galloway** *Foreign Parts* They were all too at peace with themselves, too untroubled for comfort.

coming

have it coming to you be due for retribution on account of something bad that you have done. informal

not know if you are coming or going be confused, especially as a result of being very busy. informal

where someone is coming from someone's meaning, motivation, or personality. informal

commando

go commando wear no underpants. informal

common

common or garden of the usual or ordinary type. British informal

> ❶ *Common or garden* was originally used to describe a plant in its most familiar domesticated form, e.g. 'the common or garden nightshade'.

> **1964 Leonard Woolf** *Letter* I certainly do not agree that the unconscious mind reveals deeper truths about someone else than plain common or garden common sense does.

the common touch the ability to get on with or appeal to ordinary people.

> ❶ An obsolete sense of *common* (which comes from Latin *communis* meaning 'affable') may have influenced this phrase, as

may a Shakespearean phrase used in his play about the great exponent of the common touch, King Henry V, on the eve of the battle of Agincourt: 'a little touch of Harry in the night'.

> **1910 Rudyard Kipling** *If* If you can talk with crowds and keep your virtue, Or walk with Kings—nor lose the common touch ...

company

be (*or* **err**) **in good company** be in the same situation as someone important or respected.

compare

compare notes exchange ideas, opinions, or information about a particular subject.

compliment

return the compliment ❶ give a compliment in return for another. ❷ retaliate or respond in kind.

conclusion

jump (*or* **leap**) **to conclusions** (*or* **the conclusion that**) make a hasty judgement or decision before learning or considering all the facts.

try conclusions with engage in a trial of skill or argument with. formal

> **1902 G. S. Whitmore** *The Last Maori War in New Zealand* Te Kooti's prestige enormously increased by an apparent unwillingness to try conclusions with him, even with an immensely superior force and in the open plains.

concrete

be set in concrete (of a policy or idea) be fixed and unalterable.

conjure

a name to conjure with a person who is important within a particular sphere of activity.

> ❶ The image here is of magically summoning a spirit to do your bidding by invoking a powerful name or using a spell.

> **1954 Iris Murdoch** *Under the Net* His name, little known to the public, is one to conjure with in Hollywood.

conspicuous

conspicuous by your absence obviously not present in a place where you should be.

> ❶ This phrase was coined by Lord John Russell in a speech made in 1859. He acknowledged as his source for the idea a passage in Tacitus describing a procession of images at a funeral: the fact that those of Cassius and Brutus were absent attracted a great deal of attention.

conspiracy

a conspiracy of silence an agreement to say nothing about an issue that should be generally known.

> ❶ This expression appears to have originated with the French philosopher Auguste Comte (1798–1857).

contempt

hold someone or something in contempt consider someone or something to be unworthy of respect or attention.

> ❶ In formal legal contexts, *holding someone in contempt* means that they are judged to have committed the offence of contempt of court, i.e. they are guilty of disrespect or disobedience to the authority of a court in the administration of justice.

content

to your heart's content to the full extent of your desires.

> ❶ *Heart's content* was used by Shakespeare in *Henry VI, Part 2* (1593) and in *The Merchant of Venice* (1596) in the sense of 'complete inward satisfaction'.

contention

bone of contention: *see* BONE.

contest

no contest ❶ a decision by the referee to declare a boxing match invalid on the grounds that one or both of the boxers are not making serious efforts. ❷ a competition, comparison, or choice of which the outcome is a foregone conclusion.

> ❶ This expression is mainly found in the USA, and is perhaps influenced by the plea of *nolo contendere* (I do not wish to contend) in US law, meaning that the defendant in a criminal prosecution accepts conviction but does not admit guilt.

contradiction

contradiction in terms a statement or group of words associating objects or ideas which are incompatible.

> **1994** *Toronto Life* Veggie burger?— a contradiction in terms I had no wish to argue with: vegetables are fine and necessary, but in their place.

conviction

have the courage of your convictions: *see* COURAGE.

cooee

within cooee of within reach of; near to.

> ❶ *Cooee* originated as an Aboriginal word used as a shout to attract attention, and was adopted by European settlers in Australia. The literal meaning of the phrase *within cooee of* is 'within hailing distance of'.

cook

cook the books alter records, especially accounts, with fraudulent intent or in order to mislead. informal

> ❶ *Cook* has been used since the mid 17th century in this figurative sense of 'tamper with' or 'manipulate'.

cook on the front burner be on the right lines; be on the way to rapid success. North American informal

> ❶ Another version of this phrase is *cook with gas*.

cook someone's goose spoil someone's plans; cause someone's downfall. informal

> ❶ The underlying idea of this phrase seems to be that a goose was cherished and fattened up for a special occasion, and therefore to cook it prematurely meant to spoil the plans for a feast.

too many cooks spoil the broth if too many people are involved in a task or activity, it will not be done well. proverb

> **1997** *Times* Too many cooks spoil the broth and at Apple there is now the equivalent of Marco Pierre White, Anton Mosimann and Nico Ladenis.

cookie

the way the cookie crumbles how things turn out (often used of an undesirable but unalterable situation). informal, chiefly North American with your hand in the cookie jar engaged in surreptitious theft from your employer. North American informal

cool

cool as a cucumber perfectly cool or self-possessed.

> **1992 Randall Kenan** *Let the Dead Bury Their Dead* How many men do you know, black or white, could bluff, cool as a cucumber, caught butt-naked in bed with a damn whore?

cool your heels: see HEEL.

coon

for (or in) a coon's age a very long time. North American informal

> **1951 William Styron** *Lie Down in Darkness* I haven't seen him in a coon's age.

a gone coon a person or thing in desperate straits or as good as dead. US informal

> ❶ *Coon* in these idioms is an informal abbreviation of *raccoon*. Raccoons were hunted for their fur, and *a gone coon* was one that had been cornered so that it could not escape.

coop

fly the coop: see FLY.

coot

bald as a coot: see BALD.

cop

cop hold of take hold of. British

> ❶ A slang word meaning 'catch', *cop* probably originated in northern English dialect.

cop a plea engage in plea bargaining. North American

it's a fair cop an admission that the speaker has been caught doing wrong and deserves punishment.

not much cop not very good. British informal

> ❶ *Cop* is used here in the sense of 'an acquisition'.

> **1998** *Spectator* Suddenly everyone has noticed that the rest of her album…isn't actually much cop after all.

copybook

blot your copybook: see BLOT.

cord

cut the cord cease to rely on someone or something influential or supportive and begin to act independently.

> ❶ The image here is of the cutting of a baby's umbilical cord at birth.

corn

corn in Egypt a plentiful supply.

> ❶ This expression comes from the aged Jacob's instructions to his sons in Genesis 42:2: 'Behold, I have heard that there is corn in Egypt: get you down thither, and buy for us from thence'.

corner

cut corners: see CUT.

fight your corner defend your position or interests.

the four (or far) corners of the world (or earth) remote regions of the earth, far away from each other.

> **1999 Katie Hickman** *Daughters of Britannia* In amongst the fishing boats and the caiques… sailed innumerable vessels from all four corners of the earth.

in someone's corner on someone's side; giving someone support.

> ❶ This idiom and *fight your corner* are boxing metaphors and refer to the diagonally opposite corners taken by opponents in a boxing match. Trainers and assistants are in a boxer's corner to offer support and encouragement between rounds.

paint yourself into a corner: see PAINT.

turn the corner: see TURN.

corridor

the corridors of power the senior levels of government or administration, where covert influence is regarded as being exerted and significant decisions are made.

> ❶ This expression comes from the title of C. P. Snow's novel *The Corridors of Power* (1964). Although most usual with *power*, the phrase can be more specifically applied to the most influential levels of the hierarchy within a particular place or organization, especially when they are regarded as operating covertly. The French word *coulisse* (meaning 'the wings in a theatre' and 'corridor') has a similar figurative sense of the corridor as a place of negotiation and behind-the-scenes scheming.

cost

cost an arm and a leg: *see* ARM.

count the cost: *see* COUNT.

cotton wool

wrap someone in cotton wool be over-protective towards someone.

couch

couch potato someone who watches a lot of television, eats junk food, and takes little or no physical exercise. informal

> ❶ *Couch potato* was a humorous American coinage using the image of a person with the physical shape of a potato slouching on a sofa or couch. Originally, the phrase relied on a pun with *tuber* in the slang term *boob tuber*, which referred to someone devoted to watching the *boob tube* or television.

on the couch undergoing psychoanalysis or psychiatric treatment.

counsel

a counsel of despair an action to be taken when all else fails.

> **2003** *Guardian* This is not a counsel of despair. The argument in favour of the euro can be won, as Winning From Behind, a pamphlet published today by Britain in Europe, argues.

a counsel of perfection advice that is ideal but not feasible.

> **1986** E. **Hall** in *Home Owner Manual* Twice yearly desludging has been recommended but this is probably a counsel of perfection.

count

count your chickens treat something that has not yet happened as a certainty. informal

> ❶ This phrase refers to the proverb *don't count your chickens before they're hatched*.

count the pennies: *see* PENNY.

count sheep: *see* SHEEP.

count something on the fingers of one hand used to emphasize the small number of a particular thing.

> **1992** *Fly Rod and Reel* Two decades ago one could count on the fingers of one hand the saltwater anglers who had caught a sailfish or a marlin on a fly.

count to ten count to ten under your breath in order to prevent yourself from reacting angrily to something.

out for the count unconscious or soundly asleep.

> ❶ A North American variant of the phrase is *down for the count*. In boxing, the *count* is the ten-second period, counted out loud by the referee, during which a boxer who has been knocked to the ground may regain his feet: if he fails to do so he must concede victory to his opponent. A boxer who manages to rise within the count of ten is said to 'beat the count'.

take the count (of a boxer) be knocked out.

countenance

out of countenance disconcerted or unpleasantly surprised.

> ❶ *Countenance* here has the sense of 'confidence of demeanour or calmness of expression'.

counter

go counter run or ride against the direction taken by an animal or person hunted or sought.

> ❶ In Britain, the variants *hunt counter* and *run counter* are also found.

over the counter by ordinary retail purchase, with no need for a prescription or licence.

under the counter (*or* **table**) (with reference to goods bought or sold) surreptitiously and usually illegally.

> **1994** *Coarse Fishing Today* The obvious danger is that river fish will be pinched and flogged 'under the counter'.

country

go (*or* **appeal**) **to the country** test public opinion by dissolving Parliament and holding a general election. British

line of country a subject about which a person is skilled or knowledgeable. British

unknown country an unfamiliar place or topic.

> ❶ The Latin equivalent, *terra incognita*, is also used in English.

courage

Dutch courage: *see* DUTCH.

have the courage of your convictions act on your beliefs despite danger or disapproval.

> **1998** *Times* The knives were out for us and we had to have the courage of our convictions.

take your courage in both hands nerve yourself to do something that frightens you.

course

stay the course: *see* STAY.

court

hold court: *see* HOLD.

Coventry

send someone to Coventry refuse to associate with or speak to someone. chiefly British

> ❶ This expression, which dates from the mid 18th century, is thought by some to stem from the extreme unpopularity of soldiers stationed in Coventry, who were cut off socially by the citizens. Another suggestion is that the phrase arose because Royalist prisoners were sent to Coventry during the English Civil War, the city being staunchly Parliamentarian.

cover

blow someone's cover discover or expose someone's real identity.

break cover emerge into the open; suddenly leave a place of shelter.

> ❶ *Break cover* originally referred to a hunted animal emerging from the undergrowth in which it had been hiding.

cover the waterfront cover every aspect of something. North American informal

> **1999 Tony Parsons** *Man and Boy* And I suddenly realised how many father figures Luke has, father figures who seem to cover the waterfront of parental responsibilities.

cover your back foresee and avoid the possibility of attack or criticism. informal

cover your tracks conceal evidence of what you have done.

cow

have a cow become angry, excited, or agitated. North American informal

> **1990 Susin Nielsen** *Wheels* 'Don't have a cow,' she said huffily. 'It's no big deal.'

a sacred cow an idea, custom, or institution held, especially unreasonably, to be above questioning or criticism.

> ❶ *Sacred cow* originally referred to the veneration of the cow as a sacred animal in the Hindu religion.

> **1991** *Here's Health* The British diet remains a sacred cow.

till the cows come home for an indefinitely long time. informal

crab

catch a crab (in rowing) effect a faulty stroke in which the oar is jammed under water or misses the water altogether.

crack

crack heads together: *see* bang heads together *at* BANG.

crack a book open a book and read it; study. North American informal

crack a bottle open a bottle, especially of wine, and drink it.

crack a crib break into a house. British informal

the crack of dawn very early in the morning.

> ❶ *Crack* here means the instant of time occupied by the crack of a whip.

crack of doom a peal of thunder announcing the Day of Judgement.

> ❶ The idea of thunder announcing the Last Judgement comes from several passages in the book of Revelation (e.g., 6:1, 8:5).

a fair crack of the whip fair treatment; a chance to participate or compete on equal terms. British informal

> **1989 T. M. Albert** *Tales of the Ulster Detective* You might think that the police concocted the circumstances to deny these men a fair crack of the whip.

crack wise make jokes. North American informal

paper over the cracks: *see* PAPER.

cracked

cracked up to be asserted to be (used to indicate that someone or something has been described too favourably). informal

> ❶ This expression stems from the use of *crack* as an adjective to mean 'pre-eminent', a sense dating from the late 18th century.

> **1986 Willy Russell** *Shirley Valentine* Our Brian suddenly realised that the part of Joseph wasn't as big as it had been cracked up to be.

crackers

go crackers ❶ become insane; go mad. ❷ become extremely annoyed or angry.

cracking

get cracking act quickly and energetically. informal

crackling

a bit of crackling an attractive woman regarded as a sexual object. British informal

> **1968 Peter Dickinson** *Skin Deep* 'You know her?' 'I do, sir. Nice bit of crackling, she is.'

cramp

cramp someone's style prevent a person from acting freely or naturally. informal

crash

crash and burn fail spectacularly. North American informal

> **1994** *Hispanic* But if you use Spanish, be careful not to crash and burn...the language is booby-trapped for the unwary PR professional.

craw

stick in your craw make you angry or irritated.

> ❶ Literally, this phrase means 'stick in your throat'. A *craw* is the crop of a bird or insect; the transferred sense of the word to refer to a person's gullet, originally humorous, is now almost entirely confined to this expression. Compare with **stick in your gizzard** (*at* GIZZARD).

crazy

crazy like a fox very cunning or shrewd.

creature

creature of habit a person who follows an unvarying routine.

credit

credit where credit is due praise should be given when it is deserved, even when you are reluctant to give it.

> ❶ This sentiment was earlier expressed in the form *honour where honour is due*, following the Authorized Version of the Bible: 'Render therefore to all their dues: tribute to whom tribute is due; custom to whom custom; fear to whom fear; honour to whom honour' (Romans 13:7).

creek

be up the creek without a paddle be in severe difficulty, usually with no means of extricating yourself from it. informal

> ❶ Often shortened to *be up the creek*, this expression is recorded in the mid 20th century as military slang for 'lost' (for example, while on a patrol).

creep

give someone the creeps induce a feeling of fear or revulsion in someone.

> **1996 Roddy Doyle** *The Woman Who Walked Into Doors* It's the emptiness; there's no one on the street at that time, along the river. It gives me the creeps.

make your flesh creep (or crawl): *see* FLESH.

crest

on the crest of a wave at a very successful point.

cricket

not cricket contrary to traditional standards of fairness or rectitude. British informal

> ❶ The game of cricket, with its traditional regard for courtesy and fair play, has been a metaphor for these qualities since at least the mid 19th century.

crimp

put a crimp in have an adverse effect on. informal

> **1990 Walter Stewart** *Right Church, Wrong Pew* Well, that maybe puts a crimp in my theory.

crisp

burnt to a crisp: *see* **burnt to a cinder** *at* BURNT.

crocodile

shed (or weep) crocodile tears put on a display of insincere grief.

> ❶ This expression draws on the ancient belief that crocodiles wept while luring or devouring their prey.

crook

be crook on be annoyed by. Australian & New Zealand informal

go crook ❶ lose your temper; become angry. ❷ become ill. Australian & New Zealand informal

> ❶ *Crook* in late 19th-century Australian slang meant 'bad' or 'unpleasant'.

> ❶ **1950** *Coast to Coast 1949–50* What'd you do if you were expelled? Y'r old man'd go crook, I bet.

cropper

come a cropper ❶ fall heavily. ❷ suffer a defeat or disaster. informal

> ❶ Sense 1 appears to have originated in mid 19th-century hunting jargon, and possibly came from the phrase *neck and crop* meaning 'bodily' or 'completely'.

> ❷ **1980 Shirley Hazzard** *The Transit of Venus* He had seen how people came a cropper by giving way to impulse.

cross

at cross purposes misunderstanding or having different aims from one another.

cross as two sticks very annoyed or grumpy. British informal

> ❶ This expression is a play on the two senses of *cross*, firstly 'bad-tempered' and secondly 'intersecting'.

cross your fingers (*or* **keep your fingers crossed**) hope that your plans will be successful; trust in good luck.

> ❶ The gesture of putting your index and middle fingers across each other as a sign of hoping for good luck is a scaled-down version of the Christian one of making the sign of the Cross with your whole hand and arm as a request for divine protection. It is also superstitiously employed when telling a deliberate lie, with the idea of warding off the evil that might be expected to befall a liar.

> **1998** *Spectator* Since resources were limited …the only hope the clients had was to hang in there, fingers crossed.

cross the floor join the opposing side in Parliament. British

> ❶ The floor of the House of Commons is the open space separating members of the Government and Opposition parties, who sit on benches facing each other across it.

cross my heart used to emphasize the truthfulness and sincerity of what you are saying or promising. informal

> ❶ The full version of this expression is *cross my heart and hope to die*, and is sometimes reinforced by making a sign of the Cross over your chest.

cross someone's palm with silver pay someone for a favour or service. often humorous

> ❶ *Crossing someone's palm with silver* was originally connected with the telling of fortunes, when the client would literally trace out the sign of a cross on the hand of the fortune-teller with a silver coin.

cross the Rubicon: *see* RUBICON.

cross swords have an argument or dispute.

> ❶ Originally, this expression had the literal sense of 'fight a duel'.

have your cross to bear suffer the troubles that life brings.

> ❶ The reference here is to Jesus (or Simon of Cyrene) carrying the Cross to Calvary before the Crucifixion. The image is also used metaphorically in the New Testament (for example, in Matthew 10:38: 'And he that taketh not his cross and followeth after me is not worthy of me').

crossed

get your wires (*or* **lines**) **crossed** have a misunderstanding.

> ❶ Wires being crossed originally referred to a faulty telephone connection ('a crossed line'), which resulted in another call or calls being heard.

crossfire

be caught in the crossfire suffer damage or harm inadvertently as the result of the conflict between two other people or groups.

> ❶ The literal sense of the phrase, in a military context, is 'be trapped (and possibly killed) by being between two opposing sides who are shooting at each other'.

> **1998** *New Scientist* This suggested that the corneal cells are innocent victims caught in the crossfire as T cells fight the viral infection.

crossroads

at a (*or* **the**) **crossroads** at a critical point, when decisions with far-reaching consequences must be made.

dirty work at the crossroads: *see* DIRTY.

crow

as the crow flies used to refer to a shorter distance in a straight line across country rather than the distance as measured along a more circuitous road.

eat crow: *see* EAT.

crowd

crowd the mourners exert undue pressure on someone. US informal

pass in a crowd: *see* PASS.

crowning

crowning glory ❶ the best and most notable aspect of something. ❷ a person's hair. informal

cruel

be cruel to be kind act towards someone in a way which seems harsh but will ultimately be of benefit.

> ❶ In Shakespeare's *Hamlet*, 'I must be cruel only to be kind' was Hamlet's explanation of his reasons for bullying his mother about her second marriage.

cruising

cruising for a bruising heading or looking for trouble. informal, chiefly North American

> **1998** *Times* The problem... is the unrealistic value of the Hong Kong dollar... it has been cruising for a bruising for most of last year.

crumb

crumbs from someone's (or a rich man's) table an unfair and inadequate or unsatisfactory share of something.

> ❶ Luke 16:21 describes the beggar Lazarus as 'desiring to be fed with the crumbs which fell from the rich man's table'.

crunch

when (or if) it comes to the crunch when (or if) a point is reached or an event occurs such that immediate and decisive action is required. informal

cruse

a widow's cruse: see WIDOW.

cry

cry for the moon: see MOON.

cry foul protest strongly about a real or imagined wrong or injustice.

> ❶ *Foul* in this context means *foul play*, a violation of the rules of a game to which attention is drawn by shouting 'foul!'

> **1998** *Times* She can't cry foul when subjected to fair and standard competition.

cry from the heart a passionate and honest appeal or protest.

> ❶ The French equivalent *cri de coeur* has also been in use in English since the early 20th century.

cry over spilt milk: see MILK.

cry stinking fish disparage your own efforts or products.

> ❶ This expression stems from the practice of street vendors crying their wares (i.e. shouting and praising their goods) to attract customers. If a vendor were to cry 'stinking fish', he could not expect to attract many.

> **1991** *Independent on Sunday* I want to use the Home Affairs Committee Report for those in racing to go forward together and at last to stop crying 'stinking fish'.

cry wolf: see WOLF.

in full cry expressing an opinion loudly and forcefully.

> ❶ *Full cry* originated and is still used as a hunting expression referring to a pack of hounds all baying in pursuit of their quarry.

great (or much) cry and little wool a lot of fuss with little effect; a lot of fuss about nothing.

> ❶ This expression comes from the idea of shearing pigs, where the result could be expected to be *great cry and little wool*.

crying

for crying out loud used to express your irritation or impatience. informal

> **1941 Rebecca West** *Black Lamb and Grey Falcon* For crying out loud, why did you do it?

crystal

crystal clear ❶ completely transparent and unclouded. ❷ unambiguous; easily understood.

cuckoo

cuckoo in the nest an unwelcome intruder in a place or situation.

> ❶ The female cuckoo often lays its eggs in other birds' nests. Once hatched, the cuckoo fledgling pushes the other birds' fledglings out of the nest.

cucumber

cool as a cucumber: see COOL.

cud

chew the cud ❶ (of a ruminant animal) further chew partly digested food. ❷ think or talk reflectively.

> ❷ **1992** *DJ* We chewed the cud, drank a few beers and at the end of the meal, Malu asked if I wanted to hit a club.

cudgel

cudgel your brain (or brains) think hard about a problem.

> ❶ This expression was used by Shakespeare in *Hamlet*: 'Cudgel thy brains no more about it'.

take up the cudgels start to support someone or something strongly.

cue

on cue at the correct moment.

take your cue from follow the example or advice of.

> ❶ *Cue* in both of these idioms is used in the theatrical sense of 'the word or words that signal when another actor should speak or perform a particular action'.

cuff

off the cuff without preparation. informal

> ❶ This expression refers to impromptu notes made on a speaker's shirt cuffs as an aid to memory.

on the cuff ❶ on credit. US informal ❷ beyond what is appropriate or conventional. New Zealand

> ❶ **1992 Sandra Birdsell** *The Chrome Suite* Their surveillance system keeps a beady eye open and they don't let you buy groceries on the cuff.

culture

culture vulture a person who is very interested in the arts, especially to an obsessive degree.

> ❶ The image of a *vulture* here is of a greedy and often undiscriminating eater.

cup

in your cups while drunk. informal

> ❶ *In your cups* is now used mainly to mean 'drunk', but in former times the phrase could also mean 'during a drinking bout'. Either could be intended in the passage in the Apocrypha regarding the strength of wine: 'And when they are in their cups, they forget their love both to friends and brethren, and a little after draw out swords' (1 Esdras 3:22).

> **1948 Vladimir Nabokov** *Letter* I have received your letter . . . and can only excuse its contents by assuming that you were in your cups when you wrote it.

not your cup of tea not what you like or are interested in. informal

curate

a curate's egg something that is partly good and partly bad.

> ❶ This expression stems from a *Punch* cartoon produced in 1895, showing a meek curate breakfasting with his bishop. BISHOP: I'm afraid you've got a bad egg, Mr Jones. CURATE: Oh no, my Lord, I assure you! Parts of it are excellent!

curdle

make your blood curdle: *see* BLOOD.

curiosity

curiosity killed the cat being inquisitive about other people's affairs may get you into trouble. proverb

curl

curl the mo succeed brilliantly; win. Australian informal

make someone's hair curl shock or horrify someone. informal

> ❶ This expression may have developed in the mid 20th century as a dramatic or humorous variation of **make someone's hair stand on end** (see HAIR).

out of curl lacking energy. British

> ❶ This is an early 20th-century expression based on the idea that curly hair has vitality (as in 'bouncy curls'). Therefore, hair which has become limp or *out of curl* may be thought to indicate listlessness or enervation.

current

pass current be generally accepted as true or genuine. British

> ❶ *Pass current* originally referred to the currency of a genuine coin, as opposed to a counterfeit one.

curry

curry favour ingratiate yourself with someone through obsequious behaviour.

> ❶ *Curry* here means 'groom a horse or other animal' with a coarse brush or comb. The phrase is an early 16th-century alteration of the Middle English *curry favel*, Favel (or Fauvel) being the name of a chestnut horse in an early 14th-century French romance who epitomized cunning and duplicity. From this

'to groom Favel' came to mean to use on him the cunning which he personified. It is unclear whether the bad reputation of chestnut horses existed before the French romance, but the idea is also found in 15th-century German in the phrase *den fahlen hengst reiten* (ride the chestnut horse) meaning 'behave deceitfully'.

curtain

bring down the curtain on bring to an end.

> ⓘ The curtain referred to is the one lowered at the front of the stage in a theatre at the end of a performance.

custom

old Spanish customs: *see* SPANISH.

cut

a cut above superior to. informal

> **1998** *Spectator* Samuel was a scholar . . . and his contributions are a cut above the rest.

an atmosphere that you could cut with a knife: *see* ATMOSPHERE.

be cut out for (*or* **to be**) have exactly the right qualities for a particular role, task, or job. informal

> ⓘ The sense of *cut out* here is 'formed or fashioned by cutting', as the pieces of a garment are cut out from the fabric.

> **1992 Paul Auster** *Leviathan* Whenever I stopped and examined my own behavior, I concluded that I wasn't cut out for marriage.

cut and dried (of a situation, issue, or ideas) completely settled or decided.

> ⓘ A distinction was originally made between the *cut and dried* herbs sold in herbalists' shops and growing herbs.

cut and run make a speedy or sudden departure from an awkward or hazardous situation rather than confront or deal with it. informal

> ⓘ *Cut and run* was originally an early 18th-century nautical phrase, meaning 'sever the anchor cable because of an emergency and make sail immediately'.

cut and thrust ❶ a spirited and rapid interchange of views. ❷ a situation or sphere of activity regarded as carried out under adversarial conditions.

> ⓘ In fencing, a *cut* is a slashing stroke and a *thrust* one given with the point of the weapon.

cut both ways ❶ (of a point or statement) serve both sides of an argument. ❷ (of an action or process) have both good and bad effects.

> ⓘ The image behind this expression is that of a double-edged weapon (see **double-edged sword** *at* DOUBLE-EDGED).

> ❶ **1998 Sanjida O'Connell** *Angel Bird* Words have the power to cut both ways and I was not strong enough to wield them

cut corners undertake something in what appears to be the easiest, quickest, or cheapest way, often by omitting to do something important or ignoring rules.

> ⓘ This phrase comes from *cutting (off) the corner*, which means 'taking the shortest course by going across and not round a corner'.

cut the crap get to the point; state the real situation. vulgar slang

cut a dash be stylish or impressive in your dress or behaviour.

> ⓘ As a noun, *dash* in the sense of 'showy appearance' is now found only in this expression, but this sense does also survive in the adjective *dashing*.

cut someone dead completely ignore someone.

cut a deal come to an arrangement, especially in business; make a deal. North American informal

> ⓘ *Cut* here relates to the informal sense of the noun *cut* as 'a share of profits'.

cut someone down to size deflate someone's exaggerated sense of self-worth. informal

cut a — figure present yourself or appear in a particular way.

> **1994** *Vanity Fair* David has cut a dashing figure on the international social scene.

cut from the same cloth of the same nature.

> **1999** *Washington Post* The last thing a franchise needs is for the two most important men at the top to be cut from the same cloth.

cut in line jump the queue. US

cut it meet the required standard. informal

> **1998** *Spectator* Heaven knows how such people get jobs in universities; they would not cut it on *Fifteen-to-One*.

cut it fine: *see* FINE.

cut the Gordian knot solve or remove a problem in a direct or forceful way, rejecting gentler or more indirect methods.

> **ⓘ** The knot referred to is that with which Gordius, king of ancient Phrygia (in Asia Minor), fastened the yoke of his wagon to the pole. Its complexity was such that it gave rise to the legend that whoever could undo it would become the ruler of Asia. When Alexander the Great passed that way en route to conquer the East he is said simply to have severed the knot with his sword.

cut it out used to ask someone to stop doing or saying something that is annoying or offensive. informal

cut loose ❶ distance yourself from a person, group, or system by which you are unduly influenced or on which you are over-dependent. **❷** begin to act without restraint. informal

> **❶ 1993 Isidore Okpewho** *Tides* When the time comes that I feel my friends are not sufficiently behind me in what I'm trying to do, I'm going to cut loose from them.

cut your losses abandon an enterprise or course of action that is clearly going to be unprofitable or unsuccessful before you suffer too much loss or harm.

> **ⓘ** The sense of *cut* here is probably 'sever yourself from' rather than 'reduce in size'.

> **1991 Jane Smiley** *A Thousand Acres* Ginny is eternally hopeful, you know. She never cuts her losses. She always thinks things could change.

cut the mustard come up to expectations; meet the required standard. informal

> **ⓘ** *Mustard* appears in early 20th-century US slang with the general meaning of 'the best of anything'.

> **1998** *New Scientist* But if you want to go beyond this into hypersonic flight...they just don't cut the mustard.

cut no ice have no influence or effect. informal

> **1973 Joyce Porter** *It's Murder with Dover* MacGregor remembered...that logical argument didn't cut much ice with Dover and he abandoned it.

cut someone off (or down) in their prime bring someone's life or career to an abrupt end while they are at the peak of their abilities.

the cut of someone's jib the appearance or look of a person.

> **ⓘ** This was originally a nautical expression suggested by the prominence and characteristic form of the jib (a triangular sail set forward of the foremast) as the identifying characteristic of a ship.

cut a (or the) rug dance, typically in an energetic or accomplished way. North American informal

> **1966** *Sky Magazine* The wide-open spaces around the bar...mean, as it fills up, the place soon resembles a club and the punters are itching to cut a rug.

cut someone some slack: *see* SLACK.

cut your teeth acquire initial practice or experience of a particular sphere of activity or with a particular organization.

> **ⓘ** The form *cut your eye teeth* is also found. The image is that of the emergence of a baby's teeth from its gums.

cut to the chase come to the point. North American informal

> **ⓘ** In this idiom, *cut* is being used in the cinematographic sense 'move to another shot in a film'. Chase scenes are a particularly exciting feature of some films, and the idiom expresses the idea of ignoring any preliminaries and coming immediately to the most important part.

cut up rough behave in an aggressive, quarrelsome, or awkward way. British informal

> **ⓘ** *Cut up* is here being used in the sense of 'behave'. The phrase *cut up rough* is used by Dickens and the variant *cut up savage* (now no longer in use) by Thackeray.

> **1998** *Spectator* The jury, knowing full well that Clodius' supporters could cut up rough, asked for and received state protection.

cut your coat according to your cloth undertake only what you have the money or ability to do and no more. proverb

have your work cut out: *see* WORK.

make (or miss) the cut come up to (or fail to come up to) a required standard.

> **ⓘ** In golf, a player has to equal or better a particular score in order to avoid elimination from the last two rounds of a four-round tournament. If the player succeeds, they *make the cut*.

cylinder

firing on all cylinders: *see* FIRING.

Dd

dab

be a dab hand at be expert at.

> ❶ *Dab* in this sense is recorded since the late 17th century, but its origin is unknown.

> **1998** *Bookseller* Stephanie Cabot...is apparently a dab hand at milking cows, according to one of those mystifying diary items in Skateboarders' Weekly.

dagger

at daggers drawn in a state of bitter enmity.

> ❶ The image here is of the drawing of daggers as the final stage in a confrontation before actual fighting breaks out. Although recorded in 1668, the expression only became common from the early 19th century onwards.

look daggers at glare angrily or venomously at.

> ❶ The expression *speak daggers* is also found and is used by Shakespeare's Hamlet in the scene in which he reproaches his mother.

dag

rattle your dags hurry up. Australian & New Zealand informal

> ❶ *Dags* are the excreta-clotted lumps of wool at the rear end of a sheep, which, in heavily fouled animals, rattle as they run.

daisy

fresh as a daisy very bright and cheerful. informal

> ❶ This expression alludes to a daisy reopening its petals in the early morning or to its welcome appearance in springtime. The freshness of daisies has been a literary commonplace since at least the late 14th century, when it was used by Chaucer.

pushing up the daisies dead and buried. informal

> ❶ This phrase, a humorous early 20th-century euphemism, is now the most frequently used of several daisy-related expressions for being in the grave. Other idioms include *under the daisies* and *turn your toes up to the daisies*, both dating from the mid 19th century.

damage

what's the damage? used to ask the cost of something. informal

dammit

as near as dammit (*or* **damn it**) as close to being accurate as makes no difference. informal

damn

not give a damn: *see* GIVE.

damn someone or something with faint praise praise someone or something so unenthusiastically as to imply condemnation.

> ❶ This expression comes from the poet Alexander Pope's 'Epistle to Dr Arbuthnot' (1735): 'Damn with faint praise, assent with civil leer, And without sneering, teach the rest to sneer'.

> **1994** *Canadian Defence Quarterly* True there is the occasional condescending nod to those who served, but this frequently amounts to damning with faint praise.

not be worth a damn have no value or validity at all. informal

damned

damned if you do and damned if you don't in some situations whatever you do is likely to attract criticism.

> **1998** *Spectator* Some of the media were critical of the photo...That did not stop them all running it on the front page. You're damned if you do and damned if you don't.

damnedest

do (*or* **try**) **your damnedest** do or try your utmost to do something.

> ❶ The superlative form of the adjective *damned* is used here as a noun and can mean either 'your worst' or (more usually now) 'your best', depending on the context.

Damon

Damon and Pythias two faithful friends.

> **ⓘ** Phintias (the more correct form of the name) was condemned to death for plotting against Dionysius I of Syracuse. To enable Phintias to go to arrange his affairs, Damon offered to take his friend's place in Dionysius' prison and to be executed in his stead if he failed to return. Phintias returned just in time to redeem Damon, and Dionysius was so impressed by their friendship that he pardoned and released Phintias as well.

damp

a damp squib an unsuccessful attempt to impress; an anticlimax.

> **ⓘ** This expression stems from the idea that a squib, a type of small firework, will not have the desired explosive effect if it is damp.

damper

put a (or the) damper (or dampener) on have a depressing, subduing, or inhibiting effect on someone or something.

damsel

damsel in distress a young woman in trouble. humorous

> **ⓘ** Damsel in distress makes humorous reference to the ladies in chivalric romances whose sole purpose was to be rescued from peril by a **knight in shining armour** (see KNIGHT).

dance

dance attendance on do your utmost to please someone by attending to all their needs or requests.

> **ⓘ** The expression originally referred to someone waiting 'kicking their heels' until an important person summoned them or would see them.

> **1999 Shyama Perera** I Haven't Stopped Dancing Yet Tammy and I sat on a vinyl bench seat and watched the visiting flow while Jan disappeared to dance attendance on her mother.

dance to someone's tune comply completely with someone's demands and wishes.

lead someone a (merry) dance cause someone a great deal of trouble or worry. British

> **1993 Isidore Okpewho** Tides I will be content to lead my friends at the NSS a merry dance if only to get even with them for messing me up the way they did.

dander

get your dander up lose your temper; become angry.

> **ⓘ** The sense of dander in this originally US expression is uncertain, as neither dandruff nor dunder (meaning 'the ferment of molasses') seems entirely plausible.

dangling

keep someone dangling keep someone, especially a would-be suitor, in an uncertain position.

dark

a dark horse a person, especially a competitor, about whom little is known.

> **ⓘ** The expression was originally horse-racing slang. The earliest recorded use was by Benjamin Disraeli in 1831: 'A dark horse, which had never been thought of . . . rushed past the grand stand in sweeping triumph'.

keep someone in the dark ensure that someone remains in a state of ignorance about something.

> **2003** Village Voice It's payback time for an administration that . . . has ignored lawmakers and . . . deliberately kept them in the dark.

keep something dark keep something secret from other people.

> **1993** New York Review of Books Ottoline was determined to keep her affair with Russell safe from Bloomsbury's prying eyes and she and Russell went to Feydeauesque lengths to keep their secret dark.

a shot (or stab) in the dark an act whose outcome cannot be foreseen; a mere guess.

> **ⓘ** The metaphorical use of in the dark to mean 'in a state of ignorance' dates from the late 17th century.

darken

never darken someone's door (or doorstep) keep away from someone's home permanently.

> **1988 Salman Rushdie** The Satanic Verses They couldn't lock her away in any old folks' home, sent her whole family packing when they dared to suggest it, never darken her doorstep, she told them, cut the whole lot off without a penny or a by your leave.

dash

cut a dash: see CUT.

do your dash exhaust your energies or chances. Australian informal

1973 Chester Eagle *Who Could Love the Nightingale?* 'Keep going,' she said. 'Keep going.' 'I've done my dash, Marg, in every sense of the words.'

date

a blind date: *see* BLIND.

pass your sell-by date: *see* PASS.

daunted

nothing daunted: *see* NOTHING.

Davy Jones's locker

go to Davy Jones's locker be drowned at sea.

> **ⓘ** Davy Jones is identified in Tobias Smollett's *Peregrine Pickle* (1751) as 'the fiend that presides over all the evil spirits of the deep', but the origin of the name is uncertain.

dawn

the crack of dawn: *see* CRACK.

a false dawn: *see* FALSE.

day

all in a day's work (of something unusual or problematic) accepted as part of someone's normal routine or as a matter of course.

at the end of the day: *see* END.

call it a day decide or agree to stop doing something, either temporarily or permanently.

> **ⓘ** This expression comes from the idea of having done a day's work; in the mid 19th century, the form was *call it half a day*.

carry (*or* **win**) **the day** be victorious or successful.

> **ⓘ** The sense of *day* used here is 'the day's work on the field of battle'.

day in, day out continuously or repeatedly over a long period of time.

day of reckoning the time when past mistakes or misdeeds must be punished or paid for; a testing time when the degree of your success or failure will be revealed.

> **ⓘ** This expression refers to the Day of Judgement, on which, according to Christian tradition, human beings will have to answer to God for their transgressions.

don't give up the day job used as a humorous way of recommending someone not to pursue an alternative career at which they are unlikely to be successful. informal

1996 Charlie Higson *Getting Rid of Mr Kitchen* 'You are the worst beggar I have ever encountered,' I said. 'Don't give up the day job.'

from day one from the very beginning.

1996 Christopher Brookmyre *Quite Ugly One Morning* The system churns out junior doctors who have paid bugger-all attention to the meat and two veg medicine they will find themselves up to their necks in from day one.

have had your (*or* **its**) **day** be no longer popular, successful, or influential.

if he (*or* **she**) **is a day** at least (added to a statement about the age of a person or thing).

1992 Shashi Tharoor *Show Business* Lawrence must be fifty if he's a day.

just another day at the office: *see* OFFICE.

make a day of it: *see* MAKE.

make someone's day: *see* MAKE.

not someone's day used to convey that someone has suffered a day of successive misfortunes. informal

1997 A. Sivanandan *When Memory Dies* He sighed inwardly, this was not his day.

one of those days a day when several things go wrong.

a red letter day: *see* RED.

seen (*or* **known**) **better days** be in a worse state than in the past; have become old, worn-out, or shabby.

that will be the day something is very unlikely to happen. informal

1991 Alistair Campbell *Sidewinder* 'Now for my proposal, which you'll find irresistible.' 'That'll be the day.'

those were the days used to assert that a particular past time was better in comparison with the present.

1997 Brenda Clough *How Like a God* 'Those were the days,' Rob said. 'B.C.—before children! Remember?'

daylight

beat the living daylights out of give someone a very severe beating. informal

> **ⓘ** *Daylight* or *daylights* has been used from the mid 18th century as a metaphor for 'eyes', and here has the extended sense of any vital organ of the body.

burn daylight use artificial light in daytime; waste daylight.

frighten (*or* **scare**) **the living daylights out of** give someone a very severe fright.

> ❶ This expression was a mid 20th-century development from *beat the living daylights out of*, on the premise that the effect of extreme fear is as drastic as physical violence.

1955 Frank Yerby *The Treasure of Pleasant Valley* Didn't mean to hit him... Meant to throw close to him and scare the living daylights out of him.

see daylight begin to understand what was previously puzzling or unclear.

dead

dead and buried used to emphasize that something is finally and irrevocably in the past.

dead as a (*or* **the**) **dodo** ❶ no longer alive. ❷ no longer effective, valid, or interesting. informal

> ❶ The name *dodo* comes from Portuguese *duodo* meaning 'simpleton'. It was applied to the large flightless bird of Mauritius because the bird had no fear of man and so was easily killed, being quickly wiped out by visiting European sailors. The dodo's fate has made it proverbial for something that is long dead and the name has been used metaphorically for an old-fashioned, stupid, or unenlightened person since the 19th century.

2000 John Caughie *Television Drama* The once pleasant family hour is now as dead as a dodo.

dead as a doornail (*or* **as mutton**) completely dead.

> ❶ A *doornail* was one of the large iron studs formerly often used on doors for ornamentation or for added strength; the word occurred in various alliterative phrases (e.g. *deaf as a doornail* and *dour as a doornail*) but *dead as a doornail* is now the only one in common use.

a dead cat bounce a misleading sign of vitality in something that is really moribund. informal

> ❶ A dead cat might bounce if it is dropped from a great height: the fact of it bouncing does not reliably indicate that the cat is alive after all. The expression was coined in the late 20th century by Wall Street traders to refer to a situation in which a stock or company on a long-term, irrevocable downward trend suddenly shows a small temporary improvement.

dead from the neck (*or* **chin**) **up** stupid. informal

1990 *Film Comment* Steward subscribes to the notion that all women are 'nitwits and lunkheads, dead from the neck up'.

dead in the water unable to function effectively.

> ❶ *Dead in the water* was originally used of a ship and in this context means 'unable to move'.

1997 *Times* And Oasis? Well, they are hardly dead in the water, having sold three million copies of Be Here Now.

a dead letter a law or practice no longer observed.

> ❶ This phrase was originally used with reference to passages in the biblical epistles in which St Paul compares the life-giving spirit of the New Testament with what he sees as the dead 'letter' of the Mosaic law. Later (until the late 19th century) *Dead-letter Office* was the name given to the organization that dealt with unclaimed mail or mail that could not be delivered for any reason. The expression has been used metaphorically for an obsolete or unobserved law since the mid 17th century.

1998 *Spectator* They were saying on the news... that some provision of the Stormont agreement might end up a dead letter.

dead meat in serious trouble. informal

1989 Tracy Kidder *Among Schoolchildren* You're dead meat, I'm gonna get you after school.

dead men's shoes: *see* SHOE.

the dead of night the quietest, darkest part of the night.

the dead of winter the coldest part of winter.

> ❶ The sense of *dead* here and in the previous idiom developed in the 16th century from *dead time of* —, meaning the period most characterized by lack of signs of life or activity.

dead on your feet extremely tired. informal

> ❶ This expression was a development from the phrase *dead tired*, as an exaggerated way of expressing a feeling of exhaustion. *Dead* is sometimes also used on its own to mean 'exhausted'.

dead to the world fast asleep; unconscious. informal

2000 Michael Ondaatje *Anil's Ghost* The nurse tried to wake him, but he was dead to the world.

from the dead ❶ from a state of death. ❷ from a period of obscurity or inactivity.

make a dead set at make a determined attempt to win the affections of. British

> ❶ Dating from the early 19th century, this was originally a sporting idiom, referring to the manner in which a dog such as a setter or pointer stands stock still with its muzzle pointing in the direction of game.

over my dead body used to emphasize that you completely oppose something and would do anything to prevent it from happening. informal

wouldn't be seen (or **caught**) **dead in** (or **with** or **at**) — used to express strong dislike or disinclination for a particular thing or situation. informal

> **1997** *Independent* Kate's books, said one literary editor, can be read happily by those who wouldn't be seen dead with a Catherine Cookson.

deaf

deaf as an adder (or **a post**) completely or extremely deaf.

> ❶ The traditional deafness of an adder is based on an image in Psalm 58:4: 'the deaf adder that stoppeth her ear'.

fall on deaf ears (of a statement or request) be ignored by others.

> **1990 Ellen Kuzwayo** *Sit Down and Listen* All efforts by her husband to dissuade her from wishing to leave fell on deaf ears.

deal

a big deal a thing considered important. informal

big deal! used to express contempt for something regarded as impressive or important by another person. informal

a raw (or **rough**) **deal** a situation in which someone receives unfair or harsh treatment. informal

a square deal a fair bargain or treatment.

> ❶ *Square* here has the sense of 'honest', which as an adjective was associated originally with honourable play at cards. See also **on the square** (at SQUARE).

death

at death's door so ill that you may die.

> **1994 S. P. Somtow** *Jasmine Nights* How stupid of me to trouble her with my petty problems when she's probably at death's door!

be the death of cause someone's death.

> ❶ *Be the death of* is generally used as an exaggerated or humorous way of describing the effects of laughter, embarrassment, boredom, or similar emotions.

> **1999 Chris Dolan** *Ascension Day* If her mother ever found out that William Grant was in Glasgow, it'd be the death of her.

be frightened to death be made very alarmed and fearful. informal

be in at the death ❶ be present when a hunted animal is caught and killed. ❷ be present when something fails or comes to an end.

catch your death (of cold) catch a severe cold or chill. informal

a death's head at the feast: *see* FEAST.

die a (or **the**) **death** come to an end; cease or fail to be popular or successful.

> **1999** *Linedancer* Our industry must expand … otherwise it will die a death with just a few clubs remaining.

do something to death perform or repeat something so frequently that it becomes tediously familiar.

a fate worse than death: *see* FATE.

like death warmed up extremely tired or ill. informal

> ❶ *Like death warmed up* was originally military slang, recorded from the 1930s. The North American version is *like death warmed over*.

a matter of life and death: *see* LIFE.

deck

not playing with a full deck mentally deficient. North American informal

> ❶ A *deck* in this phrase is a pack of playing cards.

on deck ready for action or work. North American

> ❶ This expression refers to a ship's main deck as the place where the crew musters to receive orders for action.

deep

dig deep ❶ give money or other resources generously. ❷ make a great effort to do something. informal

> ❶ The idea here is of thrusting your hands deep into your pockets to find money with which to pay for something.

❷ **1991** *Sports Illustrated* You really have to dig deep night after night to get up for every game.

go off (or go in off) the deep end give way immediately to anger or emotion. informal

> ❶ This expression refers to the deep end of a swimming pool, where the diving board is located. In the USA the phrase has also developed the meaning 'go mad', but in either sense the underlying idea is of a sudden explosive loss of self-control.

in deep water (or waters) in trouble or difficulty. informal

> ❶ *In deep water* is a biblical metaphor; see, for example, Psalm 69:14: 'let me be delivered from them that hate me, and out of the deep waters'.

jump (or be thrown) in at the deep end face a difficult problem or undertaking with little experience of it. informal

deliver

deliver the goods provide something promised or expected. informal

delusion

delusions of grandeur a false impression of your own importance.

> ❶ This expression is the equivalent of the French phrase *folie de grandeur*, which came into English in the late 19th century and is still used today.

demon

like a demon: *see* **like the devil** *at* DEVIL.

depth

hidden depths admirable but previously unnoticed qualities.

out of your depth unable to cope due to lack of ability or knowledge.

> ❶ Literally, if you are *out of your depth* you are in water too deep to stand in.

derry

have a derry on someone be prejudiced against someone. Australian & New Zealand

> ❶ This expression refers to the traditional song refrain *derry down*, and was a late 19th-century adaptation of **have a down on** (*see* DOWN).

1948 David Ballantyne *The Cunninghams* She didn't like the Baptists though, had a derry on that crowd ever since Hilda took her to an evening service.

deserts

get (or receive) your just deserts receive what you deserve, especially appropriate punishment.

design

have designs on aim to obtain something desired, especially in an underhand way.

> **2003** *Economist* Hardliners ... think America has designs on its oil, and will act against Iran once it has disposed of Saddam Hussein.

despite

despite yourself used to indicate that you did not intend to do the thing mentioned.

> **1995 Ginu Kamani** *Junglee Girl* Sahil chuckled, despite himself.

deuce informal

a (or the) deuce of a — something very bad or difficult of its kind.

> **1933 John Galsworthy** *The End of the Chapter* It seems there's a deuce of a fuss in the Bolivian papers.

the deuce to pay trouble to be expected.

like the deuce very fast.

> ❶ *Deuce* was first used in 17th-century English in various exclamatory expressions in which it was equated with 'bad luck' or 'mischief', because in dice-playing two (= deuce) is the lowest and most unlucky throw. From this there soon developed the sense of *deuce* as 'the devil' (i.e. bad luck or mischief personified). *Deuce* as a euphemism for the devil occurs in a number of expressions, including those above.

device

leave someone to their own devices leave someone to do as they wish without supervision.

> ❶ *Device* in the sense of 'inclination' or 'fancy' now only occurs in the plural, and is found only in this expression or in the phrase *devices and desires*, as quoted from the General Confession in the Book of Common Prayer.

devil

between the devil and the deep blue sea caught in a dilemma; trapped between two equally dangerous alternatives.

devil-may-care cheerfully or defiantly reckless.

a (or the) devil of a — something very large or bad of its kind. informal

> **1919 Katherine Mansfield** *Letter* We had the devil of a great storm last night, lasting for hours, thunder, lightning, rain & I had appalling nightmares!

the devil's in the detail the details of a matter are its most tricky or problematic aspect.

the devil's own — a very difficult or great —. informal

> **1991 Mavis Nicholson** *Martha Jane & Me* It was the devil's own job to get her to give me some money for savings.

the devil to pay serious trouble to be expected.

> ⓘ This expression refers to the bargain formerly supposed to be made between magicians and the devil, the former receiving extraordinary powers or wealth in return for their souls.

give the devil his due if someone or something generally considered bad or undeserving has any redeeming features these should be acknowledged. proverb

like the devil (or a demon) with great speed or energy.

play devil's advocate take a side in an argument that is the opposite of what you really want or think.

> ⓘ A translation of the Latin phrase *advocatus diaboli*, devil's advocate is the popular name for the official in the Roman Catholic Church who puts the case against a candidate for canonization or beatification; he is more properly known as *promotor fidei* 'promoter of the faith'.

> **1994 Jude Deveraux** *The Invitation* She had played devil's advocate with herself a thousand times.

play the devil (or Old Harry) with damage or affect greatly.

> ⓘ *Old Harry* has been a nickname for the devil in northern England since the 18th century.

raise the devil make a noisy disturbance. informal

sell your soul (to the devil): *see* SELL.

speak (or talk) of the devil said when a person appears just after being mentioned.

> ⓘ This phrase stems from the superstition that the devil will manifest himself if his name is spoken.

sup (or dine) with the devil have dealings with a cunning or malevolent person.

> ⓘ The proverb *he who sups with the devil should have a long spoon* is used especially to urge someone dealing with a person of this type to take care.

dialogue

dialogue of the deaf a discussion in which each party is unresponsive to what the others say.

> ⓘ The French equivalent *dialogue des sourds* is also sometimes used in English.

diamond

diamond cut diamond a situation in which a sharp-witted or cunning person meets their match. British

> **1863 Charles Reade** *Hard Cash* He felt ... sure his employer would outwit him if he could; and resolved it should be diamond cut diamond.

rough diamond: *see* ROUGH.

dice

dice with death take serious risks.

> ⓘ *Dice with* is used here in the general sense of 'play a game of chance with'. In the mid 20th century *dice with death* was a journalistic cliché used to convey the risks taken by racing drivers; the expression seems for some time to have been especially connected with motoring, although it is now used of other risky activities. It gave rise to the use of *dicing* as a slang word among drivers for 'driving in a race', and it can be compared with *dicey* meaning 'dangerous', a word which originated in 1950s air-force slang.

load the dice against: *see* LOAD.

no dice used to refuse a request or indicate that there is no chance of success. North American informal

> **1990 Paul Auster** *The Music of Chance* Sorry kid. No dice. You can talk yourself blue in the face, but I'm not going.

dicky bird

not a dicky bird not a word; nothing at all. informal

> ⓘ *Dicky bird* is rhyming slang for 'word'.

1988 Glenn Patterson *Burning Your Own* Sammy put his ear to where he thought its heart ought to be: not a dickybird.

dictionary

have swallowed a dictionary use long and obscure words when speaking. informal

dido

cut didoes perform mischievous tricks or deeds. North American informal

die

die a death: *see* DEATH.

die hard disappear or change very slowly.

> ❶ This expression seems to have been used first of criminals who died resisting to the last on the Tyburn gallows in London. At the battle of Albuera in 1811, during the Peninsular War, William Inglis, commander of the British 57th Regiment of Foot, exhorted his men to 'die hard'; they acted with such heroism that the regiment earned the nickname Die-hards. The name was attached later in the century to various groupings in British politics who were determinedly opposed to change. The word *diehard* is still often used of someone who is stubbornly conservative or reactionary.

die in your bed suffer a peaceful death from natural causes.

die in harness die before retirement.

> ❶ This expression is drawing a comparison between a person at work and a horse in harness drawing a plough or cart.

> **1992** *Harper's Magazine* Don't overly concern yourself with the union pension fund. Musicians mostly die in harness.

die in the last ditch die desperately defending something; die fighting to the last extremity.

> ❶ This expression comes from a remark attributed to King William III (1650–1702). Asked whether he did not see that his country was lost, he is said to have responded: 'There is one way never to see it lost, and that is to die in the last ditch'. *Last-ditch* is often used as an adjective meaning 'desperately resisting to the end'.

the die is cast an event has happened or a decision has been taken that cannot be changed.

> ❶ This expression has its origins in Julius Caesar's remark as he was about to cross the Rubicon, as reported by the Roman historian Suetonius: *jacta alea esto* 'let the die be cast'.

die like flies: *see* FLY.

die on the vine be unsuccessful at an early stage. Compare with **wither on the vine** (*at* WITHER).

die on your feet come to a sudden or premature end. informal

die with your boots on die while actively occupied.

> ❶ *Die with your boots on* was apparently first used in the late 19th century of the deaths of cowboys and others in the American West who were killed in gun battles or hanged.

never say die used to encourage someone not to give up hope in a difficult situation.

straight as a die ❶ absolutely straight. ❷ entirely open and honest.

> ❶ **1920** *Blackwood's Magazine* The ... Ganges Canal ... runs straight as a die between its wooded banks.

to die for extremely good or desirable. informal

> **1990** *Los Angeles* Farther down the street is Tutti's, an Italian deli-restaurant that serves up ... hazelnut torte to die for.

differ

agree to differ: *see* AGREE.

different

different strokes for different folks different things please or are effective with different people. proverb

> ❶ This chiefly US expression was used as a slogan in the early 1970s in a Texan drug abuse project.

dig

dig the dirt (*or* **dig up dirt**) discover and reveal damaging information about someone. informal

> ❶ *Dirt* is commonly used as a metaphor for unsavoury gossip or scandal, as in, for example, **dish the dirt** (*see* DISH).

dig in your heels resist stubbornly; refuse to give in.

> ❶ The image here is of a horse or other animal obstinately refusing to be led or ridden forwards. *Dig in your heels* is the commonest form, but *dig in your toes* and *dig in your feet* are also found.

dig yourself into a hole (*or* **dig a hole for yourself**) get yourself into an awkward or restrictive situation.

dig your own grave do something foolish which causes you to fail or leads to your downfall.

> **1995 Colin Bateman** *Divorcing Jack* Then I thought about Patricia again and how much I was missing her and how I'd dug my own grave over the phone.

dig a pit for try to trap.

> ❶ This is a common biblical metaphor: for example, in Jeremiah 18:20 we find 'they have digged a pit for my soul'.

dignity

beneath your dignity of too little importance or value for you to do it.

> ❶ The Latin equivalent is *infra dignitatem*, and the humorous abbreviation of this, *infra dig*, is sometimes used in informal contexts.

stand on your dignity insist on being treated with due respect.

dim

take a dim view of: *see* VIEW.

dime

a dime a dozen very common and of no particular value. US informal

> ❶ A dime is a small US coin worth ten cents which occurs in various US expressions as a metaphor for cheapness or smallness.

> **1998** *New Scientist* Of course, medical breakthroughs are not a dime a dozen.

drop the dime on: *see* DROP.

get off the dime be decisive and show initiative. US informal

> **2001** *U.S. News & World Report* Congress must get off the dime and redeem the commitments that President Bush made to New York City.

on a dime ❶ (of a manoeuvre that can be performed by a moving vehicle or person) within a small area or short distance. ❷ quickly or instantly. US informal

> ❶ The British equivalent to sense 1 is **on a sixpence** (*see* SIXPENCE).

diminishing

the law of diminishing returns used to refer to the point at which the level of profits or benefits to be gained is reduced to less than the amount of money or energy invested.

> ❶ This expression originated in the early 19th century with reference to the profits from agriculture.

dine

dine out on regularly entertain friends with a humorous story or interesting piece of information.

> **1998 Fannie Flagg** *Welcome to the World, Baby Girl!* I didn't have a great childhood but I'm not going to dine out on it. I hate whiners.

dinkum

fair dinkum ❶ genuine or true. ❷ (of behaviour) acceptable. Australian & New Zealand informal

> ❶ As a noun *dinkum*, recorded from the late 19th century, was an English dialect word meaning 'hard work, honest toil'; it now mainly features as an adjective in various Australian and New Zealand expressions.

dinner

done like (a) dinner utterly defeated or outwitted. Australian & Canadian informal

> **1978 C. Green** *The Sun Is Up* I had old Splinters Maloney the fishing inspector knocking on me door wanting to see me licence. Of course I was done like a dinner.

more — than someone has had hot dinners someone's experience of a specified activity or phenomenon is vastly greater than someone else's. British informal

> **1998** *Odds On* Triplett has been second more times than he's had hot dinners, and there must be a question about his bottle, but he has two qualities that will stand him in good stead at the Olympic Club.

dinner pail

hand in your dinner pail die. informal

> ❶ A *dinner pail* was the bucket in which a workman formerly carried his dinner; compare with **kick the bucket** (*at* KICK).

dint

by dint of by means of.

> ❶ *Dint* in the sense of 'blow' or 'stroke' is now archaic, and in the sense of 'application of force' survives only in this phrase.

dip

dip your pen in gall write unpleasantly or spitefully.

> ❶ *Gall* is another word for bile, the bitter secretion of the liver; it is used in many places in the Bible as a metaphor for bitterness or affliction. See also **wormwood and gall** (*at* WORMWOOD).

dip your toe into something begin to do or test something cautiously.

> ❶ The image here is of putting your toe briefly into water in order to check the temperature.

dirt

do someone dirt harm someone maliciously. informal

> **1939 Nathaniel West** *The Day of the Locust*
> I remember those who do me dirt and those who do me favors.

drag someone through the dirt: *see* DRAG.

eat dirt: *see* EAT.

treat someone like dirt treat someone contemptuously or unfairly.

> **1996** *Just Seventeen* He was only nice to me in private—as soon as he was around other people he'd treat me like dirt.

dirty

the dirty end of the stick the difficult or unpleasant part of a task or situation. informal

> **2000** *Sunday Times* (*Johannesburg*) I still feel a bit sorry for Hugh, he always seems to get the dirty end of the stick.

dirty work at the crossroads illicit or underhand dealing. humorous

> ❶ This expression is recorded from the early 20th century and may reflect the fact that crossroads, the traditional burial site for people who had committed suicide, were once viewed as sinister places.

> **1914 P. G. Wodehouse** *The Man Upstairs* A conviction began to steal over him that some game was afoot which he did not understand, that—in a word—there was dirty work at the crossroads.

do the dirty on someone cheat or betray someone. British informal

get your hands dirty (*or* **dirty your hands**)
❶ do manual, menial, or other hard work.
❷ become directly involved in dishonest or dishonorable activity. informal

> ❶ **1998** *Spectator* Unlike its sister churches in the West, the Catholic Church in the Philippines is not afraid to get its hands dirty.

play dirty act in a dishonest or unfair way. informal

talk dirty speak about sex in a way considered to be coarse or obscene. informal

wash your dirty linen in public: *see* LINEN.

disappearing

do a disappearing act go away without being seen to go, especially when someone is looking for you.

> ❶ The suggestion here is that the person has vanished as completely and inexplicably as things vanish in a magician's act.

disaster

be a recipe for disaster be almost certain to have unfortunate consequences.

discretion

discretion is the better part of valour it's better to avoid a dangerous situation than to confront it. proverb

dish

dish the dirt reveal or spread scandalous information or gossip. informal

> **1997** *New Scientist* We love revisionist biographies that dish the dirt on our icons.

dishwater

dull as dishwater: *see* DULL.

distance

go the distance complete a difficult task or endure an ordeal.

> ❶ *Go the distance* is a metaphor from boxing that means, when used of a boxer, 'complete a fight without being knocked out' or, when used of a boxing match, 'last the scheduled length'. In the USA there is an additional baseball-related sense: 'pitch for the entire length of an inning'.

> **1998** *Times* 'Everyone wants to see an amateur who can go the distance,' another spectator said. Kuchar has certainly gone the distance.

within spitting distance within a very short distance.

> **1991** *Time* His reputation as a hard-boiled novelist is within spitting distance of Hammett's and Chandler's.

within striking distance near enough to hit or achieve.

ditchwater

dull as ditchwater: *see* **dull as dishwater** *at* DULL.

dive

take a dive ❶ (of a boxer or footballer)
pretend to fall so as to deceive an opponent
or referee. **❷** (of prices, hopes, fortunes,
etc.) fall suddenly and significantly. informal

> **❷ 1998** *New Scientist* When the DOJ
> announced its action, Microsoft's stock price
> took a dive, knocking $10 billion off the firm's
> market value.

divide

divide and rule (or conquer) the policy of
maintaining supremacy over your
opponents by encouraging dissent
between them, thereby preventing them
from uniting against you.

> **ⓘ** This is a maxim associated with a number
> of rulers, and is found in Latin as *divide et
> impera* and in German as *entzwei und
> gebiete*. Since the early 17th century, English
> writers have often wrongly attributed it to
> the Italian political philosopher Niccolò
> Machiavelli (1469–1527).

divided

divided against itself (of a group which
should be a unified whole) split by factional
interests.

> **ⓘ** This expression originates in Jesus's words
> in Matthew 12:25: 'every city or house divided
> against itself shall not stand'.

Dixie

whistle Dixie engage in unrealistic fantasies;
waste your time. US

> **ⓘ** *Dixie* is an informal name for the Southern
> states of the USA. The marching song 'Dixie'
> (1859) was popular with Confederate
> soldiers in the American Civil War.

> **2001** *New York Times* These guys are just
> whistling Dixie ... They're ignoring the basic
> issues that everyone's been pointing out to
> them for a decade.

do

do a — behave in a manner characteristic of a
specified person or thing. informal

> **2001** *Times* One reporter even got the
> brigadier in charge to 'do a Blair' and come
> over all emotional while discussing the cull.

do your head (or nut) in make you feel
angry, worried, or agitated. British informal

do the honours: *see* HONOUR.

do or die persist in the face of great danger,
even if death is the result.

> **1992** *Daily Star* It's do or die for Britain's
> fearless Rugby League lads Down Under as
> they prepare to face the Aussies in the Third
> and deciding Test.

do someone proud: *see* PROUD.

do something to death: *see* DEATH.

do the trick: *see* TRICK.

dos and don'ts rules of behaviour.

> **1999** *Alumnus* Volunteers are prepared well
> on ... cultural dos and don'ts before they leave
> for the field to serve.

dock

in dock ❶ (of a ship) moored in a dock. **❷** (of a
person) not fully fit and out of action. British
informal **❸** (of a vehicle) in a garage for
repairs.

in the dock under investigation or scrutiny
for suspected wrongdoing or harm caused.
British

> **ⓘ** In a court of law, the dock is the enclosure
> where the defendant stands during a trial.

> **1995** *Times* For once, Britain was not in the
> dock as others took the heat.

doctor

be just what the doctor ordered be very
beneficial or desirable under the
circumstances. informal

> **1948** Gore Vidal *The City and the Pillar* The
> waiter brought her a drink. 'Just what the
> doctor ordered,' she said, smiling at him.

go for the doctor make an all-out effort.
Australian informal

dodge

dodge the column shirk your duty; avoid
work. British informal

> **ⓘ** *Column* is a military term which refers to
> the usual formation of troops for marching.

dodo

dead as a dodo: *see* DEAD.

dog

dog-and-pony show an elaborate display or
performance designed to attract people's
attention. North American informal

> **1998** *Spectator* Happy as I always am to help
> the Bank of England, I have ... supplied the
> script for its euro dog and pony show.

dog eat dog a situation of fierce competition
in which people are willing to harm each
other in order to succeed.

① This expression makes reference to the proverb *dog does not eat dog*, which dates back to the mid 16th century in English and before that to Latin *canis caninam non est* 'a dog does not eat dog's flesh'.

1998 Rebecca Ray *A Certain Age* It's dog eat dog, it's every man for himself... Right from the start, fighting amongst ourselves for the few decent wages left.

dog in the manger a person inclined to prevent others from having or using things that they do not want or need themselves.

① This expression comes from the fable of the dog that lay in a manger to prevent the ox and horse from eating the hay.

the dog's bollocks the best person or thing of its kind. British vulgar slang

a dog's dinner (*or* **breakfast**) a poor piece of work; a mess. British informal

① The image is of a dog's meal of jumbled-up scraps.

2000 *Independent* He was rightly sacked because he had made such a dog's dinner of an important job.

a dog's life an unhappy existence full of problems or unfair treatment.

1987 Fannie Flagg *Fried Green Tomatoes at the Whistle Stop Cafe* The judge's daughter had just died a couple of weeks ago, old before her time and living a dog's life on the outskirts of town.

dog tired extremely tired; utterly worn out. informal

① The image here, and in the variant *dog weary*, is of a dog exhausted after a long chase or hunt.

dogs of war ❶ the havoc accompanying military conflict. literary ❷ mercenary soldiers.

① This phrase is from Shakespeare's *Julius Caesar*: 'let slip the dogs of war'. The image is of hunting dogs being loosed from their leashes to pursue their prey.

❷ 1998 *Times* The good guys... may have broken the rules by employing dogs of war.

dressed (up) like a dog's dinner wearing ridiculously smart or ostentatious clothes. British informal

every dog has his (*or* **its**) **day** everyone will have good luck or success at some point in their lives. proverb

give a dog a bad name it is very difficult to

lose a bad reputation, even if it is unjustified.

① This is a shortened version of the proverb *give a dog a bad name and hang him*, which was known from the early 18th century.

go to the dogs deteriorate shockingly, especially in behaviour or morals. informal

① This idiom derives from the fact that attending greyhound races was once thought likely to expose a person to moral danger and the risk of incurring great financial loss.

1997 *Daily Telegraph* If you read the English media or watch the cretinosities of television, you would think that the country is going to the dogs.

the hair of the dog: *see* HAIR.

help a lame dog over a stile come to the aid of a person in need.

in a dog's age in a very long time. North American informal

keep a dog and bark yourself pay someone to work for you and then do the work yourself.

1991 *Purchasing and Supply Management* He does not solve the subcontractor's technical problems, keeping a dog and barking himself.

let the dog see the rabbit let someone get on with work they are ready and waiting to do. informal

① This phrase comes from greyhound racing, where the dogs chase a mechanical rabbit around a track.

let sleeping dogs lie: *see* SLEEPING.

like a dog with two tails showing great pleasure; delighted.

① The image here is of a dog wagging its tail as an expression of happiness.

not a dog's chance no chance at all.

put on the dog behave in a pretentious or ostentatious way. North American informal

① *Dog* was late 19th-century US slang for 'style' or a 'flashy display'.

1962 Anthony Gilbert *No Dust in the Attic* Matron put on a lot of dog about the hospital's responsibility.

rain cats and dogs: *see* RAIN.

sick as a dog: *see* SICK.

throw someone to the dogs discard someone as worthless.

you can't teach an old dog new tricks you cannot make people change their ways. proverb

doggo

lie doggo remain motionless or quiet. British

> ❶ *Lie doggo* is of uncertain origin, but probably arose from a dog's habit of lying motionless or apparently asleep but nonetheless alert.

doghouse

in the doghouse (*or* **dogbox**) in disgrace or disfavour. informal

> **1963 Pamela Hansford Johnson** *Night & Silence* He'd been getting bad grades, he was in the dog-house as it was.

dollar

be dollars to doughnuts that be a certainty that. North American informal

> **1936 James Curtis** *The Gilt Kid* If he were seen it was dollars to doughnuts that he would be arrested.

you can bet your bottom dollar: *see* **you can bet your boots** *at* BET.

done

a done deal a plan or project that has been finalized or accomplished.

> **1991** *New Yorker* The French are still overreacting to German unification, even though it is a done deal.

done for in a situation so bad that it is impossible to get out of it. informal

> **1993** *Catholic Herald* Don't you realise that without that contract we're done for?

done in extremely tired. informal

> **1999 Chris Dolan** *Ascension Day* Morag was too upset and Paris was too done in to try and work out what was happening.

donkey

for donkey's years for a very long time. informal

> ❶ *For donkey's years* is a pun referring to the length of a donkey's ears and playing on a former pronunciation of *years* as *ears*.

> **1998 Ardal O'Hanlon** *The Talk of the Town* He'll be no loss, that's for sure. Sure his own family haven't spoken to him for donkey's years.

doodah

all of a doodah very agitated or excited. informal

> ❶ The nonsense word *doodah* is the refrain of the song 'Camptown Races', originally sung by slaves on American plantations.

doom

doom and gloom a general feeling of pessimism or despondency.

> ❶ This expression, sometimes found as *gloom and doom*, was particularly pertinent to fears about a nuclear holocaust during the cold war period of the 1950s and 1960s. It became a catchphrase in the 1968 film *Finian's Rainbow*.

doomsday

till doomsday for ever.

> ❶ *Doomsday* means literally 'judgement day', the Last Judgement of Christian tradition.

door

as one door closes, another opens you shouldn't be discouraged by failure, as other opportunities will soon present themselves. proverb

at death's door: *see* DEATH.

close (*or* **shut**) **the door on** (*or* **to**) exclude the opportunity for; refuse to consider.

> **1999** *South China Morning Post* Fergie did not close the door on the couple reconciling some day.

door to door ❶ (of a journey) from start to finish. ❷ visiting all the houses in an area to sell or publicize something.

lay something at someone's door regard or name someone as responsible for something.

> ❶ This phrase may have arisen from the practice of leaving an illegitimate baby on the doorstep of the man who was identified as its father.

leave the door open for ensure that there is still an opportunity for something.

open the door to create an opportunity for.

> **1995** *Kindred Spirit* By recreating the space in which you live or work, Feng Shui can open the door to abundance, wellbeing and a Renewed Sense of Purpose!

show someone the door dismiss someone unceremoniously from your presence.

a toe in the door: *see* TOE.

doornail

dead as a doornail: *see* DEAD.

doorstep

on your (*or* the) doorstep very near; close at hand.

> **1998** *New Scientist* The solution to Underhill's problem was on his doorstep.

dose

a dose of your own medicine: *see* MEDICINE.

in small doses experienced or engaged in a little at a time.

> **1994** *American Spectator* In small doses, ironical detachment is as necessary for getting along in life as...any of the other human qualities.

like a dose of salts very fast and efficiently. British informal

> ⓘ The *salts* referred to in this expression are laxatives.

> **1991 Peter Carey** *The Tax Inspector* She's going to go through your old man like a dose of salts.

dot

dot the i's and cross the t's ensure that all details are correct. informal

on the dot exactly on time. informal

> ⓘ The dot referred to is that appearing on a clock face to mark the hour.

> **1998** *Oldie* The Conditions of Sale state that the buyer has to pay the auctioneer on the dot.

the year dot a very long time ago. British informal

> **1998** *Spectator* From the year dot there has been an uneasy relationship between press and police.

double

at (*or* on) the double at running speed; very fast.

> ⓘ This modern generalized sense has developed from the mid 19th-century military use of *double pace* to mean twice the number of steps per minute of *slow pace*.

double or nothing a gamble to decide whether a loss or debt should be doubled or cancelled.

> ⓘ A British variant of *double or nothing* is *double or quits*.

double-edged

a double-edged sword (*or* weapon) a course of action or situation having both positive and negative effects.

> **2000** *Investor* A rising pound is a double-edged sword when investing overseas.

doubting

a doubting Thomas a person who refuses to believe something without having incontrovertible proof; a sceptic.

> ⓘ In the Bible, the apostle Thomas said that he would not believe that Christ had risen from the dead until he had seen and touched his wounds (John 20:24–9).

dovecote

flutter the dovecotes: *see* FLUTTER.

down

down and dirty ❶ unprincipled; unpleasant. ❷ energetically earthy, direct, or sexually explicit. North American informal

down and out beaten in the struggle of life; completely without resources or means of livelihood.

> ⓘ The phrase *down and out* comes from boxing, and refers to a boxer who is knocked out by a blow. Since the early 20th century the noun *down-and-out* has been used to describe a person without money, a job, or a place to live.

down in the mouth (of a person or their expression) unhappy or dejected. informal

down on your luck experiencing a period of bad luck. informal

down the road in the future; later on. informal, chiefly North American

> ⓘ An Australian variant of this phrase is *down the track*.

down the tube (*or* tubes) lost or wasted. informal

> **2001** *High Country News* I've already lost my alfalfa crop; that's about $20,000 down the tubes.

down to the ground completely; totally. informal

> **1997** *Daily Mail* Sly's better sense of comic timing suits the tongue-in-cheek script down to the ground.

down tools stop work, typically as a form of industrial action. British informal

have (or put) someone or something down as judge someone or something to be a particular type or class of person or thing.

> **1914 M. A. Von Arnim** *The Pastor's Wife* The other excursionists were all in pairs; they thought Ingeborg was too, and put her down at first as the German gentleman's wife because he did not speak to her.

have a (or be) down on disapprove of; feel hostile or antagonistic towards. informal

downgrade

on the downgrade in decline. North American

> ❶ *Downgrade* was originally used literally of a downward slope.

> **1953 William Burroughs** *Letter* As a matter of fact the whole region is on the downgrade. The rubber business is shot, the cocoa is eat up with broom rot.

downhill

be downhill all the way ❶ be easy in comparison with what came before. ❷ become worse or less successful.

go downhill become worse; deteriorate.

downwardly

downwardly mobile: *see* MOBILE.

dozen

a baker's dozen: *see* BAKER.

talk nineteen to the dozen: *see* TALK.

drag

drag your feet (or heels) (of a person or organization) be deliberately slow or reluctant to act.

> **1994** *Nature Conservancy* We can't afford to drag our feet until a species is at the brink of extinction.

drag someone or something through the dirt (or mud) make damaging allegations about someone or something.

> **1998** *Economist* The deputy prime minister . . . is having his name dragged through the mud.

dragon

chase the dragon: *see* CHASE.

sow (or plant) dragon's teeth take action that is intended to prevent trouble, but which actually brings it about.

> ❶ In Greek legend, Cadmus killed a dragon and sowed its teeth, which sprang up as armed men; these men then killed one another, leaving just five survivors who became the ancestors of the Thebans.

drain

down the drain totally wasted or spoilt. informal

> **1930 W. Somerset Maugham** *The Breadwinner* All his savings are gone down the drain.

drama

make a drama out of exaggerate the importance of a minor problem or incident. informal

draught

feel the draught experience an adverse change in your financial circumstances. informal

> **1992** *Daily Express* Redland . . . felt the draught of George Wimpey's interim profits slide.

draw

draw a bead on: *see* BEAD.

draw a blank: *see* BLANK.

draw someone's fire attract hostility or criticism away from a more important target.

draw the (or a) line at set a limit of what you are willing to do or accept, beyond which you will not go.

> **1995 Kate Atkinson** *Behind the Scenes at the Museum* She even manages to persuade Gillian not to cheat . . . although Gillian draws the line at not screaming when she loses.

draw the short straw: *see* STRAW.

draw stumps cease doing something.

> ❶ In the game of cricket, the stumps are taken out of the ground at the close of play.

the luck of the draw: *see* LUCK.

quick on the draw: *see* QUICK.

drawer

bottom drawer the collection of linen, clothes, and household items assembled by a woman in preparation for her marriage.

> ❶ The *bottom drawer* was the traditional place for storing for such articles. The US equivalent is *hope chest*.

drawing

back to the drawing board: *see* BACK.

on the drawing board (of an idea, scheme, or proposal) under consideration; not yet put into practice.

> ❶ To get something *off the drawing board* is to put something into action or to realize the first stages of a project.

dream

beyond your wildest dreams bigger, better, or to a greater extent than it would be reasonable to expect or hope for.

dream in colour (*or* Technicolour) be wildly unrealistic.

in your dreams used to assert that something much desired is not likely ever to happen.

> **2002** *New Yorker* Before falling asleep, I try to imagine myself as ... a savvy entrepreneur with her own catering business. In your dreams, as they say.

like a dream very well or successfully. informal

> **1996** *Good Food* The spring lamb is stuffed ... laced with garlic and herbs, and carves like a dream.

never in your wildest dreams used to emphasize that something is beyond the scope of your imagination.

> **1996** *Daily Star* Never in his wildest dreams did he think the cheers were to welcome the opening goal of a match.

dressed

dressed to kill wearing attractive and flamboyant clothes in order to make a striking impression.

drink

drink like a fish drink excessive amounts of alcohol, especially habitually.

drink someone under the table consume more alcohol than your drinking companion without becoming as drunk. informal

drive

drive a coach and horses through: *see* COACH.

drive something home: *see* HOME.

let drive attack with blows, missiles, or criticism.

> **1926** *Travel* I let drive for the point of his chin, and he went down and out for a full count.

driver

in the driver's (*or* driving) seat in charge of a situation.

> **1998** *Times* The deal would propel the no-nonsense Lancastrian into the driving seat at the UK's biggest generator.

driving

what someone is driving at the point that someone is attempting to make.

> **1986** Robert Sproat *Stunning the Punters* Martin is always saying things where I can't see what he's driving at.

drop

at the drop of a hat without delay or good reason. informal

> **1991** *Independent* These days Soviet visas are issued at the drop of a hat.

drop your aitches fail to pronounce the 'h' sound, especially at the beginning of words.

> ❶ In Britain, *dropping your aitches* is considered by some to be a sign of a lack of education or of inferior social class.

> **1903** George Bernard Shaw *Man & Superman* This man takes more trouble to drop his aitches than ever his father did to pick them up.

drop the ball make a mistake; mishandle things. North American informal

drop a brick make an indiscreet or embarrassing remark. British informal

drop your bundle become very nervous or upset; go to pieces. Australian

drop a clanger make an embarrassing or foolish mistake. British informal

> ❶ Dropping something that makes a loud clang attracts attention; this mid 20th-century expression is used especially in the context of a very embarrassing or tactless act or remark made in a social situation.

> **1998** *Spectator* Yet he never escaped from his own nagging suspicion that he had somehow overachieved ... and that he was likely to drop a huge clanger at any moment.

drop dead ❶ die suddenly and unexpectedly. ❷ used as an expression of intense scorn or dislike. informal

> ❶ This idiom is the source of the adjective *drop-dead*, which is used to emphasize how attractive someone or something is, as in *drop-dead gorgeous*.

drop the (*or* a) dime on inform on someone to the police. US informal

> **1990** Scott Turow *The Burden of Proof* Dixon says he's thought it over, the best course for him is just to drop the dime on John.

drop your guard: *see* GUARD.

drop a hint (*or* **drop hints**) let fall a hint or hints, as if casually or unconsciously.

drop someone or something like a hot potato: *see* HOT.

drop someone a line send someone a note or letter in a casual manner.

a drop in the ocean (*or* **in a bucket**) a very small amount compared with what is needed or expected.

> 1995 **Ian Rankin** *Let It Bleed* A few million was a drop in the ocean, hardly a ripple.

drop names: *see* NAME.

drop the pilot: *see* PILOT.

drop your trousers deliberately let your trousers fall down, especially in a public place.

fit (*or* **ready**) **to drop** worn out; exhausted.

have the drop on have the advantage over. informal

> ℹ️ *Have the drop on* was originally a mid 19th-century US expression used literally to mean that you have the opportunity to shoot before your opponent can use their weapon.

> 2000 *Clay Shooting* He always seems to have the drop on me by one bird no matter how hard I try.

drown

drown your sorrows forget your problems by getting drunk.

drowned

like a drowned rat extremely wet and bedraggled.

drug

a drug on the market an unsaleable or valueless commodity.

> ℹ️ *Drug* in the sense of 'a commodity for which there is no demand' is recorded from the mid 17th century, but it is not clear from the word's history whether it is the same word as the medicinal substance.

> 1998 *Spectator* Merchant banks are a drug on the market these days.

drum

beat (*or* **bang**) **the drum for** (*or* **of**) be ostentatiously in support of.

march to a different drum: *see* MARCH.

drunk

drunk as a lord (*or* **skunk**) extremely drunk.

dry

come up dry be unsuccessful. North American

> 1988 **James Trefil** *The Dark Side of the Universe* Attempts to see this decay with extremely sensitive experiments have so far come up dry.

dry as dust ❶ extremely dry. ❷ extremely dull.

> ℹ️ Sense 2 is represented in the fictitious character of the antiquarian Dr Jonas Dryasdust, to whom Sir Walter Scott addressed the prefatory epistle of *Ivanhoe* and some other novels.

there wasn't a dry eye in the house everyone in the audience of a film, play, speech, etc. was moved to tears.

duck

break your duck ❶ score the first run of your innings. Cricket ❷ make your first score or achieve a particular feat for the first time. British

duck and dive use your ingenuity to deal with or evade a situation.

> 1998 *New Scientist* You don't last for over 100 million years without some capacity to duck and dive.

fine weather for ducks: *see* WEATHER.

get (*or* **have**) **your ducks in a row** get (*or* have) your facts straight; get (*or* have) everything organized. North American informal

> 1996 *Brew Your Own* You really want to have all your ducks in a row before the meeting.

like a dying duck in a thunderstorm having a dejected or hopeless expression. informal

> ℹ️ The miserable demeanour of ducks during thunder has been proverbial since the late 18th century.

> 1933 **Agatha Christie** *Lord Edgware Dies* You did look for all the world like a dying duck in a thunderstorm.

lame duck a person or thing that is powerless or in need of help. informal

> ℹ️ In the mid 18th century, *lame duck* was used in a stock-market context, with reference to a person or company that could not fulfil their financial obligations. Later, from the mid 19th century, it was used specifically with reference to US politicians in the final period of office, after the election of their successor.

> 1998 *Spectator* At some point in his second and final term, every president becomes a lame

duck: as the man himself matters less, so does the office.

take to something like a duck to water take to something very readily.

> **1960 C. Day Lewis** *Buried Day* I had taken to vice like a duck to water, but it ran off me like water from a duck's back.

like water off a duck's back a remark or incident which has no apparent effect on a person.

play ducks and drakes with trifle with; treat frivolously.

> ⓘ This expression comes from the game of *ducks and drakes*, played by throwing a flat stone across the surface of water in such a way as to make it skim and skip before it finally sinks. The game was known by this name by the late 16th century, and it was already a metaphor for an idle or frivolous activity in the early 17th century.

duckling

an ugly duckling: *see* UGLY.

dudgeon

in high dudgeon in a state of deep resentment.

> ⓘ The origin of *dudgeon* in the sense of 'ill humour' is unknown, and it is almost always found in this phrase. However, other adjectives are sometimes used instead of *high*, for example *deep* or *great*.

> **1938 Zane Grey** *Raiders of the Spanish Peaks* Neale left in high dudgeon to take his case to his court of appeal—his mother.

duff

up the duff pregnant. British informal

> **1994** *Daily Telegraph* At 19, he was married ('only because she was up the duff' he explains gallantly).

duke

duke it out fight it out. North American informal

> ⓘ *Dukes* or *dooks* are 'fists', especially when raised in a fighting position. The word comes from rhyming slang *Duke of Yorks*, 'forks' (i.e. fingers).

dull

dull as dishwater (or ditchwater) extremely dull.

dull the edge of make less sensitive, interesting, or effective.

> ⓘ The image here is of making a knife's edge blunt.

dummy

sell someone a dummy (chiefly in rugby or soccer) deceive an opponent by feigning a pass or kick.

dump

down in the dumps (of a person) depressed or unhappy. informal

> ⓘ In early 16th-century English *dump* had the meaning 'a fit of depression', a sense now surviving only in this expression.

dumper

into the dumper into a bad or worse state or condition. North American informal

> **1991** *Tucson Weekly* J. Fife III peaked well before his run for governor...and has been sliding into the dumper ever since.

dust

dry as dust: *see* DRY.

dust and ashes used to convey a feeling of great disappointment or disillusion about something.

> ⓘ Often found in the fuller form *turn to dust and ashes in your mouth*, the phrase is used in the Bible as a metaphor for worthlessness, for example in Genesis 18:27 and the Book of Job 30:19. It derives from the legend of the Sodom apple, or Dead Sea fruit, whose attractive appearance tempted people, but which tasted only of dust and ashes when eaten.

the dust settles things quieten down.

> **1998** *New Scientist* The dust is settling on the chaos which ensued when the French sold 110,000 tickets to the World Cup football matches by phone.

eat someone's dust: *see* EAT.

gather (or collect) dust remain unused.

not see someone for dust find that a person has made a hasty departure.

> **1978 Patricia Grace** *Mutuwhenua* You didn't see this Maori for dust...Out the door, on the bike, and away.

raise (or kick up) a dust create a disturbance. British

dusted

be done and dusted (of a project) be completely finished or ready. informal

dusty

a dusty answer a curt and unhelpful reply. British

> ❶ The source of this expression is probably a passage in George Meredith's *Modern Love* (1862): 'Ah, what a dusty answer gets the soul when hot for certainties in this our life!'

Dutch

Dutch courage bravery induced by drinking alcohol.

> ❶ The phrase *Dutch courage* stems from a long-standing British belief that the Dutch are extraordinarily heavy drinkers.

a Dutch uncle a kindly but authoritative figure.

> ❶ *Dutch* here probably means no more than that the person described is not a genuine blood relation. In the mid 19th century *I will talk to him like a Dutch uncle* (meaning 'I will give him a lecture') was noted as being an American expression.

> **1999** *Daily Telegraph* She was the kindest of Dutch uncles, always prepared to listen to one's troubles.

go Dutch share the cost of something equally.

> ❶ An outing or entertainment paid for in this way is a *Dutch treat* and sharing the cost of a meal in a restaurant is *eating Dutch*.

> **1993** *Vanity Fair* He insists on buying his own tickets, 'going Dutch', as he puts it.

in Dutch in trouble. US informal, dated

> **1939 Raymond Chandler** *The Big Sleep* And for that amount of money you're willing to get yourself in Dutch with half the law enforcement of this country?

that beats the Dutch that is extraordinary or startling. US

Dutchman

I'm a Dutchman used to express your disbelief or as a way of underlining an emphatic assertion. British

> **1994 Ian Botham** *My Autobiography* I read somewhere that Warne said he had been possessed by demons. Well, in that case I'm a Dutchman.

duty

duty bound morally or legally obliged to do something.

dwaal

in a dwaal in a dreamy, dazed, or absent-minded state. South African

> **1985 Paul Slabolepszy** *Saturday Night at the Palace* Yassas—Carstens!! Wake up, man. You in a real dwaal tonight.

dyed

dyed in the wool (of a person) completely and permanently fixed in a particular belief or opinion; inveterate.

> ❶ If yarn is dyed in the raw state, it produces a more even and permanent colour.

dying

to your dying day for the rest of your life.

> **1967 George Mackay Brown** *A Calendar of Love* This one always was and ever will be to his dying day a garrulous long-winded old man.

dyke

put your finger in the dyke attempt to stem the advance of something undesirable which threatens to overwhelm you. informal

> ❶ This expression stems from the story of a small Dutch boy who saved his community from flooding by placing his finger in a hole in a dyke.

Ee

eager

an eager beaver a person who is very enthusiastic about work. informal

ear

be all ears be listening eagerly and attentively. informal

bring something (down) about your ears bring something, especially misfortune, on yourself.

dry behind the ears mature or experienced.

fall on deaf ears: *see* DEAF.

have someone's ear have access to and influence with someone.

> **1993** *Olympian* About 50 of the freshman congressman's constituents had his ear for more than two hours.

have something by the ears keep or obtain a secure hold on.

> **1949 Dylan Thomas** *Letter* I am tangled in hack-work. Depression has me by the ears.

have something coming out of your ears have a substantial or excessive amount of something. informal

> **1997** *Daily Express* In terms of advice … Jill's had suggestions coming out of her ears.

have (*or* keep) an ear to the ground be well informed about events and trends.

> ❶ The idea behind this phrase is that by putting your ear against the ground you would be able to hear approaching footsteps.

in one ear and out the other heard but disregarded or quickly forgotten.

lend an ear: *see* LEND.

listen with half an ear not give your full attention to someone or something.

make a pig's ear of: *see* PIG.

make a silk purse out of a sow's ear: *see* SILK.

out on your ear dismissed or ejected ignominiously. informal

> **1997** *Accountancy* At the age of 47, he found himself out on his ear, victim of Lord Hanson's policy of taking over companies … and replacing senior management.

set by the ears cause people to quarrel.

someone's ears are flapping someone is listening intently in order to overhear something not intended for them. informal

turn a deaf ear: *see* DEAF.

up to your ears in very busy with or deeply involved in. informal

wet behind the ears immature or inexperienced.

someone's ears are burning someone is subconsciously aware of being talked about, especially in their absence.

> ❶ The superstition that your ears tingle when you are being talked about is recorded from the mid 16th century. Originally it was the left ear only that was supposed to do so.

early

early bird a person who gets up, arrives, or acts before the usual or expected time.

> ❶ This expression comes from the saying *the early bird catches the worm*, meaning that the person who takes the earliest opportunity to do something will gain an advantage over others.

early doors early on, especially in a game or contest. British informal

> ❶ Apparently this expression arose with reference to a period of admission to a music hall ending some time before the start of the performance and giving a better choice of seating.

> **2003** *Guardian* Jeremy Vine, hosting Radio 2's music industry debate last night, got a dig in early doors about his hallowed predecessor on the station.

it's early days it is too soon to be sure how a particular situation will develop. British informal

take an early bath ❶ be sent off in a game of football or other sport. ❷ fail early on in a race or contest. informal

> ❷ **1992** *Bowlers' World* Defending champion Dave Phillips took an early bath losing all his three opening qualifying games.

earn

earn your corn put in a lot of effort for your wages. British informal

earn your keep be worth the time, money, or effort spent on you.

earner

a nice little earner a profitable activity or business. British informal

> **1996** *Independent* Today's children know a nice little earner when they see one.

earth

come back (down) to earth (*or* **bring someone back (down) to earth**) return or make someone return suddenly to reality after a period of daydreaming or euphoria.

> **2003** *Guardian* When you start to believe you're in with a shout, the big boys have a nasty habit of bringing you down to earth with a bump.

cost (*or* **charge** *or* **pay**) **the earth** cost (*or* charge *or* pay) a large amount of money. British informal

the earth moved (*or* **did the earth move for you?**) you had (*or* did you have?) an orgasm. humorous

go to earth go into hiding.

> ❶ *Go to earth* is used literally of a hunted animal hiding in a burrow or earth. Compare with **go to ground** (*at* GROUND).

like nothing on earth very strange. informal

> **1994** *Mixmag* Once in a blue moon, a record tumbles down from the vinyl mountain that sounds like nothing on earth and completely knocks you for six.

promise someone the earth: *see* **promise someone the moon** *at* MOON.

run someone or something to earth: *see* RUN.

earthly

not stand (*or* **have**) **an earthly** have no chance at all. British informal

easy

an easy touch: *see* a **soft touch** *at* TOUCH.

come easy to present little difficulty to.

> **1989** Tony Parker *A Place Called Bird* College was a lot harder than High School, book work didn't come easy to me there.

easy as ABC: *see* ABC.

easy as falling off a log very easy. informal

> ❶ This expression was originally a mid 19th-century American one, but it is now in general use. It was used around the year 1880 by Mark Twain in the alternative form *rolling off a log*.

easy as pie very easy. informal

> ❶ *Pie* as a metaphor for something pleasant was originally late 19th-century US slang. Compare with **nice as pie** and **pie in the sky** (*at* PIE).

easy come, easy go used to indicate that something acquired without effort or difficulty may be lost or spent casually and without regret.

> ❶ Although recorded in this exact form only from the mid 19th century, *easy come, easy go* had parallels in medieval French and in the English sayings *light come, light go* (mid 16th century) and *quickly come, quickly go* (mid 19th century).

easy does it approach a task carefully and slowly. informal

easy meat a person or animal overcome, outwitted, or persuaded without difficulty. informal

easy on the eye (*or* **ear**) pleasant to look at (*or* listen to). informal

> ❶ *Easy on the eye* originated in the late 19th century as a US expression describing a pretty woman, a context in which it is still often used.

go (*or* **be**) **easy on someone** be less harsh on or critical of someone. informal

go easy on (*or* **with**) **something** be sparing or cautious in your use or consumption of something. informal

have it easy be free from difficulties, especially those normally associated with a particular situation or activity. informal

I'm easy said by someone when offered a choice to indicate that they have no particular preference. informal

of easy virtue (of a woman) promiscuous.

> ❶ *Easy* in the sense of 'sexually compliant' is found in Shakespeare's *Cymbeline*: 'Not a whit, Your lady being so easy'.

take the easy way out extricate yourself from a difficult situation by choosing a course of action offering the least effort, worry, or inconvenience, even though a more honourable alternative exists.

take it easy ❶ approach a task or activity gradually or carefully. ❷ relax.

eat

eat someone alive ❶ (of insects) bite someone many times. ❷ exploit someone's weakness ruthlessly. informal

eat crow be humiliated by your defeats or mistakes. North American informal

> ❶ In the USA 'boiled crow' has been a metaphor for something extremely disagreeable since the late 19th century.

eat dirt suffer insults or humiliation. informal

> ❶ In the USA *eat dirt* also has the sense of 'make a humiliating retraction' or 'eat your words'.

eat someone's dust fall far behind someone in a competitive situation. North American informal

> **1993** *Fiddlehead* She let everybody know she was moving on to True Love and they could eat her dust.

eat your heart out ❶ suffer from excessive longing, especially for someone or something unattainable. ❷ used to indicate that you think someone will feel great jealousy or regret about something.

> ❷ **1997 Christina Reid** *Clowns* Wait'll you see my new frock. Joan Collins eat your heart out.

eat someone out of house and home eat a lot of someone else's food. informal

eat humble pie: *see* HUMBLE.

eat salt with: *see* SALT.

eat your words retract what you have said, especially when forced to do so.

eating

have someone eating out of your hand have someone completely under your control.

> **1987 Bernard MacLaverty** *The Great Profundo* One of my main difficulties is that I'm not good with an audience. There's guys can come out and have a crowd eating out of their hand right away with a few jokes.

what's eating you (or him or her)? what is worrying or annoying you (or him or her)? informal

ebb

at a low ebb in an especially poor state.

ebb and flow a recurrent or rhythmical pattern of coming and going or decline and regrowth.

> ❶ This expression makes reference to the regular movement of the tides, where *ebb* means move away from the land and *flow* move back towards it.

echo

applaud (*or* cheer) someone to the echo applaud (*or* cheer) someone very enthusiastically.

eclipse

in eclipse ❶ (of a celestial object) obscured by another or the shadow of another. ❷ losing or having lost significance, power, or prominence.

> ❷ **1991** *Atlantic* Within a decade of his death... he was in eclipse: not written about, undiscussed, forgotten in architecture schools.

economical

economical with the truth used euphemistically to describe a person or statement that lies or deliberately withholds information.

> ❶ The phrase *economy of truth* was used in the 18th century by the orator Edmund Burke (1729–97), while in the 19th century Mark Twain observed 'Truth is the most valuable thing we have. Let us economize it' (*Following the Equator*, 1897). The present phrase became current after its use in the 'Spycatcher' trial in the New South Wales Supreme Court: Robert Armstrong, head of the British Civil Service, was reported as saying of a letter: 'It contains a misleading impression, not a lie. It was being economical with the truth.'

> **2003** *Observer* He is ruthless in pursuit of commercial goals, otherwise he would not have been so economical with the truth two months ago when he ruled out any notion of signing Beckham.

edge

on the edge of your seat (*or* chair) very excited and giving your full attention to something. informal

set someone's teeth on edge: *see* TEETH.

take the edge off something reduce the intensity or effect of something, especially something unpleasant or severe.

edgeways

get a word in edgeways contribute to a conversation with difficulty because the other speaker talks almost incessantly.

effing

effing and blinding using vulgar expletives; swearing.

> ❶ *Effing* and *blinding* here stand for the initial letters of taboo or vulgar slang words.

egg

a curate's egg: *see* CURATE.

don't put all your eggs in one basket don't risk everything on the success of one venture. proverb

> **1996** *Mail on Sunday* Having too many eggs in one basket—the British stock market—can be a bad idea. Overseas investments can add balance to an investment portfolio.

go suck an egg go away (used as an expression of anger or scorn). North American informal

> **1993** *Virginian Pilot & Ledger-Star* (Norfolk, Va.) A place [in the country] where you can drop a line in the water from your back yard and tell the rest of the world to go suck an egg.

kill the goose that lays the golden egg: *see* GOOSE.

lay an egg be completely unsuccessful; fail badly. North American informal

sure as eggs is eggs: *see* SURE.

with egg on your face appearing foolish or ridiculous. informal

eight

behind the eight ball at a disadvantage; baffled. North American

> ❶ The black ball is numbered eight in a variety of the game of pool known as *eight-ball pool*.

one over the eight slightly drunk. British informal

> ❶ The idea behind this idiom is that a drinker can reasonably be expected to consume eight glasses of beer without becoming drunk. The expression was originally armed forces' slang from the early 20th century.

elbow

give someone the elbow reject or dismiss someone. informal

> ❶ The image is of nudging someone aside in a rough or contemptuous manner.

lift your elbow consume alcohol to excess.

up to your elbows in ❶ with your hands plunged into something. ❷ deeply involved in. informal

element

in (or out of) your element in (or out of) your accustomed or preferred environment, where you feel confident and at ease, often in performing a particular activity.

elephant

see the elephant see the world; get experience of life. US

> ❶ An *elephant* is used here to symbolize or typify something which is extremely remarkable or exotic.

> **1994** *Fighting Firearms* These men have all seen the elephant and represent a typical cross-section of the . . . staff in general.

a white elephant: *see* WHITE.

eleventh

at the eleventh hour at the latest possible moment.

> ❶ This expression originally referred to Jesus's parable of the labourers hired right at the end of the day to work in the vineyard (Matthew 20:1–16).

Elysian

the Elysian Fields heaven. literary

> ❶ Homer describes the Elysian Fields (called *Elysium* by Latin writers) as the happy land in which the blessed spirits live in the afterlife.

empty

be running on empty have exhausted all your resources or sustenance.

> **1998** *New Scientist* Bateson concluded that a hunted deer may be running on empty for 90 minutes, but Harris argues that this period will be just a few minutes.

empty nester a person whose children have grown up and left home. informal

empty vessels make most noise (or sound) those with least wisdom or knowledge are always the most talkative. proverb

> ❶ *Vessel* here refers to a hollow container, such as a bowl or cask, rather than a ship.

enchilada

the big enchilada a person or thing of great importance. North American informal

the whole enchilada the whole situation; everything. North American informal

> **1992** *New York Times* High-tech gadgetry is best viewed as the spice, but not the whole enchilada.

> ❶ An *enchilada* is an American Spanish word for a tortilla served with chilli sauce and a filling of meat or cheese.

end

all ends up completely. informal

> **1921 A. W. Myers** *Twenty Years of Lawn Tennis* Barrett beat him 'all ends up' in an early round.

at the end of the day when everything is taken into consideration. British informal

> **1995 Jayne Miller** *Voxpop* Today I've been giving out leaflets. You don't have to, but at the end of the day, it's worth it.

at the end of your tether having no patience, resources, or energy left to cope with something.

> ❶ A North American variant of this expression is *at the end of your rope*, and in both cases the image is that of a grazing animal tethered on a rope that allows it a certain range in which to move but which at full stretch prohibits further movement.

at a loose end: see LOOSE.

at your wit's end: see WIT.

the beginning of the end: see BEGINNING.

be on the receiving end: see RECEIVING.

be thrown in at the deep end: see DEEP.

burn the candle at both ends: see BURN.

the dirty end of the stick: see DIRTY.

end in tears have an unhappy or unpleasant outcome (often used as a warning). British

> **1992 Iain Banks** *The Crow Road* Well, let them get married. The earlier the better; it would end in tears. Let them rush into it, let them repent at leisure.

end it all commit suicide.

> **1993 Ray Shell** *iCED* Quentin thought... he'd jump off the Brooklyn Bridge and make the papers. At least he'd end it all in a blaze of media glory.

the end justifies the means wrong or unfair methods may be used if the overall goal is good.

> ❶ The Roman poet Ovid expresses this concept in *Heroides* as *exitus acta probat* meaning 'the outcome justifies the actions'.

the end of civilization as we know it ❶ the complete collapse of ordered society. ❷ used to indicate that someone is being alarmist or is overreacting to a trivial inconvenience or blunder as if it were enormously significant and catastrophic.

> ❶ This expression is supposedly a cinematic cliché, and was actually used in the film *Citizen Kane* (1941): 'a project which would mean the end of civilization as we know it'.

> **1999** *Select* The giant, dreadlocked rapper's third album contains extensive deliberations on the end of civilisation as we know it.

the end of the road (*or* **line**) the point beyond which progress or survival cannot continue.

end of story used to emphasize that there is nothing more to add on the subject just mentioned. informal

> **1998** *Times* Parents are role models. Footballers are picked for teams because they are good at football. End of story.

the end of the world a complete disaster. informal

> ❶ This expression comes from the idea of the termination of life on earth as the ultimate catastrophe, but is often used with the negative as a reassurance that a mistake or setback is not that important.

> **1994** *Face* If people are buying my records that's good, but if they're not it's not the end of the world.

get (*or* **have**) **your end away** have sex. British vulgar slang

get the wrong end of the stick: see WRONG.

go off the deep end: see DEEP.

keep (*or* **hold**) **your end up** perform well in a difficult or competitive situation. informal

make (both) ends meet earn or have enough money to live on without getting into debt.

> **1996 Amitav Ghosh** *The Calcutta Chromosome* Actually I think she's having trouble making ends meet, now that she's retired.

make someone's hair stand on end: see HAIR.

a means to an end: see MEAN.

never (*or* **not**) **hear the end of something** be continually reminded of an unpleasant topic or cause of annoyance.

> **2002** *Observer* If it was Ireland or Wales we'd support them, but not England. It's a minority nations thing. If England was to win, we'd never hear the end of it.

no end to a great extent; very much. informal

> **1984 James Kelman** *The Busconductor Hines* McCulloch gives him a go at the wheel at certain remote terminuses at specific times of the late night and early morning and his confidence grows no end.

no end of something a vast number or amount of something. informal

> **1996 Frank McCourt** *Angela's Ashes* If I could have Mrs Leibowitz and Minnie for mothers at the same time I'd have no end of soup and mashed potatoes.

the sharp end: *see* SHARP.

the thin end of the wedge: *see* THIN.

to the bitter end: *see* BITTER.

a — to end all —s something so impressive of its kind that nothing that follows will have the same impact. informal

> ❶ The First World War was often referred to as *the war to end all wars*, from the mistaken belief that it would make all subsequent wars unnecessary.

> **1971 Bessie Head** *Maru* It was a wedding to end all weddings.

enemy

be your own worst enemy act contrary to your own interests; be self-destructive.

> **1993 Richard Lowe** & **William Shaw** *Travellers* We convinced ourselves that everything was against us but the truth was we were probably our own worst enemies.

public enemy number one: *see* PUBLIC.

Englishman

an Englishman's home is his castle an English person's home is a place where they may do as they please and from which they may exclude anyone they choose. British proverb

enough

enough is as good as a feast moderation is more satisfying than excess. proverb

enough is enough no more will be tolerated.

> **1997** *Earthmatters* Unless we say 'enough is enough' and start to take habitat protection seriously, the future of the world's wildlife is in jeopardy.

enough said there is no need to say more; all is understood.

enough to make a cat laugh: *see* CAT.

envelope

push the envelope (*or* **the edge of the envelope**) approach or extend the limits of what is possible. informal

> ❶ This expression was originally aviation slang and related to graphs of aerodynamic performance on which the *envelope* is the boundary line representing an aircraft's capabilities.

> **1993** *Albuquerque* These are extremely witty and clever stories that consistently push the envelope of TV comedy.

épater

épater les bourgeois shock people who have attitudes or views regarded as conventional or complacent.

> ❶ The French phrase is generally used in English, there being no exact English equivalent. 'Il faut épater le bourgeois' ('one must astonish the bourgeois') was a comment attributed to the French poet and critic Charles Baudelaire.

> **1995** *Times* Because it takes more than a urinal to *épater les bourgeois* now, the real things that are being hauled into galleries grow ever more provocative: turds, frozen foetuses and used sanitary towels.

equal

first among equals the person or thing having the highest status in a group.

> ❶ This expression is a translation of the Latin phrase *primus inter pares*, which is also used in English.

other (*or* **all**) **things being equal** provided that other factors or circumstances remain the same.

> **1996 E. D. Hirsch Jr.** *Schools We Need* Other things being equal, students from good-home schools will always have an educational advantage over students from less-good-home schools.

err

err on the right side act so that the most likely mistake to be made is the least harmful one.

err on the side of act with a specified bias towards something.

> **1999** *Nature* Der Sündenfall's message may err on the side of alarmism, but it certainly is a good read.

to err is human, to forgive divine it is human nature to make mistakes yourself while finding it hard to forgive others. proverb

escutcheon

a blot on your escutcheon: *see* BLOT.

essence

of the essence critically important.

> **1990 Louis de Bernières** *The War of Don Emmanuel's Nether Parts* Gentlemen, we have before us an important mission for which speed and efficiency are of the essence, and where surprise is the key element.

eternal

the Eternal City a name for the city of Rome.

eternal triangle a relationship between three people, typically a couple and the lover of one of them, involving sexual rivalry.

even

an even break a fair chance. informal

> ⓘ This phrase is perhaps best known from W. C. Fields's catchphrase 'Never give a sucker an even break'. It is said to have originated in the 1923 musical *Poppy*, and was also the title of one of Field's films (1941).

even Stephens (*or* **Stevens**) an even chance.

> **1990 Alan Duff** *Once Were Warriors* And I give her half. Clean down the middle. Even stevens. I don't try and cheat her out of her share.

get (*or* **be**) **even with** inflict similar trouble or harm on someone as they have inflicted on you. informal

on an even keel ❶ (of a ship or aircraft) not tilting to one side. ❷ (of a person or situation) functioning normally after a period of difficulty.

> ❷ **1991 Deirdre Purcell** *A Place of Stones* Life ran on an even keel in the house as both of them came and went and became re-immersed in their own lives.

ever

it was ever thus (*or* **so**) used as a humorous way of suggesting that despite claims of things having been better in the past nothing much alters. informal

> **1998** *Bookseller* Curious and surprising (to say the least) and depressing things happen. But it was ever so.

every

every last (*or* **single**) used to emphasize every member of a group.

> **1991 Colin Dexter** *The Jewel That Was Ours* One clue unfinished in a Listener puzzle, and he would strain the capacity of every last brain-cell to bursting point until he had solved it.

every man for himself everyone must take care of themselves and their own interests and safety.

> ⓘ This expression has been used since medieval times, but from the mid 16th century onwards it has often been expanded to *every man for himself and the devil take the hindmost* or, less commonly, *every man for himself and God for us all*.

> **1997 Daniel Quinn** *My Ishmael* Tribes survive by sticking together at all costs, and when it's every man for himself, the tribe ceases to be a tribe.

every which way in all directions; in a disorderly fashion. North American informal

evil

the evil eye a gaze or stare superstitiously believed to cause harm.

put off the evil day (*or* **hour**) postpone something unpleasant for as long as possible.

exception

the exception that proves the rule a particular case that is so unusual that it is evidence of the validity of the rule that generally applies.

> ⓘ This phrase comes from the Latin legal maxim *exceptio probat regulum in casibus non exceptis* 'exception proves the rule in the cases not excepted'. This in fact meant that the recognition of something as an exception proved the existence of a rule, but the idiom is popularly used or understood to mean 'a person or thing that does not conform to the general rule affecting others of that class'.

> **1998** *Spectator* The success of The Full Monty in the United States is an exception which proves the rule. On such lucky breaks, industries and economies are not built.

exeunt

exeunt omnes everyone leaves or goes away.

> ⓘ The Latin phrase *exeunt omnes* means 'all go out', and was used originally as a stage direction in a printed play to indicate that all the actors leave the stage.

exhibition

make an exhibition of yourself behave in a very foolish or ill-judged way in public.

expect

what can (or do) you expect? used to emphasize that there was nothing unexpected about a person or event.

> ❶ A more elaborate statement of the same sentiment is the proverb *what can you expect from a pig but a grunt?*

eye

an eye for an eye and a tooth for a tooth used to refer to the belief that retaliation in kind is the appropriate way to deal with an offence or crime.

> ❶ This expression refers to the law of retribution as set out in the Old Testament (Exodus 21:24), known as *lex talionis*.

the eye of a needle a very small opening or space (used to emphasize the impossibility of a projected endeavour).

> ❶ This phrase comes from Matthew 19:24: 'It is easier for a camel to go through the eye of a needle, than for a rich man to enter the kingdom of God'.

> **2001** *FourFourTwo* Able to thread a pass through the eye of a needle, he can play in the centre or on either flank.

the eye of the storm ❶ the calm region at the centre of a storm or hurricane. ❷ the most intense part of a tumultous situation.

> ❷ **1998** *Times* He [Mr Yeltsin] was now our heroic figure in the eye of the storm, preaching defiance...from the top of a tank outside the White House.

be all eyes be watching eagerly and attentively.

> **1958 Jessie Kesson** *The White Bird Passes* Standing there all eyes and ears. Beat it before I take the lights from you!

clap (or lay or set) eyes on see. informal

> **1992 Barry Unsworth** *Sacred Hunger* If we go by the indications of the play, these two charmers have never clapped eyes on a man before, never flirted, never known the sweets of love.

get (or keep) your eye in become (or remain) able to make good judgements about a task or occupation in which you are engaged. British

close (or shut) your eyes to refuse to notice or acknowledge something unwelcome or unpleasant.

do a person in the eye defraud, thwart, or humiliate a person.

> **1930 J. B. Priestley** *Angel Pavement* He'd invented the job five minutes before, just to do mother in the eye.

eyes out on stalks full of eager curiosity or amazement. informal

> **1999** *Escape* This breathtaking graphics accelerator takes 3D game play on PCI systems to a whole new dimension of excitement with imagery so realistic your eyes will be out on stalks.

give someone the (glad) eye look at someone in a way that clearly indicates your sexual interest in them. informal

> **1992 James Meek** *Last Orders* If it was an attractive woman, men would give her the eye.

a gleam in someone's eye: *see* GLEAM.

go eyes out make every effort. Australian informal

half an eye a slight degree of perception or attention.

> **1962 Cyprian Ekwensi** *Burning Grass* His sandals were new because it was market day; or perhaps he had half an eye to some maiden.

have an eye for be able to recognize, appreciate, and make good judgements about a particular thing.

> **2003** *Observer* Europe's oldest continually inhabited city is Cádiz, founded by the Phoenicians in 1100 BC, but those wily Phoenicians, with an eye for a good setting, founded 'Malaka' further along the Andalucian coast a few hundred years later in 800 BC.

have (or with) an eye for (or on or to) the main chance look or be looking for an opportunity to take advantage of a situation for personal gain, especially when this is financial.

> ❶ This expression is taken from the use of *main chance* in the gambling game of hazard, where it refers to a number (5, 6, 7, or 8) called by a player before throwing the dice.

have eyes bigger than your stomach have asked for or taken more food than you can actually eat.

have eyes in the back of your head observe everything that is happening even when this is apparently impossible.

> **1991 Barbara Anderson** *Girls High* They were all in Miss Royston's class who said that she had eyes in the back of her head and they half believed it, because how else did she know.

have square eyes: *see* SQUARE.

hit someone in the eye (or between the eyes) be very obvious or impressive. informal

2001 *Independent* When I saw the technology in operation, it hit me between the eyes. I was happy to give him £20,000, and became a non-executive director.

keep an eye out (*or* open) for look out for something with particular attention.

1996 *Guardian* Keep an eye open for kingklip, a delectable fish, and the superb local hake.

keep your eye on the ball: *see* BALL.

keep your eyes open (*or* peeled *or* skinned) be on the alert; watch carefully or vigilantly for something.

make eyes at someone look at someone in a way that makes it clear you find them sexually attractive.

more to someone or something than meets the eye: *see* MEET.

my eye (*or* all my eye and Betty Martin) nonsense. informal, dated

> ❶ Who or what *Betty Martin* was has never been satisfactorily explained. Another version of the saying also in use in the late 18th century was *all my eye and my elbow*.

1991 Robertson Davies *Murther & Walking Spirits* Of course many of the grievances are all my eye and Betty Martin (Anna has picked up this soldier's phrase from her husband and likes to use it to show how thoroughly British she has become).

one in the eye for a disappointment or setback for someone or something, especially one that is perceived as being well deserved.

open someone's eyes enlighten someone about certain realities; cause someone to realize or discover something.

1998 Scoular Anderson *1314 & All That* These events opened his eyes to what had happened to his country. Now his one wish was that Scotland should be independent.

pull the wool over someone's eyes: *see* WOOL.

see eye to eye have similar views or attitudes to something; be in full agreement.

1997 A. Sivanandran *When Memory Dies* We don't see eye to eye about anything—work, having children, what's going on in the country.

—'s-eye view a view from the position or standpoint of the person or thing specified.

> ❶ The most common versions of this phrase are **bird's-eye view** (see BIRD) and **worm's-eye view** (see WORM).

1982 Ian Hamilton *Robert Lowell* There is a kind of double vision: the child's eye view judged and interpreted by the ironical narrator.

shut your eyes to be wilfully ignorant of.

1993 Isidore Okpewho *Tides* In the last few weeks, it has become clear to me that this peace and quiet may elude me if I shut my eyes to the all too obvious suffering of people around me.

turn a blind eye: *see* BLIND.

up to your eyes in very busy with or deeply involved in. informal

what the eye doesn't see, the heart doesn't grieve over if you're unaware of an unpleasant fact or situation you can't be troubled by it. proverb

with one eye on giving some but not all your attention to.

1977 Craig Thomas *Firefox* With one eye on the JPT (jet-pipe temperature) gauge he opened the throttles until the rpm gauges were at fifty-five percent and the whine had increased comfortably.

with your eyes open in full awareness.

1999 Salman Rushdie *The Ground Beneath Her Feet* I've always liked to stick my face right up against the hot sweaty broken surface of what was being done, with my eyes open.

with your eyes shut (*or* closed) ❶ without having to make much effort; easily. ❷ without considering the possible difficulties or consequences.

❶ 1994 *New Scientist* I can knock off pages of eco-babble for the UN with my eyes shut.

eyeball

eyeball to eyeball face to face with someone, especially in an aggressive way.

give someone the hairy eyeball stare at someone in a disapproving or angry way, especially with your eyelids partially lowered. North American informal

1992 Guy Vanderhaeghe *Things As They Are* The commissioner giving him the hairy eyeball all through the service didn't do anything for Reg's increasing bad humour either.

up to the (*or* your) eyeballs used to emphasize the extreme degree of an undesirable situation or condition. informal

2000 *Time* Consumers are up to their eyeballs in debt, and the strain shows.

eyebrow

raise your eyebrows (*or* an eyebrow) show surprise, disbelief, or mild disapproval.

eyelash

by an eyelash by a very small margin.

eye teeth

cut your eye teeth: *see* **cut your teeth** *at*
  CUT.

give your eye teeth for go to any lengths in
  order to obtain something.

> ❶ The *eye teeth* are the two canine teeth in
> the upper jaw.

1930 W. Somerset Maugham *Cakes & Ale* He'd
give his eye-teeth to have written a book half
as good.

Ff

face

the acceptable face of: *see* ACCEPTABLE.

a face as long as a fiddle a dismal face.

face the music be confronted with the unpleasant consequences of your actions.

get out of someone's face stop harassing or annoying someone. North American informal

have the (brass) face to have the effrontery to do something. dated

in your face aggressively obvious; assertive. informal
> **1996** *Sunday Telegraph* The . . . campaign reflects a growing trend of aggressive and 'in your face' advertisement that is alarming many within the industry.

lose face suffer a loss of respect; be humiliated.

> ❶ This expression was originally associated with China and was a translation of the Chinese idiom *tiu lien*.

make (or pull) a face (or faces) produce an expression on your face that shows dislike, disgust, or some other negative emotion, or that is intended to be amusing.

not just a pretty face: *see* PRETTY.

off your face very drunk or under the influence of illegal drugs. informal
> **1998** *Times Magazine* I've been accused of being off my face many times but you just go, by osmosis, with the people that you're with.

put a brave (or bold or good) face on something act as if something unpleasant or upsetting is not as bad as it really is.

save face retain respect; avoid humiliation.
> **1994** Thomas Boswell *Cracking Show* And Rose got to save face, at least in his own eyes, with one last brassy news conference.

save someone's face enable someone to avoid humiliation.

set your face against oppose or resist with determination.

someone's face fits someone has the necessary qualities for something.
> **1992** *Looks* My face fits and I've got the job!

throw something back in someone's face reject something in a brusque or ungracious manner.

fact

a fact of life something that must be accepted and cannot be changed, however unpalatable.

the facts of life information about sexual functions and practices, especially as given to children or teenagers.

fade

do a fade run away. informal
> **1990 Stephen King** *The Stand* Two days ago, he would probably have done a fade himself if he had seen someone.

fail

without fail absolutely predictably; with no exception or cause for doubt.

> ❶ *Fail* as a noun in the sense of 'failure or deficiency' is now only found in this phrase.

faint

a faint heart timidity or lack of willpower preventing you from achieving your objective.

> ❶ *Faint heart never won fair lady* is a proverb which dates in this wording from the early 17th century; the idea, however, was around at least two centuries earlier.

faintest

not have the faintest (idea) have no idea. informal

fair

fair and square ❶ with absolute accuracy. ❷ honestly and straightforwardly.

a fair crack of the whip: *see* CRACK.

a fair deal equitable treatment.

fair dinkum: *see* DINKUM.

fair dos used to request just treatment or to accept that it has been given. British informal

a fair field and no favour equal conditions in a contest.

fair play to someone used as an expression of approval when someone has done

famous

something praiseworthy or the right thing under the circumstances.

fair's fair used to request just treatment or assert that an arrangement is just. informal

> **2000 Sallee Vickers** *Miss Garnet's Angel* Jonah, the wandering prophet, reminded her too much of her father. 'He was a bit of a misery, wasn't he?' But then, fair's fair, living in the belly of a whale must give one a different point of view.

for fair completely and finally. US informal

> **1997 John Barth** *The Sot-Weed Factor* And when the matter of hostages arose, the mother had said 'Pray God they will take Harry, for then we'd be quit of him for fair, and not a penny poorer.'

it's a fair cop: *see* COP.

no fair unfair (often used in or as a petulant protestation). North American informal

fairy

(away) with the fairies giving the impression of being mad, distracted, or in a dreamworld.

fall

fall apart at the seams: *see* **come apart at the seams** *at* SEAM.

fall between two stools: *see* STOOL.

fall from grace: *see* GRACE.

fall in (*or* into) line conform with others or with accepted behaviour.

> ❶ This phrase originally referred to soldiers arranging themselves into military formation.

fall off the back of a lorry (of goods) be acquired in illegal or unspecified circumstances.

> ❶ The traditional bogus excuse given to the police by someone caught in possession of stolen goods was that the items in question had 'fallen off the back of a lorry'.

> **1991** *Time Out* People buy so much stolen stuff that...you can...buy a video in Dixons and take it round the corner to a pub, say it fell off the back of a lorry and get 50 quid more than it cost you.

fall on deaf ears: *see* DEAF.

fall (*or* land) on your feet achieve a fortunate outcome to a difficult situation.

> ❶ This expression comes from cats' supposed ability always to land on their feet, even if they fall or jump from a very high point.

> **1996** *Sunday Post* Unlike most people in Hollywood who starved to get there, I just fell on my feet.

fall on stony ground: *see* STONY.

fall over backwards: *see* BACKWARDS.

fall prey to: *see* PREY.

fall short (of) ❶ (of a missile) fail to reach its target. ❷ be deficient or inadequate; fail to reach a required goal.

take the fall receive blame or punishment, typically in the place of another person. North American informal

> ❶ In late 19th-century criminals' slang *fall* could mean an 'an arrest', and this was later extended to mean 'a term of imprisonment'. From this the US term *fall guy* meaning 'a scapegoat' developed in the early 20th century.

false

a false dawn a misleadingly hopeful sign.

> ❶ A false dawn is literally a transient light in the sky which precedes the rising of the sun by about an hour, commonly seen in Eastern countries.

> **1992 Frank McLynn** *Hearts of Darkness* After five weeks Clapperton seemed to recover; it proved merely a false dawn for two days later Clapperton died.

family

the (*or* your) family jewels a man's genitals. informal

in the family way pregnant. informal

sell the family silver part with a valuable resource in order to gain an immediate advantage.

> ❶ In 1985, the former British prime minister Harold Macmillan made a speech to the Tory Reform Group on the subject of privatization (the selling off of nationalized industries to private companies). He likened it to the selling of heirlooms by impoverished aristocratic families: 'First of all the Georgian silver goes...'.

famous

famous for being famous having no recognizable reason for your fame other than high media exposure.

famous for fifteen minutes (especially of an ordinary person) enjoying a brief period of fame before fading back into obscurity.

> ℹ In 1968, the pop artist Andy Warhol (1927–87) predicted that 'in the future everybody will be world famous for fifteen minutes'. Short-lived celebrity or notoriety is now often referred to as *fifteen minutes of fame*.

famous last words said as an ironic comment on or reply to an overconfident assertion that may well soon be proved wrong by events.

> ℹ This expression apparently originated as a catchphrase in mid 20th-century armed forces' slang.

2000 *Canberra Sunday Times* Speaking from New York, he said 'I expect NASDAQ to fall more than another 5–10 per cent. Famous last words, but I expect it to break 3000, that is about a 20 per cent descent.'

fancy

fancy your (or someone's) chances believe that you (or someone else) are likely to be successful.

fantastic

trip the light fantastic: *see* TRIP.

far

be a far cry from be very different from.

> **1987** *National Geographic* 'I walk out and hire a helicopter...an expensive way to mine.' And a far cry from the ancient Maori canoe expeditions...to hunt for jade.

far and away by a very large amount.

> **1990** A. L. Kennedy *Night Geometry & Garscadden Trains* She enjoyed being far and away the best cook.

far be it from (or for) me to used to express reluctance, especially to do something which you think may be resented.

so far, so good progress has been satisfactory up to now.

> **1998** *New Scientist* The project has just now reached a rigorous testing phase, and the researchers say so far, so good.

fare-thee-well

to a fare-thee-well to perfection; thoroughly. US

> ℹ This expression is of late 18th-century American origin, and is also found in the form *to a fare-you-well*.

> **1911** R. D. Saunders *Colonel Todhunter* The fight's begun, and we've got to rally around old Bill Strickland to a fare-you-well.

farm

buy the farm: *see* BUY.

fast

fast and furious lively and exciting.

> **2000** *Independent* We understand that the bidding was fast and furious right up to the last minute.

play fast and loose ignore your obligations; be unreliable.

> ℹ *Fast and loose* was the name of an old fairground game, in which a punter was challenged to pin an intricately folded belt, garter, or other piece of material to a surface. The person running the game would inevitably show that the item had not been securely fastened or made 'fast', and so the punter would lose their money. The phrase came to be used to indicate inconstancy.

> **1996** *Time Out* The big MGM production typically plays fast and loose with the facts, so it's as much an action spectacular as a genuine historical chronicle.

in the fast lane where life is exciting or highly pressured.

pull a fast one try to gain an unfair advantage by rapid action of some sort. informal

> ℹ This phrase was originally early 20th-century US slang and is also found as *put over a fast one*.

> **1993** *What Mortgage* We also know what prices should be and will pull up any builder trying to pull a fast one.

fat

the fat is in the fire something has been said or done that is about to cause trouble or anger.

> ℹ This expression refers to the sizzling and spitting caused by a spillage of cooking fat into an open flame. It was first used, in the mid 16th century, to indicate the complete failure of a plan or enterprise.

live off (or on) the fat of the land have the best of everything.

> ℹ In Genesis 45:18, Pharaoh tells Joseph's brothers: 'ye shall eat the fat of the land'. *Fat* meaning 'the best part' or 'choicest produce' is now found only in this expression.

fate

a fate worse than death a terrible experience, especially that of seduction or rape.

1991 Thomas Hayden *The Killing Frost* He dominated the conversation, holding the Hackett and Townshend women spellbound as he told of how he had broken up a white-slave ring in Dublin, and how he had rescued an innocent young girl from a fate worse than death.

seal someone's fate make it inevitable that something unpleasant will happen to someone.

tempt fate: *see* TEMPT.

father

founding father: *see* FOUNDING.

how's your father sexual intercourse. British informal

> ❶ A pre-World War I music-hall catchphrase, *how's your father* was earlier used to mean 'nonsense' before acquiring its present sexual sense. It is now used also to refer to a man's penis.

like father, like son a son's character or behaviour can be expected to resemble that of his father.

> ❶ The Latin version of this expression is *qualis pater, talis filius*. The female equivalent, *like mother, like daughter*, is based on Ezekiel 16:44: 'Behold, every one that useth proverbs shall use this proverb against thee, saying, As is the mother, so is the daughter'.

fatted

kill the fatted calf produce a lavish celebratory feast.

> ❶ The allusion is to the New Testament story of the prodigal son (Luke 15:11–32), in which the forgiving father orders his best calf to be killed in order to provide a feast to celebrate the return of his wayward son. *Fatted* is an archaic form of the verb *fat* meaning 'make or become fat'. Nowadays we use the forms *fatten* and *fattened*.

fault

— to a fault (of someone or something displaying a particular commendable quality) to an extent verging on excess.

> **1995 Bill Bryson** *Notes from a Small Island* Anyway, that's the kind of place Bournemouth is—genteel to a fault and proud of it.

favour

do me a favour used as a way of expressing brusque dismissal or rejection of a remark or suggestion.

1993 Merv Grist *Life at the Tip* Do me a favour, Webley couldn't even pass a mug of tea across the counter last season, let alone pass a ball.

do someone a favour do something for someone as an act of kindness. British informal

favourite

favourite son a famous man who is particularly popular and praised for his achievements in his native area.

> ❶ In the USA, the term is used specifically of a person supported as a presidential candidate by delegates from the candidate's home state.

fear

put the fear of God in (or into) someone cause someone to be very frightened.

without fear or favour not influenced by any consideration of the people involved in a situation; impartially.

> **1996** *Japan Times* It should be possible if all officials involved in the election process are allowed to work without fear or favour and keep their impartiality.

feast

feast your eyes on gaze at with pleasure.

feast of reason intellectual talk.

> ❶ This expression comes from the poet Alexander Pope's description of congenial conversation in *Imitations of Horace*: 'The feast of reason and the flow of soul'.

feast or famine either too much of something or too little.

a ghost (or spectre) at the feast someone or something that brings gloom or sadness to an otherwise pleasant or celebratory occasion.

> ❶ The *ghost* or *spectre* of Banquo at the feast in Shakespeare's *Macbeth* is the most famous literary instance of this. There are other versions of the expression. *A skeleton at the feast* dates from the mid 19th century and probably refers to the ancient Egyptian practice of having the coffin of a dead person, adorned with a painted portrait of the deceased, present at a funeral banquet. *A death's head at the feast* alludes to the use of a *death's head* or skull as a *memento mori* (an object which serves as a reminder of death).

a movable feast an event which takes place at no regular time.

> ❶ In a religious context a movable feast is a feast day (especially Easter Day and the other Christian holy days whose dates are related to it) which does not occur on the same calendar date each year.

feather

a feather in your cap an achievement to be proud of.

> ❶ Originally (in the late 17th century), a feather in your cap was taken as a sign of foolishness. However, by the mid 18th century the phrase was acquiring its modern positive sense.

> **1998** *Times* To take six wickets in the last innings of the game was a feather in his cap.

feather your (own) nest make money, usually illicitly and at someone else's expense.

> ❶ This phrase refers to the way in which some birds use feathers (their own or another bird's) to line the interior of their nest.

> **1998** *Spectator* It won't solve a damned thing except feather the nests of a lot of dodgy pen-pushers and party hacks.

in fine (or high) feather in good spirits.

> ❶ The image here is of a bird in its breeding plumage, when it is in peak condition.

show the white feather: *see* WHITE.

fed up

fed up to the teeth (or back teeth) extremely annoyed.

feel

feel your age become aware that you are growing older and less energetic.

feel someone's collar: *see* COLLAR.

feel the draught: *see* DRAUGHT.

feel your oats: *see* OAT.

feel the pinch: *see* PINCH.

feel the pulse of: *see* PULSE.

fell

in (or at) one fell swoop all in one go.

> ❶ This expression comes from Macduff's appalled reaction to the murder of his wife and children in Shakespeare's *Macbeth* : 'Oh hell-kite! . . . All my pretty chickens, and their dam At one fell swoop?'

fence

mend fences: *see* MEND.

over the fence unreasonable or unacceptable. Australian & New Zealand informal

> **1964** *Sydney Morning Herald* Some publications which unduly emphasize sex were 'entirely over the fence'.

sit on the fence avoid making a decision or choice.

> ❶ The two sides of a fence are seen here as representing the two opposing or conflicting positions or interests involved in a particular debate or situation.

> **1995 Duncan McLean** *Bunker Man* Let's have a proper decision—goal or no goal—none of this sitting on the fence.

fetch

fetch and carry go backwards and forwards bringing things to someone in a servile fashion.

> ❶ This phrase was originally used to refer to a dog retrieving game that had been shot.

fettle

in fine fettle in very good condition.

> ❶ *Fettle* was recorded in a mid 18th-century glossary of Lancashire dialect as meaning 'dress, case, condition'. It is now seldom found outside this phrase and its variants, which include *in good fettle* and *in high fettle*.

few

few and far between scarce or infrequent.

have a few drink enough alcohol to be slightly drunk. informal

> **1991 James Kelman** *Events in Yer Life* In fact it's hard to talk politics at all down there. I tend to keep my mouth shut. Unless I've had a few.

fiddle

a face as long as a fiddle: *see* FACE.

fiddle while Rome burns be concerned with relatively trivial matters while ignoring the serious or disastrous events going on around you.

> ❶ This phrase comes from the Roman biographer and historian Suetonius' description of the behaviour of the Roman emperor Nero during the great fire that destroyed much of Rome in AD 64.

fit as a fiddle in very good health.

hang up your fiddle retire from business; give up an undertaking. chiefly US

hang up your fiddle when you come home cease to be cheerful or entertaining when you are in the company of your family. chiefly US

on the fiddle engaged in cheating or swindling. informal

> ❶ *Fiddle* was late 19th-century US slang for a 'swindle'.

play second fiddle to take a subordinate role to someone or something.

> ❶ The expression derives from the respective roles of the fiddles or violins in an orchestra. Both *play first fiddle* and *play third fiddle* are much less common. The implication of *playing second fiddle* is often that it is somewhat demeaning.
>
> **1998** *Times* In *A Yank at Oxford* she played second fiddle to Vivien Leigh, which never got anyone very far.

field

a fair field and no favour: *see* FAIR.

hold the field remain the most important.

> **1991** *Twentieth Century British History* What analyses of AIDS policies hold the field?

play the field indulge in a series of sexual relationships without committing yourself to anyone. informal

> **1936 L. Lefko** *Public Relations* He hasn't any steady. He plays the field—blonde, brunette, or what have you.

fierce

something fierce to a great and almost overwhelming extent; intensely or furiously. North American informal

> **1986 Monica Hughes** *Blaine's Way* Maud had trapped my right arm against the chair and it was getting pins and needles something fierce.

fifteen

famous for fifteen minutes: *see* FAMOUS.

fifth

fifth column an organized group of people sympathizing with and working for the enemy within a country at war or otherwise under attack.

> ❶ *Fifth column* is a translation of the Spanish phrase *quinta columna*: during the Spanish Civil War, an extra body of supporters was claimed by General Mola as being within Madrid when he besieged the city with four columns of Nationalist forces in 1936.

take the fifth (in the USA) exercise the right of refusing to answer questions in order to avoid incriminating yourself.

> ❶ The reference in this phrase is to Article V of the ten original amendments (1791) to the Constitution of the United States, which states that 'no person . . . shall be compelled in any criminal case to be a witness against himself'.

fig

in full fig wearing the smart clothes appropriate for an event or occasion. informal

> ❶ *Fig* in the sense of 'dress or equipment' is now used only in this phrase, which was first recorded in the mid 19th century.

not give (*or* **care**) **a fig** not have the slightest concern about.

> ❶ *Fig* was formerly used in a variety of expressions to signify something regarded as valueless or contemptible.

fight

fight fire with fire use the weapons or tactics of your enemy or opponent, even if you find them distasteful.

> **1998** *New Scientist* Many opponents of biotechnology might say that they are simply fighting fire with fire. After all, the biotechnology industry is not averse to misquoting people when it suits them.

fight like cat and dog: *see* CAT.

fight a losing battle be fated to fail in your efforts.

fight or flight the instinctive physiological response to a threatening situation, which readies you either to resist violently or to run away.

fight shy of be unwilling to undertake or become involved with.

> **1992** *Farmers Guardian* Welsh companies often fight shy of dealing with the big multiples.

fight tooth and nail: *see* TOOTH.

figure

figure of fun a person who is considered ridiculous.

1990 Richard Critchfield *Among the British* [Reagan] was the first American leader in my lifetime who was widely regarded over here as a figure of fun.

fill

fill the bill: *see* BILL.

fill someone's shoes (or boots) take over someone's function or duties and fulfil them satisfactorily. informal

final

the final straw: *see* **the last straw** *at* STRAW.

find

find your feet ❶ stand up and become able to walk. **❷** establish yourself in a particular situation or enterprise.

> **❷ 1990 V. S. Naipaul** *India* In Calcutta he stayed with some friend or distant relation until he found his feet.

find God experience a religious conversion or awakening.

find it in your heart to do something allow or force yourself to do something.

> **1988 Richard Rayner** *Los Angeles Without a Map* Could you find it in your heart to lend me, say, $2,500?

finder

finders keepers (losers weepers) used, often humorously, to assert that whoever finds something by chance is entitled to keep it (and the person who lost it will just have to lament its loss). informal

> ❶ This expression has been widely used since the early 19th century, although the idea goes back much further and is found in the work of the Roman dramatist Plautus. A variant sometimes heard is *findings keepings*.

fine

cut it (or things) fine allow a very small margin of something, usually time.

fine feathers beautiful clothes.

> ❶ The proverb *fine feathers make fine birds*, meaning that an eye-catching appearance makes a person seem beautiful or impressive, has been known in England since the late 19th century. It is recorded in the early 16th century in French as *les belles plumes font les beaux oiseaux*.

not to put too fine a point on it to speak bluntly.

one fine day at some unspecified or unknown time.

1990 Wilfred Sheed *Essays in Disguise* If Sydney blew away one fine day, Melbourne could easily take its place as a center of mateship and conspicuous democracy.

fine art

have (or get) something down to a fine art achieve a high level of skill, facility, or accomplishment in some activity through experience.

finer

the finer points of the more complex or detailed aspects of.

finest

your finest hour the time of your greatest success.

> **1940 W. S. Churchill** *Speech to House of Commons* Let us therefore brace ourselves to that duty, and so bear ourselves that, if the British Commonwealth and its Empire lasts for a thousand years, men will still say, 'This was their finest hour'.

—'s finest the police of a specified city. North American informal

> **2000 Nelson DeMille** *The Lion's Game* As I indicated, I was a homicide detective, one of New York's Finest.

finger

be all fingers and thumbs be clumsy or awkward in your actions. British informal

> ❶ In the mid 16th century this idea was expressed in the form *each finger is a thumb*. *All thumbs* developed in the 19th century as an expression indicating a complete lack of dexterity.

burn your fingers (or get your fingers burned/burnt) suffer unpleasant consequences as a result of your actions.

> **1998** *Times* An American buyer remains a possibility, although it is not entirely clear why any would want to risk getting their fingers burnt twice.

cross your fingers: *see* CROSS.

get (or pull) your finger out cease prevaricating and start to act. British informal

give someone the finger make a gesture with the middle finger raised as an obscene sign of contempt. North American informal

> ❶ Since 1976, this gesture has sometimes been called the *Rockefeller Gesture* after Nelson Rockefeller was seen making it on a news film.

have a finger in every pie be involved in a large and varied number of activities or enterprises.

have a finger in the pie be involved in a matter, especially in an annoyingly interfering way.

have your fingers in the till: *see* TILL.

have (or keep) your finger on the pulse be aware of all the latest news or developments.

lay a finger on touch someone, usually with the intention of harming them.

> **1993 Tony Parker** *May the Lord in His Mercy be Kind to Belfast* The one thing I'll say about my husband is he never laid a finger on the children and he never hit me in front of them.

point the finger openly accuse someone or apportion blame.

> **1998** *Spectator* Reason suggests that one should point the finger at those who whipped up the emotion in the first place.

put something on the long finger postpone consideration of something; put something off. Irish

put the finger on inform against someone to the authorities. informal

put your finger on identify something exactly.

> **1988 Glenn Patterson** *Burning Your Own* There was something about the dinette that struck him as peculiar, but he couldn't quite put his finger on it.

snap (or click) your fingers make a sharp clicking sound by bending the last joint of the middle finger against the thumb and suddenly releasing it, typically in order to attract attention in a peremptory way or to accompany the beat of music.

twist (or wind or wrap) someone around your little finger have the ability to make someone do whatever you want.

work your fingers to the bone: *see* BONE.

your fingers itch you are longing or impatient to do something.

> **1998** *Patchwork & Quilting* There's a good gallery towards the end of the book and it will make your fingers itch to get started.

fingertip

at your fingertips (especially of information) readily available.

by your fingertips only with difficulty; barely.

> **1990** *Current History* In early 1988, United States Assistant Secretary of State Elliott

Abrams said that General Noriega was clinging to power 'by his fingertips'.

to your fingertips totally; completely.

> **1991** *Sun* McMahon, a professional to his fingertips, gave it his best shot even though an injury at this delicate stage could have sabotaged the last big move of his career.

finish

a fight to the finish a fight, contest, or match which only ends with the complete defeat of one of the parties involved.

finished

the finished article something that is complete and ready for use.

fire

breathe fire be fiercely angry.

> ❶ The implied comparison in this expression is with a fire-breathing dragon.

catch fire ❶ begin to burn. ❷ become interesting or exciting.

> ❷ **1994** *Coloradoan* I do not think this is something that's going to catch fire as a trend.

fire and brimstone the supposed torments of hell.

> ❶ In the Bible, fire and brimstone are the means of divine punishment for the wicked (see, for example, Genesis 19:24 or Revelation 21:8). *Brimstone* (from the Old English word *brynstān* meaning 'burning stone') is an archaic word for 'sulphur' and is now rarely found outside this phrase.

fire in the (or your) belly a powerful sense of ambition or determination.

> **1991** *Vanity Fair* Bennett is quick to deny feeling the fire in the belly generally considered a prerequisite for tenancy at 1600 Pennsylvania Avenue.

go through fire (and water) face any peril.

> ❶ This phrase originally referred to the medieval practice of trial by ordeal, which could take the form of making an accused person hold or walk on red-hot iron or of throwing them into water.

light a fire under someone stimulate someone to work or act more quickly or enthusiastically. North American

play with fire: *see* PLAY.

set the world on fire: *see* **set the world alight** *at* SET.

under fire ❶ being shot at. ❷ being rigorously criticized.

> ❷ **1993** *Albuquerque* (*New Mexico*) *Journal* Zoe Baird, under fire for hiring illegal aliens to work in her home, has withdrawn her name as President Clinton's nominee for US Attorney General.

where's the fire? used to ask someone why they are in such a hurry or in a state of agitation. informal

> **1963** J. F. Straker *Final Witness* 'Where's the fire, dear boy?' he drawled. 'Do we really have to run for it?'

fireman

visiting fireman: *see* VISITING.

firing

firing on all (four) cylinders working or functioning at a peak level.

> ❶ This expression is a metaphor from an internal-combustion engine: a cylinder is said to be firing when the fuel inside it is ignited.

> **1998** *Entertainment Weekly* Even when his imagination isn't firing on all cylinders, Amis is still worth picking up, if only to enjoy the jazzy rhythm of his prose.

firm

be on firm ground be sure of your facts or secure in your position, especially in a discussion.

a firm hand strict discipline or control.

> ❶ Often used in the the fuller form, *a firm hand on the reins*, this phrase is employing the image of controlling a horse by using the reins.

first

first among equals: *see* EQUAL.

first blood: *see* BLOOD.

first come, first served used to indicate that people will be dealt with strictly in the order in which they arrive or apply.

first off as a first point; first of all. informal, chiefly North American

> **1991** *Globe & Mail* (*Toronto*) First off, I wouldn't worry about the 'fashionability' of any particular garment. If you'd like to wear something, then wear it.

first past the post ❶ (of a contestant, especially a horse, in a race) winning a race by being the first to reach the finishing line. ❷ denoting an electoral system whereby a candidate or party is selected by achievement of a simple majority. British

first thing early in the morning; before anything else.

first things first important matters should be attended to before anything else.

> ❶ *First Things First* was the title of a book by George Jackson, subtitled 'Addresses to young men' (1894).

first up ❶ first of all. ❷ at the first attempt. Australian

get to first base: *see* BASE.

of the first order (*or* **magnitude**) used to denote something that is excellent or considerable of its kind.

> ❶ In astronomy, magnitude is a measure of the degree of brightness of a star. Stars *of the first magnitude* are the most brilliant.

of the first water: *see* WATER.

fish

big fish: *see* **big cheese** *at* BIG.

a big fish in a small (*or* **little**) **pond** a person seen as important and influential only within the limited scope of a small organization or group.

drink like a fish: *see* DRINK.

fish in troubled waters make a profit out of trouble or upheaval.

fish or cut bait stop vacillating and decide to act on or disengage from something. North American informal

a fish out of water a person who is in a completely unsuitable environment or situation.

> **1991 Margaret Weiss** *King's Test* He realized that he was a fish out of water—a pilot in the midst of marines.

have other (*or* **bigger**) **fish to fry** have other or more important matters to attend to.

> **1985 Gregory Benford** *Artifact* Kontos can throw a fit back there, chew the rug, anything—it won't matter. His government has bigger fish to fry.

like shooting fish in a barrel done very easily.

> **1992 Laurie Colwin** *Home Cooking* I fear that's the urgency of greed. Picking cultivated berries is like shooting fish in a barrel.

neither fish nor fowl (**nor good red herring**) of indefinite character and difficult to identify or classify.

> ❶ This expression arose with reference to dietary laws formerly laid down by the Church during periods of fasting or abstinence.

a pretty kettle of fish: *see* KETTLE.

there are plenty more fish in the sea used to console someone whose romantic relationship has ended by pointing out that there are many other people with whom they may have a successful relationship in the future.

> ❶ This expression alludes to the proverb *there are as good fish in the sea as ever came out of it.*

fishing

a fishing expedition a search or investigation undertaken with the hope, though not the stated purpose, of discovering information.

> **1998** *High Country News* Agency insiders describe the inquiry as a fishing expedition to uncover evidence that Dombeck may have been a party to illegal lobbying.

fist

an iron fist in a velvet glove: *see* **an iron hand in a velvet glove** *at* IRON.

make a — fist of do something to a specified degree of success. informal

> **1998** *Times* An opening stand of 99 by Hancock and Hewson helped Gloucestershire to make a decent fist of it yesterday.

fit

fit the bill: *see* **fill the bill** *at* BILL.

fit as a fiddle: *see* FIDDLE.

fit as a flea: *see* FLEA.

fit for the gods excellent; extremely pleasing.

fit like a glove: *see* GLOVE.

fit to be tied very angry. informal

> **1988 Joan Smith** *A Masculine Ending* He was fit to be tied when I separated from Hugh, and he seems to blame me for the whole thing.

fit to bust with great energy.

> **1992 Daphne Glazer** *The Last Oasis* I'd be rushing back at night, pedalling on my bike fit to bust.

give someone a fit greatly shock, frighten, or anger someone. informal

in fits in a state of hysterical amusement. informal

in (or by) fits and starts with irregular bursts of activity.

five

take five take a short break; relax.

> ❶ *Five* here is short for 'a five-minute break'.

fix

fix someone's wagon bring about someone's downfall; spoil someone's chances of success. US

> **1951 Truman Capote** *The Grass Harp* She said her brother would fix my wagon, which he did…I've still got a scar where he hit me.

get a fix on ❶ determine the position of an aircraft, ship, etc., by visual or radio bearings or astronomical observation. ❷ assess or determine the nature or facts of; obtain a clear understanding of. informal

> ❷ **1993** *Independent on Sunday* You do not necessarily get a fix on life by fooling around with the fictive process.

flag

fly the flag ❶ (of a ship) be registered to a particular country and sail under its flag. ❷ represent or demonstrate support for your country, political party, or organization, especially when you are abroad.

> ❶ In sense 2, the forms *show the flag, carry the flag,* and *wave the flag* are also found.

> ❷ **1996** *Hello!* She flew the flag for British tennis in the Eighties.

keep the flag flying ❶ represent your country or organization, especially when abroad. ❷ show continued commitment to something, especially in the face of adversity.

> ❶ This expression comes from the practice in naval warfare of lowering the flag on a defeated ship to signify a wish to surrender.

put the flags (or flag) out celebrate publicly.

show the flag (of a naval vessel) make an official visit to a foreign port, especially as a show of strength.

wrap yourself in the flag make an excessive show of your patriotism, especially for political ends. chiefly North American

> **1993** *Globe & Mail* (*Canada*) For a politician at election time, wrapping oneself in the Canadian flag is a reflex action, as irresistible as bussing a baby.

flagpole

run something up the flagpole test the popularity of a new idea or proposal.

> ❶ The idea behind this expression is of hoisting a particular flag to see who salutes.

flame

an old flame a former lover. informal

shoot someone or something down in flames: see SHOOT.

flapping

someone's ears are flapping: see EAR.

flash

flash in the pan a thing or person whose sudden but brief success is not repeated or repeatable.

> ❶ This phrase developed from the priming of a firearm, the flash being from an explosion of gunpowder within the lock.

> **1998** *New Scientist* But Java … may turn out to be flash in the pan: books on human–computer interaction struggle to stay abreast of rapid developments in computing.

quick as a flash (especially of a person's response or reaction) happening or made very quickly.

flat

fall flat fail completely to produce the intended or expected effect.

fall flat on your face ❶ fall over forwards. ❷ fail in an embarrassingly obvious way.

flat as a pancake: see PANCAKE.

flat out ❶ as fast or as hard as possible. informal ❷ without hesitation or reservation; unequivocally. chiefly North American

> ❶ **1995** *Independent* Since August 1993 she has been working flat out on her latest three part documentary. ❷ **1993** *Coloradoan* She flat out said she didn't trust her fellow board members.

on the flat ❶ on level ground as opposed to uphill. ❷ (of a horse race) on an open course as opposed to one with jumps.

flat-footed

catch someone flat-footed take someone by surprise or at a disadvantage. informal

> ❶ The opposite of *flat-footed* in this metaphorical sense is **on your toes** (see TOE).

> **1998** *Field* Farming and forestry were both caught flat-footed when fashion changed.

flatter

flatter to deceive encourage on insufficient grounds and cause disappointment.

> **1913** *Field* Two furlongs from home Maiden Erlegh looked most dangerous, but he flattered only to deceive.

flatting

go flatting leave the family home to live in a flat. Australian & New Zealand

flavour

flavour of the month someone or something that enjoys a short period of great popularity; the current fashion.

> ❶ This phrase originated in a marketing campaign in American ice-cream parlours in the 1940s, when a particular flavour of ice cream would be singled out each month for special promotion.

flea

fit as a flea in very good health.

> ❶ The phrase makes reference to a flea's agility.

a flea in your ear a sharp reproof.

> ❶ Formerly *a flea in your ear* also meant something that agitates or alarms you, as does the French phrase *avoir la puce à l'oreille*. Nowadays, it is often found in the phrases *give someone a flea in the ear* or *send someone away with a flea in their ear*.

flesh

go the way of all flesh die or come to an end.

> ❶ In the Authorized Version of the Bible *all flesh* is used to refer to all human and animal life.

in the flesh in person rather than via a telephone, film, article, etc.

make someone's flesh creep (*or* **crawl**) cause someone to feel fear, horror, or disgust.

put flesh on (the bones of) something add more details to something which exists only in a draft or outline form.

your pound of flesh: see POUND.

flesh and blood

your (own) flesh and blood near relatives; close family.

flex

flex your muscles give a show of strength or power.

> **1998** *Times* Mr Prescott is flexing his muscles and the City is wondering just how far he is prepared to go.

flexible

flexible friend a credit card.

> ❶ This phrase comes from the advertising slogan 'Access—your flexible friend'.

flick

give someone the flick (*or* **get the flick**) reject someone (*or* be rejected) in a casual or offhand way. informal, chiefly Australian

flight

in full flight escaping as rapidly as possible.

> **1938** *Life* A week later General Cedillo was reported in full flight through the bush, with Federal troops hot on his heels.

flip

flip your lid suddenly go mad or lose your self-control. informal

> ❶ A chiefly US variant of this phrase is *flip your wig*.

flit

do a moonlight flit: *see* MOONLIGHT.

float

float someone's boat appeal to or excite someone, especially sexually. informal

flog

flog a dead horse waste energy on a lost cause or unalterable situation.

> **1971** *Cabinet Maker & Retail Furnisher* If this is the case, we are flogging a dead horse in still trying to promote the scheme.

flood

be in full flood ❶ (of a river) be swollen and overflowing its banks. ❷ have gained momentum; be at the height of activity.

> ❷ **1991** *Journal of Theological Studies* There is too much detail for comfort . . . which is somewhat confusing when exposition is in full flood.

floor

cross the floor: *see* CROSS.

from the floor (of a speech or question) delivered by an individual member at a meeting or assembly, rather than by a representative on the platform.

take the floor ❶ begin to dance on a dance floor. ❷ speak in a debate or assembly.

flotsam

flotsam and jetsam useless or discarded objects.

> ❶ *Flotsam* refers to the wreckage of a ship or its cargo found floating on or washed up by the sea, while *jetsam* is unwanted material thrown overboard from a ship and washed ashore. The two nouns are seldom used independently, almost always appearing together in this phrase.

flow

go with the flow be relaxed; accept a situation. informal

> ❶ The image here is of going with the current of a stream rather than trying to swim against it.

> **1997** *J-17* Go with the flow today. You can't change the way things are going to pan out, so just let it all happen.

in full flow ❶ talking fluently and easily and showing no sign of stopping. ❷ performing vigorously and enthusiastically.

flower

the flower of — the finest individuals out of a number of people or things.

> ❶ Middle and early modern English did not recognize the modern distinction in spelling and sense between *flower* and *flour*, and the earliest instances of this expression relate to the sense that in modern English would be spelt *flour*, referring to the finest part of the wheat.

> **1991** **Pat Robertson** *New World Order* This vainglorious conqueror wasted the flower of French youth on his own personal dreams of empire.

fluff

bit of fluff: *see* BIT.

flush

a busted flush: *see* BUSTED.

in the first flush in a state of freshness and vigour.

> ❶ The exact origins of *flush* as a noun are unknown; early senses share the idea of a sudden rush or abundance of something (e.g. water, growth of grass, or emotion).

1997 Tom Petsinis *The French Mathematician* A month ago, in the first flush of enthusiasm . . . I tackled the classic problem of trisecting an angle using only a compass and straightedge.

flutter

flutter the dovecotes alarm, startle, or upset a sedate or conventionally minded community.

> ❶ This expression may come from Shakespeare's *Coriolanus*: 'like an eagle in a dove-cote, I Fluttered your Volscians in Corioli'. Compare with **put the cat among the pigeons** (at CAT).

1992 *Daily Telegraph* It is however the arrival of Michael Heseltine at the DTI that will flutter the dovecotes most of all.

flutter your eyelashes open and close your eyes rapidly in a coyly flirtatious manner.

fly

die (*or* **drop**) **like flies** die or collapse in large numbers.

drink with the flies drink alone. Australian & New Zealand informal

1963 D. Whitington *Mile Pegs* 'Have a drink?' the larrikin invited. 'Or do you prefer drinking with the flies?'

fly the coop make your escape. informal

1991 Julia Phillips *You'll Never Eat Lunch In This Town Again* Has David left? Nah, he would want to make sure I'm really ensconced, or I might fly the coop.

fly the flag: *see* FLAG.

fly high be very successful; prosper.

> ❶ The noun *high-flyer* (or *high-flier*) meaning 'a successful and ambitious person' developed from this phrase in the mid 17th century.

a fly in amber a curious relic of the past, preserved into the present.

> ❶ The image is of the fossilized bodies of insects which are often found preserved in amber.

fly in the face of be openly at variance with what is usual or expected.

a fly in the ointment a minor irritation or other factor that spoils the success or enjoyment of something.

> ❶ This expression alludes to Ecclesiastes 10:1: 'Dead flies cause the ointment of the apothecary to send forth a stinking savour'.

1998 *Times* Before you conclude that I have become a raging Europhile, let me say that there is a fly in the ointment.

fly a kite try something out to test opinion. informal

> ❶ A historical sense of this phrase was 'raise money by an accommodation bill', meaning to raise money on credit, and this sense of testing public opinion of your creditworthiness gave rise to the current figurative sense. The US phrase *go fly a kite!* means 'go away!'.

fly the nest (of a young person) leave their parent's home to set up home elsewhere. informal

> ❶ The image here is of a young bird's departure from its nest on becoming able to fly. Compare with **empty nester** (at EMPTY).

fly off the handle lose your temper suddenly and unexpectedly. informal

> ❶ This expression uses the image of a loose head of an axe flying off its handle while the axe is being swung.

a fly on the wall an unnoticed observer of a particular situation.

> ❶ This expression is often used as an adjective, as in a *fly-on-the-wall documentary*, where it refers to a film-making technique in which events are merely observed and presented realistically with minimum interference, rather than acted out under direction.

a fly on the wheel a person who overestimates their own influence.

> ❶ This phrase stems from Aesop's fable of a fly sitting on the axletree of a moving chariot and saying, 'See what a dust I raise'.

like a blue-arsed fly in an extremely hectic or frantic way. British vulgar slang

> ❶ The 'blue-arsed fly' referred to is a bluebottle, well known for its frenetic buzzing about.

1998 Rebecca Ray *A Certain Age* I'm not going to run around like a blue-arsed fly pandering to you and your bloody room, alright?

on the fly ❶ while in motion. ❷ while busy or active. ❸ (of an addition or modification in computing) carried out during the running of a program without interrupting the run.

there are no flies on — the person mentioned is very quick and astute.

> ❶ Early instances of this expression suggest that it originated with reference to cattle who were so active that no flies settled on them. The phrase was noted in the mid 19th century as being very common in Australia as a general expression of approbation. In the USA it could also be used to convey that the person in question was of superior breeding or behaved honestly.

wouldn't hurt (or harm) a fly used to emphasize how inoffensive and harmless a person or animal is.

flyer

take a flyer take a chance. chiefly North American

> **1998** *Times* Or we [i.e. journalists] can take a flyer: share a hunch and risk coming a cropper.

flying

with flying colours with distinction.

> ❶ Formerly, in military contexts, *flying colours* meant having the regimental flag flying as a sign of success or victory; a conquered army usually had to *lower* (or *strike*) *its colours*.

Flynn

be in like Flynn seize an opportunity; be successful. Australian

> ❶ The *Flynn* referred to in this expression is Errol Flynn, the Australian-born actor, who had a reputation as a notable playboy.

> **1987** Kathy Lette *Girls' Night Out* Russell brightened. 'Really?' I'm in, he thought to himself. I'm in like Flynn. 'You really see it that way?' He slid his arms around her.

foam

foam at the mouth: *see* **froth at the mouth** *at* FROTH.

fog

in a fog in a state of perplexity; unable to think clearly or understand something.

foggiest

not have the foggiest (idea or notion) have no idea at all. informal, chiefly British

follow

follow in someone's footsteps: *see* FOOTSTEP.

follow your nose ❶ trust to your instincts. ❷ move along guided by your sense of smell. ❸ go straight ahead.

follow suit ❶ (in bridge, whist, and other card games) play a card of the suit led. ❷ conform to another's actions.

> ❷ **2002** *History of Scotland* The first Earl of Huntly was a Gordon by adoption. Many other lesser men followed suit, assuming the surname of so successful a family.

food

food for thought something that warrants serious consideration or reflection.

fool

a fool and his money are soon parted a foolish person spends money carelessly and will soon be penniless. proverb

fools rush in where angels fear to tread people without good sense or judgement will have no hesitation in tackling a situation that even the wisest would avoid. proverb

be no (or nobody's) fool be a shrewd or prudent person.

fool's gold something deceptively attractive and promising in appearance.

> ❶ *Fool's gold* is the name popularly given to any yellow metal, such as pyrite or chalcopyrite, that may be mistaken for gold.

> **2003** *Nation* Many good people have been euchred into falling for the current fool's gold—politicians and lobbyists calling for 'universal healthcare'.

more fool — used as an exclamation indicating that a specified person is unwise to behave in such a way.

> **2002** *Pride* Any self-respecting female should be wise enough to steer clear of Romeo rats and, if you don't, then more fool you.

there's no fool like an old fool the foolish behaviour of an older person seems especially foolish as they are expected to think and act more sensibly than a younger one. proverb

foot

dig in your feet: *see* **dig in your heels** *at* DIG.

drag your feet: *see* DRAG.

fall on your feet: *see* FALL.

foot the bill: *see* BILL.

get (or start) off on the right (or wrong) foot make a good (or bad) start at something, especially a task or relationship.

> **1998** *Spectator* This relationship got off on the wrong foot...when Mr Cook's scathing attack on the government over the arms-to-

Iraq affair was felt to include some officials as well.

get your feet under the table establish yourself securely in a new situation. chiefly British

get your feet wet begin to participate in an activity.

have feet of clay have a fatal flaw in a character that is otherwise powerful or admirable.

> ❶ This expression alludes to the biblical account of a magnificent statue seen in a dream by Nebuchadnezzar, king of Babylon. It was constructed from fine metals, all except for its feet which were made of clay; when these were smashed, the whole statue was brought down and destroyed. Daniel interprets this to signify a future kingdom that will be 'partly strong, and partly broken', and will eventually fall (Daniel 2:31–5).

have a foot in both camps have an interest or stake in two parties or sides without commitment to either.

> **1992** *Community Care* As EWOs [Education Welfare Officers] we have a foot in both camps. We work with the children and their families and the school and bring the two together.

have (or get) a foot in the door have (or gain) a first introduction to a profession or organization.

have one foot in the grave be near death through old age or illness. informal, often humorous

have (or keep) your feet on the ground be (or remain) practical and sensible.

have something at your feet have something in your power or command.

keep your feet: see KEEP.

put your best foot forward embark on an undertaking with as much speed, effort, and determination as possible.

put foot hurry up; get a move on. South African informal

put your foot down ❶ adopt a firm policy when faced with opposition or disobedience. ❷ make a motor vehicle go faster by pressing the accelerator pedal with your foot. British informal

put your foot in it (or put your foot in your mouth) say or do something tactless or embarrassing; commit a blunder or indiscretion. informal

> **1992 Deirdre Madden** *Remembering Light & Stone* As the evening went on, and people

made a point of not talking to me, I realized that I'd put my foot in it.

put a foot wrong make any mistake in performing an action.

> **1999** *Times* For 71 holes of the Open he didn't put a foot wrong.

be run off your feet: see RUN.

six feet under: see SIX.

sweep someone off their feet quickly and overpoweringly charm someone.

think on your feet: see THINK.

vote with your feet: see VOTE.

footloose

footloose and fancy-free without any commitments or responsibilities; free to act or travel as you please.

> ❶ *Footloose* was used literally in the late 17th century to mean 'free to move the feet'. The sense 'without commitments' originated in late 19th-century US usage. *Fancy* in *fancy-free* is used in the sense of 'love' or 'the object of someone's affections'.

footsie

play footsie with someone ❶ touch someone's feet lightly with your own feet, usually under a table, as a playful expression of romantic interest. ❷ work with someone in a cosy and covert way.

footstep

follow (or tread) in someone's footsteps do as another person did before, especially in making a journey or following an occupation.

for

be for it be in imminent danger of punishment or other trouble. British informal

> **1997 Peter Carey** *Jack Maggs* The master. He reads to me. He would be reading to me now but I said I was ill and must go back to my bed. I'm for it if he finds me gone.

there's (or that's) — for you used ironically to indicate a particularly good example of a quality or thing mentioned.

> **1982 William Least Heat-Moon** *Blue Highways* Satchel Paige—there's a name for you—old Satch could fire the pill a hundred and five miles an hour.

forbidden

forbidden fruit a thing that is desired all the more because it is not allowed.

> ❶ The original *forbidden fruit* was that forbidden to Adam in the Garden of Eden: 'But of the tree of the knowledge of good and evil, thou shalt not eat of it' (Genesis 2:17).

force

force someone's hand make someone act prematurely or do something they dislike.

force the issue compel the making of an immediate decision.

force the pace adopt a fast pace in a race in order to tire out your opponents quickly.

in force in great strength or numbers.

> **1989** Amy Wilentz *The Rainy Season* They turned out in force, armed with machetes and cocomacaques.

forelock

take time by the forelock seize an opportunity. literary

> ❶ The Latin writer Phaedrus described Opportunity or Occasion as being bald except for a long forelock, a personification that was illustrated in Renaissance emblem books and was applied also to Time.

touch (*or* **tug**) **your forelock** raise a hand to your forehead in deference when meeting a person of higher social rank.

fork

Morton's fork: *see* MORTON.

forked

with forked tongue untruthfully or deceitfully. humorous

> ❶ The image is of the forked tongue of a snake, snakes being traditional symbols of treachery and deceit.

> **2002** *New York Times* Orpheus members have long spoken with forked tongues about conductors. They...make sweeping generalizations about them.

forlorn

a forlorn hope a faint remaining hope or chance; a desperate attempt.

> ❶ This expression developed in the mid 16th century from the Dutch expression *verloren hoop* 'lost troop'. The phrase originally denoted a band of soldiers picked to begin an attack, many of whom would not survive; the equivalent French phrase is *enfants perdus* 'lost children'. The current sense, which dates from the mid 17th century, arose from a misunderstanding of the etymology.

form

a matter of form: *see* MATTER.

fortune

fortune favours the brave a successful person is often one who is willing to take risks. proverb

the fortunes of war the unpredictable events of war.

a small fortune a large amount of money. informal

soldier of fortune: *see* SOLDIER.

forty

forty winks a short sleep or nap, especially during the day. informal

> ❶ This expression dates from the early 19th century, but *wink* in the sense of 'a closing of the eyes for sleep' is found from the late 14th century.

foul

foul your own nest do something damaging or harmful to yourself or your own interests.

> ❶ The proverb *it's an ill bird that fouls its own nest*, used of a person who criticizes or abuses their own country or family, has been found in English since the early 15th century.

founding

founding father someone who establishes an institution.

> ❶ *Founding Father* is used in particular of an American statesman at the time of the Revolution, especially a member of the Federal Constitutional Convention of 1787.

four

on all fours with equal with; presenting an exact analogy with.

> **1992** *Independent* President Saddam's occupation of Kuwait was, he declared, on all fours with Hitler's aggressions.

to the four winds: *see* to the wind *at* WIND.

fourth

the fourth estate the press; the profession of journalism.

> ❶ The three traditional Estates of the Realm (the Crown, the House of Lords, and the House of Commons) are now viewed as having been joined by the press, which is

regarded as having equal power. As early as 1843 Lord Macaulay stated: 'The gallery in which the reporters sit has become a fourth estate of the realm'.

fox

crazy like a fox: *see* CRAZY.

frame

be in (or out of) the frame ❶ be (*or* not be) eligible or the centre of attention. **❷** under suspicion or wanted (*or* not) by the police.

Frankenstein

Frankenstein's monster a thing that becomes terrifying or destructive to its maker.

> ❶ *Frankenstein* was the title of a novel written in 1818 by Mary Shelley. The scientist Frankenstein creates and brings to life a manlike monster which eventually turns on him and destroys him; Frankenstein is not the name of the monster itself, as is often assumed.

1991 John Kingdom *Local Government & Politics in Britain* The factories of the bourgeoisie had created another dangerous by-product, a Frankenstein's monster posing a constant sense of threat—the working class.

free

for free without cost or payment; free of charge. informal

1957 Godfrey Smith *The Friends* Back home we pay if we're ill…You don't expect to be ill for free.

free and easy informal and relaxed.

free, gratis, and for nothing without charge. humorous

free rein: *see* REIN.

it's a free country said when asserting that a course of action is not illegal or forbidden, often in justification of it.

make free with treat without ceremony or proper respect; take liberties with.

there's no such thing as a free lunch: *see* LUNCH.

freeze

freeze the balls off a brass monkey: *see* **brass monkey** *at* BRASS.

freeze your blood fill you with feelings of fear or horror.

> ❶ According to the medieval physiological scheme of the four humours in the human

body (melancholy, phlegm, blood, and choler), blood was the hot, moist element, so the effect of horror or fear in making the blood cold was to make it unable to fulfil its proper function of supplying the body with vital heat or energy. Compare with **make your blood run cold** (*at* BLOOD).

French

excuse (or pardon) my French used to apologize for swearing. informal

> ❶ *French* has been used since the late 19th century as a euphemism for bad language.

1992 Angela Lambert *A Rather English Marriage* A loony can change a bloody toilet-roll, pardon my French.

take French leave make an unannounced or unauthorized departure.

> ❶ This expression stems from the custom prevalent in 18th-century France of leaving a reception or entertainment without saying goodbye to your host or hostess.

fresh

be fresh out of something have just sold or run out of a supply of something. informal

break fresh ground: *see* **break new ground** *at* GROUND.

a breath of fresh air: *see* BREATH.

fresh as a daisy: *see* DAISY.

fresh blood: *see* **new blood** *at* BLOOD.

friend

a fair-weather friend someone who cannot be relied on in a crisis.

1998 *Spectator* The Americans gave up supplying gold on demand to other countries' central banks at £35 an ounce…when their fair-weather friends from London threatened to turn up and clean them out.

flexible friend: *see* FLEXIBLE.

a friend at court a person in a position to use influence on your behalf.

friends in high places people in senior positions who are able and willing to use their influence on your behalf.

fright

look a fright have a dishevelled or grotesque appearance. informal

frighten

frighten the daylights out of: *see* DAYLIGHT.

frighten the life out of: see LIFE.

frightened

frightened of your own shadow: see afraid of your own shadow *at* SHADOW.

be frightened out of your wits: see WIT.

be frightened to death: see DEATH.

frightener

put the frighteners on threaten or intimidate. British informal

> ❶ Literally, a *frightener* is a thug who intimidates victims on behalf of a gang.

> **1998 John Milne** *Alive & Kicking* She decides to put the frighteners on him by hiring me as a private detective.

fritz

go (or be) on the fritz (of a machine) stop working properly. North American informal

> ❶ The nature of any connection with *Fritz*, the derogatory nickname for a German, is uncertain. The related phrase *put the fritz on* means 'put a stop to something'.

frog

have a frog in your throat lose your voice or find it hard to speak because of hoarseness or an apparent impediment in your throat. informal

front

front of house ❶ the parts of a theatre in front of the proscenium arch. ❷ the business of a theatre that concerns the audience, such as ticket sales.

on the front burner: see on the back burner *at* BURNER.

frosty

it'll be a frosty Friday (in July) used to indicate that something is very unlikely to happen. Canadian informal

> **1990 Walter Stewart** *Right Church, Wrong Pew* It would be a frosty Friday in the middle of July before he would discuss personal affairs with the press.

froth

froth (or foam) at the mouth be very angry.

> ❶ This phrase stems from the involuntary production of large amounts of saliva from the mouth during a seizure or fit.

fruit

bear fruit have good results.

> ❶ This expression is a biblical metaphor, found, for example, in Matthew 13:23: 'But he that received seed into the good ground is he that heareth the word, and understandeth it; which also beareth fruit, and bringeth forth, some an hundredfold, some sixty, some thirty'.

frying

out of the frying pan into the fire from a bad situation to one that is worse.

fudge

fudge factor a figure which is included in a calculation in order to account for some unquantified but significant phenomenon or to ensure a desired result.

> ❶ *Fudge*, apparently originating in the mid 18th century as an exclamation of disgust or irritation, later acquired a specific verbal sense in printers' jargon, meaning to 'do work imperfectly or as best you can with the materials available'.

fuel

add fuel to the fire (or flames) (of a person or circumstance) cause a situation or conflict to become more intense, especially by provocative comments.

full

at full cock (of a firearm) with the cock lifted to the position at which the trigger will act.

at full stretch: see STRETCH.

come full circle: see CIRCLE.

in full cry: see CRY.

full as a goog: see GOOG.

the full monty: see MONTY.

full of beans: see BEAN.

full of years having lived to a considerable age. archaic

> ❶ *Full of years* is an expression originating in the Authorized Version of the Bible: 'an old man, and full of years' (Genesis 25:8).

full pelt: see PELT.

full steam (or speed) ahead used to indicate that you should proceed with as much speed or energy as possible.

in full fig: see FIG.

in full flight: see FLIGHT.

in full flow: *see* FLOW.

in full swing: *see* SWING.

not the full quid: *see* QUID.

not playing with a full deck: *see* DECK.

on a full stomach: *see* STOMACH.

to the full to the greatest possible extent.

full whack: *see* **top whack** *at* WHACK.

fullness

the fullness of your (*or* the) heart great or
overwhelming emotion. literary

in the fullness of time after a due length of
time has elapsed; eventually.

fun

poke fun at: *see* POKE.

fund

in funds having money to spend. British

funeral

it's (*or* that's) someone's funeral used to
warn someone that an unwise act or
decision is their own responsibility. informal

> **1996 Amitav Ghosh** *The Calcutta Chromosome*
> I'll turn a few pages for you; but remember, it
> was you who asked. It's your funeral.

funny

see the funny side of something appreciate
the humorous aspect of a situation or
experience.

fur

be all fur coat and no knickers have an
impressive or sophisticated appearance
which belies the fact that there is nothing
to substantiate it. British informal

fur and feather game animals and birds.

the fur will fly there will be serious, perhaps
violent, trouble. informal

> ❶ This phrase originated in the early 19th
> century, in the US. The image is of a furious
> fight between dogs or cats.

furiously

give someone furiously to think: *see* THINK.

furniture

part of the furniture a person or thing that
has been somewhere so long as to seem a
permanent, unquestioned, or invisible
feature of the scene. informal

fury

like fury with great energy or effort. informal

> ❶ This expression dates from the mid
> 19th century, but *fury* has been used of things
> that operate with irresistible force since the
> late 16th century (e.g. 'the fury of the sea').

> **1994–5** *Game Gazette* I was to fish it [the
> Zambesi] for the legendary Tiger
> fish…that…has a mouth of teeth like a
> canteen of cutlery and fights like fury.

fuse

light the fuse: *see* LIGHT.

future

future shock a state of distress or
disorientation due to rapid social or
technological change.

> ❶ This phrase was coined by the American
> writer Alvin Toffler in *Horizon* (1965), where
> he defines it as 'the dizzying disorientation
> brought on by the premature arrival of the
> future'.

Gg

gad

on (or upon) the gad on the move.

> ⓘ The noun *gad* is archaic and is now used only in this expression. The verb *gad* meaning 'go from one place to another in search of pleasure', is more familiar today; both may have their origins in an obsolete word *gadling*, meaning 'a wanderer or vagabond'.

gaff

blow the gaff reveal or let out a plot or secret.

> ⓘ The word *gaff* is recorded from the early 19th century, but its origins are uncertain.

gaiety

the gaiety of nations general cheerfulness or amusement. British

> ⓘ In *The Lives of the English Poets*, Samuel Johnson wrote about the death of the great actor David Garrick (1717–79), remarking that it 'has eclipsed the gaiety of nations and impoverished the public stock of harmless pleasure'.

gait

go your (or your own) gait pursue your own course. dated

> **1940** Herbert Read *Annals of Innocence* These are qualities to be enjoyed by non-poetic people: the poet must go his own gait.

gall

dip your pen in gall: *see* DIP.

wormwood and gall: *see* WORMWOOD.

gallery

play to the gallery act in an exaggerated or histrionic manner, especially in order to appeal to popular taste.

> ⓘ From the mid 17th century the highest seating in a theatre was called the gallery, and it was here that the cheapest seats—and the least refined members of the audience—were to be found. This figurative expression dates from the late 19th century.

game

ahead of the game: *see* AHEAD.

beat someone at their own game: *see* BEAT.

as game as Ned Kelly very brave. Australian

> ⓘ Ned Kelly (1855–80) was a famous Australian outlaw, the leader of a band of horse and cattle thieves and bank raiders operating in Victoria; he was eventually hanged at Melbourne.

the game is up the plan, deception, or crime is revealed or foiled.

game on ❶ a signal for play to begin in a game or match. ❷ said when you feel that a situation is about to develop in your favour. informal

> ❷ **1999** *FHM* She soon invited me back to her place for the other. Game on!

game over said when a situation is regarded as hopeless or irreversible.

> ⓘ This expression probably comes from the use of the phrase at the conclusion of a computer game.

> **2001** *Wall Street Journal* There's a finite amount of money available, and, if it runs out, game over.

give the game away inadvertently reveal your own or another's intentions.

the name of the game: *see* NAME.

off (or on) your game playing badly (or well).

on the game involved in prostitution. British informal

> ⓘ The phrase itself apparently dates from the late 19th century, but *game* in the sense of 'sexual activity' is much older. Shakespeare talks of 'daughters of the game' in *Troilus and Cressida* (1606) and from the early 17th century *gamester* was a term used to describe a lewd person.

the only game in town the best or most important of its kind; the only thing worth concerning yourself with. informal

> **1998** *Spectator* But there is . . . a sense of resentment that the big set-piece political interviews are not now the only game in town.

play games deal with someone or something in a way that lacks due seriousness or respect or deviates from the truth.

> **2000 Mike Gayle** *Turning Thirty* I couldn't stand him at first. I'd have a conversation with him and would come away feeling like he was playing games with me.

play someone's game advance another's plans, whether intentionally or not.

play the game behave in a fair or honourable way; abide by the rules or conventions.

> **1993 Andy McNab** *Bravo Two Zero* Shorncliffe was a nightmare, but I learned to play the game. I had to—there was nothing else for me.

two can play at that game: *see* TWO.

what's your (or the) game? what's going on?; what are you up to? informal

gamut

run the gamut experience, display, or perform the complete range of something.

> ❶ *Gamut* is a contraction of medieval Latin *gamma ut*, *gamma* being the lowest note in the medieval musical scale and *ut* the first of the six notes forming a hexachord. Together, therefore, they represent the full range of notes of which a voice or an instrument is capable.

> **1996** *Europe: Rough Guide* Russia's hotels run the gamut from opulent citadels run as joint-ventures with foreign firms to seedy pits inhabited by mobsters.

gangbusters

go gangbusters proceed very vigorously or successfully. North American informal

> ❶ Literally, a *gangbuster* is 'a person who assists in the vigorous or violent break-up of criminal gangs', from which the more general sense of 'a successful person' has developed. The phrase *like gangbusters* means 'vigorously and successfully'.

> **1994** *Wall Street Journal* Sotheby's glamorous semi-annual black tie auction of contemporary art was going gangbusters.

garbage

garbage in, garbage out incorrect or poor quality input inevitably produces faulty output.

> ❶ This expression is often abbreviated as *GIGO*. The phrase originated in the mid 20th century in the field of computing, but it can now have a more general application.

> **1987** *Washington Times* The computer rule 'garbage in, garbage out' applies to the human mind just as much as it does to the computer.

garden

everything in the garden is lovely (or rosy) all is well. informal

> ❶ *Everything in the garden is lovely* was an early 20th-century catchphrase, originating in a song popularized by the English music-hall artiste Marie Lloyd (1870–1922), and is used as an expression of general satisfaction and contentment.

lead someone up the garden path give someone misleading clues or signals. informal

> ❶ The earliest (early 20th-century) examples of this phrase use just *garden* rather than *garden path*, which suggests that the original context was of someone enticing a person they wanted to seduce or flirt with out into a garden. A North American variant of the phrase is *lead someone down the garden path*.

Garnet

all Sir Garnet highly satisfactory. informal, dated

> ❶ Sir Garnet Wolseley (1833–1913), leader of several successful military expeditions, was associated with major reforms in the army. He was the model for the 'modern Major-General' in Gilbert and Sullivan's *The Pirates of Penzance*.

gas

all gas and gaiters a satisfactory state of affairs. informal, dated

> ❶ This expression was first recorded in Charles Dickens' *Nicholas Nickleby* (1839): 'All is gas and gaiters'.

> **1961 P. G. Wodehouse** *Ice in the Bedroom* She cries 'Oh, Freddie darling!' and flings herself into his arms, and all is gas and gaiters again.

run out of gas run out of energy; lose momentum. North American informal

step on the gas press on the accelerator to make a car go faster. North American informal

gasket

blow a gasket ❶ suffer a leak in a gasket of an engine. ❷ lose your temper. informal

gasp

your (or the) last gasp the point of death, exhaustion, or completion.

1996 Will Hutton *The State We're In* The failure of the 1994 rail strike was the last gasp of an old order.

gate

get (*or* **be given**) **the gate** be dismissed from a job. North American informal

gatepost

between you and me and the gatepost: *see* **between you and me and the bedpost** *at* BEDPOST.

gauntlet

run the gauntlet go through an intimidating or dangerous crowd, place, or experience in order to reach a goal.

> ❶ This phrase alludes to the former military practice of punishing a wrongdoer by forcing him to run between two lines of men armed with sticks, who beat him as he passed. *Gauntlet* here has nothing to do with a glove, but is a version of an earlier word *gantlope*, itself taken from Swedish *gatloppe*, which meant 'lane course'.

throw down (*or* **take up**) **the gauntlet** issue (*or* accept) a challenge.

> ❶ In medieval times, a person issued a challenge by throwing their gauntlet (i.e. glove) to the ground; whoever picked it up was deemed to have accepted the challenge.

gear

change gear begin to move or act differently, usually more rapidly.

> ❶ This expression derives from literally engaging a different gear of a motor vehicle in order to alter its speed. Compare with *in gear* (with a gear engaged, and so ready for action) and its opposite *out of gear*. To *move up a gear* means literally 'change to a higher gear'; the phrase is often used figuratively to mean 'put more effort into an activity'.

give someone the gears harass or pester someone. Canadian

> **1989 Guy Vanderhaeghe** *Homesick* Whenever Daniel gave him the gears about overdressing, the old man grew sulky and grouchy.

genie

let the genie out of (*or* **put the genie back in**) **the bottle** let loose (*or* bring back under control) an unpredictable force, course of events, etc.

> ❶ A *genie* or *jinnee* in Arabian stories is a spirit that can adopt various forms and take a mischievous or benign hand in human affairs. The genie generally inhabits a lamp (compare with **Aladdin's lamp** *at* ALADDIN) or bottle from which someone can release it by the appropriate words or actions. The Arabic word appears in English in various transliterations; *genie* derives from French *génie* (from Latin *genius* meaning 'a tutelary spirit'), used by the French translators of *The Arabian Nights* because it was similar in form and sense to the Arabic word.

> **2002** *Chicago Tribune* Keeping the nuclear genie in the bottle has not been easy. India and Pakistan have both developed nuclear weapons in recent years.

gentleman

a gentleman's agreement an arrangement or understanding which is based on the trust of both or all parties, rather than being legally binding.

> **1991 Charles Anderson** *Grain: Entrepreneurs* There had been a 'gentleman's agreement' by the Grain Growers not to enter the markets of Saskatchewan Wheat Pool's predecessor.

the little gentleman in the velvet coat the mole. humorous

> ❶ This expression was a toast used by the Jacobites, supporters of the deposed James II and his descendants in their claim to the British throne. It referred to the belief that the death of King William III resulted from complications following a fall from his horse when it stumbled over a molehill. The phrase is found in various other forms, including *the wee gentleman in black velvet*.

genuine

the genuine article a person or thing considered to be an authentic and excellent example of their kind.

George

let George do it let someone else do the work or take the responsibility.

get

as — as all get out to a great or extreme extent. North American informal

> **1990 M. Scott Peck** *A Bed by the Window* She could be as huffy as all get out.

be out to get someone be determined to punish or harm someone.

don't get mad, get even used to advise in

favour of revenge rather than fruitless
rage. informal

> ❶ This expression was a saying popularized
> by the US president John F. Kennedy, who
> called it 'that wonderful law of the Boston
> Irish political jungle'.

1998 *New Scientist* The Wellcome Trust doesn't
get mad, it gets even.

get it together get yourself or a situation
organized or under control. informal

get-up-and-go energy, enthusiasm, and
initiative. informal

> ❶ A mid 19th-century US colloquialism was
> 'get up and get'.

get your own back have your revenge;
retaliate British informal

ghost

the ghost in the machine the mind viewed as
distinct from the body.

> ❶ This phrase was coined by the British
> philosopher Gilbert Ryle in *The Concept of
> Mind* (1949) for a viewpoint that he
> considered completely misleading.

the ghost walks money is available and
salaries will be paid.

> ❶ This expression has been explained in
> theatrical phrasebooks by the story that an
> actor playing the ghost of Hamlet's father
> refused to 'walk again' until the cast's
> overdue salaries had been paid.

give up the ghost ❶ (of a person) die. ❷ (of a
machine) stop working; break down,
especially permanently. ❸ stop making an
effort; give up hope.

> ❶ The Old English meaning of *ghost*, 'the
> soul or spirit as the source of life', survives
> only in this idiom.

look as if you have seen a ghost look very
pale and shocked.

not have (or stand) the ghost of a chance
have no chance at all.

gift

the gift of the gab the ability to speak with
eloquence and fluency.

> ❶ *Gab*, dating from the late 18th century,
> was an informal word for 'conversation or
> chatter'. In Scotland it was associated with
> *gab*, an early 18th-century dialect variant of
> *gob* meaning 'the mouth'.

the gift of tongues: *see* TONGUE.

God's (own) gift to —: *see* GOD.

in the gift of (of a church living or official
appointment) in the power of someone to
award.

look a gift horse in the mouth find fault with
what has been given or be ungrateful for an
opportunity.

> ❶ The Latin version of the proverb *don't
> look a gift horse in the mouth* (*noli... equi
> dentes inspicere donati*) was known to St
> Jerome in the early 5th century AD. The 16th-
> century English form was *do not look a given
> horse in the mouth*.

1998 *New Scientist* The JAMA paper offers this
advice to researchers involved in industry-
funded studies: 'At times it may be prudent...
to look a gift horse in the mouth'.

gild

gild the lily try to improve what is already
beautiful or excellent.

> ❶ This phrase adapts lines from
> Shakespeare's *King John*: 'To gild refined
> gold, to paint the lily... Is wasteful and
> ridiculous excess'.

gill

green about the gills: *see* GREEN.

gilt

take the gilt off the gingerbread make
something no longer appealing.

> ❶ Gingerbread was traditionally made in
> decorative forms that were then ornamented
> with gold leaf.

ginger

ginger group a highly active faction within a
party or movement that presses for
stronger action on a particular issue. informal

> ❶ An old horse dealer's trick (recorded from
> the late 18th century) to make a broken-
> down animal look lively was to insert ginger
> into its anus. From this developed the
> metaphorical phrase *ginger up*, meaning
> 'make someone or something more lively'; in
> the early 20th century the term *ginger group*
> arose, to refer to a highly active faction in a
> party or movement that presses for stronger
> action about something.

1970 *New Society* The appearance of ginger
groups to fight specific proposals, is not
necessarily a bad thing—particularly if the
established bodies aren't prepared to fight.

gingerbread

take the gilt off the gingerbread: *see* GILT.

gird

gird (up) your loins prepare and strengthen yourself for what is to come.

> ❶ This expression is of biblical origin, the idea being that the long, loose garments worn in the ancient Orient had to be hitched up to avoid impeding a person's movement. In 1 Kings 18:45–6, we find: 'And Ahab rode, and went to Jezreel. And . . . Elijah . . . girded up his loins, and ran before Ahab to the entrance of Jezreel'. The phrase was also used metaphorically in the New Testament: 'Wherefore gird up the loins of your mind, be sober, and hope to the end for the grace that is to be brought unto you . . .' (1 Peter 1:13).

girl

page three girl: *see* PAGE.

give

give and take ❶ mutual concessions and compromises. ❷ exchange of words and views.

give as good as you get respond with equal force or vehemence when attacked.

give someone or something best: *see* BEST.

give someone furiously to think: *see* THINK.

give the game (or show) away inadvertently reveal something secret or concealed.

give it to someone scold or punish someone. informal

give me — I prefer or admire a specified thing.

> **1998** BBC Vegetarian Good Food Iceberg lettuce is a massive Eighties con—give me a round lettuce any day.

give or take — to within — (used to express the degree or accuracy of a figure). informal

> **1991 Biyi Bandele-Thomas** The Man who Came in from the Back of Beyond Aged twenty-five give or take a few years, he spoke in a detached voice, like a judge passing the death sentence.

give up the ghost: *see* GHOST.

give someone what for punish or scold someone severely. British informal

give yourself airs: *see* AIR.

not give a damn (or hoot) not care at all. informal

> **1998 Penelope Lively** Spiderweb The boys knew that the teachers didn't like them and they didn't give a damn.

gizzard

stick in your gizzard be a source of great and continuing annoyance. informal

glad

give someone the glad hand offer someone a warm and hearty, but often insincere, greeting or welcome. informal

in your glad rags in your smartest clothes; in formal evening dress. informal

> **1922 H. B. Hermon-Hodge** Up Against It In Nigeria We all turned out in our glad rags to join in the procession.

glassy

the (or just the) glassy the most excellent person or thing. Australian informal

> ❶ In mid 20th-century surfing slang, a *glassy* is an extremely smooth wave offering excellent surfing conditions.

gleam

a gleam (or twinkle) in someone's eye ❶ a barely formed idea. ❷ a child who has not yet been conceived. humorous

glitter

all that glitters is not gold the attractive external appearance of something is not a reliable indication of its true nature. proverb

gloom

doom and gloom: *see* DOOM.

glory

crowning glory: *see* CROWNING.

go to glory die or be destroyed.

in your glory in a state of extreme joy or exaltation. informal

glove

fit like a glove (of clothes) fit exactly.

> **1989 T. M. Albert** Tales of an Ulster Detective McNinch invited him to try the shoe on his foot, which he did—and it fitted him like a glove.

the gloves are off (or with the gloves off or take the gloves off) used to express the notion that something will be done in an uncompromising or brutal way, without compunction or hesitation.

> ❶ The contrast implied in this phrase is with a gloved hand handling things gently or in a civilized way.

glutton

a glutton for punishment a person who is always eager to undertake hard or unpleasant tasks.

> ❶ *Glutton of —* was used figuratively from the early 18th century for someone inordinately fond of the thing specified, especially when translating the Latin phrase *helluo librorum* 'a glutton of books'. The possible origin of the present phrase is in early 19th-century sporting slang.

gnash

gnash your teeth feel or express anger or fury.

> ❶ The gnashing of teeth, along with weeping or wailing, is used throughout the Bible to express a mixture of remorse and rage (for example, in Matthew 8:12: 'But the children of the kingdom shall be cast out into outer darkness: there shall be weeping and gnashing of teeth').

> **1998** *Times* Prepare yourself for the usual wailing and gnashing of teeth after tomorrow's retail price index figures.

gnat

strain at a gnat: see STRAIN.

gnome

gnomes of Zurich Swiss financiers or bankers, regarded as having sinister influence. derogatory

> ❶ This phrase stems from a remark made by the British politician Harold Wilson in a speech in 1956: 'all the little gnomes in Zurich … about whom we keep on hearing'.

go

all systems go: see SYSTEM.

be all go be very busy or active. informal

from go to whoa from start to finish.

from the word go from the very beginning. informal.

> **1997 Bridget O'Connor** *Tell Her You Love Her* Mr Parker was in love with me almost from the word go.

go ape: see APE.

go-as-you-please untrammelled or free.

> **1998** *Canal Boat and Inland Waterways* Enjoy a go-as-you-please cruise aboard one of our all weather self drive luxury day boats.

go ballistic: see BALLISTIC.

go bananas: see BANANA.

go down with (all) guns firing fail or be beaten, but continue to offer resistance until the end.

go figure said to express the speaker's belief that something is inexplicable. North American informal

> **1999** *Massive* In the last election, the Tories got 19 per cent of the votes in Scotland and have no MPs there at all, while the Lib Dems got 13 per cent and have 10 MPs. Go figure.

go great guns: see GUN.

go halves (or shares) share something equally.

go (to) it act in a vigorous, energetic, or dissipated way. British informal

> **1995** *Times* While there is time, become an activist, disrupt political meetings. Go to it.

go postal: see POSTAL.

go the way of all flesh: see FLESH.

go the whole hog: see HOG.

go well used to express good wishes to someone leaving. South African

have a go ❶ make an attempt; act resourcefully. ❷ take independent or single-handed action against a criminal or criminals.

have a go at attack or criticize someone. chiefly British

make a go of be successful in something. informal

> ❶ An Australian and New Zealand variant of this expression is *make a do of it*, which dates from the early 20th century.

> **1987 Evelyn E. Smith** *Miss Melville Returns* He'd been unable to make a go of life in the city, and so he'd returned to the small New England village he came from.

on the go very active or busy. informal

to go (of food or drink from a restaurant or cafe) to be eaten or drunk off the premises. North American

goal

score an own goal ❶ (in football) score a goal by mistake against your own side. ❷ do something that has the unintended effect of harming your own interests. informal

> ❷ **1991 Brian MacArthur** *Despatches from the Gulf War* Television's mission to explain was taken to its outer limit and at times scored an own goal by developing a bias against understanding.

goalpost

move the goalposts unfairly alter the conditions or rules of a procedure during its course.

> **1989** *Dimensions* Many companies have, in recent years, moved the goalposts so that those who used to qualify no longer do so.

goat

get someone's goat irritate someone. informal

> **1998 Andrea Ashworth** *Once in a House on Fire* It got his goat when he caught me ... with my nose stuck in a book turned the wrong way up.

play (or **act**) **the (giddy) goat** fool around; act irresponsibly. informal

God

God's acre a churchyard. archaic

> ❶ This phrase comes from the German word *Gottesacker* meaning 'God's seed field' in which the bodies of the dead are 'sown'.

God's (own) gift to — the ideal or best possible person or thing for someone or something (used chiefly ironically or in negative statements).

> **1998** *Spectator* Their [the English] hooligans, their pressmen, hell, even their footballers behave as if they were God's own gift to sport.

God willing used to express the wish that you will be able to do as you intend or that something will happen as planned.

> ❶ This is an expression found in many cultures: compare with Latin *deo volente* or Arabic *inshallah*.

in the lap of the gods: *see* LAP.

little tin god a self-important person.

> ❶ *Tin* is implicitly contrasted here with precious metals. The phrase seems to have originated in Rudyard Kipling's *Plain Tales from the Hills*, where he described idols that he thought were given undeserved veneration: 'Pleasant it is for the Little Tin Gods When great Jove nods; But Little Tin Gods make their little mistakes In missing the hour when great Jove wakes'.

> **1987 Fannie Flagg** *Fried Green Tomatoes at the Whistle Stop Cafe* This little tin God in the polyester suit and the three-pound shoes. So smug, so self-important, with the nurses fluttering around him like geisha girls.

play God behave as if all-powerful or supremely important.

goes

anything goes there are no rules about acceptable behaviour or dress.

> ❶ This phrase appeared earlier, in the late 19th century, as *everything goes*.

as (or **so**) **far as it goes** bearing in mind its limitations (said when qualifying praise of something).

what goes around comes around the consequences of your actions will have to be dealt with eventually. proverb

who goes there? said by a sentry as a challenge.

going

going, going, gone! an auctioneer's traditional announcement that bidding is closing or closed, and that this is the last chance to have something. informal

going on — (or **going on for —**) approaching a specified time, age, or amount. humorous

> **1994 Janice Galloway** *Foreign Parts* Cassie, carrying this bloody windsurfing board through customs. Thirty-one going on fifteen.

have — going for you have a specified factor or factors in your favour. informal

> **1997 Marian Keyes** *Rachel's Holiday* All we really had going for us was our hair; mine was long and dark and hers was long and blonde.

while the going is good while conditions are favourable.

gold

fool's gold: *see* FOOL.

go gold (of a recording) achieve sales meriting a gold disc.

pot (or **crock**) **of gold** a large but distant or illusory reward.

> ❶ This expression alludes to the traditional story that a pot of gold is to be found by anyone who succeeds in reaching the end of a rainbow.

worth your weight in gold: *see* WEIGHT.

gold dust

like gold dust very valuable and rare.

golden

a golden age a period in the past when things were at their best, happiest, or most successful.

> ❶ According to Greek and Roman mythology, the Golden Age was the earliest and best age of the world, when human beings lived in a state of perfect happiness. The Ages of Silver, Brass, and Iron represented successive stages of a descent into barbarism and misery.

a golden calf something, especially wealth, as an object of excessive or unworthy worship.

> ❶ In the Bible, the golden calf was a statue of gold in the shape of a calf, made by Aaron in response to the Israelites' plea for a god while they awaited Moses' return from Mount Sinai, where he was receiving the Ten Commandments (Exodus, chapter 32).

a golden handshake a sum of money paid by an employer to a retiring or redundant employee.

> ❶ On the same principle, the phrase *a golden hello* was coined in the late 20th century. It is explained in an Appointments section of the *New Scientist* in 1998: 'Employers...especially in the financial sector, are offering "golden hellos". These are advances of up to £2000, sometimes given on acceptance of a job offer or with the first month's salary.'

the golden mean the avoidance of extremes.

> ❶ This phrase translates the Latin phrase *aurea mediocritas*, which comes from the Roman poet Horace's *Odes*.

the golden section the division of a line so that the whole is to the greater part as that part is to the smaller part.

> ❶ This is a mathematical term for a proportion known since the 4th century and mentioned in the works of the Greek mathematician Euclid. It has been called by several names, but the mid 19th-century German one *goldene Schnitt*, translating Latin *sectio aurea*, has given rise to the current English term.

gone

gone with the wind: *see* WIND.

gong

kick the gong around: *see* KICK.

good

all to the good to be welcomed without qualification.

as good as — very nearly —.

1997 *Cosmopolitan* If you are famous, you can't allow someone to diss you without retaliating—it's as good as admitting they're more important than you.

as good as gold extremely well-behaved.

as good as new in a very good condition or state, especially close to the original state after damage, injury, or illness.

be good news: *see* NEWS.

be in good company: *see* COMPANY.

be — to the good have a specified amount of profit or advantage.

> **1992** *Guardian* By then Sheffield were a goal to the good.

come up with (or **deliver) the goods** do what is expected or required of you. informal

get (or **have) the goods on someone** obtain (*or* possess) information about a person which may be used to their detriment. informal

good and — used as an intensifier before an adjective or adverb. informal

> **1998 Barbara Kingsolver** *The Poisonwood Bible* As soon as I had her good and terrified I'd slip away.

good oil reliable information. Australian informal

> ❶ This expression has behind it the image of oil that is used to lubricate a machine and so ensure that it runs well.

good Samaritan: *see* SAMARITAN.

have a (good) mind to do something: *see* MIND.

in good time ❶ with no risk of being late. ❷ in due course but without haste.

in someone's good books: *see* **in someone's bad books** *at* BOOK.

make good be successful.

no good to gundy no good at all. Australian informal

> **1955 Nina Pulliam** *I Traveled a Lonely Land* Just cards and races and booze—and fightin'. No good to Gundy!

one good turn deserves another: *see* TURN.

take something in good part not be offended by something.

up to no good doing or intending to do something wrong. informal

> **1997 Iain Sinclair** *Lights Out for the Territory* 'Here we are then,' he said, 'two boyos from the valleys up to no good in the big, wicked city.'

goog

full as a goog very drunk. Australian informal

> ❶ *Goog* is slang for 'egg', but its origins are uncertain.

goose

all someone's geese are swans someone habitually exaggerates the merits of undistinguished people or things.

> ❶ The goose is proverbially contrasted with the swan as being the clumsier, less elegant, and less distinguished bird; compare with **turn geese into swans** below.

cook someone's goose: *see* COOK.

kill the goose that lays the golden egg(s) destroy a reliable and valuable source of income.

> ❶ One of Aesop's fables tells the tale of a man who owned a miraculous goose that laid eggs of gold. However, he grew dissatisfied with its production of just one egg a day and killed it in the deluded expectation of finding a large quantity of gold inside it.

> **1999** *New York Times* Change is needed in the nation's drug policies ... But we need to address the problem carefully in a way that doesn't kill the goose that lays the golden egg.

turn geese into swans exaggerate the merits of people.

what's sauce for the goose is sauce for the gander: *see* SAUCE.

Gordian

cut the Gordian knot: *see* CUT.

gorge

cast the gorge at reject with loathing. dated

your gorge rises you are sickened or disgusted.

> ❶ *Gorge* is an obsolete term from falconry, meaning 'a meal for a hawk'; from this derives the more general sense of 'the contents of the stomach'.

gory

the gory details the explicit details of something.

> **1988** **David Carpenter** *God's Bedfellows* She starts telling me some of the gory details ... it was cancer ... and everybody knew he was dying.

gospel

gospel truth the absolute truth. informal

> **1998** *Mirror* Any research that puts down men is accepted as gospel truth these days.

Gotham

a wise man of Gotham: *see* WISE.

gourd

out of your gourd ❶ out of your mind; crazy. ❷ under the influence of alcohol or drugs. North American informal

> ❶ **1988** **Jay McInerney** *The Story of My Life* After ten minutes I'm bored out of my gourd.
> ❷ **1993** **Stephen King** *Gerald's Game* I was 'on medication' (this is the technical hospital term for 'stoned out of one's gourd').

grab

up for grabs available; obtainable. informal

> ❶ This phrase was originally mid 20th-century US slang, relating especially to a woman who is open to sexual advances.

grace

be in someone's good (*or* bad) graces be regarded by someone with favour (*or* disfavour).

fall from grace ❶ fall into a state of sin. ❷ fall from favour.

> ❷ **1998** **Martin Booth** *The Industry of Souls* He was an officer in the local militia before he arrested a young official ... for corruption and fell from grace.

with good (*or* bad) grace in a willing and happy (*or* resentful and reluctant) manner.

grade

make the grade succeed; reach the desired standard. informal

grain

against the grain contrary to the natural inclination or feeling of someone or something.

> ❶ This phrase alludes to the fact that wood is easier to cut along the line of the grain than across or against it.

a grain of mustard seed a small thing capable of vast development.

> ❶ Black mustard seed grows to a great height. In Matthew 13:31–2 it is stated that 'mustard seed ... indeed is the least of all seeds: but when it is grown, it is the greatest among herbs'.

g

grand

a (*or* the) grand old man of a man long and highly respected in a particular field.

> ❶ Recorded from 1882, and popularly abbreviated as *GOM*, *Grand Old Man* was the nickname of the British statesman William Ewart Gladstone (1809–98), who went on to win his last election in 1892 at the age of eighty-three.

grandeur

delusions of grandeur: *see* DELUSION.

grandmother

teach your grandmother to suck eggs presume to advise a more experienced person.

> ❶ The proverb *you can't teach your grandmother to suck eggs* has been used since the early 18th century as a caution against any attempt by the ignorant or inexperienced to instruct someone wiser or more knowledgeable.

grape

sour grapes: *see* SOUR.

grapevine

hear something on the grapevine acquire information by rumour or by unofficial communication.

> ❶ This phrase comes originally from an American Civil War expression, when news was said to be passed 'by grapevine telegraph'. Compare with **bush telegraph** (*at* TELEGRAPH).

grasp

grasp at straws: *see* clutch at straws *at* STRAW.

grasp the nettle tackle a difficulty boldly. British

> ❶ This expression refers to a belief (recorded from the late 16th century onwards) enshrined in a rhyme quoted in Sean O'Casey's *Juno and the Paycock* (1925): 'If you gently touch a nettle it'll sting you for your pains; grasp it like a lad of mettle, an' as soft as silk remains'.

> 1998 *New Scientist* The problem was that governments failed to grasp the nettle and scrap the system.

grass

at the grass roots at the level of the ordinary voter; among the rank and file of a political party.

the grass is always greener other people's lives or situations always seem better than your own.

> ❶ This is a shortened form of the proverb 'the grass is always greener on the other side of the fence', usually used as a caution against dissatisfaction with your own lot in life. There are a number of sayings about the attractions of something distant or inaccessible, for example *blue are the faraway hills*.

not let the grass grow under your feet not delay in acting or taking an opportunity.

put someone or something out to grass ❶ put an animal out to graze. ❷ force someone to retire; make someone redundant. informal

grasshopper

knee-high to a grasshopper: *see* KNEE-HIGH.

grave

dig your own grave: *see* DIG.

have one foot in the grave: *see* FOOT.

silent (*or* quiet) as the grave very quiet.

take the (*or* your etc.) secret to the grave die without revealing a secret.

turn (*or* turn over) in their grave used to express the opinion that something would have caused anger or distress in someone who is now dead.

> 1998 *Spectator* There was a lot of buzz at Jeff Koons's studio . . . But the grinding noise one heard was Peter Fuller turning in his grave.

graven

a graven image a carved representation of a god used as an object of worship.

> ❶ This expression is from the second of the Ten Commandments: 'Thou shalt not make unto thee any graven image' (Exodus 20:4).

gravy

board the gravy train obtain access to an easy source of financial gain. informal

> ❶ *Gravy* is an informal term for 'money easily acquired' and *gravy train* is perhaps an alteration of *gravy boat*, a long, narrow jug used for serving gravy.

grease

grease (or oil) someone's palm bribe someone. informal

> ❶ This phrase comes from the practice of applying grease to a machine to make it run smoothly. The same expression exists in French as *graisser la patte*. The form with *palm* is now predominant but *hand* appears in the earliest recorded versions of the idiom, dating from the 16th century.

> **1998** *Economist* Licences to run a shop [in Italy] . . . have caused many an official's palm to be greased.

grease the wheels make things go smoothly, especially by paying the expenses.

greased

like greased lightning: *see* **like lightning** *at* LIGHTNING.

greasy

greasy spoon a cheap, run-down restaurant or cafe serving fried foods.

> **1968** **Len Deighton** *Only When I Larf* Bob said he was hungry and wanted to pull up at every greasy spoon we passed.

great

the great and the good distinguished and worthy people collectively. often ironic

> **1998** *New Scientist* But last year, an ad hoc committee of the Internet's great and good unveiled its own plan.

great and small of all sizes, classes, or types.

> **1997** *Times Education Supplement* You are strongly advised to keep well clear of all creatures great and small.

a great one for a habitual doer of; an enthusiast for.

> **1994** **Romesh Gunesekera** *Reef* Early on I learned the value of making lists from watching Mister Salgado. He was a great one for lists.

Greek

it's all Greek to me I can't understand it at all. informal

> ❶ *Greek* meaning 'unintelligible language or gibberish' is recorded from the 16th century. In Shakespeare's *Julius Caesar*, Casca, having noted that Cicero speaks Greek, adds 'for mine own part, it was Greek to me'.

beware (or fear) the Greeks bearing gifts if rivals or enemies show apparent generosity or kindness, you should be suspicious of their motives. proverb

> ❶ This proverb refers to the Trojan priest Laocoon's warning in Virgil's *Aeneid*: '*timeo Danaos et dona ferentes*', in which he warns his countrymen against taking into their city the gigantic wooden horse that the Greeks have left behind on their apparent departure. The fall of Troy results from their failure to heed this warning.

green

green about (or around or at) the gills looking or feeling ill or nauseous. informal

> ❶ A person's *gills* are the fleshy parts between the jaw and the ears: this sense of the word dates from the early 17th century. Other colours are occasionally used to indicate a sickly appearance; much less common is *rosy about the gills* indicating good health.

green light permission to go ahead with a project.

> ❶ The green light referred to is the traffic signal indicating that traffic is free to move forward. Red and green lights were in use from the late 19th century in railway signals, but this figurative use of green light appears to date from the mid 20th century.

> **1997** *New Scientist* Zemin even got the green light to buy nuclear power plants.

green with envy very envious or jealous.

the green-eyed monster jealousy. literary

> ❶ Green is traditionally the colour of jealousy, as shown in the previous idiom *green with envy* and in this one, where the green-eyed monster is jealousy personified. This expression is a quotation from Shakespeare's *Othello*, where Iago warns: 'O! beware my lord of jealousy; It is the green-eyed monster which doth mock The meat it feeds on'.

grey

a grey area an ill-defined situation or field not readily conforming to a category or to an existing set of rules.

> ❶ In the 1960s, *grey areas* in British planning vocabulary referred to places that were not in as desperate a state as slums but which were in decline and in need of rebuilding.

> **2001** *Rough Guide to Travel Health* In theory, it should be a cinch to diagnose appendicitis, but in practice it's much more of a grey area.

grief

come to grief have an accident; meet with disaster.

> **2000 R. W. Holden** *Taunton Cider & Langdons* The historian...will see no trace of the battlefield where Charles's grandson, the Duke of Monmouth, came to grief.

give someone grief be a nuisance to someone. informal

> **1998** *Times* One of the passengers who'd been giving the cabin crew grief started yelling, 'We've had a near miss.'

grig

merry (or lively) as a grig full of fun; extravagantly lively.

> ❶ The meaning and origin of the word *grig* are unknown. Samuel Johnson conjectured in his *Dictionary* that it referred to 'anything below the natural size'. A sense that fits in with the *lively* version of this idiom is 'a young or small eel in fresh water'. The phrases *merry grig* and *merry Greek*, meaning 'a lively, playful person', were both in use in the mid 16th century, but it is impossible to establish the precise relationship between them or to be certain which may be an alteration of the other.

grim

like (or for) grim death with intense determination.

> **1989 Jonathan Gash** *Jade Woman* Here and there a greenish scumble of vegetation hung on for grim death.

the Grim Reaper a personification of death in the form of a cloaked skeleton wielding a large scythe.

grin

grin and bear it suffer pain or misfortune in a stoical manner.

> ❶ The usual modern sense of *grin* is less sinister than its earliest senses: when it entered the language it primarily meant 'an act of showing the teeth' or 'a snarl'. From the mid 17th century to the mid 18th century, a *grin* was generally used in a derogatory way or in unfavourable contrast to a cheerful *smile*. The sense of *grin* in *grin and bear it* retains the earlier associations with showing your teeth in a grimace of pain or anger. *Grin and abide* is recorded as a proverb in the late 18th century; the modern version dates from the late 19th century.

grind

grind to a halt (or come to a grinding halt) move more and more slowly and then stop.

> **1999** *Times* Traffic is expected to grind to a halt throughout the West Country as up to a million sightseers make the trip.

grindstone

keep your nose to the grindstone work hard and continuously.

> ❶ A *grindstone* was a thick revolving disc of stone on which knives and tools were sharpened. Appearing in various forms since the mid 16th century, this idiom originally referred to getting mastery over someone else by forcing them to work without a break.

grip

come (or get) to grips with ❶ engage in physical combat with. ❷ begin to deal with or understand.

get a grip keep or recover your self-control.

> **2000 Jo-Ann Goodwin** *Danny Boy* I took a deep breath, trying desperately to get a grip, to hold myself together.

grist

grist to the mill experience, material, or knowledge which can be turned to good use.

> ❶ *Grist* in the sense of 'corn that is to be ground' is now used only in this phrase and in the proverb *all is grist that comes to the mill*. The word is related to Old Saxon *gristgrimmo* meaning 'gnashing of teeth'.

grit

true grit strength of character; stamina. informal

> ❶ *Grit* in this colloquial sense originated in early 19th-century US English.

Grody

Grody to the max unspeakably awful. US informal

> ❶ *Grody* is probably an alteration of *grotesque* and *to the max* of *to the maximum point*.

groove

in (or into) the groove ❶ performing well or confidently, especially in an established pattern. ❷ indulging in relaxed and spontaneous enjoyment, especially dancing. informal

> **ⓘ** A *groove* is the spiral track cut in a gramophone record that forms the path for the needle. *In the groove* is first found in the mid 20th century, in the context of jazz, and it gave rise to the adjective *groovy*, which initially meant 'playing or able to play jazz or similar music well'.

gross

by the gross in large numbers or amounts.

> **ⓘ** A *gross* was formerly widely used as a unit of quantity equal to twelve dozen; the word comes from the French *gross douzaine*, which literally means 'large dozen'.

ground

break new (or fresh) ground do something innovative which is considered an advance or positive benefit.

> **ⓘ** Literally, to break new ground is to do preparatory digging or other work prior to building or planting something. In North America the idiom is *break ground*.

cut the ground from under someone's feet do something which leaves someone without a reason or justification for their actions or opinions. informal

get in on the ground floor become part of an enterprise in its early stages. informal

get off the ground (or get something off the ground) start (or cause to start) happening or functioning successfully.

go to ground ❶ (of a fox or other animal) enter its earth or burrow to hide, especially when being hunted. ❷ (of a person) hide or become inaccessible, usually for a prolonged period.

have your feet on the ground: see FOOT.

on the ground in a place where real, practical work is done.

on your own ground on your own territory or concerning your own range of knowledge or experience.

prepare the ground make it easier for something to occur or be developed.

run someone or something to ground: see **run someone or something to earth** at RUN.

thick (or thin) on the ground existing (or not existing) in large numbers or amounts.

work (or run) yourself into the ground exhaust yourself by working or running very hard. informal

grove

groves of Academe the academic community. literary

> **ⓘ** This phrase alludes to the Roman poet Horace's *Epistles*, in which he says: *Atque inter silvas Academi quaerere verum* 'and seek for truth in the groves of Academe'. The Academia was a grove near ancient Athens where a number of philosophers, Plato among them, taught their pupils.

grow

grow on trees be plentiful or easily obtained.

> **1996 Nozipo Maraire** *Zenzele* Children these days think that money grows on trees!

guard

lower (or drop or let down) your guard ❶ relax your defensive posture, leaving yourself vulnerable to attack. ❷ reduce your level of vigilance or caution.

> **ⓘ** This is an expression connected in its literal sense with boxing, as is its opposite *raise your guard* meaning 'adopt a defensive posture'.

guernsey

get a guernsey ❶ be selected for a football team. ❷ gain recognition or approbation. Australian informal

> **ⓘ** A *guernsey* is a type of knitted shirt or sweater; in Australia the word is specifically applied to a football shirt.

guess

anybody's guess a totally unpredictable matter. informal

> **1999 Jason Elliot** *An Unexpected Light* The most likely scenario was a government alliance with the forces of the north, although it was anyone's guess how long such a Faustian pact might last.

by guess and by God without specific guidance or direction.

> **ⓘ** This expression was originally used in a nautical context, where it meant to steer blind, without the guidance of landmarks. The alternative *by guess and by Godfrey* is also sometimes found.

guest

be my guest please do. informal

1988 Jay McInerney *The Story of My Life* I'll hurt myself, Mannie screams. Be my guest, says Rebecca.

gullet

stick in your gullet: *see* **stick in your throat** *at* THROAT.

gum tree

up a gum tree in or into a predicament. informal

> ❶ This phrase is now found mainly in British English, but the phrase is recorded in the early 19th century in the USA, where *possum up a gum tree* was the title of a song or dance.

> **1992** *Economist* If they should end up seeking a deal with the Unionists, offers of devolution will lead ministers straight up a gum tree.

gun

a big gun: *see* **a big cheese** *at* BIG.

blow great guns be very windy. informal

go down with (all) guns firing: *see* GO.

go great guns perform forcefully, vigorously, or successfully. informal

> **1913** *Field* A moment later Louvois shot out, passed Sanquhar and Fairy King, and going great guns...beat the favourite by a head.

jump the gun: *see* JUMP.

smoking gun: *see* SMOKING.

stick to your guns refuse to compromise or change, despite criticism. informal

> ❶ The image here is of a soldier maintaining his position under enemy fire.

> **1998** *New Scientist* Researchers have bravely stuck to their guns as they went about seeking public funds.

top gun a (or the) most important person.

under the gun under great pressure. North American informal

with (all) guns blazing with great determination and energy, often without thought for the consequences. informal

gut

—your guts out perform a specified action as hard or as fully as possible. informal

> **2000 Anthony Bourdain** *Kitchen Confidential* He'll take them out, get them liquored up so they blab their guts out, and I'll have a full report by noon next.

hate someone's guts feel a strong hatred for someone. informal

have someone's guts for garters punish or rebuke someone severely. informal

gutser

come a gutser suffer a failure or defeat. informal

> ❶ *Gutser* (also spelled *gutzer*) is explained in Fraser and Gibbons' *Soldier and Sailor Words* (1925) as 'pre-war slang, and an old term among Scottish boys for falling flat on the water in diving, instead of making a clean header'. In air-force slang *come* (or *fetch*) a *gutser* meant 'crash'.

gyp

give someone gyp cause pain or severe discomfort to someone. British informal

> ❶ *Gyp* may be a dialect contraction of *gee-up*, a word of command used to urge a horse to move faster, the connection being that, in this phrase, whatever is giving someone *gyp* is preventing them from resting or taking things easy.

Hh

habit

kick the habit: *see* KICK.

hackles

make someone's hackles rise make someone angry or indignant.

> ❶ *Hackles* are the long feathers on the neck of a fighting cock or the hairs on the top of a dog's neck, which are raised when the animal is angry or excited.

hail

hail-fellow-well-met showing excessive familiarity.
> **1979 Steven Levenkron** *The Best Little Girl in the World* Harold was accustomed to hail-fellow-well-met salesmen and deferential secretaries and even irate accountants.

hair

hair of the dog a small quantity of alcohol taken as a remedy for a hangover. informal

> ❶ The full form of this phrase is *hair of the dog that bit you*. Hair from a rabid dog was at one time thought to be a remedy against the effects of its bite; in this expression, the recommended cure for a hangover is a small amount of the cause of the problem.

> **1987 Bruce Allen Powe** *The Ice Eaters* Murray, still feeling the effects of the previous evening, had suggested they go into a bar because he needed a hair of the dog.

in (*or* **out of**) **someone's hair** annoying (*or* ceasing to annoy) someone. informal

keep your hair on! used to urge someone not to panic or lose their temper. British informal

let your hair down behave wildly or uninhibitedly. informal

make someone's hair stand on end alarm or horrify someone.

neither hide nor hair of: *see* HIDE.

not turn a hair remain apparently unmoved or unaffected.

put hair (*or* **hairs**) **on your chest** (of alcoholic drink) revive your strength. informal

split hairs make small and overfine distinctions.

> ❶ This expression was first recorded in the late 17th century. *Split straws*, dating from the 19th century, is a less common version.

half

a — and a half a particular person or thing considered as an impressive example of the kind specified. informal
> **1998 Sarah Waters** *Tipping the Velvet* The daughter must be a beauty and a half...if the mother is so eager to keep her safe and close, away from young men's eyes.

at half cock when only partly ready. informal

> ❶ *At half cock* is used of a firearm with the cock lifted but not moved to the position at which the trigger will act. It is usually found in *go off at half cock* or *go off half-cocked* meaning 'go ahead without making proper preparation and therefore fail'.

half the battle: *see* BATTLE.

half a chance the slightest opportunity. informal
> **1970 Nina Bawden** *The Birds on the Trees* Give her half a chance and she'll make you think black's white.

half an eye: *see* EYE.

half a loaf not as much as you want but better than nothing.

> ❶ This phrase alludes to the proverb *half a loaf is better than no bread*, which has been in use since the mid 16th century.

the half of it the most important part or aspect of something. informal
> **1987 George Turner** *Sea & Summer* Mum...would ask, 'But is this true?' and Billy...would tell her that wasn't the half of it.

have a mind to do something: *see* MIND.

how the other half lives: *see* OTHER HALF.

not do things by halves do things thoroughly or extravagantly.

not half ❶ not nearly as. ❷ not at all. informal ❸ to an extreme degree; very much so. British informal

too — **by half** used to emphasize something bad. British

> **1994** *Independent on Sunday* The idea that moving a few pot plants around a room can bring its occupant prosperity and well-being...seems too superstitious by half.

your better half: see BETTER.

halfway

a halfway house ❶ a compromise. ❷ the halfway point in a progression. ❸ a place where ex-prisoners, mental patients, etc. can stay while they become reaccustomed to normal life.

> ❶ In the late 18th century, *a halfway house* was an inn or other establishment halfway between two places or at the midpoint of a journey.

Hamlet

Hamlet without the prince a performance or event taking place without the principal actor.

> ❶ The phrase comes from an account given in the *Morning Post* of September 1775. The member of a theatrical company who was to play Hamlet in a production of Shakespeare's play ran off with an innkeeper's daughter before the performance; when the play was announced to the audience, they were told 'the part of Hamlet [was] to be left out, for that night'.

hammer

come (*or* **go**) **under the hammer** be sold at an auction.

hammer something home: see **drive something home** at HOME.

hammer and tongs with great energy and noise.

> ❶ The image here is of a blacksmith striking the hot iron removed from the forge with a pair of tongs.

> **1996 Emma Lathen** *Brewing Up a Storm* The big fight she had with Sean Cushing. They were going at it hammer and tongs.

hammering

take a hammering ❶ be subjected to harsh treatment. ❷ be heavily defeated. informal

hand

all hands the entire crew of a ship.

> ❶ A US variant of this phrase is *all hands and the cook*, meaning 'absolutely everyone available', since the cook would not normally be expected to do the work of other team members except in cases of dire emergency. *All hands on deck* or *all hands to the pumps*, in addition to their literal shipboard senses, are also used to indicate that all members of a team are required to be involved.

be a dab hand at: see DAB.

bind (*or* **tie**) **someone hand and foot** severely restrict someone's freedom to act or make decisions.

do something with one hand (tied) behind your back do something easily.

get (*or* **keep**) **your hand in** become (*or* remain) practised in something.

get your hands dirty: see DIRTY.

give (*or* **lend**) **a hand** assist in an action or enterprise.

give someone the glad hand: see GLAD.

hand in glove in close collusion or association.

> ❶ This phrase appeared earlier (in the late 17th century) as *hand and glove*; the current form gained ground from the late 18th century.

a hand's turn a stroke of work. informal

> **1982 Rodney Hall** *Just Relations* Rich was she? A wallowing pig in jewels and wicked money she never did a hand's turn to earn for herself?

(from) hand to mouth satisfying only your immediate needs because of lack of money for future plans and investments.

> **1960 Lynne Reid Banks** *The L-Shaped Room* I'm twenty-eight years old and I'm still living from hand to mouth like a bloody tramp.

hands down (especially of winning) easily and decisively.

> ❶ Originally a horse-racing expression, *win hands down* meant that a jockey was so certain of victory in the closing stages of a race that he could lower his hands, thereby relaxing his hold on the reins and ceasing to urge on his horse.

hands off! used to warn someone against touching or interfering with something.

have your hand in the till: see **have your fingers in the till** at TILL.

make (*or* **lose** *or* **spend**) **money hand over fist** make (*or* lose *or* spend) money very rapidly. informal

ⓘ This phrase first appeared in the mid 18th century as *hand over hand*. Found in nautical contexts, it referred to the movement of a person's hands when rapidly climbing a rope or hauling it in. By the mid 19th century, *hand over hand* was being used to mean 'advancing continuously and rapidly', especially of one ship pursuing another. *Hand over fist* is first recorded in the early 19th century, also in a nautical context, but it was soon used more generally to indicate speed, especially in the handling of money.

1991 Simon Winchester *Pacific* Japan continued making money hand over fist, the American trade deficit became steadily larger and larger.

on (*or* **off**) **someone's hands** having (*or* not having) to be dealt with or looked after by the person specified.

put your hands together applaud.

put your hands up raise your hands in surrender or to signify assent or participation.

the right hand doesn't know what the left hand's doing there is a state of confusion or a failure of communication within a group or organization.

set (*or* **put**) **your hand to** start work on.

ⓘ A fuller version of this phrase is *set your hand to the plough*, which alludes to Luke 9:62: 'No man, having put his hand to the plough, and looking back, is fit for the kingdom of God'.

sit on your hands: *see* SIT.

take a hand in become influential in determining something; intervene.

1988 *Shetland Times* The amenity trust is also taking a hand in restoring two old gravestones in the Ollaberry kirkyard.

turn your hand to something undertake an activity different from your usual occupation.

1994 Barbara Anderson *All the Nice Girls* Win had always told him he was an able man, a fixer, one who could turn his hand to anything.

wait on someone hand and foot attend to all of someone's needs or requests, especially when this is regarded as unreasonable.

1955 L. P. Hartley *A Perfect Woman* He has everything he wants and servants who wait on him hand and foot.

wash your hands of: *see* WASH.

with your hand in the cookie jar: *see* COOKIE.

handshake

golden handshake: *see* GOLDEN.

handsome

handsome is as handsome does character and behaviour are more important than good looks. proverb

ⓘ In this particular form the proverb dates from the mid 17th century. When used of behaviour, *handsome* really means 'chivalrous' or 'genteel', though in this saying it is taken to refer to good looks. The original sense is made clear in the earlier version: *goodly is he that goodly dooth*.

hang

get the hang of something learn how to operate or do something. informal

1990 Roddy Doyle *The Snapper* He was pretending to time them . . . because he couldn't get the hang of the stop-watch Bertie'd got him.

hang by a thread: *see* THREAD.

hang fire delay or be delayed in taking action or progressing.

ⓘ In the late 18th century, *hang fire* was used to refer to the action of a firearm that was slow in communicating the fire through the vent to the charge and so did not go off immediately.

hang a left (*or* **right**) make a left (*or* right) turn. US informal

hang loose: *see* LOOSE.

hang of a — (*or* **a hang of**) to a very high degree; very great. South African informal

ⓘ In this expression *hang* is probably being used as a euphemism for *hell*.

1945 Frank Sargeson *When the Wind Blows* All this was because Charlie was hang of a funny to be with.

hang someone out to dry leave someone in a difficult or vulnerable situation. informal

ⓘ The image here is of hanging wet washing on a clothes line to dry. The idea of 'flapping uselessly or ineffectually' like clothes drying in the wind is also behind the cricketing metaphor *hanging your bat out to dry*, which dates from the late 19th century and means 'holding your bat away from your body at an ineffectual angle'.

1998 *Spectator* We point out that another MP . . . has been hung out to dry for failing to declare what was (relative to this) a minuscule interest.

hang tough be or remain inflexible or firmly resolved. North American informal

> **1992 Randall Kenan** *Let the Dead Bury their Dead* Obviously, he intended to hang tough at first, but apparently Miss Jesse's psychic bullwhip lashed out and snap-crackled his brain.

hang up your boots stop working; retire. informal

> ❶ *Boots* are seen in this expression as part of a person's working clothes. A common Canadian variant is *hang up your skates*.

> **1997** *Farmers Weekly* The hard fact is that all farmers, whether the pension scheme is attractive or not, are, mostly, reluctant to hang their boots up.

hang your hat be resident. North American informal

> **2001 Kevin Sampson** *Outlaws* End of the day though it ain't the Royal and that is where I want to hang my hat.

let it all hang out be uninhibited or relaxed. informal

not care (or give) a hang not care at all. informal

> ❶ *Hang* here is a late 19th-century euphemism for *damn*.

hanging

a hanging offence a fault or crime so serious that the perpetrator should be executed.

> **1998** *Spectator* It is hardly a hanging offence to overlook telegrams about a small African country, but surely the Prime Minister must read JIC reports?

happy

happy as a sandboy extremely happy; perfectly contented with your situation.

> ❶ An 1823 dictionary describes a *sandboy* as an urchin who sold sand in the streets, and according to the same source the expression *jolly as a sandboy* was already proverbial by that date for 'a merry fellow who has tasted a drop'. A common British version of the phrase is *happy as Larry*, Larry being a pet name for *Lawrence*. This saying is sometimes connected with the renowned boxer Larry Foley (1847–1917); on the other hand, it may owe something to *larry*, a dialect word used by Thomas Hardy, meaning 'a state of excitement'. The North American version is *happy as a clam*, which apparently originated in the early 19th century on the east coast, where clams are plentiful: the full version *happy as a clam at high water* explains the source of the clam's satisfaction.

happy hunting ground a place where success or enjoyment is obtained.

> ❶ This phrase originally referred to the optimistic hope of Native Americans that the afterlife will be spent in a country where there are good hunting grounds.

> **1991** *Antique Collector* With Old Master drawings still considered an undervalued genre, this should prove a happy hunting ground for those in search of a bargain.

hard

be hard put to find it very difficult to.

> **2001 Marc Blake** *24 Karat Schmooze* He wore an Armani suit with a navy shirt, a club tie (although the vintners would have been hard put to name the actual club) and a Freemasonry pin.

hard as nails ❶ very hard. ❷ (of people) insensitive or callous; without pity.

hard as the nether millstone callous and unyielding.

> ❶ The *nether millstone* is the lower of the two millstones by which corn is ground. The phrase alludes to Job 41:24: 'His heart is as firm as a stone, and as hard as a piece of the nether millstone'.

hard at it busily working. informal

> **1997** *Independent* I leave home … just after 6am each day and I'm hard at it by 7.30.

a hard case ❶ a tough or intractable person. ❷ an amusing or eccentric person. Australian & New Zealand

a hard nut to crack a person or thing that is difficult to understand or influence. informal

a hard row to hoe: *see* ROW.

the hard way through suffering or learning from the unpleasant consequences of mistakes.

> **1996 Nozipo Maraire** *Zenzele* I think she understands better than the rest of us that we are at heart one family, for she has had to learn the hard way.

play hard to get deliberately adopt an aloof or uninterested attitude, typically in order to make yourself more attractive or interesting. informal

put the hard word on ask a favour of someone, especially a sexual or financial favour. Australian & New Zealand informal

> **1997 Derek Hansen** *Sole Survivor* But if he'd come to put the hard word on her, why hadn't he picked a more appropriate time? Midmorning had never struck her as particularly conducive to romance.

a hard nut: *see* **a tough nut** *at* NUT.

hare

mad as a March hare: *see* **mad as a hatter** *at* MAD.

run with the hare and hunt with the hounds try to remain on good terms with both sides in a conflict or dispute. British

> ❶ This expression has been in use since the mid 15th century.

start a hare raise a topic of conversation. British, dated

> ❶ The rapid twisting and running of a hunted hare is here used as a metaphor for the pursuit of a topic in an animated conversation, especially one in which the participants hold strong views.

harm

out of harm's way in a safe place.

> **1996** Frank McCourt *Angela's Ashes* Take down the Pope and hide him in the coal hole . . . where he won't be seen and he'll be out of harm's way.

someone or something wouldn't harm a fly: *see* **someone or something wouldn't hurt a fly** *at* FLY.

there is no harm in — the course of action specified may not guarantee success but is at least unlikely to have unwelcome repercussions.

> **1997** Arundhati Roy *The God of Small Things* He decided that since she couldn't have a husband there was no harm in her having an education.

harness

in harness ❶ in the routine of daily work. ❷ working closely with someone to achieve something.

> ❶ The image is of a horse or other animal being used for driving or draught work.

harp

harp on the same string dwell tediously on one subject.

harrow

under the harrow in distress.

> ❶ A *harrow* is a heavy frame set with iron teeth or tines, drawn over ploughed land to break up clods and root up weeds; an animal caught under a harrow would suffer extreme pain. In the poem 'Pagett, MP' (1886),

> Rudyard Kipling alludes to such a situation: 'The toad beneath the harrow knows Exactly where each tooth-point goes'.

Harry

play Old Harry with: *see* **play the devil with** *at* DEVIL.

hash

make a hash of make a mess of; bungle. informal

> ❶ *Hash* comes from the French verb *hacher* meaning 'chop up small'. A *hash* is a dish of cooked meat cut into small pieces and recooked with gravy; from this comes the derogatory sense of *hash* meaning 'a jumble of incongruous elements; a mess'.

settle someone's hash deal with and subdue a person very forcefully. informal

sling hash: *see* SLING.

haste

more haste, less speed you make better progress with a task if you don't try to do it too quickly. proverb

> ❶ The primary meaning of 'speed' in this proverbial saying was 'success in the performance of an activity', rather than 'rapidity of movement', though it is the latter that is now generally assumed to be meant.

hat

be all hat and no cattle tend to talk boastfully without acting on your words. US informal

black hat (*or* white hat) used in reference to the bad (*or* good) party in a situation.

> ❶ This idiom refers to the colour of the hats traditionally worn by the bad (or good) characters in cowboy films.

keep something under your hat keep something a secret.

pass the hat round collect contributions of money from a number of people for a specific purpose.

pick something out of a hat select something, especially the winner of a contest, at random.

pull one out of the hat bring off an unexpected trick in an apparently desperate situation.

> ❶ The image here is of a rabbit pulled out of a magician's hat.

1971 James McClure *The Steam Pig* I must say you've really pulled one out of the hat this time.

take your hat off to state your admiration for someone who has achieved something. British

throw your hat in (*or* **into**) **the ring** indicate willingness to take up a challenge or enter a contest.

1998 *Times* We have been anticipating that South Africa would throw its hat into the ring for some time and have a high regard for the candidacy.

hatch

batten down the hatches: *see* BATTEN.

hatches, matches, and despatches the births, marriages, and deaths columns in a newspaper. humorous, dated

under (the) hatches ❶ below deck in a ship. **❷** concealed from public knowledge.

hatchet

do a hatchet job on criticize savagely.

haul

haul someone over the coals: *see* COAL.

have

have had it ❶ be in a very poor condition; be beyond repair or past its best. **❷** be extremely tired. **❸** have lost all chance of survival. **❹** be unable to tolerate someone or something any longer. informal

have it away (on your toes) leave quickly. British informal

have it away (*or* **off**) **with** have sexual intercourse with. British vulgar slang

1998 *Oldie* Today, young Billy would be having it off with all three young ladies on a rota basis.

have it both ways: *see* BOTH.

have (got) it in for have a particular dislike of someone and behave in a hostile manner towards them. informal

have (got) it in you to do something have the capacity or potential to do something. informal

have it out with someone attempt to resolve a contentious matter by confronting someone and engaging in a frank discussion or argument. informal

have (got) nothing on someone or something be not nearly as good as someone or something, especially in a particular respect.

1998 Barbara Kingsolver *The Poisonwood Bible* Those glassy museum stares have got nothing on you, my uncaptured favorite child, wild as the day is long.

have one too many: *see* MANY.

havoc

play havoc with completely disrupt; cause serious damage to.

1989 Vijay Singh *In Search of the River Goddess* I hate contractors who come from the plains, chop down trees, play havoc with our lives.

hawk

watch someone like a hawk keep a vigilant eye on someone, especially to check that they do nothing wrong.

hay

hit the hay go to bed. informal

make hay make good use of an opportunity while it lasts.

> ❶ This is a shortened version of the proverb *make hay while the sun shines*, which dates from the mid 16th century.

1998 Simon Winchester *The Surgeon of Crowthorne* The British papers, always eager to vent editorial spleen on their transatlantic rivals, made hay with this particular aspect of the story.

make hay of throw into confusion.

head

bang (*or* **knock**) **people's heads together** reprimand people severely, especially in an attempt to stop them arguing.

1998 *Community Care* There are few signs yet that the SEU has been willing to bang government heads together over social security policy.

bang (*or* **knock**) **your head against a brick wall** doggedly attempt the impossible and have your efforts repeatedly and painfully rebuffed.

1995 Jayne Miller *Voxpop* You're banging your head against a brick wall for years and still getting nowhere. It's soul-destroying.

be hanging over your head (of something unpleasant) threaten to affect you at any moment.

be on someone's (own) head be someone's sole responsibility.

bite (*or* **snap**) **someone's head off** reply sharply and brusquely to someone.

do someone's head in cause someone to feel annoyed, confused, or frustrated. British informal

1997 *Sunday Telegraph* Now psychobabble has become part of our vocabulary—and it's doing Theodore Dalrymple's head in.

do something standing on your head do something very easily.

get your head down ❶ sleep. ❷ concentrate on the task in hand. British informal

get your head round (or around) something understand or come to terms with something. informal

give someone their head allow someone complete freedom of action.

> ❶ The image is of allowing a horse to go as fast as it wants rather than checking its pace with the bit and reins. Compare with **allow free rein to** (at REIN).

1994 Charles Grant *X-Files: Goblins* Rather than try to derail him, however, it was better to give him his head and go along for the ride.

go to your head ❶ (of alcohol) make you dizzy or slightly drunk. ❷ (of success) make you conceited.

have your head screwed on: *see* SCREWED.

head and shoulders above by far superior to. informal

1996 *Time Out* The film stands head and shoulders above 99.9 per cent of post-70's Hollywood product.

head over heels upside down; turning over completely in a forward motion, as in a somersault.

> ❶ The earlier, more logical, version of this phrase was *heels over head*; the normal modern form dates from the late 18th century. It is often used figuratively in an extreme condition, as in *head over heels in love*, 'madly in love', or *head over heels in debt*, 'deeply in debt'.

heads I win, tails you lose I win whatever happens.

heads will roll there will be some people dismissed or disgraced.

1975 Sam Selvon *Moses Ascending* It appears he went back for reinforcements, and is returning to make some drastic changes in the administration of the Establishment. Heads will roll, they say.

hold (or put) a gun (or a pistol) to someone's head force someone to do something by using threats.

keep (or lose) your head remain (or fail to remain) calm.

1990 *Time* He claims that Quayle rises to the challenge, takes chances but keeps his head.

keep your head above water avoid succumbing to difficulties, especially falling into debt.

keep your head down remain inconspicuous in difficult or dangerous times. informal

1995 Edward Toman *Dancing in Limbo* All his instincts told him to keep his head down. He didn't need Lily's constant nagging to remind him he was in deep trouble.

King Charles's head: *see* KING.

knock someone or something on the head: *see* KNOCK.

make head or tail of understand at all.

1994 S. P. Somtow *Jasmine Nights* I'm . . . trying to puzzle out why he has turned his animosity on me instead of those who are clearly his enemies. I can't make head or tail of it.

need your head examined be foolishly irresponsible.

> ❶ The implication here is that the examination will reveal proof of insanity.

1992 Patrick McCabe *The Butcher Boy* Any man thinks this work is easy needs his head examined—you want to be tough to work here!

off (or out of) your head ❶ mad or crazy. ❷ extremely drunk or severely under the influence of illegal drugs. informal

off the top of your head without careful thought or investigation.

1988 Jamaica Kincaid *A Small Place* He apologises for the incredible mistake he has made in quoting you a price off the top of his head which is so vastly different (favouring him) from the one listed.

over your head ❶ beyond your ability to understand. ❷ without your knowledge or involvement, especially when you have a right to this. ❸ with disregard for your own (stronger) claim.

put your heads together consult and work together.

put something into someone's head suggest something to someone.

stand (or turn) something on its head completely reverse the principles or interpretation of an idea, argument, etc.

take it into your head to do something decide impetuously to do something.

1991 Ben Okri *The Famished Road* Fearing that the supervisor might notice me as well and take it into his head to order me to break my neck carrying cement bags, I hurried on.

turn heads attract a great deal of attention or interest.

turn someone's head make someone conceited.

with your head in the clouds: see CLOUD.

— your head off laugh, talk, shout, etc. with a complete lack of restraint or without stopping.

> **1990 Paul Auster** *The Music of Chance* Now that the kid was out of danger, he began to show his true colors, and it wasn't long before he was talking his head off.

headline

hit the headlines be written about or given attention as news.

heap

at the top (or bottom) of the heap (of a person) at the highest (or lowest) point of a society or organization.

be struck all of a heap be extremely disconcerted. informal

heap coals of fire on someone's head: see COAL.

hear

be unable to hear yourself think be unable to think clearly as a result of an excessive amount of noise. informal

heart

after your own heart of the type that you like or understand best; sharing your tastes.

> **1988 Sebastian Barry** *Boss Grady's Boys* He took away every year I had to give a man, and then took away himself for good measure. He was a man after my own heart so I will not blame him.

from the bottom of your heart (or from the heart) with sincere feeling.

have the heart be insensitive or hard-hearted enough.

> **1990 Neil Bissoondath** *On the Eve of Uncertain Tomorrows* Miguel doesn't have the heart to force her to do what he knows she should be doing.

have (or put) your heart in be (or become) keenly involved in or committed to an enterprise.

have your heart in your mouth be greatly alarmed or apprehensive.

have your heart in the right place be sincere or well intentioned.

heart and soul great energy and enthusiasm.

> **1977 Michael Frayn** *Alphabetical Order* She hasn't been here long, I know. But she's put her whole heart and soul into this place.

heart of gold a generous nature.

heart of oak a courageous nature.

> ⓘ Literally, the *heart* is the solid central part of the oak tree traditionally used for timber for ships. The phrase was popularized by the words of an 18th-century song: 'Heart of oak are our ships, Heart of oak are our men'.

heart of stone a stern or cruel nature.

heart to heart candidly or intimately.

hearts and minds used in reference to emotional and intellectual support or commitment.

> **1999** *New Yorker* In the battle between Darwinians and creationists for the hearts and minds of the uncommitted, it matters whether evolution by natural selection is spiritually suggestive.

in your heart of hearts in your innermost feelings.

my heart bleeds for you: see BLEEDS.

take something to heart take something seriously; be much affected or upset by something.

> **1992 Ian Rankin** *A Good Hanging* Suicidal, just as actors can be. He took criticism to heart. He was a perfectionist.

to your heart's content: see CONTENT.

wear your heart on your sleeve make your feelings apparent.

> ⓘ In medieval times, it was the custom for a knight to wear the name of a lady on his sleeve during a tournament; the phrase was later popularized by Shakespeare in *Othello*: 'For I will wear my heart upon my sleeve, For daws to peck at'.

> **1998** *Spectator* He ... is not suffering from compassion fatigue, yet neither does he wear his heart on his sleeve.

your heart's desire someone or something that is greatly wished for.

your heart sinks into your boots: see BOOT.

heartbeat

a heartbeat (away) from very close to; on the verge of.

hearth

hearth and home home and its comforts.

heat

if you can't stand the heat, get out of the kitchen if you can't deal with the pressures and difficulties of a situation or task, you should leave others to deal with it rather than complaining. proverb

in the heat of the moment while temporarily angry, excited, or engrossed, and without stopping for thought.

turn the heat on someone or something concentrate pressure or criticism on someone or something. informal

turn up the heat intensify pressure or criticism. informal

heather

set the heather on fire be very exciting. Scottish

heave

heave in sight (or into view) come into view. informal

> ❶ *Heave* meaning 'rise up, as on the swell of a wave' occurs in several nautical expressions; here the allusion is to the way that objects appear to rise up over the horizon at sea.

heaven

in seventh heaven in a state of ecstasy.

> ❶ In late Jewish and Muslim theology, there were considered to be seven heavens, and the seventh of these was the highest, where a state of eternal bliss was to be enjoyed.

move heaven and earth make extraordinary efforts.

> **1999** *Dogs Today* We may not be vets but we are owners who will move heaven and earth to help our dogs recover.

stink (or smell) to high heaven have a very strong and unpleasant odour.

the heavens opened it started to rain suddenly and very heavily.

heavy

heavy on using a lot of.

> **1984 Studs Terkel** *The Good War* We were heavy on the Italian feeling in America. We were more Italian than Italians.

make heavy weather: *see* WEATHER.

heck

a heck of a — used for emphasis in various statements or exclamations. informal

> ❶ Of dialect origin, *heck* is a late 19th-century euphemism for *hell*.

> **1989** *Guardian* It is not entirely true to say everyone who is anyone has been coached there, but a heck of a lot have.

hedge

hedge your bets try to minimize the risk of being wrong or incurring loss by pursuing two courses of action at the same time.

> ❶ *Hedging* your financial liabilities, especially bets or speculative investments, meant limiting your potential losses by also putting money on another outcome, in such a way as to balance, more or less, any potential loss on the initial transaction. In betting terms, this specifically means putting money on more than one runner in a race.

> **1992** *Great Lakes Fisherman* All three methods have their proponents, and most anglers are wise to hedge their bets by using more than one method.

heel

Achilles heel: *see* ACHILLES.

at (or to) heel (of a dog) close to and slightly behind its owner.

> ❶ *Bring someone to heel*, meaning 'get someone under control and make them act subserviently', is taken from this expression.

cool your heels be kept waiting.

> ❶ A British variant of this is *kick your heels*.

dig in your heels: *see* DIG.

down at heel ❶ (of a shoe) with the heel worn down. ❷ (of a person, place, or thing) with a poor, shabby appearance.

drag your heels: *see* **drag your feet** *at* DRAG.

kick up your heels have a lively, enjoyable time. chiefly North American

set (or rock) someone back on their heels astonish or discomfit someone.

take to your heels (or legs) run away.

turn on your heel turn sharply round.

under the heel of dominated or controlled by.

> **1990 Julian Fane** *Hope Cottage* The exceptional sufferings of Russia under the heel of Marxism may in the long run have a redemptive effect.

hell

all hell broke (or was let) loose suddenly there was chaos or uproar. informal

be hell on be unpleasant or harmful to.

come hell or high water no matter what difficulties may occur.

> **1995 Ian Rankin** *Let It Bleed* It was the one appointment he'd known all day he would keep, come hell or high water.

for the hell of it just for fun. informal

— from hell an extremely unpleasant or troublesome instance or example of something. informal

> **1998** *Times* As for Ellie Sykes, who calls herself 'the skating mum from hell', she's pushier still.

get the hell out (of) escape from a place or situation very quickly. informal

give someone (or get) hell reprimand someone (or be reprimanded) severely. informal

go to (or through) hell and back endure an extremely unpleasant or difficult experience.

go to hell in a handbasket undergo a rapid process of deterioration. North American informal

> ❶ This expression has been recorded since the early 20th century; variants of it include *go to hell in a handcart* and *go to hell in a basket*.

> **1990** *Nature Conservancy* I read widely on environmental issues and often feel that 'the world is going to hell in a handbasket'.

hell for leather as fast as possible.

> ❶ This phrase dates from the late 19th century, and originally referred to riding a horse at reckless speed.

a (or one) hell of a — used to emphasize something very bad or great. informal

> **1990 Stephen King** *The Stand* If someone on the committee has been leaking, we're in a hell of a jam.

hell's half acre a great distance. North American

hell hath no fury like a woman scorned a woman who has been rejected by a man can be ferociously angry and vindictive. proverb

not a hope (or chance) in hell no hope (or chance) at all. informal

> ❶ An elaboration of this phrase is *not a snowball's chance in hell*.

play (merry) hell with throw into turmoil; disrupt. informal

raise hell ❶ make a noisy disturbance. ❷ complain vociferously. informal

there will be hell to pay serious trouble will occur as a result of a previous action. informal

until (or till) hell freezes over for an extremely long time or forever. informal

hello

a golden hello: *see* a golden **handshake** *at* HANDSHAKE.

help

so help me (God) used to emphasize that you mean what you are saying.

> ❶ This phrase alludes to the oath taken by witnesses in court when they swear to tell 'the truth, the whole truth, and nothing but the truth, so help me God'.

hen

like a hen with one chick (or chicken) absurdly fussy and overanxious.

rare (or scarce) as hen's teeth extremely rare.

> ❶ As hens do not possess teeth, the implication is that something is rare to the point of non-existence. The phrase was originally a US colloquialism, dating from the mid 19th century.

her

her indoors a humorous reference to a man's wife. British informal

herd

ride herd on: *see* RIDE.

here

here today, gone tomorrow soon over or forgotten; short-lived or transient.

> **1996** *Sunday Telegraph* Apparently when people spend their money on things that are here today gone tomorrow, like flowers, food and Champagne, it tells you more about the state of the economy than when they buy solid things.

neither here nor there of no importance or relevance.

> **1993** *Independent on Sunday* The fact that American audiences haven't recognised it as a great film and appreciated its outstanding acting is neither here nor there.

Herod

out-Herod Herod behave with extreme cruelty or tyranny.

> ❶ Herod, the ruler of Judaea at the time of Jesus's birth and the man responsible for ordering the massacre of boy babies in his realm, was portrayed in medieval miracle plays as a blustering tyrant. The phrase is from Shakespeare's *Hamlet*: 'I would have such a fellow whipp'd for o'erdoing Termagant; it out-herods Herod'.

herring

a red herring: *see* RED.

hewer

hewers of wood and drawers of water menial drudges; labourers.

> ℹ️ This expression refers to Joshua 9:21, which tells the story of how the Israelites were tricked into sparing the lives of some of the indigenous inhabitants of the Promised Land: 'And the princes said unto them, Let them live; but let them be hewers of wood and drawers of water unto all the congregation'.

hidden

a hidden agenda a person's real but concealed aims and intentions.

> **1993** *New Scientist* I hear that the physics community is fearful the government has a hidden agenda and intends eventually to close the Daresbury Laboratory.

hide

hide your light under a bushel keep quiet about your talents or accomplishments.

> ℹ️ A *bushel* is a unit of measurement equal to eight gallons: in former times the word also referred to a container able to hold this amount. The expression has its source in Matthew 5:15: 'neither do men light a candle, and put it under a bushel, but on a candlestick'.

> **1997** *Spectator* Actors are not naturally people who believe in hiding their light under a bushel.

neither hide nor hair of someone not the slightest trace of someone.

hiding

on a hiding to nothing unlikely to succeed, or in a position to gain no advantage if you do. British

> **1998** *Spectator* Which only goes to show that even the most reflexive liberal panderer is on a hiding to nothing in this territory.

high

be for the high jump be about to be severely punished. British informal

> ℹ️ This expression was first recorded in the early 20th century as a military term meaning 'be put on trial before your commanding officer'. The image behind it is that of an execution by hanging.

from on high ❶ from a very high place. ❷ from remote high authority or heaven.

high and dry ❶ (especially of ships left stranded by the sea as the tide ebbs) out of the water. ❷ in a difficult position, especially without resources.

> ❷ **1996 Frank McCourt** *Angela's Ashes* I hear he left you high and dry, eh? I don't know how a man in his right mind can go off and leave a wife and family to starve and shiver in a Limerick winter.

high and low in many different places.

> **1993** *Independent* As the world's press hunted for him high and low, he was holed up in a country hotel.

high and mighty ❶ important and influential. ❷ thinking or acting as though you are more important than others; arrogant. informal

high as a kite intoxicated.

high days and holidays special occasions. informal

> ℹ️ In the Church's calendar a *high day* was the day of an important festival. A *holiday* (originally *holy day*) was similar but less specific. *Holiday* now refers to any day off, without any sacred significance, and so *holy day* is used if a specifically religious occasion is intended.

> **1998 Pamela Jooste** *Dance with a Poor Man's Daughter* I was too busy looking out for all of you. I only danced on high days and holidays.

high old (of a time or state) most enjoyable or remarkable. informal

> **1955 Jean Potts** *Death of a Stray Cat* You probably had a high old time chasing blondes.

high on the hog: *see* HOG.

high, wide, and handsome expansive and impressive; stylish and carefree in manner. informal

> ℹ️ This phrase originated in the USA, and *Yankee Slang* (1932) identifies 'Ride him, Cowboy, high, wide and handsome' as a shout commonly heard at rodeos.

> **1990** *Times Education Supplement* Your eyes are often distracted by high quality displays of work, and the library is high, wide and handsome.

hit the high spots visit places of entertainment. informal

in high feather: *see* **in fine feather** *at* FEATHER.

on a high in a state of euphoria. informal

> ℹ️ This expression was originally mid 20th-century US slang, referring specifically to the euphoria induced by drugs.

on your high horse used to refer to someone behaving in an arrogant or pompous manner. informal

run high: *see* RUN.

hike

take a hike go away (used as an expression of irritation or annoyance). informal

> **1998 Dennis Danvers** *Circuit of Heaven* I'm going to bed now. Why don't you take a hike?

hill

a hill of beans: *see* BEAN.

ancient (*or* old) as the hills of very long standing or very great age.

> ❶ *Hills* are used in the Bible as a metaphor for permanence.

over the hill past your best; declining. informal

up hill and down dale: *see* UP.

hilt

(up) to the hilt completely.

> ❶ The image is that of plunging the blade of a knife deeply into something, so that only the hilt is visible.

hind

on your hind legs: *see* LEG.

hint

drop a hint: *see* DROP.

hip pocket

in someone's hip pocket completely under someone's control. North American

hire

hire and fire engage and dismiss, especially as indicating a position of established authority over other employees.

> **1992 Martin Anderson** *Impostors in the Temple* Usually the trustees, and they alone, hire and fire the president. They have fiduciary responsibility.

history

be history ❶ be perceived as no longer relevant to the present. ❷ used to indicate imminent departure, dismissal, or death. informal

> ❷ **1995** *Country* If Ducas does get the girl, you can lay odds that she'll be history by the end of the song.

the rest is history used to indicate that the events succeeding those already related are so well known that they need not be recounted again.

hit

hit and miss done or occurring at random; succeeding by chance rather than through planning.

> **1998** *New Scientist* But not all species of mosquitoes carry malaria and identifying the culprits is difficult, making control hit and miss.

hit-and-run ❶ (of a person) causing accidental or wilful damage and escaping before being discovered or stopped. ❷ (of an incident or accident) in which damage is caused in this way.

hit someone below the belt behave deviously towards someone, especially so as to gain an unfair advantage.

> ❶ In boxing, delivering a blow below an opponent's waistline is against the rules.

hit someone for six: *see* SIX.

hit the bottle: *see* BOTTLE.

hit the bricks go on strike. US informal

hit the ground running start something and proceed at a fast pace with enthusiasm. informal

> ❶ This late 20th-century expression achieved the status of a cliché in the 1990s. It seems likely to refer to military personnel disembarking rapidly from a helicopter, though it cannot be definitely traced back to any particular 20th-century war.

> **1997** *Independent* Some targets move too fast, even for a government that makes it clear it has hit the ground running.

hit the hay: *see* HAY.

hit the headlines: *see* HEADLINE.

hit home: *see* HOME.

hit it off with feel a liking for; be friendly with. informal

hit the jackpot: *see* JACKPOT.

hit the mark be successful in an attempt or accurate in a guess.

> ❶ The *mark* referred to here is a target in shooting.

hit the nail on the head state the truth exactly; find exactly the right answer.

> **1998** *Spectator* Yet his conceit and knack of hitting nails on heads meant that even his best performances made him as many enemies as friends.

hit or miss as likely to be unsuccessful as successful.

hit the right note: *see* NOTE.

hit the road set out on a journey; depart. informal

> ⓘ A US variant of this expression is *hit the trail.*

hit the sack: *see* SACK.

hit the spot: *see* SPOT.

hit where you live strike at your vital point.

> **2002** *New York Times* The movies hit [teenagers] where they live—in their own state of desperation and doubt.

hitch

hitch horses together get on well together; act in harmony. US

hitch your wagon to a star make use of powers higher than your own.

> ⓘ This phrase was used by the American philosopher and poet Ralph Waldo Emerson in 1870 in the context of idealistic aspiration; modern usage generally has the more cynical implication of attaching yourself to someone successful or famous in order to profit from the association.

> **1998** *Spectator* [Francis Bacon] was among the first to hitch his wagon to the star of the repulsive George Villiers... James I's next favourite.

hob

play (*or* **raise**) **hob** cause mischief; make a fuss. North American

> ⓘ *Hob* is short for *hobgoblin* and is used in this mid 19th-century expression to mean *the devil*. Compare with **raise Cain** (*at* CAIN) and **raise the devil** (*at* DEVIL).

> **1993** *Canadian Living* When rain finally came, it wouldn't stop and played hob with the lentils that were growing there for the first time in a big way.

Hobson

Hobson's choice: *see* CHOICE.

hock

in hock ❶ having been pawned. ❷ in debt.

> ⓘ *Hock* here comes from the Dutch word *hok* meaning 'hutch' or 'prison'. Originally mid 19th-century US slang, this sense of *hock* is now found only in this phrase or, occasionally, in *out of hock*.

❷ **1998** *Spectator* Our conservatoires are still in hock to the Germano-Austrian symphonic tradition.

hog

go the whole hog do something completely or thoroughly. informal

> ⓘ The origin of the phrase is uncertain, but a fable in William Cowper's *The Love of the World: Hypocrisy Detected* (1779) is sometimes mentioned: certain Muslims, forbidden to eat pork by their religion but tempted to indulge in some, maintained that Muhammad had had in mind only one particular part of the animal. They could not agree which part that was, and as 'for one piece they thought it hard From the whole hog to be debarred' between them they ate the whole animal, each salving his conscience by telling himself that his own particular portion was not the one that had been forbidden. *Go the whole hog* is recorded as a political expression in the USA in the early 19th century; an 1835 source maintains that it originated in Virginia 'marking the democrat from a federalist'.

live high on (*or* **off**) **the hog** have a luxurious lifestyle. North American

> **1991 Norman Mailer** *Harlot's Ghost* Even the Joint Chiefs' flunkies live high on the military hog.

hog in armour a person who is ill at ease.

hog on ice an insecure person. North American informal

hoist

hoist with your own petard: *see* PETARD.

hold

don't hold your breath: *see* BREATH.

hold someone or something at bay: *see* BAY.

hold the clock on time a sporting contest or similar event.

hold court be the centre of attention amidst a crowd of your admirers.

hold the field: *see* FIELD.

hold the fort take responsibility for a situation while someone is absent.

hold someone's hand give a person comfort, guidance, or moral support in a sad or difficult situation.

hold hard used to exhort someone to stop or wait. British

> ⓘ *Hold hard* was originally an exclamation warning riders in the hunting field to pull hard on the reins to make their horses stop, similar to **hold your horses** *below.*

hold the line ❶ not yield to the pressure of a difficult situation. **❷** maintain a telephone connection during a break in the conversation.

> ❶ Sense 1 is a military metaphor, from the idea of a line of soldiers withstanding an attack without moving from their positions.

> **❶ 1980 Shirley Hazzard** *The Transit of Venus* But if we made one exception we would naturally be in no position to hold the line on similar cases.

hold your horses wait a moment; restrain your enthusiasm. informal

> **1999 Colin Dexter** *The Remorseful Day* Hold your horses! One or two things I'd like you to check first, just to make it one hundred per cent.

hold your own: *see* OWN.

hold your peace: *see* PEACE.

hold the stage: *see* STAGE.

hold your thumbs fold your fingers over your thumbs to bring good luck; hope for luck or success. South African

> **1987** *Sunday Times (South Africa)* They say they are holding thumbs for her and praying that the pregnancy will be trouble-free.

hold your tongue remain silent. informal

hold someone or something to ransom: *see* RANSOM.

hold water (of a statement, theory, or line of reasoning) appear to be valid, sound, or reasonable.

no holds barred no rules or restrictions apply in a particular conflict or dispute.

> ❶ *No holds barred* was originally a phrase used only in wrestling, where it indicated that there were no restrictions on the kinds of holds used.

holding

be left holding the baby be left with an unwelcome responsibility, often without warning.

> ❶ A US variant of this expression is *be left holding the bag*.

there is no holding someone someone is particularly determined or cannot be prevented from doing something.

hole

blow a hole in ruin the effectiveness of something.

hole in the wall ❶ a small dingy place, especially a business or, in the USA, a place where alcoholic drinks are sold illegally. **❷** an automatic cash dispenser installed in the outside wall of a bank.

in a hole in an awkward situation from which it is difficult to escape. informal

> ❶ This figurative use of *hole* has been in use since the mid 18th century (compare with **dig yourself into a hole** at DIG). The English politician Denis Healey described the first law of politics as 'when you are in a hole, stop digging'.

in the hole in debt. North American

money burns a hole in your pocket: *see* MONEY.

need something like a hole in the head used to emphasize that someone has absolutely no need or desire for something. informal

pick holes criticize.

a square peg in a round hole: *see* PEG.

holiday

a Roman holiday: *see* ROMAN.

holier

holier than thou characterized by an attitude of self-conscious virtue and piety.

> ❶ This phrase comes from Isaiah 65:5: 'Stand by thyself, come not near to me; for I am holier than thou'.

hollow

beat someone hollow defeat or surpass someone completely or thoroughly.

in the hollow of your hand entirely in your power.

holy

holy of holies a place or thing regarded as sacrosanct.

> ❶ The reference here is to the Hebrew phrase for the inner chamber of the sanctuary in the Jewish Temple at Jerusalem, separated by a veil from the outer chamber.

home

bring something home to someone make someone realize the full significance of something.

close (*or* near) to home (of a remark or topic of discussion) relevant or accurate to the point that you feel uncomfortable or embarrassed.

come home to someone (of the significance of something) become fully realized by someone.

> **1981 Fannie Flagg** *Daisy Fay & the Miracle Man* It came home to me that night that Momma has certainly lost her sense of humour.

drive something home make something clearly and fully understood by the use of repeated or forcefully direct arguments.

> ❶ The verbs *hammer*, *press*, and *ram* are also used in place of *drive*.

hit (*or* **strike**) **home** ❶ (of a blow or a missile) reach an intended target. ❷ (of a person's words) have the intended, often unsettling or painful, effect on their audience. ❸ (of the significance or true nature of a situation) become fully realized by someone.

home and dry successful in achieving your objective. chiefly British

> ❶ A fuller version of this phrase, which dates from the mid 20th century, is *home and dry on the pig's back*.

home and hosed successful in achieving your objective. chiefly Australian & New Zealand

> **1998** *Times* The championship was over, Manchester United were home and hosed.

home free successful in achieving your objective. North American

a home from home a place where you are as happy, relaxed, or at ease as in your own home.

> ❶ The North American version of this expression is *a home away from home*.

home, James (and don't spare the horses)! used as a humorous way of exhorting the driver of a vehicle to drive home quickly. dated

> ❶ This was the title of a popular song by F. Hillebrand in 1934; it represents a parody of the instruction given to a coachman in the days of the horse and carriage.

who's — when —'s at home a humorously emphatic way of asking about someone's identity. British

> **1991 Joseph O'Connor** *Mothers Were All the Same* The old lady said to tell that to Yuri Gagarin, but the hostess just giggled and said, 'Who's he when he's at home?'

honest

earn (*or* **turn**) **an honest penny** earn money by fair means, especially by hard work.

an honest broker a disinterested intermediary or mediator.

> ❶ This expression is a translation of the German *ehrlicher Makler*. In a speech in 1878 the German statesman Bismarck (1815–98) recommended adopting this role in peace-making, and the phrase became one of his sobriquets.

make an honest woman of marry a woman, especially to avoid scandal if she is pregnant. dated or humorous

> ❶ *Honest* here originally meant 'respectable', but was probably associated with the archaic sense 'chaste or virtuous'.

honour

do the honours perform a social duty or small ceremony for others.

honours are even there is equality in the contest. British

(in) honour bound obliged by your sense of honour.

hoof

on the hoof ❶ (of livestock) not yet slaughtered. ❷ without great thought or preparation.

> ❷ **1997** *Times* Are we not witnessing an example of Tony Blair making policy on the hoof… with a decision to match the circumstances, not the principle?

hook

by hook or by crook by one means or another; by fair means or foul.

> ❶ The *hook* referred to here is probably a billhook or heavy curved pruning knife; one of the earliest recorded instances of this phrase is in Gower's *Confessio Amantis* (1390), which uses the rare word *hepe* (meaning 'a pruning knife') in place of *hook*. Various folk etymologies for the expression have been put forward, none of them entirely convincing. In 1822 William Cobbett wrote of people who lived near woodland being allowed, under the ancient forest law of England, to gather dead branches for fuel, which they may have brought down from the trees literally *by hook* or *by crook*.

> **1998 Adèle Geras** *Silent Snow, Secret Snow* Till then, she would hang on. By hook or by crook. Come what may.

get (*or* **give someone**) **the hook** be dismissed

from a job (*or* dismiss someone from a job). North American informal

hook it run away. British informal

hook, line, and sinker used to emphasize that someone has been completely tricked or deceived. informal

> ℹ This phrase is a fishing metaphor: all three are items attached to a fishing rod and likely to be gulped down by a greedy fish. The phrase has been in use since the mid 19th century.

> **1996 Colin Bateman** *Of Wee Sweetie Mice & Men* Patricia wouldn't know what had hit her. She'd fall for me hook, line and sinker once I'd reminded her what we were all about.

off the hook ❶ no longer in trouble or difficulty. informal ❷ (of a telephone receiver) not on its rest, and so not receiving incoming calls.

> ℹ *Hook* in sense 1 is a long-standing (mid 15th-century) figurative use of the word to mean 'something by which a person is caught and trapped', as a fish hook catches a fish. Sense 2 is a fossilized expression from the late 19th century, the early years of telephony, when the receiver literally hung on a hook.

on the hook for (in a financial context) responsible for. North American informal

> **2001** *High Country News* Taxpayers are currently on the hook for anywhere from $32 billion to $72 billion in abandoned mine cleanup costs.

off the hooks dead. British informal

sling your hook leave; go away. British informal

> ℹ *Sling your hook* appears in a slang dictionary of 1874, where it is defined as 'a polite invitation to move on'.

> **1998** *Times* I now realise that Sylvia hasn't heard from him since she told him to sling his hook.

hookey

play hookey stay away from school without permission or explanation; play truant. North American informal

hoop

put someone (*or* go) through the hoops make someone undergo (*or* be made to undergo) a difficult and gruelling test or series of tests.

> **1994** *Legion* The crew was as fast and efficient as any they had put through the hoops.

hoot

not care (*or* give) a hoot (*or* two hoots) not care at all. informal

> **1990 Karen Lawrence** *Springs of Living Water* Never think about anybody but yourself, do you? Never give two hoots about your poor little sister following you around.

hop

hop the twig (*or* stick) ❶ depart suddenly. ❷ die. British informal

on the hop unprepared. British informal

> **1991 M. S. Power** *Come the Executioner* He went down to the dining-room, catching the staff on the hop, but they greeted him cheerfully enough.

hope

hope chest a chest containing linen, clothes, and household items stored by a woman in preparation for her marriage. North American

> ℹ The British equivalent of this expression is **bottom drawer** (see DRAWER).

hope against hope cling to a mere possibility.

> **1995 Bill Bryson** *Notes from a Small Island* I plodded on, hoping against hope that there would be a pub or cafe in Kimmeridge.

hope springs eternal it is human nature always to find fresh cause for optimism.

> ℹ This is a shortened version of Alexander Pope's line in *An Essay on Man* (1733): 'Hope springs eternal in the human breast'.

> **1992 Angela Lambert** *A Rather English Marriage* Hope springs eternal—she smiled wryly—even in Tunbridge Wells.

horizon

on the horizon just imminent or becoming apparent.

Horlicks

make a Horlicks of make a mess of. British informal

> **1988 Joanna Trollope** *The Choir* He thought privately that they would make a fearful horlicks of running the choir.

horn

blow (*or* toot) your own horn talk boastfully about yourself or your achievements. North American

draw (*or* pull) in your horns become less assertive or ambitious; draw back.

❶ The image here is of a snail drawing in its retractile tentacles when disturbed.

1991 Paul Grescoe *Flesh Wound* Hollywood's major studios were pulling in their horns in the wake of a disastrous Christmas season.

on the horn on the telephone. North American informal

on the horns of a dilemma faced with a decision involving equally unfavourable alternatives.

❶ A mid 16th-century source described a *dilemma* as 'a horned argument' (after Latin *argumentum cornutum*), the idea being that if you avoided one 'horn' of the argument you ended up impaled on the other.

hornet

a hornets' nest a situation fraught with trouble, opposition, or complications.
1992 *New Scientist* The notion of these 'life patents' has opened up a hornets' nest of moral, legal, social and scientific concerns.

horse

a dark horse: see DARK.

don't change horses in midstream choose a sensible moment to change your mind. proverb

❶ This expression is quoted by Abraham Lincoln in 1864 as the saying of 'an old Dutch farmer'. Early versions of it used *swap* instead of *change*.

eat like a horse eat heartily and greedily.

frighten the horses cause consternation or dismay; shock.
1996 *Independent* No matter the inadvertent hurt or crass provocation or outright insult, bite your tongue, be pleasant, be polite, don't frighten the horses.

(straight) from the horse's mouth from the person directly concerned or another authoritative source.

❶ This expression refers to the presumed ideal source for a racing tip and hence for other useful information.

1998 *New Scientist* PhD students will be able to learn these subjects direct from the horse's mouth.

hitch horses together: see HITCH.

a horse of another (or different) colour a thing significantly different.
1975 Sam Selvon *Moses Ascending* Two or three is okay, but when you start bringing in a battalion, it is a horse of a different colour.

horses for courses different people are suited to different things or situations.

❶ The earliest recorded instance of this expression, in A. E. T. Watson's *Turf* (1891), suggests its origin: 'A familiar phrase on the turf is "horses for courses" … the Brighton Course is very like Epsom, and horses that win at one meeting often win at the other'.

1989 *Guardian* It's a question of horses for courses, finding the best route forward and adopting the practices to fit that rather than bulldozing your way through without perhaps realising the wider environment in which this needs to work.

a Trojan horse: see TROJAN.

wild horses won't drag someone to something (or something from someone) nothing will make someone go to a particular place (or divulge particular information). informal
1998 *Times* As things stand, wild horses wouldn't drag [children] to a symphony concert.

hostage

a hostage to fortune an act, commitment, or remark which is regarded as unwise because it invites trouble or could prove difficult to live up to.

❶ The original *hostages to fortune* were a man's family, the allusion being to Francis Bacon's essay on marriage (1625): 'He that hath wife and children hath given hostages to fortune'.

hot

blow hot and cold: see BLOW.

drop someone or something like a hot potato quickly abandon someone or something. informal

❶ *Drop* here is used literally, but also in the figurative sense of 'end a social acquaintance with someone'. A *hot potato* can be used independently as a metaphor for a controversial or awkward issue or problem that no one wants to deal with.

go hot and cold experience sudden feelings of fear, embarrassment, or shock.
1973 Anthony Price *October Men* His wife had said … that she had gone 'all hot and cold' after nearly being run over.

have the hots for be sexually attracted to. informal
1996 Janette Turner Hospital *Oyster* One summer night, there was a man with a knife, a

man on my own surveying team, a man I fancied, a man I knew had the hots for me.

hot air empty talk that is intended to impress.

> **1998** *Times* If a chief executive is convinced that a day spent hot-air ballooning is a more effective way of motivating the troops than a lot of hot air from him or her, then anything goes.

hot and heavy intense; with intensity. North American informal

hot on the heels of following closely.

hot to trot ready and eager to engage in an activity. informal

hot under the collar angry, resentful, or embarrassed.

> **1995 Edward Toman** *Dancing in Limbo* It seems that the gentleman in question has been getting very hot under the collar of late about our public image.

in hot water in a situation of difficulty, trouble, or disgrace.

> **1997** *TV Quick* Hunter finds himself in hot water when a local TV reporter accuses him of police brutality—and is later found dead.

make it (or things) hot for someone make life difficult for someone.

sell like hot cakes: *see* CAKE.

too hot to hold you (of a place) not safe to remain in because of your past misconduct.

> **1984 Gwyn Jones** *A History of the Vikings* Of Naddod we read that he was . . . a viking of note who seems to have made Norway and other Norse settlements too hot to hold him.

hour

keep late (or regular) hours do the same thing, typically getting up and going to bed, late (or at the same time) every day.

the small hours: *see* SMALL.

till all hours till very late. informal

house

eat someone out of house and home: *see* EAT.

get on (or along) like a house on fire have a very good and friendly relationship.

go round (or all round) the houses ❶ take a circuitous route to your destination. ❷ take an unnecessarily long time to get to the point.

house and home a person's home (used for emphasis).

a house divided a group or organization weakened by internal dissensions.

> ❶ This phrase alludes to Matthew 12:25: 'Every city or house divided against itself shall not stand', that is, will be unable to withstand external pressures.

a house of cards an insecure or over-ambitious scheme.

> ❶ Literally, a *house of cards* is a structure of playing cards balanced together.

> **1992** *New York Times Book Review* Integrated Resources later proved to be a house of cards, costing Drexel customers many millions when it collapsed.

on the house (of drinks or a meal in a bar or restaurant) free.

put (or set or get) your house in order make necessary reforms.

> **2002** *New York Times* There will be no moral credibility for the bishops to speak about justice, truth, racial equality, war or immigration if they can't get their own house in order.

safe as houses thoroughly or completely safe. British

houseroom

not give something houseroom be unwilling to have or consider something. British

> ❶ The word *houseroom*, dating from the late 16th century, literally means 'lodging or accommodation in a house'.

> **1986 Liz Lochhead** *True Confessions* Course I do get the Woman and the Woman's Own plus I swap Options for the Cosmopolitan off our Joy. I wouldn't give Woman's Realm houseroom.

housetop

proclaim (or shout) something from the housetops announce something publicly.

Hoyle

according to Hoyle according to plan or the rules.

> ❶ Edmond Hoyle (1672–1769) wrote a number of authoritative books about whist and other card games; his name, at first synonymous with expert opinion on card games, became a metaphor for the highest authority in all fields.

> **1989 Tom Bodett** *The End of the Road* His divinely inspired plan had gone exactly according to Hoyle. He'd fooled them.

huff

huff and puff ❶ breathe heavily with exhaustion. ❷ express your annoyance in an obvious or threatening way.

hum

hum and haw (*or* ha) hesitate; be indecisive.
British

> ❶ The word *hum* has been used as an
> inarticulate syllable in hesitant speech since
> Chaucer; *ha* appears in a similar role from the
> early 17th century.

humble

eat humble pie make a humble apology and
accept humiliation.

> ❶ *Humble pie* is from a mid 19th-century
> pun based on *umbles*, meaning 'offal',
> which was considered to be an inferior
> food.

> **1998** *Spectator* A white youth behind us did
> shout racial abuse. But...after the game was
> over his companions forced him to come up to
> Darcus to eat humble pie.

hump

live on your hump be self-sufficient. informal

> ❶ The image here is of the camel, which is
> famous for surviving on the fat in its hump
> without feeding or drinking.

over the hump over the worst.

hurt

someone or something wouldn't hurt a fly:
see FLY.

hustle

hustle your butt move or act quickly. North
American informal

> ❶ Other variants of this phrase include
> *hustle your buns* and, in vulgar slang, *hustle
> your ass*.

I

dot the i's and cross the t's: *see* DOT.

ice

break the ice do or say something to relieve tension or get conversation started at the start of a party or when people meet for the first time.

on ice ❶ (especially of a plan or proposal) held in reserve for future consideration. ❷ (of wine or food) kept chilled by being surrounded by ice. ❸ (of an entertainment) performed by skaters.

> ❶ **1995** *Times Education Supplement* In Kent plans for 10 more nursery classes next year are on ice.

(skating) on thin ice in a precarious or risky situation.

iceberg

the tip of an (*or* the) iceberg the small perceptible part of a much larger situation or problem which remains hidden.

> ❶ This phrase refers to the fact that only about one fifth of the mass of an iceberg is visible above the surface of the sea.

> **1998** *New Scientist* This leaves pressure groups wondering whether there are further breaches still waiting to be discovered. Sue Mayer of Gene Watch asks: 'Is it the tip of the iceberg?'

icing

the icing on the cake an attractive but inessential addition or enhancement.

> ❶ A North American variant of this phrase is *the frosting on the cake*.

> **1996** *Independent* State education is no longer always free. The jumble sale and the summer fair, which used to provide the icing on the school cake, are now providing the staple fare.

idea

get (*or* give someone) ideas become (*or* make someone) ambitious, big-headed, or tempted to do something against someone else's will, especially make a sexual advance. informal

if

if anything used to suggest tentatively that something may be the case (often the opposite of something previously implied).

illusion

be under the illusion that wrongly believe that.

> **1998** *Independent* The keening harmonies of the Brothers Gibb, a million naff dance routines by medallion men under the illusion that they were John Travolta.

be under no illusion (*or* illusions) be fully aware of the true state of affairs.

> **1992** *Christian Scientist Monitor* It is crucial to the nation's security ... that we be under no illusions about reasons for this zero-loss rate.

image

a graven image: *see* GRAVEN.

imitation

imitation is the sincerest form of flattery copying someone or something is an implicit way of paying them a compliment. proverb

improve

improve the shining hour make good use of time; make the most of your time. literary

> ❶ This expression comes from Isaac Watts's *Divine Songs for Children* (1715): 'How doth the little busy bee Improve each shining hour'.

in

be in for have good reason to expect (typically something unpleasant).

> **1988** **Hugh Scott** *The Shaman's Stone* The weather will break soon, then we'll be in for a storm.

be in on be privy to a secret.

have it in for someone have hostile feelings towards someone. informal

in with enjoying friendly relations with. informal

> **1990 Jeffrey Masson** *Final Analysis* I was in demand everywhere...simply because I was in with the right people.

the ins and outs all the details of something.

inch

give someone an inch once concessions have been made to someone they will demand a great deal.

> ❶ The full form of the saying is the proverb *give someone an inch and he will take a mile*. In former times, *ell* (an obsolete measure of length equal to a little over a metre) was sometimes substitued for *mile*.

within an inch of your life almost to the point of death.

> **1997 Marian Keyes** *Rachel's Holiday* He kept touching his hair, which, as well as being dyed to within an inch of its life, was blowdried, flicked and rigid with spray.

incline

incline your ear listen favourably. literary

> ❶ *Incline thine ear* is an expression used throughout the Bible, for example in Psalms 17:6: 'I have called upon thee, for thou wilt hear me, O God: incline thine ear unto me, and hear my speech'.

Indian

Indian summer ❶ a period of dry, warm weather occurring in late autumn. ❷ a tranquil or productive period in someone's later years.

> ❷ **1930 Vita Sackville-West** *The Edwardians* Meanwhile she was quite content that Sebastian should become tanned in the rays of Sylvia's Indian summer.

influence

under the influence affected by alcoholic drink, especially beyond the legal limits for driving a vehicle; drunk. informal

Injun

honest Injun honestly; really. dated

injury

do yourself an injury suffer physical harm or damage. informal

innings

have had a good innings have had a long and fulfilling life or career. British informal

> ❶ In cricket, an *innings* is the period that a team or batsman spends batting, and a *good innings* is one during which a lot of runs are scored.

> **2002** *Oldie* He keeps dropping heavy hints when he visits: he...said the other evening I have had a good innings (I am 86).

innocence

in all innocence without knowledge of something's significance or possible consequences.

> **1992 Jeff Torrington** *Swing Hammer Swing!* I'd given him the matches in all innocence but that didn't let me off the hook.

inside

on the inside in a position affording private information. informal

> **1932** *Daily Express* I have chatted with men who are believed to be on the inside, and they have informed me that there will certainly be changes at forward and in the three-quarter line.

inside out

know someone or something inside out know someone or something very thoroughly.

turn something inside out ❶ turn the inner surface of something outwards. ❷ change something utterly.

> ❷ **2002** *New Republic* My every preconception about Renaissance tapestry had been turned inside out.

insult

add insult to injury do or say something that makes a bad or displeasing situation even worse.

> ❶ This phrase comes from Edward Moore's play *The Foundling* (1748): 'This is adding insult to injuries'.

intent

to all intents and purposes in all important respects.

> **1992** *London Review of Books* For if in 1976 pianists really were about to lose the skill of polyphonic piano-playing, then to all intents and purposes the skill of playing the piano was at an end.

interest

declare an (or your) interest make known your financial interests in an undertaking before it is discussed.

interference

run interference intervene on someone's behalf, typically so as to protect them from distraction or annoyance. North American informal

> ℹ *Run interference* is a metaphor from American football, where it refers to the legal blocking of an opponent to clear a way for the ball carrier.

iron

have many (or other) irons in the fire have many (or a range of) options or courses of action available or be involved in many activities or commitments at the same time.

> ℹ Various tools and implements made (or formerly made) of iron are called *irons*, for example grappling irons or branding irons. The metaphor is of a blacksmith or other worker who heats iron objects in a fire until they reach the critical temperature at which they can be shaped or used.

an iron curtain an impenetrable barrier, especially *the Iron Curtain*, the physical and other barriers preventing the passage of people and information between the Soviet bloc and the West during the cold war.

> ℹ In the late 18th century, an *iron curtain* was literally a fire curtain in a theatre, but the figurative sense was in use from the early 19th century, well before Winston Churchill observed in a speech in March 1946 that 'an iron curtain has descended across the Continent [of Europe]'.

the iron entered into someone's soul someone became deeply and permanently affected by imprisonment or ill-treatment. literary

> ℹ This expression comes from a phrase in the Latin Vulgate version of the Bible, *ferrum pertransit animam ejus*, a mistranslation of the Hebrew which literally translates as 'his person entered into the iron', meaning 'he was placed in fetters'.

an iron hand (or fist) in a velvet glove firmness or ruthlessness masked by outward gentleness.

iron out the wrinkles resolve all minor difficulties and snags.

> ℹ *Iron out* has been in figurative use since the mid 19th century; it often occurs with other nouns, especially *differences*.

> **1984** *New Yorker* Willa had sold her story to Universal Pictures and was in California ironing out some wrinkles in the deal.

new off the irons newly made or prepared; brand new. dated

> ℹ The *irons* here are engraved stamps used for impressing a design or figure on something, as in coining money, striking a medal, or embossing paper. This sense is now obsolete and survives only in this phrase.

strike while the iron is hot: *see* STRIKE.

itching

an itching palm an avaricious or greedy nature.

> **1937 Wyndham Lewis** *The Revenge for Love* Had Alvaro been bribed? Had such a man an itching palm like the rest of them?

itchy

get (or have) itchy feet be restless; have a strong urge to travel or move from place to place. informal

item

be an item (of a couple) be involved in an established romantic or sexual relationship. informal

> **1997** *Independent* 'It is fair to say they are an item but they are not engaged,' said one of Mr Brown's closest confidantes.

ivory

tickle (or tinkle) the ivories play the piano. informal

> ℹ The *ivories* are the white keys of the piano, traditionally made of ivory.

Jj

jack

before you can say Jack Robinson very quickly or suddenly. informal

> ⓘ This expression was in use in the late 18th century, but neither an early 19th-century popular song about Jack Robinson nor some mid 19th-century attempts to identify the eponymous Jack Robinson shed any light on its origins.

every man Jack each and every person. informal

> ⓘ Jack is a pet name form of the forename John. It was sometimes used in informal American speech as a form of address to a man whose name you did not know, and as a generic name for any ordinary or working-class man.

I'm all right, Jack used to express or comment upon selfish complacency. informal

> ⓘ I'm all right, Jack was an early 20th-century catchphrase which became the title of a 1959 British film.

jack of all trades (and master of none) a person who can do many different types of work (but has special skill in none).

> ⓘ Jack is used here to mean a 'general labourer' or 'odd-job man', a sense dating from the mid 19th century.

on your Jack on your own. British informal

> ⓘ This an abbreviation of the rhyming slang expression on your Jack Jones.

jackpot

hit the jackpot ❶ win a jackpot. ❷ have great or unexpected success, especially in making a lot of money quickly. informal

> ⓘ Originally, in the late 19th century, jackpot was a term used in a form of poker, where the pot or pool accumulated until a player could open the betting with a pair of jacks or higher cards. It is now used of any large money prize that accumulates until it is won.

jam

have jam on it have some additional pleasure, ease, or advantage.

> **1974 Olivia Manning** Rain Forest Hugh... was free to leave at six...Pedley...said: 'You've got jam on it: walking home in the sunset.'

jam tomorrow a pleasant thing which is often promised but rarely materializes. British

> ⓘ This expression comes from Lewis Carroll's Through the Looking-Glass (1871): 'The rule is jam tomorrow and jam yesterday—but never jam today'.

Jane

plain Jane an unattractive girl or woman.

> **2002** Guardian [The film] assembles its stereotypes (the sexy exchange student, the plain Jane who's really a fox, the jock who is only dating her for a bet) then proceeds to gunk them all with a ton of scatalogical prankery.

jazz

and all that jazz and such similar things. informal

> ⓘ Of unknown origin, jazz was used informally to mean 'meaningless talk' within a decade of the word's first appearance in its musical sense, in the early 20th century. This phrase was a mid 20th-century development.

> **1960** Punch Politics, world affairs, film stars' babies and all that jazz, the things that the adult world seems obsessed with, do not interest us at all.

Jekyll

Jekyll and Hyde a person alternately displaying opposing good and evil personalities.

> ⓘ The Strange Case of Dr Jekyll and Mr Hyde (1886) is a novel by Robert Louis Stevenson, in which the physician Jekyll, in order to indulge his evil instincts, uses a drug to create the persona of Hyde, which at first he can assume at will but which gradually gains control of him.

jerk

put a jerk in it act vigorously, smartly, or quickly. informal, dated

> **1939 C. Day Lewis** *Child of Misfortune* Put a jerk in it. I'm meeting my boy at the second house at the Royal.

jewel

the jewel in the (or someone's) crown the most attractive or successful part of something.

> ❶ In the early 20th century, this was used as a term for the British imperial colonies as a whole. *The Jewel in the Crown* was subsequently used by Paul Scott as the title of the first novel of his Raj Quartet, which is set in the last days of British rule in India.

jib

the cut of someone's jib: see CUT.

jig

in jig time extremely quickly; in a very short time. North American informal

the jig is up the scheme or deception is revealed or foiled. North American informal

> ❶ The sense of *jig* here dates from the late 16th century and means 'jest' or 'trick'. *The jig is over* is recorded from the late 18th century in the USA and the usual modern version with *up* appeared only slightly later.

jingbang

the whole jingbang the whole lot. informal

> ❶ The origins of *jingbang* and its variant *jimbang*, both found only in this phrase, are uncertain.

Job

a Job's comforter a person who aggravates distress under the guise of giving comfort.

> ❶ In the Bible, Job was a prosperous man whose patience and piety was tested by a series of undeserved misfortunes. The attempts of his friends to comfort him only add to his sense of despair and he tells them: 'miserable comforters are ye all' (Job 16:2). Despite his ordeals, he remains confident of the goodness and justice of God and in the end he is restored to his former situation.

job

do a job on someone do something which harms or defeats an opponent. informal

jobs for the boys used in reference to the practice of giving paid employment to your friends, supporters, or relations. British derogatory

> **2002** *Guardian* The James Report found the unit operated a 'jobs for the boys' recruitment policy favouring Reed's friends and political acquaintances.

just the job exactly what is needed. British informal

make the best of a bad job: see **make the best of it** at BEST.

more than your job's worth not worth risking your job for.

> ❶ This phrase has given rise to the term *Jobsworth*, which is applied to the kind of person, usually a minor official, who says 'it's more than my job's worth' as a way of justifying an insistence on petty rules, even at the expense of common sense.

join

join the club: see CLUB.

join the great majority die. euphemistic

> ❶ This expression was first used by the poet Edward Young (1683–1765): 'Death joins us to the great majority'. However, the idea of the dead being 'the majority' is a very old one; it is found, for example, in the writings of the Roman satirist Petronius as *abiit ad plures*: 'he's gone to join the majority'.

joint

out of joint ❶ (of a specified joint) out of position; dislocated. ❷ in a state of disorder or disorientation.

> ❷ **1601 William Shakespeare** *Hamlet* The time is out of joint.

joke

get (or be) beyond a joke become (or be) something that is serious or worrying. informal

> **2002** *Guardian* The rogue animal is believed to have attacked at least six residents in the past week, and his antics are now described by residents as 'well beyond a joke'.

the joke is on someone someone looks foolish, especially after trying to make someone else look so. informal

> **1998** *Spectator* He turned out to be as right as rain ... so the joke was on us.

joker

the joker in the pack a person or factor

likely to have an unpredictable effect on events.

> ❶ In a pack of playing cards, a *joker* is an extra card which does not belong to one of the four suits (clubs, diamonds, hearts, and spades) and usually bears the figure of a jester. It is used in some card games as a trump and in poker as a wild card.

> **1973 George Sims** *Hunters Point* Fred Wheeler may be the joker in the pack. He might have got Dave involved in something wild.

Joneses

keep up with the Joneses try to maintain the same social and material standards as your friends or neighbours.

> ❶ This phrase originated as a comic-strip title, 'Keeping up with the Joneses—by Pop' in the New York *Globe* (1913). *Jones*, one of the most common British family names, is used as a generic name for neighbours or presumed social equals.

journey

a sabbath day's journey: *see* SABBATH.

joy

full of the joys of spring lively and cheerful.

wish someone joy used to congratulate someone on something. British, chiefly ironic
> **2001** *Daily Telegraph* I . . . wish Lord Hamlyn, Tony and Cherie every possible joy of sex, money, and all the rest of it.

Judas

a Judas kiss an act of betrayal, especially one disguised as a gesture of friendship.

> ❶ Judas Iscariot was the disciple who betrayed Jesus to the authorities in return for thirty pieces of silver: 'And he that betrayed him gave them a sign, saying, Whomsoever I shall kiss, that same is he: hold him fast' (Matthew 26:48).

judgement

against your better judgement contrary to what you feel to be wise or sensible.

jugular

go for the jugular be aggressive or unrestrained in making an attack.
> **1997** *Cosmopolitan* Once she decides she wants a man, she goes for the jugular and doesn't give a hoot about any other woman (such as his girlfriend).

jump

get (*or* **have) the jump on** get (*or* have) an advantage over someone as a result of your prompt action. North American informal
> **1912 George Ade** *Knocking the Neighbors* Rufus was sinfully Rich . . . his Family had drilled into him the low-down Habit of getting the Jump on the Other Fellow.

go (and) jump in the lake go away and stop being a nuisance. informal
> **1998** *New Scientist* He is in some unexplained way independent of his genes . . . if they don't like what he does, his genes can go jump in the lake.

jump someone's bones have sex with someone. North American vulgar slang

jump down someone's throat respond to what someone has said in a sudden and angrily critical way. informal

jump the gun act before the proper or appropriate time. informal

> ❶ In athletics, a competitor who *jumps the gun* sets off before the starting pistol has been fired. The expression appears in the early 20th century as *beat the gun*.

jump on the bandwagon: *see* BANDWAGON.

jump out of your skin be extremely startled. informal

jump the queue ❶ push into a queue of people in order to be served or dealt with before your turn. ❷ take unfair precedence over others.

> ❶ The US version of this expression is *jump in line*.

jump the rails (*or* **track)** (of a train) become dislodged from the track; be derailed.

jump the shark (of a television series or film) reach a point at which far-fetched events are included merely for the sake of novelty, indicative of a decline in quality. US informal

> ❶ This phrase is said to refer to an episode of the long-running US television series *Happy Days*, in which the central character (the Fonz) jumped over a shark while waterskiing.

jump ship ❶ (of a sailor) leave the ship on which you are serving without having obtained permission to do so. ❷ suddenly abandon an organization, enterprise, etc.

jump through hoops be obliged to go through an elaborate or complicated procedure in order to achieve an objective.

2002 *Guardian* For the Going Underground single in 1980, the producer made Weller jump through hoops to deliver a convincing vocal performance.

jump (or leap) to conclusions (or the conclusion) form an opinion hastily, before you have learned or considered all the facts.

jump to it take prompt and energetic action.

> **1974 Marian Babson** *The Stalking Lamb* When you hear my signal—jump to it!

on the jump ❶ moving quickly. **❷** abruptly; swiftly. informal

> **❷ 1972 Judson Philips** *The Vanishing Senator* Get over here on the jump... Step on it, will you?

one jump ahead one step or stage ahead of someone else and so having the advantage over them.

jumping

be jumping up and down be very angry, upset, or excited. informal

jungle

the law of the jungle the principle that those who are strong and apply ruthless self-interest will be most successful.

> **1989 Bessie Head** *Tales of Tenderness & Power* And at the beer tank the law of the jungle prevailed, the stronger shoving the weaker.

jury

the jury is out a decision has not yet been reached on a controversial subject.

> **1998** *New Scientist* The jury is still out, but it looks as if there are no significant changes in the cosmic dust flux during past climate cycles.

justice

do someone or something justice (or do justice to someone or something) treat or represent someone or something with due fairness or appreciation.

do yourself justice perform as well as you are able to.

poetic justice: *see* POETIC.

rough justice: *see* ROUGH.

kangaroo

have kangaroos in the (*or* your) top paddock be mad or eccentric. Australian informal

> **1985 Peter Carey** *Illywacker* 'And he was a big man too, and possibly slow-witted.' 'Leichhardt?' 'No, Bourke...He had kangaroos in his top paddock.'

keen

keen as mustard extremely eager or enthusiastic. British informal

> ❶ *Keen* is used here to mean 'operating on the senses like a sharp instrument'.

keep

keep the ball rolling: *see* BALL.

keep open house provide general hospitality.

> **1950 Elizabeth Goudge** *Gentian Hill* All well-to-do Devon farmhouses keep open house on Christmas Eve.

keep something under wraps: *see* WRAP.

keep up with the Joneses: *see* JONESES.

keep your eye on the ball: *see* BALL.

keep your feet (*or* legs) manage not to fall.

keep someone on their toes: *see* on your toes *at* TOE.

you can't keep a good man (*or* woman) down a competent person will always recover well from setbacks or problems. informal

kettle

a different kettle of fish a completely different matter or type of person from the one previously mentioned. informal

> **1993** *Empire* Meryl is the finest actress of her generation but Arnold is, er, a different kettle of fish.

the pot calling the kettle black: *see* POT.

a pretty (*or* fine) kettle of fish an awkward state of affairs. informal

> ❶ In late 18th-century Scotland, *a kettle of fish* was a large saucepan of fish, typically freshly caught salmon, cooked at Scottish picnics, and the term was also applied to the picnic itself. By the mid 18th century, the novelist Henry Fielding was using the phrase to mean 'a muddle'.

key

in (*or* out of) key in (*or* out of) harmony.

kibosh

put the kibosh on put an end to; thwart the plans of. informal

> ❶ The meaning and origin of *kibosh* is uncertain. 'Put the kye-bosh on her' is used by 'a pot-boy' in Charles Dickens's *Sketches by Boz* (1836).

kick

kick against the pricks hurt yourself by persisting in useless resistance or protest.

> ❶ In the Bible, on the road to Damascus Saul heard the words: 'It is hard for thee to kick against the pricks' (Acts 9:5). The image is that of an ox or other beast of burden fruitlessly kicking out when it is pricked by a goad or spur.

kick someone's ass (*or* butt) dominate, beat, or defeat someone. North American vulgar slang

kick (some) ass (*or* butt) act in a forceful or aggressive manner. North American vulgar slang

> **1995 Martin Amis** *Information* You got to come on strong. Talk big and kick ass.

a kick at the can (*or* cat) an opportunity to achieve something. Canadian informal

kick the bucket die. informal

> ❶ The *bucket* in this phrase may be a pail on which a person committing suicide might stand, kicking it away before they hanged themselves. Another suggestion is that it refers to a beam on which something can be hung up; in Norfolk dialect the beam from which a slaughtered pig was suspended by its heels could be referred to as a *bucket*.

kick someone down the ladder reject or disown the friends or associates who have helped you to rise in the world, especially with the idea of preventing them from attaining a similar position.

kick the gong around smoke opium. informal

> ❶ *Gong* is early 20th-century US slang for a narcotic drug, especially opium.

kick the habit stop engaging in a habitual practice. informal

> **1992** *Economist* Perhaps it is time for ex-French West Africa to choose its own forms of government...and kick the habit of turning to France whenever trouble starts.

a kick in the pants (*or* up the arse *or* backside) something that prompts or forces fresh effort. informal

> **1996** *Southern Cross* On Saturday night, Mr Groom said the party understood the electorate had given the Liberals a kick in the pants.

a kick in the teeth a grave setback or disappointment, especially one seen as a betrayal. informal

> **1994** *Daily Mirror* The rates rise was a kick in the teeth for the housing market, which had been showing signs of recovery.

kick over the traces become insubordinate or reckless.

> ❶ *Traces* are the straps by which a draught horse is attached to the vehicle it is pulling. If the animal kicked out over these straps, the driver would no longer be able to control it.

kick someone upstairs remove someone from an influential position in a business by giving them an ostensible promotion. informal

kick someone when they are down cause further misfortune to someone who is already in a difficult situation.

kick something into touch remove something from the centre of attention or activity. British informal

> ❶ In football and rugby, the touchlines mark the sides of the playing area and if the ball is kicked beyond these (*into touch*), it is no longer in play.

> **1998** *New Scientist* The British public is more interested in these matters than many politicians think. Such issues cannot be kicked into touch.

kick up a fuss (*or* a stink) register strong disapproval; object loudly to something. informal

kick up your heels: *see* HEEL.

kick your heels: *see* **cool your heels** *at* HEEL.

kick yourself be annoyed with yourself for doing something foolish or missing an opportunity.

more kicks than halfpence more harsh treatment than rewards. informal, dated

kid

handle (*or* treat) someone or something with kid gloves deal with someone or something very gently or tactfully.

> ❶ *Kid gloves* are those made with leather from a young goat's skin.

kids' stuff something that is childishly simple or naive. informal

> **1982** **Vivien Alcock** *The Sylvia Game* He had grown out of the game; it was kid's stuff. Besides it always landed him in trouble.

a new kid on the block: *see* BLOCK.

kill

be in at the kill be present at or benefit from the successful conclusion of an enterprise.

dressed to kill: *see* DRESSED.

go (*or* move in *or* close in) for the kill take decisive action to turn a situation to your advantage.

if it kills you whatever the problems or difficulties involved. informal

> **2001** **Nancy Hope Wilson** *Mountain Pose* I'm cracking that code if it kills me.

kill the fatted calf: *see* FATTED.

kill the goose that lays the golden egg: *see* GOOSE.

kill or cure (of a remedy for a problem) likely to either work well or fail catastrophically, with no possibility of partial success. British

> **1998** **Richard Gordon** *Ailments through the Ages* Mackenzie complained that the Germans' policy was 'kill or cure': if they tried an elaborate laryngectomy, it would turn them from surgeons into assassins.

kill two birds with one stone achieve two aims at once.

kill someone with (*or* by) kindness spoil someone by overindulging them.

> ❶ This expression dates back to the mid 16th century; it famously appears in the title of Thomas Heywood's play *A Woman Killed with Kindness* (1607).

kill yourself laughing be overcome with laughter.

killing

make a killing have a great financial success, especially on a stock exchange.

kilter

out of kilter out of harmony or balance.

> ❶ *Kilter*, dating from the early 17th century, was a dialect word meaning 'frame or order'. It is now used only in this phrase.

king

King Charles's head an obsession.

> ❶ This expression alludes to the character of 'Mr Dick', in Charles Dickens's novel *David Copperfield*, who could not write or speak on any matter without the subject of King Charles's head intruding.

king of beasts the lion.

king of birds the eagle.

king of kings ❶ a king who has lesser kings under him. ❷ God.

king of terrors death personified.

King or Kaiser any powerful earthly ruler.

a king's ransom a huge amount of money; a fortune.

> ❶ In feudal times prisoners of war were freed for sums in keeping with their rank, so a king, as the highest-ranking individual, commanded the greatest ransom.

take the King's shilling: *see* SHILLING.

kingdom

come into (or to) your kingdom achieve recognition or supremacy.

till (or until) kingdom come forever. informal

to kingdom come into the next world. informal

> ❶ *Kingdom come* is the next world or eternity; it comes from the clause in the Lord's Prayer *thy kingdom come*.

> **1996** *Total Sport* Graham Gooch may be fast approaching his mid-forties but the old boy still clatters most bowlers to Kingdom come.

kiss

have kissed the blarney stone: *see* BLARNEY.

a Judas kiss: *see* JUDAS.

kiss and make up become reconciled.

> **1991** *Economist* [China] and Vietnam are preparing to kiss and make up in the cause of socialist solidarity.

kiss and tell recount your sexual exploits, especially to the media concerning a famous person. chiefly derogatory

kiss someone's arse (or ass) behave obsequiously towards someone. vulgar slang

kiss ass behave in an obsequious or sycophantic way. North American vulgar slang

kiss my arse go away!; go to hell! vulgar slang

kiss of death an action or event that causes certain failure for an enterprise.

> ❶ This expression may refer to the kiss of betrayal given by Judas Iscariot to Jesus in the Garden of Gethsemane (Matthew 26:48–9).

> **1998** *Spectator* I commend the Commission's recent Green Paper and its efforts to introduce an enlightened, evolutionary discussion—although I hope my saying so will not be the kiss of death.

kiss of life ❶ mouth-to-mouth resuscitation. ❷ an action or event that revives a failing enterprise.

> ❷ **1997 Anthony Barnett** *This Time* She gave a decrepit institution the kiss of life, when she became its adversary.

kiss the dust submit abjectly; be overthrown.

kiss the ground prostrate yourself as a token of respect.

> ❶ This phrase refers to the practice, found particularly in courts of the ancient Eastern world, of throwing yourself on the ground in front of a monarch.

kiss the rod accept punishment meekly or submissively.

> ❶ This idiom refers to a former practice of making a child kiss the rod with which it was beaten. It is used by Shakespeare in *Two Gentlemen of Verona*: 'How wayward is this foolish love That, like a testy babe, will scratch the nurse And presently all humbled kiss the rod'.

kiss something goodbye (or kiss goodbye to something) accept the certain loss of something. informal

kissy-face

play kissy-face (or kissy-kissy) behave in an excessively friendly way in order to gain favour. informal

kit

get your kit off take off all your clothes. British informal

kitchen

everything but the kitchen sink everything imaginable. informal, humorous

> ❶ This expression was identified by Eric Partridge in his *Dictionary of Forces' Slang* (1948) as being used in the context of an intense bombardment in which the enemy fired everything they had *except the kitchen sink* (or *including the kitchen sink*).

> **1965 Ed McBain** *Doll* Brown began searching. 'Everything in here but the kitchen sink,' he said.

kite

high as a kite intoxicated with drugs or alcohol. informal

> ❶ This expression is a play on *high* meaning 'lofty' and its informal sense 'intoxicated'.

kith

kith and kin your relations.

> ❶ *Kith*, an Old English word meaning 'native land' or 'countrymen', is now only used in this phrase, which itself dates back to the late 14th century. The variant *kith or kin* is also sometimes found.

kitten

have kittens be extremely nervous or upset. British informal

kitty

scoop the kitty be completely successful; gain everything.

> ❶ In gambling games, the *kitty* is the pool of money that is staked.

knee

at your mother's (or father's) knee at an early age.

bring someone or something to their knees reduce someone or something to a state of weakness or submission.

> **1997** *Sunday Times* Doom and gloom merchants everywhere are predicting all kinds of plagues befalling the world's computer systems anytime now, bringing business to its knees.

on bended knee: *see* BENDED.

on your knees ❶ in a kneeling position. ❷ on the verge of collapse.

weak at the knees overcome by a strong emotion.

knee-high

knee-high to a grasshopper very small or very young. informal, humorous

> ❶ In this form the phrase apparently dates from the mid 19th century, but early 19th-century US versions include *knee-high to a toad* and *knee-high to a mosquito*.

knell

ring the knell of announce or herald the end of.

> ❶ The image here is of the tolling of a bell to announce a death or funeral.

knickers

get your knickers in a twist become upset or angry. British informal

> ❶ This expression was originally used specifically of women, the humorous masculine equivalent being *get your Y-fronts in a twist*.

> **1998** *Times* I'm not as anxious as I was ... Most things these days, I'm really not going to get my knickers in a twist about.

knife

an atmosphere that you could cut with a knife: *see* ATMOSPHERE.

before you can say knife very quickly; almost instantaneously. informal

get (or stick) the knife into (or in) someone do something hostile or aggressive to someone. informal

go (or be) under the knife have surgery. informal

like a (hot) knife through butter very easily; without any resistance or difficulty.

twist (or turn) the knife deliberately make someone's grief or problems worse.

> **1991 Mavis Nicholson** *Martha Jane & Me* While she and I were playing the cat-and-mouse game of these stories, I would sometimes, just to twist the knife a little further, ask about the little girl's father.

the knives are out (for someone) there is open hostility (towards someone). informal

knife-edge

on a knife-edge (or razor's edge) in a tense situation, especially one finely balanced between success and failure.

> **2000** *South African Times UK* With the game poised on a knife-edge, the Wallabies won a

ruck and George Gregan's pass was floated to the flyhalf, who picked his line perfectly.

knight

a knight in shining armour an idealized or heroic person, especially a man who comes to the rescue of a woman in distress or in a difficult situation.

> ❶ This expression, a variant of which is *a knight on a white charger*, is often used ironically of someone who presents himself in this guise but is in fact inadequate to the role. Compare with **a white knight** (*at* WHITE).

knight of the road a man who frequents the roads, for example a travelling sales representative, lorry or taxi driver, or tramp.

> ❶ Originally, in the mid 17th century, this phrase was ironically applied to a highwayman.

a white knight: *see* WHITE.

knitting

stick to the (*or* your) knitting (of an organization) concentrate on a known core area of business activity rather than diversify into other areas in which it has no experience. informal

knob

with knobs (*or* brass knobs) on and something more. British informal

> **1998** *Pi Magazine* But all this would count for zilch if the music didn't stand the test of time. But it does, with knobs on.

knock

knock someone's block off hit someone very hard in anger. informal

> ❶ *Block* is used here in its informal sense of 'head'.

knock someone dead greatly impress someone. informal

> **1991** Julia Philips *You'll Never Eat Lunch In This Town Again* I'm good at public speaking. I've been knocking them dead at seminars.

knock someone into the middle of next week hit someone very hard. informal

knock it off used to tell someone to stop doing something that you find annoying or foolish. informal

knock on (*or* at) the door seek to join a particular group or sphere of action.

knock someone for six: *see* hit someone for six *at* SIX.

knock someone or something on the head decisively prevent an idea, plan, or proposal from being held or developed. British informal

> ❶ The image in this phrase is of stunning or killing a person or an animal by a blow to their head.

knock someone sideways affect someone very severely; make someone severely depressed or unable to cope. informal

> **1998** Penelope Lively *Spiderweb* It's always knocked me sideways—the thought of what we carry around, stashed away.

knock someone's socks off: *see* SOCK.

knock something into a cocked hat: *see* COCKED HAT.

knock spots off easily outdo. informal

> ❶ This expression may refer to shooting out the pips (spots) on a playing card in a pistol-shooting competition. Although it is now found chiefly in British English, the phrase originated in America.

> **1997** *Spectator* [Walter Laut Palmer's] 'Morning in Venice' is a tour-de-force . . . It knocks spots off the neighbouring, deeply unattractive, Monet of a gondola.

knock them in the aisles amaze and impress people. informal

knock your head against a brick wall: *see* bang your head against a brick wall *at* HEAD.

knock someone or something into shape: *see* lick someone or something into shape *at* SHAPE.

the school of hard knocks: *see* SCHOOL.

take a knock suffer a material or emotional setback.

knock on wood: *see* touch wood *at* WOOD.

knocked

you could have knocked me (*or* her, him, etc.) down with a feather I (*or* she, he, etc.) was greatly surprised. informal

> ❶ A similar idiom is found in Samuel Richardson's novel *Pamela* (1741) ('you might have beat me down with a feather'); the modern form of the expression with *knock* dates from the mid 19th century.

knocker

on the knocker ❶ going from door to door,

knot

usually canvassing, buying, or selling. ❷ (of
payment) immediately; on demand.
Australian & New Zealand informal

up to the knocker in good condition; to
perfection. informal

knot

at a rate of knots very fast. British informal

> ❶ A *knot* here is a nautical unit of speed,
> equal to one nautical mile per hour.

cut the knot: see CUT.

tie the knot get married. informal

tie someone (up) in knots make someone
completely confused. informal

> **1996** *Daily Star* It looks like an open and shut
> case until the brilliant QC starts getting the
> prosecution witnesses tied up in knots.

know

— as we know it as is familiar or customary
in the present.

> **1991** *Scientific American* Now that all-out
> nuclear war seems to be receding as an
> imminent threat to life as we know it,
> the National Aeronautics and Space
> Administration has come up with something
> else to keep us worried: doomsday asteroids.

be in the know be aware of something
known only to a few people.

**before you know where you are (or before
you know it)** with baffling speed. informal

know a thing or two be experienced or
shrewd.

> **1993** *Rolling Stone* Andy Shernoff . . . knows a
> thing or two about great glam punk.

know better than be wise, well-informed, or
well-mannered enough to avoid doing
something specified.

> **1989** **Anne Fine** *Goggle-Eyes* Inspector McGee
> knows better than to tangle with Beth's
> granny.

know (or not know) from nothing be totally
ignorant, either generally or concerning
something in particular. North American
informal

know little (or nothing) and care less
be completely unconcerned about
something; be studiously ignorant.

know someone in the biblical sense have
sex with someone. informal, humorous

> ❶ *Know* in this sense is an old use which is
> particularly associated with language in the
> Bible, e.g. Genesis 4:1: And Adam knew Eve
> his wife; and she conceived, and bare Cain'.

know something like the back of your hand:
see BACK.

know the ropes be thoroughly acquainted
with the way in which something is done.
informal

> ❶ In its literal sense, this expression goes
> back to the days of sailing ships, when skill in
> handling ropes was essential for any sailor.
> The idiom is found in various forms, from the
> mid 19th century onwards, e.g. *learn* or
> *understand the ropes* and *show* or *teach
> someone the ropes*

know the score be aware of what is going on.

> **2002** *New York Times Magazine* Nowadays,
> everyone knows the score. Aside from
> discovering, say, that Tom Hanks is mean,
> what story of show business ugliness would
> scandalize us?

know too much be in possession of too much
important information to be allowed to live
or continue as normal.

know what's what have enough knowledge
or experience. informal

> **1992** *More* I know what's what at work, so no-
> one's going to trip me up.

know what you like have fixed or definite
tastes, without necessarily having the
knowledge or informed opinion to support
them.

> **2002** *Sunday Herald* We adjourn to Starbucks
> where . . . I know what I like (grand skinny
> latte, £2.15).

know where the bodies are buried: *see*
BODY.

know where you are (or stand) with know
how you are regarded by someone; know
the opinions of someone on an issue.

> **1991** **Julian Barnes** *Talking It Over* Good old
> Stuart, he's so reliable. You know where you
> are with Stuart.

know who's who be aware of the identity
and status of each person.

know your own mind be decisive and
certain.

not know someone from Adam: *see* ADAM.

not know what hit you be hit, killed, or
attacked by someone or something
without warning.

not know what to do with yourself be at a
loss as to what to do, typically through
boredom, embarrassment, or anxiety.

not know where (or which way) to look feel
great embarrassment and not know how to
react.

knowing

there is no knowing no one can tell.

known

have known better days: *see* **have seen better days** *at* DAY.

knows

for all someone knows used to express the limited scope or extent of someone's information.

knuckle

go the knuckle fight with the fists. Australian informal

near the knuckle verging on the indecent or offensive. British informal

> ❶ In the late 19th century this expression was used more generally to mean 'close to the permitted limit of behaviour'.

labour

a labour of Hercules a task requiring enormous strength or effort.

> ⓘ In Greek mythology, Hercules was a man of superhuman strength and courage who performed twelve immense tasks or labours imposed on him as a penance for killing his children in a fit of madness. After his death he was ranked among the gods.

a labour of love a task done for the love of a person or for the work itself.

labour the point explain or discuss something at excessive or unnecessary length.

ladder

kick someone down the ladder: see KICK.

lady

it isn't over till the fat lady sings there is still time for a situation to change.

> ⓘ This phrase comes from the saying *the opera isn't over till the fat lady sings*, which originated in the 1970s in the USA; it is doubtful whether any particular operatic production or prima donna was ever intended.

ladies who lunch women with the money and free time to meet for social lunches. informal

> ⓘ This expression comes from the title of a 1970s song by Stephen Sondheim: 'A toast to that invincible bunch ... Let's hear it for the ladies who lunch'. While it is often used of women who raise money for charity by organizing fashionable lunches, it is also often used in a derogatory way of women with the money and leisure to lunch at expensive restaurants.

Lady Bountiful a woman who engages in ostentatious acts of charity to impress others.

> ⓘ Lady Bountiful is the name of a character in *The Beaux' Stratagem* (1707), a play by the Irish Restoration dramatist George Farquhar.

Lady Luck chance personified as a controlling power in human affairs.

Lady Muck a haughty or socially pretentious woman. British informal

laldy

give it laldy do something with vigour or enthusiasm. Scottish

> ⓘ *Laldy* or *laldie*, as in *give someone laldy*, means 'a punishment or beating'.
>
> **1993** Irvine Welsh *Trainspotting* A chorus ... echoes throughout the pub. Auld, toothless Willie Shane is giein it laldy.

lam

on the lam in flight, especially from the police. North American informal

lamb

like a lamb to the slaughter as a helpless victim.

> ⓘ This expression is found in the Bible in Isaiah 53:7: 'he is brought as a lamb to the slaughter', an image later applied to Jesus.

lame

lame duck: see DUCK.

lamp

smell of the lamp: see SMELL.

land

land on your feet: see *fall on your feet at* FALL.

how the land lies what the state of affairs is.

in the land of the living alive or awake. humorous

> ⓘ This is a biblical idiom: see, for example, Job 28:13: 'Man knoweth not the price thereof; neither is it found in the land of the living' or Psalms 52:5: 'God shall likewise destroy thee for ever, he shall take thee away, and pluck thee out of thy dwelling place, and root thee out of the land of the living'.

land of Nod a state of sleep.

> ⓘ In the Bible, the Land of Nod was the place to which Cain was exiled after the

murder of his brother Abel (Genesis 4:16). It has been used punningly to refer to sleep since the 18th century, notably by Jonathan Swift in *Polite Conversation* (1731–8): 'I'm going to the Land of Nod'.

live off the land (*or* **the country**) live on whatever food you can obtain by hunting, gathering, or subsistence farming.

> **1995** *Empire* Harrison Ford is the frazzled father who ups his family from cosy suburbia in an effort to live off the land, get back to nature, etc.

no man's land: *see* NO.

landscape

a blot on the landscape: *see* BLOT.

language

speak the same language understand one another as a result of shared opinions and values.

> **1990** *New Age Journal* I translate between Greenpeace-speak and record industry-speak, because the two groups just don't speak the same language.

lap

fall (*or* **drop**) **into someone's lap** (of something pleasant or desirable) come someone's way without any effort having been made.

in the lap of luxury in conditions of great comfort and wealth.

in the lap of the gods (of the success of a plan or event) open to chance; depending on factors that you cannot control.

> ❶ This expression comes from one used in several passages in the works of the Greek epic poet Homer. The original Greek refers to the 'knees' of the gods, possibly because suppliants laid gifts on the knees of those who were sitting in judgement upon them.

lares

lares and penates the home.

> ❶ In ancient Rome, the *lares* and *penates* were the protective gods of a household, and they came to be used to signify the home itself. The phrase *lares and penates* is generally used to refer to those things that are considered to be the essential elements of someone's home; in 1775 Horace Walpole wrote in a letter 'I am returned to my own Lares and Penates—to my dogs and cats'.

large

give (*or* **have**) **it large** go out and enjoy yourself, typically with drink or drugs. British informal

> **1999** *London Student* Clubbers had it large to Americans Josh Wink and long-time Detroit supremo Derrick May.

large as life: *see* LIFE.

lark

up with the lark up very early in the morning.

> ❶ References to the early-morning singing of the lark date back to the 16th century: the first recorded instance is found in John Lyly's *Euphues*. Early risers are often referred to as *larks*, while their late-to-bed counterparts may be described as *owls*. The phrase also employs a play on the word *up*, since the lark sings on the wing while flying high above its nest.

Larry

happy as Larry: *see* **happy as a sandboy** *at* HAPPY.

lash

have a lash at make an attempt at; have a go at. Australian & New Zealand

last

be the last word be the most fashionable or up-to-date.

> **1989** *Life* Thanks to a built-in microchip, Teddy Ruxpin became the last word in talking dolls.

die in the last ditch: *see* DIE.

famous last words: *see* FAMOUS.

have the last word ❶ make or have the right to make the final decision or pronouncement about something. ❷ carry out a final and conclusive action in a process or course of events.

(drinking) in the last chance saloon having been allowed one final opportunity to improve or get something right. informal

> **1998** *Times* Gascoigne has finally found himself in the Last Chance Saloon.

last but not least last in order of mention or occurrence but not of importance.

the last of the Mohicans the sole survivor(s) of a particular race or kind.

> ❶ *The Last of the Mohicans* is the title of an 1826 novel by James Fenimore Cooper (1789–1851). The Mohicans, also spelled *Mohegans*, were an Algonquian people who

formerly inhabited the western parts of the US states of Connecticut and Massachusetts.

the last straw: *see* STRAW.

last thing late in the evening, especially as a final act before going to bed.

on your last legs: *see* LEG.

pay your last respects: *see* PAY.

late

late in the day at a late stage in proceedings, especially too late to be useful.

> ❶ A North American variant of this expression is *late in the game*.

the late unpleasantness: *see* UNPLEASANTNESS.

laugh

enough to make a cat laugh: *see* CAT.

good for a laugh guaranteed to amuse or entertain.

> **1998** *Spectator* I'm now ashamed to admit it, but the fact remains that in 1979 voting Tory did seem good for a laugh.

have the last laugh be finally vindicated, thereby confounding earlier scepticism.

> ❶ There are various proverbial sayings expressing this idea, such as *he laughs best who laughs last* and *he who laughs last, laughs longest*.

laugh all the way to the bank make a great deal of money with very little effort. informal

> **1998** *Country Life* In the Taw Valley they don't need to say 'cheese' to raise a smile—they just whisper 'environment' and laugh all the way to the bank.

laugh in someone's face show open contempt for someone by laughing rudely at them in their presence.

the laugh is on me (*or* **you** *or* **him, etc.**) the situation is reversed and now the other person is the one who appears ridiculous.

laugh like a drain laugh raucously; guffaw. British informal

a laugh a minute very funny.

laugh yourself silly (*or* **sick**) laugh uncontrollably or for a long time.

laugh on the other side of your face be discomfited after feeling satisfaction or confidence about something.

> ❶ A North American variant of this expression is *laugh out of the other side of your mouth*.

laugh someone or something out of court dismiss someone or something with contempt as being obviously ridiculous.

laugh someone or something to scorn ridicule someone or something.

> ❶ This is a biblical idiom: see, for example, Job 12:4: 'I am as one mocked of his neighbour, who calleth upon God, and he answereth him: the just upright man is laughed to scorn' or Matthew 9:24: 'He said unto them, Give place: for the maid is not dead, but sleepeth. And they laughed him to scorn.'

laugh up your sleeve be secretly or inwardly amused.

> ❶ The use of *up* in this expression is a relatively recent development; the phrase dates from the mid 16th century in the form *laugh in your sleeve*.

play something for laughs (of a performer) try to arouse laughter in an audience, especially in inappropriate circumstances.

laughing

be laughing be in a fortunate or comfortable situation. informal

> **2000** Ian Pattison *A Stranger Here Myself* I spotted a card in the window of a Lyons Tearoom. *Dishwashers Wanted. No Exp. Nec.* 'That's it,' I said to Cotter, 'we're laughing.'

no laughing matter something serious that should not be joked about.

laurels

look to your laurels be careful not to lose your superior position to a rival.

rest on your laurels be so satisfied with what you have already done or achieved that you make no further effort.

> ❶ In ancient Greece, a wreath made of bay-tree (laurel) leaves was awarded as a mark of distinction and, in particular, to victors at the Pythian Games held at Delphi.

lavender

lay something up in lavender: *see* LAY.

law

be a law unto yourself behave in a manner that is not conventional or predictable.

the law of the jungle: *see* JUNGLE.

the law of the Medes and Persians: *see* MEDES.

lay down the law issue instructions to other people in an authoritative or dogmatic way.

take the law into your own hands punish someone for an offence according to your own ideas of justice, especially in an illegal or violent way.

take someone to law initiate legal proceedings against someone.

there's no law against it used in spoken English to assert that you are doing nothing wrong, especially in response to an actual or implied criticism. informal

lay

lay rubber: see **burn rubber** at RUBBER.

lay eyes on: see **clap eyes on** at EYE.

lay a charge make an accusation.

> **1989 Tony Parker** *A Place Called Bird* We have domestic assaults. The complainant lays a charge.

lay down the law: see LAW.

lay a (or the) ghost get rid of a distressing, frightening, or worrying memory or thought.

> ❶ The image here is of exorcizing an unquiet or evil spirit.

lay it on the line: see LINE.

lay someone low ❶ (of an illness) reduce someone to inactivity. ❷ bring to an end the high position or good fortune formerly enjoyed by someone.

lay something at someone's door: see DOOR.

lay something on the table: see TABLE.

lay something on thick (or with a trowel) grossly exaggerate or overemphasize something. informal

lay something to rest soothe and dispel fear, anxiety, grief, and similar unpleasant emotions.

lay something up in lavender preserve something carefully for future use.

> ❶ The flowers and stalks of lavender were traditionally used as a preservative for stored clothes.

lay store by: see **set store by** at STORE.

lead

get the lead out move or work more quickly; hurry up. North American informal

> ❶ This expression originated as mid 20th-century jazz slang, meaning 'play at a brisk speed'. A fuller version is *get the lead out of your pants*. Renowned for its weight, the metal *lead* appears in a number of expressions as a metaphor for inertness or heaviness (see, for example, **go down like a lead balloon** below and **swing the lead** at SWING).

go down (or over) like a lead balloon (especially of a speech, proposal, or joke) fail; be a flop. informal

> **1996** *Prospect* Simon Jenkins's book, *Accountable to None*, has gone down like a lead balloon with most Conservative reviewers.

lead someone a dance: see DANCE.

lead someone by the nose control someone totally, especially by deceiving them. informal

> ❶ The image here is of an animal being controlled by a restraint round or in the nose. Shakespeare used this expression in *Othello* (1604): 'The Moor... will as tenderly be led by th'nose As asses are'.

lead from the front take an active role in what you are urging and directing others to do.

lead in your pencil vigour or energy, especially sexual energy in a man. informal

> **1972 Dan Lees** *Zodiac* The couscous is supposed to put lead in your pencil but with Daria I needed neither a talking point nor an aphrodisiac.

lead someone up the garden path: see GARDEN.

lead with your chin behave or speak incautiously. informal

> ❶ This expression originated as mid 20th-century boxing slang, referring to a boxer's stance that leaves his chin unprotected.

swing the lead: see SWING.

leaf

shake (or tremble) like a leaf tremble greatly, especially from fear.

take a leaf out of someone's book closely imitate or emulate someone in a particular way.

> **1999** *London Student* Maybe the other colleges should take a leaf out of Imperial's book and try pub games instead of sports.

turn over a new leaf improve your conduct or performance.

> ℹ The *leaf* referred to here is a page of a book. The phrase has been used in this metaphorical sense since the 16th century, and while it now always means 'change for the better', it could previously also mean just 'change' or even 'change for the worse'.

leak

have (*or* take) a leak urinate. informal

spring a leak (of a boat or container) develop a leak.

> ℹ The expression was originally a nautical one, referring to the timbers of a wooden ship springing out of position and so letting in water.

lean

lean over backwards: *see* **bend over backwards** *at* BACKWARDS.

leap

a leap in the dark a daring step or enterprise whose consequences are unpredictable.

leap to the eye (especially of writing) be immediately apparent.

by leaps and bounds with startlingly rapid progress.

lease

a new lease of (*or* on) life a substantially improved prospect of life or use after rejuvenation or repair.
> **1997** *BBC Vegetarian Good Food* Give salads, sandwiches and jacket spuds a new lease of life with a spoonful of flavoured mayonnaise.

leash

strain at the leash: *see* STRAIN.

least

least said, soonest mended a difficult situation will be resolved more quickly if there is no discussion of it.

not least notably; in particular.

to say the least (*or* the least of it) used as an understatement or euphemism to imply that the reality is more extreme, usually worse.
> **1997** *Spectator* References in Mr Cole's letter to the 'bottle' were, to say the least, distasteful.

leave

leave someone cold fail to interest someone.
> **1993** James Merril *A Different Person* I might have waxed sentimental over the ruins of Catullus's garçonnière but places that 'breathe History' have always left me cold.

leave much (*or* a lot) to be desired be highly unsatisfactory.

take French leave: *see* FRENCH.

take leave of your senses: *see* SENSE.

leech

like a leech persistently or clingingly present.

> ℹ This idiom refers to the way in which a leech attaches itself by suction to the person or animal from which it is drawing blood: the parasites are very difficult to remove once they are attached to the skin and feeding.

leeway

make up (the) leeway struggle out of a bad position, especially by recovering lost time. British

> ℹ *Leeway*, which dates from the mid 17th century, was the nautical term for the drift of a ship towards the side downwind of its course. The figurative use of this phrase dates from the early 19th century.

left

be left at the post fail to compete. informal

> ℹ The image here is of a racehorse that fails to leave the starting post along with its rivals.

be left holding the baby: *see* HOLDING.

hang a left: *see* HANG.

have two left feet be clumsy or awkward.

left, right, and centre (*also* left and right *or* right and left) on all sides.
> **1996** *Loaded* She relocated to New York... quickly finding herself heralded left, right and centre as The Face Of The '80s.

leg

feel (*or* find) your legs become able to stand or walk.

get your leg over (of a man) have sexual intercourse. vulgar slang

have the legs of be able to go faster or further than a rival. British

keep your legs: *see* **keep your feet** *at* KEEP.

not have a leg to stand on have no facts or sound reasons to support your argument or justify your actions.

on your hind legs standing up to make a speech. British informal

on your last legs near the end of life, usefulness, or strength.

> **1987 Eric Newby** *Round Ireland in Low Gear* It is certainly difficult to imagine how anyone who is in any way infirm, and some of the pilgrims who make the climb are literally on their last legs, can reach the top.

take to your legs: *see* **take to your heels** *at* HEEL.

legend

a legend in their own lifetime a very famous or notorious person.

legit

go legit begin to behave honestly after a period of illegal activity. informal

> ❶ *Legit* was originally a late 19th-century theatrical abbreviation meaning 'a legitimate actor', that is, one who acts in 'legitimate theatre' (conventional or serious drama).

leisure

lady (or man or gentleman) of leisure a person who does not need to earn a living or whose time is free from obligations to others.

lemon

the answer's a lemon the response or outcome is unsatisfactory. informal

> ❶ A *lemon* here is used to represent a bad, unsatisfactory, or disappointing thing, possibly because the lemon is the least valuable symbol that can be achieved by playing a fruit machine.

hand someone a lemon pass off a substandard article as good; swindle someone.

lend

lend an ear (or your ears) listen to someone sympathetically or attentively.

lend your name to something allow yourself to be publicly associated with something.

Lenten

Lenten fare meagre rations that do not include meat.

> ❶ Lenten fare is literally food appropriate to *Lent*, the Christian season of fasting between Ash Wednesday and Easter Saturday in commemoration of Jesus's forty days of fasting in the wilderness.

leopard

a leopard can't change his spots people can't change their basic nature. proverb

less

in less than no time very quickly or soon. informal

lesser

the lesser evil (or the lesser of two evils) the less harmful or unpleasant of two bad choices or possibilities.

let

let someone down gently seek to give someone bad news in a way that avoids causing them too much distress or humiliation.

let it drop (or rest) say or do no more about a matter or problem.

let it go (or pass) choose not to react to an action or remark.

let off steam: *see* STEAM.

let yourself go ❶ act in an unrestrained or uninhibited way. ❷ neglect yourself or your appearance; become careless or untidy in your habits.

let or hindrance obstruction or impediment. formal

> ❶ *Let* in its Middle English sense of 'something that impedes' is now archaic and rarely occurs outside this phrase, in which it duplicates the sense of *hindrance*. It is, however, used in sports such as badminton and tennis.

> **1999 Marion Shoard** *A Right to Roam* Citizens can claim routes as new public paths on the grounds that they have been used without let or hindrance for at least twenty years.

let rip: *see* RIP.

let slip: *see* SLIP.

let something drop (or fall) casually reveal a piece of information.

letter

a dead letter: *see* DEAD.

a man (or woman) of letters a scholar or writer.

to the letter with adherence to every detail.

> ❶ The French equivalent of this phrase is *au pied de la lettre*, which has been used in English since the late 18th century.

level

do your level best do your utmost; make all possible efforts.

a level playing field a situation in which everyone has a fair and equal chance of succeeding.

> **1998** *Times* Most damagingly, the Brussels-centred concept of 'the level playing field' had also proved a wonderfully convenient alibi for protectionist lobbies.

on the level honest and truthful. informal

liberty

take liberties ❶ behave in an unduly familiar manner towards a person. ❷ treat something freely, without strict faithfulness to the facts or to an original.

take the liberty venture to do something without first asking permission.

licence

licence to print money a very lucrative commercial activity, typically one perceived as requiring little effort.

lick

at a lick at a fast pace. informal

a lick and a promise a hasty performance of a task, especially of cleaning something. informal

> **2001 Andrew O'Hare** *Green Eyes* Trying to scrub my teeth was just as disastrous as before, washing the face was no more than a lick and a promise but it would have to do.

lick someone's boots be excessively obsequious towards someone, especially to gain favour.

lick someone or something into shape: *see* SHAPE.

lick your lips (*or* chops) look forward to something with eager anticipation.

> **1997** *Guardian* Headhunting agencies licked their chops at the prospect of the fat placement fees.

lick your wounds retire to recover your strength or confidence after a defeat or humiliating experience.

lid

blow the lid off remove means of restraint and allow something to get out of control. informal

> **1995** *Daily Express* Fleiss was taken to court on prostitution charges and threatened to blow the lid off Hollywood by revealing names of all her superstar clients.

flip your lid: *see* FLIP.

keep a (*or* the) lid on ❶ keep an emotion or process from going out of control. ❷ keep something secret. informal

put the (*or* a) lid on put a stop to. informal

> **1996** *Observer* Nothing's final. I haven't put the lid on anything.

put the (tin) lid on be the culmination of a series of acts or events that makes things unbearable. British informal

> **1999 Chris Dolan** *Ascension Day* Mum found she was pregnant a month before the wedding, then Dad put the tin lid on it by getting himself laid off.

take (*or* lift) the lid off (*or* lift the lid on) reveal unwelcome secrets about. informal

lie

give the lie to something serve to show that something previously stated or believed to be the case is not true.

I tell a lie (*or* that's a lie) an expression used to immediately correct yourself when you realize that you have made an incorrect remark. informal

let sleeping dogs lie: *see* SLEEPING.

let something lie take no action regarding a controversial or problematic matter.

lie in state (of the corpse of a person of national importance) be laid in a public place of honour before burial.

lie like a trooper tell lies constantly and flagrantly. Compare with **swear like a trooper** (at SWEAR).

lie through your teeth (*or* in your throat) tell an outright lie without remorse. informal

live a lie lead a life that conceals your true nature or circumstances.

nail a lie: *see* NAIL.

lies

as far as in me lies to the best of my power.

how the land lies: *see* LAND.

life

do anything for a quiet life make any concession to avoid being disturbed.

the facts of life: *see* FACT.

for dear (*or* your) life as if or in order to escape death.

> **1992** *Independent* I made for the life raft and hung on for dear life.

for the life of me however hard I try; even if my life depended on it. informal

1998 Robert Newman *Manners* I cannot for the life of me think what the name of the lead singer was.

frighten the life out of terrify.

get a life start living a fuller or more interesting existence. informal

1997 *J-17* All anybody seems to be talking about today is school. These people need to get a life.

large as life (of a person) conspicuously present. informal

> ⓘ This expression was originally used literally, with reference to the size of a statue or portrait relative to the original: in the mid 18th century Horace Walpole described a painting as being 'as large as the life'. The humorous mid 19th-century elaboration of the expression, *large as life and twice as natural*, used by Lewis Carroll and others, is still sometimes found; it is attributed to the Canadian humorist T. C. Haliburton (1796–1865).

larger than life ❶ (of a person) attracting attention because their appearance or behaviour is more flamboyant than that of ordinary people. ❷ (of a thing) seeming disproportionately important.

1996 *Face* I feel that Keith from The Prodigy has been your best cover this year—he is London, in your face, loud and larger than life.

life and limb life and all bodily faculties.

1993 *Vanity Fair* Castro is particularly irked by the bad press Cuba gets concerning... the rafters who risk life and limb to get to Florida.

the life and soul of the party a person whose vivacity and sociability makes a party enjoyable.

life in the fast lane an exciting and eventful lifestyle, especially a wealthy one. informal

a matter of life and death a matter of vital importance.

a new lease of life: *see* LEASE.

not on your life said to emphasize your refusal to comply with some request. informal

see life gain a wide experience of the world, especially its more pleasurable aspects.

take your life in your hands risk being killed.

this is the life an expression of contentment with your present circumstances.

1995 Nicholas Whittaker *Platform Souls* This is the life, nothing to do but read and look out of the window.

to the life exactly like the original.

to save your life even if your life were to depend on it.

walk of life: *see* WALK.

within an inch of your life: *see* INCH.

lifeline

throw a lifeline to (*or* **throw someone a lifeline**) provide someone with a means of escaping from a difficult situation.

lifetime

of a lifetime (of a chance or experience) such as does not occur more than once in a person's life; exceptional.

lift

lift (*or* **stir**) **a finger** (*or* **hand**) make the slightest effort to do something, especially to help someone.

1992 *Daily Telegraph* If the public does not care much for the interests of the press, it will not lift a finger to save a politician from sexual embarrassment.

light

be light on be rather short of.

be light on your feet be quick or nimble.

go out like a light fall asleep or lose consciousness suddenly. informal

hide your light under a bushel: *see* HIDE.

in (the) light of drawing knowledge or information from; with regard to.

1990 *Times Education Supplement* Proposals to build problem-solving into all A-level subjects may have to be re-examined in the light of new research commissioned by the Government.

light at the end of the tunnel a long-awaited indication that a period of hardship or adversity is nearing an end.

light a fire under someone: *see* FIRE.

light the (*or* **a**) **fuse** (*or* **touchpaper**) do something that creates a tense or exciting situation.

> ⓘ The image here is of lighting a fuse attached to gunpowder, fireworks, etc. in order to cause an explosion. A *touchpaper*, which is used in the same way as a fuse, is a twist of paper impregnated with saltpetre to make it burn slowly.

1998 *Times* The rejection of global capitalism may light a touchpaper in all those countries battered by the crisis.

the light of your life a much-loved person.

make light (*or* **little**) **of** treat as unimportant.

1990 *Vanity Fair* Ian says they still hope to marry someday, and tries to make light of their non-wedding.

make light work of accomplish a task quickly and easily.

punch someone's lights out beat someone up.

lightning

lightning never strikes twice the same calamity never occurs twice.

> ❶ This expression refers to the popular belief that lightning never strikes the same spot twice.

> **1983** Penelope Lively *Perfect Happiness* It's nasty, isn't it?...Having to go to the same airport. Though in a way you can't help thinking well lightning never strikes twice.

like lightning (or like greased lightning) very quickly.

like

like it or not used to indicate that someone has no choice in a matter. informal
> **1998** *New Scientist* Like it or not, people expect more honesty from those who claim to be on the side of the environment.

like —, like — as — is, so is —.

> ❶ Two familiar sayings which appear in this form are *like father, like son*, recorded in this form from the early 17th century onwards, and *like mother, like daughter*.

> **1982** Anita Desai *A Village by the Sea* Did he teach you to tell me that—that rogue, your father? Like father, like daughter. A family full of liars, no-goods.

the likes of a similar type of person or thing. informal

> **1989** Charles Shaar Murray *Crosstown Traffic* They specialized in an odd combination of funk workouts and soulish adaptations of folk-rock hits by the likes of James Taylor and the Doobie Brothers.

likely

a likely story used to express disbelief of an account or excuse.

lily

gild the lily: *see* GILD.

limb

life and limb: *see* LIFE.

out on a limb ❶ isolated or stranded. ❷ without support.

> ❶ A *limb* here is the projecting branch of a tree. A related expression is *go out on a limb*, meaning 'take a risk' or 'act boldly and uncompromisingly'.

> **1991** *Times Education Supplement* I don't always want to go out on a limb, or sound confrontational by flatly saying that the child has done this or that.

tear someone limb from limb violently dismember someone.

limit

be the limit be intolerably troublesome or irritating. informal

line

the bottom line the final reality; the important conclusion.

> ❶ Literally, *the bottom line* is the final total in an account or balance sheet.

> **1991** *Sun* The bottom line is that we would rather have Venables and Sugar than Gazza, Maxwell and Scholar.

come down to the line (of a race) be closely fought right until the end.

come (or bring someone or something) into line conform (or cause someone or something to conform).

do a line with someone have a regular romantic or sexual relationship with someone. Irish & New Zealand informal

end of the line the point at which further effort is unproductive or you can go no further.

get a line on learn something about. informal
> **1939** Raymond Chandler *The Big Sleep* I was trying to get a line on you, sure.

lay (or put) it on the line speak frankly.

(draw) a line in the sand (state that you have reached) a point beyond which you will not go.

the line of least resistance: *see* RESISTANCE.

line your pocket (or pockets) make money, usually by dishonest means.

out of line behaving in a way that breaks the rules or is considered disreputable or inappropriate.

toe the line: *see* TOE.

linen

wash your dirty linen in public: *see* WASH.

lion

a lion in the way a danger or obstacle, especially an imaginary one. literary

> ❶ This expression developed from a biblical phrase in Proverbs 22:13: 'The slothful man saith, There is a lion without, I shall be slain in the streets'.

the lion's den a demanding, intimidating, or unpleasant place or situation.

the lion's mouth a place of great peril.

the lion's share the largest part of something.

> **1998** *Times* Rich countries generally seize the lion's share of trade.

throw someone to the lions cause someone to be in an extremely dangerous or unpleasant situation.

> ❶ In ancient Rome, Christians and other religious or political dissidents were thrown to the lions in the arena to be killed.

lip

bite your lip repress an emotion; stifle laughter or a retort.

curl your lip raise a corner of your upper lip to show contempt; sneer.

hang on someone's lips listen attentively to someone.

lick (*or* **smack**) **your lips** look forward to something with relish; show your satisfaction.

pass someone's lips be eaten, drunk, or spoken by someone.

pay lip service to something express approval of or support for something without taking any significant action.

> **1998** *New Scientist* Green organisations are having great difficulty maintaining their membership, and politicians pay lip service to environmental problems.

someone's lips are sealed a person is obliged to keep a secret.

lists

enter the lists issue or accept a challenge.

> ❶ In medieval times, the *lists* were the enclosed area in which knights fought each other in tournaments.

little

make little of: *see* **make light of** *at* LIGHT.

quite the little — used when ironically or condescendingly recognizing that someone has a particular quality or accomplishment.

> **1995 John Banville** *Athena* She was being quite the little home-maker, all bustle and frown.

live

live and breathe something be extremely interested in or enthusiastic about a particular subject or activity; spend a great deal of your time pursuing a particular interest.

live and learn used, especially in spoken English, to acknowledge that a fact is new to you.

> **1998 Barbara Kingsolver** *The Poisonwood Bible* A man who leaves his wife for his mistress is no catch, I was sorry to find out. Well, live and learn

live and let live you should tolerate the opinions and behaviour of others so that they will similarly tolerate your own.

> ❶ On its first appearance in English in 1622, this was referred to as a Dutch proverb (*Leuen ende laeten leuen*).

live by your wits: *see* WIT.

live in the past ❶ have old-fashioned or outdated ideas and attitudes. ❷ dwell on or reminisce at length about past events.

live it up spend your time in an extremely enjoyable or extravagant way. informal

live a lie: *see* LIE.

live off the fat of the land: *see* FAT.

live off the land: *see* LAND.

live out of a suitcase live or stay somewhere on a temporary basis and with only a limited selection of your belongings, typically because your occupation requires a great deal of travelling.

live over the shop live on the premises where you work.

live your own life follow your own plans and principles; be independent of others.

live rough live and sleep outdoors as a consequence of having no proper home.

live to fight another day survive a certain experience or ordeal.

> ❶ This idea, found in the works of the Greek comic playwright Menander, is expressed in the English proverbial rhyme *He who fights and runs away Lives to fight another day.*

live to tell the tale survive a dangerous experience and be able to tell others about it.

where you live at, to, or in the right, vital, or most vulnerable spot. North American

> **2002** *New York Times* The movies hit them where they live—in their own state of desperation and doubt.

lively

look lively: see LOOK.

lively as a grig: see **merry as a grig** *at* GRIG.

living

be (the) living proof that (or of) show by your or something's existence and qualities that something is the case.

live on borrowed time: see BORROWED.

in (or within) living memory within or during a time that is remembered by people still alive.

the living image of an exact copy or likeness of.

load

get a load of used to draw attention to someone or something. informal

> **1994 Quentin Tarantino** *Pulp Fiction* It's legal to carry it, but ... get a load of this, alright—if the cops stop you, it's illegal for them to search you.

get (or have) a load on become drunk. US informal

load the dice against (or in favour of) someone put someone at a disadvantage (or advantage).

> **1995** *Maclean's* What global warming has done is load the dice in favor of warmer-than-normal seasons and extreme climatic events.

take a (or the) load off your feet sit or lie down.

take a load off someone's mind bring someone relief from anxiety.

loaded

loaded for bear: see BEAR.

loaf

half a loaf: see HALF.

loaves and fishes personal profit as a motive for religious profession or public service.

> ❶ This idiom developed from a biblical passage in John 6:26: 'Jesus answered them and said, Verily, verily, I say unto you, Ye seek me, not because ye saw the miracles, but because ye did eat of the loaves, and were filled'.

use your loaf use your common sense. British informal

> ❶ This expression probably comes from *loaf of bread*, rhyming slang for 'head'.

loath

nothing loath: see NOTHING.

lock

have a lock on have an unbreakable hold or total control over. North American informal

> ❶ *Lock* is here used in the sense of a hold in wrestling that prevents an opponent from moving a limb.

> **1974 Paul Erdman** *Silver Bears* He would sooner see the whole bank go down the drain ... than get beaten by us. Unless we develop an even better lock on him—and that won't be easy.

lock horns engage in conflict.

> ❶ The image here is of two bulls fighting head-to-head with their horns. Both the literal and figurative senses of the phrase originated in the USA, in the mid 19th century.

lock, stock, and barrel including everything; completely.

> ❶ *Lock, stock, and barrel* refers literally to the complete mechanism of a firearm.

under lock and key securely locked up.

locker

go to Davy Jones's locker: see DAVY JONES'S LOCKER.

a shot in the locker: see SHOT.

log

easy as falling off a log: see EASY.

loggerheads

at loggerheads in violent dispute or disagreement.

> ❶ This expression is possibly a use of *loggerhead* in the late 17th-century sense of 'a long-handled iron instrument for heating liquids and tar'; the tool was perhaps also used as a weapon.

loins

gird your loins: see GIRD.

loiter

loiter with intent stand or wait around with the intention of committing an offence. British

> ❶ This is a legal phrase which derives from an 1891 Act of Parliament; it is also used figuratively and humorously of anyone who is waiting around for some unspecified purpose.

Lombard

all Lombard Street to a China orange great wealth against one ordinary object; virtual certainty. dated

> ❶ *Lombard Street* in London was originally occupied by bankers from Lombardy, and it still contains a number of London's principal banks. This idiom dates from the early 19th century, but the use of a *China orange* to mean 'a worthless thing' is recorded earlier.

London

a London particular a dense fog formerly affecting London. dated

> ❶ This expression originated in Charles Dickens's *Bleak House* (1853).

lonesome

by (or on) your lonesome all alone. informal

long

by a long chalk: *see* CHALK.

by a long shot: *see* SHOT.

in the long run (or term) over a long period of time; eventually.

> **1997** *New Scientist* But as the economist Maynard Keynes pointed out, in the long run we are all dead.

the long and the short of it all that can or need be said.

> **1999 Tim Lott** *White City Blue* His mother takes a lot of looking after, his wage is worse than Nodge's, and the long and short of it is he hasn't got a pot to piss in.

long in the tooth rather old.

> ❶ This phrase was originally used of horses, referring to the way their gums recede with age.

long time no see it's a long time since we last met (used as a greeting). informal

> ❶ This idiom developed as a humorous imitation of broken English spoken by a Native American.

not be long for this world have only a short time to live.

> **1996 Frank McCourt** *Angela's Ashes* Mrs. Finucane...says she's not long for this world and the more Masses said for her soul the better she'll feel.

not by a long chalk: *see* CHALK.

not by a long shot: *see* SHOT.

over the long haul over an extended period of time. chiefly North American

longbow

draw the longbow make exaggerated claims or statements. dated

> ❶ The longbow was the national weapon of England from the 14th century until the introduction of firearms, and prowess in its use was highly prized. The phrase has been used in this metaphorical sense since the mid 17th century.

look

look before you leap you shouldn't act without first considering the possible consequences or dangers. proverb

look daggers: *see* DAGGER.

look down your nose at despise. informal

look lively used to tell someone to be quick in doing something. informal

> ❶ A variant of this phrase is *look alive*, but this is now rather dated.

look someone in the eye (or face) look directly at someone without showing embarrassment, fear, or shame.

look someone up and down scrutinize someone carefully.

look the other way deliberately ignore wrongdoing by others.

> **1998** *Economist* The Greek government looked the other way as lorries...switched documents the minute they crossed the border.

look sharp be quick.

> **1953 Margaret Kennedy** *Troy Chimneys* I had...begun an idle flirtation with Maria, ...then, perceiving that I should be caught if I did not look sharp, I kept out of her way.

lookout

be on the lookout ❶ keep searching for someone or something that is wanted. ❷ be alert to danger or trouble.

> ❶ The word *lookout*, which originated in naval and military contexts, was first applied, in the late 17th century, to sentries or other people employed to keep watch. The sense of 'the action of keeping watch', as used in this expression, dates from the mid 18th century.

loop

in (or out of) the loop aware (or unaware) of information known to only a limited number of people. informal

1998 *Times* An insider suggests to a favoured, helpful journalist that the said minister is out of the loop and on the skids.

throw (*or* **knock**) **someone for a loop** surprise or astonish someone; catch someone off guard. North American

loose

hang (*or* **stay**) **loose** be relaxed; refrain from taking anything too seriously. informal

a loose cannon a unpredictable person or thing likely to cause unintentional damage.

> ❶ A *loose cannon* was originally a cannon that had broken loose from its fastening or mounting, an accident especially dangerous on wooden ships of war.

loose end

at a loose end having nothing to do; not knowing what to do.

> ❶ A North American variant of this expression is *at loose ends*.

lord

Lord of the Flies the Devil.

> ❶ This expression is often used with allusive reference to the title of the 1954 novel by William Golding (1911–93), in which a group of schoolboys marooned on an uninhabited tropical island revert to savagery and primitive ritualistic behaviour.

lorry

fall off a lorry: *see* FALL.

lose

lose face: *see* FACE.

lose sleep worry.

lose your mind (*or* **your marbles**) become insane or irrational. informal

lose your rag: *see* RAG.

lose your shirt: *see* SHIRT.

lose your touch: *see* TOUCH.

lose your (*or* **the**) **way** no longer have a clear idea of your purpose or motivation in an activity or business.

loser

be on (*or* **on to**) **a loser** be involved in a course of action that is bound to fail.

losing

a losing battle a struggle that is bound to end in failure.

lost

all is not lost used to suggest that there is still some chance of success or recovery.

be lost (*or* **at a loss**) **for words** be so surprised, confused, or upset that you cannot think what to say.

be lost in the shuffle: *see* SHUFFLE.

be lost on someone fail to influence or be noticed or appreciated by someone.

> **1990 Katherine Frank** *Emily Brontë* Charlotte's lovely surroundings and the steady unfurling of one glorious summer day after the next were lost on her.

give someone up for lost stop expecting that a missing person will be found alive.

a lost soul: *see* SOUL.

make up for lost time do something faster or more often in order to compensate for not having done it quickly or often enough before.

lot

all over the lot in a state of confusion or disorganization. US informal

fall to someone's lot become someone's task or responsibility.

throw in your lot with decide to ally yourself closely with and share the fate of a person or group.

> ❶ Both this and the previous idiom come from the process of deciding something by drawing or casting lots.

> **1992 Michael Medved** *Hollywood vs. America* Yuppie physician Michael J. Fox decides to give up his dreams of glitz and glory in L.A. and to throw in his lot with the lovable locals.

love

for the love of Mike used to accompany an exasperated request or to express dismay. British informal

> ❶ *Mike* is perhaps used here as a generic name for an Irishman; compare with *mickey* in **take the mickey out of** (*at* MICKEY).

love me, love my dog if you love someone, you must accept everything about them, even their faults. proverb

love's young dream ❶ the relationship of young lovers. ❷ the object of someone's love. ❸ a man regarded as a perfect lover.

not for love or money not in any circumstances. informal

> **1998** *Spectator* I am told that you cannot get a plasterer for love or money, but that the going rate is a big kiss and £1,000 a week.

there's no (or little or not much) love lost between there is mutual dislike between two or more people mentioned.

lower

lower the boom on ❶ treat someone severely. ❷ put a stop to an activity. informal

> ❶ It has been suggested that this phrase originally meant 'knocking out an adversary with one punch' in a fight.

lower the tone diminish the spirit or moral character of a conversation, place, etc.

> ❶ *Tone* here is used to mean the general character or attitude of a conversation, place, piece of writing, etc.

lower your sights: *see* **raise your sights** *at* SIGHT.

lowest

the lowest of the low those regarded as the most immoral or socially inferior of all.

> **1995 Nicholas Whittaker** *Platform Souls* And fare dodgers, well, they're the lowest of the low, and should be strung up.

luck

as luck would have it used to indicate the fortuitousness of a situation.

> **1994 Beryl Gilroy** *Sunlight on Sweet Water* As luck would have it, one day they met in the door of the rum shop.

the luck of the draw the outcome of chance rather than something you can control.

the luck of the Irish very good luck.

make your own luck be successful through your own efforts and opportunism.

ride your luck let favourable events take their course without taking undue risks.

try your luck (at something) do something that involves risk or luck, hoping to succeed.

> **1964 Mary Stewart** *This Rough Magic* I finally decided, after three years of juvenile leads in provincial rep that it was time to try my luck in London.

your luck is in (or out) you are fortunate (or unfortunate) on a particular occasion.

lucky

you, he, etc. will be lucky (or should be so lucky) used to say that someone's wishes or expectations are unlikely to be fulfilled.

lull

the lull before the storm: *see* STORM.

lump

a lump in the throat a feeling of tightness or dryness in the throat caused by strong emotion, especially grief.

take (or get) your lumps suffer punishment; be attacked or defeated. informal, chiefly North American

> **1971 Bernard Malamud** *The Tenants* Now I take my lumps, he thought. Maybe for not satisfying Mary.

lunch

do lunch meet for lunch. informal, chiefly North American

ladies who lunch: *see* LADY.

out to lunch: *see* OUT.

there's no such thing as a free lunch you never get something for nothing; any benefit received has eventually to be paid for.

> **1996** *Washington Times* Europeans are now learning some hard facts of life about socialized medicine: there's no such thing as a free lunch.

lurch

leave someone in the lurch leave an associate or friend abruptly and without assistance or support when they are in a difficult situation.

> ❶ *Lurch* as a noun meaning 'a state of discomfiture' dates from the mid 16th century but it is now used only in this idiom.

> **1987 Eileen Dunlop** *The House on the Hill* What have Gilmores ever done but leave her in the lurch? Poor Jane, she just can't run the risk of being hurt again.

lying

take something lying down accept an insult or injury without attempting retaliation.

> **1989 Shimmer Chinodya** *Harvest of Thorns* She's boasting in front of me, laughing at me for being weak. Today she'll know I'm not going to take it lying down any longer.

lyrical

wax lyrical about (or over) talk in an

effusive or enthusiastic way about
something.

> ❶ *Wax* (from Old English *weaxan*) was used
> to mean 'increase in size' right through until
> early modern English, but since then it has
> been superseded in all general contexts by
> *grow*. It now survives only in certain
> expressions, especially with reference to the
> moon's monthly increase and decrease
> (*waxing and waning*).

1998 *New Scientist* Even as they wax lyrical
about the perils of a changing climate, Clinton
and Gore are presiding over the most massive
expansion of oil exploration and drilling
since . . . the Trans-Alaska Pipeline twenty
years ago.

Mm

mad

mad as a hatter (*or* **a March hare**) completely crazy. informal

> ⓘ In this expression, a *hatter* refers to Lewis Carroll's character, the Mad Hatter, in *Alice's Adventures in Wonderland* (1865). It is thought that hatters suffered from the effects of mercury poisoning because of the fumes arising from the use of mercurous nitrate in the manufacture of felt hats. The *March hare* version refers to the way hares leap about during the breeding season.

mad as a (cut) snake crazy or eccentric. Australian informal

madding

far from the madding crowd secluded or removed from public notice.

> ⓘ The phrase was originally used in Thomas Gray's 'Elegy Written in a Country Churchyard' (1751). It is now better known as the title of one of Thomas Hardy's novels.

madness

that way madness lies it is ill-advised to pursue a particular course of action as it will cause distress or anxiety.

> ⓘ This phrase is a quotation from *King Lear*, taken from the speech in which Lear shies away from contemplating the ingratitude of his daughters Regan and Goneril.

maggot

act the maggot behave in a foolishly playful way. Irish informal

magic

a magic carpet: *see* CARPET.

magnitude

of the first magnitude: *see* **of the first order** *at* FIRST.

main

by main force through sheer strength.

> ⓘ *Main* derives from the Old English word *mægen* meaning 'physical force'. As an

adjective meaning '(of strength or force) exerted to the full', it is a very ancient usage: *mægenstrengo* occurs in the Anglo-Saxon epic *Beowulf*.

majority

join the great majority: *see* JOIN.

the silent majority: *see* SILENT.

make

make a beeline for: *see* BEELINE.

make the cut: *see* CUT.

make someone's day make an otherwise ordinary or dull day pleasingly memorable for someone.

make a day (*or* night) of it devote a whole day (*or* night) to an activity, typically an enjoyable one.

make do manage with the limited or inadequate means available.

> ⓘ This phrase can be used alone or in *make do and mend*, a UK slogan from the 1940s.

make like pretend to be; imitate. North American informal

> **1939 John Steinbeck** *The Grapes of Wrath* This rich fella . . . makes like he's poor.

make or break be the factor which decides whether something will succeed or fail.

> ⓘ A variant of this phrase, found chiefly in British English, is *make or mar*. The use of *make* together with *mar* is recorded from the early 15th century, but since the mid 19th century *break* has become more common.

> **1998** *Your Garden* Neighbours can make or break a home and there's certainly no keeping up with the Jones's mentality here.

on the make ❶ intent on gain, typically in a rather unscrupulous way. ❷ looking for a sexual partner. informal

put the make on make sexual advances to. North American informal

> **1993 Anne River Siddons** *Hill Towns* Put the make on you, did she, Joe? I should have warned you. Past a certain blood alcohol level Yolie gets snuggly.

maker

meet your maker die. humorous or euphemistic

> ⓘ This expression alludes to the Christian belief that, after death, the soul goes to be judged by God, its creator.

making

be the making of someone ensure someone's success or favourable development.

malice

malice aforethought the intention to kill or harm which is held to distinguish unlawful killing from murder.

mammon

the mammon of unrighteousness wealth ill-used or ill-gained.

> ⓘ This biblical expression comes from Luke 16:9: 'And I say unto you, Make to yourselves friends of the mammon of unrighteousness; that, when ye fail, they may receive you into everlasting habitations'. *Mammon* ultimately comes from Hebrew *māmōn* meaning 'money or wealth'. In early use, it was used to refer to the devil of covetousness; it later was used as the personification of wealth regarded as an idol or an evil influence.

man

as — as the next man as — as the average person.

> **1998 Tom Clancy** *Rainbow Six* I like red meat as much as the next man.

be your own man (*or* **woman**): *see* OWN.

every man for himself: *see* EVERY.

every man has his price: *see* PRICE.

man about town a fashionable male socialite.

man and boy throughout life from youth.

> ⓘ The Scottish poet William Dunbar used the phrase *baith man and lad* in the early 16th century, but the modern usage follows Shakespeare's *Hamlet*: 'I have been sexton here, man and boy, thirty years'.

a man for all seasons a man who is ready to cope with any contingency and whose behaviour is always appropriate to every occasion.

> ⓘ Robert Whittington applied this description to the English statesman and scholar Sir Thomas More (1478–1535), and it was used by Robert Bolt as the title of his 1960 play about More.

the man in the moon ❶ the imagined likeness of a face seen on the surface of a full moon. ❷ used, especially in comparisons, to refer to someone regarded as out of touch with real life.

> ❷ **1991** *Sight & Sound* You thought...you could mention even the most famous classic films as reference points in script meetings and not be looked at like the man in the moon.

the man in (*or* **on**) **the street** an ordinary person, usually with regard to their opinions, or as distinct from an expert.

> ⓘ A specifically British variation of this expression is **the man on the Clapham omnibus** (*see below*).

man of the cloth a clergyman.

> ⓘ Jonathan Swift used *cloth* as an informal term for the clerical profession in the early 18th century, but it was earlier applied to several other occupations for which distinctive clothing was worn, e.g. the legal or military professions.

man of God ❶ a clergyman. ❷ a holy man or saint.

a man of letters: *see* LETTER.

man of the moment a man of importance at a particular time.

man of straw (*or* **straw man**) ❶ a person compared to an effigy stuffed with straw; a sham. ❷ a sham argument set up to be defeated, usually as a means of avoiding having to tackle an opponent's real arguments.

> ❷ **1991** *Past & Present* By making the representativeness of the case-studies into the crucial issue, Rubinstein is erecting a straw man which he can easily demolish without addressing the basic criticisms of his sources and methodology.

a man of the world: *see* WORLD.

the man on the Clapham omnibus the average man, especially with regard to his opinions. British

> ⓘ This expression is attributed to the English judge Lord Bowen (1835–94), who used it as a metaphor for any ordinary reasonable person—such as a juror is expected to be. Clapham is a district in south London.

man's best friend an affectionate or humorous way of referring to a dog.

a man's man a man whose personality is such that he is more popular and at ease with other men than with women.

ⓘ This expression was apparently first used in George Du Maurier's story *The Martian* (1897), where the *man's man* is defined as 'a good comrade par excellence, a frolicsome chum, a rollicking boon-companion, a jolly pal'. A *man's woman*, which dates from the early 20th century, is a woman who is more at ease with men than with other women.

1991 *Men's Health* Masculinity used to be simple to define. If you had hair on your chest and a deep voice, and belonged to a club that excluded women, you were masculine, or, as was the phrase of the time, 'a man's man'.

man to man in a direct and frank way between two men; openly and honestly.

men in (grey) suits powerful men within an organization who exercise their influence or authority anonymously.

men in white coats psychiatrists or psychiatric workers (used to imply that someone is mad or mentally unbalanced). humorous

> **1995** *Economist* Mrs Thatcher was removed from Ten Downing Street by men in grey suits. Judging by her hyperthyroidic performance this week, it would now take men in white coats.

separate (or sort out) the men from the boys show or prove which people in a group are truly competent, brave, or mature.

> **1968** *House & Garden* The Dry Martini...is a drink that will quickly separate the men from the boys and the girls from their principles.

twelve good men and true: *see* TWELVE.

mangle

put someone through the mangle: *see* **put someone through the wringer** *at* WRINGER.

manner

in a manner of speaking in some sense; so to speak.

ⓘ *Manner of speaking* is recorded in the mid 16th century; compare with French *façon de parler*, which has been in use in English since the early 19th century.

to the manner born naturally at ease in a specified way of life, job, or situation.

ⓘ This comes from Shakespeare's *Hamlet*: 'though I am native here And to the manner born'. Punning on this expression, *to the manor born* is used to refer to someone who has aristocratic origins.

manse

son (or daughter) of the manse the child of a minister, especially a Presbyterian.

many

be too (or one too) many for outwit or baffle.

have one too many become slightly drunk.

many's the — used to indicate that something happens often.

> **2000** *Taxi News* Many's the happy hour I've spent listening to cabbies thrash that one out.

map

all over the map *see* **all over the place** *at* ALL.

off the map (of a place) very distant or remote. Compare with **off the beaten track** (*at* BEATEN).

put something on the map make something prominent or important.

wipe something off the map obliterate something totally.

marble

lose your marbles go insane; become irrational or senile. informal

ⓘ *Marbles* as a term for 'a person's mental faculties' probably originated as early 20th-century American slang. The underlying reference is apparently to the children's game played with multicoloured glass balls.

> **1998** *Spectator* At least, that is how I recall the event, but I am losing my marbles.

pick up your marbles and go home withdraw petulantly from an activity after having suffered a setback. informal, chiefly US

ⓘ The image here is of a child who refuses sulkily to continue playing the game of marbles.

March

mad as a March hare: *see* **mad as a hatter** *at* MAD.

march

march to (the beat of) a different tune (or drum or drummer) consciously adopt a different approach or attitude to the majority of people; be unconventional. informal

ⓘ The version with *drummer* comes ultimately from Henry David Thoreau's *Walden* (1854): 'If a man does not keep pace with his companions, perhaps it is because he hears a different drummer'.

1997 *New Scientist* In formulating his ideas about the composition of the fundamental building blocks of matter...Sternglass has marched to the beat of an entirely different drum.

mare

a mare's nest a wonderful discovery which proves or will prove to be illusory.

> ❶ A *mare's nest* is here being used to symbolize something that does not exist, as horses do not make nests. The phrase is first recorded in the late 16th century, as is the variant *a horse's nest*, although the latter is now no longer in use.

marines

tell that to the marines (*or* **the horse marines**) a scornful expression of incredulity.

> ❶ This saying may have originated in a remark made by Charles II, recommending that unlikely tales should be referred to sailors who, from their knowledge of distant places, might be the people best qualified to judge their truthfulness. *Horse marines*, dating from the early 19th century, were an imaginary cavalry corps, soldiers mounted on horseback on board ship being a humorous image of ineptitude or of people out of their natural element. In 1823 Byron noted that *That will do for the marines, but the sailors won't believe it* was an 'old saying', and the following year Walter Scott used *Tell that to the marines—the sailors won't believe it!* in his novel *Redgauntlet*.

> **1998** *Times* Truth is the issue, say the apologists, not the grope. You can tell that to the marines. The issue is the grope.

mark

be quick (*or* **slow**) **off the mark** be fast (*or* slow) in responding to a situation or understanding something.

> ❶ The *mark* here is the line or marker from which a competitor starts a race, as is also the case in **get off the mark** and **on your marks**.

a black mark: *see* BLACK.

get off the mark get started.

leave (*or* **make**) **its** (*or* **your** *or* **a**) **mark** have a lasting or significant effect.

make your mark become famous and successful.

mark someone's card give someone information. informal

> ❶ This idiom, which dates from the mid 20th century, derives from the world of horse racing. The *card* is a *race card*, the list of runners at a race meeting, so to *mark someone's card* is to give them tips for possible winners.

the mark of Cain the stigma of a murderer; a sign of infamy.

> ❶ According to the book of Genesis, God placed a mark on Cain after the murder of his brother Abel, originally as a sign that he should not be killed or harmed; this was later taken to identify him as a murderer (Genesis 4:15).

mark time ❶ (of troops) march on the spot without moving forward. ❷ pass your time in routine activities until a more interesting opportunity presents itself.

mark something with a white stone: *see* WHITE.

near (*or* **close**) **to the mark** almost correct or accurate.

> ❶ The *mark* in this and the two following idioms is a target or goal.

off (*or* **wide of**) **the mark** ❶ a long way away from an intended target. ❷ incorrect or inaccurate.

on the mark correct or accurate.

on your marks used to instruct competitors in a race to prepare themselves in the correct starting position.

up to the mark ❶ of the required standard. ❷ (of a person) as healthy or cheerful as usual.

market

be in the market for wish to buy.

a drug on the market: *see* DRUG.

marriage

marriage of convenience a marriage concluded to achieve a practical purpose.

> ❶ This expression was used by Joseph Addison in the early 18th century, translating the French *mariage de convenance*, which has itself been current in English since the mid 19th century.

> **1949 George Bernard Shaw** *Buoyant Billions* The proportion of happy love marriages to happy marriages of convenience has never been counted.

marrow

to the marrow to your innermost being.

> ℹ *Marrow* is the soft, fatty substance found in the cavities of bones.

1994 Maurice Gee *Crime Story* Moral corruption, the lawyer said. Men who are greedy to the marrow of their bones.

marry

marry money marry a rich person. informal

mat

go to the mat vigorously engage in an argument or dispute, typically on behalf of a particular person or cause.

> ℹ The *mat* referred to is the thick mat in a gym on which wrestling is practised.

1924 P. G. Wodehouse *Leave it to Psmith* I ... heard ... you and Aunt Constance going to the mat about poor old Phyllis.

on the mat being reprimanded by someone in authority. informal

> ℹ This idiom is a military reference: the orderly room mat was where a soldier accused of some misdemeanour would stand before the commanding officer.

match

meet your match encounter your equal in strength or ability.

the whole shooting match: *see* SHOOTING.

Matilda

waltz (or walk) Matilda carry a bundle of your personal possessions as you travel the roads. Australian

> ℹ The name *Matilda* was one of a number of names given to the swag or pack carried by bushmen in Australia. The expression was famously used by A. B. ('Banjo') Paterson (1864–1941) in his 1903 song 'Waltzing Matilda'.

matter

a matter of form a point of correct procedure.

Matthew

the Matthew principle the principle that more will be given to those who are already provided for.

> ℹ This phrase stems from the gospel passage: 'Unto every one that hath shall be given, and he shall have abundance' (Matthew 25:29).

max

to the max to the highest degree possible. informal

McCoy

the real McCoy the real thing; the genuine article. informal

> ℹ The origin is of this phrase is unknown, but it appears in the form 'the real Mackay' in a letter by Robert Louis Stevenson in 1883. *McCoy* is glossed as 'genuine liquor' in a 1930 edition of the *American Mercury*.

1992 Jeff Torrington *Swing Hammer Swing!* 'How d'you know the armour's real?' 'Oh, I'm sure it's the real McCoy.'

meal

make a meal of treat a task or occurrence with more attention or care than necessary, especially for effect. British informal

1961 Colin Willock *Death in Covert* Dyson ... was making a meal of everything. He had carefully paced the distance ... He had stuck sticks in the ground.

mean

the golden mean: *see* GOLDEN.

mean business be in earnest.

1992 *New York Times* The protest is a matter of principle ... and also a necessary act of assertiveness by the delegates to show they mean business.

mean to say really admit or intend to say.

1977 Jennifer Johnston *Shadows on our Skin* I mean to say, Joe Logan, where are you if you can't resist putting a small white tube of poison into your mouth every half an hour?

a means to an end a thing that is not valued or important in itself but is useful in achieving an aim.

> ℹ *End* and *means* are compared or contrasted in several proverbial sayings, for example **the end justifies the means** (*see* END) and *he who wills the end wills the means.*

no mean — a very good —.

> ℹ This expression was famously used by St Paul: 'I am ... a Jew of Tarsus ... a citizen of no mean city' (Acts 21:39).

1990 *L.A. Style* Surviving the rise and fall of art trends is no mean trick.

meaning

not know the meaning of the word behave

as if unaware of the concept referred to or implied. informal

measure

for good measure in addition to what has already been done, said, or given.

get (*or* **take** *or* **have**) **the measure of** assess or have assessed the character, nature, or abilities of someone or something.

measure your length (of a person) fall flat on the ground. dated

meat

be meat and drink to be a source of great pleasure or encouragement to.

> **2002** *Total Film* Sex, conspiracy theories, top hats and 'orrible murder, the elements of the Jack The Ripper story are meat and drink to film-makers.

dead meat: *see* DEAD.

easy meat: *see* EASY.

meat and potatoes ordinary but fundamental things; basic ingredients.

> **1993** *New York Times* Mainstream rock acts like Van Halen and Bruce Springsteen are the meat and potatoes of A.O.R.

medal

the reverse of the medal (*or* **shield**) the opposite view of a matter.

Medes

the law of the Medes and Persians something which cannot be altered.

> ⓘ This expression refers to Daniel 6:12: 'The thing is true, according to the law of the Medes and Persians, which altereth not'.

medicine

a dose (*or* **taste**) **of your own medicine** the same bad treatment that you have given to others.

> ⓘ The idea of taking or receiving *your own medicine* has been in metaphorical use since the mid 19th century.

> **1994 Eoin McNamee** *Resurrection Man* Every time you turn on the telly there's some politician talking the mouth off himself, dose of their own medicine's what they want.

meek

meek as Moses (*or* **a lamb**) very meek.

> ⓘ This expression is a biblical allusion to Numbers 12:3: 'Now the man Moses was very meek'.

meet

meet the case be adequate.

meet your eye (*or* **ear**) be visible (*or* audible).

meet someone's eye (*or* **eyes** *or* **gaze**) look directly at someone.

meet someone halfway make a compromise with someone.

meet your maker: *see* MAKER.

meet your match: *see* MATCH.

meet your Waterloo: *see* WATERLOO.

there's more to someone or something than meets the eye a person or situation is more complex or interesting than they appear.

meeting

a meeting of minds an understanding or agreement between people.

megillah

the whole megillah something in its entirety, especially a complicated set of arrangements or a long-winded story. North American informal

> ⓘ *Megillah* is the Hebrew word for a 'scroll' and refers particularly to each of five books of the Jewish Scriptures (the Song of Solomon, Ruth, Lamentations, Ecclesiastes, and Esther) appointed to be read in the synagogue on certain important days.

Melba

do a Melba ❶ return from retirement. ❷ make several farewell appearances. Australian & New Zealand informal

> ⓘ The Australian operatic soprano Nellie Melba (the stage name of Helen Mitchell, 1861–1931) made repeated 'farewell' appearances.

melt

melt in the mouth (of food) be deliciously light or tender and need little or no chewing.

memory

take a trip (*or* **walk**) **down memory lane** deliberately recall pleasant or sentimental memories.

mend

mend (your) fences make peace with a person.

> ❶ This expression originated in the late 19th century in the USA, with reference to a member of Congress returning to his home town to keep in touch with the voters and to look after his interests there. Similar notions are conjured up by the saying *good fences make good neighbours*.

> **1994 Louis de Bernières** *Captain Corelli's Mandolin* He knew assuredly he should go and mend his fences with the priest.

mend your pace go faster; alter your pace to match another's.

on the mend improving in health or condition; recovering.

mentioned

be mentioned in dispatches be commended for your actions. British

> ❶ In official military reports from the front line any soldiers who have been responsible for particular acts of bravery are commended by name.

mercy

be thankful (*or* **grateful**) **for small mercies** be relieved that an unpleasant situation is alleviated by minor advantages.

merry

lead someone a merry dance: *see* DANCE.

merry as a grig: *see* GRIG.

mess

mess with someone's head cause someone to feel frustrated, anxious, or upset. US informal

sell something for a mess of pottage: *see* POTTAGE.

message

get the message infer an implication from a remark or action. informal

> **1993 Isidore Okpewho** *Tides* I think he got the message, because he flashed me a look from the corner of his eye.

send the right (*or* **wrong**) **message** make a significant statement, either implicitly or by your actions.

messenger

shoot (*or* **kill**) **the messenger** treat the bearer of bad news as if they were to blame for it.

> ❶ Being the bearer of bad tidings has been a traditionally thankless task, as indicated in Sophocles' *Antigone*, 'No man loves the

messenger of ill' and Shakespeare's *Antony and Cleopatra*, 'The nature of bad news infects the teller'.

method

there is method in someone's madness there is a sensible foundation for what appears to be foolish or strange behaviour.

> ❶ This expression comes from the scene in *Hamlet* in which Hamlet feigns madness, causing Polonius to remark: 'Though this be madness, yet there is method in't'.

mettle

be on your mettle be ready or forced to prove your ability to cope well with a demanding situation.

put someone on their mettle (of a demanding situation) test someone's ability to face difficulties in a spirited and resilient way.

> ❶ Originally the same word as *metal*, *mettle* was no more than a variant spelling that gradually became particularly associated with figurative uses of the word, meaning 'quality of temperament', and from that 'natural spirit' or 'courage'. These senses eventually developed so far from the literal senses that it was no longer apparent that they were originally the same word. The distinctive spellings *metal* and *mettle* to distinguish the two were in use by the early 18th century, though not necessarily universally applied until the following century.

Mexican

Mexican overdrive the neutral gear position used when coasting downhill. US informal

> ❶ This expression originated in the mid 20th century, especially in language used by long-distance truck drivers.

mickey

take the mickey tease or ridicule someone, especially in an unkind or persistent way. informal, chiefly British

> ❶ The origin of this phrase is unknown; *take* (or *extract*) *the Michael* is a humorously formal variant.

Mickey Finn

slip someone a Mickey Finn give someone a drugged or otherwise adulterated drink.

❶ Recorded from the 1920s, this expression is of unknown origin, but it is sometimes said to be the name of a notorious Chicago barkeeper (c.1896–1906).

microscope

under the microscope under critical examination.

Midas

the Midas touch the ability to make money out of anything that you undertake.

❶ In classical legend, *Midas* was a king of Phrygia (in Asia Minor) who had the power to turn everything he touched into gold.

middle

the middle of nowhere somewhere very remote and isolated. informal

❶ This is one example of several derogatory expressions concerning rural life as viewed from an urban perspective: compare with **the back of beyond** (at BACK) and **in the sticks** (at STICK).

steer (or take) a middle course adopt a policy which avoids extremes.

midnight

burn the midnight oil: *see* BURN.

midstream

in midstream ❶ in the middle of a stream or river. ❷ (of an activity or process, especially one that is interrupted) part-way through its course; unfinished.

might

might is right those who are powerful can do what they wish unchallenged, even if their action is in fact unjustified.

❶ This was an observation made by both Greek and Latin writers and it was known in this form in English as far back as the early 14th century.

with might and main with all your force.

❶ *Main* derives from the Old English word *mægen* meaning 'physical strength' (see also **by main force** at MAIN). The use of the two nouns *might* and *main* together dates from the mid 15th century; *main* in this sense is no longer used in modern English except in this phrase.

Mike

for the love of Mike: *see* LOVE.

mile

be miles away be lost in thought and so unaware of what is happening around you. informal

go the extra mile be especially assiduous in your attempt to achieve something.

❶ This origins of this expression can be traced back to the New Testament injunction 'And whosoever shall compel thee to go a mile, go with him twain' (Matthew 5:41). The revue song of 1957 by Joyce Grenfell, 'Ready . . . To go the extra mile', may have popularized its use.

a mile a minute very quickly. informal

❶ As a noun, *mile a minute* is a popular nickname for the quick-growing climbing plant Russian Vine.

run a mile used to show that someone is frightened by or very unwilling to do something. informal

1999 Chris Dolan *Ascension Day* She'll run a mile if you contact her direct. I'll do my go-between bit, for you and her, if you do the same for me.

see (or tell or spot) something a mile off recognize something very easily. informal

stand (or stick) out a mile be very obvious or incongruous. informal

milk

cry over spilt (or spilled) milk lament or make a fuss about a misfortune that has happened and that cannot be changed or reversed.

milk and honey prosperity and abundance.

❶ This expression alludes to the prosperity of the Promised Land of Israel in the Bible (Exodus 3:8).

milk and water feeble, insipid, or mawkish.

milk the bull (or ram) engage in an enterprise doomed to failure.

the milk in the coconut a puzzling fact or circumstance.

the milk of human kindness care and compassion for others.

❶ This phrase comes from *Macbeth*. In Lady Macbeth's soliloquy on the subject of her husband's character, she remarks: 'Yet I do fear thy nature; It is too full o' the milk of human kindness To catch the nearest way'.

mill

go (or put someone) through the mill undergo (or cause someone to undergo) an unpleasant experience.

run of the mill: see RUN.

million

gone a million (of a person) completely defeated or finished. Australian informal
  1976 Australian (Sydney) Gough's gone. Gone a million. He's had it.

look (or feel) (like) a million dollars (of a person) look (or feel) extremely good. informal

millstone

hard as the nether millstone: see HARD.

a millstone round your neck a very severe impediment or disadvantage.

> ❶ A *millstone* was a large circular stone used to grind corn. The phrase alludes to a method of executing people by throwing them into deep water with a heavy stone attached to them, a fate believed to have been suffered by several early Christian martyrs.

mince

not mince words (or matters) speak candidly and directly, especially when criticizing someone or something.

mincemeat

make mincemeat of defeat decisively or easily in a fight, contest, or argument. informal

mind

be in (or of) two minds be unable to decide between alternatives.

cast your mind back think back; recall an earlier time.

close (or shut) your mind to (or against) refuse to consider or acknowledge.

come (or spring) to mind (of a thought or idea) occur to someone; be thought of.

give someone a piece of your mind: see PIECE.

have a mind of your own ❶ be capable of independent opinion or action. ❷ (of an inanimate object) seem capable of thought and desire, especially by behaving contrary to the will of the person using it.

have a (or a good or half a) mind to do something be very much inclined to do something.

have something on your mind be troubled by the thought of something.

in your mind's eye in your imagination or mental view.

mind over matter the power of the mind asserted over the physical universe; the use of willpower to overcome physical problems.

mind your Ps and Qs be careful to behave well and avoid giving offence.

> ❶ Various suggestions have been made concerning the significance of *P* and *Q*. One obvious one is that a child learning to read or write might have difficulty in distinguishing between the two tailed letters *p* and *q*. Another is that printers had to be very careful not to confuse the two letters when setting type.

mind the shop be temporarily in charge of affairs.

mind your back (or backs) used to warn inattentive bystanders that someone wants to get past. informal

not pay someone any mind not pay someone any attention. North American

on someone's mind preoccupying someone, especially in a disquieting way.

open your mind to be prepared to consider or acknowledge; be receptive to.

out of your mind ❶ having lost control of your mental faculties; insane. ❷ used to express a belief in someone's foolishness or mental turmoil. ❸ suffering from the specified condition to a very high degree. informal

put your mind to something start to concentrate on something.

minor

in a minor key (especially of a literary work) understated.
  1995 Independent He was a moralist in a minor key.

mint

in mint condition (of an object) new or as if new; in pristine condition.

> ❶ The image behind this phrase is of a newly minted coin.

minute

one minute to midnight the last moment or opportunity. informal

1998 *New Scientist* It's one minute to midnight for the discredited WHO.

mirror

all done with mirrors achieved with an element of trickery.

> ❶ This phrase alludes to the fact that conjuring tricks are often explained as being achieved through the skilful use of mirrors; compare with **smoke and mirrors** (at SMOKE).

mischief

do someone (*or* yourself) a mischief injure someone or yourself. informal

make mischief create trouble or discord.

misery

put someone out of their misery release someone from suspense or anxiety, especially by telling them something they are anxious to know. informal

put something out of its misery end the suffering of a creature in pain by killing it.

miss

give something a miss decide not to do or have something. British informal

miss the cut: *see* **make the cut** at CUT.

miss a beat hesitate or falter, especially in demanding circumstances or when making a transition from one activity to another.

miss the boat (*or* bus) be too slow to take advantage of an opportunity. informal

> **1987 Kathy Lette** *Girls' Night Out* He'll never get divorced and marry her. She'll miss the boat.

not miss much be alert to or aware of everything that is happening around you. informal

not miss a trick never fail to take advantage of a situation. informal

> **1965** *Harper's Bazaar* Fenwicks... never misses a trick when it comes to picking up a new accessory idea.

mistake

and no mistake without any doubt. informal

> **1993 Sam McAughtry** *Touch & Go* He was a headcase and no mistake.

make no mistake (about it) do not be deceived into thinking otherwise. informal

> **1974** *Times* Make no mistake. We had a major work of television last night.

mistaking

there is no mistaking someone or something it is impossible not to recognize someone or something.

mite

a widow's mite: *see* WIDOW.

mitt

get your mitts on obtain possession of. informal

> ❶ *Mitt*, an abbreviation of *mitten,* is an informal term for a person's hand that dates back to the late 19th century.

mix

mix and match select and combine different but complementary items, such as clothing or pieces of equipment, to form a coordinated set.

mixed

a mixed blessing something good which nevertheless has some disadvantages.

mixture

the mixture as before the same treatment repeated. British

> ❶ *The mixture as before* was an instruction which was formerly written on medicine bottles.

mobile

downwardly (*or* upwardly) mobile moving to a lower (*or* higher) social position; losing (*or* gaining) wealth and status.

mocker

put the mockers on ❶ put an end to; thwart. ❷ bring bad luck to.

> ❶ This expression originated as early 20th-century British slang. An Australian variant is *put the mocks* on.

> ❶ **1966 Lionel Davidson** *A Long Way to Shiloh* Shimshon and the judo both seemed to have put the mockers on this particular idyll. We left soon after. ❷ **1970 Joyce Porter** *Dover Strikes Again* This investigation had got the mockers on it from the start.

mockery

make a mockery of something make something seem foolish or absurd.

> **1998** *New Scientist* In some fisheries, waste makes up about half of the landed catch,

which makes a mockery of most population models.

molehill

make a mountain out of a molehill: *see* MOUNTAIN.

moment

have your (or its) moments have short periods that are better or more impressive than others.

moment of truth a crisis; a turning point when a decision has to be made or a crisis faced.

> ❶ This expression is a translation of the Spanish *el momento de la verdad*, which refers to the final sword thrust in a bullfight.

Monday

Monday morning quarterback a person who is wise after the event. North American

> ❶ In American football, a *quarterback* is the player stationed behind the centre who directs the team's attacking play. In North American English the word has also developed the sense of 'a person who directs or coordinates an operation or project'. A *Monday morning quarterback* is someone who passes judgement on something or criticizes it when it is too late for their comments to be of any use, since the particular game or project in question has finished or been completed.

money

be in the money have or win a lot of money. informal

for my money ❶ in my opinion or judgement. ❷ for my preference or taste.

have money to burn have so much money that you can spend as lavishly as you want.

money burns a hole in your pocket (or purse) you have an irresistible urge to spend money as soon as you have it.

money for jam (or old rope) ❶ money earned for little or no effort. ❷ an easy task. British informal

> ❶ These expressions, which date back to the early 20th century, may have originated as military slang. In 1919, the *Athenaeum* stated that *money for jam* arose as the result of the 'great use of jam in the Army'.

money talks wealth gives power and influence to those who possess it. proverb

on the money accurate; correct. chiefly North American

put money (or put your money) on ❶ place a bet on something. ❷ have confidence in the truth or success of something.

put your money where your mouth is take action to support your statements or opinions. informal

see the colour of someone's money: *see* COLOUR.

throw good money after bad incur further loss in a hopeless attempt to recoup a previous loss.

throw money at something try to solve a problem by recklessly spending more money on it, without due consideration of what is required.

monkey

as artful (or clever) as a wagonload (or cartload) of monkeys extremely clever or mischievous. British informal

have a monkey on your back ❶ have a burdensome problem. ❷ be dependent on drugs. informal

> ❶ Sense 2 originated as mid 20th-century US slang; it can also mean 'experience withdrawal symptoms after ceasing to take a drug'.

have (or get) your monkey up be angry.

like a monkey on a stick restless and agitated.

> ❶ The image here is of a child's toy which consists of a figure of a monkey attached to a stick up and down which it can be moved.

make a monkey of (or out of) someone humiliate someone by making them appear ridiculous.

not give a monkey's be completely indifferent or unconcerned. informal

put a person's monkey up make someone angry.

monster

Frankenstein's monster: *see* FRANKENSTEIN.

the green-eyed monster: *see* GREEN-EYED.

month

a month of Sundays a very long, seemingly endless period of time.

> ❶ This expression may be a reference to the traditionally slow passage of Sundays as a result of religious restrictions on activity or entertainment. In a letter written in 1849,

monty

G. E. Jewsbury talked of the absence of mail deliveries on Sundays, remarking: 'If I don't get a better letter from you . . . you may pass "a month of Sundays" at breakfast without any letter from me'.

1998 *Country Life* All in all, the Ministry of Agriculture is gaining the no-nonsense, get-your-coats-off atmosphere that Jack Cunningham could not have managed in a month of Sundays.

monty

the full monty the full amount expected, desired, or possible. informal

> ❶ The origin of this expression is unclear. Among various, though unsubstantiated theories, one cites as the source the phrase *the full Montague Burton*, apparently meaning 'a complete three-piece suit' (from the name of a tailor of made-to-measure clothing in the early 20th century). Another theory recounts the possibility of a military origin, with *the full monty* being 'the full cooked English breakfast' insisted upon by Field Marshal Montgomery.

moon

bark at the moon clamour or make an outcry to no effect.

> ❶ The barking of dogs at a full moon has been a metaphor for futile activity since the mid 17th century.

cry (or ask) for the moon ask for what is unattainable or impossible. British

> ❶ The *moon* in this expression, which dates from the mid 16th century, stands for something distant and unattainable, as it does in **promise someone the moon** below.

many moons ago a long time ago. informal

> ❶ The reference here is to the phases of the moon marking out the months.

once in a blue moon: *see* BLUE.

over the moon extremely happy; delighted. informal

> ❶ This phrase comes from an old nursery rhyme which includes the lines *Heigh diddle diddle, the cat and the fiddle, the cow jumped over the moon*.

promise someone the moon (or earth) promise something that is unattainable. British

1998 *New Scientist* Scientists tend to promise taxpayers the moon, and then not deliver.

moonlight

do a moonlight flit make a hurried, usually nocturnal, removal or change of abode, especially in order to avoid paying your rent. informal

> ❶ **Make a moonlight flitting** is recorded from the early 19th century and appears to have originated in northern England or Scotland. The expression is now often shortened to *do a moonlight*.

morning

morning, noon, and night all of the time; constantly.

1993 Tony Parker *May the Lord in His Mercy be Kind to Belfast* It was the sort [of relationship] where nothing else matters for you except to be with that other person morning, noon and night.

mortal

shuffle off this mortal coil: *see* COIL.

Morton

Morton's fork a situation in which there are two choices or alternatives whose consequences are equally unpleasant.

> ❶ John Morton (c.1420–1500) was Archbishop of Canterbury and chief minister of Henry VII. *Morton's fork* was the argument used by him to extract contributions to the royal treasury: the obviously rich must have money and the frugal must have savings, so neither could evade his demands.

mote

a mote in someone's eye a trivial fault in someone which is less serious than one in someone else who is being critical.

> ❶ A *mote* is a tiny speck of dust or a similar substance. The phrase comes from Matthew 7:3–5: 'Why beholdest thou the mote that is in thy brother's eye, but considerest not the beam that is in thine own eye?': the implication is that someone is ignoring a glaring fault of their own while criticizing a smaller one in someone else.

moth

like a moth to the flame irresistibly attracted to someone or something.

mothball

in mothballs unused but kept in good condition for future use.

motion

go through the motions ❶ do something perfunctorily, without any enthusiasm or commitment. **❷** simulate an action; act out something.

motley

wear motley play the fool.

> **ℹ** *Motley* was the name given to the particoloured clothes worn by a court jester in former times.

mould

break the mould put an end to a pattern of events or behaviour, especially one that has become rigid and restrictive, by doing things in a markedly different way.

> **ℹ** Originally this phrase referred to casting artefacts in moulds: destroying a mould ensured that no further identical examples could be produced. The expression became a catchphrase in Britain in the early 1980s with the foundation of the Social Democratic Party. Its founders promoted the party as breaking the 'out-of-date mould' of British politics, a phrase used by Roy Jenkins in a speech in 1980.

mountain

have a mountain to climb be facing a very difficult task.

if the mountain won't come to Muhammad, Muhammad must go to the mountain if one party will not compromise, the other party will have to make the extra effort.

> **ℹ** The story behind this expression is that Muhammad was once challenged to demonstrate his credentials as a prophet by summoning Mount Safa to come to him. When the mountain did not move in response to the summons, Muhammad observed that had the mountain moved it would undoubtedly have overwhelmed him and all his followers and that therefore he would go to the mountain to give thanks to God for his mercy in not allowing this disaster to happen.

make a mountain out of a molehill foolishly or pointlessly exaggerate the importance of something trivial.

> **ℹ** The contrast between the size of molehills and that of mountains has been made in this and related expressions since the late 16th century.

move mountains ❶ achieve spectacular and apparently impossible results. **❷** make every possible effort.

> **ℹ** In sense 1, the phrase alludes to 1 Corinthians 13:2: 'And though I have the gift of prophecy, and understand all mysteries, and all knowledge; and though I have all faith, so that I could remove mountains, and have not charity, I am nothing'.

mousetrap

a better mousetrap an improved version of a well-known article.

> **ℹ** This expression comes from an observation attributed to Ralph Waldo Emerson in 1889, though also claimed by Elbert Hubbard: 'If a man write a better book, preach a better sermon, or make a better mousetrap than his neighbour, tho' he build his house in the woods, the world will make a beaten path to his door'.

mouth

be all mouth (and no trousers) tend to talk boastfully without any intention of acting on your words. informal

> **1998** *Oldie* What was the point of the Sitwells?... The image was the point, transcending mere achievement... The Sitwells were all mouth and no trousers.

make someone's mouth water ❶ cause someone to salivate at the prospect of appetizing food. **❷** cause someone to feel an intense desire to possess something.

put words in (*or*** into) someone's mouth ❶** falsely report what someone has said. **❷** prompt or encourage someone to say something.

take the words out of someone's mouth say what someone else was about to say.

mouthful

give someone a mouthful talk to or shout at someone in an angry, abusive, or severely critical way; swear at someone. British informal

say a mouthful make a striking or important statement; say something noteworthy. North American informal

movable

a movable feast: *see* FEAST.

move

move up a gear: *see* **change gear** *at* GEAR.

get a move on hurry up. informal

> 1992 **Lisa Tuttle** *Lost Futures* So stop worrying, sweetheart, and let's get a move on...I don't want to be late.

make a move ❶ take action. **❷** start on a journey; leave somewhere. British

make a move on (*or* **put the moves on**) make a proposition to someone, especially of a sexual nature. informal

move the goalposts: *see* GOALPOST.

move heaven and earth: *see* HEAVEN.

move mountains: *see* MOUNTAIN.

move with the times keep abreast of current thinking or developments.

the spirit moves someone: *see* SPIRIT.

mover

a mover and shaker someone at the centre of events who makes things happen; a powerful person.

> ❶ *Movers and shakers* is first recorded in Arthur O'Shaughnessy's 1874 poem 'Ode'.

> 1998 *Times* Ten years from now his name will again be high on the list of movers and shakers to watch in the decade.

much

not much in it little difference between things being compared.

so much the better (*or* **worse**) it is better (*or* worse) for that reason.

> 1995 *Guardian* If you can get a tropical fruit juice...so much the better.

muchness

much of a muchness very similar; nearly the same. informal

> ❶ *Muchness*, used in Middle English in the sense 'large size, bigness', is now very seldom used outside this expression, which dates from the early 18th century.

muck

as common as muck of low social status. British informal

make a muck of handle incompetently; bungle. British informal

where there's muck there's brass dirty or unpleasant activities are also lucrative. proverb

mud

clear as mud: *see* CLEAR.

drag someone through the mud: *see* **drag someone through the dirt** *at* DRAG.

fling (*or* **sling** *or* **throw**) **mud** make disparaging or scandalous remarks or accusations. informal

> ❶ The proverb *throw dirt* (or *mud*) *enough, and some will stick*, to which this phrase alludes, is attributed to the Florentine statesman Niccolò Machiavelli (1469–1527).

someone's name is mud someone is in disgrace or unpopular. informal

> ❶ *Mud* was a colloquial term for a fool from the early 18th century to the late 19th century.

> 1998 *Times* Just because I smoked a few lousy cigarettes every hour for 25 years, my name is mud in the insurance business.

muddy

muddy the waters make an issue or a situation more confusing and harder to understand by introducing complications.

> ❶ The figurative use of *muddy* to mean 'make something hard to perceive or understand' occurs in Shakespeare; *muddy the waters* dates from the mid 19th century.

mug

a mug's game an activity which it is stupid to engage in because it is likely to be unsuccessful or dangerous. informal

> ❶ *Mug* was mid 19th-century slang for a fool, in particular someone who has been duped by a card sharper or criminal. *Mug's game* appeared in the early 20th century and has been applied to a wide variety of activities, especially horse racing and betting on horses.

> 1992 *Economist* From the way many western businessmen talk, you would think investing in eastern Germany was a mug's game.

mullock

poke mullock at ridicule someone. Australian & New Zealand informal

> ❶ In Middle English, *mullock* meant 'refuse or rubbish', a sense which only survives in dialect use. In Australian English it came to be used of rock that either did not contain gold or from which the gold had been extracted, and it then developed the extended sense of 'worthless information or nonsense'. This phrase dates from the early 20th century; compare with **poke borak at** (*at* BORAK).

multitude

cover a multitude of sins conceal or gloss over a lot of problems or defects.

> **ⓘ** This phrase refers to 1 Peter 4:8: 'For charity shall cover the multitude of sins'.

mum

keep mum remain silent about something; not reveal a secret. informal

mum's the word say nothing; don't reveal a secret. informal

> **ⓘ** In both of these idioms, *mum* stands for an inarticulate sound made with pursed lips indicating either unwillingness or inability to speak.

> **1991** *Atlantic City* Mum's the word on who will play the major figures in this tale of woe.

murder

get away with murder succeed in doing whatever you choose without being punished or suffering any disadvantage. informal

murder will out murder cannot remain undetected.

> **ⓘ** This expression was used by Chaucer in *The Prioress's Tale*: 'Mordre wol out, certeyn, it wol nat faille'.

scream (or yell) blue murder make an extravagant and noisy protest. informal

> **ⓘ** A North American variant of this phrase is *scream bloody murder*.

> **1995 Iain Banks** *Whit* I was now left with the ticklish problem of how to let my great-aunt know there was somebody there in the room with her without . . . causing her to scream blue murder.

Murphy

Murphy's law if anything can go wrong it will.

> **ⓘ** *Murphy's law* is said to have been the inspiration of a Californian project manager for the firm Northrop, referring to a remark made in 1949 by a colleague, Captain Edward Murphy of the Wright Field-Aircraft Laboratory. In 1955, *Aviation Mechanics Bulletin* explained Murphy's Law as 'If an aircraft part can be installed incorrectly, someone will install it that way'.

muscle

flex your muscles: *see* FLEX.

mushroom

like mushrooms suddenly and in great numbers.

music

music to your ears something that is very pleasant or gratifying to hear or discover.

mustard

cut the mustard: *see* CUT.

a grain of mustard seed: *see* GRAIN.

muster

pass muster be accepted as adequate or satisfactory.

> **ⓘ** This was originally a military expression, meaning 'come through a review or inspection without censure'. It is found earlier (late 16th century to late 17th century) in the now obsolete form *pass (the) musters* and has been in figurative use since the late 16th century.

mutton

dead as mutton: *see* **dead as a doornail** *at* DEAD.

mutton dressed as lamb a middle-aged or old woman dressed in a style suitable for a much younger woman. British informal

> **ⓘ** *Mutton* occurs in various derogatory contexts relating to women. It has been used as a slang term for prostitutes from the early 16th century, for example, while the phrase *hawk your mutton* means 'flaunt your sexual attractiveness' or (of a prostitute) 'solicit for clients'.

> **1988 Salman Rushdie** *The Satanic Verses* Mutton dressed as lamb, fifty plus and batting her eyelashes like an eighteen-year-old.

Nn

nail

hard as nails: *see* HARD.

hit the nail on the head: *see* HIT.

nail your colours to the mast: *see* COLOURS.

a nail in the coffin an action or event regarded as likely to have a detrimental or destructive effect on a situation, enterprise, or person.

> **1981 R. Lancaster** *Plant Hunting in Nepal* A major nail in the coffin of the plant hunter, so some people believe, is the growing importance placed on plant conservation in the wild.

nail a lie expose something as a falsehood or deception.

> ❶ The reference here is to shopkeepers nailing forged coins to their shop counter to expose them and put them out of circulation, or to farmers pinning dead vermin to a barn door as a deterrent to others.

on the nail (of payment) without delay.

> ❶ The origins of this expression are uncertain. It may be related to the obsolete phrase *to the nail*, meaning 'to perfection' or 'to the utmost', which derived from the habit of sculptors giving a finishing touch to their work with a fingernail, or to joiners testing the accuracy of a joint in the same way. A North American equivalent is *on the barrelhead*.

> **1993 Jonathan Gash** *Paid and Loving Eyes* Illegal syndicates pay cash on the nail.

right on the nail with complete accuracy.

naked

the naked truth the plain truth, without concealment or embellishment.

> ❶ This phrase may originally have developed as a translation of the Latin phrase *nudaque veritas*, found in Horace's *Odes*, or to any of various fables that personify Truth as a naked woman in contrast to the elaborate dress and artifice of Falsehood.

name

call someone names insult someone verbally.

drop names refer frequently to well-known people in such a way as to imply that they are close acquaintances.

give your name to invent, discover, or found something which then becomes known by your name.

have to your name have in your possession.

have your name in lights ❶ (of an actor or performer) have their name displayed in lights outside a theatre, concert hall, etc. ❷ be famous.

in all but name existing in a particular state but not formally recognized as such.

> **1999 Chris Hulme** *Manslaughter United* He had spent twenty-one out of twenty-five years in segregation (solitary confinement in all but name).

in name only by description but not in reality.

> **1993** *Harper's Magazine* In Western Europe the Communist parties shrank year after year...they had become small-bourgeois capitalist parties, Communist in name only.

make a name for yourself become famous.

name and shame identify wrongdoers by name with the intention of embarrassing them into improving their behaviour.

> **1998** *New Scientist* I'm all for naming and shaming, as this is worth many times more than fines.

name names mention specific names, especially of people involved in something wrong or illegal.

name no names refrain from mentioning the names of people involved in an incident.

> **1999** *New York Times* Naming no names, two familiar Presidential candidates...recently sought to get at the son by condemning the father's promise of a 'kinder and gentler' nation.

the name of the game the main purpose or most important aspect of a situation. informal

no names, no pack drill punishment or blame cannot be meted out if names and details are not mentioned.

> ❶ *Pack drill* is a form of military punishment in which an offender has to perform parade-ground exercises while carrying a heavy pack. This early 20th-century expression is often

used as an aside to recommend reticence about a particular subject.

put a name to know or manage to remember what someone or something is called.

someone's name is mud: *see* MUD.

something has your name on it you are destined or particularly suited to receive or experience a specified thing.

take someone's name in vain: *see* VAIN.

to name (but) a few giving only these as examples, even though more could be cited.

> **1996** *Mail on Sunday* A choice of sundried tomato bread, honey and walnut knots, dill and sesame knots, peppercorn rolls and croissants to name but a few.

what's in a name? names are arbitrary labels.

> ❶ This phrase comes from Shakespeare's *Romeo and Juliet*: 'What's in a name? that which we call a rose By any other name would smell as sweet'.

you name it whatever you can think of (used to express the extent or variety of something). informal

> **1991 Angela Carter** *Wise Children* The streets of tall, narrow houses were stuffed to the brim with stand-up comics; adagio dancers; soubrettes; conjurers; fiddlers; speciality acts with dogs, doves, goats, you name it.

nana

do (*or* lose) your nana lose your temper. Australian

off your nana mentally deranged. Australian

> ❶ *Nana* in these idioms is probably short for *banana*; compare with **go bananas** *at* BANANA.

nap

go nap ❶ win all the matches or games in a series. ❷ risk everything in one attempt.

not go nap on not be too keen on; not care much for. Australian informal

> ❶ *Nap* is the name of a card game resembling whist in which a player attempts to take all five tricks. Its original name was *Napoleon*.

napping

catch someone napping (of an action or event) find someone off guard and unprepared to respond. informal

nasty

a nasty taste in the mouth: *see* **a bad taste in the mouth** *at* TASTE.

a nasty piece (*or* bit) of work an unpleasant or untrustworthy person. informal

something nasty in the woodshed: *see* WOODSHED.

nation

one nation a nation not divided by social inequality.

> ❶ *One nation* was a political slogan of the 1990s, associated especially with the debate between the right and left wings of the British Conservative Party.

native

go native (of a person living away from their own country or region) abandon their own culture, customs, or way of life and adopt those of the country or region they are living in.

nature

call of nature used euphemistically to refer to a need to urinate or defecate.

get (*or* go) back to nature return to the type of life (regarded as being more in tune with nature) that existed before the development of complex industrial societies.

in the nature of things inevitable or inevitably.

> **2002** *Economist* The IMF sometimes makes mistakes. It is in the nature of things: the Fund practises battlefield medicine.

in a state of nature ❶ in an uncivilized or uncultivated state. ❷ totally naked. ❸ (in Christian theology) in a morally unregenerate condition, unredeemed by divine grace.

nature red in tooth and claw: *see* RED.

the nature of the beast the inherent or essential quality or character of something, which cannot be changed and must be accepted. informal

your better nature the good side of your character; your capacity for tolerance, generosity, or sympathy.

> **1995** *Daily Mail* Pollard is thrown out of the Woolpack and tries to weasel his way back in by appealing to Caroline's better nature.

navel

contemplate your navel spend time complacently considering yourself or your own interests; concentrate on one issue at the expense of a wider view.

near

so near and yet so far a rueful comment on a situation in which you have narrowly failed to achieve an aim.

nearest

your nearest and dearest your close friends and relatives.

necessary

a necessary evil something that is undesirable but must be accepted.

> **1997** *Internet World* Advertising may be a necessary evil. After all, someone has to support Internet ventures.

neck

break your neck to do something exert yourself to the utmost to achieve something. informal

get (or catch) it in the neck be severely criticized or punished. informal

have the (brass) neck to do something have the impudence or nerve to do something. informal

neck and neck level in a race, competition, or comparison.

> ❶ This phrase, together with **win by a neck** below, originally developed with reference to horse racing. A *neck* is the length of the head and neck of a horse as a measure of its lead in a race.

> **1998** *Spectator* The Republicans had a 30-point lead over the Democrats; today, the Democrats are neck and neck on what's supposed to be a bedrock conservative issue.

neck or nothing risking everything on success.

> **1934 Leslie Charteris** *The Saint Intervenes* In broad daylight, there was no chance of further concealment; and it was neck or nothing at that point.

the same neck of the woods the same small geographical area or community.

> ❶ *Neck* in the sense of 'narrow strip of woodland' is recorded from the late 18th century.

> **1998** *Spectator* Both [letters] come from the same neck of the woods, both are on the same subject and both are cries for help which are being ignored.

stick your neck out: *see* STICK.

up to your neck in ❶ heavily involved in something onerous or unpleasant. ❷ very busy with. informal

win by a neck succeed by a small margin.

Ned Kelly

game as Ned Kelly: *see* GAME.

needle

a needle in a haystack something that is almost impossible to find because it is concealed by so many other similar things.

> **2002** *New York Times Magazine* Terrorists don't fit a consistent profile: you're looking for a needle in a haystack, but the color and shape of the needle keep changing.

sharp as a needle: *see* SHARP.

needs

must needs do something ❶ cannot avoid or help doing something. ❷ foolishly insist on doing something.

needs must sometimes you are forced to take a course of action that you would have preferred to avoid.

> ❶ This is a shortened form of the proverb *needs must when the Devil drives*, which is first found in a work by the medieval author John Lydgate.

nelly

not on your nelly certainly not.

> ❶ This expression, modelled on the phrase *not on your life*, originated as *not on your Nelly Duff*, which is British rhyming slang for 'puff', meaning 'breath of life'.

nerve

a bag of nerves: *see* BAG.

get on someone's nerves irritate or annoy someone. informal

have nerves of steel not be easily upset or frightened.

live on your nerves (or your nerve ends) be extremely anxious or tense.

strain every nerve make every possible effort.

> ❶ *Nerve* is used here in an earlier sense of 'tendon or sinew'.

touch (or hit) a (raw) nerve provoke a reaction by referring to a sensitive topic.

a war of nerves: *see* WAR.

Nessus

the shirt of Nessus used to refer to a destructive force or influence. literary

> ❶ In Greek mythology, Nessus was a centaur killed by Hercules. While dying, Nessus told Deianira, Hercules' wife, that if she ever had cause to doubt her husband's love, she should wrap him in a shirt soaked in Nessus' blood as this would ensure his constancy. Deianira followed these instructions, but the centaur's blood was in fact a powerful poison that corroded Hercules' body and as he tried to remove the shirt chunks of his flesh were ripped away.

> **1922 Edith Wharton** *The Glimpses of the Moon* It was as if a sickness long smouldering in him had broken out and become acute, enveloping him in the Nessus shirt of his memories.

nest

a mare's nest: *see* MARE.

nester

empty nester: *see* EMPTY.

net

slip (or fall) through the net escape from or be missed by something organized to catch or deal with you.

> **1977 Margaret Drabble** *The Ice Age* Britain is, after all, a welfare state, and not many slip through its net.

surf the net: *see* SURF.

nettle

grasp the nettle: *see* GRASP.

network

the old boy network: *see* OLD.

never

never-never land an imaginary utopian place or situation.

> ❶ This expression is often used with allusion to the imaginary country in J. M. Barrie's *Peter Pan* (1904). The term was used earlier to denote the remote and unpopulated northern part of the Northern Territory and Queensland in Australia (from which, it is implied, a person might never return).

never say die: *see* DIE.

new

a new broom: *see* BROOM.

a new kid on the block: *see* BLOCK.

new off the irons: *see* IRON.

a new one on (me, him, etc.) an account, idea, or joke not previously encountered by me, him, etc. informal

turn over a new leaf: *see* LEAF.

a whole new ball game: *see* BALL.

news

be bad news be a problem or handicap. informal

> **1996** *City Paper (Baltimore)* From the moment we see Mark Wahlberg... surrounded by pool-hall scumbags, we know he's bad news.

be good news be an asset; be commendable or admirable. informal

no news is good news without information to the contrary you can assume that all is well. proverb

New York

a New York minute a very short time; a moment. US informal

next

next in line immediately below the present holder of a position in order of succession.

next door

the boy (or girl) next door a person or the type of a person perceived as familiar, approachable, and dependable, typically in the context of a romantic partnership.

nibs

his nibs a mock title used to refer to a self-important man, especially one who is in authority. informal

> **1989 Guy Vanderhaege** *Homesick* Whatever his nibs prefers. I see that hasn't changed either. He still expects things to be organized to suit him and only him.

nice

make nice (or nice-nice) be pleasant or polite to someone, typically in a hypocritical way. North American informal

nice one used to express approval. British informal

> **2001** *Searcher* Waving it aloft with delight, I shouted a 'Howzat!' that merely elicited grudging grunts of 'Nice one' from the Mexborough duo.

nice work if you can get it used to express envy of what is perceived to be another person's more favourable situation, especially if they seem to have reached it with little effort. informal

> **ⓘ** *Nice work if you can get it* was the title of an Ira Gershwin song from 1937.

nicety

to a nicety precisely.

nick

in — nick in a specified condition. British informal

> **1997 Ian Rankin** *Black & Blue* Don't be fooled by the wheezing old pensioner routine. Eve's around fifty, still in good nick.

in the nick of time only just in time; just at the critical moment.

> **ⓘ** *Nick* is used here in the sense of 'the precise moment of an occurrence or an event'. This form of the phrase dates from the mid 17th century, but *in the (very) nick* is recorded from the late 16th century.

> **1985 Nini Herman** *My Kleinian Home* Time and again, when all seemed lost, I somehow won through in the nick of time.

nick someone for cheat someone out of something, typically a sum of money. North American informal

> **1962** *Washington Daily News* Taxpayers… have heard rumblings that they might be nicked for about a million dollars each year to subsidize professional sports here.

nickel

accept a wooden nickel be fooled or swindled. US

> **ⓘ** A *wooden nickel* is a worthless or counterfeit coin.

not worth a plugged nickel of no value. US

> **ⓘ** A *plugged* coin has had a part removed and the space filled with base material.

> **1991 R. Hawkey & R. Bingham** *Wild Card* If as much as a whisper gets out… none of our lives are going to be worth a plugged nickel.

night

make a night of it: *see* **make a day of it** *at* MAKE.

night and day all the time; constantly.

night of the long knives a treacherous betrayal or ruthless action.

> **ⓘ** *Night of the long knives* is especially associated with the massacre of the Brownshirts on Hitler's orders in 1934. Traditionally, the phrase referred to the legendary massacre of the Britons by Hengist in 472, described by Geoffrey of Monmouth in his *Historia Regum Britanniae*. In Britain it has been particularly used of the occasion in 1962 on which Harold Macmillan dismissed a third of his cabinet at the same time, of which the Liberal politician Jeremy Thorpe remarked 'Greater love hath no man than this, that he lay down his friends for his life'.

nine

dressed (up) to the nines dressed very smartly or elaborately.

> **ⓘ** This expression may come from the 99th Wiltshire Regiment, a military unit who were noted for their smart appearance.

a nine days' wonder: *see* WONDER.

nine to five typical office hours.

nine times out of ten on nearly every occasion.

on cloud nine: *see* CLOUD.

ninepence

no more than ninepence in the shilling of low intelligence. dated

> **ⓘ** Since the decimalization of the British coinage, this phrase has gradually fallen out of use, but there are numerous other humorous variations on the theme of someone not possessing their proper share of brains or intelligence, for example **a sandwich short of a picnic** (*see* SANDWICH).

ninepin

go down (or drop or fall) like ninepins topple or succumb in large numbers.

> **1994 Beryl Gilroy** *Sunlight on Sweet Water* They were falling like ninepins to the wizardry of our fast bowler, Bachan.

nineteen

talk nineteen to the dozen: *see* TALK.

nip

in the nip naked. Irish informal

nip something in the bud suppress or destroy something at an early stage.

> ℹ This phrase refers to the horticultural practice of pinching out plant buds to prevent the development of shoots or flowers. *Nip* in this sense was used figuratively in the late 16th century, and *nip in the bud* in the early 17th century.

put in the nips cadge, borrow, or extort money. Australian & New Zealand informal

nit

keep nit keep watch or act as a guard. Australian

> ℹ *Nit* here is possibly an alteration of *nix*, a warning signal by schoolchildren that a teacher is approaching.

pick nits look for and criticize small or insignificant faults or errors.

> ℹ The image here is of the painstaking removal of tiny parasitic *nits* (lice or lice eggs) from someone's hair. The phrase originated in the mid 20th century, chiefly in North American usage.

no

no man's land an intermediate or ambiguous area of thought or activity.

> ℹ This phrase was used literally in the late 16th century for a piece of land without an owner, but it is particularly associated with the terrain between the German trenches and those of the Allied forces in World War I. The figurative use of the phrase dates from the late 19th century.

the noes have it the negative votes are in the majority. Compare with **the ayes have it** (*at* AYE).

no two ways about it used to convey that there can be no doubt about something.

not (*or* **never**) **take no for an answer** persist in spite of refusals.

no worries all right; fine. informal

— or no — regardless of the person, thing, or quality specified.
> **1995 Kazuo Ishiguro** *The Unconsoled* I was thinking there's no reason we can't start doing all sorts of things together now, house or no house.

noble

the noble art boxing. chiefly archaic

> ℹ A fuller version of this phrase is *the noble art* (or *science*) *of self-defence*.

noblesse

noblesse oblige privilege entails responsibility.

nobody

be nobody's fool: *see* FOOL.

like nobody's business: *see* BUSINESS.

nod

get (*or* **give someone or something**) **the nod** ❶ be selected or approved (*or* select or approve someone or something). ❷ get (*or* give someone) a signal or information.

a nod's as good as a wink there's no need for further elaboration or explanation.

> ℹ This is a shortened form of the proverb, dating from the late 18th century, *a nod is as good as a wink to a blind horse*, used to convey that a mere hint or suggestion can be or has been understood. *A nod and a wink* is also used to mean 'a hint or innuendo'.

on the nod by general agreement and without discussion. British informal

nodding

be on nodding terms know someone slightly.

have a nodding acquaintance with someone or something know someone slightly; know a little about something.
> **1989 Donnie Radcliffe** *Simply Barbara Bush* Their families had lived less than ten miles apart as they were growing up, and their fathers almost certainly had a nodding acquaintance on the golf course.

no-go

a no-go area an area which is dangerous or impossible to enter or to which entry is restricted or forbidden.

> ℹ As a noun, *no-go* was first used in the late 19th century in the sense of 'an impracticable situation'. Its use in this phrase, with the sense of 'no entry', is particularly associated with Northern Ireland in the 1970s.

> **1971** *Guardian* For journalists and others, the Bogside and Creggan estates are 'no-go areas', with the IRA in total effective control.

noise

a big noise: *see* **a big cheese** *at* BIG.

make a noise speak or act in a way designed to attract a lot of attention or publicity.

none

be none the wiser: *see* WISER.

none the worse: *see* WORSE.

will have (*or* want) none of something
refuse to accept something (especially with
reference to behaviour).

> **2000 Joe Pemberton** *Forever & Ever Amen* It
> wasn't James's idea to board the *Christina*. He'd
> told Aunty Mary that it had sunk on the telly
> but she would have none of it.

non-linear

go non-linear become very excited or angry,
especially about a particular obsession.
informal

> ⓘ This expression may have originated as a
> humorous play on the phrase **go off the rails**
> (*see* RAIL).

nonsense

make nonsense (*or* a nonsense) of reduce
the value of something to a ridiculous
degree.

nook

every nook and cranny every part or aspect
of something.

noose

put your head in a noose bring about your
own downfall.

north

up north to or in the north of a country.
informal

nose

by a nose (of a victory) by a very narrow
margin.

> ⓘ In horse racing, *by a nose* is the narrowest
> margin by which a horse can win.

cannot see further than your nose be
unwilling or fail to consider different
possibilities or to foresee the consequences
of your actions.

count noses count people, typically in order
to determine the numbers in a vote.

cut off your nose to spite your face
disadvantage yourself in the course of
trying to disadvantage another.

> ⓘ This idea was proverbial for self-
> defeating malice in both medieval Latin and
> medieval French, and has been found in
> English since the mid 16th century.

get up someone's nose irritate or annoy
someone. informal

give someone a bloody nose inflict a
resounding defeat on someone.

keep your nose clean stay out of trouble.
informal

keep your nose out of refrain from
interfering in someone else's affairs.

keep your nose to the grindstone: *see*
GRINDSTONE.

lead someone by the nose: *see* LEAD.

on the nose ❶ to a person's sense of smell.
❷ precisely. informal, chiefly North American
❸ distasteful; offensive. Australian informal

put someone's nose out of joint upset or
annoy someone. informal

turn up your nose at show distaste or
contempt for something. informal

under someone's nose (of an action)
committed openly and boldly, but without
someone noticing or noticing in time to
prevent it. informal

with your nose in the air haughtily.

> **1994** *Time* Charles de Gaulle arrived in the U.S.
> with his nose in the air; he considered Jackie
> empty and much too beau monde.

not

not half: *see* HALF.

not in my back yard expressing an objection
to the siting of something regarded as
undesirable in your own neighbourhood,
with the implication that it would be
acceptable elsewhere.

> ⓘ This expression originated in the USA in
> derogatory references to anti-nuclear
> campaigners. In Britain it is particularly
> associated with reports of the then
> Environment Secretary Nicholas Ridley's
> opposition in 1988 to housing developments
> near his own home. More recently, it has
> been used in association with the siting of
> housing for refugees and asylum seekers.
> The phrase has given rise to the acronym
> *nimby* as a term for someone with these
> attitudes.

not least: *see* LEAST.

note

hit (*or* strike) the right (*or* wrong) note say
or do something in exactly the right (*or*
wrong) way.

strike (*or* sound) a — note express a feeling
or view of a particular kind.

2000 *Times* John McCain... was expected to strike a hawkish note last night, calling for the upgrading of the Armed Forces.

nothing

be as nothing (compared) to be insignificant in comparison with.

1998 *Oldie* Believe me, being pronounced anathema is as nothing compared to the earful you get from a liberal who considers himself insufficiently appreciated.

have nothing on someone or something
❶ have much less of a particular quality or ability than someone or something; be inferior to someone or something in a particular respect. ❷ (especially of the police) have no incriminating information about someone. informal

nothing daunted without having been made fearful or apprehensive.

> ❶ This use of *nothing* to mean 'not at all' is now archaic and is almost always found either in this phrase or in **nothing loath** below.

1992 **Robert Black** *Orkney: A Place of Safety?* Nothing daunted, the committee members set to.

nothing doing ❶ there is no prospect of success or agreement. ❷ nothing is happening. informal

there's nothing (or nothing else) for it there's no alternative. British

2002 *Which?* If there's nothing for it other than to get a shiny new appliance, the next question to ask is: 'Where does the old one go?'

nothing less than used to express how extreme something is.

1990 **Katherine Frank** *Emily Brontë* Nothing less than the ultimate feminine destiny of marriage had been within her reach, and Charlotte had almost immediately spurned it.

nothing loath quite willing.

> ❶ This expression was used by John Milton in *Paradise Lost*: 'Her hand he seis'd, and to a shadie bank... He led her nothing loath'.

nothing much in it: *see* MUCH.

nothing to it very simple to do. informal

stop at nothing: *see* STOP.

sweet nothings words of affection exchanged by lovers.

think nothing of it do not apologize or feel bound to show gratitude (used as a polite response).

you ain't seen nothing yet there is something even more extreme or impressive in store. informal

> ❶ This expression was popularized by Al Jolson's aside in the 1927 film *The Jazz Singer*, 'you ain't heard nuttin' yet'.

notice

at short (or a moment's) notice with little warning or time for preparation.

put someone on notice (or serve notice) warn someone of something about or likely to occur, often in a formal or threatening way.

now

now or never used to convey urgency.

1994 **James Kelman** *How Late It Was, How Late* It's now or never, know what I'm saying; he's out this once, there's no gony be a second time.

now you're talking an expression of enthusiastic agreement or approval.

nowhere

in the middle of nowhere: *see* MIDDLE.

a road to nowhere: *see* ROAD.

nth

to the nth degree to any extent; to the utmost.

> ❶ In mathematics, *nth* denotes an unspecified member of a series of numbers or enumerated items.

1994 *i-D* Along the way they argue, get harassed by ignorant locals, sing along to their favourite tunes and camp it up to the nth degree.

nudge

a nudge and a wink encouragement given secretly or implicitly; covert support.

> ❶ Both a *nudge* and a *wink* are covert signs of complicity, with *wink* also having the implication of 'shutting your eyes' to something.

1998 *Times* There was a nudge and a wink at some mercenary help that in the end proved unnecessary.

nudge nudge (wink wink) used to draw attention to an innuendo, especially a sexual one, in the previous statement. informal

> ⓘ This expression is a catchphrase from *Monty Python's Flying Circus*, a British television comedy programme.

nuff

nuff said there is no need to say any more.

> ⓘ *Nuff* is an informal or dialect shortening of *enough*.

nuisance

make a nuisance of yourself cause trouble and annoyance, usually deliberately or avoidably.

number

a back number: see BACK.

by numbers following simple instructions identified by numbers; mechanically.

> ⓘ This phrase alludes to *painting by numbers*, a painting kit with a canvas on which numbers have been marked to indicate which colour of paint should be applied at which place.

1992 *Canadian Yachting* We discovered navigation by numbers as our beamy flotilla floated from buoy to buoy reading off the charts like a road map.

do a number on treat someone badly, typically by deceiving, humiliating, or criticizing them in a calculated and thorough way. North American informal

have someone's number understand a person's real motives or character and thereby gain some advantage. informal

have someone's (name and) number on it (of a bomb, bullet, or other missile) be destined to hit a specified person. informal

make your number report your arrival, pay a courtesy call, or report for duty.

> ⓘ This expression has nautical origins: when ships *made their number*, they signalled to others the number by which they were registered. The literal sense was first recorded in the mid 19th-century, with the figurative extension developing soon afterwards.

public enemy number one: see PUBLIC.

someone's number is up the time has come when someone is doomed to die or suffer some other disaster or setback. informal

> ⓘ This phrase may allude to a lottery number or to the various biblical passages referring to the 'number of your days', i.e. the

length of your life, for example in Job 38:21: 'Knowest thou it, because thou wast then born? or because the number of thy days is great?'

take care of (or look after) number one be selfishly absorbed in protecting your own person and interests. informal

without number too many to count.

1990 Bill Bryson *Mother Tongue* The varieties of wordplay available in English are almost without number—puns, tongue-twisters, anagrams, riddles, cryptograms.

numbered

someone's or something's days are numbered someone or something will not survive or remain in a particular position for much longer.

nut

be nuts about (or on) be very enthusiastic about or fond of. informal

1934 Dashiell Hammett *The Thin Man* She told me she had this job with Wynant and he was nuts about her and she was sitting pretty.

do your nut be extremely angry or agitated. British informal

> ⓘ In this phrase and in **off your nut** below, *nut* means 'head'.

for nuts even tolerably well. British informal

1934 Angela Thirkell *Wild Strawberries* That Miss Stevenson can't play for nuts.

nuts and bolts the basic practical details of something. informal

off your nut out of your mind; crazy. informal

take (or use) a sledgehammer to crack a nut: see SLEDGEHAMMER.

a tough (or hard) nut (to crack) someone who is difficult to deal with or hard to beat; a formidable person. informal

nutmeg

a wooden nutmeg a false or fraudulent thing. US

> ⓘ A *wooden nutmeg* was a piece of wood shaped to resemble a nutmeg and fraudulently sold as the real thing. This deception was particularly associated with the inhabitants of Connecticut, giving rise to the nickname 'the Nutmeg State'.

nutshell

in a nutshell in the fewest possible words.

> ❶ A *nutshell* is a traditional metaphor for a very small space. It is used by Shakespeare in *Hamlet*: 'I could be bounded in a nutshell, and count myself a king of infinite space, were it not that I have bad dreams'.

nutty

be nutty about like very much. informal

nutty as a fruitcake completely crazy. informal

> ❶ *Nutty* meaning 'mad or crazy' dates from the late 19th century, and this phrase, punning on the sense of 'full of nuts', from the 1930s. *Fruitcake* is also used on its own to mean 'a crazy or eccentric person'.

Oo

oar

rest on your oars ❶ cease rowing by leaning on the handles of your oars, thereby lifting them horizontally out of the water. ❷ relax your efforts.

> ℹ️ A US variant of this phrase is *lay on your oars*.

stick (or poke or put) your oar in give an opinion or advice without being asked. informal

> **1992** *Daily Telegraph* My only minor fault is I sometimes like putting my oar in…and my advice can be a little brutal.

oat

feel your oats feel lively and buoyant. US informal

> ℹ️ Oats are used as feed for horses, making them friskier and more energetic.

get your oats have sexual intercourse. informal

> **1965 William Dick** *A Bunch of Ratbags* I was kissing her excitedly and passionately …Cookie, you're gonna get your oats tonight for sure, I thought to myself.

off your oats lacking an appetite. informal

sow your wild oats go through a period of wild or promiscuous behaviour while young.

> ℹ️ *Wild oats* are weeds found in cornfields which resemble cultivated oats: spending time sowing them would be a foolish or useless activity. The expression has been current since the late 16th century; from the mid 16th to the early 17th century, *wild oat* was also used as a term for a dissolute young man.

object

no object not influencing or restricting choices or decisions.

> **1998** *Independent* I'm a very impulsive buyer, if I see something I buy it, money no object.

Occam

Occam's razor the principle that in explaining something no more assumptions should be made than are necessary.

> ℹ️ This principle takes its name from to the English philosopher and Franciscan friar William of Occam (c.1285–1349): the image is that of the razor cutting away all extraneous assumptions.

odd

odd one (or man) out ❶ someone or something that is different to the others. ❷ someone who is not able to fit easily or comfortably into a group or society.

odds

ask no odds ask no favours. US

by all odds certainly. North American

it makes no odds it does not matter. informal, chiefly British

> ℹ️ This phrase and **what's the odds** below come from an earlier use of *odds* to mean 'difference in advantage or effect'.

lay (or give) odds ❶ offer a bet with odds favourable to the other person betting. ❷ be very sure about something.

> ℹ️ The opposite of *lay odds* in sense 1 is *take odds* which means 'offer a bet with odds unfavourable to the other person betting'.

over the odds above what is generally considered acceptable, especially for a price. British

shout the odds talk loudly and in an opinionated way.

what's the odds? what does it matter? informal

odour

be in good (or bad) odour with someone be in (or out of) favour with someone.

odour of sanctity ❶ a state of holiness. ❷ sanctimoniousness. derogatory

> ℹ️ This expression is a translation of the French idiom *odeur de sainteté*. It refers to a sweet or balsamic odour which was reputedly emitted by the bodies of saints at or after death, and which was regarded as evidence of their sanctity.

off

off and on intermittently; now and then.

off and running making good progress.

offence

a hanging offence: *see* HANGING.

office

good offices help and support, often given by exercising your influence.

> **2002** *Daily Telegraph* Mr Blair will demonstratively use his good offices to bring round the German and French leaders, thereby gaining prestige in Washington.

just another day at the office boring routine.

> **1997** *Times* Professional cricket has been reduced to just another day at the 'office'.

offing

in the offing nearby; likely to happen or appear soon.

> ⓘ This expression originated as a nautical term for a distance offshore, beyond a harbour or anchoring ground. It has been used figuratively since the late 18th century.

oil

burn the midnight oil: *see* BURN.

oil someone's palm: *see* **grease someone's palm** *at* GREASE.

no oil painting not very attractive. British informal

oil and water two elements, factors, or people that do not agree or blend together.

> ⓘ Water and oil are two liquid substances that repel each other and cannot be mixed together.

oil the wheels help something go smoothly.

pour oil on troubled waters: *see* POUR.

old

any old how in no particular order.

come the old soldier: *see* SOLDIER.

make old bones: *see* BONE.

of the old school traditional or old-fashioned.

> **1998 Imogen de la Bere** *The Last Deception of Palliser Wentwood* He came of the old school, in which men did not weep in front of other men.

the old Adam: *see* ADAM.

old as the hills: *see* **ancient as the hills** *at* HILL.

the old boy network mutual assistance, especially preferment in employment, shown among those with a shared social and educational background.

the old days a period in the past, often seen as significantly different from the present, especially noticeably better or worse.

old enough to be someone's father (*or* **mother)** of a much greater age than someone. informal

> **1997 Nelson DeMille** *Plum Island* He was probably old enough to be their father, but girls paid attention to money, pure and simple.

an old one a familiar joke.

the old school tie the attitudes of group loyalty and traditionalism associated with wearing the tie of a particular public school. British

old Spanish customs: *see* SPANISH.

an old wives' tale a widely held traditional belief that is now thought to be unscientific or incorrect.

> ⓘ The phrase (and its earlier variant *old wives' fable*) is recorded from the early 16th century, with the earliest example being from Tyndale's translation of the Bible.

play Old Harry with: *see* **play the devil with** *at* DEVIL.

olive

hold out (*or* **offer) an olive branch** offer a token of peace or goodwill.

> ⓘ A branch of an olive tree is an emblem of peace. In the Bible, it was the token brought by a dove to Noah to indicate that God's anger was assuaged and that the flood had abated (Genesis 8:11).

on

be on about talk about tediously and at length. British informal

be on at someone nag or grumble at someone. British informal

be on to someone be close to discovering the truth about an illegal or undesirable activity that someone is engaging in. informal

be on to something have an idea or information that is likely to lead to an important discovery. informal

it's not on it's impractical or unacceptable. informal

on and off intermittently; now and then.

on it drinking heavily. *Australian informal*

on side supporting or part of the same team as someone else.

> **1997** *Spectator* And while clearly 'on side' with New Labour, he has never been a closely quartered insider.

you're on said by way of accepting a challenge or bet. *informal*

once

once a —, always a — a person cannot change their fundamental nature.

> **1993** Margaret Atwood *The Robber Bride* She was once a Catholic...and once a Catholic, always a Catholic, according to her mother.

once and for all (*or* **once for all**) now and for the last time; finally.

once and future denoting someone or something that is eternal, enduring, or constant.

> ❶ This expression comes from T. H. White's *The Once and Future King* (1958), a series of novels about the Arthurian legends.

once bitten, twice shy a bad experience makes you wary of the same thing happening again.

> ❶ This expression dates from the late 19th century. A variant common in the USA is *once burned, twice shy*.

once (*or* **every once**) **in a while** from time to time; occasionally.

> **1989** Annie Dillard *The Writing Life* Every once in a while Rahm saw a peephole in the clouds and buzzed over for a look.

one

get something in one understand or succeed in guessing something immediately. *informal*

one on one (*or* **one to one**) denoting or referring to a situation in which two parties come into direct contact, opposition, or correspondence.

> **1995** *Represent* I wanna speak to God one on one me and him.

the one that got away something desirable that has eluded capture.

> ❶ This phrase comes from the angler's traditional way of relating the story of a large fish that has managed to escape after almost being caught: 'you should have seen the one that got away'.

public enemy number one: *see* PUBLIC.

rolled into one: *see* ROLLED.

take care of number one: *see* NUMBER.

one-horse

one-horse race a contest in which one candidate or competitor is clearly superior to all the others and seems certain to win.

> **1995** *Sun* (Baltimore) The Rangers, who have won six of their last seven, could make it a one-horse race in a hurry.

one-horse town a small town with few and poor facilities. *informal*

onion

know your onions be fully knowledgeable about something. *informal*

> ❶ *Onions* is perhaps short for rhyming slang *onion rings*, meaning 'things'. The phrase dates from the 1920s.

open

be open with speak frankly to; conceal nothing from.

an open book: *see* **a closed book** *at* CLOSED.

in (*or* **into**) **the open** ❶ out of doors; not under cover. ❷ not subject to concealment or obfuscation; made public.

open-and-shut (of a case or argument) admitting no doubt or dispute; straightforward and conclusive.

open sesame a marvellous or irresistible means of achieving access to what would normally be inaccessible.

> ❶ In the tale of Ali Baba and the Forty Thieves in the *Arabian Nights*, the door of the robbers' cave was made to open by uttering this magic formula.

with your eyes open (*or* **with open eyes**) fully aware of the risks and other implications of an action or situation.

opener

for openers to start with; first of all. *informal*

opium

the opium of the people (*or* **masses**) something regarded as inducing a false and unrealistic sense of contentment among people.

ⓘ This idiom is a translation of the German phrase *Opium des Volks*, used by Karl Marx in 1844 in reference to religion.

opportunity

opportunity knocks a chance of success occurs.

ⓘ This expression comes from the proverb *opportunity never knocks twice at any man's door* or *opportunity knocks but once*. The form of the saying with *opportunity* dates from the late 19th century, but *fortune* was used in the early 19th century and a version of the saying is recorded in medieval French.

option

keep (*or* **leave**) **your options open** avoid committing yourself.

> **1996 Colin Bateman** *Of Wee Sweetie Mice and Men* Have it your way. We'll go to Princetown. But I'm keeping my options open. If there's any more trouble...we're out, we're home.

orange

all Lombard Street to a China orange: *see* LOMBARD.

squeeze (*or* **suck**) **an orange** take all that is profitable out of something.

orbit

into orbit into a state of heightened activity, performance, anger, or excitement. informal

> **1988 Candia McWilliam** *A Case of Knives* I am a greedy girl, not merely swayed but waltzed into orbit by appearances.

order

orders are orders commands must be obeyed, however much you may disagree with them.

out of order ❶ not in normal sequence. ❷ (of a machine) not working. ❸ (of behaviour) improper or unacceptable. informal

a tall order: *see* TALL.

other half

how the other half lives used to express or allude to the way of life of a different group in society, especially a wealthier one. British informal

out

at outs at variance or enmity.

ⓘ A North American variant of this expression is *on the outs*.

> **1997 A. Sivanandran** *When Memory Dies* Now the land had been taken from him...He was at outs with the world.

out and about (of a person, especially after an illness) engaging in normal activity.

out and away by far.

out at elbows: *see* ELBOW.

out for having your interest or effort directed to; intent on.

out-Herod Herod: *see* HEROD.

out of it ❶ not used or included in something. ❷ astray or distant from the centre or heart of anything. ❸ extremely drunk. informal

out of order: *see* ORDER.

out of pocket: *see* POCKET.

out to lunch crazy; insane. informal

out with someone or something an exhortation to expel or dismiss someone or something unwanted.

out with it say what you are thinking.

> **1993 Margaret Atwood** *The Robber Bride* She would be so squirrelly with desire—out with it, lust, capital L, the best of the Seven Deadlies —that she'd scarcely be able to sit still.

outdoors

the great outdoors the open air; outdoor life. informal

outside

get outside of eat or drink something. informal

> **1981 Sam McAughtry** *Belfast Stories* We'll get outside of a feed of bacon and egg and black pudding.

on the outside looking in (of a person) excluded from a group or activity.

over

over and done with completely finished.

overboard

go overboard ❶ be highly enthusiastic. ❷ behave immoderately; go too far.

ⓘ The idea behind this idiom is that of recklessly jumping over the side of a ship into the water.

throw something overboard abandon or discard something.

ⓘ The idea here is that something thrown over the side of a ship is lost forever.

overdrive

Mexican overdrive: *see* MEXICAN.

over-egg

over-egg the pudding (*or* cake) go too far in embellishing, exaggerating, or doing something.

> ❶ Excessive quantities of egg in a pudding could either make it too rich or cause it not to set or cook correctly.

> **1998** *Spectator* This is a noble end, but in her eagerness to reach it Duffy somewhat over-eggs the cake.

overplay

overplay your hand spoil your chance of success through excessive confidence in your position.

> ❶ In a card game, if you overplay your hand, you play a hand on the basis of an overestimate of your likelihood of winning.

overshoot

overshoot (*or* overstep) the mark go beyond what is intended or proper; go too far.

owe

owe someone one feel indebted to someone. informal

> **1990 Paul Auster** *The Music of Chance* 'I guess I owe you one,' Floyd said, patting Nashe's back in an awkward show of gratitude.

own

as if you own the place in an overbearing or self-important manner. informal

be your own man (*or* woman *or* person) act independently and with confidence.

come into its (*or* your) own become fully effective, used, or recognized.

get your own back take action in retaliation for a wrongdoing or insult. informal

hold your own retain a position of strength in a challenging situation; not be defeated or weakened.

> **1953 Margaret Kennedy** *Troy Chimneys* A young man so gifted may hold his own very well.

oyster

the world is your oyster: *see* WORLD.

Pp

P

mind your Ps and Qs: *see* MIND.

pace

change of pace a change from what you are used to. chiefly North American

off the pace behind the leader or leading group in a race or contest.

put someone or something through their paces make someone or something demonstrate their qualities or abilities.

set the pace ❶ start a race as the fastest. **❷** lead the way in doing or achieving something.

stand (*or* stay) the pace be able to keep up with another or others.

pack

go to the pack deteriorate; go to pieces. Australian & New Zealand informal

> **1980** Frank Moorhouse *Days of Wine and Rage* All the places overseas where the British have pulled out are going to the pack.

pack your bag (*or* bags) put your belongings in a bag or suitcase in preparation for your imminent departure.

pack heat carry a gun. North American informal

pack it in stop what you are doing. informal

pack a punch ❶ be capable of hitting with skill or force. **❷** have a powerful effect.

packing

send someone packing make someone leave in an abrupt or peremptory way. informal

paddle

paddle your own canoe be independent and self-sufficient. informal

> ❶ This expression has been in figurative use from the early 19th century: it was the title of a popular song by Sarah T. Bolton in 1854.

page

on the same page (of two or more people) in agreement. US

page three girl a model whose nude or semi-nude photograph appears as part of a regular series in a tabloid newspaper.

> ❶ This sort of photograph is featured on page three of the British tabloid newspaper *The Sun*.

paid

put paid to stop abruptly; destroy. informal

pain

no pain, no gain suffering is necessary in order to achieve something.

> ❶ There has been a proverbial association between *pain* and *gain* since at least the late 16th century, and 'No Paines, no Gaines' was the title of a 1648 poem by Robert Herrick. The modern form, which dates from the 1980s, probably originated as a slogan used in fitness classes.

> **1997** *American Spectator* As the cliché goes, no pain, no gain. In fact, in our confessional age, you can make quite a lot of gains for very little pain.

a pain in the neck an annoying or tedious person or thing. informal

> ❶ There are a number of vulgar slang alternatives to *neck* in this idiom, such as *a pain in the arse* or, in the USA, *ass*.

paint

like watching paint dry (of an activity or experience) extremely boring.

paint the Forth Bridge used to indicate that a task can never be completed.

> ❶ The steel structure of the Forth Railway Bridge in Scotland has required continuous repainting: it is so long that once the painters reach one end, they have to begin again at the other.

paint the town red go out and enjoy yourself flamboyantly. informal

paint yourself into a corner leave yourself no means of escape or room to manoeuvre.

painting

no oil painting: *see* OIL.

pair

another pair of shoes: *see* SHOE.

pair of hands a person seen in terms of their participation in a task.

pale

beyond the pale outside the bounds of acceptable behaviour.

> ❶ A *pale* (from Latin *palus* meaning 'a stake') is a pointed wooden post used with others to form a fence; from this it came to refer to any fenced enclosure. So, in literal use, *beyond the pale* meant the area beyond a fence. The term *Pale* was applied to various territories under English control and especially to the area of Ireland under English jurisdiction before the 16th century. The earliest reference (1547) to the *Pale* in Ireland as such draws the contrast between the English Pale and the 'wyld Irysh': the area *beyond the pale* would have been regarded as dangerous and uncivilized by the English.

pale into insignificance lose importance or value.

palm

cross someone's palm with silver: *see* CROSS.

grease someone's palm: *see* GREASE.

have (or hold) someone in the palm of your hand have someone under your control or influence.

read someone's palm tell someone's fortune by looking at the lines on their palm.

pan

go down the pan reach a stage of abject failure or uselessness.

> **1997 Ian Rankin** *Black & Blue* My company's just about given up trying to sell to the oil industry. They'd rather buy Yank or Scandinavian...no wonder Scotland's down the pan.

pancake

flat as a pancake completely flat.

Pandora

a Pandora's box a process that once begun generates many complicated problems.

> ❶ In Greek mythology, Pandora was the first mortal woman. One story recounts that she was created by Zeus and sent to earth with a box or jar of evils in revenge for the fact that Prometheus had disobediently given the gift of fire to the earth. She let all the evils out of the container to infect the earth; only hope remained to ease the lot of humankind. In another account, the box contained all the blessings of the gods which, with the exception of hope, escaped and were lost when the box was opened.

> **1997** *Spectator* Drummond's series...has opened a Pandora's box of complaints... about the tide of mediocrity engulfing the art.

panic button

press (or push or hit) the panic button respond to a situation by panicking or taking emergency measures. informal

> ❶ A *panic button* is a security device which can be used to raise the alarm in an emergency.

pants

beat the pants off: *see* BEAT.

by the seat of your pants: *see* SEAT.

catch someone with their pants (or trousers) down catch someone in an unprepared state or sexually compromising situation. informal

scare (or bore etc.) the pants off someone make someone extremely scared, bored, etc. informal

wearing (or in) short pants very young. informal

> ❶ A little boy was traditionally dressed in shorts before attaining a certain age, when he would be allowed to wear long trousers.

paper

make the papers be written about or given attention as news.

not worth the paper it is written on (of an agreement, promise, etc.) of no value or validity whatsoever.

on paper ❶ in writing. ❷ in theory rather than in reality.

paper over the cracks disguise problems or divisions rather than trying to solve them.

> ❶ The phrase is a translation of a German expression used by the statesman Otto von Bismarck in a letter of 1865, and early uses refer to this.

a paper tiger an apparently dangerous but actually ineffectual person or thing.

> ❶ This expression became well known in the West from its use by Mao Zedong, the Chinese Communist leader. In an interview in 1946, he expressed the view that 'all reactionaries are paper tigers'.

1998 *Oldie* We fear that the Rail Regulator and the Consultative Committee are paper tigers and a waste of time.

paper bag

someone couldn't — their way out of a paper bag a person is completely unable to do something, either through ineptitude or weakness. informal

> **1999** *Time Out N.Y.* The problem is, he also, at the time, loved Victoria Tennant, and she can't act her way out of a paper bag even if you soak it with a hose first.

par

above par ❶ at a premium. **❷** better than average.

> ❶ *Above par* is a stock exchange idiom. In this and the following idioms, *par* is the Latin for 'equal'.

at par at face value.

below (*or* under) par ❶ at a discount. **❷** worse than usual, often in relation to a person's health.

> ❶ As a golfing term, *under par* means 'better than usual': *see* **par for the course** below.

on a par with equal in importance or quality to; on an equal level with.

> **1998** *Spectator* Imagine learning that the MCC had been used for 200 years as a front for procuring under-age boys ... The scandal of the Tour de France is roughly on a par with such a revelation.

par for the course what is normal or expected in any given circumstances.

> ❶ In golf, *par* is the number of strokes that a first-class player would normally require to get round a particular course.

up to par at an expected or usual level or quality.

> **1989** **Randall Kenan** *A Visitation of Spirits* Why not him? Did he not look okay? Did he smell bad? Have bad breath? Were his clothes not up to par?

parcel

pass the parcel a situation in which movement or exchange takes place, but no one gains any advantage.

> ❶ *Pass the parcel* is the name of a children's game in which a parcel is passed round to the accompaniment of music. When the music stops, the child holding the parcel is allowed to open it.

1998 *Times* People who won the initial franchises have made the money ... Any movement from now on is just a game of pass the parcel, really.

pare

pare something to the bone: *see* **cut something to the bone** *at* BONE.

parenthesis

in parenthesis as a digression or after-thought.

part

be part and parcel of be an essential feature or element of.

> ❶ Both *part* and *parcel* ultimately come from Latin *pars* meaning 'part' and in this phrase they have virtually identical senses. The phrase is first recorded in mid 16th-century legal parlance; it is now used in general contexts to emphasize that the item mentioned is absolutely integral to the whole.

> **1998** *Spectator* It's not enough for people just to shrug their shoulders and say, 'Well, that is part and parcel of being in public life'.

a man of (many) parts a man showing great ability in many different areas.

part brass rags with: *see* RAG.

part company ❶ (of two or more people) cease to be together; go in different directions. **❷** (of two or more parties) cease to associate with each other, usually as the result of a disagreement.

take something in good part: *see* GOOD.

particular

a London particular: *see* LONDON.

parting

a (*or* the) parting of the ways a point at which two people must separate or at which a decision must be taken.

> ❶ This phrase has its origins in Ezekiel 21:21: 'the king of Babylon stood at the parting of the way, at the head of the two ways'.

party

the party's over a period of success, good fortune, or happiness has come to an end. informal

> **1998** *Independent* Until the Government decided yesterday that the party's over, it was seemingly routine procedure for our hospital consultants to have ... the Committee on

Distinction Awards, which is dominated by the consultants, look after their interests.

pass

come to a pretty pass: *see* PRETTY.

head (or cut) someone or something off at the pass forestall someone or something, especially at a critical moment or at the last possible moment.

> ⓘ *Pass* is used here in the sense of a narrow route through mountains.

pass the baton: *see* BATON.

pass the buck: *see* BUCK.

pass by on the other side avoid having anything to do with something that should demand your attention or concern.

> ⓘ This expression refers to the parable of the good Samaritan, recounted in Luke 10. A man travelling from Jerusalem to Jericho was attacked and robbed during the course of his journey. He was left lying by the road and the first two people who saw him 'passed by on the other side' of the road. It was the third traveller, the Samaritan (a man from Samaria) who helped him.

pass the hat round: *see* HAT.

pass in a crowd be not conspicuously below the average, especially in terms of appearance.

pass in your ally die. Australian informal

> ⓘ In this phrase, an *ally* is a toy marble made of marble, alabaster, or glass.

pass muster: *see* MUSTER.

pass someone's lips: *see* LIP.

pass the parcel: *see* PARCEL.

pass the time of day: *see* TIME.

pass your sell-by date reach a point where you are useless or worn out. informal

> ⓘ A sell-by date is that stamped on perishable goods indicating the latest date on which they may be sold.

> **1998** *Spectator* He would probably have to turn on them [his colleagues] when, in his view, they had passed their sell-by date.

sell the pass betray a cause. British

> ⓘ As in **head someone off at the pass** above, *pass* is here used in the sense of a narrow route through mountains, viewed as a strategic point in time of war. *Selling the pass* was supplying information to the enemy that would enable them to circumvent or

otherwise get through the obstacle (*turn the pass*). In the mid 19th century it was considered to be an Irish expression meaning 'betray your fellow countrymen by selling information to the authorities'.

> **1996** *Economist* Having sold the pass on the referendum, will he really be able to hold the pass on responsible economics?

passage

passage of (or at) arms a fight or dispute.

work your passage work in return for a free place on a voyage.

past

not put it past someone believe someone to be psychologically capable of doing something, especially something you consider wrong or rash.

past it too old to be of any use or any good at anything. informal

pasture

put someone out to pasture force someone to retire.

pat

have something off (or down) pat have something memorized perfectly.

on your pat on your own. Australian informal

> ⓘ This expression is from rhyming slang, *Pat Malone* meaning 'alone'.

pat someone on the back express approval of or admiration for someone.

stand pat stick stubbornly to your opinion or decision. chiefly North American

> ⓘ In the card games poker and blackjack, *standing pat* involves retaining your hand as dealt, without drawing other cards.

patch

not a patch on greatly inferior to. British informal

> **1991** Mavis Nicholson *Martha Jane & Me* We thought the uniform of our soldiers was 'pathetic', not a patch on the American soldiers' uniform.

a purple patch: *see* PURPLE.

path

lead someone up the garden path: *see* GARDEN.

the path of least resistance: *see* **the line of least resistance** *at* RESISTANCE.

patter

the patter of tiny feet used to refer to the expectation of the birth of a baby.

> **2002** *Pride* If, like me, you find yourself single in the penultimate year of your twenties and the only patter of tiny feet is your neighbour's cat, then chop, chop ladies—so much to do so little time.

pause

give pause to someone (*or* **give someone pause for thought**) cause someone to think carefully or hesitate before doing something.

pave

pave the way for create the circumstances to enable something to happen or be done.

pay

it (always) pays to — it produces good results to do a particular thing.

> **1994** *Guns & Shooting* A custom handgun can be a big investment so it always pays to choose the right pistolsmith.

pay its (*or* their) way (of an enterprise or person) earn enough to cover its or their costs.

pay the piper pay the cost of an enterprise. informal

> ❶ This expression comes from the proverb *he who pays the piper calls the tune*, and is used with the implication that the person who has paid expects to be in control of whatever happens.

pay your respects make a polite visit to someone.

> ❶ A similar expression is *pay your last respects*, meaning 'show respect towards a dead person by attending their funeral'.

pay through the nose pay much more than a fair price. informal

> **1998** *Country Life* We pay a lot of money for a fairly ordinary garment in order to advertise a name that is only well-known because we pay through the nose for the huge advertising budget.

you pays your money and you takes your choice used to convey that there is little to choose between one alternative and another.

> ❶ Both *pays* and *takes* are non-standard, colloquial forms, retained from the original version of the saying in a *Punch* joke of 1846.

pea

like peas (*or* **like as two peas**) **in a pod** so similar as to be indistinguishable or nearly so.

peace

hold your peace remain silent about something.

keep the peace refrain or prevent others from disturbing civil order.

no peace for the wicked: *see* WICKED.

peach

a peach of a — a particularly excellent or desirable thing of the kind specified. informal

> ❶ *Peach* has been used since the mid 18th century as a colloquial term for an attractive young woman and more generally since the mid 19th century for anything of exceptional quality.

> **1998** *Spectator* Neil Pollard … rode a peach of a race … to win the two-mile marathon.

peaches and cream (of a girl's complexion) of a cream colour with downy pink cheeks.

pearl

cast (*or* **throw**) **pearls before swine** give or offer valuable things to people who do not appreciate them.

> ❶ This expression is a quotation from Matthew 7:6: 'Give not that which is holy unto the dogs, neither cast ye your pearls before swine, lest they trample them under their feet, and turn again and rend you'.

pearly

pearly whites a person's teeth. British informal

pear-shaped

go pear-shaped go wrong. informal

> ❶ This phrase originated as RAF slang, as a humorously exaggerated allusion to the shape of an aircraft that has crashed nose first. Today, however, people probably assume it derives from the idea of a woman gaining weight on her hips.

> **1998** *Spectator* Unfortunately it all went pear-shaped because the programme to which I was going to peg my babblings … just wasn't interesting enough to sustain a whole review.

pebble

not the only pebble on the beach not the

only person to be considered in a particular situation; (of a former lover) not unique or irreplaceable.

> ℹ This expression is from an 1897 song title: *You're Not The Only Pebble On The Beach*. The original context was that of courtship: the way to advance your suit was to make it plain to the lady that 'she's not the only pebble on the beach'. It is now often used more generally as a warning against selfish egocentricity.

pecker

keep your pecker up remain cheerful. British informal

> ℹ *Pecker* is probably being used here in the sense of 'a bird's beak or bill', and by extension 'a person's face or expression'. The phrase has been current in British English since the mid 19th century, but it has rather different connotations in the US, where *pecker* is an informal term for *penis*.

pedal

with the pedal to the metal with the accelerator of a car pressed to the floor. North American informal

peed

peed off annoyed or irritated. informal

> ℹ *Pee* represents the initial letter of *piss*, and the phrase is used euphemistically as a slightly less vulgar expression than *pissed off*.

peg

off the peg (of clothes) ready-made as opposed to specially made for a particular person. chiefly British

> ℹ A North American variant of this phrase is *off the rack*.

a peg to hang a matter on something used as a pretext or occasion for the discussion or treatment of a wider subject.

a square peg in a round hole a person in a situation unsuited to their abilities or character.

> ℹ The variant *a round peg in a square hole* is also found, although it is less common.

take someone down a peg or two make someone realize that they are less talented or important than they think they are.

Pelion

pile (or heap) Pelion on Ossa add an extra difficulty or task to an already difficult situation or undertaking. literary

> ℹ In Greek mythology, the mountain Pelion was held to be the home of the centaurs, and the giants were said to have piled Mounts Olympus and Ossa on its summit in their attempt to reach the heavens and destroy the gods.

pelt

at full pelt with great speed; as fast as possible.

in your pelt naked. Irish informal

pen

dip your pen in gall: *see* DIP.

the pen is mightier than the sword writing is more effective than military power or violence. proverb

penny

count the (or your) pennies be careful about how much you spend.

> ℹ Variants of this expression are *watch the pennies* and, in the USA, *pinch the pennies*.

earn an honest penny: *see* HONEST.

in for a penny, in for a pound used to express someone's intention to see an undertaking through, however much time, effort, or money this entails.

not have a penny to bless yourself with be completely impoverished. dated

> ℹ This expression refers either to the cross on the silver pennies which circulated in England before the reign of Charles II or to the practice of crossing a person's palm with silver for luck.

the penny drops someone finally realizes or understands something. informal, chiefly British

> ℹ The image here is of the operation of a coin-operated slot machine.

not have two pennies to rub together lack money; be very poor.

a penny for your thoughts used to ask someone what they are thinking about. informal

pennies from heaven unexpected benefits, especially financial ones.

> ❶ *Pennies from Heaven* was the title of a 1936 song by the American songwriter Johnny Burke (1908–64). The expression is also well known as the title of a BBC drama series by Dennis Potter in the late 1970s.

penny wise and pound foolish careful and economical in small matters while being wasteful or extravagant in large ones.

a pretty penny: *see* PRETTY.

spend a penny urinate. British informal

> ❶ At one time coin-operated locks were commonly found on the doors of public lavatories. The phrase is now rather dated.

turn up like a bad penny (of someone or something unwelcome) inevitably reappear or return.

> ❶ A *bad penny* is a counterfeit coin which circulates rapidly as people try to pass it on to someone else.

two (or ten) a penny plentiful or easily obtained and consequently of little value. chiefly British

percentage

play the percentages (or the percentage game) choose a safe and methodical course of action when calculating the odds in favour of success. informal

perch

knock someone off their perch cause someone to lose a position of superiority or pre-eminence. informal

perish

perish the thought used, often ironically, to show that you find a suggestion or idea completely ridiculous or unwelcome. informal

1993 *Tablet* Is he one of those people who file their own press cuttings and who even, perish the thought, write down their own witticisms?

permitting

— permitting if the specified thing does not prevent you from doing something.

1997 *Classic Boat* Time and weather permitting rudderless sailing is also taught, along with spinnaker and trapezing.

person

be your own person: *see* **be your own man** *at* OWN.

perspective

in (or out of) perspective ❶ (of a work of art) showing the right (or wrong) relationship between visible objects. ❷ correctly (or incorrectly) regarded in terms of relative importance.

petard

hoist with (or by) your own petard have your plans to cause trouble for others backfire on you.

> ❶ The phrase is from Shakespeare's *Hamlet*: 'For 'tis the sport to have the enginer Hoist with his own petard'. In former times, a *petard* was a small bomb made of a metal or wooden box filled with explosive powder, while *hoist* here is the past participle of the dialect verb *hoise,* meaning 'lift or remove'.

phut

go phut fail to work properly or at all. informal

> ❶ *Phut* is usually considered to be imitative of a dull, abrupt sound, like that made by a rifle or a machine breaking down. In fact, its earliest recorded use is by Rudyard Kipling in the late 19th century, and the context makes it likely that it was an Anglo-Indian word from Hindi and Urdu *phaṭnā* meaning 'to burst'.

physical

get physical ❶ become aggressive or violent. ❷ become sexually intimate with someone. ❸ take exercise. informal

physician

physician, heal thyself before attempting to correct others, make sure that you aren't guilty of the same faults yourself. proverb

> ❶ This expression alludes to Luke 4:23: 'And he said unto them, Ye will surely say unto me this proverb, Physician, heal thyself: whatsoever we have heard done in Capernaum, do also here in thy country'.

pick

pick and choose select only the best or most desirable or appropriate from among a number of alternatives.

pick someone's brains (or brain) question someone who is better informed about a subject than yourself in order to obtain information. informal

pick something clean completely remove the flesh from a bone or carcass.

pick up the pieces restore your life or a situation to a more normal state, typically after a shock or disaster.

pick up the threads resume something that has been interrupted.

picnic

be no picnic be difficult or unpleasant. informal

> **2001** *Rant* While Cheung looks elegant...in the 25 different versions of the *cheongsam* dress she wears in the film, moving in the garments was no picnic.

picture

be (or look) a picture (of a person or thing) be beautiful.

get the picture understand a situation. informal

in the picture fully informed about something.

out of the picture no longer involved; irrelevant.

a (or the) picture of — the embodiment of a specified state or emotion.

> **1989** *Woman's Realm* The...little girl looks a picture of health in her blue dungarees and red boots.

pretty as a picture: *see* PRETTY.

pie

easy as pie: *see* EASY.

eat humble pie: *see* HUMBLE.

nice (or sweet) as pie extremely nice or agreeable.

a piece (or slice) of the pie a share in an amount of money or business regarded as something to be divided up.

pie in the sky something that is agreeable to contemplate but very unlikely to be realized. informal

> ℹ️ This phrase comes from a 1911 song by the American labour leader Joe Hill (1879–1915), in which a preacher tells a slave: 'Work and pray, live on hay, You'll get pie in the sky when you die'.

piece

all of a piece with something entirely consistent with something.

> **1997 Edmund White** *The Farewell Symphony* This new disease seemed all of a piece with the hate promulgated by know-nothing American fundamentalists.

give someone a piece of your mind tell someone what you think, especially when you are angry about their behaviour.

go to pieces become so nervous or upset that you are unable to behave or perform normally.

in one piece unharmed or undamaged, especially after a dangerous journey or experience.

pick (or pull or tear) someone or something to pieces criticize someone or something in a severe or detailed way.

a piece (or slice) of the action ❶ a share in the excitement of something. **❷** a share in the profits from something. informal

a piece of ass (or tail) a woman regarded in sexual terms. vulgar slang

a piece of cake: *see* CAKE.

say your piece give your opinion or a prepared statement.

pierce

pierce someone's heart affect someone keenly or deeply.

pig

bleed like a (stuck) pig bleed copiously.

bring (or drive) your pigs to market succeed in realizing your potential.

in a pig's eye expressing scornful disbelief at a statement. informal, chiefly North American

> **1987 Evelyn E. Smith** *Miss Melville Returns* Under other circumstances I think we could have been friends. 'In a pig's eye,' Susan thought.

make a pig of yourself overeat. informal

> **1991 Francis King** *The Ant Colony* I do love chocolates. Always make a pig of myself over them.

make a pig's ear of bungle; make a mess of. British informal

> ℹ️ This probably developed with humorous reference to the phrase **make a silk purse out of a sow's ear** (*see* SILK).

on the pig's back living a life of ease and luxury; in a very fortunate situation. Irish informal

pig (or piggy) in the middle a person who is placed in an awkward situation between two others. chiefly British

> ℹ️ This expression comes from the name of a game in which two people attempt to throw a ball to each other without a third person in the middle catching it.

a pig in a poke something that is bought or accepted without knowing its value or seeing it first.

> ❶ In this expression, a *poke* is a small sack or bag, a sense which is now found chiefly in Scottish use.

> **1996 John Doran** *Red Doran* I didn't want to sell the fellow a pig in a poke, so I explained that the ducks were bred only for laying.

pigs might (or can) fly used ironically to express disbelief. chiefly British

> ❶ *Pigs fly in the air with their tails forward* was a proverbial saying in the 17th century; the current version dates back to the late 19th century, and the first recorded use is by Lewis Carroll.

> **1973 Jack Higgins** *A Prayer for the Dying* 'Something could come out of that line of enquiry.' 'I know...Pigs might also fly.'

squeal (or yell) like a stuck pig squeal or yell loudly and shrilly.

> ❶ A *stuck pig* is one that is being butchered by having its throat cut; compare with **bleed like a stuck pig** above.

sweat like a pig sweat profusely. informal

pigeon

be someone's pigeon be someone's concern or affair.

> ❶ In this phrase, the word *pigeon* derives from *pidgin*, as in *pidgin English*, the term for a grammatically simplified form of a language used for communication between people not sharing a common language. *Pidgin* itself represents a Chinese alteration of the English word 'business': it entered the English language with the meaning 'occupation' or 'affair(s)' in the early 19th century, emerging from the hybrid of English and other languages used at that time between Europeans and the Chinese for trading purposes.

pike

come down the pike appear on the scene; come to notice. North American

> ❶ In this expression, a *pike* is short for 'turnpike', the American term for a motorway on which a toll is charged.

> **1983 Ed McClanahan** *The Natural Man* He was, in a word, the most *accomplished* personage who'd yet come down the pike in all the days of Harry's ladhood.

pile

at the top of the pile: *see* **at the top of the heap** *at* HEAP.

make a (or your) pile become rich. informal

> ❶ *Pile* here means 'a pile of money'.

pile it on exaggerate for effect. informal

pile on the agony exaggerate or aggravate a bad situation. informal

pill

a bitter pill (to swallow) an unpleasant or painful necessity (to accept).

> **1996** *European* The move, while not entirely unexpected, has been a bitter pill to swallow.

sugar (or sweeten) the pill make an unpleasant or painful necessity more acceptable.

> ❶ The image here is of making bitter-tasting medicine more palatable by adding sugar.

pillar

from pillar to post from one place to another in an unceremonious or fruitless manner.

> ❶ This expression may have developed with reference to the rebounding of a ball in a real-tennis court. It has been in use in this form since the mid 16th century, though its earlier form, *from post to pillar*, dates back to the early 15th century.

> **2002** *Independent* There will be 'a single door to knock on' so people with a point to make are not passed endlessly from pillar to post.

a pillar of society a person regarded as a particularly responsible citizen.

> ❶ The use of *pillar* to mean 'a person regarded as a mainstay or support for something' is recorded from medieval times; *Pillars of Society* was the English title of an 1888 play by the Norwegian dramatist Henrik Ibsen.

pilot

drop the pilot abandon a trustworthy adviser.

> ❶ *Dropping the Pilot* was the caption of a famous cartoon by John Tenniel, published in *Punch* in 1890. It depicted Bismarck's dismissal as German Chancellor by the young Kaiser Wilhelm II.

pin

clean (or neat) as a new pin extremely clean or neat.

p

for two pins I'd, she'd, etc. — used to indicate that you are very tempted to do something, especially out of annoyance.

> **1997** *Spectator* Certainly it is a fierce dog... What is more, for two pins it would bite us again.

pin your colours to the mast: *see* COLOURS.

on pins and needles in an agitated state of suspense.

> ❶ *Pins and needles* is the pricking or tingling sensation in a limb recovering from numbness.

you could hear a pin drop there was absolute silence or stillness.

pin your ears back listen carefully.

pinch

at a pinch if necessary; in an emergency.

> ❶ A North American variant of this expression is *in a pinch*.

feel the pinch experience hardship, especially financial.

take something with a pinch of salt: *see* SALT.

pineapple

the rough end of the pineapple bad treatment. Australian & New Zealand informal

> **1981** Peter Barton *Bastards I Have Known* There was no way that I was going to get 'the rough end of the pineapple' from Wally, so I kept out of his way.

pink

in the pink in extremely good health and spirits. informal

> ❶ Literally, a *pink* is a plant with sweet-smelling pink or white flowers and slender leaves. In figurative use, *the pink* came to mean 'a supreme example of something', as in Shakespeare's *Romeo and Juliet*: 'I am the very pink of courtesy'. This led to the development of the phrase *in the pink of condition*, of which *in the pink* is a shortened version.

pip

give someone the pip make someone irritated or depressed. informal, dated

> ❶ *Pip* is a disease of poultry or other birds. In the late 15th century the word came to be used, often humorously, of various ill-defined or minor ailments suffered by people and so the informal sense of 'ill humour' developed.

> **1976** *Scotsman* I feel it's my duty but I'm not keen. My grandchildren give me the pip.

pip someone at (*or* to) the post defeat someone at the last moment.

> ❶ *Pip* was an informal late 19th-century term for 'defeat', but it is uncertain from which sense of the noun *pip* it derives. *Post* here is the winning post in a race.

squeeze someone until the pips squeak extract the maximum amount of money from someone. British

> ❶ This expression alludes to a speech made in 1918 by the British politician Sir Eric Geddes on the subject of Germany's payment of indemnities after World War I: 'The Germans ... are going to pay every penny; they are going to be squeezed as a lemon is squeezed—until the pips squeak'. More recently, in the 1970s, the Labour Chancellor Denis Healey declared his intention to squeeze the rich until the pips squeaked.

pipe

put that in your pipe and smoke it used to indicate that someone should accept what has been said, even if it is unwelcome. informal

> **1947** W. Somerset Maugham *Creatures of Circumstance* I'm engaged to her, so put that in your pipe and smoke it.

pipeline

in the pipeline being planned or developed; about to happen.

> **1992** *Sunday Times of India* In effect, this means that two bio-pics on Buddha are in the pipeline for release in 1993.

piping

piping hot very hot.

> ❶ *Piping* describes the hissing or sizzling noise made by food taken very hot from the oven. The phrase was earliest used by Chaucer in *The Miller's Tale*: 'And wafres, pipyng hoot out of the gleede' ('gleede' is an obsolete word for a fire).

> **1997** *Sunday Times* Try the chilli cakes... served piping hot from food stalls on the beach.

piss vulgar slang

not have a pot to piss in be very poor. North American

a piece of piss a very easy thing to do. British

piss in the wind do something that is ineffective or a waste of time.

take the piss (out of) mock someone or something. British

> **1998** *Spectator* It must be admitted, however, that any child who tried nowadays to follow my priggish example would, probably rightly, be accused at once of taking the piss.

pissed vulgar slang

pissed as a newt (or fart) very drunk.

pissed off annoyed; irritated.

pit

be the pits be extremely bad or the worst of its kind. informal

> **ⓘ** *Pits* is a mid 20th-century informal term for 'armpits' and has connotations of body odour; from this it came to refer generally to something regarded as bad or unpleasant.

dig a pit for: *see* DIG.

the pit of your (or the) stomach an ill-defined region of the lower abdomen seen as the seat of strong feelings, especially anxiety.

pitch

make a pitch make a bid to obtain a contract or other benefit.

> **ⓘ** *Pitch* is used here in the late 19th-century colloquial sense of a sales pitch.

pitched

a pitched battle a fierce fight.

> **ⓘ** Literally, *a pitched battle* is one fought on a predetermined ground (the *pitch*), as opposed to either a casual skirmish or a **running battle** (see RUNNING).

pitchfork

rain pitchforks: *see* **rain cats and dogs** *at* RAIN.

pity

more's the pity used to express regret about a fact that has just been stated. informal

> **1994** *Amstrad Action* The full version of this game never got released. More's the pity, as if the demo's anything to go by, it would have been a stormer.

place

go places ❶ travel. ❷ be increasingly successful. informal

> **❷ 1991 Francis King** *The Ant Colony* Guido is going to go places, I'm sure of it. He's not going to be a labourer forever.

place in the sun a position of favour or advantage.

> **ⓘ** In 1897 the German Chancellor, Prince Bernhard Von Bülow, made a speech in the Reichstag in which he declared: 'we desire to throw no one into the shade [in East Asia], but we also demand our place in the sun'. As a result, the expression has become associated with German nationalism; it is in fact recorded much earlier and is traceable to the writings of the French mathematician and philosopher Blaise Pascal (1623–62).

> **2002** *India Weekly* I think it is a great feeling, to know that after years of derision from the world, the Hindi film industry is achieving its place in the sun.

plain

plain as day (or the nose on your face) very obvious. informal

plain as a pikestaff ❶ very obvious. ❷ ordinary or unattractive in appearance.

> **ⓘ** This phrase is an alteration of *plain as a packstaff*, which dates from the mid 16th century, the staff being that of a pedlar, on which he rested his pack of goods for sale. The version with *pikestaff* had developed by the end of the 16th century

plan

plan B: *see* B.

planet

what planet are you on? used to indicate that someone is out of touch with reality. British informal

plank

thick as two planks: *see* THICK.

walk the plank lose your job or position.

> **ⓘ** The image here is of the traditional fate of the victims of pirates: being forced to walk blindfold along a plank over the side of a ship to your death in the sea.

plate

on a plate with little or no effort from the person concerned. informal

> **1986 Max Egremont** *Dear Shadows* They were handed an asset on a plate and treated it in a totally uncreative way.

on your plate occupying your time or energy. chiefly British

1999 Vikram Seth *Equal Music* At the moment, I may as well tell you, it'll be a relief not to do it. I've got a lot on my plate—too much.

platinum

go platinum (of a recording) achieve sales meriting a platinum disc.

play

play your cards close to your chest: *see* **keep your cards close to your chest** *at* CARD.

make a play for attempt to attract or attain. informal

1999 *Independent* Tracie was seen... heading out for a club to make a play for a cute barman.

make (great) play of (*or* **with**) draw attention to in an ostentatious manner, typically to gain prestige or advantage.

2002 *Daily Telegraph* With the tabloids leading the way, reporters digging into their backgrounds made great play of their unorthodox pasts.

play your ace: *see* ACE.

play ball: *see* BALL.

play a blinder perform very well. informal

> ❶ Dating from the 1950s, *blinder* is a colloquial term for 'a dazzlingly good piece of play' in sport, especially in rugby or cricket.

2001 *Sun* Gilles will start and I would just love him to play a blinder and score a couple of goals to knock Southampton out of the cup.

play both ends against the middle keep your options open by supporting or favouring opposing sides.

play by the rules follow what is generally held to be the correct line of behaviour.

play your cards right: *see* CARD.

play the devil with: *see* DEVIL.

play ducks and drakes with: *see* DUCK.

play fair observe principles of justice; avoid cheating.

play someone false prove treacherous or deceitful towards someone; let someone down.

play fast and loose behave irresponsibly or immorally.

1998 *Spectator* Fingers may point at those custodians playing fast and loose with the national treasure.

play favourites show favouritism towards someone or something. chiefly North American

play the field: *see* FIELD.

play for time use specious excuses or unnecessary manoeuvres to gain time.

play the game: *see* GAME.

play the goat: *see* GOAT.

play God: *see* GOD.

play havoc with: *see* HAVOC.

play hell with: *see* HELL.

play hookey: *see* HOOKEY.

play a (*or* **your**) **hunch** make an instinctive choice.

play into someone's hands act in such a way as unintentionally to give someone an advantage.

play it cool make an effort to be or appear to be calm and unemotional. informal

play the market speculate in stocks.

play possum: *see* POSSUM.

play (*or* **play it**) **safe** (*or* **for safety**) take precautions; avoid risks.

play something by ear ❶ perform music without having to read from a score. ❷ proceed instinctively according to results and circumstances rather than according to rules or a plan. informal

> ❷ **1992 Paul Auster** *Leviathan* The only condition was that Sachs arrive at Maria's house promptly at ten o'clock, and from then on they would play it by ear.

play to the gallery: *see* GALLERY.

play with fire take foolish risks.

play yourself in become accustomed to the circumstances and conditions of a game or activity; get into a rhythm or pattern of working or performing. British

playing

a level playing field: *see* LEVEL.

not playing with a full deck: *see* DECK.

please

as — as you please used to emphasize the degree to which someone or something possesses the specified quality, especially when this is seen as surprising. informal

1989 Marilynne Robinson *Mother Country* Hearing themselves expound as slick as you please on every great question of the age... they must feel that their gift to the world of enlightenment exculpates the racism.

pleased

pleased as punch: *see* PUNCH.

pleasure

at Her (or His) Majesty's pleasure detained in a British prison.

pledge

sign (or take) the pledge make a solemn undertaking to abstain from alcohol.

plight

plight your troth pledge your word in marriage or betrothal.

> ❶ The verb *plight* is now virtually obsolete except in this particular phrase, as is the noun *troth*.

plot

lose the plot lose your ability to understand what is happening; lose touch with reality. informal

> **1997** *Spectator* The truth is that we've lost the plot of great painting and have entered a new phase in which the criteria for judging work are…demonstrably shallow and trivial.

the plot thickens the situation becomes more difficult and complex.

> ❶ This expression comes from *The Rehearsal* (1671), a burlesque drama by George Villiers, 2nd Duke of Buckingham: 'now the plot thickens very much upon us'.

plough

plough a lonely (or your own) furrow follow a course of action in which you are isolated or in which you can act independently.

plough the sand labour uselessly.

> ❶ *Ploughing the sand* has been a proverbial image of fruitless activity since the late 16th century.

put (or set) your hand to the plough embark on a task.

> ❶ This phrase alludes to Luke 9:62: 'And Jesus said unto him, No man, having put his hand to the plough, and looking back, is fit for the kingdom of God'.

plug

pull the plug: *see* PULL.

plughole

go down the plughole be unsuccessful, lost, or wasted. informal

plum

have a plum in your mouth have a rich-sounding voice or affected accent. British

like a ripe plum (or ripe plums) used to convey that something can be obtained with little or no effort.

plumb

out of plumb not exactly vertical.

> **1984** T. Coraghessan Boyle *Budding Prospects* His bad eye, I noticed, had gone crazy. Normally it was just slightly out of plumb.

plumb the depths ❶ reach the extremes of evil or unhappiness. ❷ inquire into the most obscure or secret aspects of something.

plume

borrowed plumes: *see* BORROWED.

plunge

take the plunge commit yourself to a course of action about which you are nervous. informal

plus

plus-minus more or less; roughly. South African

> **1992** *Weekend Post* He expected 'plus-minus' 1000 files would eventually be forwarded for 'possible prosecution'.

poach

poach on someone's territory encroach on someone else's rights.

poacher

poacher turned gamekeeper someone who now protects the interests which they previously attacked.

pocket

have deep pockets have large financial resources. informal

> **1998** *Spectator* In any case, it was never in any danger of going out of business…there were several other putative proprietors with deep pockets waiting in the wings.

in pocket ❶ having enough money or money to spare; having gained in a transaction. ❷ (of money) gained by someone from a transaction.

in someone's pocket dependent on someone financially and therefore under their influence; closely involved with someone.

out of pocket having lost money in a transaction.

pay out of pocket pay for something with your own money. US

put your hand in your pocket spend or provide your own money.

poetic

poetic justice the fact of experiencing a fitting or deserved retribution for your actions.

> ❶ This phrase is from Alexander Pope's satire *The Dunciad*: 'Poetic Justice, with her lifted scale'.

point

the finer points of: *see* FINER.

point the bone at: *see* BONE.

point of no return the point in a journey or enterprise at which it becomes essential or more practical to continue to the end.

score points (off) deliberately make yourself appear superior to someone else by making clever remarks.

> **1986 Jack Batten** *Judges* There's nothing condescending or cruel about his wit. He doesn't score points off the people in the prisoners' box. He doesn't take advantage.

take someone's point accept the validity of someone's idea or argument. chiefly British

win on points win by accumulating a series of minor gains rather than by a single dramatic feat.

> ❶ In boxing, a fighter wins *on points* by having the referee and judges award him more points than his opponent, rather than by a knockout.

point-blank

ask (or tell, etc.) someone point-blank ask (or tell, etc.) someone something very directly, abruptly, or rudely.

> ❶ In its literal sense *point-blank* describes a shot or bullet fired from very close to its target. One of the earliest senses of the noun *blank* was 'the white spot in the centre of a target'.

poisoned

a poisoned chalice something that is apparently desirable but likely to be damaging to the person to whom it is given.

> **1998** *New Scientist* Anyone who discovers a superconductor that works at room temperature may be handing the world a poisoned chalice ... the material might be too toxic to be usable.

poke

poke fun at tease or make fun of.

> **1989 Basile Kerblay** *Gorbachev's Russia* They used to poke fun at his boorish ways.

poke your bib in: *see* **stick your bib in** *at* BIB.

poke your nose into take an intrusive interest in; pry into. informal

poke your oar in: *see* **stick your oar in** *at* OAR.

take a poke at someone ❶ hit or punch someone. ❷ criticize someone.

pole

be poles apart differ greatly in nature or opinion.

in pole position in an advantageous position.

> ❶ In motor racing, *pole position* is the position on the front row of the starting grid which will allow the driver to take the first bend on the inside. The phrase originated in the 19th century as a horse-racing term, referring to the starting position nearest the inside boundary rails.

politics

play politics act for political or personal gain rather than from principle. derogatory

pomp

pomp and circumstance the ceremonial formality surrounding a public event.

pony

on Shanks's pony: *see* SHANKS'S PONY.

poor

poor as a church mouse (or as church mice) extremely poor.

> ❶ *Church mice* may be considered to be particularly poor or deprived in that they do not have the opportunity to find pickings from a kitchen or larder.

poor little rich girl (or boy) a wealthy young person whose money brings them no contentment (often used as an expression of mock sympathy).

> ❶ 'Poor Little Rich Girl' was the title of a 1925 song by Noel Coward.

the poor man's — an inferior or cheaper substitute for the thing specified.

> **1991** *Canberra Times* Just as alarming is the prospect of FAEs, Fuel-Air Explosives ... known as the poor man's atom bomb.

poor relation a person or thing that is considered inferior or subordinate to others of the same type or group.

> **1997** *Independent on Sunday* Many downhillers think of Nordic skiing as a poor relation—fit only for wimps who can't take speed.

take a poor view of: *see* **take a dim view of** *at* VIEW.

pop

— **a pop** costing a specified amount per item. North American informal

> **1999 Tim Lott** *White City Blue* I never thought I'd see the day when a curry house would do Margaritas. The waiter looks delighted. I'm not surprised at six pounds a pop.

have (or take) a pop at ❶ physically attack. ❷ criticize. informal

> ❷ **1995** *Musik* Two of the girls we rumbled were so outraged that they put up flyers all over the country taking a pop at us.

in pop in pawn. British informal

pop the question propose marriage. British informal

pop your clogs die. informal

> **1998** *Oldie* We cannot claim any credit for foreseeing that Enoch was about to pop his clogs.

pope

Is the Pope (a) Catholic? used to indicate that something is blatantly obvious. informal

poppy

a tall poppy: *see* TALL.

port

any port in a storm in adverse circumstances any source of relief or escape is welcome.

> ❶ Literally, this expression applies to a ship seeking shelter from rough weather; it has been in use as a proverb from at least the mid 18th century.

pose

strike a pose: *see* STRIKE.

possessed

like someone possessed very violently or wildly, as if under the control of an evil spirit.

possum

play possum ❶ pretend to be asleep or unconscious when threatened. ❷ feign ignorance.

> ❶ This expression, recorded from the early 19th century in the USA, refers to the opossum's habit of feigning death when threatened or attacked (*possum* is an informal US term for an opossum).

stir the possum stir up controversy; liven things up. Australian informal

post

beaten at the post: *see* BEATEN.

be left at the post: *see* LEFT.

deaf as a post: *see* **deaf as an adder** *at* DEAF.

first past the post: *see* FIRST.

from pillar to post: *see* PILLAR.

pip someone at the post: *see* PIP.

postal

go postal go mad, especially from stress. US informal

> ❶ This expression arose as a result of several recorded cases in the USA in which postal-service employees ran amok and shot colleagues.

> **1999** *New Yorker* A man two seats away 'went postal' when the battery on his cell phone gave out. A heavyset passenger had to sit on the man until the train finally pulled into Grand Central.

posted

keep someone posted keep someone informed of the latest developments.

> ❶ *Posted-up* was a mid 19th-century Americanism meaning 'well informed'.

pot

for the pot for food or cooking.

> **1992 Doris Lessing** *African Laughter* That was when we shot for the pot, just shooting what we needed.

go to pot deteriorate through neglect. informal

> ❶ The idea here is of chopping ingredients up into small pieces before putting them in the pot for cooking, and from this comes the sense 'be ruined or destroyed'.

keep the pot boiling: *see* BOILING.

the pot calling the kettle black someone making criticisms about someone else which could equally well apply to themselves.

> **1998** *Times* Yet as Guardian insiders point out, the pot can't call the kettle black. She can't cry foul when subjected to fair and standard competition.

pot of gold: see GOLD.

put someone's pot on inform on a person. Australian & New Zealand informal

shit (or piss) or get off the pot used to convey that someone should stop wasting time and get on with something. vulgar slang

potato

couch potato: see COUCH.

drop someone or something like a hot potato: see HOT.

small potatoes: see SMALL.

Potemkin

a Potemkin village a sham or unreal thing.

> ❶ Count Potemkin (1739–91), a favourite of Empress Catherine II of Russia, reputedly ordered a number of fake villages to be built for the empress's tour of the Crimea in 1787.

pot luck

take pot luck take a chance that whatever is available will be good or acceptable.

pottage

sell something for a mess of pottage sell something for a ridiculously small amount.

> ❶ This expression comes from the biblical story of Esau, who sold his birthright to his brother Jacob in return for a dish of lentil broth (Genesis 25:29–34). *Mess* is a term for a serving of semi-liquid food and *pottage* is an archaic word for soup or stew. Although the phrase is recorded from 1526 it does not occur in the Authorized Version of the Bible (1611); it does, however, appear in chapter headings in the Bibles of 1537 and 1539 and in the Geneva Bible of 1560.

pound

your pound of flesh an amount you are legally entitled to, but which it is morally offensive to demand.

> ❶ The allusion here is to Shylock's bond with the merchant Antonio in Shakespeare's *The Merchant of Venice* and to the former's insistence that he should receive it, even at the cost of Antonio's life.

pound the pavement move about on foot at a steady, regular pace in a town or city.

> **1992** *New York Times* Put yourself in the shoes of someone who . . . is now out pounding the pavement wondering what to settle for in a low-wage job.

pour

it never rains but it pours: see RAIN.

pour cold water on: see COLD.

pour it on progress or work quickly or with all your energy. North American informal

pour oil on troubled waters try to settle a disagreement or dispute with words intended to placate or pacify those involved.

powder

keep your powder dry be ready for action; remain alert for a possible emergency.

> ❶ When his troops were about to cross a river, the English statesman and general Oliver Cromwell (1599–1658) is said to have exorted them: 'Put your trust in God; but mind to keep your powder dry'. The *powder* referred to is gunpowder.

> **1998** *Independent* Instead of keeping its powder dry for the important things, New Labour's political fate is being inextricably bound up with events over which mere politicians can have no control.

powder your nose (of a woman) go to the lavatory.

> ❶ This is an early 20th-century euphemism, which is now rather dated. The term *powder room* has been used since the 1940s to refer to a ladies' toilet in a hotel, restaurant, or similar public building.

> **1972** L. P. Davies *What Did I Do Tomorrow?* I'll use your bathroom. To powder my nose, as nice girls say.

take a powder depart quickly, especially in order to avoid a difficult situation. North American informal

> **2002** *New York Times* Why don't you take a powder, jerk, or how'd you like a knuckle sandwich?

power

do someone or something a power of good be very beneficial to someone or something. informal

more power to your elbow! said to encourage someone or express approval of their actions. British

power behind the throne a person who exerts authority or influence without having formal status.

the powers that be the authorities.

> ❶ This phrase comes from Romans 13:1: 'the powers that be are ordained of God'.

practice

old Spanish practices: see **old Spanish customs** at SPANISH.

practice makes perfect regular exercise of an activity or skill is the way to become proficient in it.

practise

practise what you preach do what you advise others to do.

prawn

come the raw prawn: see RAW.

prayer

not have a prayer have no chance at all of succeeding at something. informal

> **1998** *Oldie* Show them you can re-programme the computer to eliminate the Millennium Problem and you are in. Confess that you don't even know how to turn it on, and you haven't a prayer.

preach

preach to the converted advocate something to people who already share your convictions about its merits or importance.

precious

precious little (*or* **few**) extremely little (*or* few).

pregnant

a pregnant pause (*or* **silence**) a pause or silence that is laden with meaning or significance.

premium

put (*or* **place**) **a premium on** regard as or make particularly valuable or important.

> **1998** *New Scientist* Enormous forces would have acted upon the skull and neck, putting a premium on size and strength.

presence

presence of mind the ability to remain calm and take quick, sensible action when faced with difficulty or danger.

present

all present and correct used to indicate that not a single thing or person is missing.

> **1982** **Bernard MacLaverty** *A Time to Dance* She began to check it, scraping the coins towards her quickly and building them into piles. 'All present and correct,' she said.

(there is) no time like the present used to suggest that something should be done now rather than later.

present company excepted excluding those who are here now.

press

press something home: see **drive something home** at HOME.

press (the) flesh (of a celebrity or politician) greet people by shaking hands. informal, chiefly North American

> **2000** *New Yorker* Clinton seemed . . . a figure from the past—a politician made to press the flesh, to give speeches in large halls and negotiate with his opponents in small rooms.

pretty

come to a pretty pass reach a bad or regrettable state of affairs.

not just a pretty face intelligent as well as attractive.

a pretty penny a large sum of money. informal

> **1989** **Russell Banks** *Affliction* You can probably get a pretty penny for that place in a year or two.

pretty as a picture very pretty.

sitting pretty in an advantageous position or situation. informal

prey

fall prey to ❶ be hunted and killed by. ❷ be vulnerable to or overcome by.

price

everyone has their price everyone can be won over by money.

a price on someone's head a reward offered for someone's capture or death.

price yourself out of the market be unable to compete commercially.

what price —? ❶ used to ask what has become of something or to suggest that something has or would become worthless. ❷ used to state that something seems unlikely.

> ❶ **1991** *New Scientist* What price modern medicine with its reliance on the prescription pad, and the slavish devotion to pills?

prick

kick against the pricks: see KICK.

prick up your ears ❶ (especially of a horse or dog) make the ears stand erect when on the alert. ❷ (of a person) become suddenly attentive.

p

a spare prick at a wedding a person who is out of place or has no role in a particular situation. British vulgar slang

pricking

a pricking in your thumbs a premonition or foreboding.

> ❶ This expression comes from a speech by the Second Witch in Shakespeare's *Macbeth*: 'By the pricking of my thumbs, Something wicked this way comes'.

pride

pride goes (or comes) before a fall if you're too conceited or self-important, something will happen to make you look foolish.

> ❶ This phrase is adapted from Proverbs 16:18: 'Pride goeth before destruction, and an haughty spirit before a fall'. *Goes before* here means 'precedes'.

pride of place the most prominent or important position amongst a group of things.

> **1995 Abdulrazak Gurnah** *Paradise* He was brought up in a devout Sikh household in which the writings of the great Gurus had pride of place in the family shrine.

your pride and joy someone or something of which you are very proud and which is a source of great pleasure.

prime

prime the pump stimulate or support the growth or success of something, especially by supplying it with money.

> ❶ This phrase is used literally of a mechanical pump into which a small quantity of water needs to be poured before it can begin to function.

> **1977 Tom Sharpe** *The Great Pursuit* Significance is all... Prime the pump with meaningful hogwash.

primrose

the primrose path the pursuit of pleasure, especially when it is seen to bring disastrous consequences.

> ❶ The allusion here is to 'the primrose path of dalliance' to which Ophelia refers in *Hamlet*.

prince

prince (or princess) of the blood a man (or woman) who is a prince (or princess) by right of their royal descent.

prisoner

prisoner of conscience a person detained or imprisoned because of their religious or political beliefs.

> ❶ This phrase is particularly associated with the campaigns of Amnesty International, a human-rights organization.

take no prisoners be ruthlessly aggressive or uncompromising in the pursuit of your objectives.

> **1998** *Times* The transition from Formula One to front-wheel drive saloon cars was never going to be easy... especially in a series where drivers are not known for taking prisoners.

pro

the pros and cons the arguments for and against something; the advantages and disadvantages of something.

> ❶ *Pro* is Latin for 'for'; *con* is an abbreviation of Latin *contra*, meaning 'against'.

Procrustean

a Procrustean bed something designed to produce conformity by unnatural or violent means.

> ❶ In Greek mythology, Procrustes was a robber who tied his victims to a bed, either stretching or cutting off their legs in order to to make them fit it.

> **1998** *Spectator* Intellectuals often employ their intellects for foolish purposes, forcing facts onto a Procrustean bed of theory.

prod

on the prod looking for trouble. North American informal

prodigal

prodigal son a person who leaves home to lead a spendthrift and extravagant way of life but later makes a repentant return.

> ❶ The biblical parable of the prodigal son in Luke 15: 11–32 tells the story of the spendthrift younger son of a wealthy man who leaves home and wastes all his money. When he repents of his extravagant ways and returns home, he is joyfully welcomed back by his father. See also **kill the fatted calf** (at FATTED).

production

make a production of do something in an unnecessarily elaborate or complicated way.

profession

the oldest profession the practice of working as a prostitute. humorous

> **ⓘ** Politics or the law is sometimes humorously awarded the status of 'second oldest profession', with the sarcastic implication that their practitioners are as immoral and mercenary as society traditionally considered prostitutes to be.

prolong

prolong the agony cause a difficult or unpleasant situation to last longer than necessary.

promise

on a promise (of a person) confidently assured of something, especially of having sexual intercourse with someone. informal

promise someone the moon: see MOON.

promises, promises used to indicate that the speaker is sceptical about someone's stated intention to do something. informal

proof

above proof (of alcohol) having a stronger than standard strength.

the proof of the pudding is in the eating the real value of something can be judged only from practical experience or results and not from appearance or theory.

> **ⓘ** *Proof* here means 'test', rather than 'verification'.

> **1998 Nigella Lawson** *How to Eat* Don't hide the fact that you're microwaving it: they do say the proof of the pudding is in the eating.

prop

prop up the bar spend a considerable time drinking in a pub. informal

protest

under protest after expressing your objection or reluctance; unwillingly.

> **1997** *Independent* Jon Benet would come to the Griffin house for her lessons on deportment, disappearing into the basement—sometimes under protest—to practise Dior turns.

proud

do someone proud ❶ act in a way that gives someone cause to feel pleased or satisfied. **❷** treat someone with lavish generosity or honour. informal

providence

tempt providence: see **tempt fate** at TEMPT.

prune

prunes and prisms used to denote a prim and affected speech, look, or manner.

> **ⓘ** In Charles Dickens's *Little Dorrit* (1857), Mrs General advocates speaking this phrase aloud in order to give 'a pretty form to the lips'.

public

go public ❶ become a public company. **❷** reveal details about a previously private concern.

in the public eye the state of being known or of interest to people in general, especially through the media.

public enemy number one ❶ a notorious wanted criminal. **❷** a person or thing regarded as the greatest threat to a group or community.

> **❷ 1995** *Independent* So foods that pile on the pounds are seen as Public Enemy Number One.

publish

publish or perish used to refer to an attitude or practice existing within academic institutions, whereby researchers are under pressure to publish material in order to retain their positions or to be deemed successful.

pudding

in the pudding club pregnant. British informal

puff

in all your puff in your whole life. informal, chiefly British

pull

like pulling teeth extremely difficult or laborious to do. informal

> **2002** *Independent* It was like pulling teeth in the first half. I thought we were never going to score.

pull a face: see **make a face** at FACE.

pull a fast one: *see* FAST.

pull in your horns: *see* **draw in your horns** *at* HORN.

pull someone's leg deceive someone playfully; tease someone.

pull the other one used to express a suspicion that you are being deceived or teased. British informal

> ❶ A fuller form of this expression is *pull the other one, it's got bells on.*

> **1994** *Sunday Times* Michael Foot receive a warm ovation from the CBI? Norman Tebbit address a TUC conference? Pull the other one.

pull out all the stops: *see* STOP.

pull the plug prevent something from happening or continuing; put a stop to something. informal

> ❶ This phrase alludes to an older type of lavatory flush which operated by the pulling out of a plug to empty the contents of the pan into the soil pipe.

> **1997** *New Scientist* And with the first elements of the ISS set for launch next year, it's hardly likely Congress will pull the plug on the project.

pull rank: *see* RANK.

pull strings make use of your influence and contacts to gain an advantage unofficially or unfairly.

> ❶ An American variant of this expression is **pull wires**: the image here and in the next idiom is of a puppeteer manipulating a marionette by means of its strings.

> **1998** *New Scientist* Behind the scenes, there is invariably a democratic government or two pulling strings to keep the cigarette barons in power.

pull the strings be in control of events or of other people's actions.

pull together cooperate in a task or undertaking.

pull the wool over someone's eyes: *see* WOOL.

pull your punches be less forceful, severe, or violent than you could be.

pull your socks up: *see* SOCK.

pull your weight do your fair share of work.

pull yourself together recover control of your emotions.

pulp

beat (*or* **smash) someone to a pulp** beat someone severely.

pulse

feel (*or* **take) the pulse of** ascertain the general mood or opinion of.

> ❶ The image here is of literally determining someone's heart rate by feeling and timing the pulsation of an artery.

> **1994** *Daily Mirror* Our new Housing Monitor...will take the pulse of the housing market to keep you informed about the value of your most precious asset—your home.

pump

pump iron exercise with weights. informal

punch

beat someone to the punch anticipate or forestall someone's actions.

pleased (*or* **proud) as Punch** feeling great delight or pride.

> ❶ This expression alludes to the self-congratulatory glee displayed by the grotesque, hook-nosed Punch, anti-hero of the Punch and Judy puppet show.

pull punches: *see* PULL.

punch above your weight engage in an activity or contest perceived as being beyond your capacity or abilities.

> ❶ This is a metaphor from boxing, in which contests are arranged between opponents of nearly equal weight.

> **1998** *Spectator* Post-imperial Britain retains an imperial habit of mind...we entertain...an ambition to 'punch above our weight'.

punch the (time) clock ❶ (of an employee) clock in or out. ❷ be employed in a conventional job with regular hours. North American

punch someone's lights out: *see* LIGHT.

punch your ticket: *see* TICKET.

roll with the punches: *see* ROLL.

punt

take (*or* **have) a punt at** have a go at; attempt. Australian & New Zealand informal

> **1998** *Times: Magazine* However cheerfully positive I can be about the future, the man from the Pru isn't going to take a punt on me living the full term.

pup

sell someone a pup swindle someone, especially by selling them something that is worthless. British informal

> ❶ This phrase originated in the early 20th century; the idea behind it is presumably that of dishonestly selling someone a young and inexperienced dog when an older, trained animal had been expected.

> **1930 W. Somerset Maugham** *Cakes and Ale* The public has been sold a pup too often to take unnecessary chances.

purdah

in purdah in seclusion.

> ❶ *Purdah* comes from the curtain (*parda*) used in traditional Hindu and Muslim households, especially in the Indian subcontinent, to conceal women from the eyes of strangers. The transferred use of this expression to refer to seclusion generally dates from the 1920s.

> **1998** *Times* Treasury ministers are, of course, in purdah.

pure

pure and simple and nothing else.

> **1991** *Alabama Game & Fish* They are bred for waterfowling, pure and simple.

pure as the driven snow completely pure.

> ❶ When used of snow, *driven* means that it has been piled into drifts or made smooth by the wind. The phrase was famously parodied by the actress Tallulah Bankhead in 1947: 'I'm as pure as the driven slush'.

the real Simon Pure: *see* SIMON PURE.

purler

come (*or* **go**) **a purler** fall heavily, especially head first.

> ❶ The verb *purl* was in dialect or colloquial use in the mid 19th century in the senses 'turn upside down', 'capsize', or 'go head over heels'.

purple

born in (*or* **to**) **the purple** born into a reigning family or privileged class.

> ❶ In ancient times, purple garments were worn only by royal and imperial families because of the rarity and costliness of the dye. *Born in the purple* (rather than *to*) may have specific reference to the fact that Byzantine empresses gave birth in a room in the palace at Constantinople whose walls were lined with the purple stone porphyry. The title 'the Porphyrogenitos' or 'Porphyrogenita' was used for a prince or princess born in this room.

a purple patch an ornate or elaborate passage in a literary composition.

> ❶ This term is a translation of Latin *purpureus pannus*, and comes from the Roman poet Horace's *Ars Poetica*: 'Works of serious purpose and grand promises often have a purple patch or two stitched on, to shine far and wide'.

purpose

accidentally on purpose apparently by accident but in fact intentionally. humorous

purse

hold the purse strings have control of expenditure.

make a silk purse out of a sow's ear: *see* SILK.

push

at a push if necessary; in an emergency. British
> **1997** *Trail* It's roomy for one person, but can take two at a push.

give someone (*or* **get**) **the push** (*or* **shove**) dismiss someone (*or* be dismissed) from a job; reject someone (*or* be rejected) in a relationship. British informal

push at (*or* **against**) **an open door** have no difficulty in accomplishing a task; fail to realize how easy something is.

push the boat out: *see* BOAT.

push someone's buttons: *see* BUTTON.

push your luck act rashly or presumptuously on the assumption that you will continue to be successful or in favour. informal

when push comes to shove when action must be taken; if the worst comes to the worst. informal
> **2001** *Financial Director* When push comes to shove, investors are not always impressed with promises of jam tomorrow.

pushing

pushing up the daisies: *see* DAISY.

put

not know where to put yourself feel deeply embarrassed. informal
> **1986 Robert Sproat** *Stunning the Punters* He was begging and pleading with me . . . with tears rolling down his cheeks so I didn't know where to put myself.

put backbone into someone: *see* BACKBONE.

put the boot in: *see* BOOT.

put a brave face on something: *see* FACE.

put the finger on: *see* FINGER.

put it (*or* **yourself) about** be sexually promiscuous. British informal

put it to someone make a statement or allegation to someone and challenge them to deny it.

put one over on deceive someone into accepting something false. informal

put the screws on: *see* SCREW.

put a sock in it: *see* SOCK.

put something behind you get over a bad experience by distancing yourself from it.

put two and two together: *see* TWO.

put up or shut up defend or justify yourself or remain silent. informal

> **2003** *New York Times* Iraq's unexpected willingness to grant access to United Nations weapons inspectors presented American intelligence with a challenge to put up or shut up.

put the wind up: *see* WIND.

put someone wise: *see* WISE.

put words in someone's mouth: *see* MOUTH.

put your best foot forward: *see* FOOT.

put your finger on something: *see* FINGER.

put your foot down: *see* FOOT.

put your foot in it: *see* FOOT.

put your hands together: *see* HAND.

put your hands up: *see* HAND.

put your mind to: *see* MIND.

putty

be like putty (*or* **wax) in someone's hands** be easily manipulated or dominated by someone.

> **1975 Sam Selvon** *Moses Ascending* Bob was there, and I gave him a little bit of crumpet, and afterwards he was like putty in my hands.

Pyrrhic

Pyrrhic victory a victory gained at too great a cost.

> ❶ Pyrrhus was a king of Epirus, who defeated the Romans at Asculum in 279 BC, but in doing so sustained heavy losses and lost his finest troops.

Qq

q.t.

on the q.t. secretly or secret; without anyone noticing. informal

> ℹ️ *q.t.* is a humorous abbreviation of *quiet*.

quake

quake in your shoes: *see* **shake in your shoes** *at* SHAKE.

quart

get (or fit) a quart into a pint pot attempt to do the impossible, especially when this takes the form of trying to fit something into a space that is too small. British

quarter

a bad quarter of an hour: *see* BAD.

queen

take the Queen's shilling: *see* **take the King's shilling** *at* SHILLING.

Queensberry

the Queensberry Rules standard rules of polite or acceptable behaviour.

> ℹ️ The *Queensberry Rules* are the code of rules which were drawn up in 1867 under the supervision of Sir John Sholto Douglas (1844–1900), ninth Marquis of Queensberry, to govern the sport of boxing in Great Britain.

queer

in Queer Street in difficulty, especially by being in debt. British informal, dated.

> ℹ️ *Queer Street* was an imaginary street where people in difficulties were supposed to live. The phrase has been used since the early 19th century to indicate various kinds of misfortune, but its predominant use has been to refer to financial difficulty. The use of 'queer' to mean 'a male homosexual' is a separate development.

> **1952 Angus Wilson** *Hemlock and After* He enjoys a little flutter...and if he finds himself in Queer Street now and again, I'm sure no one would grudge him his bit of fun.

queer someone's pitch spoil someone's chances of doing something, especially secretly or maliciously. British

> ℹ️ This phrase originated as 19th-century slang; early examples of its use suggest that the *pitch* referred to is the spot where a street performer stationed themselves or the site of a market trader's stall.

> **1973 Elizabeth Lemarchand** *Let or Hindrance* He's a decent lad...he would never have risked queering Wendy's pitch with Eddy.

question

be a question of time be certain to happen sooner or later.

the sixty-four thousand dollar question: *see* SIXTY-FOUR.

quick

be quick off the mark: *see* MARK.

cut someone to the quick cause someone deep distress by a hurtful remark or action.

> ℹ️ *Quick* means an area of flesh that is well supplied with nerves and therefore very sensitive to touch or injury.

quick and dirty makeshift; done or produced hastily. informal, chiefly US

quick as a flash: *see* FLASH.

quick on the draw very fast in acting or reacting.

> ℹ️ The *draw* is the action of taking a pistol or other weapon from its holster.

quid

be quids in be in a position where you have profited or are likely to profit from something. British informal

> ℹ️ *Quids* is only found in this phrase, the normal plural being *quid*.

not the full quid not very intelligent. Australian & New Zealand informal

> ℹ️ As an informal term for a pound sterling (or, in former times, a sovereign or guinea) *quid* dates from the late 17th century: its

q

origins are unknown. Compare with **not the full shilling** (*at* SHILLING).

quiet

anything for a quiet life: *see* LIFE.

quiet as a mouse (*or* **lamb**) (of a person or animal) extremely quiet or docile.

> **1982 Robertson Davies** *The Rebel Angels* I shall be as quiet as a mouse. I'll just tuck my box…in this corner, right out of your way.

quiet as the grave: *see* **silent as the grave** *at* GRAVE.

quince

get on someone's quince irritate or exasperate someone. Australian informal

quits

call it quits ❶ agree or acknowledge that terms are now equal, especially on the settlement of a debt. ❷ decide to abandon an activity or venture, especially so as to cut your losses.

> ❶ The origin of the -s in *quits* is uncertain: the word may be an abbreviation of the medieval Latin *quittus*, meaning 'discharged', which was used on receipts to indicate that something had been paid for.

The phrase is recorded from the late 19th century, but an earlier form, *cry quits*, dates back to the mid 17th century.

quiver

an arrow in the quiver: *see* ARROW.

qui vive

on the qui vive on the alert or lookout.

> ❶ The French expression *qui vive?* (used in English since the late 16th century) means literally '(long) live who?' In former times a sentry would issue this challenge to someone approaching his post so as to ascertain where their allegiance lay.

> **1976 J. E. Weems** *Death Song* They came in groups of four, five, or six—'all on the *qui vive*, apprehensive of treachery, and ready to meet it'.

quote

quote — unquote used parenthetically when speaking to indicate the beginning and end (or just the beginning) of a statement or passage that you are repeating, especially to emphasize the speaker's detachment from or disagreement with the original. informal

q

Rr

R

the three Rs reading, (w)riting, and (a)rithmetic, regarded as the fundamentals of elementary education.

rabbit

breed like rabbits reproduce prolifically. informal

buy the rabbit fare badly; come off worse. informal

pull (or bring) a rabbit out of the (or a) hat used to describe an action that is fortuitous, and may involve sleight of hand or deception.

work the rabbit's foot on cheat or trick. US

> ❶ A *rabbit's foot* is traditionally carried as a good-luck charm.

race

be in the race have a chance of success. Australian & New Zealand informal

> **1953 T. A. G. Hungerford** *Riverslake* 'See that bloke?' He pointed down the road after the vanished car. 'A few years ago he wouldn't have been in the race to own a car like that.'

a race against time a situation in which someone attempts to do or complete something before a particular time or before something else happens.

rack

at rack and manger amid abundance or plenty.

> ❶ A *rack* is a frame in which hay is placed, and a *manger* also holds food for horses. The use of *rack* and *manger* together dates from the late 14th century in both literal and figurative senses.

go to rack and ruin gradually deteriorate in condition because of neglect; fall into disrepair.

> ❶ *Rack* is a variant spelling of the word *wrack*, meaning 'destruction', but it is the standard one in this expression, which has been in use since the late 16th century.

1998 *Oldie* The allotment below mine looks set to go to rack and ruin from its previous well-tended state.

off the rack: *see* **off the peg** *at* PEG.

on the rack suffering intense distress or strain.

rack your brains (or brain) make a great effort to think of or remember something.

> ❶ A *rack* was a medieval instrument of torture consisting of a frame on which a victim was stretched by turning rollers to which their wrists and ankles were tied. To *rack* someone was to torture them on this device and the image in this idiom is of subjecting one's brains to a similar ordeal in the effort to remember something.

1998 *Spectator* If I rack my brains for something nice to say about our weather, I suppose it does at least enable us to grow better grass than they do in California.

raft

a (whole) raft of — a large collection of something.

> ❶ *Raft* here is an alteration of a dialect word *raff*, meaning 'a great quantity'.

1998 *Housing Agenda* Since the election of Labour last May, the social inclusion agenda has come to span a whole raft of Government initiatives.

rag

chew the rag: *see* **chew the fat** *at* CHEW.

(from) rags to riches used to describe a person's rise from a state of extreme poverty to one of great wealth.

> **2000 Imogen Edwards-Jones** *My Canapé Hell* Much was made of his East End roots, his chance discovery on Oxford Street. He was truly a modern day tale of rags to riches.

in your glad rags: *see* GLAD.

lose your rag lose your temper. informal

> **1998** *New Scientist* In boxing as in medieval theology, anger is a sin. Lose your rag and you are likely to lose the match.

part brass rags with quarrel and break off a friendship with.

> ℹ This expression is explained in W. P. Drury's short story *The Tadpole of an Archangel* (1898): 'When [sailors] desire to prove the brotherly love . . . with which each inspires the other, it is their . . . custom to keep their brasswork cleaning rags in a joint ragbag. But should relations . . . become strained between them, the bag owner casts forth upon the deck . . . his sometime brother's rags; and with the parting of the brassrags hostilities begin'. The phrase originated as late 19th-century nautical slang.

rag, tag, and bobtail a group of people perceived as disreputable or undesirable.

> ℹ A *bobtail* is a horse or dog with a docked tail, while *rag* and *tag* both express the idea of 'tattered clothes': the phrase literally means 'people in ragged clothes together with their dogs and horses'. The forms *tag, rag, and bobtail*, *ragtag and bobtail*, and *tagrag and bobtail* are also found.

a red rag to a bull: *see* RED.

take the rag off the bush (*or* **hedge**) surpass everything or everyone. chiefly US

rage

all the rage very popular or fashionable.

> ℹ *Rage* is used here in the sense of a widespread (and often temporary) enthusiasm or fashion.

1998 *New Scientist* The weather people call this repetition 'ensemble forecasting', and it has been all the rage since an unexpected storm blew in late one evening and ripped through southern Britain in October 1987.

ragged

run someone ragged exhaust someone by making them undertake a lot of physical activity.

rail

go off the rails begin behaving in a strange, abnormal, or wildly uncontrolled way. informal

1998 *New Scientist* If you had . . . asked him what he was doing, you might have thought he'd gone off the rails.

on the rails ❶ behaving or functioning in a normal or regulated way. informal **❷** (of a racehorse or jockey) in a position on the racetrack nearest the inside fence.

ride the rails: *see* RIDE.

rain

it never rains but it pours misfortunes or difficult situations tend to follow each other in rapid succession or to arrive all at the same time.

rain cats and dogs rain very hard.

> ℹ Despite much speculation, there is no consensus as to the origin of *rain cats and dogs*. Suggestions range from the supernatural (cats being associated with witches who were credited with raising storms, dogs being attendants upon Odin, the Scandinavian storm god) to the down-to-earth (animals in medieval times drowning in flooded streets in times of heavy rain and their bodies being assumed by the credulous to have fallen from the skies). Other versions of the saying are *rain pitchforks* and, in Britain, *rain stair rods*, which date from the early 19th century and mid 20th century respectively, and reflect the shaft-like appearance of heavy rain. *Rain cats and dogs* is first recorded in Jonathan Swift's *Polite Conversation* (1738).

rain on somone's parade prevent someone from enjoying an occasion or event; spoil someone's plans. informal, chiefly North American

(come) rain or shine whether it rains or not; whatever the circumstances.

1994 *BBC Top Gear Magazine* But come rain or shine, there is a torrent of new convertibles about to reach the UK.

right as rain (of a person) perfectly fit and well, especially after a minor illness or accident. informal

1995 Patrick McCabe *The Dead School* You just make sure to give him this medicine and come tomorrow night he'll be right as rain.

rainbow

at the end of the rainbow used to refer to something much sought after but impossible to attain.

> ℹ This phrase refers to the story of a crock of gold supposedly to be found by anyone who succeeds in reaching the end of a rainbow.

chase rainbows (*or* **a rainbow**) pursue an illusory goal.

rain check

take a rain check said when politely refusing an offer, with the implication that you may take it up at a later date. North American

> ⓘ A *rain check* is a ticket given to spectators at US sporting events enabling them to claim a refund of their entrance money or gain admission on another occasion if the event is cancelled because of rain. The rain-check system is mentioned as operating in US sports grounds in the late 19th century; the figurative use of the word dates from the early 20th century.

rainy

a rainy day a possible time of need, usually financial need, in the future.

> ⓘ The expression may originate from the days when casual farm labourers needed to save a proportion of their wages 'for a rainy day', i.e. for occasions when bad weather might prevent them from working and earning money.

> **2002** *New York Times Book Review* The Russian walked out of K.G.B. headquarters with 'insurance against a rainy day'—the K.G.B.'s file on its secret mole inside the F.B.I.

raise

raise Cain: *see* CAIN.

raise the devil: *see* DEVIL.

raise a dust ❶ cause turmoil. ❷ obscure the truth. British

raise your eyebrows: *see* EYEBROW.

raise your hat to someone admire or applaud someone.

> ⓘ The image here is of the gesture of briefly removing your hat as a mark of courtesy or respect to someone.

raise hell: *see* HELL.

raise the roof make or cause someone to make a lot of noise inside a building, for example through cheering.
> **1995** *Daily Mail* The fans were patient and understanding and when I finally scored against Swansea they raised the roof.

raise the wind obtain money for a purpose. British

> ⓘ When it first entered the language in medieval times, this phrase referred to the belief that spirits or witches were able to cause the winds to blow in order to help or hinder ships; the figurative use dates from the late 18th century.

rake

rake over (old) coals (*or* **rake over the ashes**) revive the memory of a past event which is best forgotten. chiefly British

a rake's progress a progressive deterioration, especially through self-indulgence.

> ⓘ A *rake* is a fashionable or wealthy man with dissolute or promiscuous habits. *A Rake's Progress* was the title of a series of engravings by William Hogarth (1697–1764). They depicted the rake's life progressing from wealthy and privileged origins to debt, despair, and death on the gallows.

thin as a rake (of a person or animal) very thin.

ram

ram something home: *see* **drive something home** *at* HOME.

rank

break rank (*or* **ranks**) ❶ (of soldiers or police officers) fail to remain in line. ❷ fail to maintain solidarity.

close ranks ❶ (of soldiers or police officers) come closer together in a line. ❷ unite in order to defend common interests.
> ❷ **1998** *Country Life* The farming community stands to lose those privileges unless it closes ranks against the few who let the side down.

pull rank take unfair advantage of your seniority or privileged position.

rise through (*or* **from**) **the ranks** ❶ (of a private or a non-commissioned officer) receive a commission. ❷ advance from a lowly position in an organization by your own efforts.

ransom

hold someone or something to ransom ❶ hold someone prisoner and demand payment for their release. ❷ demand concessions from a person or organization by threatening damaging action.

a king's ransom: *see* KING.

rap

beat the rap escape punishment for or be acquitted of a crime. North American informal

rap someone on (*or* **over**) **the knuckles** rebuke or criticize someone.

take the rap be punished or blamed, especially for something that is not your fault or for which others are equally responsible.

> ⓘ The late 18th-century use of *rap* to mean 'criticism' or 'rebuke' was extended in early

20th-century American English to include 'a criminal charge' and 'a prison sentence'. Compare with **take the fall** (at FALL).

raspberry

blow a raspberry make a derisive or contemptuous sound with your lips.

> ❶ This expression is from rhyming slang, where *raspberry tart* means a fart.

> **1996** *Observer* It is unthinkable that, this close to a general election, the party is going to blow a raspberry at its leader.

rat

rats deserting a sinking ship people hurrying to get away from an enterprise or organization that is failing. informal

ration

come up (*or* **be given**) **with the rations** (of a medal) be awarded automatically and without regard to merit. military slang

rattle

rattle someone's cage make someone feel angry or annoyed, usually deliberately. informal

> ❶ A humorous comparison is implied between the person annoyed in this way and a dangerous animal taunted by spectators outside its cage.

rattle sabres threaten to take aggressive action.

raw

come the raw prawn attempt to deceive someone. Australian informal

> ❶ In Australian English, a stupid person can be referred to as a *prawn*.

> **1959** Eric Lambert *Glory Thrown In* Don't ever come the raw prawn with Doc, mate. He knows all the lurks.

in the raw ❶ in its true state; not made to seem better or more palatable than it actually is. ❷ (of a person) naked. informal

touch someone on the raw upset someone by referring to a subject about which they are extremely sensitive.

ray

ray of sunshine someone or something that brings happiness into the lives of others.

> **1997** *Trail* Don't worry … let our Knowledge experts bring a ray of sunshine into your lives with their radiant personalities and shining answers.

razor

Occam's razor: *see* OCCAM.

on a razor's edge: *see* **on a knife-edge** *at* KNIFE-EDGE.

read

read between the lines look for or discover a meaning that is hidden or implied rather than explicitly stated.

> **1994** *American Spectator* Those familiar with the virulent animosity in this element of black racism can read between the lines to get a fuller picture.

read someone like a book be able to understand someone's thoughts and motives clearly or easily.

read my lips listen carefully (used to emphasize the importance of the speaker's words or the earnestness of their intent). North American informal

> ❶ This expression was most famously used by the US Republican president George Bush in an election campaign pledge in 1988: 'Read my lips: no new taxes'.

read the riot act give someone a strong warning that they must improve their behaviour.

> ❶ The Riot Act was passed by the British government in 1715 in the wake of the Jacobite rebellion of that year and was designed to prevent civil disorder. The Act made it a felony for a group of twelve or more people to refuse to disperse after being ordered to do so and having being read a certain part of the Act by a person in authority. It was not repealed until 1967.

take something as read assume something without the need for further discussion.

you wouldn't read about it used to express incredulity, disgust, or ruefulness. Australian & New Zealand informal

ready

ready for the off (of a person or vehicle) fully prepared to leave. informal

ready to roll (of a person or machine) fully prepared to start functioning or moving. informal

real

for real used to assert that something is

genuine or is actually the case. North American informal

> **1992 Michael Bishop** *Count Geiger's Blues* The man . . . radiated only bluster and uncertainty. If challenged, he'd run. The other man facing Xavier was for real. He'd fight.

get real! used to convey that an idea or statement is foolish or overly idealistic. informal, chiefly North American

> **1995 Jayne Miller** *Voxpop* You might think living in a garret and starving for your art is wonderful, but get real!

the real McCoy: *see* MCCOY.

the real Simon Pure: *see* SIMON PURE.

the real thing a thing that is absolutely genuine or authentic. informal

ream

ream someone's ass (*or* butt) criticize or rebuke someone. North American vulgar slang

reap

reap the harvest (*or* fruits) of suffer the results or consequences of.

you reap what you sow you eventually have to face up to the consequences of your actions.

> ℹ This proverbial saying exists in various forms. Its biblical source is Galatians 6:7: 'Be not deceived; God is not mocked: for whatsoever a man soweth, that shall he also reap'.

rear

rear its head (of an unpleasant matter) emerge; present itself.

reason

for reasons best known to himself (*or* herself, etc.) used when recounting someone's behaviour to suggest that it is puzzling or perverse. chiefly humorous

see reason (*or* sense) realize that you have been wrong and adopt a sensible attitude.

(it) stands to reason it is obvious or logical.

theirs (*or* ours) not to reason why it is not someone's place to question a situation, order, or system.

> ℹ This phrase comes from Tennyson's poem 'The Charge of the Light Brigade' (1854), which describes how, in a notorious incident in the Crimean War, the British cavalry unquestioningly obeyed a suicidal order to ride straight at the Russian guns.

rebel

a rebel without a cause a person who is deeply dissatisfied with society in general but does not have a specific aim to fight for.

> ℹ *Rebel Without A Cause* was the title of a US film starring James Dean, released in 1955.

rebound

on the rebound while still affected by the emotional distress caused by the ending of a romantic or sexual relationship.

receiving

be at (*or* on) the receiving end be subjected to something unpleasant. informal

recharge

recharge your batteries regain your strength and energy by resting and relaxing for a time.

reckoned

a — to be reckoned with (*or* to reckon with) a thing or person of considerable importance or ability that is not to be ignored or underestimated.

> **2002** *New Internationalist* Now nearly 80, the ex-Harvard Pro is still full of brio and a force to be reckoned with.

record

for the record so that the true facts are recorded or known.

> **1992** *Sun* There was no need to ask if I had gone to the flat. For the record I have never been to the flat. The questions were calculated to make me look bad.

a matter of record something that is established as a fact through being officially recorded.

off the record not made as an official or attributable statement.

> **1990 Charles Allen** *The Savage Wars of Peace* I went to see him very much as somebody going in just to have a chat with him off the record after the interrogation.

on (the) record ❶ used in reference to the making of an official or public statement. ❷ officially measured and noted. ❸ recorded on tape and reproduced on a record or another sound medium.

put (*or* set) the record straight give the true version of events that have been reported incorrectly; correct a misapprehension.

red

better dead than red the prospect of nuclear war is preferable to that of a Communist society.

> ❶ This expression was a cold-war slogan; it was reversed by the nuclear disarmament campaigners of the late 1950s as *better red than dead*.

in the red in debt, overdrawn, or losing money.

> ❶ *Red* ink was traditionally used to indicate debit items and balances in accounts. Compare with **in the black** (AT BLACK).

paint the town red: *see* PAINT.

red as a beetroot (of a person) red-faced, typically through embarrassment.

a red herring something, especially a clue, which is or is intended to be misleading or distracting.

> ❶ This expression derives from the former practice of using the pungent scent of a dried smoked herring to teach hounds to follow a trail (smoked herrings were red in colour as a result of the curing process).

red in tooth and claw involving savage or merciless conflict or competition.

> ❶ This phrase originated as a quotation from Tennyson's 'In Memoriam' (1850): 'Nature, red in tooth and claw'.

> **1998** *Spectator* Life is sharper on the shop floor, too; and for small business it is red in tooth and claw.

a red letter day a pleasantly memorable, fortunate, or happy day.

> ❶ In Church calendars, a saint's day or church festival was traditionally distinguished by being written in red letters.

(like) a red rag to a bull an object, utterance, or act which is certain to provoke or anger someone.

> ❶ The colour red was traditionally supposed to provoke a bull, and is the colour of the cape used by matadors in bullfighting.

> **1998** *Times* Such talk is like a red rag to a bull at the Soil Association.

reds under the bed used during the cold war with reference to the feared presence and influence of Communist sympathizers in a society.

see red become very angry suddenly. informal

red-light

red-light district an area of a city or town containing many brothels, strip clubs, and other sex businesses.

redress

redress the balance take action to restore equality in a situation.

reduced

in reduced circumstances used euphemistically to refer to the state of being poor after being relatively wealthy.

reed

a broken reed a weak or ineffectual person, especially one on whose support it is foolish to rely.

> ❶ This expression refers to Isaiah 36:6, in which the Assyrian general taunts King Hezekiah of Jerusalem about the latter's supposed ally, the Egyptian pharaoh: 'Lo, thou trustest in the staff of this broken reed, on Egypt'.

rein

(a) free rein complete freedom of action or expression.

> ❶ The image here is of loosening grip on the reins of a horse, allowing it to choose its own course and pace, in contrast to the greater control implied by the next idiom.

keep a tight rein on exercise strict control over; allow little freedom to.

reinvent

reinvent the wheel waste a great deal of time or effort in creating something that already exists or doing something that has already been done.

relieve

relieve your feelings use strong language or vigorous behaviour when annoyed.

religion

get religion be converted to religious belief and practices. informal

remain

it remains to be seen something is not yet known or certain.

> **1996** *Scientific American* It remains to be seen how well Russian and U.S. spacefarers will work together … in the more demanding

environment of a space station under construction.

residence

— **in residence** a person with a specified occupation (especially an artist or writer) paid to work for a time in a college or other institution.

> **2002** *Ashmolean Annual Report* Artist in Residence, Sarah Mulhall, demonstrates print-making techniques.

resistance

the line (*or* path) of least resistance an option which avoids difficulty or unpleasantness; the easiest course of action.

resort

in the last resort whatever else happens or is the case; ultimately.

> **1991** John Caldwell *Oxford History of English Music* In the last resort it was only Italian singers who could command the attention of the public in a large theatre.

respect

pay your respects: *see* PAY.

respecter

be no respecter of persons treat everyone the same, without being influenced by their status or wealth.

> ❶ This expression refers to Acts 10:34: 'God is no respecter of persons'.

rest

give it a rest used to ask someone to stop doing or talking about something that the speaker finds irritating or tedious. informal

no rest for the wicked: *see* **no peace for the wicked** *at* WICKED.

rest your case ❶ conclude your presentation of evidence and arguments in a lawsuit. ❷ used humorously to show that you believe you have presented sufficient evidence for your views.

the rest is history: *see* HISTORY.

rest on your laurels: *see* LAURELS.

retreat

beat a retreat: *see* BEAT.

revenge

revenge is a dish best served (*or* eaten)

cold vengeance is often more satisfying if it is not exacted immediately. proverb

reverse

the reverse of the medal: *see* MEDAL.

reward

go to your reward die.

> ❶ This euphemisistic expression is based on the idea that people receive their just deserts after death.

rewrite

rewrite history select or interpret events from the past in a way that suits your own particular purposes.

rewrite the record books (of a sports player) break a record or several records.

rhyme

rhyme or reason logical explanation or reason.

ribbon

cut a (*or* the) ribbon perform an opening ceremony, usually by formally cutting a ribbon strung across the entrance to a building, road, etc.

cut (*or* tear) something to ribbons ❶ cut (*or* tear) something so badly that only ragged strips remain. ❷ damage something severely.

rich

a bit rich used to refer to something that causes ironic amusement or indignation.

> **1998** *Times* It is also a bit rich for Mr Hames to reprove Buckingham Palace for its 'new, slick, emphasis on presentation', while speaking for the organisation that invented 'rebranding Britain'.

Richard

have had the Richard be irreparably damaged. Australian

> ❶ This expression comes from rhyming slang *Richard the Third*, meaning 'bird'. In the theatre, *get the bird* means 'be booed and hissed at'.

rid

be well rid of be in a better state for having removed or disposed of a troublesome or unwanted person or thing.

r

riddance

good riddance said to express relief at having got free of a troublesome or unwanted person or thing.

> ❶ Sometimes a fuller form is used: *good riddance to bad rubbish!*

riddle

talk (*or* **speak**) **in riddles** express yourself in an ambiguous or puzzling manner.

ride

for the ride for pleasure or interest, rather than any serious purpose.

> **2002** *New York Times* Women are now the primary force behind an explosion in new cocktail concoctions, and men are simply going along for the ride, say bartenders and liquor marketing executives.

let something ride take no immediate action over something.

ride bodkin: *see* BODKIN.

ride for a fall act in a reckless or arrogant way that invites defeat or failure. informal

> ❶ This phrase originated as a late 19th-century horse-riding expression, meaning to ride a horse, especially in the hunting field, in such a way as to make an accident likely.

ride herd on keep watch over.

> ❶ Literally, this North American expression means 'guard or control a herd of cattle by riding round its edge'.
>
> **1999** *Coloradoan* (Fort Collins) That, in turn, would detract from his ability to ride herd on Washington special interests, allowing deficits to grow like mushrooms under a rotten log.

ride high be successful.

ride off into the sunset achieve a happy conclusion to something.

> ❶ In the closing scenes of westerns, the characters are often seen riding off into the sunset after everything has been resolved satisfactorily.

ride on someone's coat-tails: *see* COAT-TAIL.

ride the pine (*or* **bench**) (of an athlete) not participate in a game or event, typically because of poor form. North American informal

ride the rails travel by rail, especially without a ticket. North American

ride roughshod over: *see* ROUGHSHOD.

someone or something rides again used to indicate that someone or something has reappeared unexpectedly and with new vigour.

ride shotgun ❶ travel as a guard in the seat next to the driver of a vehicle. ❷ ride in the passenger seat of a vehicle. ❸ act as a protector. chiefly North American

a rough (*or* **easy**) **ride** a difficult (*or* easy) time doing something.

take someone for a ride deceive or cheat someone. informal

rig

(in) full rig (wearing) smart or ceremonial clothes. informal

right

bang to rights (of a criminal) with positive proof of guilt. informal

> ❶ A North American variant of this expression is *dead to rights*.
>
> **1993 G. F. Newman** *Law & Order* He hadn't got the most vital piece of information he needed in order to capture the blaggers bang to rights.

put (*or* **set**) **someone right** ❶ restore someone to health. ❷ make someone understand the true facts of a situation.

right as a trivet: *see* TRIVET.

right enough certainly; undeniably. informal

a right one a silly or foolish person. British informal

> **1988 Salman Rushdie** *The Satanic Verses* Quite soon they burst out into uproarious guffaws, we've got a right one here and no mistake.

she's (*or* **she'll be**) **right** that will be all right; don't worry. Australian informal

somewhere to the right of Genghis Khan holding right-wing views of the most extreme kind.

> ❶ Genghis Khan (1162–1227), the founder of the Mongol empire, is used here as a supreme example of a repressive and tyrannical ruler. The name of the early 5th-century warlord Attila the Hun is sometimes substituted for that of Ghengis Khan in this expression.

Riley

the life of Riley (*or* **Reilly**) a luxurious or carefree existence. informal

> ❶ *Reilly* or *Riley* is a common Irish surname. A popular song of the early 20th century entitled 'My Name is Kelly' included the lines

'Faith and my name is Kelly Michael Kelly, But I'm living the life of Reilly just the same'. This may be the source of the expression but it is possible that the songwriter, H. Pease, was drawing on an already existing catchphrase.

1978 *Daily Telegraph* It is simply not true that we don't pay tax and are living the life of Riley.

Rimmon

bow down in the house of Rimmon: *see* BOW.

rinderpest

before (or since) the rinderpest a long time ago (or for a very long time). South African

> ❶ *Rinderpest* is a contagious viral disease of cattle that periodically caused heavy losses in much of Africa. The 1896 epidemic was so devastating that it was treated as a historical landmark, so giving rise to this expression.

ring

hold the ring monitor a dispute or conflict without becoming involved in it.
> **1991 Mark Tully** *No Full Stops in India* The police no longer attempt to hold the ring between the farmers and landless labourers fighting for just the paltry minimum wage.

ring a bell: *see* BELL.

ring the changes: *see* CHANGE.

ring down (or up) the curtain mark the end (or the beginning) of an enterprise or event.

> ❶ The reference here is to the ringing of a bell in a theatre as the signal to raise or lower the stage curtain at the beginning or end of a perfomance. Compare with **bring down the curtain on** (at CURTAIN).

ring in your ears (or head) linger in the memory.

ring the knell of: *see* KNELL.

ring off the hook (of a telephone) be constantly ringing due to a large number of incoming calls. North American

run (or make) rings round someone outclass or outwit someone very easily. informal

throw your hat in the ring: *see* HAT.

riot

read the riot act: *see* READ.

rip

let rip ❶ do something or proceed vigorously or without restraint. ❷ express yourself vehemently or angrily. informal

let something rip ❶ allow something, especially a vehicle, to go at full speed. ❷ allow something to happen forcefully or without interference. ❸ express something forcefully and noisily. informal

rise

get (or take) a rise out of provoke an angry or irritated response from someone, especially by teasing them. informal

rise and shine get out of bed smartly; wake up. informal

rise from the ashes be renewed after destruction.

> ❶ In classical mythology, the phoenix was a unique bird resembling an eagle that lived for five or six centuries in the Arabian desert. After this time it burned itself on a funeral pyre ignited by the sun and fanned by its own wings and was then born again from the ashes with renewed youth to live through another cycle of life. The simile *like a phoenix from the ashes* is used of someone or something that has made a fresh start after apparently experiencing total destruction.

rise to the bait react to a provocation or temptation exactly as intended.

> ❶ The image here is of a fish coming to the surface to take a bait or fly.

> **1966** *Listener* I should perhaps apologise for having risen to the bait of Mr Wilkinson's provocative letter.

rise with the sun (or lark) get up early in the morning.

rising

someone's star is rising: *see* STAR.

rite

rite of passage a ceremony or event marking an important stage in someone's life, especially birth, initiation, marriage, and death.

Ritz

put on the Ritz make a show of luxury or extravagance.

> ❶ The hotels in Paris, London, and New York founded by the Swiss-born hotelier César Ritz (1850–1918) became synonymous with great luxury. This expression dates from the heyday of these grand hotels in the early 20th century.

r

river

sell someone down the river betray someone, especially so as to benefit yourself. informal

> ❶ This expression originated in the USA, with reference to the practice in the slave-owning states of selling troublesome slaves to owners of sugar-cane plantations on the lower Mississippi, where conditions were harsher than those in the more northerly states.

1998 *Bookseller* Once you have lost it with the first three the last lot will sell you down the river so fast it isn't true.

up the river to or in prison. informal, chiefly North American

> ❶ This phrase originated with reference to Sing Sing prison, which is situated up the Hudson River from the city of New York.

road

all roads lead to Rome: *see* ROME.

down the road in the future. informal

the end of the road: *see* END.

hit the road: *see* HIT.

in (or out of) the (or your) road in (or out of) someone's way. informal

one for the road a final drink, especially an alcoholic one, before leaving for home. informal

a road to nowhere a situation or course of action offering no prospects of progress or advancement.

take to the road (or take the road) set out on a journey or series of journeys.

roaring

do a roaring trade (or business) sell large amounts of something; do very good business. informal

rob

rob Peter to pay Paul take something away from one person to pay another, leaving the former at a disadvantage; discharge one debt only to incur another.

> ❶ This expression probably arose in reference to the saints and apostles Peter and Paul, who are often shown together as equals in Christian art and who therefore may be presumed to be equally deserving of honour and devotion. It is uncertain whether a specific allusion is intended; variants of the

phrase include *unclothe Peter and clothe Paul* and *borrow from Peter to pay Paul*.

1997 *New Scientist* So far, NASA has been able to rob Peter to pay Paul, taking money from the shuttle and science programmes to keep the ISS on track.

rob someone blind get a lot of money from someone by deception or extortion. informal

Robin Hood

round Robin Hood's barn by a circuitous route.

> ❶ Robin Hood is the semi-legendary English medieval outlaw reputed to have robbed the rich and helped the poor. In this expression, *Robin Hood's barn* represents an out-of-the-way place of a kind that might be used by an outlaw or fugitive such as Robin Hood. Recorded from the mid 19th century, the phrase seems to have originated in the dialect speech of the English Midlands, the area in which Robin Hood is said to have operated.

rock

between a rock and a hard place in a situation where you are faced with two equally difficult or unpleasant alternatives. informal

1998 *Times* They are saying now, as they once said of Richard Nixon, that Bill Clinton is 'between a rock and a hard place'.

get your rocks off ❶ have an orgasm.
❷ obtain pleasure or satisfaction. vulgar slang

on the rocks ❶ (of a relationship or enterprise) experiencing difficulties and likely to fail.
❷ (of a drink) served undiluted and with ice cubes. informal

rock the boat: *see* BOAT.

rocker

off your rocker crazy. informal

> ❶ A *rocker* in this expression is a concave piece of wood or metal placed under a chair or cradle enabling it to rock back and forth.

1932 Evelyn Waugh *Black Mischief* It's going to be awkward for us if the Emperor goes off his rocker.

rocket

not rocket science used to indicate that something is not very difficult to understand. humorous

rise like a rocket (and fall like a stick) rise suddenly and dramatically (and subsequently fall in a similar manner).

> ⓘ The origin of this phrase is a jibe made by Thomas Paine about Edmund Burke's oratory in a 1792 House of Commons debate on the subject of the French Revolution. Paine remarked: 'As he rose like a rocket, he fell like the stick'.

rocky

the rocky road to — a difficult progression to something.

> **2001** *Star* So far A1 haven't put a foot wrong on the rocky road to superstardom.

rod

kiss the rod: *see* KISS.

make a rod for your own back do something likely to cause difficulties for yourself later.

a rod in pickle a punishment in store.

> ⓘ *In pickle* means 'preserved ready for future use'. This form, which dates from the mid 17th century, has superseded an earlier mid 16th-century variant *a rod in piss*.

rule someone or something with a rod of iron control or govern someone or something very strictly or harshly.

> ⓘ This expression comes from Psalm 2:9: 'Thou shalt break them with a rod of iron; thou shalt dash them in pieces like a potter's vessel'.

spare the rod and spoil the child if children are not physically punished when they do wrong their personal development will suffer. proverb

Roland

a Roland for an Oliver an effective or appropriate retort or response; tit for tat. archaic

> ⓘ The phrase alludes to the evenly matched single combat between Roland, the legendary nephew of Charlemagne, and Oliver, another of Charlemagne's knights (paladins). Neither man was victorious and a strong friendship subsequently developed between them. According to the French medieval epic the *Chanson de Roland*, Roland was in command of the rearguard of Charlemagne's army when it was ambushed at Roncesvalles (now Roncevaux) in the Pyrenees in 778; despite the urging of Oliver that he should blow his horn to summon aid, Roland refused to do so until too late, and they were slain along with the rest of the rearguard.

roll

on a roll experiencing a prolonged spell of success or good luck. informal

> **1998** *Oldie* Western economists cottoned on to basic 'flaws' in the [Indonesian] economy which they hadn't noticed (or didn't want to notice) while it was on a roll.

a roll in the hay (*or* **the sack**) an act of sexual intercourse. informal

> **1998 Barbara Kingsolver** *The Poisonwood Bible* He just treats me like his slave-girlfriend-housemaid, having a roll in the hay when he feels like it and then running off doing God knows what for months at a time.

a roll Jack Rice couldn't jump over a large quantity of money. Australian informal

roll of honour ❶ a list of those who have died in battle. ❷ a list of people whose deeds or achievements, typically in sport, are honoured.

roll up your sleeves prepare to fight or work.

roll with the punches ❶ (of a boxer) move their body away from an opponent's blows so as to lessen the impact. ❷ adapt yourself to difficult or adverse circumstances.

strike someone off the rolls (*or* **roll**) debar a solicitor from practising after dishonesty or other misconduct.

> ⓘ The *rolls* here are the official lists or records, so called from the time when such records were kept on parchment or paper scrolls.

rolled

(all) rolled into one (of characteristics drawn from different people or things) combined in one person or thing.

> **1907 George Bernard Shaw** *Major Barbara* My methods . . . would be no use if I were Voltaire, Rousseau, Bentham, Mill, Dickens, Carlyle, Ruskin, George, Butler, and Morris all rolled into one.

rolling

be rolling (**in it** *or* **in money**) be very rich. informal

> ⓘ *Rolling in* (i.e. 'turning over and over in') here has the sense of 'luxuriating in'. The idea of wallowing in riches has been current since the late 16th century.

have people rolling in the aisles: *see* AISLE.

a rolling stone a person who does not settle in one place for long.

> ⓘ This expression comes from the proverb *a rolling stone gathers no moss*, meaning that a person who is always moving on will not

accumulate wealth or status, or responsibilities or commitments.

rolling drunk so drunk as to be swaying or staggering.

Roman

a Roman holiday an occasion on which enjoyment or profit is derived from the suffering or discomfort of others.

> ℹ This expression comes from the poet Byron's description of the dying gladiator in *Childe Harold's Pilgrimage* as having been 'butchered to make a Roman holiday'.

Rome

all roads lead to Rome there are many different ways of reaching the same goal or conclusion.

> ℹ This is an ancient saying which was based on the fact that Rome was the point of convergence of all the main roads of the Roman empire, and after that of the medieval pilgrimage routes through Europe. It can be compared with the medieval Latin phrase *mille vie ducunt hominem per secula Romam*, meaning 'a thousand roads lead a man forever towards Rome'.

Rome was not built in a day a complex or ambitious task is bound to take a long time and should not be rushed.

> ℹ This warning against rashness and impatience has been current in English since the mid 16th century.

when in Rome (do as the Romans do) when abroad or in an unfamiliar environment you should adopt the customs or behaviour of those around you.

> ℹ This proverbial expression may ultimately derive from St Ambrose of Milan (*d.* 397), who is quoted in one of St Augustine's letters as saying that when he was in Rome he fasted as they did there, on a Saturday, although when he was in Milan he did not do this. A medieval Latin saying expresses the idea as *si fueris Romae, Romano vivito more; si fueris alibi, vivito sicut ibi*, 'if you are at Rome, live in the Roman manner; if elsewhere, live as they do there'.

> **1998 Pat Chapman** *1999 Good Curry Guide* Cutlery is still for wimps (though you no longer have to ask for it). But when in Rome, eat the correct way, please, using a piece of Roti to scoop up your curry, in your right hand only.

roof

go through (or hit) the roof ❶ (of prices or figures) reach extreme or unexpected heights; become exorbitant. ❷ suddenly become very angry. *informal*

raise the roof: *see* RAISE.

the roof falls in a disaster occurs; everything goes wrong.

rooftop

shout something from the rooftops talk about something openly and jubilantly, especially something previously kept secret.

> ℹ This phrase is adapted from Luke 12:3: 'that which ye have spoken in the ear in closets shall be proclaimed upon the housetops'.

room

in a smoke-filled room (of political bargaining or decision-making) conducted privately by a small group of influential people rather than more openly or democratically.

> ℹ This expression comes from a 1920 news report about the selection of the Republican presidential candidate: '[Warren] Harding of Ohio was chosen by a group of men in a smoke-filled room'.

no (or not) room to swing a cat used in reference to a very confined space. *humorous*

> ℹ The *cat* in this expression is probably a 'cat-o'-nine-tails', a form of whip with nine knotted cords. In former times these whips were used to flog wrongdoers, especially at sea.

room at the top opportunity to join an elite or the top ranks of a profession.

> ℹ The expression is attributed to the American politician Daniel Webster (1782–1852), who was cautioned against attempting to enter the overcrowded legal profession and is said to have replied: 'There is always room at the top'.

root

put down roots begin to lead a settled life in a particular place.

root and branch used to express the thorough or radical nature of a process or operation.

1999 *Which?* Last year, the government undertook a root and branch examination of the home-buying process in England and Wales.

strike at the root (or roots) of have a potentially destructive effect on.

take root become fixed or established.

rope

give someone enough rope (or plenty of rope) give a person enough freedom of action to bring about their own downfall.

> ❶ The fuller form of this expression is the proverb *give a man enough rope and he will hang himself*, which has been in use in various forms since the mid 17th century.

know the ropes: *see* KNOW.

money for old rope: *see* **money for jam** *at* MONEY.

on the ropes in a desperate position; in a state of near collapse or defeat.

> ❶ This is an idiom from boxing, alluding to the situation of a losing boxer who is forced back by his opponent against the ropes that mark the sides of the boxing ring. First recorded, in its literal sense, in the early 19th century, the phrase has been in figurative use since at least the 1920s.

a rope of sand used in allusion to something that provides only illusory security or coherence. literary

rose

bed of roses: *see* BED.

come up roses (of a situation) develop in a very favourable way. informal

come up smelling of roses: *see* SMELLING.

everything's (or it's all) roses everything is going well. informal

(there is) no rose without a thorn every apparently desirable situation has its share of trouble or difficulty.

> ❶ This expression has been proverbial since the mid 15th century. The earliest recorded instance is in a work by John Lydgate (1430–40): 'There is no rose . . . in garden, but there be sum thorne'.

not all roses not entirely perfect or agreeable. informal

> **1938 Graham Greene** *Brighton Rock* Sometimes he's bad to me . . . it's not all roses.

roses, roses, all the way very successful or pleasant.

> ❶ This expression is taken from the first line of Robert Browning's poem 'The Patriot' (1855), where it describes the throwing of roses at a popular hero as he passed through the streets.

> **1977** *World of Cricket Monthly* Although Australia lost the Ashes, it was roses, roses, all the way for him.

smell the roses: *see* SMELL.

under the rose in confidence; under pledge of secrecy. archaic

> ❶ The origin of the rose as an emblem of secrecy is uncertain; the concept may have originated in Germany and there was a similar expression in early modern Dutch. *Under the rosse* appears in a 1546 State Paper of Henry VIII, with a gloss that suggests that it was then a new or unfamiliar expression. The Latin equivalent *sub rosa* has also been very commonly used in English since the mid 17th century in this metaphorical sense.

rot

the rot sets in a rapid succession of (usually unaccountable) failures begins.

rough

bit of rough a (usually male) sexual partner whose toughness or lack of sophistication is a source of attraction. informal

> **1998** *Spectator* The programme dwelt at length on the maestro's interest in extramarital sex, particularly with below-stairs women—what would be called these days a bit of rough.

rough and ready ❶ rough or crude but effective. ❷ (of a person or place) unsophisticated or unrefined.

rough around the edges having a few imperfections.

rough as bags lacking refinement; coarse. Australian & New Zealand informal

a rough diamond a person who has genuinely fine qualities but uncouth manners. informal

> ❶ Literally, *a rough diamond* is a diamond before it has been cut and polished. A North American variant of this expression is *a diamond in the rough*.

the rough edge (or side) of your tongue a scolding.

rough edges slight imperfections in someone or something that is basically satisfactory.

rough justice ❶ treatment, especially

punishment, that is approximately fair. ❷ treatment that is not at all fair or not in accordance with the law.

a rough passage (or ride) a difficult time or experience.

sleep rough sleep in uncomfortable conditions, usually out of doors. British

take the rough with the smooth accept the difficult or unpleasant aspects of life as well as the good.

roughshod

ride roughshod over carry out your own plans or wishes with arrogant disregard for others.

> **1977** *Times Literary Supplement* Sociologists are notorious for their use of generalizing terms that ride roughshod over the particularities of history.

round

go the round (or rounds) (of a story or joke) be passed on from person to person.

in the round ❶ (of sculpture) standing free with all sides shown, rather than carved in relief against a ground. ❷ treated fully and thoroughly; with all aspects shown or considered. ❸ (of a theatrical performance) with the audience placed on at least three sides of the stage.

round the bend: *see* BEND.

a square peg in a round hole: *see* PEG.

row

a hard (or tough) row to hoe a difficult task.

> ❶ Hoeing a row of plants is used here as a metaphor for very arduous work.

royal

royal road to a way of attaining or reaching something without trouble.

> ❶ This expression alludes to a remark attributed to the Greek mathematician Euclid (c.300 BC). When the Egyptian ruler Ptolemy I asked whether geometry could not be made easier, Euclid is said to have replied: 'There is no royal road to geometry'.

rub

not have two — to rub together have none or hardly any of the specified items, especially coins. informal

> **1999** *Independent* Soon you realise you have as many troubles when you are rich as when you haven't two pennies to rub together.

rub your hands show keen satisfaction or expectation.

rub someone's nose in something (or rub it in) emphatically or repeatedly draw someone's attention to an embarrassing or painful fact. informal

> ❶ This expression comes from the mistaken belief that the way to house-train a puppy or kitten is to rub their noses in their faeces or urine if they have made a mess indoors.

> **1963** P. M. Hubbard *Flush as May* I'm sorry. I've said I'm sorry...Don't rub my nose in it.

rub shoulders associate or come into contact with another person.

> ❶ A US variant of this expression is *rub elbows*.

> **1943 Graham Greene** *The Ministry of Fear* It wasn't exactly a criminal world, though eddying along its dim and muted corridors you might possibly rub shoulders with genteel forgers.

rub someone (up) the wrong way irritate or repel someone.

> ❶ The image here is of stroking an animal against the lie of its fur.

there's (or here's) the rub that is the crucial difficulty or problem. literary

> ❶ This expression comes from Shakespeare's *Hamlet*: 'To sleep: perchance to dream: ay, there's the rub; For in that sleep of death what dreams may come When we have shuffled off this mortal coil, Must give us pause'. In the game of bowls, a *rub* is an impediment that prevents a bowl from running smoothly.

> **1998** *Times* Even worse, and here is the rub, nobody could say who put what paper in which tier of whose red box.

rubber

burn rubber drive very quickly. informal

> **1998** *Times* Monsanto is burning rubber on a racetrack to become world leader in life sciences.

Rubicon

cross the Rubicon take an irrevocable step.

> ❶ The Rubicon was a small river in north-east Italy which in the first century BC marked the boundary of Italy proper with the province of Cisalpine Gaul. By taking his army across the Rubicon into Italy in 49 BC, Julius Caesar broke the law forbidding a general to lead an army out of his own province, and so committed himself to war against the Senate and Pompey.

ruffle

ruffle someone's feathers cause someone to become annoyed or upset.

ruffled

smooth someone's ruffled feathers make someone less angry or irritated by using soothing words.

rug

cut a rug: *see* CUT.

pull the rug (from under someone) abruptly withdraw support from someone.

rule

rule of thumb a broadly accurate guide or principle, based on experience or practice rather than theory.

> **1998** *New Scientist* The best forecast of tomorrow's weather in any one place often comes not from a supercomputer, but from the rule of thumb that says: tomorrow it will be similar to today.

— rule(s), OK? used to express your enthusiasm for a particular person or thing. informal, humorous

> **2000** *Elle* Here at ELLE we've always been big fans of Kerrigan's urban babewear, and this season . . . she really rocked. Daryl K rules, OK?

rule the roost be in complete control.

> ❶ The original expression was *rule the roast*, which was common from the mid 16th century onwards. Although none of the early examples of its use shed any light on its source, we can surmise that it originally referred to someone being the most important person at a banquet or feast. *Rule the roost*, found from the mid 18th century, has now replaced the earlier version.

run the rule over examine cursorily for correctness or adequacy. British

> **1998** *Spectator* A committee of directors will run the rule over would-be bidders.

rumour

rumour has it it is rumoured.

> **1993** Margaret Atwood *The Robber Bride* It's a good thing Roz didn't invest in that one, rumour has it that the backers are losing a shirt or two.

run

be run off your feet be kept extremely busy. informal

run it fine: *see* **cut it fine** *at* FINE.

give someone or something a (good) run for their money provide someone or something with challenging competition or opposition.

> **1997** *Rugby World* Beaten Welsh Cup finalists Swansea gave them a good run for their money for much of the campaign before fading away.

run to seed: *see* **go to seed** *at* SEED.

have a (good) run for your money derive reward or enjoyment in return for your outlay or efforts.

(try to) run before you can walk attempt something difficult before you have grasped the basic skills required.

run someone close almost defeat a person or team in a contest.

run dry (especially of a source of money or information) be completely used up.

(make a) run for it attempt to escape someone or something by running away.

run foul of come into conflict with; go against.

> ❶ This expression is nautical in origin: when used of a ship it means 'collide or become entangled with an obstacle or another vessel'. Both literal and figurative uses were current by the late 17th century.

run the gauntlet: *see* GAUNTLET.

run high be strong or tumultuous.

> ❶ The image here is of waves or tides rising above their normal height, especially in stormy conditions.

> **1993** *Wall Street Journal Europe* Everybody knows it is an exercise, but emotions nevertheless run high as the Army 'augmentees' warm to their roles.

run into the sand come to nothing.

> **1994** *Sunday Times* The Ulster Unionists . . . are angry because they gave reluctant support to December's initiative and it now seems to be running into the sand.

run a mile: *see* MILE.

run off at the mouth talk excessively or indiscreetly. North American informal

run of the mill the ordinary or undistinguished type.

> ❶ In this expression, the *run* is literally the material produced from a mill before it has been sorted or inspected for quality.

run someone out of town force someone to leave a place. chiefly North American

run rings round: *see* RING.

run someone or something to earth (or ground) find someone or something, usually after a long search.

> ❶ This is an idiom from hunting, especially foxhunting, its literal meaning being 'chase a hunted animal to its lair and corner it there'.

run with the hare and hunt with the hounds: *see* HARE.

run yourself into the ground: *see* **work yourself into the ground** *at* GROUND.

runaround

give someone the runaround deceive and confuse someone; avoid answering someone's questions directly. informal

rune

read the runes try to forecast the outcome of a situation by analysing all the significant factors involved. British

> ❶ The *runes* were an ancient Germanic alphabet once used in northern Europe, each character of which was supposed to have a secret magical significance. Small stones and pieces of bone engraved with these characters were used to try to foretell the future.

runner

do a runner leave hastily, especially to avoid paying for something or to escape from somewhere. British informal

> **1997 Iain Sinclair** *Lights Out For The Territory* Nobody seemed to know if the absentee landlord had done a runner.

running

in (or out of) the running in (or no longer in) contention for an award, victory, or a place in a team.

make the running set the pace in a race or activity.

a running battle a confrontation that has gone on for a long time.

> ❶ Literally, a *running battle* is one that is constantly changing its location, the opposite of **a pitched battle** (see PITCHED). The expression *running fight* was used in the late 17th century to describe a naval engagement in which the fight was continued as one party retreated or fled. *Running battle* appears to have originated in the mid 20th century.

take a running jump used when angrily rejecting or disagreeing with someone.

> **1998** *Oldie* Get back to the studio and tell the focus groups to take a running jump!

take up the running take over as pacemaker in a race.

rush

give someone the bum's rush: *see* BUM.

rush your fences act with undue haste. British

> ❶ This is a metaphor from horse riding: in the hunting field if you *rush your fences*, rather than tackling the obstacles steadily, you risk a fall.

a rush of blood (to the head) a sudden attack of wild irrationality in your thinking or actions.

rut

in a rut following a fixed (especially tedious or dreary) pattern of behaviour that is difficult to change.

> ❶ The *rut* in this expression is the deep groove worn by a wheel travelling many times along the same track.

> **1995 Nick Hornby** *High Fidelity* I should have spotted that we were in a rut, that I had allowed things to fester to such an extent that she was on the lookout for someone else.

Ss

sabbath

a sabbath day's journey a short and easy journey.

> ❶ Rabbinical law allowed a Jew to travel a certain distance on the Sabbath (about a kilometre); in the Bible, Mount Olivet is described as being 'from Jerusalem a sabbath day's journey' (Acts 1:12).

sack

hit the sack go to bed. informal

hold the sack bear an unwelcome responsibility. North American

a roll in the sack: *see* **a roll in the hay** *at* ROLL.

sackcloth

in sackcloth and ashes manifesting grief or repentance.

> ❶ In the Bible, the wearing of sackcloth and the sprinkling ashes on your head were signs of penitence or mourning.

> **1999** *Athletics Weekly* It was their first focal point, the moment of truth when their season could blossom further in Seville or end in sackcloth and ashes.

sacred

a sacred cow: *see* COW.

saddle

in the saddle ❶ on horseback. ❷ in a position of control or responsibility.

safe

better safe than sorry: *see* BETTER.

safe as houses: *see* HOUSE.

a safe bet: *see* BET.

a safe pair of hands: *see* HAND.

to be on the safe side in order to have a margin of security against risks.

> **2000 Tom Clancy** *The Bear and the Dragon* To be on the safe side, the messages were super-encrypted with a 256-bit system specially made at the National Security Agency.

safety

there's safety in numbers being in a group of people makes you feel more confident or secure about taking action. proverb

sail

sail close to (or near) the wind ❶ sail as nearly against the wind as possible. ❷ come close to breaking a rule or the law; behave or operate in a risky way.

take the wind out of someone's sails: *see* WIND.

salad

your salad days ❶ the period when you are young and inexperienced. ❷ the peak or heyday of something.

> ❶ This is a quotation from Shakespeare's *Anthony and Cleopatra*. Cleopatra is commenting on her previous relationship with Julius Caesar: 'My salad days, When I was green in judgement, cold in blood To say as I said then!'

saloon

in the last chance saloon: *see* LAST.

salt

eat salt with be a guest of. British dated

like a dose of salts: *see* DOSE.

put salt on the tail of capture.

> ❶ This phrase alludes to the humorous advice traditionally given to young children about the best way to catch a bird.

rub salt into the (or someone's) wound make a painful experience even more painful for someone.

salt the books fraudulently increase the apparent value of an invoice or account. informal

salt a mine fraudulently make a mine appear to be a paying one by placing rich ore into it. informal

the salt of the earth a person or group of people of great kindness, reliability, or honesty.

> ❶ This phrase comes from Matthew 5:13: 'Ye are the salt of the earth: but if the salt have lost his savour, wherewith shall it be salted?'

sit below the salt be of lower social standing or worth.

> ❶ This expression derives from the former custom of placing a large salt cellar midway down a long dining table at which people were seated in order of rank.

take something with a pinch (*or* grain) of salt regard something as exaggerated; believe only part of something.

> **1998** *Bookseller* Meanwhile...readers should take the quotes they see with a pinch of salt.

worth your salt good or competent at the job or profession specified.

> **2000** *Saga Magazine* Every place setting is measured with a ruler because no butler worth his salt wants to get to the end of a table with say, four settings left, and nowhere to put them.

Samaritan

good Samaritan a charitable or helpful person.

> ❶ In the Bible, Jesus tells the parable of a man who 'went down from Jerusalem to Jericho and fell among thieves' (Luke 10). The first two people who came across him lying stripped and wounded by the side of the road 'passed by on the other side'. It was the third man, a Samaritan (i.e. a man from Samaria) who took pity on him and helped him.

same

by the same token: *see* TOKEN.

one and the same the same person or thing (used for emphasis).

> **1999 David Mitchell** *Ghostwritten* Everybody both in heaven and hell wanted one and the same thing: meat in their bellies.

same difference used to express the speaker's belief that two or more things are essentially the same, in spite of apparent differences. informal

same here the same applies to me. informal

> **1993 Andy McNab** *Bravo Two Zero* 'I've still got my map and compass,' I said. 'Yeah, same here.'

sand

built on sand: *see* BUILT.

bury your head in the sand: *see* BURY.

rope of sand: *see* ROPE.

run into the sand: *see* RUN.

the sands (of time) are running out the allotted time is nearly at an end.

> ❶ The image here is of the sand in an hourglass moving from the upper chamber to the lower.

sandboy

happy as a sandboy: *see* HAPPY.

sandwich

the meat (*or* filling) in the sandwich a person who is awkwardly caught between two opposing factions.

a sandwich (*or* two sandwiches) short of a picnic (of a person) stupid or crazy. informal

sardine

packed like sardines crowded very close together.

sauce

what's sauce for the goose is sauce for the gander what is appropriate in one case is also appropriate in the other case in question. proverb

> ❶ This expression is often used as a statement that what is right or wrong for one sex is right or wrong for the other as well. John Ray, who was the first to record this saying (in his *English Proverbs* of 1670), remarked 'This is a woman's Proverb'.

> **1998** *New Scientist* What is sauce for the US goose is sauce for the Iraqi gander!

saucer

have eyes like saucers have your eyes opened wide in amazement.

sausage

not a sausage nothing at all. British informal

save

be unable to do something to save your life used to indicate that the person in question is very incompetent at doing something.

> ❶ The first recorded use of this expression is by Anthony Trollope in *The Kellys and O'Kellys* (1848): 'If it was to save my life and theirs, I can't get up small talk for the rector and his curate'.

save your breath: *see* BREATH.

save the day (*or* situation) find or provide a solution to a difficulty or disaster.

> **1990 Richard Critchfield** *Among the British* When the postwar social fabric started to tear, amid a stagnant economy and global

decline...Edward Heath...was supposed to save the day. He failed to deliver.

save face: *see* FACE.

save someone's skin (*or* neck *or* bacon) rescue someone from danger or difficulty.

saved

saved by the bell preserved from danger narrowly or by an unexpected intervention.

> ❶ In boxing matches a contestant who has been knocked to the floor can be saved from being counted out by the ringing of the bell to mark the end of a round.

say

have something (*or* nothing) **to say for yourself** contribute (*or* fail to contribute) to a conversation or discussion.

say the word give permission or instructions to do something.

saying

go without saying be too well known or obvious to need to be mentioned.

there is no saying it is impossible to know.

scabbard

throw away the scabbard abandon all thought of making peace.

> ❶ This expression derives from the proverb *he who draws his sword against his prince must throw away the scabbard*. It implies that the person in question has no choice but to fight

scalded

like a scalded cat at a very fast speed.

> **1997** T3 If you're in a desperate hurry you can bury the accelerator...and take off like a scalded cat.

scale

the scales fall from someone's eyes someone is no longer deceived.

> ❶ In the Bible, this expression described how St Paul, blinded by his vision on the road to Damascus, received his sight back at the hand of God (Acts 9:18).

throw something on (*or* into) **the scale** emphasize the relevance of something to one side of an argument or debate.

tip (*or* turn) **the scales at** have a weight of a specified amount.

turn the scales (*or* balance) alter the probability of the outcome.

scarce

make yourself scarce surreptitiously disappear; keep out of the way. informal

scare

scare the daylights out of: *see* **frighten the daylights out of** *at* DAYLIGHT.

scene

behind the scenes in private; secretly.

> ❶ This expression alludes to the area out of sight of the public at the back of a theatre stage.

change of scene (*or* scenery) a move to different surroundings.

not your scene not something you are interested in. informal

set the scene ❶ describe a place or situation in which something is about to happen. ❷ create the conditions for a future event.

scenery

chew the scenery: *see* CHEW.

scent

on the scent ❶ (of an animal) following the scent of its quarry. ❷ in possession of a useful clue in a search or investigation.

put (*or* throw) **someone off the scent** mislead someone in the course of a search or investigation.

scheme

the scheme of things the organization of things in general; the way the world is.

schmear

the whole schmear everything possible or available; every aspect of something. North American informal

> ❶ *Schmear* (also spelled *schmeer*, *shmear*, or *shmeer*) means 'bribery' or 'flattery', and comes from the Yiddish verb *schmirn* meaning 'grease' or 'flatter'.

> **1970 Lawrence Sanders** *The Anderson Tapes* I want a complete list...Any thing and everything...The whole shmear.

school

of the old school: *see* OLD.

the old school tie: *see* OLD.

the school of hard knocks painful or difficult experiences that are seen to be useful in teaching someone about life.

school of thought a particular way of thinking, especially one not followed by the speaker.

science

blind someone with science: *see* BLIND.

score

know the score be aware of the essential facts about a situation. informal

on that (or this) score so far as that (or this) is concerned.

score an own goal: *see* GOAL.

score points: *see* POINT.

settle (or pay) a (or the) score take revenge on someone for something damaging that they have done in the past.

Scout

Scout's honour used to indicate that you have the honourable standards associated with Scouts, and so will stand by a promise or tell the truth. informal

> ❶ A Scout is a member of the Scout Association, an organization for boys founded in 1908 by Lord Baden-Powell with the aim of developing their character by training them in self-sufficiency and survival techniques in the outdoors.

scrape

scrape acquaintance with contrive to get to know. dated

> **1992** *Atlantic* I thought how lucky the Crimms were to have scraped acquaintance with me, for I seldom reveal my identity to ordinary people on my jaunts around the world.

scrape the barrel (or the bottom of the barrel) be reduced to using things or people of the poorest quality because there is nothing else available. informal

scratch

from scratch from the very beginning, especially without utilizing or relying on any previous work for assistance.

> ❶ In certain sports, the *scratch* was originally the line or mark drawn to indicate the point from which competitors had to start a race unless they had been awarded an advantage and were able to start ahead of this line. So, a competitor starting *from scratch*

would start from a position without any advantage. The expression **up to scratch** (see below) also comes from this sense of the noun *scratch*: a competitor who was up to scratch was of a good enough standard to start a race.

scratch a — and find a — an investigation of someone or something will soon reveal their true nature.

> ❶ The first version of this expression used in English, in the early 19th century, was a translation of a remark attributed to Napoleon: *grattez le Russe et vous trouverez le Tartare*, 'scratch the Russian and you will find the Tartar'.

> **1924 George Bernard Shaw** *St Joan* Scratch an Englishman and find a Protestant.

scratch your head ❶ think hard in order to find a solution to something. ❷ feel or express bewilderment. informal

scratch the surface ❶ deal with a matter only in the most superficial way. ❷ initiate the briefest investigation to discover something concealed.

up to scratch up to the required standard; satisfactory.

you scratch my back and I'll scratch yours if you do me a favour, I will return it. proverb

screw

have a screw loose be slightly eccentric or mentally disturbed. informal

put the screws on exert strong psychological pressure on someone so as to intimidate them into doing something. informal

tighten (or turn) the screw (or screws) exert strong pressure on someone. informal

a (final or last) turn of the screw an additional amount of pressure or hardship applied to a situation that is already extremely difficult to bear. informal

screwed

have your head screwed on (the right way) have common sense. informal

Scylla

Scylla and Charybdis used to refer to a situation involving two dangers in which an attempt to avoid one increases the risk from the other. literary

> ❶ In classical mythology, *Scylla* was a female sea monster who devoured sailors when they tried to navigate the narrow channel

between her and the whirlpool *Charybdis*. In later legends, *Scylla* was a dangerous rock, located on the Italian side of the Strait of Messina, a channel which separates the island of Sicily from the 'toe' of Italy.

sea

(all) at sea confused or unable to decide what to do.

> **1993 Sheila Stewart** *Ramlin Rose* She had a lot of bodily sufferin. Mr Statham and the Girls couldn't stand it; they was all at sea.

seal

put (or set) the seal on put the finishing touch to.

set (or put) your seal to (or on) mark with your own distinctive character.

> ❶ The reference in both of these idioms is to the former practice of stamping your personal seal on a completed letter or other document.

sealed

someone's lips are sealed: *see* LIP.

seam

bursting (or bulging) at the seams (of a place or building) full to overflowing. informal

come (or fall) apart at the seams ❶ (of a thing) fall to pieces. ❷ (of a person); have an emotional breakdown; collapse. informal

> ❶ *Seams* are the lines along which pieces of fabric or the planks of a boat are joined, perceived as the points most likely to be damaged or weakened.

season

a man for all seasons: *see* MAN.

seat

by the seat of your pants by instinct rather than logic or knowledge. informal

> ❶ This expression was first used by pilots in the mid 20th century, in the form *fly by the seat of your pants*, meaning 'fly a plane by relying on human judgement rather than navigational instruments'.

> **1977 Martin Walker** *National Front* Mussolini had governed by the seat of his pants, guided in part by his early Socialism, in part by his ... bombastic nationalism.

second

play second fiddle to: *see* FIDDLE.

second childhood a state of childishness that sometimes occurs in old age.

second to none surpassed by no other.

> **1961 Joseph Heller** *Catch-22* He would stand second to none in his devotion to country.

section

the golden section: *see* GOLDEN.

see

see the back of: *see* BACK.

see someone coming recognize a person who can be fooled or deceived. informal

see eye to eye: *see* EYE.

see a man about a dog used euphemistically when leaving to go to the lavatory or if you do not wish to disclose the nature of the errand you are about to undertake. humorous

see reason: *see* REASON.

see someone right make sure that a person is appropriately rewarded or looked after. British informal

see something coming foresee or be prepared for an event, typically an unpleasant one.

see your way clear to do (or doing) something find that it is possible or convenient to do something.

seed

go (or run) to seed ❶ (of a plant) cease flowering as the seeds develop. ❷ deteriorate in condition, strength, or efficiency.

sow the seed: *see* SOW.

seeing

be seeing things be hallucinating.

> **1987 Rohinton Mistry** *Tales from Firozsha Baag* How much fun they made of me. Calling me crazy, saying it is time for old ayah to go back to Goa ... she is seeing things.

seeing is believing you need to see something before you can accept that it really exists or occurs. proverb

seen

have seen better days: *see* DAY.

seize

seize the day make the most of the present moment.

> ❶ This expression is a translation of Latin *carpe diem*, originally a quotation from the Roman poet Horace.

sell

sell someone or something short fail to recognize or state the true value of someone or something.

> **1998** *Times* Mr Ashdown may secure his seat in the Cabinet, but he will have bought it by selling liberal principles short.

sell someone a bill of goods: *see* BILL.

sell someone a dummy: *see* DUMMY.

sell someone a pup: *see* PUP.

sell someone down the river: *see* RIVER.

sell like hot cakes: *see* CAKE.

sell the pass: *see* PASS.

sell your soul (to the devil) do or be willing to do anything, no matter how wrong, in order to achieve your objective.

> ❶ The reference here is to a contract supposedly made with the devil by certain people: in return for granting them all their desires in this life, the devil would receive their souls for all eternity. The most famous person reputed to have entered into such a contract was the 16th-century German astronomer and necromancer Faust, who became the subject of plays by Goethe and Marlowe and a novel by Thomas Mann.

send

send someone flying cause someone to be violently flung to the ground.

send someone packing: *see* PACKING.

send someone to Coventry: *see* COVENTRY.

sense

bring someone to their senses cause someone to think and behave reasonably after a period of folly or irrationality.

come to your senses become reasonable after acting foolishly.

see sense: *see* see reason *at* REASON.

take leave of your senses go mad.

separate

go your separate ways ❶ leave in a different direction from someone with whom you have just travelled or spent time. ❷ end a romantic, professional, or other relationship.

separate the men from the boys: *see* MAN.

separate the sheep from the goats: *see* SHEEP.

separate the wheat from the chaff: *see* WHEAT.

serve

serve your time ❶ hold office for the normal period. ❷ spend time in office, an apprenticeship, or prison.

serve two masters take orders from two superiors or follow two conflicting or opposing principles or policies at the same time.

> ❶ This phrase alludes to the warning given in the Bible against trying to serve both God and Mammon (Matthew 6:24).

sesame

open sesame: *see* OPEN.

set

be set in stone: *see* be carved in stone *at* STONE.

set eyes on: *see* clap eyes on *at* EYE.

make a dead set at: *see* DEAD.

set your face against: *see* FACE.

set your hand to: *see* HAND.

set your heart (*or* hopes) on have a strong desire for or to do.

set little (*or* much *or* a great deal) by consider to be of little (*or* great) value.

set out your stall ❶ display or show off your abilities, attributes, or experience in order to convince someone of your suitability for something. ❷ make your position on an issue very clear. British

set the scene: *see* SCENE.

set store by: *see* STORE.

set your teeth ❶ clench your teeth together. ❷ become resolute.

set the wheels in motion do something to begin a process or put a plan into action.

set the world alight (*or* on fire) achieve something sensational. informal

> ❶ A British variant of this expression is *set the Thames on fire*.

> **1976** **Dick Francis** *In the Frame* He was the same sort of man my father had been, middle-aged, middle-of-the-road, expert at his chosen job but unlikely to set the world on fire.

settle

settle someone's hash: *see* HASH.

settle a score: *see* SCORE.

seven

seven-league boots: *see* BOOT.

seventh

in seventh heaven: see HEAVEN.

shade

a shade — a little —. informal

> **1984 Armistead Maupin** *Babycakes* Shall we go a shade lighter...Pink it up a bit?

shades of — used to suggest reminiscence of or comparison with someone or something specified.

> ❶ The sense of *shade* alluded to here is 'shadow' or 'ghost'.

> **1991 Cordelia Mansall** *Discover Astrology* Perhaps it is shades of the way your mother had to reject her own brilliance. You have a very fine brain which you tend to put down.

shadow

be frightened of your own shadow be unreasonably timid or nervous.

wear yourself to a shadow completely exhaust yourself through overwork.

shaggy

a shaggy-dog story a long, rambling story or joke, especially one that is amusing only because it is absurdly inconsequential or pointless.

> ❶ The expression, dating back to the 1940s, comes from the subject of one such anecdote, a dog with shaggy hair.

> **1993** *New York Times Book Review* The book has the unhurried pace of the best of the shaggy dog stories; the pleasure is all in the journey rather than the destination.

shake

get (or give someone) a fair shake get (or give someone) just treatment or a fair chance. informal

in two shakes (of a lamb's tail) very quickly.

more — than you can shake a stick at used to emphasize the largeness of an amount. informal

> **1996** *Hong Kong & Macau: Rough Guide* There are more organised tours of Hong Kong than you can shake a stick at and...some are worth considering.

no great shakes not very good or significant. informal

> **1989 Guy Vanderhaeghe** *Homesick* I got specs now. Catch better with them than before, but still am no great shakes at ball.

shake the dust off your feet leave a place indignantly or disdainfully.

> ❶ This expression comes from Jesus's instructions to his disciples: 'And whosoever shall not receive you ... when ye depart out of that house or city, shake off the dust of your feet' (Matthew 10:14).

shake (or quake) in your shoes (or boots) tremble with apprehension.

shake a leg make a start; rouse yourself. informal

> **1995 Trevor Ferguson** *The Fire Line* Shake a leg. We're outta here.

shamrock

drown the shamrock drink, or go drinking on St Patrick's day.

> ❶ The *shamrock* with its three-lobed leaves was said to have been used by St Patrick, the patron saint of Ireland, to illustrate the doctrine of the Trinity. It is now used as the national emblem of Ireland.

Shanks's pony

on Shanks's pony using your own legs as a means of transport.

> ❶ *Shanks* (from the Old English word *sceanca*, 'leg bone') is now used as an informal term for 'legs'. The original form of the expression was *on Shanks's mare*.

shape

get into shape (or get someone into shape) become (or make someone) physically fitter by exercise.

lick (or knock or whip) someone or something into shape act forcefully to bring someone or something into a fitter, more efficient, or better-organized state.

> ❶ This expression originally referred to the belief, expressed in some early bestiaries, that bear cubs were born as formless lumps and were literally licked into shape by their mother. A bestiary was a treatise about different types of animal, popular especially in medieval times.

the shape of things to come the way the future is likely to develop.

shape up or ship out used as an ultimatum to someone to improve their performance or behaviour or face being made to leave. informal, chiefly North American

share

share and share alike have or receive an equal share; share things equally.

sharp

look sharp: *see* LOOK.

sharp as a needle extremely quick-witted.

> ❶ A North American variant is *sharp as a tack*.

the sharp end ❶ the most important or influential part of an activity or process. **❷** the side of a system or activity which is the most unpleasant or suffers the chief impact. **❸** the bow of a ship. British humorous

she

who's she — the cat's mother? ❶ used as a mild reproof, especially to a child, for impolite use of the pronoun *she* when a person's name would have been more well mannered. **❷** expressing the speaker's belief that a woman or girl has a high opinion of herself or is putting on airs. British informal

sheep

the black sheep: *see* BLACK.

count sheep count imaginary sheep jumping over a fence one by one in an attempt to send yourself to sleep.

> **1977 Harvey Pitcher** *When Miss Emmie was in Russia* Did you know that if you count sheep, it is watching the sheep jump that sends you off?

make sheep's eyes at someone look at someone in a foolishly amorous way.

separate the sheep from the goats divide people or things into superior and inferior groups.

> ❶ This expression alludes to the parable of the Last Judgement in Matthew 25:32–3: 'And before him shall be gathered all nations: and he shall separate them one from another, as a shepherd divideth his sheep from the goats: and he shall set the sheep on his right hand, but the goats on the left'.

sheet

two (or three) sheets to (or in) the wind drunk. informal

> ❶ The origins of this expression are nautical. *Sheets* here are the ropes attached to the corners of a ship's sail, used for controlling the extent and direction of the sail; if they are hanging loose in the wind, the vessel is likely to be out of control or taking an erratic course.

shelf

off the shelf not designed or made to order but taken from existing stock or supplies.

on the shelf ❶ (of people or things) no longer useful or desirable. **❷** (of a woman) past an age when she might expect to have the opportunity to marry. **❸** (of a music recording or a film) awaiting release on the market after being recorded.

shell

come out of (or retreat into) your shell become less (or more) shy and retiring.

shield

the other side of the shield: *see* **the other side of the coin** at COIN.

the reverse of the shield: *see* **the reverse of the medal** at MEDAL.

two sides of a shield two ways of looking at something; two sides to a question.

shift

make shift do what you want to do in spite of not having ideal conditions; get along somehow.

shift for yourself manage as best you can without help.

shift your ground say or write something that contradicts something you have previously written or said.

shilling

not the full shilling not mentally alert or quick-thinking.

take the King's (or Queen's) shilling enlist as a soldier. British

> ❶ It was once the practice to pay a shilling to a man who enlisted as a soldier.

shine

take the shine off spoil the brilliance or excitement of; overshadow.

take a shine to take a fancy to; develop a liking for. informal

shingle

hang out your shingle begin to practise a profession. North American

> ❶ The main and oldest sense of *shingle* is 'a wooden roofing tile', but in the early 19th century the word developed the more general sense of 'a piece of board', while in the USA it also acquired the particular

meaning 'a small signboard'. Literally, *hanging out your shingle* refers to hanging up a sign that advertises your profession.

ship

rats deserting a sinking ship: *see* RAT.

run a tight ship: *see* TIGHT.

ships that pass in the night transitory acquaintances.

> ❶ This expression comes from Henry Wadsworth Longfellow's poem *Tales of a Wayside Inn* (1874).

when someone's ship comes in (*or* home) when someone's fortune is made.

> ❶ This expression dates back to the period of Britain's maritime empire, when the safe arrival of a valuable cargo meant an instant fortune for the owner and those who had shares in the enterprise.

shipshape

shipshape and Bristol fashion with everything in good order.

> ❶ Recorded from the mid 19th century, this term originally referred to the commercial prosperity of the port of Bristol and the good condition of its shipping.

shirt

keep your shirt on don't lose your temper; stay calm. informal

lose your shirt lose all your possessions, especially as the result of unwise financial transactions. informal

put your shirt on bet all you have on; be sure of. British informal

the shirt off your back your last remaining possessions as offered to another person.

shit vulgar slang

be shitting bricks be extremely nervous or frightened.

not know shit from Shinola be very ignorant or innocent. US

> ❶ *Shinola* is the proprietary name of a US brand of boot polish.

up shit creek in an awkward predicament.

when the shit hits the fan when a situation becomes critical; when the disastrous consequences of something become public.

shithouse vulgar slang

be built like a brick shithouse (of a person) have a very solid physique.

shitless vulgar slang

be scared (*or* bored) shitless be extremely frightened (*or* bored).

shock

future shock: *see* FUTURE.

short, sharp shock ❶ a brief but harsh custodial sentence imposed on offenders in an attempt to discourage them from committing further offences. ❷ a severe measure taken in order to effect quick results.

> ❶ The Home Secretary William Whitelaw advocated the *short sharp shock* as a form of corrective treatment for young offenders at the 1979 Conservative Party Conference; the deterrent value of such a regime was to be its severity rather than the length of time served.

shoe

another pair of shoes quite a different matter or state of things.

be in another person's shoes be in another person's situation or predicament.

dead men's shoes property or a position coveted by a prospective successor but available only on a person's death.

if the shoe fits, wear it: *see* **if the cap fits, wear it** *at* CAP.

wait for the other shoe to drop wait for the next or final thing to happen. North American

where the shoe pinches where your difficulty or trouble is.

shoot

shoot the breeze (*or* the bull) have a casual conversation. North American informal

shoot your cuffs pull your shirt cuffs out to project beyond the cuffs of your jacket or coat.

shoot someone or something down in flames forcefully destroy an argument or proposal.

> **1999** *BBC Top Gear Magazine* I've been shot down in flames by the boys in the *Top Gear* office for saying this, but I reckon the Porsche Boxster has to be one of the most beautifully sculpted bits of artwork going.

shoot from the hip react suddenly or without careful consideration of your words or actions. informal

shoot it out engage in a decisive confrontation, typically a gun battle. informal

shoot a line describe something in an exaggerated, untruthful, or boastful way. British informal

shoot your mouth off talk boastfully or indiscreetly. informal

shoot yourself in the foot inadvertently make a situation worse for yourself; demonstrate gross incompetence. informal

> **1997** *Spectator* The only thing the Royal Opera seems to have done successfully is shoot itself in the foot.

shooting

the whole shooting match everything. informal

> **1989 Patrick O'Brian** *The Thirteen Gun Salute* I have seen all the great houses brought down, Coutts, Drummonds, Hoares, the whole shooting match.

shop

all over the shop (or **show**) ❶ everywhere; in all directions. ❷ in a state of disorder or confusion. ❸ wildly or erratically. informal

> ❶ *All over the shop* was first recorded as British 'pugilistic' slang in Hotten's *Slang Dictionary* of 1874: to inflict severe punishment on an opponent was 'to knock him all over the shop'.

live over the shop: see LIVE.

talk shop discuss matters concerning your work, especially in circumstances where this is inappropriate.

> **1990 G. Gordon Liddy** *The Monkey Handlers* Lawyers talk shop, bounce ideas off one another all the time.

short

be caught (or **taken**) **short** ❶ be put at a disadvantage. ❷ urgently need to urinate or defecate. British informal

a brick short of a load: see BRICK.

bring (or **pull**) **someone up short** make someone check or pause abruptly.

get (or **have**) **someone by the short and curlies** (or **short hairs**) have complete control of a person. informal

in short order immediately; rapidly. chiefly North American

in the short run (or **term**) over a brief period of time.

make short work of accomplish, consume, or destroy quickly.

a sandwich short of a picnic: see SANDWICH.

short and sweet brief and pleasant.

the short end of the stick the disadvantage in a situation; a bad deal.

> **1994** *Hispanic* Latinas are getting the 'short end of the stick' when it comes to equality in the business world and seeking financing for their businesses.

short, sharp shock: see SHOCK.

shot

a big shot: see **a big cheese** *at* BIG.

by a long shot by far; outstandingly. informal

call the shots: see CALL.

get (or **be**) **shot of** get (or be) rid of. British informal

give it your best shot try as hard as you can to do something. informal

like a shot without hesitation; willingly. informal

not a shot in your locker no money or chances left. British

> ❶ The *locker* referred to in this expression is a compartment in which ammunition is kept.

not by a long shot by no means.

> **1991 Zee Edgell** *In Times Like These* Even though we had a very good crowd at the meeting tonight we weren't at full strength, not by a long shot.

a shot in the arm stimulus or encouragement. informal

a shot in the dark: see DARK.

shot to pieces (or **to hell**) ruined. informal

shotgun

ride shotgun: see RIDE.

shoulder

be on someone's shoulder keep a close check on someone. informal

> **1998** *Times* No England manager can control his players ... I can't be on their shoulder week in and week out.

look over your shoulder be anxious or insecure about a possible danger.

> **1990** *Daily Star* The chief executive ... toasted the lifting of the takeover threat. 'Now they can get on with running the business while not looking over their shoulders,' says one city analyst.

put your shoulder to the wheel set to work vigorously.

> ❶ The image here is of pushing with your shoulder against the wheel of a cart or other vehicle that has become stuck.

rub shoulders with: *see* RUB.

a shoulder to cry on someone who listens sympathetically to another person's problems.

shoulder to shoulder ❶ side by side. ❷ acting together towards a common aim.

> ❶ Sense 2 developed from the idea of soldiers standing side by side in unbroken ranks.

straight from the shoulder: *see* STRAIGHT.

shout

in with a shout having a good chance. informal

shout the odds talk loudly and in an opinionated way.

shouting

all over bar the shouting (of a contest) almost finished and therefore virtually decided. informal

shove

if push comes to shove: *see* PUSH.

show

all over the show: *see* **all over the shop** *at* SHOP.

get (*or* keep) the show on the road start (*or* keep going) an enterprise or organization. informal

> **1997** *Spectator* Much rarer . . . is the journalist who helps to keep the national show on the road.

give the (whole) show away demonstrate the inadequacies or reveal the truth of something.

the only show in town the only or most significant thing.

> **1998** *New Scientist* This should scupper the laser idea, and yet, with no other explanations on offer, it's the only show in town.

show someone a clean pair of heels retreat speedily; run away. informal

show your colours: *see* COLOURS.

show the flag: *see* FLAG.

show your hand (*or* cards) disclose your plans.

> ❶ The image here is of players revealing their cards in a card game.

show a leg get out of bed; get up. British informal, dated

show of hands the raising of hands among a group of people to indicate a vote for or against something, with numbers typically being estimated rather than counted.

show your teeth reveal your strength; be aggressive. British

show someone the door dismiss or eject someone from a place.

> **1991 Michael Curtin** *The Plastic Tomato Cutter* Mr Yendall, would you credit I had applicants who scorned the wages? I showed them the door.

shower

send someone to the showers fail early on in a race or contest. North American informal

shred

a thing of shreds and patches something made up of scraps of fabric patched together. literary

> ❶ In the third act of *Hamlet*, the prince describes his uncle Claudius, who has usurped the throne, as 'a king of shreds and patches'; this description was parodied by W. S. Gilbert in *The Mikado* as 'a thing of shreds and patches'.

shuffle

be (*or* get) lost in the shuffle be overlooked or missed in a confused or crowded situation. North American informal

shuffle the cards change policy or direction.

shuffle off this mortal coil: *see* COIL.

shut

be (*or* get) shut of be (*or* get) rid of. informal

shut the door on: *see* **close the door on** *at* DOOR.

shut your mind to: *see* **close your mind to** *at* MIND.

shut the stable door after the horse has bolted: *see* STABLE.

shut up shop ❶ cease trading, either temporarily or permanently. ❷ stop some activity. informal

shutter

put up the shutters (of a business) cease trading either for the day or permanently.

shy

have a shy at try to hit something, especially with a ball or stone.

sick

sick and tired annoyed about or bored with something and unwilling to put up with it any longer. informal

sick as a dog extremely ill. informal

sick as a parrot extremely disappointed. humorous

> ❶ This expression is a late 20th-century British catchphrase, often associated with disappointed footballers or football managers.

> **1998** *New Scientist* Many of my MP colleagues are as sick as the proverbial parrot that Lord Sainsbury has been appointed to succeed John Battle as Britain's science minister.

the sick man of — a country that is politically or economically unsound, especially in comparison with its neighbours in the region specified.

> ❶ In the late 19th century, following a reported comment by Tsar Nicholas I of Russia about the moribund state of the Turkish empire, the Sultan of Turkey was described as *the Sick Man of Europe*. The term was later extended to Turkey itself and subsequently applied to other countries.

> **1992** *Independent* He vilified the West as 'the sick man of the modern world' and attacked its institutions as 'the dictatorship of the majority dressed up as democracy'.

sick to death very annoyed by something and unwilling to put up with it any longer. informal

sick to your stomach ❶ feeling nauseous. ❷ disgusted.

worried sick so anxious as to make yourself ill.

side

let the side down fail to meet the expectations of your colleagues or friends, especially by mismanaging something. British

on the — side rather —.

> **1996** *Wanderlust* This is a serious jacket with big pockets and a well thought out design, though a little on the heavy side.

on the side ❶ in addition to your regular job or as a subsidiary source of income. ❷ secretly, especially with regard to a sexual relationship in addition to your legal or regular partner. ❸ served separately from the main dish.

the other side of the coin: *see* COIN.

sidelines

on (*or* from) the sidelines in (*or* from) a position where you are observing a situation but are unable or unwilling to be directly involved in it.

> ❶ In sports such as football and basketball, the *sidelines* mark the long edges of a playing area, behind which spectators, coaches, and other non-players must remain.

sideways

knock someone sideways: *see* KNOCK.

sight

heave in sight: *see* HEAVE.

in (*or* within) your sights within the scope of your ambitions or expectations.

> ❶ The image in this phrase and in **raise your sights** and **set your sights on** below is of a target visible through the sights of a gun.

out of sight, out of mind you soon forget people or things that are no longer visible or present. proverb

raise (*or* lower) your sights become more (*or* less) ambitious; increase (*or* lower) your expectations.

set your sights on have as an ambition; hope strongly to achieve or reach.

> **1996** *Home* Within ten minutes I had made an offer ... But another couple has also set their sights on the cottage, so sealed bids were submitted.

a sight for sore eyes a person or thing that is very attractive or that you are extremely pleased or relieved to see. informal

a sight more — (*or* **a sight — than** *or* **a sight too —**) someone or something has a great deal or too much of a particular specified quality. informal

> **1994** *New Scientist* Some did bottle experiments in the lab, under tightly controlled conditions but usually involving just two species; real life is a sight more complicated than that.

sign

sign of the times something typical of the nature or quality of a particular period, typically something undesirable.

sign on the dotted line agree formally.

1921 P. G. Wodehouse *Indiscretions of Archie*
I spoke to him as one old friend to
another...and he sang a few bars from
'Rigoletto', and signed on the dotted line.

signed

**signed, sealed, and delivered (or signed and
sealed)** formally and officially agreed and
in effect.

silence

silence is golden it's often wise to say
nothing. proverb

> ❶ The fuller form of the saying is *speech is
> silver, but silence is golden.*

silent

silent as the grave: *see* GRAVE.

the silent majority the majority of people,
regarded as holding moderate opinions but
rarely expressing them.

> ❶ This phrase was first particularly
> associated with the US President Richard
> Nixon, who claimed in his 1968 presidential
> election campaign to speak for this segment
> of society.

> **1998** *Spectator* Independent-thinking
> columnists claimed a silent majority loathed
> Di mania and maybe they were right.

the silent treatment a stubborn refusal to
talk to someone, especially after a recent
argument or disagreement.

> **2000** *Independent* Since the complaint, Ms
> Thomas, who has worked for the City police
> since 1994, claims she has been given the
> silent treatment.

silk

make a silk purse out of a sow's ear turn
something inferior into something of top
quality.

> ❶ The observation that *you can't make a silk
> purse out of a sow's ear* has been proverbial
> since the late 16th century; there was an
> earlier version which featured *a goat's fleece*
> instead of *a sow's ear.*

silly

— yourself silly be unable to act rationally
because of doing something to excess.

> **1998** *Time Out N.Y.* Drink yourself silly at the
> long bar or chow down at the large tables in
> the back.

the silly season the months of August
and September regarded as the time

when newspapers often publish trivia
because of a lack of important news.
chiefly British

> ❶ This concept and phrase date back to the
> mid 19th century. In high summer Victorian
> London was deserted by the wealthy and
> important during the period in which
> Parliament and the law courts were in recess.

silver

be born with a silver spoon in your mouth
be born into a wealthy family of high social
standing.

have a silver tongue be eloquent or
persuasive.

on a silver platter (or salver) without having
been asked or sought for; without
requiring any effort or return from the
recipient.

> ❶ The image here is of a butler or waiter
> presenting something on a silver tray.

a silver lining a positive or more hopeful
aspect to a bad situation, even though this
may not be immediately apparent.

> ❶ The full form of the phrase is the proverb
> *every cloud has a silver lining.*

the silver screen the cinema industry;
cinema films collectively.

> ❶ In the early days of cinematography, a
> projection screen was covered with metallic
> paint to give a highly reflective, silver-
> coloured surface.

Simon Pure

the real Simon Pure the real or genuine
person or thing.

> ❶ Simon Pure is a character in Susannah
> Centlivre's *A Bold Stroke for a Wife* (1717),
> who for part of the play is impersonated by
> another character.

sin

— as sin having a particular undesirable
quality to a high degree. informal

> **1991 Robert R. McCammon** *Boy's Life*
> Everybody knew Saxon's Lake was as deep as
> sin.

for your sins used to suggest that a task or
duty is so onerous or unpleasant that it
must be a punishment. chiefly British

> **1994 John Birmingham** *He Died With Felafel In
> His Hand* Then the extended family that is

s

Brisbane sent some people along to keep me company, and for my sins, I took them in.

like sin vehemently or forcefully. informal

sing

sing a different tune (*or* **song**) change your opinion about or attitude towards someone or something.

sing for your supper: *see* SUPPER.

sing from the same hymn (*or* **song**) **sheet** present a united front in public by not disagreeing with one another. British informal

> **2000** *South China Morning Post* We're all singing from the same hymn sheet and there is a real will to clean up the game, though it may take a life ban to restore cricket's credibility.

singe

singe your wings suffer harm, especially in a risky attempt.

singing

all-singing, all-dancing: *see* ALL.

sink

everything but the kitchen sink: *see* KITCHEN.

sink or swim fail or succeed entirely by your own efforts.

sinking

a (*or* **that**) **sinking feeling** an unpleasant feeling caused by the realization that something unpleasant or undesirable has happened or is about to happen.

siren

siren song (*or* **call**) the appeal of something that is also considered to be harmful or dangerous.

> ❶ In classical mythology, the Sirens were sea nymphs whose beautiful singing lured sailors to their doom on submerged rocks.

sit

sit at someone's feet be someone's pupil or follower.

sit loosely on not be very binding.

sit on the fence: *see* FENCE.

sit on your hands take no action.

> **1998** *Times* The England selectors, historically, find reasons to sit on their hands.

sit (heavy) on the stomach (of food) take a long time to be digested.

sit on someone's tail drive extremely close behind another vehicle, typically while waiting for a chance to overtake.

sit tight ❶ remain firmly in your place. ❷ refrain from taking action or changing your mind. informal

> ❶ **1984 Studs Terkel** *The Good War* Our colonel told everyone to sit tight, don't leave the camp.

sit up (and take notice) suddenly start paying attention or have your interest aroused. informal

six

at sixes and sevens in a state of total confusion or disarray.

> ❶ This phrase originated as gambling slang and may be an alteration or corruption of Old French *cinque* (five) and *sice* (six), these being the highest numbers on dice. The idea of risking all your goods on the two highest numbers led to the idea of carelessness and neglect of your possessions and eventually to the development of the phrase's current meaning.

> **1998** *Oldie* But if you arrive in the afternoon we may be a bit at sixes and sevens as we're doing a wedding reception.

hit (*or* **knock**) **someone for six** affect someone very severely; utterly overwhelm someone. British informal

> ❶ In this expression, *six* stands for six runs, referring to a hit in cricket which sends the ball clear over the boundary of the ground for a score of six runs.

six feet under dead and buried. informal

> ❶ Six feet is the traditional depth of a grave.

six of one and half a dozen of the other used to convey that there is no real difference between two alternatives.

sixpence

on a sixpence (of a stop or turn) within a small area or short distance. British informal

> ❶ The old sixpenny coin was one of the smallest in circulation prior to decimalization in 1971.

sixty-four

the sixty-four thousand dollar question something that is not known and on which a great deal depends.

> ❶ This expression dates from the 1940s and was originally *the sixty-four dollar question*,

from a question posed for the top prize in a broadcast quiz show.

1996 *Independent* Will conversion make the society a better business? That is the $64,000 question.

size

that's about the size of it said to confirm a person's assessment of a situation, especially one regarded as bad. informal

skate

get your skates on make haste; hurry up. British informal

skating

(skating) on thin ice: see ICE.

skeleton

a skeleton at the feast: see **a ghost at the feast** *at* FEAST.

a skeleton in the cupboard a discreditable or embarrassing fact that someone wishes to keep secret.

> ❶ A US variant of this expression is *a skeleton in the closet.*

skid

hit the skids begin a rapid decline or deterioration. informal

> ❶ The origin of *skid* is uncertain, but it may be connected with the Old Norse word from which English *ski* is derived. It is used here and in the next two entries in the sense of a plank or roller on which a heavy object may be placed in order to move it easily.

on the skids (of a person or their career) in a bad state; failing. informal

1989 Thomas Berger *The Changing Past* Jackie arrived at middle age with a career on the skids.

put the skids under hasten the decline or failure of. informal

skin

be skin and bone be very thin.

by the skin of your teeth by a very narrow margin; only just.

get under someone's skin ❶ annoy or irritate someone intensely. ❷ fill someone's mind in a compelling and continual way. ❸ reach a deep understanding of someone. informal

❸ **1998** *Times* A student of the Method school, he has to get under the skin of the character he portrays.

give someone (some) skin shake or slap hands together as a gesture of friendship or solidarity. US black slang

have a thick (or thin) skin be insensitive (or oversensitive) to criticism or insults.

it's no skin off my nose it's a matter of indifference to me; I am unaffected by something. informal

there's more than one way to skin a cat there's more than one way of achieving your aim.

> ❶ There are several traditional proverbs along these lines, for example *there are more ways of killing a cat than choking it with cream.*

under the skin in reality, as opposed to superficial appearances.

skirt

a bit of skirt: see **a bit of fluff** *at* BIT.

skull

out of your skull ❶ out of your mind; crazy. ❷ very drunk. informal

sky

the sky is the limit there is practically no limit.

1991 *Nation* He proudly proclaims that today in Russia the sky is the limit to what a person can earn.

to the skies very highly; enthusiastically.

1989 Gay Daly *Pre-Raphaelites in Love* Gabriel wrote to his little sister praising Lizzie to the skies.

slack

cut someone some slack allow someone some leeway; make allowances for someone's behaviour. North American informal

1998 *Times* Most, though, are willing to cut Spielberg some slack for the sake of cinematic interpretation.

take (or pick) up the slack ❶ pull on the loose end or part of a rope in order to make it taut. ❷ use up a surplus or improve the use of resources to avoid an undesirable lull in business.

slap

a slap in the face (or eye) an unexpected rejection or affront.

1996 *Independent* The move was seen as another slap in the face for the monarchy in Australia.

slap on the wrist a mild reprimand or punishment.

> **1997** *New Scientist* Last week, in a Washington district court, [a judge] ordered software giant Microsoft to stop forcing PC-makers to install both Windows 95 and its Web browser, Internet Explorer. So far, though, it is just a slap on the wrist.

slap someone on the back congratulate someone heartily.

slate

on the (*or* your) slate to be paid for later; on credit. British

> ❶ Shops and bars formerly kept a record of what a customer owed by chalking it on a tablet made of slate.

wipe the slate clean: *see* WIPE.

sledgehammer

take (*or* use) a sledgehammer to crack a nut use disproportionately forceful means to achieve a simple objective.

> ❶ A *sledgehammer* is a large, heavy hammer used for such jobs as breaking up rocks and driving in fence posts.

> **1998** *New Scientist* Fighting tooth decay by annihilating mostly harmless bacteria in your mouth is like taking a sledgehammer to crack a nut.

sleep

sleep easy: *see* EASY.

sleep like a log (*or* top) sleep very soundly.

the sleep of the just a deep, untroubled sleep.

> ❶ The idea here is that only those with clear consciences can expect to have a peaceful night's sleep.

sleep rough: *see* ROUGH.

sleep with one eye open sleep very lightly so as to be aware of what is happening around you.

someone could do something in their sleep someone could do or accomplish something with no effort or conscious thought. informal

sleeping

let sleeping dogs lie avoid interfering in a situation that is currently causing no problems, but may well do so as a consequence of such interference. proverb

> ❶ In the early 14th century the French phrase *n'esveillez pas lou chien qui dort* advised 'do not wake the sleeping dog', while Chaucer remarks in *Troilus and Criseyde* 'it is nought good a slepyng hound to wake'. The present form of the proverb seems to be traceable to Walter Scott's novel *Redgauntlet* (1824).

sleeve

have an ace up your sleeve: *see* ACE.

have a card up your sleeve: *see* CARD.

laugh up your sleeve: *see* LAUGH.

roll up your sleeves: *see* ROLL.

up your sleeve (of a strategy, idea, or resource) kept secret and in reserve for use when needed.

wear your heart on your sleeve: *see* HEART.

sleigh ride

take someone for a sleigh ride mislead someone.

> ❶ A *sleigh ride* here is an implausible or false story or a hoax: if you *take someone for a sleigh ride* you mislead or cheat them. *Sleigh ride* can also mean 'a drug-induced high', so *take a sleigh ride* means 'take drugs, especially cocaine'.

sleight

sleight of hand the display of skilful, especially deceptive, dexterity or cunning.

> ❶ Literally, the expression means 'manual dexterity in performing a conjuring trick'.

slice

a slice of the action: *see* **a piece of the action** *at* PIECE.

a slice of the cake a share of the benefits or profits. informal

> **1991 Robert Reiner** *Chief Constables* Perhaps it's because they're such good spenders that our slice of the cake is sufficient for all we want.

slide

let something slide negligently allow something to deteriorate.

sling

put someone's (*or* have your) ass in a sling land someone (*or* be) in trouble. North American vulgar slang

sling beer work as a bartender. North American informal

sling hash (*or* **plates**) serve food in a cafe or diner. North American informal

sling your hook: *see* HOOK.

slings and arrows adverse factors or circumstances.

> ❶ This expression is taken from the 'to be or not to be' speech in *Hamlet*: 'Whether tis nobler in the mind to suffer the slings and arrows of outrageous fortune, Or to take arms against a sea of troubles, And by opposing end them'.

> **2001 Ian J. Deary** *Intelligence* The genetic lottery and the environmental slings and arrows influence the level of some of our mental capabilities.

slip

give someone the slip evade or escape from someone. informal

let something slip ❶ reveal something inadvertently in the course of a conversation. ❷ fail to take advantage of an opportunity.

let something slip through your fingers (*or* **grasp**) ❶ lose hold or possession of something. ❷ miss the opportunity of gaining something.

> ❷ **1925 W. Somerset Maugham** *Of Human Bondage* He was mad to have let such an adventure slip through his fingers.

a slip of a — a young, small, and slim person.

> **1980 Philip Larkin** *Letter* After all you are a very young 51! Hardly 51 at all! A slip of a thing!

slip of the pen (*or* **the tongue**) a minor mistake in writing (*or* speech).

> ❶ The equivalent Latin phrases, *lapsus calami* and *lapsus linguae*, are also sometimes used in formal English.

slip on a banana skin make a silly and embarrassing mistake.

there's many a slip ('twixt cup and lip) many things can go wrong between the start of something and its completion; nothing is certain until it has happened. proverb

slippery

slippery slope an idea or course of action which will lead inevitably to something unacceptable, wrong, or disastrous.

> **1998** *Spectator* Those of us who feared that devolution would not assuage nationalist sentiment but turn out to be the slippery slope to separatism have a good chance of being proved right.

slow

slow but (*or* **and**) **sure** not quick but achieving the required result eventually. proverb

smack

have a smack at make an attempt at or attack on. informal

a smack in the face (*or* **eye**) a strong rebuff. informal

small

the (wee) small hours the early hours of the morning immediately after midnight.

small is beautiful the belief that something small-scale is better than a large-scale equivalent.

> ❶ *Small is Beautiful* is the title of a book by E. F. Schumacher, published in 1973. The phrase is best known through its adoption as a slogan by environmentalists.

small potatoes something insignificant or unimportant.

> ❶ This phrase originated in mid 19th-century American use, especially in the form *small potatoes and few in the hill*.

> **2002** *Science* Turner calls this budget a start but says it's 'small potatoes' compared to what will be needed to get fuel cell cars to market.

smart

look smart be quick. chiefly British

smell

live (*or* **survive**) **on the smell of an oil rag** live in conditions of extreme want. Australian

smell blood discern weakness or vulnerability in an opponent.

smell of the lamp show signs of laborious study and effort.

> ❶ The *lamp* here is an oil lamp, formerly used for night-time work or study.

smell a rat begin to suspect trickery or deception. informal

smell the roses enjoy or appreciate what is often ignored. North American informal

smelling

come up (or out) smelling of roses (or violets) make a lucky escape from a difficult situation with your reputation intact. informal

> ❶ The fuller form of this expression, *fall in the shit and come up smelling of roses*, explains the idea behind it.

smiling

come up smiling recover from adversity and cheerfully face the future. informal

> **1989** *Woman's Realm* But despite her ordeal courageous Kelly has come up smiling and is now looking forward to a bright future.

smoke

go up in smoke ❶ be destroyed by fire. ❷ (of a plan) come to nothing. informal

no smoke without fire (or where there's smoke there's fire) there's always some reason for a rumour. proverb

> **1998** *Times* This is not saying that there is no smoke without fire—which sentiment underlines why bogus claims can do so much irrevocable damage—but that this is always, necessarily, going to be an incendiary issue.

smoke and mirrors the obscuring or embellishing of the truth of a situation with misleading or irrelevant information. chiefly North American

> **1998** *Sunday Telegraph* Ministers accused the Conservatives of a 'smoke and mirrors' con trick.

smoke like a chimney smoke tobacco incessantly.

watch someone's smoke observe another person's activity.

> ❶ The implication of this phrase is that the activity in question will be so fast and furious that smoke will be generated.

> **1947** P. G. Wodehouse *Full Moon* Look at Henry the Eighth . . . And Solomon. Once they started marrying, there was no holding them—you just sat back and watched their smoke.

smoking

a smoking gun (or pistol) a piece of incontrovertible evidence.

> ❶ This phrase draws on the assumption, a staple of detective fiction, that the person found with a recently fired gun must be the guilty party. The use of the phrase in the late 20th century was particularly associated with the Watergate scandal in the early 1970s

involving the US President Richard Nixon. When one of the Watergate tapes revealed Nixon's wish to limit the FBI's role in the investigation, Barber B. Conable famously commented: 'I guess we have found the smoking pistol, haven't we?'

> **1998** *New Scientist* This genetic smoking gun is evidence of a migration out of Asia that is hard to refute.

smooth

in smooth water in quiet and serene circumstances, especially after difficulties.

smooth someone's ruffled feathers: *see* RUFFLED.

snake

a snake in the grass a treacherous or deceitful person.

> ❶ Since the late 17th century this expression has entirely superseded the earlier idiom a *pad in the straw*. *Pad* is an old dialect term for a toad, an animal that was formerly thought to be poisonous.

snaky

go (or drive someone) snaky lose (or cause someone to lose) their self-control. Canadian

snap

bite someone's head off: *see* HEAD.

in a snap in a moment; almost immediately. informal, chiefly North American

snap your fingers at: *see* FINGER.

snappy

make it snappy be quick about it.

> **1994** Pete Hamill *A Drinking Life* Into bed! he said. Make it snappy! I retreated into the darkness of the second floor from the kitchen.

sneezed

not to be sneezed at not to be rejected without careful consideration; worth having or taking into account. informal

snook

cock a snook openly show contempt or a lack of respect for someone or something. informal, chiefly British

> ❶ Literally, if you cock a snook, you place your hand so that your thumb touches your nose and your fingers are spread out, in order to express contempt. Recorded from the late 18th century, the expression's origins are uncertain—as are those of the gesture itself,

which occurs under a variety of names and in many countries, the earliest definite mention of it being by Rabelais in 1532.

snow

pure as the driven snow: *see* PURE.

snowball

not a snowball's chance in hell: *see* **not a hope in hell** *at* HELL.

snuff

up to snuff ❶ up to the required standard. **❷** in good health. informal

snug

snug as a bug (in a rug) extremely comfortable. humorous

soap

no soap no chance of something happening or occurring. North American informal

> ❶ The origin of this expression, used to refuse a request, may lie in the mid 19th-century US informal use of *soap* to mean 'money'.

> **1929 Edmund Wilson** I Thought of Daisy If he tries to cut in on you, don't letum—I'll just tellum, no soap.

sober

sober as a judge completely sober.

sock

knock (or blow) someone's socks off amaze or impress someone. informal

> **1991 Barbara Anderson** Girls High Years ago she saw a Hockney...the few lines which sketched the owlish face knocked her socks off.

knock the socks off someone beat or surpass someone. informal

pull your socks up make an effort to improve your work, performance, or behaviour. informal

put a sock in it stop talking. British informal

sock it to someone attack someone vigorously or make a forceful impression on them in some other way. informal

> **1991** Baseball Today Chicago socked it to the other teams in the American league.

— **your socks off** do something with great energy or enthusiasm. informal

> **1996** Premiere Ray Liotta strikes perfect notes as Hill while Joe Pesci blows your socks off as sociopathic side-kick Tommy.

soda

from soda to hock from beginning to end. dated

> ❶ In the card game faro, the *soda* is the exposed top card at the beginning of a deal, while the *hock* is the last card remaining in the box after all the others have been dealt.

soft

have a soft spot for be fond of or affectionate towards.

soldier

come (or play) the old soldier use your greater age or experience of life to deceive someone or to shirk a duty. informal

> ❶ In US nautical slang a *soldier* or an *old soldier* was an incompetent seaman.

soldier of fortune an adventurous person ready to take service under any person or state in return for money; a mercenary.

some

and then some and plenty more than that. informal, chiefly US

> **1998** New Scientist But by simply sitting still and digesting, a chick could double this rate and then some.

something

thirty-something (or forty-something, etc.) an unspecified age between thirty and forty (forty and fifty, etc.). informal

son

son of a gun a humorous or affectionate way of addressing or referring to someone. informal

> ❶ The term arose with reference to the guns carried on board ships: it is said to have been originally applied to babies born at sea by women accompanying their husbands.

song

for a song very cheaply. informal

> ❶ The ultimate origin of this phrase is probably the practice, in former times, of selling written copies of ballads very cheaply at fairs. The expression was in common use by the mid 17th century.

> **1985 Nini Herman** My Kleinian Home The place was going for a song, since anyone in his right mind would have steered well clear of it.

s

on song performing well; in good form. British informal

> **1996** *Times* The horse is in pretty good shape. I rode him out at Haydock and he felt on song.

song and dance ❶ a fuss or commotion. informal **❷** a long explanation that is pointless or deliberately evasive. North American informal

sop

a sop to Cerberus something offered to appease someone.

> ❶ In Greek mythology, Cerberus was the three-headed watchdog which guarded the entrance of Hades. In the *Aeneid* Virgil describes how the Sibyl guiding Aeneas to the underworld threw a drugged cake to Cerberus, thus enabling the hero to pass the monster in safety.

sorcerer

sorcerer's apprentice a person who having instigated a process is unable to control it.

> ❶ This is a translation of the French *l'apprenti sorcier*, the title of an 1897 symphonic poem by Paul Dukas based on *der Zauberlehrling*, a 1797 ballad by Goethe. In this ballad the apprentice's use of magic spells sets in motion a series of events which he cannot control.

sore

stand (or stick) out like a sore thumb be very obviously different from the surrounding people or things.

sorrow

more in sorrow than in anger with regret or sadness rather than with anger.

> ❶ This is taken from *Hamlet*. When Hamlet asks Horatio to describe the expression on the face of his father's ghost, Horatio replies 'a countenance more in sorrow than in anger'.

sort

it takes all sorts people vary greatly in character, tastes, and abilities. proverb

> ❶ The complete form of this expression is *it takes all sorts to make a world*, often used as a comment on what the speaker feels to be unconventional behaviour.

> **1999 David Mitchell** *Ghostwritten* We're a chat show. It takes all sorts. You complain when they're too dull. You complain when they're too colourful.

out of sorts ❶ slightly unwell. **❷** in low spirits; irritable.

sort the men from the boys: *see* **separate the men from the boys** *at* MAN.

soul

the life and soul of the party: *see* LIFE.

a lost soul ❶ a soul that is damned. **❷** a person who seems unable to cope with everyday life.

sell your soul: *see* SELL.

work the soul case out of put someone under severe stress.

soup

from soup to nuts from beginning to end; completely. North American informal

> ❶ Soup is likely to feature as the first course of a formal meal, while a selection of nuts may be offered as the final one.

in the soup in trouble. informal

sour

sour grapes an attitude in which someone disparages or pretends to despise something because they cannot have it themselves.

> ❶ In Aesop's fable *The Fox and the Grapes*, the fox, unable to reach the tempting bunch of grapes, comforts himself with the thought that they were probably sour anyway.

> **1998** *New Scientist* At 66, I can be acquitted of any sour grapes, but I feel sorry for younger MPs...[who] have all been passed over.

south

down south to or in the south of a country. informal

> **1995 Bill Bryson** *Notes from a Small Island* 'Ah, you're the chap from down south,' he said, remembering, which threw me a little. It isn't often you hear Yorkshire referred to as down south.

sow

have the right sow by the ear have the correct understanding of a situation.

make a silk purse out of a sow's ear: *see* SILK.

sow the seed (or seeds) of do something which will eventually bring about a particular result.

> **1991 Philip Slater** *A Dream Deferred* Each authoritarian government, groping toward

modernization, would thereby sow the seeds of its own destruction.

space

watch this space used to indicate that further developments are expected and more information will be given later. informal

> ❶ The *space* referred to here is a section of a newspaper available for a specific purpose, especially for advertising.

> **1979 Julian Rathbone** *The Euro-Killers* Where is he? Watch this space for exciting revelations in the next few days.

spade

call a spade a spade speak plainly or bluntly, without avoiding issues which are unpleasant or embarrassing.

> ❶ A variation on this phrase, dating from the early 20th century and used for humorous emphasis, is *call a spade a shovel*.

> **1998** *Spectator* A man whom I might not agree with where politics are concerned, but one who calls a spade a spade.

in spades to a very high degree; as much as or more than could be desired. informal

> ❶ This expression derives from the fact that spades are the highest-ranking suit in the card game bridge.

> **1996** *Time Out* Wit, vitality, heart, story-telling flair: the movie has each in spades.

Spanish

old Spanish customs (*or* **practices**) long-standing though unauthorized or irregular work practices.

> ❶ This expression has been in use in printing circles since the 1960s; it is often used humorously to refer to practices in the British newspaper printing houses in Fleet Street, London, formerly notorious for their inefficiency. The reason for describing such practices as 'Spanish' is not known.

> **1998** *Spectator* [Outsourcing] can do much for flexibility and more for costs and it is a proven cure for quaint old Spanish customs.

spanner

a spanner in the works an event, person, or thing that prevents the smooth or successful implementation of a plan; a drawback or impediment.

> ❶ A variant, found chiefly in North American English, is *a monkey wrench in the works*, a *monkey wrench* being a spanner or wrench with adjustable jaws: to *throw a spanner* (or *a monkey wrench*) *into the works* is to deliberately wreck someone's plans or activities. In his 1974 novel *The Monkey Wrench Gang*, Edward Abbey used this as a metaphor for systematic industrial sabotage, and *monkey-wrenching* is now a colloquial term for such activity.

> **1997** *Spectator* Pretty well all the newspapers... are now adversarial in tone, conceiving their basic purpose as throwing spanners in the works almost as a matter of principle.

spare

go spare become extremely angry or distraught. British informal

> **1991 Roddy Doyle** *The Van* Remind me to replace this one... Veronica'll go spare if she goes to get it on Sunday and it's not there.

spare someone's blushes: *see* BLUSH.

to spare left over.

spark

sparks fly a discussion becomes heated or lively.

strike sparks off each other (*or* **one another**) (of two or more people) creatively inspire each other while working on something.

speak

it speaks well for something places someone or something in a favourable light.

speak for yourself give your own opinions.

> ❶ The exclamation *speak for yourself!* indicates to someone that an opinion they have expressed is not shared by yourself and is resented.

speak in tongues speak in an unknown language during religious worship.

> ❶ Speaking in (or with) tongues is a phenomenon known more formally as *glossolalia*, which is regarded by some as a gift of the Holy Spirit. The Bible records that the apostles demonstrated this ability (e.g. Acts 10:46, 19:6), and it is a component of present-day charismatic Christian worship.

speak your mind express your feelings or opinions frankly.

> **1982 Marion Z. Bradley** *The Mists of Avalon* Someday she would be too weary or too unguarded to care, and she would speak her mind to the priest.

speak of the devil: *see* DEVIL.

speak volumes ❶ (of a gesture, circumstance, or object) convey a great deal. **❷** be good evidence for.

> **❷ 1998** *New Scientist* It was a minor scandal... but it spoke volumes about the world's shifting relationship with its favourite illicit drug.

speak as you find base your opinion of someone or something purely on personal experience.

> **1988 Hilary Mantel** *Eight Months on Ghazzah Street* Look, I don't have any theories. I just go issue by issue. I just speak as I find.

spec

on spec in the hope of success but without any specific plan or instructions. informal

> **❶** The informal abbreviation of *speculation* to *spec* was originally American, but it has been used in British English since the early 19th century, and the phrase *on spec* itself dates from the mid 19th century.

> **2000** *Times* As large sculpture is commissioned before being produced, Barbara's routine became the opposite of Ben's, whose work was produced on spec.

spectre

a spectre at the feast: *see* **a ghost at the feast** *at* FEAST.

speed

up to speed ❶ operating at full speed. **❷** (of a person or company) performing at an anticipated rate or level. **❸** (of a person) fully informed or up to date. informal

> **❷ 1998** *Times Magazine* Penati advises on menus and drops in occasionally to check that everything is up to speed. **❸ 1998** *New Scientist* It's well known to anyone who is up to speed with e-mail.

spell

under someone's spell so devoted to someone that they seem to have magic power over you.

spend

spend a penny: *see* PENNY.

spike

spike someone's guns take steps to thwart someone's intended course of action.

> **❶** First recorded in English in the late 17th century, the expression referred literally to the practice of hammering a metal spike into a captured enemy cannon so that it could not be fired.

spill

spill the beans reveal secret information, especially unintentionally or indiscreetly. informal

spill your guts reveal copious information to someone in an uninhibited way. informal

spin

spin your wheels: *see* WHEEL.

spin a yarn: *see* YARN.

spirit

enter into the spirit join wholeheartedly in an event.

> **1994 Jonathan Coe** *What a Carve Up!* His sarcasm was mischievous rather than icy, so I tried to enter into the spirit.

the spirit is willing (but the flesh is weak) someone has good intentions (but yields to temptation and fails to live up to them).

> **❶** This expression quotes Jesus's words in Matthew 26:41, on finding his disciples asleep in the Garden of Gethsemane despite his instructions that they should stay awake.

the spirit moves someone someone feels inclined to do something.

> **❶** This was a phrase originally used by Quakers, with reference to the inspiration of the Holy Spirit.

spit

be the spit (*or* the dead spit) of look exactly like. informal

> **❶** The full form of the phrase is *be the spit and image of*, perhaps coming from the idea of a person apparently being formed from the spit of another, so great is the similarity between them. This fuller form also lies behind the expression *spitting image*.

spit and polish extreme neatness or smartness.

spit and sawdust (of a pub) old-fashioned, run-down, or dirty. British informal

> **❶** Until the mid 20th century, the general bar of a pub would often have sawdust sprinkled on the floor, on to which the customers could spit.

spit blood be very angry.

spit (out) the dummy behave in a petulant way. Australian informal

spit in the eye (*or* face) of show contempt or scorn for.

spitting

spitting in (*or* **into**) **the wind** a futile or pointless activity.

> **1996** *Daily Telegraph* Both the Church report and the atheist professor are spitting in the wind, of course, because the incoming tide of superstition has a long way to rise yet.

splash

make a splash attract a great deal of attention.

> **1996** Amitav Ghosh *The Calcutta Chromosome* This was just about the time that new sciences like bacteriology and parasitology were beginning to make a splash in Europe.

split

split hairs: *see* HAIR.

split your sides be convulsed with laughter. informal

split the ticket (*or* **your vote**) vote for candidates of more than one party. US

split the vote (of a candidate or minority party) attract votes from another candidate or party with the result that both are defeated by a third. British

spoil

too many cooks spoil the broth: *see* COOK.

spoilt

be spoilt for choice have so many attractive possibilities to choose from that it is difficult to make a selection. British

spoke

put a spoke in someone's wheel prevent someone from carrying out a plan. British

> ❶ It is not clear why a *spoke*, a normal component of many wheels, should have such a negative effect. It has been suggested that *spoke* here is a mistranslation of the Dutch word *spaak*, meaning 'a bar' or 'a stave', which is found in the identical Dutch idiom.

sponge

throw in the sponge: *see* THROW.

spoon

greasy spoon: *see* GREASY.

make a spoon or spoil a horn make a determined effort to achieve something, whatever the cost.

> ❶ This phrase alludes to the former practice of making spoons out of the horns of cattle or sheep.

win the wooden spoon be the least successful contestant; win the booby prize.

> ❶ A wooden spoon was originally presented to the candidate coming last in the Cambridge University mathematical tripos (the final honours examination for a BA degree).

sport

the sport of kings horse racing.

sporting

a sporting chance some possibility of success.

spot

a blind spot: *see* BLIND.

hit the spot be exactly what is required. informal

knock spots off: *see* KNOCK.

put someone on the spot force someone into a situation in which they must make a difficult decision or answer a difficult question. informal

spout

up the spout ❶ no longer working or likely to be of use or successful. ❷ (of a woman) pregnant. British informal

sprat

a sprat to catch a mackerel a small expenditure made, or a small risk taken, in the hope of a large or significant gain. British

> ❶ A *sprat* is a small sea fish, while a *mackerel* is rather larger. The phrase has been in use since the mid 19th century and is also found with *whale* in the place of *mackerel*.

spread

spread like wildfire: *see* WILDFIRE.

spread yourself too thin be involved in so many different activities or projects that your time and energy are not used to good effect.

spread your wings: *see* WING.

spur

on the spur of the moment on a momentary impulse; without premeditation.

1988 Rodney Hall *Kisses of the Enemy* Now that was a witticism, an inspiration on the spur of the moment.

win your spurs: *see* WIN.

square

back to square one: *see* BACK.

get square with pay a creditor.

have square eyes habitually watch television to excess.

on the square ❶ honest; straightforward. **❷** having membership of the Freemasons.

> **❷ 1997** *Guardian* One non-Masonic officer...claims he was moved sideways... and subsequently he discovered that the corrupt officers and the commander were all 'on the square'.

square accounts with: *see* **settle accounts with** *at* ACCOUNT.

square the circle do something that is considered to be impossible.

> ❶ In its literal sense, *square the circle* means 'construct a square equal in area to a given circle'. Since this problem is incapable of a purely geometrical solution, the phrase has developed a more general application and is used to refer to an attempt to do something impossible.

squeeze

put the squeeze on someone coerce or pressurize someone. informal

> **1993 Jonathon Green** *It: Sex Since the Sixties* One day two characters walked into my studio and tried to put the squeeze on me for protection money.

squeeze someone until the pips squeak: *see* PIP.

squib

a damp squib: *see* DAMP.

stab

a stab in the dark: *see* **a shot in the dark** *at* DARK.

a stab in the back a treacherous act or statement; a betrayal.

stable

shut (*or* lock) the stable door after the horse has bolted try to avoid or prevent something bad or unwelcome when it is already too late to do so. proverb

> ❶ This saying dates back to medieval times. Until the late 19th century it was used in the form *shut the stable door after the steed is stolen*.

stage

hold the stage dominate a scene of action or forum of debate.

set the stage for prepare the conditions for the occurrence or beginning of something.

> **1998** *High Country News* Udall had ruffled uniforms, but he had also set the stage for the glory years of the agency.

stair rod

rain stair rods: *see* **rain cats and dogs** *at* RAIN.

stake

go to the stake for do anything to defend a specified belief, opinion, or person.

> ❶ In the past, especially during times of religious persecution, heretics were liable to be tied to a wooden stake and burned alive if they refused to recant their beliefs.

pull up stakes (of a person) move or go to live elsewhere. North American

> ❶ The *stakes* are the pegs or posts which secure a tent or which are put up as a palisade around a temporary settlement.

> **2000 Anthony Bourdain** *Kitchen Confidential* Steven...has chosen to leave New York for Florida with his girlfriend, pulling up stakes, giving up his apartment, even bringing along his goldfish.

stake a claim declare your right to something.

> ❶ This expression refers to the practice of putting stakes around the perimeter of a piece of land to which a claim is laid. It is American in origin, dating from the California gold rush of 1849, when the prospectors registered their claims to individual plots of land in this way.

stall

set out your stall: *see* SET.

stand

stand someone in good stead: *see* STEAD.

stand on your own (two) feet be or become self-reliant or independent.

stand out like a sore thumb: *see* SORE.

stand out a mile: *see* MILE.

stand pat: *see* PAT.

stand up and be counted state publicly your support for someone or something.

will the real — please stand up used rhetorically to indicate that the specified person should clarify their position or reveal their true character. informal

> **1996** *Maclean's* There have been moments when I wanted to ask, 'Would the real Mr. Arafat please stand up', but these have been fleeting.

standing

leave someone or something standing (of a person or thing) be much better or faster than someone or something else.

stands

it stands to reason: *see* REASON.

star

have stars in your eyes be idealistically hopeful or enthusiastic, especially about a possible future in entertainment or sport.

reach for the stars have high or ambitious aims.

see stars see flashes of light, especially as a result of being hit on the head.

someone's star is rising someone is becoming ever more successful or popular.

starch

take the starch out of someone shake someone's confidence, especially by humiliating them. US

staring

be staring someone in the face (of a fact or object) be glaringly apparent or obvious.

be staring something in the face (of a person) be on the verge of defeat, death, or ruin.

start

start a hare: *see* HARE.

starter

under starter's orders (of horses, runners, or other competitors) ready to start a race on receiving the signal from the starter.

state

state of the art the most recent stage in the development of a product, incorporating the newest ideas and the most up-to-date features.

state of grace a condition of being free from sin.

state of play ❶ the score at a particular time in a cricket or football match. ❷ the current situation in an ongoing process, especially one involving opposing or competing parties. British

stay

stay loose: *see* **hang loose** *at* LOOSE.

stay the course (*or* **distance**) ❶ hold out to the end of a race or contest. ❷ pursue a difficult task or activity to the end.

stay your hand: *see* HAND.

a stay of execution a delay in carrying out a court order.

stay put (of a person or object) remain somewhere without moving or being moved.

> **1994** *Sunday Times* Despite firm intentions to explore, campers tend to stay put, especially if there are lots of activities and a good pool.

stead

stand someone in good stead (of something learned or acquired) be advantageous or useful to someone over time or in the future.

steady

go steady have a regular romantic or sexual relationship with a particular person. informal

> **1905** *Edith Wharton The House of Mirth* I thought we were to be married: he'd gone steady with me six months and given me his mother's wedding ring.

steady as she goes keep on with the same careful progress. informal

> ⓘ In nautical vocabulary, *steady* is the instruction given to the helmsman to keep the ship on the same course.

> **1998** *Bookseller* His boss set him one task: 'steady as she goes, but more so'.

steal

steal someone blind rob or cheat someone in a comprehensive or merciless way. informal

steal someone's clothes appropriate someone's ideas or policies. British informal

steal a march on gain an advantage over someone, typically by acting before they do.

steal the show attract the most attention and praise.

steal someone's thunder win praise for

yourself by pre-empting someone else's attempt to impress.

> ❶ The critic and playwright John Dennis (1657–1734) invented a new method of simulating the sound of thunder in the theatre, which he employed in his unsuccessful play *Appius and Virginia*. Shortly after his play had finished its brief run, Dennis attended a performance of *Macbeth* in which the improved thunder effect was used, and he is reported to have exclaimed in a fury: 'Damn them! They will not let my play run, but they steal my thunder.'

steam

get up (*or* **pick up**) **steam** ❶ generate enough pressure to drive a steam engine. ❷ (of a project, plan, or process in its early stages) gradually gain more impetus and driving force.

have steam coming out of your ears be extremely angry or irritated. informal

let (*or* **blow**) **off steam** get rid of pent-up energy or emotion. informal

> ❶ The image here is of the release of excess steam from a steam engine through a valve.

run out of (*or* **lose**) **steam** lose impetus or enthusiasm. informal

> **1992 Jeff Torrington** *Swing Hammer Swing!* Eventually I ran out of steam and came to a halt.

under your own steam without assistance from others.

> **1996 Colin Bateman** *Of Wee Sweetie Mice & Men* She was starting to move under her own steam, hesitant Bambi steps which weren't helped by being hurried along, but a good sign nevertheless.

steer

steer a middle course: *see* MIDDLE.

stem

from stem to stern from the front to the back, especially of a ship.

step

mind (*or* **watch**) **your step** be careful.

step into the breach: *see* BREACH.

step on it ❶ make a motor vehicle go faster by pressing down on the accelerator pedal with your foot. ❷ hurry up. informal

> ❶ A US variant of this expression is *step on the gas*.

step out of line behave inappropriately or disobediently.

step on someone's toes: *see* **tread on someone's toes** at TREAD.

sterner

be made of sterner stuff (of a person) have a stronger character and be more able to overcome problems than others.

> ❶ This expression comes from Shakespeare's *Julius Caesar*: 'When that the poor have cried, Caesar hath wept; Ambition should be made of sterner stuff: Yet Brutus says he was ambitious; And Brutus is an honourable man'.

> **1998** *Spectator* Unlike the Americans, who are inclined to pull all their personnel out of a country at the first hint of trouble, the British foreign service is made of sterner stuff.

stew

stew in your own juice suffer the unpleasant consequences of your own actions or temperament without the consoling intervention of others. informal

stick

in the sticks in a remote rural area. informal

stick out like a sore thumb: *see* **stand out like a sore thumb** at SORE.

stick out a mile: *see* **stand out a mile** at MILE.

stick at nothing allow nothing to deter you from achieving your aim, even if it means acting wrongly or dishonestly.

stick your bib in: *see* BIB.

stick your chin out show firmness or fortitude.

stick in your craw: *see* CRAW.

stick in your gizzard: *see* GIZZARD.

stick in your throat: *see* THROAT.

stick it on ❶ make high charges. ❷ tell an exaggerated story. informal

stick it to someone treat someone harshly or severely. informal, chiefly US

stick your neck out risk incurring criticism, anger, or danger by acting or speaking boldly. informal

> **1969 Bessie Head** *When Rain Clouds Gather* Things are so bad that if anyone sticks his neck out for a refugee, he's not likely to get promoted for five years.

stick your oar in: *see* OAR.

stick one (*or* it) on someone hit someone. informal

a stick to beat someone or something with a fact or argument held over someone or something as a threat or an advantage.

stick to someone's fingers (of money) be embezzled by a person. informal

stick to your guns: *see* GUN.

stick to your ribs (of food) be very filling.

up sticks go to live elsewhere. British informal

sticky

sticky fingers a propensity to steal. informal

a sticky wicket: *see* WICKET.

stiff

a stiff upper lip a quality of uncomplaining stoicism.

> ❶ This is a characteristic particularly associated with the British but the phrase is apparently North American in origin, dating back to the mid 19th century. It is used, for example, in Harriet Beecher Stowe's novel *Uncle Tom's Cabin*, published in 1852.

> **1998** *Spectator* The Princess . . . as her final gift to the British people, had unstarched their stiff upper lips.

still

still small voice the voice of your conscience.

> ❶ In 1 Kings 19:12, the voice of God is described as a *still small voice*.

still waters run deep a quiet or placid manner may conceal a passionate nature. proverb

sting

sting in the tail an unpleasant or problematic end to something.

> **1992 Ronald Wright** *Stolen Continents* At last Hendrick came to the sting in the tail of his speech.

stink

like stink extremely hard or intensely. informal

> **2000 Steven Heighton** *The Shadow Boxer* Let him tire out a bit and then go to work on him upstairs. Jabs and straight rights now, got it? Go on. Get on him like stink.

stir

stir a finger: *see* **lift a finger** *at* LIFT.

stir your stumps (of a person) begin to move or act. British informal, dated

> ❶ *Stump* has been used as an informal term for 'leg' since the 15th century; the expression itself dates from the mid 16th century.

stitch

a stitch in time if you sort out a problem immediately, it may save a lot of extra work later. proverb

> ❶ The fuller form of the expression is *a stitch in time saves nine*. *Nine* here has no particular significance as a number but was chosen because of its similarity in sound with the word *time*.

in stitches laughing uncontrollably. informal

> ❶ *Stitch*, in the sense of 'a sudden localized jabbing pain', such as might be caused by a needle, is recorded in Old English. It is now generally used of a muscle spasm in the side caused especially by exertion. Shakespeare seems to have been the first to describe *stitches* brought on by laughter; in *Twelfth Night* (1601) Maria invites her fellow conspirators to observe the lovelorn Malvolio with the words: 'If you . . . will laugh yourselves into stitches, follow me'.

> **1981 D. M. Thomas** *The White Hotel* She had them in stitches with her absurd—but true—anecdotes.

stock

on the stocks in construction or preparation.

> ❶ During construction, a ship is supported on a frame or scaffolding known as the *stocks*.

put (*or* take) stock in believe or have faith in.

> ❶ The earliest example so far recorded of this expression is by Mark Twain in *Galaxy* (1870): 'The "chance" theory . . . is . . . calculated to inflict . . . pecuniary loss upon any community that takes stock in it'.

take stock ❶ make an inventory of the merchandise in a shop. ❷ review or make an assessment of a particular situation, typically as a prelude to making a decision.

stomach

an army marches on its stomach soldiers or workers can only fight or function effectively if they have been well fed.

> ❶ The saying has been attributed to both Frederick the Great and Napoleon I. It is a version of the French phrase *c'est la soupe qui fait la soldat*.

on a full (*or* **an empty**) **stomach** having (*or* without having) eaten beforehand.

a strong stomach an ability to see or do unpleasant things without feeling sick or squeamish.

stompie

pick up stompies break into a conversation of which you have heard only the end. South African

> ❶ In Afrikaans, a *stompie* is a cigarette butt.

stone

be carved (*or* **set** *or* **written**) **in stone** be fixed and unchangeable.

> ❶ The reference here is to the biblical Ten Commandments, written on tablets of stone by God and handed down to Moses on Mount Sinai (Genesis 31:18).

cast (*or* **throw**) **the first stone** be the first to accuse or criticize.

> ❶ The phrase comes from an incident recorded in St John's Gospel. A group of men preparing to stone an adulterous woman to death were addressed by Jesus with the words: 'He that is without sin among you, let him first cast a stone at her' (John 8:7).

have kissed the blarney stone: *see* BLARNEY.

leave no stone unturned try every possible course of action in order to achieve something.

mark something with a white stone: *see* WHITE.

a stone's throw a short distance.

> **1989** Joanna Trollope *Village Affairs* Can't tell you the difference it will make, having you a stone's throw away.

stony

fall on stony ground (of words or a suggestion) be ignored or badly received.

> ❶ The reference here is to the parable of the sower recounted in both St Mark's and St Matthew's Gospels, in which some of the seed scattered by the sower fell on stony places where it withered away.

stool

fall between two stools fail to be or to take one of two satisfactory alternatives. British

> ❶ This phrase comes from the proverb *between two stools one falls to the ground*, first referred to in English by the medieval writer John Gower in *Confessio Amantis* (c.1390).

stop

pull out all the stops make a very great effort; go to elaborate lengths.

> ❶ The stops referred to here are those of an organ. Although this is an early 20th-century expression, Matthew Arnold, in the Preface to *Essays in Criticism* (1865) refers to an attempt on his behalf 'to pull out a few more stops in that...somewhat narrow-toned organ, the modern Englishman'.

stop at nothing recognize no obstacles or reasons for not doing something; be utterly ruthless or determined.

> **1991** *Time* Seen simplistically and from afar, Saddam Hussein comes across as ...the villain who will stop at nothing.

stop your ears ❶ put your fingers in your ears to avoid hearing. ❷ refuse to listen.

stop a gap serve to meet a temporary need.

stop someone's mouth bribe or otherwise induce a person to keep silent about something.

stop the show (of a performer) provoke prolonged applause or laughter, causing an interruption.

stopper

put a (*or* **the**) **stopper on** cause something to end or become quiet.

store

set (*or* **lay** *or* **put**) **store by** (*or* **on**) consider something to be of a particular degree of importance or value.

storm

go down a storm be enthusiastically received by an audience.

the lull (*or* **calm**) **before the storm** a period of unusual tranquillity or stability that seems likely to presage difficult times.

a storm in a teacup great excitement or anger about a trivial matter.

> ❶ A North American variant of this expression is *a tempest in a teapot*.

> **1998** *Times* A storm in a teacup? Who cares about a bunch of seeds?

take something by storm ❶ capture a place by a sudden and violent attack. **❷** have great and rapid success in a particular place or with a particular group of people.

> **1998** *Times* Round-up Ready soya has taken America by storm.

— **up a storm** perform a particular action with great enthusiasm and energy. chiefly North American

> **1990** *Harper's Magazine* What I fear is that we talk up a storm and never better the situation for the exploited or the poor.

story

end of story: *see* END.

it's (*or* **that's**) **the story of my life** used to lament the fact that a particular misfortune has happened too often in your experience. informal

to cut (*or* **make**) **a long story short** used to end an account of events quickly.

stout

a stout heart courage or determination. literary

stove

slave over a hot stove work very hard preparing a meal. informal

straight

keep a straight face manage to not show any facial expression, even though you are amused.

the straight and narrow morally correct behaviour.

> ❶ The full form of the expression is *the straight and narrow path* or *way*. It developed from a misunderstanding of Matthew 7:14, 'strait is the gate, and narrow is the way, which leadeth unto life', where *strait* is in fact being used as another word for *narrow*.

a straight arrow: *see* ARROW.

straight as a die: *see* DIE.

a straight fight a contest between just two opponents, especially in an election. British

straight from the shoulder ❶ (of a blow) well delivered. **❷** (of a verbal attack) frank or direct.

straight off (*or* **out**) without hesitation or deliberation. informal

straight up truthfully; honestly. informal

strain

strain at a gnat make a difficulty about accepting something trivial. literary

> ❶ The phrase derives from Matthew 23:24, 'Ye blind guides, which strain at a gnat, and swallow a camel'. The word *strain* here appears to mean 'make a violent effort', but it may in fact refer to the straining of a liquid to remove unwanted particles: the image is of a person quietly accepting a difficulty or problem of significant proportions while baulking at something comparatively trivial.

strain at the leash be eager to begin or do something.

strain every nerve: *see* NERVE.

strange

make strange (of a baby or child) fuss or be shy in company. Canadian

> **1987** *Alice Munro* The Progress of Love Her timid-looking fat son . . . usually liked Violet, but today he made strange.

straw

clutch (*or* **grasp** *or* **catch**) **at straws** do, say, or believe anything, however unlikely or inadequate, which seems to offer hope in a desperate situation.

> ❶ This expression comes from the proverb *a drowning man will clutch at a straw*, which is recorded in various forms since the mid 16th century.

draw the short straw be the unluckiest of a group of people, especially in being chosen to perform an unpleasant task.

> ❶ One method of drawing lots involves holding several straws of varying lengths with one end concealed in your hand and then inviting other members of the group to take one each.

the last (*or* **final**) **straw** a further difficulty or annoyance, typically minor in itself but coming on top of a whole series of difficulties, that makes a situation unbearable.

> ❶ The full version of this is the proverb *the last straw breaks the camel's back*. The modern form is traceable to Charles Dickens in *Dombey and Son* (1848), but earlier versions are recorded, including a mid 17th-century reference to *the last feather breaking a horse's back*.

a straw in the wind a slight but significant hint of future developments.

s

straws in your hair a state of insanity.

> ⓘ In former times, the floors of mental institutions were covered with straw, and so having straw in the hair came to be regarded as a characteristic of a deranged person.

streak

like a streak (of lightning) very fast. informal

stream

against (or with) the stream against (or with) the prevailing view or tendency.

on stream in or into operation or existence; available.

street

not in the same street far inferior in terms of ability. British informal

streets ahead greatly superior. British informal

> **1991 Alistair Campbell** *Sidewinder* He has his shortcomings, sure, but he's streets ahead of Dr Nada.

up (or right up) your street well suited to your tastes, interests, or abilities. informal

> ⓘ A North American variant of this expression is *up your alley*.

strength

go from strength to strength develop or progress with increasing success.

a tower (or pillar) of strength a person who can be relied upon to be a source of strong support and comfort.

> ⓘ This phrase may come from the Book of Common Prayer: 'O Lord... be unto them a tower of strength'.

strengthen

strengthen someone's hand (or hands) enable or encourage a person to act more vigorously or effectively.

stretch

at full stretch ❶ with a part of your body fully extended. ❷ using the maximum amount of your resources or energy.

at a stretch ❶ in one continuous period. ❷ with much effort or difficulty.

by no (or not by any) stretch of the imagination used to emphasize that something is definitely not the case.

> **1996 New Statesman** Though it is by no stretch of the imagination a political paper, its owner

has a reputation as an outspoken critic of China.

stretch your legs go for a short walk, typically after sitting in one place for some time.

stretch a point allow or do something not usually acceptable, typically as a result of particular circumstances.

> **1998 Penelope Lively** *Spiderweb* I seem to recall that you are agnostic, but I would suggest, with all respect, that you stretch a point and attend Sunday Matins, at least on occasion.

stretch your wings: *see* WING.

stricken

stricken in years used euphemistically to describe someone old and feeble.

stride

take something in your stride deal with something difficult or unpleasant in a calm and competent way.

strike

strike at the root of: *see* ROOT.

strike it rich find a source of abundance or success. informal

strike lucky (or strike it lucky) have a lucky success. British

strike oil attain prosperity or success.

> **1994 Nature** S. P. Goldman... seems to have struck oil in the search for better ways of computing electronic states.

strike while the iron is hot make use of an opportunity immediately.

> ⓘ Iron can only be hammered into shape at a blacksmith's forge while it is hot.

striking

within striking distance: *see* DISTANCE.

string

have a second string to your bow have an alternative resource that you can make use of if the first one fails. British

> ⓘ This is a metaphor from archery; related expressions include *have several strings to your bow* and *add another string to your bow*. *Second string* can also be used on its own to mean simply 'an alternative resource or course of action'.

how long is a piece of string? used as a rejoinder to indicate that it is unreasonable for someone to expect the speaker to be more precise about something. informal

no strings attached no special conditions or restrictions apply to an opportunity or offer. informal

on a string under your control or influence.

> ⓘ The idea here is of a puppeteer manipulating a puppet by its strings.

pull strings: *see* PULL.

pull the strings: *see* PULL.

stroke

different strokes for different folks: *see* DIFFERENT.

not (or never) do a stroke of work do no work at all.

put someone off their stroke disconcert someone so that they do not work or perform as well as they might; break the pattern or rhythm of someone's work.

stroke of genius an outstandingly brilliant and original idea.

stroke of luck (or good luck) a fortunate occurrence that could not have been predicted or expected.

stroke someone (or someone's hair) the wrong way irritate a person.

strong

come it strong indulge in exaggeration. British informal

come on strong ❶ behave aggressively or assertively. ❷ make great efforts or advances. informal

going strong continuing to be healthy, vigorous, or successful. informal

strong meat ideas or language likely to be found unacceptably forceful or extreme. British

strong on ❶ good at; expert in. ❷ possessing large quantities of; rich in.

strut

strut your stuff dance or behave in a lively, confident way. informal

> 1998 *Country Life* London is a place to hide in, to get lost in; New York is a stage on which to strut your stuff.

stubborn

stubborn as a mule extremely stubborn. informal

stuck

get stuck in (or into) start doing something enthusiastically or with determination. British informal

study

in a brown study: *see* BROWN.

stuffing

knock (or take) the stuffing out of someone severely impair someone's confidence or strength. informal

stump

beyond the black stump beyond the limits of settled, and therefore civilized, life. Australian

> ⓘ This phrase comes from the custom of using a fire-blackened stump of wood as a marker when giving directions to travellers.

on the stump going about the country making political speeches or canvassing. chiefly North American

> ⓘ In rural America in the late 18th century, the *stump* of a felled tree was often used as an impromptu platform for someone making a speech.

up a stump in a situation too difficult for you to manage. US

succeeds

nothing succeeds like success success leads to opportunities for further and greater successes. proverb

suck

suck someone dry exhaust someone's physical, material, or emotional resources.

suck it and see the only way to know if something will work or be suitable is to try it. British informal

sudden

(all) of a sudden suddenly.

> ⓘ As a noun *sudden* is now found only in this phrase, but from the mid 16th century to the early 18th century it was in regular use in the sense 'an unexpected danger or emergency'.

suffer

not suffer fools gladly be impatient or intolerant towards people you regard as unwise or unintelligent.

> ❶ This expression refers to 2 Corinthians 11:19: 'For ye suffer fools gladly, seeing ye yourselves are wise'.

2001 *Daily Telegraph* Such was her expertise as a Victorianist that her advice was widely sought, though she did not suffer fools gladly.

sugar

sugar the pill: see PILL.

suit

follow suit: see FOLLOW.

men in suits: see MAN.

suit the action to the word carry out your stated intentions at once.

> ❶ The expression comes from the scene in *Hamlet* in which a troupe of actors arrive to present a play to the king and queen. Hamlet instructs them to 'suit the action to the word, the word to the action'.

suit someone down to the ground be extremely convenient or appropriate for a particular person. British

summer

Indian summer: see INDIAN.

sun

catch the sun: see CATCH.

make hay while the sun shines: see HAY.

someone's sun is set the time of someone's prosperity is over.

the sun is over the yardarm it is the time of day when it is permissible to drink alcohol. informal

> ❶ This was originally a nautical expression: a *yardarm* is the outer extremity of a *yard*, a cylindrical spar slung across a ship's mast for a sail to hang from. The time of day referred to is noon, rather than 6 o'clock in the evening, as is often supposed.

1992 Angela Lambert *A Rather English Marriage* Have a snifter? Sun's over the yardarm, as they say in the senior service.

under the sun on earth; in existence.

sunny side

sunny side up (of an egg) fried on one side only. North American

sunset

ride off into the sunset: see RIDE.

sup

sup with the devil: see DEVIL.

supper

sing for your supper earn a benefit or favour by providing a service in return.

> ❶ This phrase comes from the nursery rhyme *Little Tommy Tucker*.

sure

sure as eggs is eggs (*also* **sure as fate**) without any doubt; absolutely certain.

sure thing ❶ a certainty. **❷** certainly; of course. informal

> ❶ **2001** *Business Week* Any potential legal challenge to Microsoft's bundling decisions in XP is no sure thing. ❷ **1995 Chitra Banerjee Divakaruni** *Arranged Marriage* 'Would you?' I said gratefully. 'That would make me feel so much better.' ... 'Sure thing!' said Sharmila hurriedly as she hung up.

surf

surf the net move from site to site on the Internet.

> ❶ *Surf* here comes from *channel-surfing*, the practice of switching frequently between channels on a television set in an attempt to find an interesting programme.

survival

survival of the fittest the continued existence of organisms which are best adapted to their environment, with the extinction of others, as a concept in the Darwinian theory of evolution.

> ❶ The phrase was coined by the English philosopher and sociologist Herbert Spencer (1820–1903) in *Principles of Biology* (1865). Besides its formal scientific use, the phrase is often used loosely and humorously in contexts relating to physical fitness (or the lack of it).

suss

on suss on suspicion of having committed a crime. British informal

> ❶ *Suss* is an abbreviation of *suspicion*, earlier and more correctly spelled *sus*. Until its abolition in 1981, a law nicknamed the *sus law* allowed the police to arrest a person on the suspicion that they were likely to commit a crime.

swallow

one swallow doesn't make a summer a single fortunate event does not mean that what follows will also be good. proverb

1998 *Spectator* One swallow doesn't make a summer . . . nor one instance of police dereliction of duty, incompetence, laziness and stupidity a complete breakdown in law and order.

swathe

cut a swathe through pass through something causing great damage, destruction, or change.

> ❶ A *swathe* was the area cut by a single sweep of a mower's scythe, and so the width of a strip of grass or corn cut in this way.

swear

swear blind affirm something in an emphatic manner. British informal

> ❶ A North American variant of this expression is *swear up and down*.

swear like a trooper swear a great deal.

> ❶ A *trooper* was originally a private soldier in a cavalry unit. Troopers were proverbial for their coarse behaviour and bad language at least as early as the mid 18th century: in *Pamela* (1739–40), Samuel Richardson writes 'she curses and storms at me like a Trooper'. Compare with **lie like a trooper** (*at* LIE).

sweat

by the sweat of your brow by your own hard work, typically manual labour.

> ❶ This idiom is often used with reference to God's sentence on Adam after the Fall, condemning him to work for his food: 'In the sweat of thy face shalt thou eat bread' (Genesis 3:19).

don't sweat it don't worry. US

no sweat without any difficulty or problem. informal

> **1998** *GQ* Give me a date and I'll take it, no sweat. No problem. If I'm available.

sweat blood ❶ make an extraordinarily strenuous effort to do something. ❷ be extremely anxious. informal

sweat bullets be extremely anxious or nervous. North American informal

sweat it out ❶ endure an unpleasant experience, typically one involving extreme physical exertion in great heat. ❷ wait in a state of extreme anxiety for something to happen or be resolved. informal

sweat the small stuff worry about trivial things. US

sweep

make a clean sweep: *see* CLEAN.

sweep the board win all the money in a gambling game; win all possible prizes or rewards.

sweep something under the carpet: *see* CARPET.

sweet

keep someone sweet keep someone well disposed towards yourself, especially by favours or bribery. informal

she's sweet all's well. Australian informal

> **1964 Kylie Tennant** *Summer's Tales* 'Everything O.K.?' 'Yep,' said the scrawny man beneath us. 'She's sweet.'

sweet Fanny Adams absolutely nothing at all. informal

> ❶ Fanny Adams was the youthful victim in a famous murder case in 1867, her body being mutilated and cut to pieces by the killer. With gruesome black humour, her name came to be used as a slang term for a type of tinned meat or stew recently introduced to the Royal Navy; the current meaning developed early in the 20th century. *Sweet Fanny Adams* is often abbreviated in speech to *sweet FA*, which is understood by many to be a euphemism for *sweet fuck all*.

the sweet spot a particularly fortunate or beneficial circumstance or factor.

> ❶ The *sweet spot* on a tennis racket is the point believed by players to deliver the maximum power to the ball. In 1997 a physicist in Australia claimed to have disproved its existence.

> **1997** *Times* Enjoy the 'sweet spot' now, but don't expect a boom.

sweeten

sweeten the pill: *see* sugar the pill *at* PILL.

sweetness

sweetness and light ❶ social or political harmony. ❷ a reasonable and peaceable person.

> ❶ This is a phrase used by Jonathan Swift in *The Battle of the Books* (1704) and taken up by Matthew Arnold in *Culture and Anarchy* (1869): 'The pursuit of perfection, then, is the pursuit of sweetness and light'.

swim

swim with the tide: *see* go with the tide *at* TIDE.

in the swim involved in or aware of current affairs or events.

swing

get (back) into the swing of things get used to (or return to) being easy and relaxed about an activity or routine you are engaged in. informal

go with a swing (of a party or other event) be lively and enjoyable. informal

in full swing (of an activity) proceeding vigorously.

swing the lead malinger; shirk your duty. British informal

> ℹ This phrase originated in the armed forces and the *lead* in question is probably a sounding lead, a lump of lead attached to a line and slowly lowered to determine the depth of a stretch of water. The connection between this process and shirking one's duty is not entirely clear.

swings and roundabouts a situation in which different actions or options result in no eventual gain or loss. British

> ℹ This expression comes from the proverbial saying *you lose on the swings what you gain on the roundabouts.*

> **1983 Penelope Lively** *Perfect Happiness* I have always reckoned on a fair share of that—swings and roundabouts, rough with smooth.

swollen

have a swollen head be conceited.

sword

beat (or turn) swords into ploughshares devote resources to peaceful rather than aggressive or warlike ends.

> ℹ The reference here is to the biblical image of God's peaceful rule: 'they shall beat their swords into plowshares, and their spears into pruning hooks' (Isaiah 2:4).

cross swords: *see* CROSS.

a double-edged sword: *see* DOUBLE-EDGED.

he who lives by the sword dies by the sword those people who commit violent acts must expect to suffer violence themselves. proverb

> ℹ The phrase was originally used with allusion to an incident in the Garden of Gethsemane. When the men came to arrest Jesus, one of his disciples drew his sword and cut off the ear of 'the servant of the high priest', earning this rebuke from Jesus: 'all they that take the sword shall perish with the sword' (Matthew 26:52). In contemporary versions *sword* is sometimes replaced by *gun, bomb*, etc.

put someone to the sword kill someone, especially in war.

sword of Damocles an imminent danger.

> ℹ When the courtier Damocles described Dionysius I, ruler of Syracuse (405–367 BC), as the happiest of men, Dionysius gave him a graphic demonstration of the fragility of his happiness: he invited Damocles to a banquet, in the middle of which he looked up to see a naked sword suspended over his head by a single hair.

Sydney

Sydney or the bush all or nothing. Australian

syllable

in words of one syllable using very simple language; expressed plainly.

> **1994** *Canal & Riverboat* Bear with me then, if I use words of one syllable now and again, in this series of articles for L drivers.

sync

in (or out of) sync working well (or badly) together; in (or out of) agreement.

> ℹ *Sync* (or *synch*) is an informal abbreviation of *synchronization*.

> **1997** *Sunday Times* The most serious obstacle is the fact that the British economy's cycle is out of sync with Europe.

system

all systems go everything functioning properly, ready to proceed.

get something out of your system get rid of a preoccupation or anxiety. informal

> **1988 Erich Segal** *Doctors* First she let her get the crying out of her system.

Tt

T

to a T (*or* **tee**) exactly; to perfection. informal

> ❶ This origin of this idiom, which dates back to the late 17th century, is uncertain. Attempts to link *T* with either a golfer's tee or a builder's T-square are unconvincing. It is possible that the underlying idea is that of completing the letter T by putting in the cross stroke, but the early 17th-century expression *to a tittle* was identical in meaning, and it is possible that *T* may be an abbreviation of *tittle*.

> **2000** *Post* (*Denver*) He's got Ralphie's same non-charismatic charisma down to a T.

tab

keep tabs (*or* **a tab**) **on** monitor the activities or development of; keep under close observation. informal

> **1978 Mario Puzo** *Fools Die* Jordan knew that Merlyn the Kid kept tabs on everything he did.

pick up the tab pay for something. informal, chiefly North American

table

lay something on the table ❶ make something known so that it can be freely and sensibly discussed. ❷ postpone something indefinitely. chiefly US

turn the tables reverse your position relative to someone else, especially by turning a position of disadvantage into one of advantage.

> ❶ Until the mid 18th century, *tables* was the usual name for the board game backgammon. Early instances of the use of this phrase, dating from the mid 17th century, make it clear that it comes from the practice of turning the board so that a player had to play what had previously been their opponent's position.

under the table drunk to the point of unconsciousness. informal

> **1921 W. Somerset Maugham** *The Trembling of a Leaf* Walker had always been a heavy drinker, he was proud of his capacity to see men half his age under the table.

tack

come down to brass tacks: *see* BRASS.

tackie South African informal

a piece of old tackie an easy task.

> **1979** *Cape Times* Getting the news of the Zimbabwe Rhodesian ceasefire to the … guerillas might well make Paul Revere's famous midnight ride look like a piece of old tackie.

tread tackie drive or accelerate.

> **1989** *Daily Dispatch* By the time they finally trod tackie on the road out, a full week had gone by.

> ❶ *Tackies* are plimsolls. The origin of the word is uncertain, though there may be a connection with the English adjective *tacky*, meaning 'slightly sticky', perhaps referring to the effect of extreme heat on the plimsolls' rubber soles.

tag

tag, rag, and bobtail: *see* **rag, tag, and bobtail** *at* RAG.

tail

chase your (own) tail keep on doing something futile. informal

a piece of tail: *see* **a piece of ass** *at* PIECE.

the tail wags the dog the less important or subsidiary factor or thing dominates a situation; the usual roles are reversed.

> **1997** *Spectator* What is wrong is the almost total lack of artistic leadership, the administrative tail wagging the dog.

with your tail between your legs in a state of dejection or humiliation. informal

with your tail up in a confident or cheerful mood. informal

take

have what it takes have the necessary qualities for success. informal

on the take taking bribes. informal

> **1990 Morley Torgov** *St. Farb's Day* I seen plenty of cops drive Mercedes. The ones that're on the take.

take someone or something apart ❶ dismantle something. ❷ defeat someone or something conclusively. ❸ criticize someone or something severely. informal

take something as read accept something without reading or discussing it. British

take the biscuit (or bun or cake) be the most remarkable. informal

> **1925 P. G. Wodehouse** *Letter* Of all the poisonous, foul, ghastly places, Cannes takes the biscuit with absurd ease.

take it into your head: *see* HEAD.

take it on the chin: *see* CHIN.

take it or leave it said to convey that the offer you have made is not negotiable and that you are indifferent to another's reaction to it.

take someone's name in vain: *see* VAIN.

take no prisoners: *see* PRISONER.

take someone's point: *see* POINT.

take something lying down: *see* LYING.

take stock: *see* STOCK.

take something to heart: *see* HEART.

take to your heels: *see* HEEL.

take someone to the cleaners: *see* CLEANER.

take up the gauntlet: *see* **throw down the gauntlet** *at* GAUNTLET.

taking

for the taking (of a person or thing) ready or available for someone to take advantage of.

> **1994 Jane Hamilton** *A Map of the World* I try to imagine the land for the taking, and what it must have meant to have space for as far as the eye can see.

tale

herein (or therein) lies a tale there is a story connected with this.

> **1998** *Spectator* Now it has decided to fight back and clear its name. And herein lies a tale, however ludicrous.

an old wives' tale: *see* OLD.

talk

chalk and talk: *see* CHALK.

talk big talk confidently or boastfully. informal

talk of the devil: *see* **speak of the devil** *at* DEVIL.

talk a blue streak: *see* BLUE.

talk dirty: *see* DIRTY.

talk a good game talk convincingly yet fail to act effectively. US informal

> **2000** *Sunday Times* There were two types of people in the industry: the consultants who talk a good game but deliver little, and the wide boys and girls who get bums on seats but sacrifice standards.

talk the hind leg off a donkey talk incessantly. British informal

> ❶ In 1808 *talking a horse's hind leg off* was described as an 'old vulgar hyperbole' in *Cobbett's Weekly Political Register*, but the version with *donkey* was current by the mid 19th century. In 1879 Anthony Trollope mentioned *talk the hind legs off a dog* as an Australian variant.

> **1970 Nina Bawden** *The Birds on the Trees* Talk, talk—talk the hind leg off a donkey, that one.

talk nineteen to the dozen talk incessantly. British

> ❶ No convincing reason has been put forward as to why nineteen should have been preferred in this idiom rather than twenty or any other number larger than twelve.

> **1998 Pamela Jooste** *Dance with a Poor Man's Daughter* He hasn't even got his foot in the door before she's talking nineteen to the dozen and hanging round his neck and asking if he's got sweets in his pocket.

talk shop: *see* SHOP.

talk the talk speak fluently or convincingly about something or in a way intended to please or impress others. informal

> **1997** *Beautiful British Columbia* We may not look like true rock jocks yet, but we talk the talk.

talk through your hat talk foolishly, wildly, or ignorantly. informal

> ❶ Vulgar variants of this expression include talking through your *backside*, *arse*, and *ass*.

talk turkey: *see* TURKEY.

tall

a tall order something that is difficult to accomplish.

> **1998** *Times* But the UK economy had to slow down somewhat, and gliding it down to exactly the right spot was a tall order.

a tall poppy a privileged or distinguished person.

> ❶ The Roman tyrant Tarquin was reputed to have struck off the heads of poppies as a gruesomely graphic demonstration of the way in which the important men of a captured city should be treated. In recent years, the term *tall poppy syndrome* has also developed, referring to a tendency to discredit or disparage people who have become rich, famous, or socially prominent.

1991 Lynn Barber *Mostly Men* Journalists on the whole tend to be egalitarian-minded and contemptous of tall poppies, but I prefer the prima donnas.

tandem

in tandem ❶ one behind another.
❷ alongside each other; together.

> ❶ The Latin word *tandem* means 'at length': it was originally used in English as a term for a carriage drawn by two horses harnessed one in front of the other. Sense 1 preserves this late 18th-century sense, but since the mid 20th century the phrase has been commonly used to mean simply 'functioning as a team'.

tangled

a tangled web a complex, difficult, and confusing situation or thing.

> ❶ This phrase comes from Sir Walter Scott's epic poem *Marmion* (1808); 'O what a tangled web we weave, When first we practise to deceive!'

tango

it takes two to tango both parties involved in a situation or argument are equally responsible for it. informal

> ❶ *Takes Two to Tango* was the title of a 1952 song by Al Hoffman and Dick Manning.

1996 *Washington Post* It takes two to tango in this ... business. Both your computer's video card and your monitor must be capable of a given rate to achieve it.

tap

on tap ❶ ready to be poured from a tap.
❷ freely available whenever needed. informal **❸** on schedule to happen or occur. North American informal

taped

have (or get) someone or something taped understand someone or something fully. British informal

> ❶ Early examples of the phrase, dating from the early 20th century, do not make its development clear: the sense could derive either from the action of measuring someone with a tape measure or from that of tying someone or something up with tape (and thereby getting them under control).

2001 John Diamond *C: Because Cowards Get Cancer Too* After a few false starts you've learned how to do sending the meal back, dropping the girlfriend, getting through the job interview, making the marriage proposal: you think you've got it taped.

tapis

on the tapis (of a subject) under consideration or discussion.

> ❶ This expression is a partial translation of the French phrase *sur le tapis*, meaning literally 'on the carpet'. A carpet in this context is a covering for a table rather than a floor, as indeed it is in the English idiom **on the carpet**. It refers to the covering of the council table around which a matter would be debated.

tar

beat (or whale) the tar out of beat or thrash severely. North American informal

tar and feather smear with tar and then cover with feathers as a punishment.

> ❶ This practice was introduced in Britain in 1189, when Richard I decreed that it should be the punishment for members of the navy found guilty of theft. It seems to have been intermittently imposed on other wrongdoers in Britain and has sometimes been inflicted on an unpopular or scandalous individual by a mob.

1981 Anthony Price *Soldier No More* The Russians ... wouldn't have cared less if we'd tarred and feathered Nasser and run him out of Suez on a rail.

tar people with the same brush consider specified people to have the same faults.

Tartar

catch a Tartar: *see* CATCH.

taste

a bad (or bitter or nasty) taste in the (or someone's) mouth a strong feeling of distress or disgust following an experience. informal

a taste of your own medicine: *see* a dose of your own medicine *at* MEDICINE.

taste blood: *see* BLOOD.

tea

not for all the tea in China not at any price; certainly not! informal

tea and sympathy hospitality and consolation offered to a distressed person.

team

a whole team and the dog under the wagon a person of superior ability; an outstandingly gifted or able person. US

tear

shed crocodile tears: *see* CROCODILE.

tear your hair out act with or show extreme desperation. informal

> **1991 Jill Churchill** *A Farewell to Yarns* Someplace people were having nervous breakdowns and tearing their hair out in a desperate effort to please Phyllis.

tear someone off a strip (or tear a strip off someone) rebuke someone angrily. informal

> ❶ This expression was originally RAF slang, first recorded in the 1940s.

tear someone or something to shreds (or pieces) criticize someone or something aggressively. informal

without tears (of a subject) presented so as to be learnt or achieved easily.

> **1991 William Fox** *Willoughby's Phoney War* [They] are going to be given their first lesson this afternoon. Skiing without tears, I hardly think.

teeter

teeter on the brink (or edge) be very close to a difficult or dangerous situation.

> **1997 James Ryan** *Dismantling Mr Doyle* Letting her secret teeter on the brink of becoming public was a game Eve played more and more.

teeth

armed to the teeth: *see* ARMED.

cast something in someone's teeth: *see* CAST.

rare as hen's teeth: *see* HEN.

set someone's teeth on edge cause someone to feel intense discomfort or irritation.

> ❶ This is an expression used in the Bible to describe the unpleasant sensation caused by eating something bitter or sour: 'every man that eateth the sour grape, his teeth shall be set on edge' (Jeremiah 31:30).

> **1997 Kate O'Riordan** *The Boy in the Moon* Julia's voice sustained a quavery note that set Brian's teeth on edge.

sow dragon's teeth: *see* DRAGON.

telegraph

bush telegraph a rapid informal spreading of information or rumour; the network through which this takes place.

> ❶ This expression originated in the late 19th century, referring to the network of informers who kept bushrangers informed

> about the movements of the police in the Australian bush or outback. Compare with **hear something on the grapevine** (*at* GRAPEVINE).

tell

tell it like it is describe the true facts of a situation no matter how unpleasant they may be. informal

tell something a mile off: *see* **see something a mile off** *at* MILE.

tell tales (out of school) gossip about or reveal another person's secrets, wrong-doings, or faults.

> ❶ As telling tales to school authorities is a terrible offence in the eyes of schoolchildren, this expression is often used in the context of *declining* to supply information or gossip.

> **1991 Mark Tully** *No Full Stops in India* Indira trusted me throughout her life, and just because she's dead it's not right that I should break that trust and tell tales about her.

tell that to the marines: *see* MARINES.

tell someone where to get off (or where they get off) angrily rebuke someone. informal

tell someone where to put (or what to do with) something angrily or emphatically reject something. informal

telling

that would be telling that would be divulging confidential information. informal

> **2000 Imogen Edwards-Jones** *My Canapé Hell* 'Are you propositioning me?' I say, attempting to look provocative in my Devonshire home-knit and Angora Dutch cap. 'Now that would be telling,' he smiles.

there's no telling it's impossible to know what has happened or will happen.

tempest

a tempest in a teapot: *see* **a storm in a teacup** *at* STORM.

tempt

tempt fate (or providence) act rashly. informal

tenterhook

on tenterhooks in a state of suspense or agitation because of uncertainty about a future event.

> ℹ A *tenter* is a framework on which fabric can be held taut for drying or other treatment during the manufacturing process; in the past *tenterhooks* were hooks or bent nails fixed in the tenter to hold the fabric in position. The metaphorical use of the phrase for an agitated state of mind dates from the mid 18th century.

term

in no uncertain terms: *see* UNCERTAIN.

on terms ❶ in a state of friendship or equality. **❷** (in sport) level in score or on points.

territory

go (*or* come) with the territory be an unavoidable result of a particular situation.

> ℹ *Territory* is probably used here in its early 20th-century US sense of 'the area in which a sales representative or distributor has the right to operate'.

test

the acid test: *see* ACID.

test the water judge people's feelings or opinions before taking further action.

tether

at the end of your tether: *see* END.

thank

thank your lucky stars feel grateful for your good fortune.

> **1998** *Times* All Alec Stewart can do is thank his lucky stars that his main strike bowler is fit again.

thanks

no thanks to not because of; despite.

> **1993 Carl MacDougall**. *The Lights Below* 'How's your mother?' 'Our mother's fine. No thanks to you. She was worried sick.'

thanks for the buggy ride used as a way of thanking someone for their help. North American dated

> ℹ A *buggy* was a light horse-drawn vehicle for one or two people.

that

and all that (*or* and that) and that sort of thing; and so on. informal

> **1982 Simon Brett** *Murder Unprompted* I know he's the star and all that, but I'm damned if I'm going to be upstaged, even by him.

there

been there, done that used to express past experience of or familiarity with something. informal

> ℹ This is often used as a flippant expression of boredom or world-weariness. A late 20th-century elaboration parodies the blasé tourist's attitude to experience: *been there, done that, got the T-shirt*.

> **1996** *United Church Observer* Having no partner to pick up after me—been there, done that—I tend to, well, let things accumulate.

be there for someone be available to provide support or comfort for someone, especially at a time of adversity.

> **1998** *Spectator* Elegant, determined and intelligent, she was the perfect tycoon's wife: always there for her husband and ready to defend him.

have been there (*or* here) before know all about a situation as a result of previous experience. informal

thereby

thereby hangs a tale used to indicate that there is more to say about something.

> **1948 Christopher Bush** *The Case of the Second Chance* He and Manfrey were Brutus and Cassius respectively in that historic show at the Coliseum and thereby hangs a tale, or rather a piece of scandal.

thick

a bit thick more than you can tolerate; unfair or unreasonable. British informal

> **1991 Alistair Campbell** *Sidewinder* I thought this was a bit thick, and to begin with I tried to defend myself.

give someone (*or* get) a thick ear punish someone (*or* be punished) with a blow, especially on the ear. British informal

have a thick skin: *see* SKIN.

the thick of something the busiest or most crowded part of something.

> **1999 Christopher Brookmyre** *One Fine Day in the Middle of the Night* They'd been in the thick of it, sharing God-knows-what experiences together, from foreplay to gunplay.

thick and fast rapidly and in great numbers.

thick as thieves (of two or more people) very close or friendly; sharing secrets. informal

thick as two (short) planks very stupid. informal

> ℹ Variants of this expression include *thick as a plank* and *thick as a brick*. There is a play on

t

thick in its basic sense 'of relatively great depth from side to side' and its colloquial sense 'stupid'.

thick on the ground: *see* GROUND.

through thick and thin under all circumstances, no matter how difficult.

thin

have a thin skin: *see* **have a thick skin** *at* SKIN.

have a thin time have a wretched or uncomfortable time. British informal

into (or out of) thin air into (or out of) a state of being invisible or nonexistent.

on thin ice: *see* ICE.

thin on the ground: *see* **thick on the ground** *at* GROUND.

the thin end of the wedge an action or procedure of little importance in itself, but which is likely to lead to more serious developments. informal

thin on top balding.

thing

be all things to all men (or people) ❶ please everyone, typically by regularly altering your behaviour or opinions in order to conform to those of others. ❷ be able to be interpreted or used differently by different people to their own satisfaction.

> ❶ This expression probably originated in reference to 1 Corinthians 9:22: 'I am made all things to all men'.

be on to a good thing have found a job or other situation that is pleasant, profitable, or easy. informal

a close (or near) thing a narrow avoidance of something unpleasant.

do the — thing engage in the particular form of behaviour typically associated with someone or something. informal, chiefly North American

> **1999 Tim Lott** *White City Blue* I was going to ask Tony there, oil us all with a few bevvies, and then do the best-man thing.

do your own thing follow your own interests or inclinations regardless of others. informal

have a thing about be obsessed with or prejudiced about. informal

make a thing of ❶ regard as essential. ❷ cause a fuss about. informal

teach (or tell) someone a thing or two

impart useful information or experience. informal

> **1998** *Spectator* A docker of the 1950s . . . a sailor of any previous age could tell you a thing or two about job insecurity.

a thing of shreds and patches: *see* SHRED.

things that go bump in the night ghosts; supernatural beings. informal

> ❶ This expression comes from *The Cornish or West Country Litany*: 'From ghoulies and ghosties and long-leggety beasties And things that go bump in the night, Good Lord deliver us!' The phrase is used as a humorous way of referring to nocturnal disturbances of all sorts.

think

give someone furiously to think give a person cause to think hard.

> ❶ This is a literal translation of the French phrase *donner furieusement à penser*.

have (got) another think coming used to express the speaker's disagreement with or unwillingness to do something suggested by someone else. informal

> **2000** *Sunday Herald* (Glasgow) The accelerating pretender has another think coming if it imagines that it has an easy shot at becoming world number one.

think on your feet react to events quickly and effectively.

think twice consider a course of action carefully before embarking on it.

think the world of: *see* WORLD.

thinking

put on your thinking cap meditate on a problem. informal

third

third time lucky after twice failing to accomplish something, the third attempt may be successful.

> ❶ *Third time lucky* has been proverbial since the mid 19th century; a US variant is *third time is the charm*.

Thomas

a doubting Thomas: *see* DOUBTING.

thorn

no rose without a thorn: *see* ROSE.

a thorn in someone's side (or flesh) a source of continual annoyance or trouble.

> ❶ *A thorn in the side* comes from the biblical book of Numbers (33:55): 'those which ye let remain of them shall be pricks in your eyes, and thorns in your sides, and shall vex you in the land wherein ye dwell'. *A thorn in the flesh* quotes 2 Corinthians 12:7: 'And lest I should be exalted above measure through the abundance of the revelations, there was given to me a thorn in the flesh, the messenger of Satan to buffet me, lest I should be exalted above measure'.

on thorns continuously uneasy, especially in fear of being detected.

thought

a second thought a moment's further consideration; any worry or concern.

thread

hang by a thread be in a highly precarious state.

lose the (or your) thread be unable to follow what someone is saying or remember what you are going to say next.

three

three musketeers three close associates or inseparable friends.

> ❶ *The Three Musketeers* is a translation of *Les Trois Mousquetaires*, the title of a novel by the 19th-century French writer Alexandre Dumas père.

threescore

threescore and ten the age of seventy.

> ❶ In the Bible, threescore and ten amounts to the allotted span of a person's life: 'The days of our age are threescore years and ten' (Psalm 90:10).

thrill

thrills and spills the excitement of dangerous sports or entertainments, especially as experienced by spectators.

throat

be at each other's throats (of people or organizations) quarrel or fight persistently.

> **1990** Rian Malan *My Traitor's Heart* 'It's not only difficult for people outside to understand why blacks are at each others' throats,' he says. 'It's difficult for ourselves.'

cut your own throat bring about your own downfall by your actions.

force (or ram or shove) something down someone's throat force ideas or material

on a person's attention by repeatedly putting them forward.

stick in your throat (or gullet) be difficult or impossible to accept; be a source of continuing annoyance.

> ❶ The literal sense refers to something lodged in your throat which you can neither swallow nor spit out. See also **stick in your craw** (at CRAW) and **stick in your gizzard** (at GIZZARD).

throw

throw cold water on: *see* **pour cold water on** *at* COLD.

throw the baby out with the bathwater: *see* BABY.

throw down the gauntlet: *see* GAUNTLET.

throw dust in someone's eyes mislead someone by misrepresentation or diverting attention from a point.

throw good money after bad: *see* MONEY.

throw your hand in give up; withdraw from a contest.

> ❶ In card games, especially poker, if you *throw your hand in* you retire from the game.

throw in your lot with: *see* LOT.

throw in the towel (or sponge) abandon a struggle; admit defeat.

> ❶ Boxers or their trainers traditionally signal defeat by throwing the towel or sponge used to wipe a contestant's face into the middle of the ring.

throw stones criticize someone or something.

> ❶ This expression is often used with reference to the proverbial saying *those who live in glass houses should not throw stones*, the earliest variant of which is recorded in the mid 17th century.

throw someone to the dogs: *see* DOG.

throw someone to the wolves: *see* WOLF.

throw your weight behind someone use your influence to help support someone. informal

> **2000** *South African Times U.K.* Tony Blair and … Bill Clinton have thrown their weight behind a South African-engineered 'Marshall Plan' to rescue the developing world from deepening poverty.

thumb

be all fingers and thumbs: *see* FINGER.

thumb your nose at show disdain or contempt for. Compare with **cock a snook** (*at* SNOOK).

thumbs up (*or* **down**) an indication of satisfaction or approval (*or* of rejection or failure). informal

> ❶ The thumbs were used to signal approval or disapproval by spectators at a Roman amphitheatre, though they used 'thumbs down' to signify that a beaten gladiator had performed well and should be spared, and 'thumbs up' to call for his death.

twiddle your thumbs: *see* TWIDDLE.

under someone's thumb completely under someone's influence or control.

thunder

steal someone's thunder: *see* STEAL.

tick

on tick on credit. informal

> ❶ *Tick* is an abbreviation of *ticket*, a note recording money or goods received on credit.

tight as a tick: *see* TIGHT.

what makes someone tick what motivates someone. informal

ticket

be tickets be the end. South African informal

have tickets on yourself be excessively vain or proud of yourself. Australian informal

punch your ticket deliberately undertake particular assignments that are likely to lead to promotion at work. US informal

split the ticket: *see* SPLIT.

work your ticket contrive to obtain your discharge from prison or the army.

write your (own) ticket dictate your own terms. North American informal

tickey

on a tickey in a very small area. South African

> ❶ In the period before South African coinage was decimalized, a *tickey* was a very small silver coin worth three pennies.

tickled

be tickled pink (*or* **to death**) be extremely amused or pleased. informal

> 1992 **Guy Vanderhaeghe** *Things As They Are* She made a big show of not being taken in by him, but I could see that all six feet... of her was tickled pink by his attentions.

tide

go (*or* **swim**) **with** (*or* **against**) **the tide** act in accordance with (*or* against) the prevailing opinion or tendency.

tie

tie someone hand and foot: *see* **bind someone hand and foot** *at* HAND.

the old school tie: *see* OLD.

tie the knot: *see* KNOT.

tie one on get drunk. North American informal

tie yourself in knots: *see* KNOT.

tied

fit to be tied: *see* FIT.

tiger

have a tiger by the tail have embarked on a course of action which proves unexpectedly difficult but which cannot easily or safely be abandoned.

> ❶ An alternative way of referring to the same predicament is *ride a tiger*, which alludes to the Chinese saying *he who rides a tiger cannot dismount*. A similar difficulty confronts those who **have a wolf by the ears** (*see* WOLF).

a tiger in your tank energy, spirit, or animation.

> ❶ This expression originated as a 1960s advertising slogan for Esso petrol: 'Put a tiger in your tank'.

tight

run a tight ship be very strict in managing an organization or operation.

tight as a tick extremely drunk. informal

> ❶ The simile *as full as a tick* occurs in a late 17th-century proverb collection, referring to the way in which the blood-sucking insects swell as they gorge themselves. In the modern expression, there is a play on *tight* as an informal synonym for 'drunk' and its literal meaning 'stretched taut', like a tick satiated with blood.

a tight corner (*or* **spot** *or* **place**) a difficult situation.

> 1994 *Interzone* The temptation to also invent some kind of magical McGuffin to get his hero out of a tight corner is something he works hard to avoid.

tighten

tighten your belt: *see* BELT.

tighten the screw: *see* SCREW.

tile

on the tiles away from home having a wild or enjoyable time and not returning until late in the evening or early in the morning. informal, chiefly British

> ❶ The image here is of a cat out on the rooftops at night. The expression has been in use since the late 19th century.

till

have (*or* with) your fingers (*or* hand) in the till stealing from your employer. Compare with **with your hand in the cookie jar** (*at* COOKIE).

tilt

(at) full tilt with maximum energy or force; at top speed.

> **1912 Edith Wharton** *Letter* Just after we left Modena a crazy coachman drove full tilt out of a side road.

tilt at windmills attack imaginary enemies or evils.

> ❶ In Cervantes' 17th-century mock-chivalric novel *Don Quixote*, the eponymous hero attacked windmills in the deluded belief that they were giants.

time

ahead of your (*or* its) time: *see* AHEAD.

give someone the time of day be pleasantly polite or friendly to someone.

> **1999 Salman Rushdie** *The Ground Beneath Her Feet* You can greet her courteously but she won't give you the time of day, you can speak to her nice as pie but she won't act polite.

in the nick of time: *see* NICK.

know the time of day be well informed about something.

pass the time of day exchange a greeting or casual remarks.

take time by the forelock: *see* FORELOCK.

time and tide wait for no man if you don't make use of a favourable opportunity, you may never get the same chance again. proverb

> ❶ Although the *tide* in this phrase is now usually understood to mean 'the tide of the sea', it was originally just another way of saying 'time', used for alliterative effect.

time immemorial used to refer to a point of time so long ago that people have no knowledge or memory of it.

> ❶ In legal terms in Britain, *time immemorial* refers to the time up to the beginning of the reign of Richard I in 1189. A variant of the phrase is *time out of mind*.

time is money time is a valuable resource, therefore it's better to do things as quickly as possible. proverb

> ❶ The present form of the expression seems to originate in a speech made by Benjamin Franklin in 1748, but the sentiment is much older. The saying 'the most costly outlay is time' is attributed to the 5th-century BC Athenian orator and politician Antiphon.

time was there was a time.

> **1998** *Times* Time was when venture capital was shunned by self-respecting, ambitious corporate financiers…No longer.

(only) time will tell the truth or correctness of something will only be established at some time in the future.

tin

have a tin ear be tone-deaf.

little tin god: *see* GOD.

put the tin lid on: *see* **put the lid on** *at* LID.

tinker

not give (*or* care) a tinker's curse (*or* cuss *or* damn) not care at all. informal

> ❶ In former times, tinkers (itinerant menders of pots, pans, and other metal utensils) had a reputation for using bad language. The expression is often shortened to *not give a tinker's*.

> **1984 Patrick O'Brian** *The Far Side of the World* When I was a squeaker nobody gave a tinker's curse whether my daily workings were right or wrong.

tip

be on the tip of your tongue ❶ be almost but not quite able to bring a particular word or name to mind. ❷ be about to utter a comment or question but then think better of it.

> **1977 Bernard MacLaverty** *Between Two Shores* It was on the tip of his tongue to ask her but he didn't have the courage.

tip your hand (*or* mitt) reveal your intentions inadvertently. US informal

> ❶ This expression is the opposite of **keep your cards close to your chest** (*see* CARD).

1966 Martin Woodhouse *Tree Frog* We couldn't very well oppose it without tipping our hand.

tip your hat (or **cap)** raise or touch your hat or cap as a way of greeting or acknowledging someone.

tip someone off give someone information about something, typically in a discreet or confidential way. informal

the tip of an iceberg: *see* ICEBERG.

tip (or **turn) the scales (**or **balance)** (of a circumstance or event) be the deciding factor; make the critical difference.

tip someone the wink give someone private information; secretly warn someone of something. British informal

tired

tired and emotional drunk.

> ❶ This is a humorous euphemism, used originally in newspapers in contexts where the word *drunk* would lay the publication open to a libel charge. It is particularly associated with the British satirical magazine *Private Eye*.

tit

tit for tat a situation in which an injury or insult is given in return or retaliation.

toast

be toast be or be likely to become finished, defunct, or dead. informal, chiefly North American

1998 *Times* A new star has entered the financial firmament. Look to your laurels, George Soros, Warren Buffett, you're toast.

have someone on toast be in a position to deal with someone as you wish. British informal

1993 *Esquire* The more he thought, the more I knew I had him on toast.

tod

on your tod on your own; alone. British informal

> ❶ In rhyming slang, *on your Tod Sloan* means 'on your own'. The Tod Sloan in question was a famous American jockey who made his name in horse racing in the 1890s.

toe

dig in your toes: *see* **dig in your heels** *at* DIG.

make someone's toes curl bring about an extreme reaction in someone, either of pleasure or disgust. informal

1984 Paul Prudhomme *Louisiana Kitchen* This is so good it'll make your toes curl!

on your toes ready for any eventuality.

1921 John Dos Passos *Three Soldiers* If he just watched out and kept on his toes, he'd be sure to get it.

a toe in the door a (first) chance of ultimately achieving what you want; a position from which further progress is possible. informal

> ❶ The image here is of placing your foot in a doorway in such a way as to prevent the door being closed in your face.

toe the line accept the authority, principles, or policies of a particular group, especially under pressure.

> ❶ Competitors in a race *toe the line* by placing their toes on the starting line.

1998 *Times* An insider suggests . . . that the said minister is . . . on the skids. The minister smarts, and toes the line.

turn up your toes die. informal

> ❶ This originated as a mid 19th-century expression, a more elaborate version being *turn your toes up to the daisies*.

toffee

not be able to do something for toffee be totally incompetent at doing something. British informal

2000 *Times* Wordsworth himself couldn't spell for toffee, and his punctuation was extraordinarily bad.

token

by the same token in the same way; for the same reason.

1975 Frederick Exley *Pages from a Cold Island* The student could ask anything he chose, and by the same token Wilson could if he elected choose not to answer.

Tom

Tom, Dick, and Harry used to refer to ordinary people in general.

> ❶ This expression is first recorded in an 18th-century song: 'Farewell, Tom, Dick, and Harry. Farewell, Moll, Nell, and Sue'. It is generally used in mildly derogatory contexts (*he didn't want every Tom, Dick, and Harry knowing their business*) to suggest a large number of ordinary or undistinguished people.

Tom Tiddler's ground a place where money or profit is readily made.

> ❶ *Tom Tiddler's ground* was the name of a children's game in which one of the players, named Tom Tiddler, marked out their

territory by drawing a line on the ground. The other players ran over this line calling out 'We're on Tom Tiddler's ground, picking up gold and silver'. They were then chased by Tom Tiddler and the first (or, sometimes, the last) to be caught took his or her place.

tomorrow

as if there was (or as though there were) no tomorrow with no regard for the future consequences.

> **1980** *Guardian Weekly* Oil supplies that Americans at home continue to consume as though there were no tomorrow.

tomorrow is another day the future will bring fresh opportunities.

> ⓘ This phrase was in use as long ago as the early 16th century, in the form *tomorrow is a new day*.

tongue

the gift of tongues the power of speaking in unknown languages, regarded as one of the gifts of the Holy Spirit.

> ⓘ When the disciples of Jesus were filled with the Holy Spirit after Pentecost (Acts 2:1–4), the *gift of tongues* was one of the ways in which this phenomenon manifested itself; compare with **speak in tongues** (*at* SPEAK).

have a silver tongue: *see* SILVER.

someone's tongue is hanging out someone is very eager for something, especially a drink.

(with) tongue in cheek speaking or writing in an ironic or insincere way.

> ⓘ This expression originated in the fuller form *put* or *thrust your tongue in your cheek*, meaning 'speak insincerely'. At one time, putting your tongue in your cheek could also be a gesture of contempt, but that shade of meaning has disappeared from the modern idiom.

with forked tongue: *see* FORKED.

tooth

fight tooth and nail fight very fiercely.

top

from top to bottom completely; thoroughly.

off the top of your head: *see* HEAD.

on top of the world happy and elated. informal

over the top to an excessive or exaggerated degree, in particular so as to go beyond reasonable or acceptable limits.

> ⓘ The phrase *go over the top* originated in the First World War, when it referred to troops in the trenches charging over the parapets to attack the enemy. In modern use *over the top* is often abbreviated to *OTT*.

top and tail ❶ remove the top and bottom of a fruit or vegetable while preparing it as food. ❷ wash the face and bottom of a baby or small child. British

top the bill: *see* BILL.

top dollar a very high price. North American informal

> **2000** *Ralph* Klein has invested millions in building a non-conformist image … an image that has enabled the company to charge top dollar.

the top of the tree the highest level of a profession or career.

torch

carry a torch for feel (especially unrequited) love for.

> **1996** *TV Times* A dentist carrying a torch for the local 'strawberry blonde' wonders if he married the right woman.

hand on (or pass) the torch pass on a tradition, especially one of learning or enlightenment.

> ⓘ The image here is that of the runners in a relay passing on the torch to each other, as was the custom in the ancient Greek Olympic Games. The tradition of the torch relay is preserved as a prelude to the modern Olympics, with a team of runners carrying the Olympic torch vast distances across various countries until the site of the Games is reached.

put to the torch (or put a torch to) destroy by burning.

toss

give (or care) a toss care at all. British informal

> **1998** *Country Life* I have swum in the Dart only a few yards from a mink, and the mink has not given a toss.

toss your cookies vomit. North American informal

touch

lose your touch not show your customary skill.

> **1991** *Times* The guv'nor is a former pork butcher who has clearly not lost his touch.

the Midas touch: *see* MIDAS.

a soft (*or* easy) touch someone who is easily manipulated; a person or task easily handled. informal

> ❶ A *touch* was mid 19th-century criminal slang for the act of getting money from a person, either by pickpocketing or by persuasion. *Touch* was later extended to refer to the person targeted in this way, and a *soft touch* was specifically a person from whom money could easily be obtained.

> **1998** *Times* Henman can be something of a soft touch. For every leading player who touts his potential, two from the basement would relish his name in the draw.

touch base: *see* BASE.

touch bottom ❶ reach the bottom of water with your feet. ❷ be at the lowest or worst point. ❸ be in possession of the full facts. British

a touch of the sun a slight attack of sunstroke.

touch wood: *see* WOOD.

would not touch someone or something with a bargepole: *see* BARGEPOLE.

touchpaper

light the touchpaper: *see* light a fuse *at* LIGHT.

tough

tough as old boots very sturdy or resilient.

> ❶ Leather, of which boots are traditionally made, is notably strong and resistant to wear and tear. As *tough as leather* was in fact the earliest version of this phrase, although it has now been superseded by the current form.

> **1967** *Listener* This is no sweet old dolly ... She is tough as old boots, working for a living.

tough it out endure a period of difficult conditions. informal

> **1998** *Cosmopolitan* Hang in there and tough it out. If you don't, you might be left with permanent fears about starting in new jobs, and that will stifle your career.

towel

throw in the towel: *see* THROW.

tower

tower of strength: *see* STRENGTH.

town

go to town do something thoroughly or extravagantly, with a great deal of energy and enthusiasm. informal

> **1996** *Dougie Brimson & Eddie Brimson Everywhere We Go: Behind the Matchday Madness* When there is a major incident, the press still go to town and we are bombarded with graphic images of bloody faces.

on the town enjoying the entertainments, especially the nightlife, of a city or town. informal

paint the town red: *see* PAINT.

town and gown non-members and members of a university in a particular place.

> ❶ The *gown* is the academic dress worn by university members, now required only on ceremonial or formal occasions. The distinction between *town and gown* was made in these specific terms in early 19th-century Oxford and Cambridge, but the traditional hostility between the native inhabitants of the two cities and the incoming students has been a long-standing phenomenon, as is evidenced by the St Scholastica's Day riot in Oxford in 1354.

trace

kick over the traces: *see* KICK.

track

cover your tracks: *see* COVER.

jump the track: *see* JUMP.

make tracks (for) leave (for a place). informal

> **1984** *David Brin Practice Effect* We have another big climb ahead of us and another pass to get through. Let's make tracks.

off the beaten track: *see* BEATEN.

the wrong side of the tracks a poor or less prestigious part of town. informal

> ❶ The expression, American in origin, comes from the idea of a town divided by a railroad track. In 1929, Thorne Smith wrote 'In most commuting towns ... there are always two sides of which the tracks serve as a line of demarcation. There is the right side and the wrong side. Translated into terms of modern American idealism, this means, the rich side and the side that hopes to be rich.'

> **1977** *Listener* Eva Duarte Peron ... came from the wrong side of the tracks.

traffic

as much as the traffic will bear as much as the trade or market will tolerate; as much as is economically viable.

tragedy

tragedy of the commons the inevitable damage done to a limited resource when too many people try to avail themselves of it.

> ❶ This phrase arose from the ancient English custom by which villagers were allowed to graze their animals on common land; thoughtless or greedy people put too many animals on the commons, impoverishing the land and thereby the whole community.

1998 *New Scientist* All Web users are modern players in an old social dilemma known as the tragedy of the commons. By blindly acting in their own interests they are spoiling a valuable common resource.

trail

blaze a trail: *see* BLAZE.

trail (or drag) your coat deliberately provoke a quarrel or fight.

> ❶ If you trail your coat behind you someone is likely to step on it, either intentionally or unintentionally, so enabling you to pick a fight. This behaviour was traditionally associated with Irishmen at Donnybrook Fair, an annual fair once held in what is now a suburb of Dublin. Charlotte M. Yonge, in the novel *Womankind* (1877), alludes to this association: 'Party spirit is equally ready to give offence and to watch for it. It will trail its coat like the Irishman in the fair.'

1980 James Ditton *Copley's Hunch* I was trailing my coat . . . Trying to get the Luftwaffe to come up and fight.

transom

over the transom offered or sent without prior agreement; unsolicited. US informal

> ❶ A *transom* is a crossbar set above a door or window, and the word can also be used, especially in American English, as a term for a small window set above this crossbar. In former times, before the advent of air conditioning, many offices would leave these windows open for the purposes of ventilation, thereby allowing an aspiring author to take their manuscript to an editor's office and slip it through the open window to land on the floor inside. So, a manuscript that arrived *over the transom* was one that was unexpected. The phrase is still often used in publishing contexts, although it is no longer confined to them.

1976 Piers Anthony *But What of Earth?* Editors claim to be deluged with appallingly bad material 'over the transom' from unagented writers.

tread

tread (or step) on someone's toes offend someone, especially by encroaching on their privileges.

tread water ❶ maintain an upright position in the water by moving the feet with a walking movement and the hands with a downward circular motion. ❷ fail to advance or make progress.

> ❷ **1996** *Financial Post* The NAPM index . . . has been treading water since the spring, and that is making a lot of people nervous.

tread on air: *see* **walk on air** *at* AIR.

treat

— a treat used to indicate that someone or something does something specified very well or satisfactorily. British informal

> **1988 Ray Pickernell** *Yanto's Summer* A flared cream pleated skirt that complemented those long perfect brown legs, and a powder blue tee shirt that matched her eyes a treat.

tree

grow on trees: *see* GROW.

out of your tree completely stupid; mad. informal

up a tree in a difficult situation without escape; cornered. informal, chiefly North American

trial

trial and error the process of experimenting with various methods of doing something until you find the most successful.

trial by television (or the media) discussion of a case or controversy on television or in the media involving or implying accusations against a particular person.

trice

in a trice in a moment; very quickly.

> ❶ In late Middle English, *at a trice* meant 'at one pull or tug', and it soon developed the figurative meaning of 'in a moment, immediately'. By the late 17th century the original form of the expression had given way to the more familiar *in a trice*. *Trice* itself comes from a Middle Dutch verb meaning 'hoist'.

trick

a bag of tricks: *see* BAG.

a box of tricks: *see* BOX.

do the trick achieve the required result. informal

> **1990 Niki Hill** *Death Grows On You* I figured a box of candy would do the trick, would bring some colour back.

t

every trick in the book every available method of achieving what you want. informal

not miss a trick: *see* MISS.

the oldest trick in the book a ruse so hackneyed that it should no longer deceive anyone.

a trick worth two of that a much better plan or expedient. informal

> ❶ This phrase is from Shakespeare's *Henry the Fourth, Part 1*: 'I know a trick worth two of that i' faith'.

tricks of the trade special ingenious techniques used in a profession or craft, especially those that are little known by outsiders.

turn a trick (of a prostitute) have a session with a client. informal

up to your (old) tricks misbehaving in a characteristic way. informal

tried

tried and true proved effective or reliable by experience.

> 1967 *Listener* Miss Aukin had the good sense to use the tried and true concealment gambit by which eventually two young officers, bent on cuckolding a greengrocer, were compelled to hide in the same grandfather clock.

trim

in trim slim and healthy.

trim your sails make changes to suit your new circumstances.

> ❶ Literally, *trim a sail* means 'adjust the sail of a boat to take advantage of the wind'.

trip

trip the light fantastic dance. humorous

> ❶ This expression comes from the invitation to dance in John Milton's poem 'L'Allegro' (1645): 'Come, and trip it as ye go On the light fantastic toe'.

trivet

right as a trivet perfectly all right; in good health. British informal

> ❶ A trivet is an iron tripod placed over a fire for a cooking pot or kettle to stand on. It is used in this expression to represent firmness and steadiness.

Trojan

work like a Trojan work extremely hard.

> 1974 **Winifred Foley** *A Child in the Forest* She put me to clean out all the fowls' cotes, and I worked at it like a Trojan.

a Trojan horse ❶ a person or device intended to undermine an enemy or bring about their downfall. ❷ a program designed to breach the security of a computer system, especially by ostensibly functioning as part of a legitimate program, in order to erase, corrupt, or remove data.

> ❶ In Greek mythology, the Trojan horse was a huge hollow wooden statue of a horse in which Greek soldiers concealed themselves in order secretly to enter and capture the city of Troy, an action which brought the ten-year siege of the city to an end.

trolley

off your trolley crazy. informal

> ❶ The *trolley* in this case is a pulley running on an overhead track that transmits power from the track to drive a tram; the idea is similar to that in **go off the rails** (*see* RAIL).

> 1983 **Nathaniel Richard Nash** *The Young and Fair* If you suspect Patty, you're off your trolley.

trooper

lie like a trooper: *see* LIE.

swear like a trooper: *see* SWEAR.

trot

on the trot ❶ in succession. ❷ continually busy. British informal

troth

plight your troth: *see* PLIGHT.

trouble

meet trouble halfway distress yourself unnecessarily about what may happen.

trousers

catch someone with their trousers down: *see* **catch someone with their pants down** *at* PANTS.

wear the trousers be the dominant partner in a marriage or the dominant person in a household. informal

trout

old trout an unattractive or bad-tempered old woman. informal

1972 Victor Canning. *The Rainbird Pattern* She wasn't such a bad old trout. For all her money and position, life hadn't been all good to her.

trowel

lay something on with a trowel: *see* **lay something on thick** *at* LAY.

truck

have (*or* want) no truck with ❶ avoid dealing or being associated with. ❷ be unsympathetic or opposed to.

> ❶ The earliest sense of *truck* was 'trading by the exchange of commodities' (from French *troquer*, meaning 'barter'), from which developed the sense 'communication or dealings'.

true

out of true (*or* the true) not in the correct or exact shape.

> **1984 Jonathan Gash** *The Gondola Scam* They all look scarily out of true, and I do mean a terrible angle. Pisa's got one sloper.

true as Bob (*or* God) absolutely true. South African informal

trumpet

blow your own trumpet talk openly and boastfully about your achievements.

> **1998** *Spectator* I only mention this to blow my own trumpet . . . it was a source of great pride to be reinstated at the specific behest of Britain's most distinguished black radical journalist.

trump

come (*or* turn) up trumps ❶ (of a person or situation) have a better performance or outcome than expected. ❷ (of a person) be especially generous or helpful. informal, chiefly British

> ❶ In bridge, whist, and similar card games, trumps are cards of the suit that has been chosen to rank above the other suits. The word *trump* is an alteration of *triumph*, which was once used in card games in the same sense.

trust

not trust someone as far as you can throw them not trust or hardly trust a particular person at all. informal

truth

economical with the truth: *see* ECONOMICAL.

gospel truth: *see* GOSPEL.

naked truth: *see* NAKED.

the truth, the whole truth, and nothing but the truth the full and unvarnished truth.

> ❶ These words are part of the statement sworn by witnesses giving evidence in court. They are often used informally to emphasize the absolute veracity of a statement.

try

try conclusions with: *see* CONCLUSION.

try a fall with contend with.

try something for size try out or test something for suitability.

try your hand see how skilful you are, especially at the first attempt.

> **1994 John Barth** *Once Upon a Time* Since such dreaminess appeared to be my nature . . . why didn't I try my hand at writing fiction?

tube

go down the tube (*or* tubes) be completely lost or wasted; fail utterly. informal

tug

tug of love a dispute over the custody of a child. British informal

tune

call the tune: *see* **call the shots** *at* CALL.

change your tune: *see* CHANGE.

there's many a good tune played on an old fiddle someone's abilities do not depend on their age. proverb

> **1997** *Times* Old Star remained as cool and collected as if he had been training for this day for months. Which only goes to show that there is many a good tune played on an old fiddle.

to the tune of amounting to or involving the considerable sum of. informal

> **1996** *LSE Magazine* The average student also leaves in debt to the tune of several thousand pounds to the bank or the Student Loan Company.

tuned

tuned in aware of or able to understand something. informal

> **1994** *Today's Parent* It is more important to be tuned in to your child's needs than to be the boss.

tunnel

light at the end of the tunnel: *see* LIGHT.

turkey

go cold turkey: see COLD.

like turkeys voting for Christmas used to suggest that a particular action or decision is hopelessly self-defeating. informal

talk turkey talk frankly and straight-forwardly; get down to business. North American informal

> ❶ This phrase was first recorded in the mid 19th century, when it generally had the rather different sense of 'say pleasant things or talk politely'. Although several theories have been put forward, its origins are not clear.

turn

Buggins's turn appointment in rotation rather than by merit.

> ❶ *Buggins* is used here to represent a typical or generic surname.

not turn a hair: see HAIR.

one good turn deserves another if someone does you a favour, you should take the chance to repay it.

to a turn to exactly the right degree (used especially in relation to cooking).
> **1931** *Good Housekeeping* The meal began with a magnificent bass, broiled to a turn over heart-wood coals.

turn cat in pan: see CAT.

turn the corner pass the critical point and start to improve.

turn your hand to: see HAND.

turn someone's head: see HEAD.

turn an honest penny: see HONEST.

turn in your grave: see GRAVE.

turn on your heel: see HEEL.

turn the other cheek: see CHEEK.

turn over a new leaf: see LEAF.

turn the scales: see SCALE.

turn the tables: see TABLE.

turn to ashes: see ASH.

turn a trick: see TRICK.

turn turtle: see TURTLE.

turn up your nose: see NOSE.

turn-up

a turn-up for the book a completely unexpected event or occurrence; a surprise.

> ❶ In this expression, *turn-up* refers to the turning up or over of a particular card in a game, while the *book* in question is one kept by a bookie to record bets made on a race.

turtle

turn turtle turn upside down.

> ❶ If a turtle is flipped over on to its back, it becomes helpless and unable to move. The phrase has long been used figuratively of inanimate objects, especially boats, that have turned upside down or overturned.

> **1990** Stephen King *The Stand* His tractor turned turtle on him and killed him.

twain

never the twain shall meet two people or things are too different to exist alongside or understand each other.

> ❶ This phrase comes from Rudyard Kipling's poem 'The Ballad of East and West' (1892): 'Oh, East is East and West is West, and never the twain shall meet'.

twelve

twelve good men and true a jury. dated

> ❶ A jury in a court of law was traditionally composed of twelve men. Nowadays, of course, women also sit on juries, and so this phrase is falling out of use.

twice

be twice the man or woman that someone is be much better or stronger than someone.

think twice: see THINK.

twiddle

twiddle your thumbs be bored or idle because you have nothing to do.

twinkling

in a twinkling (*or* **the twinkling of an eye**) in an instant; very quickly.

> ❶ A *twinkling* is the time taken to wink or blink an eye. The phrase can be traced back to 1 Corinthians 15:52: 'In a moment, in a twinkling of an eye, at the last trump: for the trumpet shall sound, and the dead shall be raised incorruptible, and we shall be changed', and it has been in figurative sense since medieval times.

twist

round the twist: see **round the bend** *at* BEND.

twist someone's arm persuade someone to do something that they are or are thought to be reluctant to do. informal

twist in the wind be left in a state of suspense or uncertainty.

twist someone round your little finger: *see* FINGER.

twist the lion's tail provoke the resentment of the British. US

two

for two pins: *see* PIN.

in two shakes: *see* SHAKE.

it takes two to tango: *see* TANGO.

put two and two together draw an obvious conclusion from what is known or evident.

> ❶ An extension of this phrase is *put two and two together and make five*, meaning 'draw a plausible but incorrect conclusion from what is known or evident'.

that makes two of us you are in the same position or hold the same opinion as the previous speaker.

two can play at that game used to assert that one person's bad behaviour can be copied to that person's disadvantage.

two heads are better than one it's helpful to have the advice or opinion of a second person. proverb

> **1994 James Kelman** *How Late It Was, How Late* Cause it's hard to do it yerself Keith, two heads are better than one.

two a penny: *see* PENNY.

two-edged

a two-edged sword: *see* **a double-edged sword** *at* DOUBLE-EDGED.

twopenn'orth

add (*or* put in) your twopenn'orth contribute your opinion. informal

> ❶ The literal meaning of *twopenn'orth* is 'an amount of something that is worth or costs two pence'; by extension it can also be used to mean 'a small or insignificant amount of something'.

two-way

two-way street a situation or relationship between two people or groups in which action is required from both parties; something that works both ways.

Uu

ugly

an ugly duckling a young person who turns out to be beautiful or talented against all expectations.

> **ⓘ** *The Ugly Duckling* is a fairy tale by Hans Christian Andersen in which the 'ugly duckling', mocked and jeered at by his peers, eventually develops into a beautiful swan.

uncertain

in no uncertain terms clearly and forcefully.

> **1991** Kaye Gibbons *A Cure for Dreams* My mother got the doctor back out to our house and told him in no uncertain terms to do what he was paid to do.

uncle

cry (or say or yell) uncle surrender or admit defeat. North American informal

> **1989** Guy Vanderhaeghe *Homesick* Beat him six ways to Sunday and he still would never cry uncle or allow that there was an outside chance of his ever being wrong.

Uncle Tom Cobley (or Cobleigh) and all used to denote a long list of people. British informal

> **ⓘ** *Uncle Tom Cobley* is the last of a long list of men enumerated in the ballad 'Widdicombe Fair', which dates from around 1800.

> **1966** *Guardian* It seems clear that a compromise, half-way solution had equally been ruled out by Government, Opposition, economists, press, TV, Uncle Tom Cobleigh and all.

unco

the unco guid strictly religious and moralistic people. Scottish, chiefly derogatory

> **ⓘ** *Unco*, a Scottish alteration of *uncouth*, means 'remarkably or extremely', while *guid* is the Scottish form of *good*. The expression comes from Robert Burns's *Address to the Unco Guid, or the Rigidly Righteous* (1787), and it generally carries an implicit charge of hypocrisy.

under

under age not yet adult according to the law.

university

the university of life the experience of life regarded as a means of instruction.

unpleasantness

the late unpleasantness the war that took place recently.

> **ⓘ** This phrase was originally used of the American Civil War (1861–5).

untracked

get untracked get into your stride or find your winning form, especially in sporting contexts. US

unwashed

the (great) unwashed the mass or multitude of ordinary people. derogatory

> **1997** *Spectator* Early piers tried to be rather socially exclusive, but the need to maintain revenue soon opened the gates to the great unwashed.

up

it is all up with it is the end or there is no hope for someone or something. informal

> **2002** *Guardian* The underlying problem is not the science itself, but the fact that the science is telling politicians something they are desperate not to hear: that it's all up with our current model of gung-ho globalisation.

be up on be well informed about a matter or subject.

on the up and up ❶ steadily improving. informal ❷ honest or sincere. informal, chiefly North American

something is up something unusual or undesirable is afoot or happening. informal

> **1994** Marianne Williamson *Illuminata* It feels as though something is up, as though something significant and big is about to happen.

up against it facing some serious but unspecified difficulty. informal

up and about (or doing) having risen from bed; active.

up and running taking place; active.

> **1998** *New Scientist* The arms race may be up and running again.

up the ante: *see* ANTE.

up for it ready to take part in a particular activity. informal

> **2003** *Observer* If the chance ever arose to do my singing and play football for Southampton, I'd be well up for it.

up hill and down dale all over the place.

> **2001** *Observer* Why get ourselves bogged down with trials which may last many months and see our staff cross-examined up hill and down dale as defence counsel play the game of hunt the informant?

up in arms: *see* ARM.

up the spout: *see* SPOUT.

up sticks: *see* STICK.

up to the mark: *see* MARK.

up to your tricks: *see* TRICK.

upgrade

on the upgrade improving or progressing.

upper

have (or gain) the upper hand have (or gain) advantage or control over someone or something.

on your uppers extremely short of money. informal

> ❶ In this expression, worn-out shoes are taken as an indication of someone's poverty; the *upper* is the part of a shoe above the sole, which is all that is left after the sole has been worn away.

the upper crust the aristocracy and upper classes. informal

> ❶ In Anne Elizabeth Baker's *Glossary of Northamptonshire Words and Phrases* (1854) 'Mrs Upper Crust' is explained as the nickname for 'any female who assumes unauthorized superiority'. The term was also current in informal American speech in the mid 19th century. The French word *gratin* has a similar pair of literal and metaphorical senses, being literally 'a crust of crumbs and cheese on top of a cooked dish' and metaphorically 'the highest class of society'.

upset

upset the apple cart: *see* APPLE CART.

uptake

be quick (or slow) on the uptake be quick (or slow) to understand something. informal

upwardly

upwardly mobile: *see* **downwardly mobile** *at* MOBILE.

Vv

vain

take someone's name in vain use someone's name in a way that shows a lack of respect.

> ❶ The third of the biblical Ten Commandments is: 'Thou shalt not take the name of the Lord thy God in vain' (Exodus 20:7).

vale

vale of tears the world regarded as a scene of trouble or sorrow. literary

> ❶ This phrase dates from the mid 16th century; earlier variants included *vale of trouble*, *vale of weeping*, and *vale of woe*.

> **1997** *Shetland Times* Then by God's grace we'll meet again, Beyond this vale of tears.

the vale of years the declining years of a person's life; old age.

> ❶ This expression comes from Shakespeare's *Othello*: 'for I am declin'd into the vale of yeares'.

vanishing

do a vanishing act: *see* **do a disappearing act** *at* DISAPPEARING.

variety

variety is the spice of life new and exciting experiences make life more interesting.

> ❶ This proverbial expression comes from William Cowper's poem 'The Task' (1785): 'Variety's the very spice of life, That gives it all its flavour'.

veil

beyond the veil in a mysterious or hidden place or state, especially the unknown state of existence after death.

> ❶ The phrase was originally a figurative reference to the veil which concealed the innermost sanctuary of the Temple in Jerusalem; it was later taken as referring to the mysterious division between the next world and this.

draw a veil over avoid discussing or calling attention to something, especially because it is embarrassing or unpleasant.

take the veil become a nun.

vengeance

with a vengeance in a higher degree than was expected or desired; in the fullest sense.

vent

vent your spleen give free expression to your anger or displeasure.

> **2003** *Guardian* Woodgate's clumsy challenge on the striker was not contested, though the visitors wasted little time in venting spleen at both the culpable Danish midfielder and, erroneously, the young pretender.

vest

keep your cards close to your vest: *see* **keep your cards close to your chest** *at* CARD.

victory

Pyrrhic victory: *see* PYRRHIC.

view

take a dim (or poor) view of regard someone or something with disapproval.

> **1996** C. J. Stone *Fierce Dancing* He says that...the Home Office...take a dim view of lifers talking to the press.

village

a Potemkin village: *see* POTEMKIN.

villain

the villain of the piece the main culprit.

> **1928** P. G. Wodehouse *Money for Nothing* I'm sure you're on the right track. This bird Twist is the villain of the piece.

viper

a viper in your bosom a person you have helped but who behaves treacherously towards you.

> ❶ The phrase comes from one of Aesop's fables, in which a viper reared in a person's bosom eventually bites its nurturer. The idea is also found in Latin (*in sinu viperam habere*) and the expression appears in various forms in English from the late 16th century.

Virginia

make a Virginia fence walk crookedly because you are drunk. US

> ❶ A *Virginia fence* is a fence made of split rails or poles joined in a zigzag pattern with their ends crossing.

virtue

make a virtue of necessity derive some credit or benefit from an unwelcome obligation.

> ❶ This is a concept found in Latin in the writings of St Jerome: *facis de necessitate virtutem* 'you make a virtue of necessity'. It passed into Old French (*faire de necessité vertu*) and was apparently first used in English around 1374 by Chaucer in *Troilus and Criseyde*.

> **1997** *Spectator* How important it is for humanity always to make a virtue out of necessity.

visiting

visiting fireman a visitor to an organization given especially cordial treatment on account of their importance. US

voice

still small voice: *see* STILL.

a voice in the wilderness an unheeded advocate of reform.

> ❶ The phrase was originally used with reference to the words of John the Baptist, who proclaimed the coming of the Messiah: 'I am the voice of one crying in the wilderness' (John 1:23).

vote

split the vote: *see* SPLIT.

vote with your feet indicate an opinion by being present or absent.

> **1982** *Christian Order* Uncounted thousands have 'voted with their feet', i.e., have left the Church.

v

wag

the tail wags the dog: *see* TAIL.

wagon

fix someone's wagon: *see* FIX.

hitch your wagon to a star: *see* HITCH.

on the wagon teetotal. informal

> ❶ This expression originated in early 20th-century American use in the form *on the water wagon*, the implication being that a person *on the water wagon* would eschew alcohol in favour of water.

1989 Michael Norman *These Good Men* I'll just have a club soda with a twist of lime . . . I'm on the wagon.

a whole team and the dog under the wagon: *see* TEAM.

wake

wake up and smell the coffee become aware of the realities of a situation, however unpleasant. informal, chiefly North American

wake-up

be a wake-up (or awake up) be fully alert or aware. Australian & New Zealand informal

walk

run before you can walk: *see* RUN.

walk all over ❶ defeat easily. **❷** take advantage of. informal

walk before you can run grasp the basic skills before attempting something more difficult.

walk the chalk have your sobriety tested.

> ❶ A traditional method of ascertaining whether someone is sober or not is to see whether they can walk along a line chalked on the ground without wobbling.

walk someone off their feet (or legs) exhaust a person with walking.

walk of life the position within society that a person holds or the part of society to which they belong as a result of their job or social status.

walk on air: *see* AIR.

walk on eggs (or eggshells) be extremely cautious about your words or actions.

walk the plank: *see* PLANK.

walk Spanish be made to walk under compulsion. informal

> ❶ The origins of this expression are not clear. It may refer to the practice of pirates on the Spanish Main, who forced their captives to walk in a particular direction by gripping their collar and trousers tightly.

walk your (or the) talk suit your actions to your words. informal, chiefly North American

> ❶ This expression is also found as *walk the walk*.

walk tall feel justifiable pride. informal

1992 *Woman* This week stop wishing you were somehow different. Start to walk tall!

walk Matilda: *see* **waltz Matilda** *at* MATILDA.

walkabout

go walkabout wander around from place to place in a protracted or leisurely way.

> ❶ In Australian English, a *walkabout* is a journey into the bush undertaken by an Aboriginal in order to live in a traditional manner and re-establish contact with spiritual sources.

walkies

go walkies go missing, especially as a result of theft. informal

walking

a walking — someone who notably embodies the characteristics of some-thing. informal

1989 Charles Shaar Murray *Crosstown Traffic* He is . . . a dubious political philosopher and a walking disaster area as a businessman.

wall

between you and me and the wall: *see* **between you and me and the bedpost** *at* BEDPOST.

drive someone up the wall make someone very irritated or angry. informal

go to the wall ❶ (of a business) fail; go out of business. ❷ support someone or something, no matter what the cost to yourself. informal

off the wall ❶ eccentric or unconventional. ❷ (of a person) crazy or angry. ❸ (of an accusation) without basis or foundation. North American informal

up against the wall in an inextricable situation; in great trouble or difficulty.

> ❶ The image here is of someone facing execution by a firing squad.

wall-to-wall ❶ (of a carpet or other floor covering) fitted to cover an entire floor. ❷ of great extent or number; allowing no unfilled space or interval. informal

> ❷ **1982 Sara Paretsky** *Indemnity Only* Why would he agree to see me? He'd never heard of me, he has wall-to-wall appointments.

walls have ears used to warn someone to be careful what they say as people may be eavesdropping. proverb

wallaby

on the wallaby (or **wallaby track**) (of a person) unemployed and having no fixed address. Australian informal

waltz

waltz Matilda: *see* MATILDA.

war

a war of nerves a struggle in which opponents try to wear each other down by psychological means.

a war of words a prolonged debate which is conducted by means of the spoken or printed word.

have been in the wars have been hurt or injured. informal

a war to end all wars a war, especially the First World War, regarded as making subsequent wars unnecessary.

warm

keep something warm for someone hold or occupy a place or post until another person is ready to do so.

make it (or **things**) **warm for someone** cause trouble or make things unpleasant for someone.

warm as toast pleasantly warm.

> **1991 W. P. Kinsella** *Box Socials* Scrunched down, warm as toast, between the cookstove and the woodbox, I couldn't see that getting something for nothing could be all that bad.

warm the cockles of someone's heart: *see* COCKLE.

warn

warn someone off tell someone forcefully to keep at a distance.

> ❶ This expression comes from horse racing. Prior to 1969, the British Jockey Club had a rule empowering it to *warn someone off the course*, i.e. prohibit someone who had broken Jockey Club regulations from riding or running horses at meetings under the club's jurisdiction.

warpath

on the warpath ready and eager for confrontation.

> ❶ The phrase originated with reference to American Indians heading towards a battle with an enemy.

> **1999** *Cricketer* This summer, England are on the warpath against New Zealand in a four test series.

wart

warts and all including features or qualities that are not appealing or attractive. informal

> ❶ This expression is said to stem from a request made by Oliver Cromwell to the portrait painter Peter Lely: 'Remark all these roughnesses, pimples, warts, and everything as you see me'.

> **1998** *Times* We painted Fayed, warts and all; Fleet Street denounces us for not painting just the warts.

wash

come out in the wash be resolved eventually with no lasting harm. informal

> **1993** *Canadian Living* We could all benefit from borrowing her philosophy: be cheerful and worry sparingly. In the end, it will all come out in the wash.

wash your dirty linen in public discuss or argue about your personal affairs in public.

> ❶ This expression dates from the early 19th century in English; a similar French expression about *linge sale* is attributed to Napoleon.

wash your hands of disclaim responsibility for.

w

> ⓘ This phrase originally alluded to the biblical description of Pontius Pilate, who, when he was forced to condemn Jesus to death, sent for a bowl of water and ritually washed his hands before the crowd as a sign that he was innnocent of 'this just person' (Matthew 27:24).

won't wash will not be believed or accepted. informal

> **1998** *New Scientist* In the end, however, this argument won't wash.

waste

waste not, want not if you use a commodity or resource carefully and without extravagance you will never be in need. proverb

> ⓘ In this expression, *want* can be understood to mean either 'lack' or 'desire' according to the context.

waste of space a person perceived as useless or incompetent. informal

watch

watch someone's smoke: *see* SMOKE.

watch this space: *see* SPACE.

watch the time ensure that you are aware of the time, typically in order to avoid being late.

watch the world go by spend time observing other people going about their business.

> **1996** *Europe: Rough Guide* Outdoor seating allows you to watch the world go by or to play a game of chess with giant chess pieces under the trees.

watch your step: *see* **mind your step** *at* STEP.

watch your (*or* someone's) back protect yourself (*or* someone else) against danger from an unexpected quarter.

the watches of the night the hours of night, especially viewed as a time when you cannot sleep. literary

> ⓘ A *watch* was originally each of the three or four periods of time into which the night was divided, during which a guard would be stationed to keep a lookout for danger or trouble.

water

cast your bread upon the waters: *see* BREAD.

like water in great quantities.

> **1991 Mark Tully** *No Full Stops in India* Digvijay's supporters allege that George spent money like water to bribe the local leaders.

like water off a duck's back: *see* DUCK.

of the first water extreme or unsurpassed of kind.

> ⓘ The sense of *water* referred to in this expression is 'the quality of brilliance and transparency of a diamond or other gem': if a diamond or pearl is *of the first water* it possesses the greatest possible degree of brilliance and transparency. In its transferred use, however, the phrase often refers to someone or something regarded as undesirable, e.g. *a bore of the first water*.

on the wagon: *see* WAGON.

water under the bridge used to refer to events or situations in the past that are no longer to be regarded as important or a source of concern.

> ⓘ The related expression *there's been a lot of water under the bridge since —* is used to indicate that a lot of time has passed and a great many events have occurred since a particular event. A North American variant is *water over the dam*.

Waterloo

meet your Waterloo experience a final and decisive defeat.

> ⓘ The battle of Waterloo in 1815 marked the final defeat of Napoleon's army by the British and the Prussians.

wave

make waves ❶ create a significant impression. ❷ cause trouble. informal

> ❶ **1997** *Spectator* Perhaps unsurprisingly, it is the old pros disguised as new boys and girls who are making the biggest waves.

wax

be wax in someone's hands: *see* **be putty in someone's hands** *at* PUTTY.

wax and wane undergo alternate increases and decreases.

> **2002** *New York Times* The level of security that people are psychologically able to accept changes as crisis situations wax and wane.

wax lyrical about: *see* LYRICAL.

way

have it both ways: *see* BOTH.

go out of your way make a special effort to do something.

on the way out ❶ going down in status, estimation, or favour; going out of fashion. ❷ dying. informal

put someone in the way of give a person the opportunity of. dated

the way of the world the manner in which people typically behave or things typically happen (used to express your resignation to it).

way to go used to express pleasure, approval, or excitement.

> **1990** Robert Oliver *Making Champions* You had Bechard shakin'. He wasn't gonna mess with you. Way to go!

ways and means the methods and resources at someone's disposal for achieving something.

> ❶ In the British parliamentary system this phrase is used specifically of the various methods of raising government revenue.

> **1982** Frank McGuinness *The Factory Girls* He said too he couldn't afford opposition and there were ways and means of getting rid of it. Everybody thinks there's definitely going to be redundancies and pay-offs.

wayside

fall by the wayside ❶ fail to persist in an endeavour or undertaking. ❷ be left without attention or help.

> ❶ In sense 1 the phrase alludes to the biblical parable of the sower in Mark 4:3–20, and in particular to verse 4: 'And it came to pass, as he sowed, some fell by the way side, and the fowls of the air came and devoured it up'.

wazoo

up (or out) the wazoo in great quantities. informal

> ❶ *Wazoo* is an informal American term for the buttocks or anus. Its origins are unknown.

> **2000** Eric Garcia *Anonymous Rex* The guy in the movie had business contacts up the wazoo.

weak

weak at the knees: *see* KNEE.

the weak link the point at which a system, sequence, or organization is most vulnerable; the least dependable element or member.

wear

wear your heart on your sleeve: *see* HEART.

wear the trousers: *see* TROUSERS.

wear (or wear your years) well remain young-looking.

weather

fine (or lovely) weather for ducks wet, rainy weather. humorous

keep a weather eye on observe a situation very carefully, especially for changes or developments.

make good (or bad) weather of it (of a ship) cope well (or badly) in a storm.

make heavy weather (or work) of have unnecessary difficulty in dealing with a task or problem. informal

> ❶ In a nautical context, *heavy weather* means 'violent wind accompanied by heavy rain or rough sea'.

under the weather ❶ slightly unwell. ❷ in low spirits. informal

weaving

get weaving set briskly to work; begin action. British informal

> **1992** George MacDonald Fraser *Quartered Safe Out Here* Come on, come on, come on!... Let's get weaving!

wedge

the thin end of the wedge: *see* THIN.

weigh

weigh something in the balance: *see* BALANCE.

weight

be a weight off your mind come as a great relief after you have been worried.

be worth your (or its) weight in gold be extremely useful or helpful.

throw your weight about: *see* THROW.

welcome

welcome to the club: *see* **join the club** *at* CLUB.

outstay your welcome stay as a visitor longer than you are wanted.

welkin

make the welkin ring make a very loud sound.

> ❶ *Welkin* is a poetic term for 'the sky or heaven', which is now found only in literary contexts and in this expression.

welly

give it some welly exert more effort or strength. informal

w

> **ⓘ** *Welly* or *wellie*, an informal abbreviation of *Wellington boot*, acquired an informal sense of 'power or vigour' in the 1970s.

1997 *BBC Top Gear Magazine* Drop down a gear, give it some welly and that long bonnet rises towards the horizon in the best traditions of...a traditional British Sports Car.

west

go west be killed or lost; meet with disaster. British informal

> **ⓘ** The image here is of the sun setting in the west at the end of the day.

wet

all wet mistaken; completely wrong. North American

wet the baby's head celebrate a baby's birth with a drink, usually an alcoholic one. British informal

wet behind the ears lacking experience; immature. informal

> **ⓘ** The image is of a baby or young animal which is still damp after it has been born.

a wet blanket someone who has a depressing or discouraging effect on others.

> **ⓘ** A dampened blanket can be used to smother a fire; the image here is of a person extinguishing a lively or optimistic mood by their gloominess or negativity.

1991 Michael Curtin *The Plastic Tomato Cutter* When in the company of those of us who do succumb to the occasional dram Father Willie was never a wet blanket.

wet your whistle have a drink. informal

whack

out of whack out of order; not working. North American & Australian

1998 *Bookseller* There's been a fair amount of jeering...at the Sunday Times for getting its figures so comprehensively out of whack, by a factor of about 100 if memory serves.

top (*or* full) whack the maximum price or rate.

1989 *Holiday Which?* Tour prices vary; you pay top whack if you book in large hotels.

whale

a whale of a — an extremely good example of a particular thing. informal

1993 *Chicago Tribune* This stuffed-shirt epitome of the East Coast Establishment of his day had a whale of a time at Chicago's World's Fair.

wham-bam

wham-bam-thank-you-ma'am used in reference to sexual activity conducted roughly and quickly, without tenderness.

what

and (*or* or) what have you and (*or* or) anything else similar. informal

1997 Jonathan Coe *The House of Sleep* Most of the time he's out there, risking his life for his country and defeating Communism and what have you.

and what not and other similar things. informal

1992 Nalinaksha Bhattacharya *Hem & Football* Has anyone ever seen such a selfish daughter? Gorging herself on eggs, milk and what not while others in the house don't even get two square meals?

know what's what: see KNOW.

what with because of (used typically to introduce several causes of something).

1990 Rosamund Clay *Only Angels Forget* She's had a difficult life, what with my father skiving off when I was three and leaving her without a penny.

wheat

separate (*or* sort) the wheat from the chaff distinguish valuable people or things from worthless ones.

> **ⓘ** Chaff is the husks of corn or other seed separated out when the grain is winnowed or threshed. The metaphorical contrast between wheat and chaff is drawn in several passages in the Bible, for example in Matthew 3:12: 'he will thoroughly purge his floor, and gather his wheat into the garner; but he will burn up the chaff with unquenchable fire'.

wheel

a big wheel: see a big cheese at BIG.

reinvent the wheel: see REINVENT.

grease the wheels: see GREASE.

silly as a wheel very silly. Australian

1985 John Clanchy *The Lie of the Land* Father Tierney was mad. Cracked as an egg, some boys said, silly as a wheel.

spin your wheels waste your time or efforts. North American informal

2001 *Time* As long as our national energy policy is demand-driven...we will continue to spin our wheels.

wheel and deal engage in commercial or political scheming.

> ❶ The verb *wheel* is here used to mean 'control events'. The sense is related to the noun *a big wheel*, meaning 'an important person who makes things happen'.

the wheel of Fortune the wheel which the goddess Fortune is said to turn as a symbol of random luck or change.

wheels within wheels used to indicate that a situation is complicated and affected by secret or indirect influences.

> ❶ The image here is of the cogs found in pieces of intricate machinery.

whip

a fair crack of the whip: *see* CRACK.

whip the cat ❶ complain or moan. ❷ be sorry; show remorse. Australian & New Zealand informal

whips of large quantities of. Australian & New Zealand

whirl

give it a whirl give it a try. informal

> **1979 Snoo Wilson** *A Greenish Man* You've nothing to lose. Give it a whirl, try it for a month.

whirlwind

reap the whirlwind suffer serious consequences as a result of your actions.

> ❶ This expression alludes to the proverb *they that sow the wind shall reap the whirlwind*, which is taken from Hosea 8:7.

> **1998** *Spectator* A [political] party that thought all it had to do to keep Scotland happy was deliver devolution is instead reaping the whirlwind it sowed in the Eighties.

whisker

have (*or* **have grown**) **whisker**s (especially of a story) be very old. informal

within a whisker of extremely close or near to doing, achieving, or suffering something. informal

whistle

blow the whistle on bring an illicit activity to and end by informing on the person responsible. informal

> ❶ This idiom comes from football, in which the referee blows a whistle to indicate that a player has broken the rules. Those who inform on others engaged in an illicit activity are now referred to as *whistle-blowers*.

clean as a whistle: *see* CLEAN.

wet your whistle: *see* WET.

whistle in the dark pretend to be confident or unafraid.

> **1996 Bernard Connolly** *The Rotten Heart of Europe* Swedish authorities had, whistling in the dark, spoken of ERM 'association'—but nothing had come of it.

whistle in the wind try unsuccessfully to influence something that cannot be changed.

whistle something down the wind let something go; abandon something.

> ❶ This phrase comes from falconry. It originally referred to the action of letting a trained hawk loose by casting it off with the wind instead of against the wind in pursuit of prey.

white

big white chief: *see* CHIEF.

bleed someone white: *see* **bleed someone dry** at BLEED.

mark something with a white stone regard something as especially fortunate or happy.

> ❶ In ancient times a white stone was traditionally used as a memorial of a happy event.

show the white feather appear cowardly. British, dated

> ❶ A white feather in a game bird's tail was considered to be an indication of bad breeding.

a white elephant a possession that is useless or troublesome, especially one that is expensive to maintain or difficult to dispose of.

> ❶ In former times, the rare albino elephant was regarded as holy. It was highly prized by the kings of Siam (now Thailand) and its upkeep was extremely expensive. It was apparently the practice for a king of Siam to give one of the elephants to a courtier they disliked: the unfortunate recipient would usually be financially ruined by the attempt to maintain the animal.

a white knight a company that makes a welcome bid for a company facing an unwelcome takeover bid.

> ❶ The image here is of the traditional figure from chivalric romances, who rides to the

w

rescue of someone in danger. See also **a knight in shining armour** (*at* KNIGHT).

whited

a whited sepulchre a hypocrite; someone who is ostensibly virtuous but inwardly corrupt. literary

> ❶ This expression comes from Matthew 23:27: 'Woe unto you . . . for ye are like unto whited sepulchres, which indeed appear beautiful outward, but are within full of dead men's bones, and of all uncleanness'. A *sepulchre* is a room or monument, cut in rock or built of stone, in which a dead body is laid or buried.

whiter

whiter than white ❶ extremely white. ❷ morally beyond reproach.

who

who goes there?: *see* GOES.

whole

go the whole hog: *see* HOG.

out of (the) whole cloth wholly fabricated; with no basis in fact or reality. North American informal

> **1991 Ron Rosenbaum** *Travels with Dr. Death* The fact that her murder is officially 'unsolved' is irritating, yes, but no justification for creating conspiracy theories out of the whole cloth.

a whole new ball game: *see* BALL.

the whole nine yards everything possible or available. North American informal

> **1999 Salman Rushdie** *The Ground Beneath Her Feet* Then the lovers throw a party, and what a party! Dancing, wine, the whole nine yards.

whoop

whoop it up ❶ enjoy yourself or celebrate in a noisy way, usually in a group. ❷ create or show excitement or enthusiasm. US informal

whoopee

make whoopee ❶ celebrate wildly. ❷ make love. informal

why

the whys and wherefores the reasons for or details of something.

> **1991** *Gramophone* At this time I was desperate to know all the whys and wherefores of a really advanced technique.

wick

dip your wick (of a man) have sexual intercourse. vulgar slang

get on someone's wick annoy someone. British informal

wicked

no peace (*or* **rest**) **for the wicked** someone's heavy workload or lack of tranquillity is punishment for a sinful life. humorous

> ❶ This expression come from Isaiah 48:22: 'There is no peace, saith the Lord, unto the wicked'.

wicket

a sticky wicket ❶ a pitch that has been drying out after rain and is therefore difficult to bat on. Cricket ❷ a tricky or awkward situation. informal

wide

give a wide berth to: *see* BERTH.

widow

a widow's cruse an apparently small supply that proves inexhaustible.

> ❶ In the Bible, 1 Kings 17 tells the story of the widow to whom Elijah was sent for sustenance. When he asked her for bread, she replied that all she had for herself and her son was 'an handful of meal in a barrel and a little oil in a cruse' (a *cruse* was a small earthenware pot or jar). Elijah told her to make him a cake from these ingredients and then to make food for herself and her son as God had decreed that the containers should be continually replenished.

a widow's mite a small monetary contribution from someone who is poor.

> ❶ This phrase comes from a story recounted in Mark 12:41–4. A poor widow donated two mites (coins of very low value) to the treasury of the Temple in Jerusalem, a sum which constituted all the money she possessed. Witnessing this act, Jesus told his disciples that she had given more than the richest contributor because she had given all that she had.

wig

flip your wig: *see* **flip your lid** *at* FLIP.

wigs on the green violent or unpleasant developments; ructions.

> ❶ The image here is of wigs becoming dislodged or being pulled off during a brawl.

1996 Frank McCourt *Angela's Ashes* Mam threatens us from the bed that we're to help our small brother. She says, If ye don't fix yeer brother's shoes an' I have to get out of this bed there will be wigs on the green.

wiggle

get a wiggle on get moving; hurry. informal

wild

sow your wild oats: *see* OAT.

wild and woolly uncouth in appearance or behaviour.

> ❶ This phrase was originally applied to the American West. The adjective *woolly* probably refers to sheepskin clothing worn with the wool still attached to it, seen as characteristic clothing of the pioneers and cowboys who opened up the western US.

wilderness

a voice in the wilderness: *see* VOICE.

wildfire

spread like wildfire spread with great speed.

wild goose

a wild goose chase a foolish and hopeless search for or pursuit of something unattainable.

> ❶ This expression is first recorded in the late 16th century. It was then the term for a kind of equestrian sport in which all the competitors had to follow accurately the course of the leader at definite intervals, like a flight of wild geese. Later, the term was applied to an erratic course taken by one person or thing and followed by another.

> **1998** *Spectator* The 'struggle to align the clock and the heavens', then, is ultimately the story of mortal vanity, or at least a wild goose chase.

will

where there's a will there's a way determination will overcome any obstacle. proverb

> ❶ This form of the saying was quoted by William Hazlitt in 1822, but George Herbert recorded a variant as one of his *Outlandish Proverbs* in 1640: *To him that will, wais are not wanting.*

will o' the wisp ❶ a phosphorescent light seen hovering or floating over marshy ground, perhaps due to the combustion of methane. ❷ an elusive or deceptive person, idea, or goal.

> ❷ **1996** *Guardian* We're pursuing that old will o' the wisp, Pacific Rim cooking, again.

with the best will in the world however good your intentions (used to imply that success in a particular undertaking, although desired, is unlikely).

with a will energetically and resolutely.

> **1984 Bernard MacLaverty** *Cal* Dunlop told Cal to muck out the byre and because it was something he could do he went at it with a will.

willow

wear the green willow ❶ grieve for the loss of a loved one. ❷ suffer unrequited love. literary

> ❶ A willow branch or leaves traditionally symbolized grief or unrequited love. In *Othello*, Desdemona sings the mournful 'willow song', about a maid forsaken by her lover, shortly before she is murdered.

win

win the day: *see* **carry the day** at DAY.

win by a neck: *see* NECK.

win (or earn) your spurs gain your first distinction or honours. informal

> ❶ In the Middle Ages a knight who had *won his spurs* had attained knighthood by performing an act of bravery: a pair of gilt spurs were the distinguishing mark of a knight.

win the wooden spoon: *see* SPOON.

you can't win them all (or win some, lose some) said to express consolation or resignation after failure in a contest. informal

wind

between wind and water at a vulnerable point.

> ❶ This is a nautical metaphor referring to the part of a ship's side near the waterline that is sometimes above the water and sometimes submerged; damage to the ship at this level is particularly dangerous. The phrase is first recorded in its literal sense at the time of the Spanish Armada (1588): 'One of the shot was betweene the winde and the water, whereof they thought she would haue sonke'. By the mid 17th century, it was also being used of people.

> **1967 Michael Gilbert** *The Dust and the Heat* Mallinson *must* have guessed what was coming. Nevertheless, it hit him between wind and water.

get wind of begin to suspect that something is happening; hear a rumour of. informal

gone with the wind gone completely; having disappeared without trace.

> ❶ This expression comes from Ernest Dowson's poem 'Cynara' (1896): 'I have forgot much, Cynara, gone with the wind', but it is best known as the title of Margaret Mitchell's 1936 novel about the American Civil War.

it's an ill wind few things are so bad that no one profits from them. proverb

> ❶ The full form of this nautical saying is *it's an ill wind that blows nobody any good* or *that profits nobody*. Recorded since the mid 16th century, it is used especially as a comment on a situation in which one person's bad luck is the cause of another's good fortune.

put (or have) the wind up alarm or frighten (or be alarmed or frightened). British informal

> ❶ One of the earliest recorded uses of this expression was in a letter from the poet Wilfred Owen in 1918: 'Shells so close that they thoroughly put the wind up a Life Guardsman in the trench with me'.

raise the wind: see RAISE.

sail close to (or near) the wind verge on indecency, dishonesty, or disaster. informal

> ❶ This originated as a nautical expression, meaning 'sail as nearly against the wind as is possible'. It has been in figurative use since the mid 19th century.

> **1996 Martin Dove** *How To Win Any Consumer Competition* I like the extra thrill of writing to a tight deadline but sometimes I do sail a bit close to the wind with closing dates.

take the wind out of someone's sails frustrate a person by unexpectedly anticipating an action or remark.

> **1977 Eva Figes** *Nelly's Version* She could so easily have taken the wind out of my sails and put me in my place for good.

to the wind(s) (or the four winds) ❶ in all directions. ❷ so as to be abandoned or neglected.

> ❶ **1995 Kate Atkinson** *Behind the Scenes at the Museum* My little flock scatters to the four winds and are hugged and congratulated by their respective parents for being so pretty, charming, cute, delightful, and so on.

wind someone round your little finger: see **twist someone round your little finger** at FINGER.

windmill

fling (or throw) your cap over the wind- mill(s) act recklessly or unconventionally. dated

> **1933 John Galsworthy** *One More River* I suggest that both of you felt it would be mad to fling your caps over the windmill like that?

tilt at windmills: *see* TILT.

window

go out (of) the window (of a plan or pattern of behaviour) no longer exist; disappear. informal

> **1998** *Economist* In the ensuing struggle between the two groups [of councillors], the public interest goes out of the window.

window of opportunity a favourable opportunity for doing something that must be seized immediately if it is not to be missed.

window of vulnerability an opportunity to attack something that is at risk.

> ❶ This expression is especially associated with a cold-war claim that America's land-based missiles were easy targets for a Soviet first strike.

windward

to windward of in an advantageous position in relation to. dated

wine

new wine in old bottles something new or innovatory added to an existing or established system or organization.

> ❶ The proverb *you can't put new wine into old bottles* is a reference to Matthew 9:17: 'Neither do men put new wine into old bottles: else the bottles break, and the wine runneth out, and the bottles perish'.

wine and dine someone entertain someone by offering them drinks or a meal.

wine, women, and song the hedonistic life of drinking, sexual pleasure, and carefree entertainment proverbially required by men.

wing

in the wings ready to do something or to be used at the appropriate time.

> ❶ This idiom comes from the theatre, in which the *wings* here are the areas screened from public view where actors wait for their cue to come on stage.

on a wing and a prayer with only the slightest chance of success.

> ℹ This expression comes from the title of a 1943 song by the American songwriter Harold Adamson, 'Comin' in on a Wing and a Prayer'. He himself took it from a contemporary comment made by a wartime pilot speaking to ground control before making an emergency landing.

spread (or stretch or try) your wings extend your activities and interests or start new ones.

under your wing in or into your protective care.

> **1991 Mickey Mantle** *My Favorite Summer* He kind of took me under his wing and showed me the ropes in my first year.

winged

winged words highly significant or apposite words. literary

> ℹ The image, taken from Homer's *Iliad*, is of the words travelling as directly as arrows to their intended target.

wink

forty winks: *see* FORTY.

in the wink of an eye (or in a wink) very quickly.

not sleep (or get) a wink (or not get a wink of sleep) not sleep at all.

winking

as easy as winking very easy or easily. informal

wipe

wipe someone's eye get the better of a person. British informal, dated

wipe the floor with inflict a humiliating defeat on. informal

wipe the slate clean forgive or forget past faults or offences; make a fresh start.

> ℹ In former times, shopkeepers and pub landlords would keep a record of what was owing to them by writing the details on a tablet of slate; a *clean slate* was one on which no debts were recorded.

wire

down to the wire used to denote a situation whose outcome is not decided until the very last minute. informal

> ℹ This expression comes from horse racing and originated in North America, where a *wire* is stretched across and above the finishing line on a racecourse.

get your wires crossed: *see* CROSSED.

under the wire at the last possible opportunity, just before a time limit. North American informal

wisdom

in someone's wisdom used ironically to suggest that an action is not well judged.

> **1992** *Rugby World & Post* In their wisdom Ciaran Fitzgerald and his selectors decided to dispense with the incumbent, Rob Saunders, and bring Aherne back for his thirteenth Irish cap.

wise

be wise after the event understand and assess an event or situation only after its implications have become obvious.

> ℹ The French version of this expression can be traced back to the late 15th century: the chronicler Philippe de Commynes used the phrase *saiges après le coup* in his *Mémoires*, remarking of it 'comme l'on dit des Bretons' (as the Bretons say).

put someone wise give someone important information. informal

> **1950 Graham Greene** *The Third Man* He was a year older and knew the ropes. He put me wise to a lot of things.

a wise man of Gotham a foolish person. dated

> ℹ *Gotham* is a village in Nottinghamshire which is associated with the folk story *The Wise Men of Gotham*, in which the inhabitants of the village demonstrate their cunning by feigning stupidity. *Gotham* is now a nickname for New York City, used originally by Washington Irvine but later linked particularly with the Batman stories.

wiser

be none (or not any) the wiser know no more than before.

wish

if wishes were horses, beggars would ride if you could achieve your aims simply by wishing for them, life would be very easy. proverb

> ℹ This expression was first recorded in the early 17th century as a Scottish proverb.

the wish is father to the thought we believe a thing because we wish it to be true.

w

ⓘ This expression is used by Shakespeare in *2 Henry IV*: 'Thy wish was father, Harry, to that thought'. However, observations on this kind of self-delusion are found in much earlier writings, including those of Julius Caesar and Demosthenes.

1980 Alice Thomas Ellis *The Birds of the Air* Somewhere in that area of the human mind where the wish is father to the thought activity was taking place. Hunter, Barbara decided, had wangled this invitation in order to be with her.

wit

be at your wits' end be overwhelmed with difficulties and at a loss as to what to do next.

be frightened (or scared) out of your wits be extremely frightened.

gather (or collect) your wits bring yourself back to a state of equanimity.

1984 Geraldine McCaughrean *The Canterbury Tales* Poor old man, he was too astonished to speak. And before he could collect his wits, he was sitting at table . . . with his lord on one side and his daughter on the other.

have (or keep) your wits about you be constantly alert and vigilant.

live by your wits earn money by clever and sometimes dishonest means, having no regular occupation.

pit your wits against compete with someone or something.

1996 Earl Lovelace *Salt* Michael . . . would be the one to make money . . . there was no greater cause or adversary to pit his wits and slickness and spite against.

witching

the witching hour midnight.

ⓘ In Shakespeare's *Hamlet*, Hamlet declares: ''Tis now the very witching time of night, When churchyards yawn and hell itself breathes out contagion to this world'. He is referring to the popular superstition that witches and other supernatural powers are active at midnight.

wither

wither on the vine fail to be implemented or dealt with because of neglect or inaction.

ⓘ The image of grapes failing to grow is probably a reference to various passages in the Bible in which a withered vine is used as a metaphor for a state of physical or spiritual impoverishment.

wolf

cry wolf call for help when it is not needed; raise a false alarm.

ⓘ An old fable tells the tale of a shepherd boy who constantly raised false alarms with cries of 'Wolf!', until people no longer took any notice of him. When a wolf did actually appear and attack him, his genuine cries for help were ignored and no one came to his aid.

have (or hold) a wolf by the ears be in a precarious position.

ⓘ The saying became current in English in the mid 16th century, but the Roman comic dramatist Terence (195–159 BC) mentions its Latin equivalent, *lupum auribus tenere*, as already being an old saying in his time. *Compare with* **have a tiger by the tail** (at TIGER).

1990 George Will *Suddenly* A Communist Party administering an economy is holding a wolf by the ears.

keep the wolf from the door have enough money to avert hunger or starvation.

ⓘ The phrase has been used in this sense since the mid 16th century, but the image of the wolf as a symbol of a devouring and destructive force is found much earlier than this. In Matthew 10:16, for example, Jesus tells his disciples: 'Behold I send you forth as sheep in the midst of wolves: be ye therefore wise as serpents, and harmless as doves'.

throw someone to the wolves leave someone to be roughly treated or criticized without trying to help or defend them. informal

ⓘ This phrase probably arose in reference to tales about packs of wolves pursuing travellers in horse-drawn sleighs, in which one person was pushed off the sleigh to allow it to go faster, so enabling the others to make their escape.

1958 *Listener* This able and agreeable doctor was thrown to the wolves by a Prime Minister who had good reason to know that his own position was desperate.

a wolf in sheep's clothing a person or thing that appears friendly or harmless but is really hostile and dangerous.

ⓘ This expression comes from Jesus's words in Matthew 7:15: 'Beware of false prophets, which come to you in sheep's clothing, but inwardly they are ravening wolves'.

woman

a woman of letters: *see* **a man of letters** *at* LETTER.

a woman of the world: *see* **a man of the world** *at* WORLD.

wonder

a nine days' wonder something that attracts enthusiastic interest for a short while but is then ignored or forgotten.

work (*or* **do**) **wonders** have a very beneficial effect on someone or something.

> **1997 Paul Wilson** *Calm at Work* While it is true that holidays work wonders for the relief of stress, the relief is only temporary.

wood

cannot see the wood for the trees fail to grasp the main issue because of over-attention to details.

> ❶ The North American version of this expression is *cannot see the forest for the trees*.

out of the wood (*or* **woods**) out of danger or difficulty.

> ❶ A proverbial warning against *hallooing before you are out of the wood* dates from the late 18th century.

touch wood said in order to prevent a confident statement from bringing bad luck.

> ❶ A North American variant is *knock on wood*. The phrase refers to the traditional custom of touching something wooden to avert possible bad luck.

> **1991 Rohinton Mistry** *Such a Long Journey* Sohrab and Gustad did not shout or argue like they used to, touch wood.

wooden

accept a wooden nickel: *see* NICKEL.

win the wooden spoon: *see* SPOON.

wooden nutmeg: *see* NUTMEG.

woodshed

something nasty in the woodshed a shocking or distasteful thing kept secret. British informal

> ❶ This expression is taken from Stella Gibbons's comic novel *Cold Comfort Farm* (1933), in which Aunt Ada Doom's dominance over her family is maintained by constant references to her having seen *something nasty in the woodshed* in her youth. The details of the experience are never explained.

take someone to the woodshed reprove or punish someone, especially discreetly. US informal, dated

> ❶ This expression referred to the former practice of taking a naughty child to a woodshed to be punished, out of sight of other people.

woodwork

vanish into (*or* **come** *or* **crawl out of**) **the woodwork** (of an unpleasant person or thing) disappear into (*or* emerge from) obscurity. informal

> ❶ The implication here is that the people or things concerned are like cockroaches or other unpleasant creatures living in the crevices of skirting boards and cupboards.

wool

all wool and a yard wide of excellent quality; thoroughly sound.

> ❶ Literally, this expression refers to cloth of the finest quality.

> **1974 Anthony Gilbert** *A Nice Little Killing* No one will ever catch her . . . with an alibi all wool and a yard wide.

pull the wool over someone's eyes deceive someone, especially by telling untruths.

> **1997** *Spectator* On no occasion do I remember Ridsdale trying to pull the wool over my eyes but rather trying always to remove the wool that journalists . . . pull over their own eyes.

word

eat your words: *see* EAT.

have a word in someone's ear speak to someone privately and discreetly, usually to give them a warning. informal

in words of one syllable: *see* SYLLABLE.

a man (*or* **woman**) **of few words** a taciturn person.

a man (*or* **woman**) **of his** (*or* **her**) **word** a person who keeps the promises that they make.

not the word for it not an adequate or appropriate description.

> **1992** *European Travel & Life* The landscape of Alaska has the power to overwhelm. 'Beautiful' is not the word for it.

put words into someone's mouth: *see* MOUTH.

someone's word is law someone must be obeyed without question.

someone's **word is their bond** someone keeps their promises.

> ❶ A variant of this expression, now rather dated, is *an Englishman's word is his bond.*

take someone at their word interpret a person's words literally or exactly, especially by believing them or doing as they suggest.

take someone's word (for it) believe what someone says or writes without checking for yourself.

too — for words extremely —. informal

> **1990 Rosamund Pilcher** *September* I'm not saying 'Isn't it beautiful' all the time, because if I do, it'll just sound too banal for words.

winged words: *see* WINGED.

word of mouth spoken language; informal or unofficial discourse.

> **1987 Bruce Duffy** *The World As I Found It* His ideas were repeated by word of mouth or passed around as transcripts of the shorthand notes that his students doggedly took down during his lectures.

the word on the street a rumour or piece of information currently being circulated. informal

> **1992 Victor Headley** *Yardie* The word on the street was that Roy was hooked and had smoked a fair amount of the crack himself.

a word to the wise a hint or brief explanation given, that being all that is required.

> ❶ The equivalent Latin phrase is *verbum sapienti sat est* (a word to the wise is enough); the abbreviation of this, *verb. sap.,* is sometimes used in English.

> **1983 Penelope Lively** *Perfect Happiness* A word to the wise. If you don't know the place I'm told the thing to do is steer clear of the guided tours.

work

give someone the works ❶ give someone everything. ❷ treat someone harshly. informal

have your work cut out be faced with a hard task.

in the works being planned, worked on, or produced. chiefly North American

> **2003** *N. Y. Magazine* Movie-star-of-the-moment Jennifer Lopez . . . is in talks to star in *Monster in Law*, a new comedy in the works at New Line Cinema.

work your ass (or butt) off work extremely hard. North American vulgar slang

work your fingers to the bone: *see* BONE.

work like a beaver: *see* BEAVER.

work to rule (especially as a form of industrial action) follow official working regulations exactly in order to reduce output and efficiency. chiefly British

work your ticket: *see* TICKET.

workman

a bad workman blames his tools someone who has done something badly will seek to lay the blame on the equipment rather than admit to their own lack of skill. proverb

> ❶ A similar 13th-century French proverb observed *mauveés ovriers ne trovera ja bon hostill*, 'bad workmen will never find a good tool', and variants of this early saying can be found in English until the mid 19th century until the emergence of the modern version.

world

the best of both (or all possible) worlds the benefits of widely differing situations, enjoyed at the same time.

> ❶ The variant *all possible worlds* alludes to the catchphrase of the eternally optimistic philosopher Dr Pangloss in Voltaire's *Candide* (1759): *Dans ce meilleur des mondes possibles . . . tout est au mieux*, usually quoted in English as 'Everything is for the best in the best of all possible worlds'.

carry the world before you have rapid and complete success.

come up in the world rise in status, especially by becoming richer.

go down in the world drop in status, especially by becoming poorer.

look for all the world like look precisely like.

> **1993** *New Scientist* Fossil imprints that look for all the world like motorcycle tracks have been explained.

a man (or woman) of the world a person who is experienced and practical in human affairs.

not be long for this world: *see* LONG.

out of this world extremely enjoyable or impressive. informal

> **1995** *Daily Express* I thought the rest of the team, and especially the defence, were out of this world.

set the world alight: *see* ALIGHT.

think the world of have a very high regard for.

the world and his wife everyone; a large number of people. British

> ❶ This expression is first recorded in Jonathan Swift's *Polite Conversation* (1738).

the world, the flesh, and the devil all forms of temptation to sin.

the world is your oyster you are in a position to take the opportunities that life has to offer.

> ❶ This expression may come from Shakespeare's *The Merry Wives of Windsor*: 'Why, then the world's mine oyster, Which I with sword will open'.

> **1998** *Times* I was never brought up thinking, 'You are an Asian woman so you can't do things.' I was always given the impression that the world was my oyster.

a (*or* **the**) **world of** a very great deal of.

worm

a worm's-eye view the view looking up at something from ground level.

> ❶ This expression was formed on the pattern of **bird's-eye view** (*see* BIRD). It usually refers to the viewpoint of a humble or insignificant person who is witnessing important events or people.

(even) a worm will turn even a meek person will resist or retaliate if pushed too far. proverb

food for worms a dead person.

wormwood

wormwood and gall a source of bitter mortification and grief. literary

> ❶ *Gall* is bile, a substance secreted by the liver and proverbial for its bitterness, while *wormwood* is an aromatic plant with a bitter taste. The expression originated in reference to various passages in the Bible, for example Lamentations 3:19: 'Remembering mine affliction and my misery, the wormwood and the gall'.

worse

none the worse for ❶ not adversely affected by. ❷ not to be considered inferior on account of.

> ❶ **1991 Alistair Campbell** *Sidewinder* Two days have passed, and I am up and about, feeling none the worse for my attack of sunstroke.

so much the worse for used to suggest that a problem, failure, or other unfortunate event or situation is the fault of a person specified and that the speaker does not feel any great concern about it.

the worse for wear ❶ damaged by use or weather over time; battered and shabby. ❷ (of a person) feeling rather unwell, especially as a result of drinking too much alcohol. informal

worst

be your own worst enemy: *see* ENEMY.

do your worst do as much damage as you can (often used to express defiance in the face of threats).

get (*or* **have**) **the worst of it** be in the least advantageous or successful position; suffer the most.

if the worst comes to the worst if the most serious or difficult circumstances arise.

worth

be worth your weight in gold: *see* WEIGHT.

for all someone is worth ❶ as energetically or enthusiastically as someone can. ❷ so as to obtain everything you can from someone. informal

> ❶ **1995 Kate Atkinson** *Behind the Scenes at the Museum* In the kitchen, Brian, Adrian's lover, is wearing Bunty's pink rubber gloves and washing up for all he's worth.

not worth a plugged nickel: *see* NICKEL.

worth your salt: *see* SALT.

wrap

keep something under wraps conceal or be secretive about something. informal

> **1998** *New Scientist* The key to the fuel is a catalyst that the Navy is keeping under wraps.

wrap someone round your little finger: *see* **twist someone round your little finger** *at* FINGER.

wrap it up be quiet. British informal

wring

wring someone's withers stir someone's emotions or conscience.

> ❶ This phrase is taken from *Hamlet*. In the play-within-the-play scene, Hamlet remarks ironically that there is no need for King

Claudius, his usurping uncle, to feel troubled by the plot, remarking: 'let the galled jade wince, our withers are unwrung'. The *withers* are the bony ridge between the shoulders of a horse which is liable to be chafed by an ill-fitting saddle.

wring your hands show great distress.

wringer

put someone through the wringer (or the mangle) subject someone to a very stressful experience, especially a severe interrogation. informal

> **1984 Louise Erdrich** *Love Medicine* I saw that he had gone through the wringer. He was red-eyed, gaunt, and he was drunk.

wrinkle

iron out the wrinkles: *see* IRON.

writ

writ large clear and obvious.

> ❶ The literal sense of *written in large characters* has long fallen out of use. As the past participle of *write*, *writ* has been superseded by *written* except in this phrase and analogous phrases such as *writ small*.

> **1994** *Time* Voters fear the future, which looks to them like the present writ large: more concern about crime, more economic pressure on their families, more of that unnerving sound of something eating away at the edges of their lives.

your writ runs you have authority of a specified extent or kind.

write

nothing to write home about of little interest or value. informal

> **1970 Nina Bawden** *The Birds on the Trees* I daresay what I did was nothing to write home about, but it put food in her belly and shoes on her feet!

write your ticket: *see* TICKET.

writing

the writing is on the wall there are clear signs that something unpleasant or unwelcome is going to happen.

> ❶ This phrase comes from the biblical story of Belshazzar's feast, at which a disembodied hand appeared and wrote a message on the wall foretelling the fall of the Babylonian kingdom to the Medes and Persians (Daniel 5:5, 25–8). A North American variant is *the handwriting is on the wall*.

> **1998** *Spectator* We ought to have spotted the writing on the wall when the dear old Ministry of Works became 'English Heritage', packaging the past as a set of limited-edition, special-offer collectables.

written

be (or have something) written all over your face used to convey that the presence of a particular quality or feeling is clearly revealed by a person's expression. informal

wrong

born on the wrong side of the blanket: *see* BLANKET.

get in wrong with (or on the wrong side of) someone incur the dislike or disapproval of someone. informal

get out of bed on the wrong side: *see* BED.

get someone wrong misunderstand someone, especially by falsely imputing malice to them.

get (hold of) the wrong end of the stick misunderstand someone or something completely.

go down the wrong way (of food) enter the windpipe instead of the gullet.

in the wrong box: *see* BOX.

the wrong side of the tracks: *see* TRACK.

wrote

(and) that's all she wrote used to convey that there is or was nothing more to be said about a matter. North American informal

> **2001** *Chicago Tribune* The snap was a little high, and ... I tilted up for a second and that's all she wrote ... I took my eye off the ball.

Yy

yard

by the yard in large numbers or quantities.

> **2002** *Guardian* Culture became a commodity: painters sold landscapes cut up by the foot for home decoration; booksellers offered books by the yard; publishers traded copyrights.

yarn

spin a yarn tell a story, especially a long and complicated one.

> ⓘ A *yarn* is one of the long fibres from which a rope is made. The expression is nautical in origin and has been used in this figurative sense since the early 19th century.

year

for donkey's years: *see* DONKEY.

put years on (*or* take years off) someone make someone feel or look older (*or* younger).

the vale of years: *see* VALE.

the year dot: *see* DOT.

yes

yes and no partly and partly not.

> **1981 Brian Murphy** *The Enigma Variations* 'Do you believe that if you continue seeing me you'll be damned?' 'Yes and no.'

yesterday

yesterday's man a man, especially a politician, whose career is finished or past its peak.

yesterday's news a person or thing that is no longer of interest.

yonder

the wide blue yonder: *see* BLUE.

you

you and yours you together with your family and close friends.

> **1937** *American Home* So it's natural…to take good care of the home that gives you and yours this steadfast protection.

Index

This section contains groups of idioms which are linked by a common theme or subject. The themes are listed in alphabetical order and the word in bold print indicates where individual idioms may be found in the dictionary itself. For example, the idiom 'take the **plunge**' is listed in the dictionary at the main entry **plunge**.

Action

start the **ball** rolling
get the **bit** between your teeth
at the **coalface**
get **cracking**
go for the **doctor**
get (or pull) your **finger** out
keep your nose to the **grindstone**
hammer and tongs
hit the ground running
hot to trot
have many **irons** in the fire
rest on your **laurels**
lead from the front
put your money where your **mouth** is
rest on your **oars**
put your hand to the **plough**
take the **plunge**
press the button
roll up your sleeves
set the wheels in motion
shake a leg
put your **shoulder** to the wheel
get the **show** on the road
watch someone's **smoke**
stir your stumps
strike while the iron is hot
get **weaving**
no peace for the **wicked**

Age

out of the **ark**
have seen **better** days
the **bloom** is off the rose
you can't teach an old **dog** new tricks
there's no **fool** like an old fool
have one **foot** in the grave
full of years
ancient (or old) as the **hills**
over the **hill**
have had a good **innings**
on your last **legs**
long in the tooth
pass your sell-by date
past it
second childhood
stricken in years
threescore years and ten
there's many a good **tune** played on an old fiddle
the **vale** of years
put **years** on someone

Ambition

think **big**
bite off more than you can chew
fire in the belly
fly high
punch above your weight
room at the top
try to **run** before you can walk
set your heart on
raise your **sights**
set your **sights** on
reach for the **stars**
punch your ticket

Anger and annoyance

bent out of shape
get off your **bike**
make your **blood** boil
blow your top

have a **cob** on
count to ten
have a **cow**
go **crook**
get your **dander** up
give someone the hairy **eyeball**
breathe **fire**
fit to be tied
flip your lid
fly off the handle
froth (*or* foam) at the mouth
blow a **gasket**
make someone's **hackles** rise
hot under the collar
have your **monkey** up
do your **nana**
go **non-linear**
put someone's **nose** out of joint
do your **nut**
get on someone's **quince**
give someone the **pip**
lose your **rag**
rattle someone's cage
a **red** rag to a bull
see **red**
go through the **roof**
rub someone up the wrong way
keep your **shirt** on
go **spare**
spit blood
vent your **spleen**
have **steam** coming out of your ears
get on someone's **wick**

Anxiety and worry

screaming **abdabs**
bag (*or* bundle) of nerves
with **bated** breath
hot and **bothered**
have **butterflies** in your stomach
have a **cadenza**
like a **cat** on a hot tin roof
have your **heart** in your mouth
like a **hen** with one chick
having **kittens**
like a **monkey** on a stick
live on your **nerves**
on **pins** and needles
sweat blood
sweat bullets
on **tenterhooks**

on **thorns**
meet **trouble** halfway
twist in the wind
be a **weight** off your mind

Appearance

the **acceptable** face of
someone's **bark** is worse than their bite
bells and whistles
borrowed plumes
look as if **butter** wouldn't melt in your
   mouth
all **cats** are grey in the dark
like something the **cat** brought in
the **cut** of someone's jib
dressed like a dog's dinner
a **false** dawn
fool's gold
be all **fur** coat and no knickers
take the **gilt** off the gingerbread
all that **glitters** is not gold
handsome is as handsome does
mutton dressed as lamb
a **paper** tiger
pass in a crowd
like **peas** in a pod
a **Potemkin** village
under the **skin**
be the **spit** of
still waters run deep

Argument and conflict

agree to differ
apple of discord
battle of the giants
a **bone** of contention
have a **bone** to pick with someone
fight like **cat** and dog
chop logic
at **cross** purposes
cross swords
take up the **cudgels**
cut and thrust
at **daggers** drawn
play **devil**'s advocate
divide and rule
add **fuel** to the fire
lock horns
at **loggerheads**
go to the **mat**
passage of arms

pour oil on troubled waters
part brass **rags** with
hold the **ring**
a **running** battle
shoot it out
sparks fly
be at each others' **throats**
fight **tooth** and nail
trail your coat
try a fall with
a **war** of nerves
on the **warpath**
wigs on the green

Beauty

the body **beautiful**
belle of the ball
easy on the eye
plain **Jane**
no **oil** painting
peaches and cream
be (or look) a **picture**
plain as a pikestaff
not just a **pretty** face
pretty as a picture
a **sight** for sore eyes
an **ugly** duckling

Boastfulness and conceit

above yourself
talk **big**
too **big** for your boots
little tin **god**
be all **hat** and no cattle
turn someone's **head**
hide your light under a bushel
blow your own **horn**
draw the **longbow**
be all **mouth** and no trousers
drop **names**
pride goes before a fall
shoot a line
shoot your mouth off
have a **swollen** head
have **tickets** on yourself
blow your own **trumpet**

Bribery, corruption, and extortion

put the **bite** on

bleed someone dry
take someone to the **cleaners**
cook the books
with your hand in the **cookie** jar
dirty work at the crossroads
grease someone's palm
feather your own nest
on the **fiddle**
line your pockets
every **man** has his price
put in the **nips**
rob someone blind
salt the books
stick to someone's fingers
sticky fingers
keep someone **sweet**
on the **take**
have your fingers in the **till**

Caution

belt and braces
better safe than sorry
a **bird** in the hand
see which way the **cat** jumps
throw **caution** to the winds
dip your toe in something
discretion is the better part of valour
don't put all your **eggs** in one basket
lower your **guard**
look before you leap
steer a **middle** course
play it safe
to be on the **safe** side
let **sleeping** dogs lie
a **stitch** in time
one **swallow** doesn't make a summer
think twice
walk on eggs (or eggshells)

Certainty

an **article** of faith
you can **bet** your boots
a safe **bet**
a **bird** in the hand
in your **bones**
I should **cocoa**
count your chickens
be **dollars** to doughnuts that
I'm a **Dutchman**
gospel truth

all **Lombard** Street to a China orange
put your **money** on
no two ways about it
lay **odds**
open-and-shut
put your **shirt** on
as **sure** as eggs is eggs

Change

the **boot** is on the other foot
a **breath** of fresh air
a new **broom**
ring the **changes**
chop and change
cross the floor
future shock
don't change **horses** in midstream
Jekyll and Hyde
turn over a new **leaf**
a **leopard** can't change his spots
the law of the **Medes** and the Persians
break the **mould**
poacher turned gamekeeper
rise from the ashes
rite of passage
turn the **scales**
shuffle the cards
sing a different tune (*or* song)
be carved (*or* set) in **stone**
turn the **tables**
trim your sails
variety is the spice of life
new **wine** in old bottles

Chaos and disorder

alarms and excursions
upset the **apple** cart
raise **Cain**
put the **cat** among the pigeons
raise the **devil**
the **dust** settles
every which way
flutter the dovecotes
play **havoc** with
make **hay** of
all **hell** broke loose
play merry **hell** with
play **hob**
make a **Horlicks** of
a **hornet**'s nest

out of **joint**
out of **kilter**
all over the **lot**
raise a dust
rock the boat
come apart at the **seams**
shipshape and Bristol fashion
all over the **shop**
be lost in the **shuffle**
at **sixes** and sevens

Class

tug your **forelock**
keep up with the **Joneses**
downwardly (*or* upwardly) **mobile**
as common as **muck**
one **nation**
noblesse oblige
born to the **purple**
sit below the **salt**
be born with a **silver** spoon in your
    mouth
a **tall** poppy
the wrong side of the **tracks**
the great **unwashed**
the **upper** crust

Clothes

your best **bib** and tucker
dressed to kill
dressed up like a **dog**'s dinner
fine feathers
in your **glad** rags
fit like a **glove**
in full **fig**
mutton dressed as lamb
off the **peg**
in full **rig**
shoot your cuffs

Cooperation

be **art** and part of
play **ball**
if you can't **beat** them, join them
in **cahoots**
make common **cause** with
cheek by jowl
circle the wagons
play **footsie** with someone
give and take

a **halfway** house
hand in glove
put your **heads** together
hitch horses together
meet someone halfway
a **meeting** of minds
oil and water
the **old** school tie
the **old** boy network
on the same **page**
close **ranks**
you **scratch** my back, and I'll scratch yours
shoulder to shoulder
sing from the same hymn sheet
it takes two to **tango**
go with the **tide**
two-way street

Courage

beard the lion in his den
bell the cat
bite the bullet
have a lot of **bottle**
take the **bull** by the horns
bury your head in the sand
pull someone's **chestnuts** out of the fire
cold feet
face the music
as **game** as Ned Kelly
gird your loins
grasp the nettle
heart of oak
stick your **neck** out
have **nerves** of steel
a **stout** heart
whistle in the dark
show the **white** feather

Crime and punishment

the long **arm** of the law
six of the **best**
do **bird**
bring someone to **book**
throw the **book** at
the **boys** in blue
feel someone's **collar**
crack a crib
a **hanging** offence
take the **law** into your own hands
at Her Majesty's **pleasure**

public enemy number one
beat the **rap**
up the **river**
a **rod** in pickle
rough justice
short sharp **shock**
a **slap** on the wrist
tar and feather
twelve **good** men and true

Crisis

when the **balloon** goes up
when the **band** begins to play
burn your boats (*or* bridges)
when the **chips** are down
at the **crossroads**
when it comes to the **crunch**
at the **eleventh** hour
the **fat** is in the fire
on a **knife-edge**
make or break
moment of truth
neck or nothing
the **parting** of the ways
head someone or something off at the **pass**
point of no return
when **push** comes to shove
cross the **Rubicon**
the last (*or* final) **straw**
turn the corner

Critics and criticism

an **armchair** critic
a **back-seat** driver
if the **cap** fits, wear it
be on someone's **case**
bust someone's **chops**
a sacred **cow**
damned if you do and damned if you don't
dip your pen in gall
under **fire**
have a **go** at
do a **hatchet** job on
pick **holes**
jump down someone's throat
not **mince** words
Monday morning quarterback
give someone a **mouthful**
get it in the **neck**

pick **nits**
have a **pop** at
the **pot** calling the kettle black
rap someone over the knuckles
cast the first **stone**
straight from the shoulder
tear someone off a **strip**

Danger

put your head on the **block**
a warning shot across the **bows**
chance your arm
close shave
dice with death
go through **fire**
too **hot** to hold you
(skating) on thin **ice**
a **lion** in the way
the **lion**'s den
the **lion**'s mouth
live to tell the tale
a **loose** cannon
play with fire
ride for a fall
sail close to the wind
saved by the bell
Scylla and Charybdis
siren song
the **sword** of Damocles
hang by a **thread**
have a **tiger** by the tail
have a **wolf** by the ears
a **wolf** in sheep's clothing
out of the **woods**

Death

in **Abraham**'s bosom
bite the big one
bite the dust
go **bung**
cash in your chips
shuffle off this mortal **coil**
pushing up the **daisies**
go to **Davy Jones's** locker
hand in your **dinner pail**
buy the **farm**
go the way of all **flesh**
give up the **ghost**
have one foot in the **grave**
the **Grim** Reaper
off the **hooks**

hop the twig
join the great majority
kick the bucket
king of terrors
meet your **maker**
pass in your ally
pop your clogs
go to your **reward**
six feet under
turn up your **toes**
beyond the **veil**
go **west**
not be long for this **world**
food for **worms**

Debt

on the **cuff**
flexible friend
in **hock**
in the **hole**
your **pound** of flesh
in **Queer** Street
in the **red**
rob Peter to pay Paul
on the **slate**
get **square** with
on **tick**

Deception and lying

sell someone a **bill** of goods
be caught with **chaff**
sail under false **colours**
sell someone a **dummy**
with **forked** tongue
lead someone up the **garden** path
beware the **Greeks** bearing gifts
hook, line, and sinker
hand someone a **lemon**
all done with **mirrors**
nail a lie
accept a wooden **nickel**
do a **number** on
a wooden **nutmeg**
sell someone a **pup**
work the **rabbit**'s foot on
come the **raw** prawn
take someone for a **ride**
the **scales** fall from someone's eyes
take someone for a **sleigh ride**
sleight of hand
smell a rat

one **nation**
ask no **odds**
the **pot** calls the kettle black
redress the balance
be no **respecter** of persons
share and share alike
six of one and half a dozen of the other
on **terms**

Excess and extravagance

break a butterfly on a wheel
burn the candle at both ends
coals to Newcastle
too many **cooks** spoil the broth
have something coming out of your **ears**
enough is as good as a feast
feast or famine
gild the lily
the **golden** mean
jump the shark
lay something on with a trowel
the **Matthew** principle
sow one's wild **oats**
go **overboard**
over-egg the pudding
pile **Pelion** on Ossa
prodigal son
take a **sledgehammer** to crack a nut
in **spades**
over the **top**
waste not, want not

Expense

cost an **arm** and a leg
bang for your buck
break the bank
not worth the **candle**
cheap at the price
what's the **damage**?
go **Dutch**
cost the **earth**
on the **house**
a **king**'s ransom
pay through the **nose**
over the **odds**
pay the piper
a **pretty** penny
for a **song**
time is money
top dollar

top (*or* full) **whack**
a **white** elephant

Experience

babes in the wood
know something like the **back** of your hand
cut your teeth
be thrown in at the **deep** end
see the **elephant**
find your feet
get your feet wet (*at* **foot**)
teach your **grandmother** to suck eggs
grist to the mill
live and learn
once bitten, twice shy
the **school** of hard knocks
spread your wings
been **there**, done that
the **university** of life
wet behind the ears
a man (*or* woman) of the **world**

Family

the **angel** in the house
tied to someone's **apron** strings
born on the wrong side of the **blanket**
blood is thicker than water
blood will tell
charity begins at home
a **chip** off the old block
a **cuckoo** in the nest
empty nester
like **father**, like son
your own **flesh and blood**
hatches, matches, and despatches
hearth and home
her indoors
kith and kin
your **nearest** and dearest
tug of love
you and **yours**

Fate and chance

accidents will happen
the long **arm** of coincidence
that's the way the **cookie** crumbles
in the **lap** of the gods
lightning never strikes twice
have someone's (name and) **number** on it

someone's **number** is up
the **wheel** of Fortune

Food

break **bread** with
man cannot live by **bread** alone
eat someone out of house and home
have **eyes** bigger than your stomach
kill the **fatted** calf
eat like a **horse**
ladies who lunch (*at* **lady**)
Lenten fare
melt in the mouth
off your **oats**
get **outside** of
make a **pig** of yourself
stick to your ribs
an army marches on its **stomach**
wine and dine

Fools and foolishness

there's one **born** every minute
a **brick** short of a load
bright spark
dead from the neck up
not playing with a full **deck**
empty vessels make most noise
fools rush in where angels
    fear to tread
play the giddy **goat**
need your **head** examined
act the **maggot**
wear **motley**
no more than **ninepence** in
    the shilling
not the full **quid**
a **right** one
a **sandwich** short of a picnic
not the full **shilling**
thick as two (short) planks
silly as a **wheel**
a **wise** man of Gotham

Foresight and the future

cross someone's palm with silver
lay something up in **lavender**
a **pricking** in your thumbs
the **shape** of things to come
a **straw** in the wind
time will tell
the **writing** is on the wall

Forgiveness and reconciliation

bury the hatchet
let **bygones** be bygones
turn the other **cheek**
to **err** is human, to forgive divine
kiss and make up
mend your fences
hold out an **olive** branch
prodigal son
water under the bridge
wipe the slate clean

Friends and acquaintances

Damon and Pythias
hail-fellow-well-met
man's best friend
part brass **rags** with
rub shoulders with
scrape acquaintance with
ships that pass in the night
give someone **skin**
thick as thieves
three musketeers

Futility

a **blind** alley
like getting **blood** out of a stone
waste your **breath**
make **bricks** without straw
Buckley's chance
not a **cat** in hell's chance
go round in **circles**
whistle **Dixie**
fight a losing battle
flog a dead horse
bang your **head** against a brick wall
cry over spilt **milk**
milk the bull
bark at the **moon**
a **needle** in a haystack
painting the Forth Bridge
cast **pearls** before swine
plough the sand
a **Pyrrhic** victory
get a **quart** into a pint pot
chase **rainbows**
reinvent the wheel
a **rope** of sand
spitting in the wind

shut the **stable** door after the horse has
bolted
chase your **tail**
tilt at windmills
spin your **wheels**
whistle in the wind
a **wild goose** chase

Gossip and rumour

dish the dirt
someone's **ears** are burning
hear something on the **grapevine**
no **smoke** without fire
tell **tales** out of school
bush **telegraph**
get **wind** of
the **word** on the street

Happiness, pleasure, and enjoyment

walk on **air**
have a **ball**
beer and skittles
push the **boat** out
be a **box** of birds
bread and circuses
cakes and ale
a bowl of **cherries**
the **cherry** on the cake
on **cloud** nine
warm the **cockles** of someone's heart
like a **dog** with two tails
forbidden fruit
the **gaiety** of nations
everything in the **garden** is lovely
merry as a **grig**
in seventh **heaven**
kick up your **heels**
full of the **joys** of spring
over the **moon**
music to your ears
paint the town red
the **party**'s over
the **primrose** path
ray of sunshine
a **red** letter day
roses, roses, all the way
with your **tail** up
be **tickled** pink
on the **tiles**

on **top** of the world
walk on air
whoop it up
wine, women, and song

Haste and speed

like a **bat** out of hell
in the **blink** of an eye
like the **clappers**
rattle your **dags**
like a **dose** of salts
at the **double**
at the **drop** of a hat
put **foot**
hell for leather
hold your horses
hustle your butt
before you can say **Jack** Robinson
put a **jerk** in it
in **jig** time
on the **jump**
before you can say **knife**
at a rate of **knots**
get the **lead** out
at a **lick**
like greased **lightning**
at full **pelt**
quick and dirty
burn **rubber**
rush your fences
like a **scalded** cat
in two **shakes** (of a lamb's tail)
in **short** order
get your **skates** on
in a **trice**
in a **twinkling**
get a **wiggle** on
in the **wink** of an eye

Health and illness

the big **C**
catch your **death**
like **death** warmed up
in fine **fettle**
fit as a **fiddle**
fit as a **flea**
green about the gills
give someone **gyp**
in the **pink**
right as **rain**

sick as a dog
up to **snuff**
sick to your **stomach**
right as a **trivet**
under the **weather**

Honesty

a straight **arrow**
above **board**
put your **cards** on the table
make a **clean** breast of something
Mr **Clean**
cross my heart
straight as a **die**
fair and square
on the **level**
play fair
the **salt** of the earth
Scout's honour
on the **square**
on the **up** and up

Hope and optimism

brave new world
look on the **bright** side
count your chickens
cross your fingers
hope springs eternal
light at the end of the tunnel
a **silver** lining
come up **smiling**
have **stars** in your eyes
clutch at **straws**
third time lucky
it's an ill **wind**
the **wish** is father to the thought
the best of both (*or* all possible) **worlds**

Hypocrisy

shed **crocodile** tears
holier than thou
Lady Bountiful
pay **lip** service to something
make **nice**
physician, heal thyself
the **unco** guid
a **whited** sepulchre

Indecision and prevarication

beat about the bush

blow hot and cold
see which way the **cat** jumps
sit on the **fence**
put something on the long **finger**
fish or cut bait
run with the **hare** and hunt with the
    hounds
hedge your bets
hum and haw
the **jury** is still out
be in two **minds**
play both ends against the middle
all at **sea**

Intelligence and knowledge

know how many **beans** make five
blind someone with science
the **chattering** classes
too **clever** by half
culture vulture
feast of reason
there are no flies on (*at* **fly**)
a man (*or* woman) of **letters**
know your **onions**
not just a **pretty** face
be **quick** on the uptake
not **rocket** science
have your head **screwed** on
sharp as a needle
not **suffer** fools gladly
hand on the **torch**

Jealousy and envy

eat your heart out
the **grass** is always greener
the **green**-eyed monster
keep up with the **Joneses**
nice work if you can get it
how the **other half** lives
sour grapes

Justice

day of reckoning
get your just **deserts**
give the **devil** his due
what **goes** around comes around
murder will out
you **reap** what you sow
a **Roland** for an Oliver
what's **sauce** for the goose
    is sauce for the gander

get a fair **shake**
one good **turn** deserves another

Language, speech, and conversation

have kissed the **blarney** stone
talk a **blue** streak
chew the fat
have swallowed a **dictionary**
the **gift** of the gab
start a **hare**
say a **mouthful**
in a **nutshell**
the **pen** is mightier than the sword
have a **plum** in your mouth
prunes and prisms
a **purple** patch
run off at the mouth
shoot the breeze
have a **silver** tongue
call a **spade** a spade
speak in tongues
pick up **stompies**
in words of one **syllable**
talk the hind leg off a donkey
talk nineteen to the dozen
the gift of **tongues**

Laziness

a **bone** in your leg
eat the **bread** of idleness
couch potato
cut corners
dodge the column
rest on your **oars**
come the old **soldier**
swing the lead
twiddle your thumbs

Love

bill and coo
set your **cap** at
eternal triangle
an old **flame**
wear your **heart** on your sleeve
hell hath no fury like a woman scorned
the **light** of your life
love's young dream
the boy (or girl) **next door**
sweet **nothings**

not the only **pebble** on the beach
make **sheep**'s eyes at someone
carry a **torch** for
wear the green **willow**

Madness

have **bats** in the belfry
round the **bend** (or twist)
off your **chump**
away with the **fairies**
have **kangaroos** in the top paddock
mad as a hatter
lose your **marbles**
men in white suits (see **man**)
out of your **mind**
nutty as a fruit cake
out to lunch
off your **nana**
go **postal**
off your **rocker**
have a **screw** loose
take leave of your **senses**
straws in your hair
out of your **tree**
off your **trolley**

Marriage

your **better** half
bottom **drawer**
her indoors
make an **honest** woman of
hope chest
tie the **knot**
plight your troth
pop the question
on the **shelf**

Misfortune and adversity

with your **back** against the wall
a **bad** quarter of an hour
bed of nails
catch a Tartar
a **chapter** of accidents
be caught in a **cleft** stick
be up the **creek** without a paddle
have your **cross** to bear
between the **devil** and the deep blue sea
the **dirty** end of the stick
sow **dragon**'s teeth
behind the **eight** ball
out of the **frying pan** into the fire

up a **gum** tree
under the **harrow**
come **hell** or high water
in **hot** water
the **iron** entered someone's soul
a pretty (or fine) **kettle** of fish
go through the **mill**
a **millstone** round your neck
a **nail** in the coffin
go **pear-shaped**
the rough end of the **pineapple**
any **port** in a storm
buy the **rabbit**
on the **rack**
it never **rains** but it pours
be on the **receiving** end
between a **rock** and a hard place
roll with the punches
a hard **row** to hoe
the **short** end of the stick
slings and arrows
a **slippery** slope
a **spanner** in the works
draw the short **straw**
up a **stump**
a **thorn** in someone's side

Mistakes

throw the **baby** out with the bathwater
back the wrong horse
bark up the wrong tree
off **base**
off **beam**
up the **booay**
put the **cart** before the horse
chickens come home to roost
get your wires **crossed**
drop a clanger
to **err** is human, to forgive divine
put your **foot** in it
score an own **goal**
kill the **goose** that lays the golden egg
shoot yourself in the foot
slip of the pen (or tongue)
slip on a banana skin
get hold of the **wrong** end of the stick

Money, wealth, and prosperity

an **Aladdin**'s cave
a **bed** of roses

have one's **bread** buttered on both sides
in **clover**
corn in Egypt
feel the **draught**
have it **easy**
live off the **fat** of the land
board the **gravy** train
live high on the **hog**
in the **lap** of luxury
the **Mammon** of unrighteousness
the **Midas** touch
milk and honey
where there's **muck** there's brass
pennies from heaven
a **piece** of the action
on the **pig**'s back
make your **pile**
have deep **pockets**
be **quids** in
at **rack** and manger
the life of **Riley**
a **roll** Jack Rice couldn't jump over
be **rolling** in it
be born with a **silver** spoon in your
  mouth
Tom Tiddler's ground

Nakedness

in the **altogether**
in your **birthday** suit
in the **buff**
go **commando**
in a state of **nature**
in the **nip**
in your **pelt**
in the **raw**

Opportunity

an **arrow** in the quiver
the **ball** is in someone's court
play your **cards** right
a bite at the **cherry**
a fair **crack** of the whip
every **dog** has his day
as one **door** closes, another opens
take time by the **forelock**
not let the **grass** grow under your feet
half a chance
make **hay** while the sun shines
a **kick** at the can (or cat)
kill two birds with one stone

a new **lease** of life
miss the boat
not **miss** a trick
in **pole** position
room at the top
seize the day
not a **shot** in your locker
there's more than one way to **skin** a cat
let something **slip** through your fingers
steal a march on
strike while the iron is hot
have a second **string** to your bow
time and tide wait for no man
a **toe** in the door
window of vulnerability
the **world** is your oyster

Poverty

on your **beam** ends
not have a **bean**
keep **body** and soul together
from **clogs** to clogs in three generations
down and out
from **hand** to mouth
not have a **penny** to bless yourself with
not have two **pennies** to rub together
poor as a church mouse
in **Queer** Street
from **rags** to riches
in **reduced** circumstances
live on the **smell** of an oil rag
on your **uppers**
keep the **wolf** from the door

Power

top **banana**
get someone over a **barrel**
at someone's **beck** and call
beggar on horseback
a **big** cheese
know where the **bodies** are buried
in the **box** seat
call the shots (or tune)
hold all the **cards**
play **cat** and mouse with
in the **catbird** seat
big white **chief**
cock of the walk
dance to someone's tune
in the **driver**'s seat

have someone **eating** out of your hand
in the **hollow** of your hand
men in grey suits (at **man**)
a **mover** and shaker
have someone in the **palm** of your hand
in someone's **pocket**
pull the strings
hold the **purse** strings
rule the roost
in the **saddle**
under someone's **thumb**
have someone on **toast**
wear the **trousers**
twist someone round your little finger

Pregnancy

have a **bun** in the oven
in the (pudding) **club**
up the **duff**
in the **family** way
a **gleam** (or twinkle) in someone's eye
the **patter** of tiny feet
up the **spout**

Preparation and readiness

armed at all points
asleep at the wheel
keep your eye on the **ball**
batten down the hatches
loaded for **bear**
off the **cuff**
dot the i's and cross the t's
get all your **ducks** in a row
at your **fingertips**
firing on all (four) cylinders
gird your loins
grease the wheels
at **half** cock
on the **hoof**
jump the gun
catch someone with their **pants** down
keep your **powder** dry
prime the pump
shoot from the hip
on **spec**
on the **spur** of the moment
set the **stage** for
on the **stocks**
all **systems** go
on your **toes**

keep a **weather** eye on
in the **wings**

Reputation and fame

a **black** sheep
not as **black** as you are painted
blot your copybook
a **blot** on the escutcheon
Caesar's wife
claim to fame
under a **cloud**
give a **dog** a bad name
look to your **laurels**
a **legend** in their own lifetime
the **mark** of Cain
someone's name is **mud**
have your **name** in lights
no **smoke** without fire
a nine days' **wonder**

Revenge and retribution

settle **accounts** with someone
bay for blood
the **biter** bit
pay someone back in their own **coin**
have it **coming** to you
day of reckoning
get your just **deserts**
get **even** with
an **eye** for an eye and a tooth for a tooth
don't **get** mad, get even
a dose (*or* taste) of your own **medicine**
get your **own** back
poetic justice
revenge is a dish best served cold
settle a **score**
tit for tat

Secrecy

an **ace** up your sleeve
between you and me and the **bedpost**
keep your **cards** close to your chest
sweep something under the **carpet**
let the **cat** out of the bag
behind **closed** doors
a **closed** book
cover your tracks
a **dark** horse
a **fly** on the wall
blow the **gaff**
give the **game** away

keep something under your **hat**
under the **hatches**
a **hidden** agenda
keep the **lid** on
someone's **lips** are sealed
mum's the word
on the **q.t.**
shout something from the **rooftops**
in a smoke-filled **room**
under the **rose**
behind the **scenes**
show your hand
a **skeleton** in the cupboard
spill the beans
tip your hand
blow the **whistle** on
something nasty in the **woodshed**

Self-Interest

have an **axe** to grind
bite the hand that feeds you
bow down in the house of Rimmon
know which side your **bread** is buttered
fight your **corner**
curry favour
dog in the manger
be your own worst **enemy**
every man for himself
have an **eye** for the main chance
feather your nest
take the **fifth**
foul your own nest
I'm all right, **Jack**
the law of the **jungle**
contemplate your **navel**
put your head in a **noose**
cut off your **nose** to spite your face
not in my back yard
take care of **number** one
paint yourself into a corner
hoist with your own **petard**
make a **rod** for your own back
sell your soul to the devil
cut your own **throat**

Sex

the **birds** and the bees
a **bit** on the side
pop someone's **cherry**
of **easy** virtue

root and branch
from **soda** to hock
from **soup** to nuts
stay the course
leave no **stone** unturned
pull out all the **stops**

Time

arrow of time
once in a **blue** moon
turn back the **clock**
till the **cows** come home
in a **dog**'s age
donkey's years
the year **dot**
a movable **feast**
a **fly** in amber
till **hell** freezes over
till **kingdom** come
many **moons** ago
a **month** of Sundays
a **New York** minute
before the **Rinderpest**
round the clock
time immemorial
the **watches** of the night
the **witching** hour

Traitors and treachery

point the **bone** at
turn **cat** in pan
do the **dirty** on someone
fifth column
a fair-weather **friend**
beware the **Greeks** bearing gifts
a **Judas** kiss
night of the long knives
sell the **pass**
a **poisoned** chalice
play someone false
put someone's **pot** on
sell someone down the **river**
a **snake** in the grass
a **stab** in the back
a **Trojan** horse
a **viper** in your bosom

Travel and transport

a **bird** of passage
ride **bodkin**
seven-league **boots**
a magic **carpet**
as the **crow** flies
on the **gad**
hit the road
go round the **houses**
get **itchy** feet
knight of the road
live out of a suitcase
waltz **Matilda**
Mexican overdrive
ride the rails
ride shotgun
round **Robin Hood**'s barn
a **rolling** stone
put down **roots**
a **sabbath** day's journey
on **Shanks's** pony
pull up **stakes**
up **sticks**
on the **stump**
go **walkabout**

Unhappiness and disappointment

your heart sinks into your **boots**
beat your **breast**
a **dog**'s life
down in the mouth
down in the dumps
dust and ashes
eat your heart out
end in tears
a ghost at the **feast**
a **kick** in the teeth
a **lump** in your throat
sick as a parrot
a **slap** in the face
vale of tears
wear the green **willow**
wormwood and gall
wring your hands

Violence

blood and guts
blood and thunder
have **blood** on your hands
give someone **Bondi**
bunch of fives
tap someone's **claret**

beat the living **daylights** out of
duke it out
the **gloves** are off
go the **knuckle**
punch someone's **lights** out
tear someone **limb** from limb
get **physical**
take a **pop** at
a **Procrustean** bed
he who lives by the **sword** dies by the sword
beat the **tar** out of
have been in the **wars**

Warfare

a call to **arms**
blood and iron
the **dogs** of war
the **pen** is mightier than the sword
a **pitched** battle
rattle sabres
a **roll** of honour
throw away the **scabbard**
take the King's (or Queen's) **shilling**
beat **swords** into ploughshares
the late **unpleasantness**
the **war** to end all wars

Weakness

an **Achilles** heel
besetting sin
big girl's **blouse**
built on sand
a **chink** in someone's armour
a **faint** heart
have feet of clay (see **foot**)
hit where you live
a **house** of cards
a **house** divided
man of straw
milk and water
a **paper** tiger
a broken **reed**
fall apart at the **seams**
knock the **stuffing** out of

Weather

blow great guns
brass monkey

chuck it down
the **eye** of the storm
the **heavens** opened
Indian summer
a **London** particular
rain cats and dogs
lovely **weather** for ducks

Work and employment

get the **boot**
hang up your **boots**
someone's **bread** and butter
on the **broo**
burn the midnight oil
a **busman**'s holiday
get your **cards**
get the **gate**
a **golden** handshake
put someone out to **grass**
hit the bricks
jobs for the boys
live over the shop
put someone out to **pasture**
walk the **plank**
the oldest **profession**
punch the time clock
give someone the **push**
hang out your **shingle**
talk **shop**
put up the **shutters**
the **smell** of the lamp
old **Spanish** customs
by the **sweat** of your brow
Buggins' **turn**
walk of life
on the **wallaby** track

Youth

angry young man
the **awkward** age
babes in the wood
bright young thing
a **broth** of a boy
at your mother's (or father's) **knee**
knee-high to a grasshopper
poor little rich girl (or boy)
your **salad** days
ugly ducking
take **years** off someone

Oxford Paperback Reference

The Concise Oxford Dictionary of English Etymology
T. F. Hoad

A wealth of information about our language and its history, this
reference source provides over 17,000 entries on word origins.

'A model of its kind'

Daily Telegraph

A Dictionary of Euphemisms
R. W. Holder

This hugely entertaining collection draws together euphemisms from all
aspects of life: work, sexuality, age, money, and politics.

Review of the previous edition
'This ingenious collection is not only very funny but extremely
instructive too'

Iris Murdoch

The Oxford Dictionary of Slang
John Ayto

Containing over 10,000 words and phrases, this is the ideal reference for
those interested in the more quirky and unofficial words used in the
English language.

'hours of happy browsing for language lovers'

Observer

Oxford Paperback Reference

The Concise Oxford Companion to English Literature
Margaret Drabble and Jenny Stringer

Based on the best-selling *Oxford Companion to English Literature*, this is
an indispensable guide to all aspects of English literature.

Review of the parent volume
'a magisterial and monumental achievement'

Literary Review

The Concise Oxford Companion to Irish Literature
Robert Welch

From the ogam alphabet developed in the 4th century to Roddy Doyle,
this is a comprehensive guide to writers, works, topics, folklore, and
historical and cultural events.

Review of the parent volume
'Heroic volume ... It surpasses previous exercises of similar nature in the
richness of its detail and the ecumenism of its approach.'

Times Literary Supplement

A Dictionary of Shakespeare
Stanley Wells

Compiled by one of the best-known international authorities on the
playwright's works, this dictionary offers up-to-date information on all
aspects of Shakespeare, both in his own time and in later ages.

OXFORD

More Literature titles from OUP

Shakespeare: An Oxford Guide
Stanley Wells and Lena Cowen Orlin

This comprehensive guide to Shakespeare comprises over 40 specially commissioned essays by an outstanding team of contemporary Shakespeare scholars.

Literature in the Modern World
Dennis Walder

A unique perspective for students on literary studies from the 1920s to the present day.

The Poetry Handbook
John Lennard

A lucid and entertaining guide to the poet's craft, and an invaluable introduction to practical criticism.

VISIT THE HIGHER EDUCATION LITERATURE WEB SITE AT
www.oup.com/uk/best.textbooks/literature

Ask Oxford .COM

Oxford Dictionaries Passionate about language

For more information about the background to Oxford Quotations and Language Reference Dictionaries, and much more about Oxford's commitment to language exploration, why not visit the world's largest language learning site, www.AskOxford.com

Passionate about English?

What were the original 'brass monkeys'? **Ask**Oxford.COM

How do new words enter the dictionary? **Ask**Oxford.COM

How is 'whom' used? **Ask**Oxford.COM

Who said, 'For also knowledge itself is power?' **Ask**Oxford.COM

How can I improve my writing? **Ask**Oxford.COM

If you have a query about the English language, want to look up a word, need some help with your writing skills, are curious about how dictionaries are made, or simply have some time to learn about the language, bypass the rest and ask the experts at www.AskOxford.com.

Passionate about language?

If you want to find out about writing in French, German, Spanish, or Italian, improve your listening and speaking skills, learn about other cultures, access resources for language students, or gain insider travel tips from those **Ask**Oxford.COM in the know, ask the experts at

OXFORD

Oxford Paperback Reference

The Concise Oxford Dictionary of Quotations
Edited by Elizabeth Knowles

Based on the highly acclaimed *Oxford Dictionary of Quotations*, this
paperback edition maintains its extensive coverage of literary and
historical quotations, and contains completely up-to-date material. A
fascinating read and an essential reference tool.

The Oxford Dictionary of Humorous Quotations
Edited by Ned Sherrin

From the sharply witty to the downright hilarious, this sparkling
collection will appeal to all senses of humour.

Quotations by Subject
Edited by Susan Ratcliffe

A collection of over 7,000 quotations, arranged thematically for easy
look-up. Covers an enormous range of nearly 600 themes from 'The
Internet' to 'Parliament'.

The Concise Oxford Dictionary of Phrase and Fable
Edited by Elizabeth Knowles

Provides a wealth of fascinating and informative detail for over 10,000
phrases and allusions used in English today. Find out about anything
from the 'Trojan horse' to 'ground zero'.

Great value ebooks from Oxford!

An ever-increasing number of Oxford subject reference dictionaries, English and bilingual dictionaries, and English language reference titles are available as ebooks.

All Oxford ebooks are available in the award-winning Mobipocket Reader format, compatible with most current handheld systems, including Palm, Pocket PC/Windows CE, Psion, Nokia, SymbianOS, Franklin eBookMan, and Windows. Some are also available in MS Reader and Palm Reader formats.

Priced on a par with the print editions, Oxford ebooks offer dictionary-specific search options making information retrieval quick and easy.

For further information and a full list of Oxford ebooks please visit: www.askoxford.com/shoponline/ebooks/